1987

# The Transformation of Israeli Society

# The Transformation of Israeli Society

An Essay in Interpretation

S. N. Eisenstadt

Westview Press
Boulder, Colorado

First published in Great Britain by
George Weidenfeld and Nicolson Ltd
91 Clapham High Street, London sw4 7TA

Published in 1985 in the United States by
WESTVIEW PRESS
Frehderick A. Praeger, Publisher
5500 Central Avenue
Boulder, Colorado 80301

ISBN 0–8133–0306–0
LC 85–51253

Printed in Great Britain

To the Memory of my Parents
Michael and Rosa
and for
Shulamit,
Michael and Mimi; Irit and Ronny; Alik and Dalia;
Ido; Karin and Lee

**From Generation to Generation**

# Contents

# Tables

# Preface

This book, although close in title and to some degree in contents, is not an updating of my *Israeli Society*,* but basically, with the exception of some descriptive parts, an almost entirely new book.

It does not intend, as the former one, to present a detailed picture of the development and organization of the major spheres of life of Israeli society. Rather, its major aim is to analyse – in the vein of a long interpretative essay, yet an essay based on data – some of the major aspects and trends of development of Israeli society which have been taking place continuously since its beginning, from the early period of Zionist settlement in Eretz Israel up to today.† It analyses these processes and changes in a comparative–analytical framework. It stresses that Israel has to be seen as a modern post-revolutionary society similar in some ways to other such modern societies – be they the United States, Russia or Mexico – and yet also quite different from them, and it is the juxtaposition of these similarities and differences that provides the crucial clue to the dynamism of Israeli society.

The first such specific characteristic of the Yishuv and of Israeli society is that it developed as a colonizatory, pioneering and ideological society, rather akin to the puritan settlement in North America.

The second distinctive characteristic of Israeli society is that its development took place in the reality of an alien, later quite hostile, environment, which has made the security dilemma a central one in the construction of life in Israel.

The third – and in a way perhaps most distinctive – characteristic of Israeli society, which distinguishes it from those of other such societies, is that its origins are rooted in attempts to reconstruct Jewish national life, Jewish civilization – as articulated in the Zionist vision.

Accordingly, in order to understand the dynamics of Israeli society, we have to take into account the whole background of Jewish history in the framework of which the Zionist movement developed. Within this framework the Zionist movement constituted also a rebellion – thus creating the revolutionary component of this society. This rebellion has, at the same time, taken up, continued and reconstructed many of the elements of the premises of the Jewish civilizational vision – one of the first such visions to develop in the history of mankind, and the first on the eastern shores of the Mediterranean and among the monotheistic religions.

The fourth such distinguishing characteristic of Israeli society is the fact of its

* S. N. Eisenstadt, *Israeli Society* (London and New York 1965).
† September 1983.

being a small society – sharing many characteristics with other small modern societies, but at the same time, because of the attempt at the implementation of the Zionist vision, aspiring to become a centre of special cultural creativity, closely related to this vision. Hence the crucial importance of the analysis of the relations between Israeli society and the Jewish communities in the Diaspora, which constitute one of the major objects of this special creative vision, one of its major external markets with which all small societies are very closely interrelated, and towards which Israeli society has developed a great variety of relations, ranging from rebellion through ambivalence up to acceptance as sources of various types of support.

Throughout our analysis we have attempted to provide an interpretation of the dynamics of Israeli society in light of these comparative, analytical considerations.

Accordingly the book contains two topics which were not included in *Israeli Society*. First, the book starts not only with the analysis of the specific historical background of the Zionist movement, but with an overview, an interpretation, of Jewish history.

Second, the book also contains a special chapter on developments in Jewish communities in the Diaspora – as they share with Israel, even if in a very fraught and ambivalent relation, some of the problems of implementation of such a vision in the context of modern life.

The book does not pretend to present a history of the Jewish people or even of the Zionist movements, of the settlement in Eretz Israel or of the State of Israel itself. There are by now many books – presented in the bibliography – which deal with these topics; but rather, as indicated, it attempts to provide an interpretation from the point of view of the analytical considerations outlined above.

Given the nature of the work, I have given only minimal footnotes – mostly references to direct quotations or sources – in the text, and at the same time have provided general bibliographical indications at the end of the book.

The interpretation attempted in this book could not, however, be attempted without relying on very diversified and abundant historical, sociological and anthropological research – even if some rather severe lacunae can sometimes be found in many areas of such research.

Jewish historical research has indeed burgeoned in the last four decades and has become very extensive. I was fortunate to be introduced to it by my teachers at the Hebrew University – the late Professors Itzhak Baer and B. Dinur, pioneers in the modern Eretz-Israeli Jewish historiography – as well as to follow closely the work of the late Professor Gershon Scholem, who has pioneered the work of Jewish mysticism. I am also especially indebted to the work of my colleague Professor J. Katz and his innovative works on Jewish history in general and to his modern one in particular, as well as, of course, to the many works of younger scholars in Israel and abroad.

I owe also a great debt to Arnaldo Momigliano – to many of his works which (as for instance in *Alien Wisdom*) add some crucial dimensions in the understanding of Jewish civilizations in late antiquity, and to many conversations with him.

The same is obviously true of comparative studies and approaches which have been at the centre of my work in sociological analysis in general. Here I am greatly indebted to my late teachers, the late Professor Martin Buber and Professor R. Koebner, as well as to the late Professor M. Ginsberg, for raising my interest in this direction, to Professor Edward Shils for our continuous dialogue ranging by now for more than thirty-five years, and to many of my colleagues, contemporaries and students for continuous stimuli and co-operation in these directions of sociological analysis.

In this context I would like also to mention the seminars on Max Weber, conducted since 1976 by Professor W. Schluchter of the University of Heidelberg, the first one of which was indeed devoted to Ancient Judaism, as noted in the bibliography.

Above all I am, of course, immensely indebted to the manifold research on different aspects of Israeli society, which has indeed burgeoned since the publication of *Israeli Society* – much of it, to my great satisfaction, by my former students, students of my students and many of them my contemporary colleagues. I have indeed often directly drawn on their work, by quoting from them and referring to them – but I am indebted to them far beyond this. Without their work my attempt at an interpretation would have been much more speculative, and the numerous discussions in seminars and workshops, in the meetings of the Israeli Sociological Association, as well as more personal discussions with many of them over more than thirty years, have been of immense help and stimulus.

Beyond my general indebtedness to my colleagues and students, I have incurred more specific debts during the preparation of this book. First of all I am greatly indebted to Yehuda Elkana and Moshe Lissak, who read through an earlier draft of the manuscript and whose remarks were very helpful in the preparation of the final version – as were those of Michel Abutboul, Yoram Ben Porath, Nathan Glazer, Seymour Martin Lipset and Seymour Fox, who read parts of the earlier version.

I am very grateful to Aryeh Shachar and E. Razin for preparing the section on the settlement map of Israel (Chapter 9, I), and to Aryeh Shachar for preparing the section on the settlement policy in Judea and Samaria under the Likud governments, and to my son Michael for the section on sport activities.

Haim Barkai and Yoram Ben Porath have greatly helped me in the preparation of the chapter on the political economy, Reuven Kahane the chapter on education, Meir Zadok and S. Katz with the materials on higher education, and Yosef Bashi in respect to some aspects of the educational policies. Yaakov Nahon was kind enough to prepare most of the tables for Chapter 11.

I am indebted to many colleagues, and especially to Rivka Bar-Yosef, Moshe Davis, Eric Cohen, Chaim Adler, Yael Azmon, Dan Horowitz, Baruch Kimmerling and Dov Weintraub, for discussions of many problems analysed in this book. I am also very indebted to Edward Shils for many comments on the whole book and for very great help in editing several of the chapters.

The first, very preliminary draft of this book was started at Harvard in 1978 and I owe much to discussions at that stage with Henry Rosovsky and Nur Yalman.

My two daughters-in-law have greatly helped me – Mimi, who was a very patient research assistant, and Dalia, who provided and checked many points of information.

The typing of the various drafts and of the final version of the manuscript was done by Krista Page at Harvard, and by Dany Gargman, Suzy Shabtai, Cary Ehrenberg, Anna Katoff, Barbara Piperno, David Kruss, especially by my then secretary Norma Schapira and above all by Moshe Levy who, as throughout the years, has shown great devotion and patience in the preparation of the drafts and final manuscripts.

Sabena Honigwachs, the administrative assistant of the Department of Sociology, has greatly helped in organizational matters; Ilana Stav has helped in various technical matters; Zeev Shavit and Sara Helman have helped with the preparation of the bibliography. Above all Hilary Walford has done wonders copy editing the manuscript. I would also like to thank Mrs E. Sass and Mrs Hannah Levy for reading the proofs.

Throughout the preparation of the book I was greatly helped by the facilities provided me by the Department of Sociology and the Truman Research Institute of the Hebrew University in Jerusalem, by the Jerusalem Van Leer Foundation, and by the Department of Sociology and Center of Middle Eastern Studies of Harvard University.

Above all, I would like to thank Lord Weidenfeld, who for many years has urged me to write this book – and without whose urging the book might not have been written.

The writing of the manuscript was finished more or less in September 1983, by accident together with the resignation of Menachem Begin from the Premiership. I have not attempted to go in detail beyond this period, except for writing a brief postscript in which some comments on more recent developments, especially the 1984 elections, are presented.

S. N. Eisenstadt
*Jerusalem*
*August 1984*

# PART ONE

## The Historical Background

# CHAPTER 1
# The Emergence of Jewish Civilization

## Introduction
### *The Zionist movement and Israeli society*
### *against the background of Jewish history*

It is impossible to understand the transformations of Israeli society without reference to its relationship with the Jewish nation, people and communities, to its place – as seen from within itself and by others – in Jewish history. It is not only that its origins – the origins of the Zionist movement and of the settlement in Palestine – were rooted in a rebellion against the realities of Jewish life as they existed in different Jewish communities, above all in Europe, in the second half of the nineteenth century. Equally important is the fact that this very rebellion was to a very large extent constructed in terms of some basic, perennial themes or orientations of Jewish civilization – themes relating to the Jews themselves, to their ways of life and civilization, and to their relations to other nations. The concrete implementation of this rebellion, the crystallization of Jewish society in Eretz Israel and the development of Israeli society, have been continuously related both to these themes and to the reality of Jewish life throughout the world, in the Jewish communities in the Diaspora. It would therefore be appropriate to start our exploration with a very brief survey – not of the history of the Jewish people, something which would be beyond the scope of this book – but of some of these basic themes, realities and problems of Jewish civilization as they have developed and changed through the history of the Jewish people.

A good starting-point for such an analysis is the apparent contradiction between two aspects of Jewish existence as it could have been, and often was, portrayed in that very period in which the Zionist movement started to crystallize – the second half of the nineteenth century.

On the one hand there were the great – what today would be called 'traditional' – Jewish masses concentrated in Eastern Europe and beyond in the various countries of the Ottoman Empire. The internal life of these communities centred around the institutions of the synagogue, the places of learning, and the various communal organizations led by a combination of community leaders and rabbis; it was seemingly ruled by centuries-old traditions of learning, of ritual observance and legal prescriptions, and of prayer; and it was characterized by strong cohesive family life, and by inter-family and inter-community networks and organizations. Externally the life of these communities was shaped by the attitudes of their 'host' people: they usually lived in a situation of political powerlessness, of an almost total dependence on the will of the rulers; they had no political or citizen rights beyond the privileges or immunities granted to them by the rulers, and were indeed, until the attainment of emancipation, seen as strangers in the lands which they inhabited.

Economically they were always confined to relatively distinct and special niches allowed to them within the encompassing economic structure – above all, with some spectacular exceptions, in petty finance and commerce, in various middlemen positions such as handicraft and to a much smaller degree in the field of agriculture. Most of them – with the exception of those in special communities or special sectors, like those attached to the courts of kings or engaged in international commerce or finance – were not very affluent; many were rather poor although probably better off, even if less secure, than the peasantry which constituted the bulk of the population.

They were seen by the majority – especially in the Christian, but also in the Muslim lands – not only as an alien minority, but also as the carriers of a faith, of a civilization which denied the validity of the basic premises of the 'host' civilization; hence, by their very existence, they presented a constant threat to the dominant faith. At the same time, however, the very apparent shabbiness and precariousness of their existence, evident in the persecutions, pogroms and expulsions of which Jewish history was full, was taken by their 'host' people as proof of the inferiority of the Jewish people – but an inferiority to which those who remained within the fold of the Jewish faith and community (and there were always many who left) would never admit.

However, against this picture of apparent stagnation – later depicted by Arnold Toynbee as a 'fossil', in which the only realm of cultural creativity in which Jews could excel was the sphere of legal-ritual prescriptions – in the beginning of the second half of the nineteenth century, especially in Western Europe, there existed the kernels of a different picture, which yet had their roots in the past, as we shall see later on.

When the gates of the crystallizing modern European society and nation-states were – albeit slowly and ambivalently – opened before the Jews, there was an outburst of creativity in almost all spheres of social and especially cultural activity. In Western and Central Europe – and much more haltingly in Eastern Europe – large numbers of Jews made a rapid advance economically. They quickly transformed themselves educationally and occupationally, moving into modern educational institutions – those of the wider societies or those of their own – most of which were already shaped according to the premisses of the general society. In two or three generations they became highly prominent in many new fields of economic activity and in higher learning, in the arts, in journalism and also in some, above all the more radical, political, intellectual and social movements.

Names like Heine, Moses Hess, Mendelssohn-Bartholdy or Lassalle – to mention but a few – became part of the general cultural scene. Attitudes remained ambivalent towards them. But the strong, new, modern anti-

Semitism was no longer only religious, but more and more racial. The Jews were no longer seen as a small seemingly stagnant minority holding on to its faith and ways of life in a hostile environment. They were penetrating some of the central arenas of social and political life and becoming very visible within them, some becoming baptized, some assimilated. Yet very often they were unable to shed, at least in the eyes of their hosts, the imprint of their Jewish origins. Moreover, among the Jews in Western Europe, but above all in Eastern Europe, there were the beginnings of the creation of new types of Jewish institutions and organizations, as well as activities within the institutional frameworks of the general societies.

The Zionist movement developed (as we shall see in greater detail later on) as one of the reactions – the most radical and revolutionary one – to these two poles of Jewish existence as they developed above all in Europe, in the second half and especially the last third of the nineteenth century. But in order to understand fully the nature of this rebellion or revolution we have first to understand how it was possible for these two poles to exist and develop side by side. This brings us back to the search for some of the basic realities, constellations, problems and themes of Jewish history and civilization. In the following chapters we shall pursue such a search – without, of course, pretending to write the history of the Jewish people. Given the long – in some ways unique – continuity of this history which we shall explicate to some degree later, we shall start by going back to its origins, when some of its basic characteristics began to take shape.

# The Biblical Period
# and the Period of the Second Commonwealth
## *Historical background*

The external facts of Jewish history are, of course, well known. Jewish history emerged sometime in the middle of the second millennium before the Christian era (BCE). Its first decisive encounter was the conquest of the Land of Canaan by the tribes of Israel, under the leadership of Joshua but presumably already bearing the stamp of legislation attributed to Moses; and then the settlement of these tribes in Canaan. Such conquest, quite natural in those times in that part of the world, necessarily entailed a continuous encounter and conflict with their neighbours – the various nations or tribes which had also settled in that territory. This settlement was initially, in the period of the Judges, a relatively dispersed one, with the different tribes leading relatively separate existences, yet with some common sacred places, coming together to some degree in times of war, and maintaining some continuous common trans-tribal identity.

From the very beginning of this period the Israeli tribes were characterized by several special social characteristics, which we shall analyse in greater detail later on. At this stage of our discussion suffice it to point out that the most important of these characteristics were their relative multiplicity, and the heterogeneity of social, economic and cultural forms and elements of which they were composed. Most important among the latter were, of course, the priest and prophets who had acquired as we shall see some very outstanding characteristics in Israel which distinguished them from their seeming counterparts in the neighbouring societies.

Then in the tenth century BCE came the period of the unification and establishment of the monarchy, first under Saul, then under David and Solomon; the erection of the Temple and the attempts at the centralization of the cult; the continuation and intensive development of groups of prophets; the division of the realm after the death of Solomon, under his son Rehoboam, into the two Kingdoms of Judea (composed mostly of the tribes of Juda and Benjamin) and of Israel (composed of the other ten tribes); the continuous involvement of these Kingdoms in the international conflicts of the region, especially in the conflicts between the great Empires, the Egyptian on the one hand and the Assyrian and Babylonian on the other, as well as various kingdoms in the north, such as for instance the Akkadians; the destruction by the Assyrians of the Kingdom of Israel in 722 and the almost total disappearance of the ten tribes as a distinct cultural and political entity; the continuation of the Davidic monarchy, the priestly cults and the prophetic tradition in Judea with its centre in Jerusalem, the ultimate destruction of this monarchy in 587; the exile of large parts of the population – especially of the leadership – to Babylon, and the first movements of dispersion to other lands, especially to Egypt.

Until this point, the story, although very dynamic and to some degree dramatic, was not unique, and the Israeli nation – the Jewish people – would have disappeared from the face of subsequent history as did so many other nations in this region at that time. But they did not disappear, and it is in this fact that they are unique. Large parts, and probably the more active leadership elements, of the population of Judea went to Babylon. Many of course remained there, but many of the exiles in Babylon kept up the dream of returning to Zion, and, after the Persian conquests of Babylon under Cyrus (550–530), and later in 525 of Egypt by Cyrus's son Cambyses, they – or rather some of them – started to return to Eretz Israel and joined those who remained there in a state of decline. They came here first as rather small dispersed groups; then under the vigorous leadership of Ezra and Nehemia they re-established and reconstructed their religious and communal-political institutions, rebuilt the Temple and forged a new national identity (yet one based on continuous reference to the former period and its symbols) and new political organizations. From this a new independent political entity emerged after the Hasmonean revolt. The external story of this period is very well known and needs no more than a brief recapitulation.

With the fall of the Persian Empire in 330 BCE and the rise of the Hellenistic monarchies in the Middle East, there developed a much stronger confrontation of the Jewish people with the new expanding civilizations. The Jewish communities in general, and that in Eretz Israel in particular, became increasingly entangled in the political struggles of the region. At the same time

Jewish settlement expanded beyond the Temple City State of Jerusalem, with the consequent possibility of confrontation between the Jews and the Hellenistic – and later also Roman – rulers.

This culminated in the first dramatic encounter in the second century BCE with the Seleucid King Antiochus IV, giving rise to the Hasmonean (Maccabean) revolt and to the rise of the Hasmonean theocratic monarchy in which the office of High Priest and ruler (ethnarch-Nasi) were combined. This dynasty lasted till about the middle of the first century BCE. It was characterized, especially during the reign of Alexander Iannai (Ianneas) (103–76 BCE) and his successors, by a policy of far-reaching expansion, bringing the Jews into continuous encounter with both various local populations and the 'super powers'. During Alexander Iannai's reign there broke out an intensive civil war led against him by groups of the Pharisees. After his death Judea became strongly entangled in the Roman expansion in the Near East and in Roman–Parthian wars. The end of the Hasmonean dynasty came about 37 BCE, when Herod, the son of the Edomite adviser to Hyrcanos, Alexander's son, was declared King of Judea by the Romans and reigned till 4 BCE as a Roman client – and as a secular king.

Under Herod's successor the Kingdom was divided between his three sons, and in year 6 of the Christian era (CE) the Roman government assumed direct rule in Judea – a fact even welcomed by those more religious sectors of the Jewish population who strongly opposed the reign of a non-Jewish king. This direct subjugation to the Romans was interrupted under the brief reign of Herod's grandson Agrippa (41–4 CE), a friend of the Roman Emperor Caligula, who attempted to re-establish some sort of a unified Jewish monarchy and was on the whole accepted by most sectors of the Jewish population. But with his death there developed a continuously growing tension between the Roman procurators and the Jewish people, as well as increasing division within the latter, giving rise to the great war or rebellion against the Romans (66–7 CE), the destruction of the Temple in 70 CE and loss of political autonomy, and the move of the Sanhedrin under the leadership of Rabbi Yohanan Ben-Zakai – the leader of the Pharisees – to Yavneh.

## Cultural activity

But the period of the Second Temple did not only see the emergence and crystallization of a new independent political entity. It was also a period of great cultural transformations.

The Prophets, so predominant in the period of the First Temple, gradually disappeared; the priests, at least in the beginning of this period, became much more predominant; kings from priestly families emerged and also, perhaps most important, some entirely new types of leadership, based to a large degree on new traditions of learning as well as a multiplicity of sects.

There were the first encounters with mighty pagan Empires and a multiplicity of pagan nations, and also with a new type of civilization – the Hellenistic

– and with the Hellenistic and Roman Empires whose claims to some universal validity were rooted not just in conquest or in the mightiness of their gods but in their philosophical and legal tradition.

At the same time there was great internal cultural creativity, giving rise within the Jewish nation to many new religious, cultural and social visions – one of them, connected with Jesus, destined to reshape in the form of Christianity the whole course of history in the West and later on in the world.

The combination of internal and external turbulence culminated, as we have seen, in the destruction of the Second Temple in 70 CE, the loss of political independence and, ultimately, dispersion. But at the same time there emerged here a new institutional mould which evinced rather special frameworks of civilization, religion and collective identity despite loss of independence and continuous dispersion. Later on these continuous frameworks were to be confronted with Christianity, and then with Islam, as the dominant religions in most of the lands in which the Jews lived.

These developments created a situation in which the Jews were not just a national or religious minority in some 'alien' environment. They became such a minority in civilizations whose historical roots and basic premises were closely interwoven with Jewish history and faith; which not only developed historically out of the Jewish fold, but for whom continuous Jewish existence always constituted an ideological challenge and an ambivalent and negative reference point; for whom the Jews' adherence to their faith and modes of life was not just a curious and strange fact, but an ideological threat to the very legitimacy of their own civilizations.

There were two poles to the continuity of Jewish civilization: first, the development of institutional and cultural frameworks which made possible the continuity of the Jewish people and civilization in a situation of dispersion of Jews in many lands; and secondly the strong, ambivalent attitude of the 'host' civilizations, reciprocated by a parallel ambivalent attitude among the Jews towards these civilizations. These poles shaped the course of the Jewish history of exile.

# The Problem of the Continuity of Jewish History
## The origins of Jewish civilization

How can the puzzle of such continuity be explained – if it can be explained at all? A first approach to such an explanation necessitates the analysis of the basic realities and themes of Jewish civilization to which we have referred above.

The roots of these themes and realities do, of course, lie in those situations – about which relatively little is known – in which the Israeli tribes started to differentiate themselves from the other nations in the Near and Middle East. It was not, of course, the fact of such distinctiveness or differentiation that is unique. There was an abundance of distinct tribes or nations in that period in the Near East, each with different language and customs, worshipping different gods and organized in different political structures. The Bible is full of reference to them – be they the Aramites, the Moabites, the Philistines, the Assyrians or Babylonians, or many others.

Many of them, especially the Assyrians or Babylonians – and of course the Egyptians – were mighty Empires, but they did not create the type of civilizational, cultural distinctiveness – and continuity – that the Jewish people did. Thus it is not the mere distinctiveness of the Jewish people, but the nature of such distinctiveness and of its continuity that is of crucial importance – and which constitutes the unique quality of Jewish civilization.

This differentiation was based on a combination of some special character- istics of social structure, religious beliefs, cultural orientation, civilizational framework and symbols and modes of collective identity.

Thus, first of all, this distinctiveness can be seen in the basic characteristics of the social structure and organization of the Israeli tribes – some aspects of which seemed to persist throughout Jewish history, and which were first evident in the special pattern of the decomposition of relatively closed and semi-egalitarian tribal units. The settlement of the people of Israel in Israel was connected – as were many parallel processes among other peoples and in other parts of the world – with the breaking up of the relatively closed tribal, and to some degree territorial, communities. But this process was characterized in ancient Israel by several specific features.

One such feature was the great structural heterogeneity of the different tribal, local and socio-economic groups that coexisted here within some common frameworks. They were composed of peasants, nomads and urban dwellers. Among these different groups there developed continuous en- counters in the same or in ecologically mutually impinging settings and there took place also, within such settings, a continuous process of social differenti- ation and concomitant tensions between all these various groups. A second feature of the breaking up of the tribal communities was the fact that there developed between these various groups some common bonds – especially that of a common national or religious identity – the symbols and loci of which were not entirely embedded within any one of the local or tribal groups. Third, these common bonds were not organized within any clear-cut, fully organized political or religious framework, and were not located in any fixed centre. Indeed their most important symbol was the Ark which was, during the period of the Judges, constantly on the move. Until the establishment of the monarchy, and to some degree even afterwards, there was lacking any continuous, single organizational or even symbolic focus for such common orientations.

Finally, there was the absence of compact political boundaries and the volatile micro- and macro-political ecological settings. The micro-setting was, of course, that of Palestine itself, of repeated encounters with other settled and migratory peoples; the macro-setting was that of Palestine at the crossroads of great empires of antiquity. The net results of this volatility were the continuous fluidity and openness of political boundaries; the constant flow and mobility of people; and difficulties in the maintenance of a stable, compact political entity and even of a distinct cultural identity.

## Cultural and religious orientations

Closely related to these social conditions or characteristics was the unique complex of religious orientations and cultural moulds that developed in Ancient Israel. Of special importance was, of course, the development of the monotheistic creed – the new conception of God, the specific religious, cultic and legal frameworks that developed in connection with this conception and the combination of all these with the self-definition of the Jewish nation, with the crystallization of Jewish collective identity.

Within Ancient Israel there developed a multiplicity of modes of cultural and religious orientations, activities and organizations – such as various cultic ritual prescriptions, the strong emphasis on legal rules and codices and on ethical injunctions. Each of these cultural and religious orientations could probably be found among many of the neighbouring peoples, but the way in which they became combined in ancient Israel was probably unique. This combination was connected to the conception of one God – in the beginning probably a tribal or national God – of a type which initially could probably also be found in many other civilizations, but which among Israeli tribes became transformed into a more dynamic conception of a trans-national and ultimately transcendental God – giving rise to the first full monotheistic religion.

This conception of a transcendental God, of a God who is beyond the world, who has created it and commands it, connected with a conception of a basic tension or chasm between the transcendental and the mundane order, differed greatly from the perception of the nature of deities that was prevalent among the neighbouring pagan nations and against which it was strongly orientated. This conception had several far-reaching institutional implications – implications which have had a profound impact on the course not only of Jewish but of world history.

It gave rise to attempts to reconstruct the mundane world – human personality, the socio-political and economic orders – according to the basic conceptions of the proper relations between God and His people of Israel, between God and man.

One focus of such restructuring was that of the relation between the political and the higher, transcendental order. The political order – as the central locus of the mundane order – was conceived of as lower than the transcendental one and accordingly had to be restructured according to the precepts of the latter, according to the basic religious conceptions, and it was the rulers who were usually held to be responsible for assuming such structuring of the political order.

Thus there emerged the conception of the accountability of the rulers and of the community to a higher authority – God, Divine Law and the like.

The second focus of such attempts at restructuring the world was the development or construction of new types of 'cultural' or 'religious' collect- ivities – as distinct from ethnic or political ones. While some embryonic elements of such construction existed in many of the neighbouring societies and probably in those tribes from which the Israeli ones developed, it was only with the development and institutionalization of the new religious conceptions that those elements became transformed into a new, potentially fully-fledged civilizational collectivity or framework – that of the people of Israel, later on of the Jewish nation – with autonomous criteria of membership, channels of recruitment and loci of authority.

The membership in this collectivity tends to become imbued with a strong ideological dimension and becomes a focus of ideological contention and struggle. Such struggle, carried by the different elites and sub-elites, focused around the definition of the boundaries of these collectivities, of who is inside and who is outside, as well as around the relation between these collectivities and the 'older' political, ethnic–primordial ones.

Third, and closely related to the construction of such collectivity, there developed a tendency towards the structuring of autonomous societal centres, conceived as the major loci or embodiments of the charismatic transcendental vision and of the attempts to reconstruct the world. The development of such distinctiveness and symbolic differentiation of the centre gave rise to the tendency of such a centre to permeate the periphery, to restructure it according to the visions prevalent in the centre, and it was thus natural that the struggle among various elites for predominance in the centre, and for the consequent mode of shaping of the social order, became one of the most fundamental aspects of this civilization.

## *Visions of civilization*

Many of these institutional features and dynamics were not, in their most general characteristics, unique to Ancient Israel – although it was probably there, as well as in a different way in Ancient Greece, that they first developed institutional orientations and implications. The attempts to reconstruct the mundane world according to a transcendental vision, the development of a conception of the accountability of rulers, the construction of specific civilizational frameworks and new types of societal centres were, in their broad outlines, common to all those civilizations which the German philosopher Karl Jaspers called the Axial Age civilizations. These were those civilizations within which there emerged and became institutionalized in the first millennium, and in the beginning of the Christian era, conceptions of a basic tension between the transcendental and the mundane orders. The most important of these civilizations – often also called the Great Civilizations – were Ancient Israel, and later on in Christianity, Ancient Greece, to a certain extent Zoroastrian- ism in Persia, China in the early Imperial period, Hinduism and Buddhism and, much later, beyond the Axial Age proper, Islam.

These transcendental visions and attempts at the restructuring of the world were carried in all these civilizations by a relatively new social element – namely by autonomous cultural elites, autonomous intellectuals. These elites differed greatly from their 'ancestors' (the specialists in various technical, ritual, magical and sacral activities of the pre-Axial Age civilizations which, of course, abounded in the pagan nations in the Near East and in sectors of Ancient Israel society) and it was against them that the wrath of prophets and some of the more autonomous priests was directed.

The new transcendental orientations which they articulated transformed such specialized technical activities into attempts at a relatively autonomous construction of the cultural and social order. At the same time these elites became more autonomous and independent, recruited and legitimated in terms of distinct autonomous criteria and channels different from those of the basic ascriptive units, and they tended to become potentially independent of other elites and social groups and categories – but necessarily in strong competition with them.

Such competition between the different elites became very intensive in these civilizations because, with the institutionalization of such transcendental conceptions, a parallel transformation took place in the structure of other elites – be they political, military, educational or in some cases economic. These various elites also tended to see themselves as performing not only specific technical, functional activities, but as being potentially autonomous carriers of the models of distinct cultural and social order closely related to the transcendental vision prevalent in their respective societies – and accordingly there tended to develop a strong competition between them and the more specifically religious or cultural elites.

Moreover, within these societies, the elites themselves were not homo-geneous. There developed a multiplicity of secondary elites – cultural, political or educational – each often carrying a different transcendental vision and a different conception of the cultural and social order.

It was these various competing elites in general, and the new types of cultural and political elites in particular, that were the most active in the attempts to restructure the world – and such restructuring involved, in all Axial Age civilizations, at least three crucial dimensions or aspects: the restructuring of personality, of collectivities and of institutional formations.

# The Specific Characteristics of Jewish Civilization
## *Religious beliefs*

But while these processes were common to all the Axial Age civilizations, their concrete contents varied greatly between these different civilizations. They varied, above all, first of all with respect to the specific conception of the transcendental world and of its relation to the mundane world that developed in each of them, and second – and in close relation to them – according to the composition, structure and organization of the carriers of this conception: the major autonomous elites.

The conception of tension between the transcendental and the mundane world and of its possible resolutions that developed in Ancient Israel was focused around four central poles: first, around the conception, as we have seen, of a transcendental, universal God; second, around covenantal, semi-contractual relations between Him and His chosen people of Israel; third, around the combination in these covenantal relations of ethical, legal and cultic elements; and, fourth, around the infusion of a strong historical consciousness in the definition of these relations and consequently in the self-identity of the people of Israel, of the Jewish people.

Thus, out of the various nations of the Middle East, in Ancient Israel there developed the conception not of a 'particularistic' tribal deity but rather of a universal God, independent of any particular tribe or nation, who is not immanent in the world, but beyond it and is its Creator, with claims to rule over all the nations.

Second there developed a very strong emphasis, a covenantal, semi-contractual conception of the relationship between God and the tribes of Israel, the people of Israel; of the covenant with God as being the central focus of the tribal confederation; of the very construction of the Israeli tribes as a specific, distinct nation, as God's chosen people.

This covenant between God and the people of Israel established a semi-contractual relation between them, based on God's selecting of His free will the people of Israel as His chosen people – but contingent on their acceptance of His commandments. This covenantal relation made the people of Israel not just a passive object of God's will, but also an active, responsible agent in shaping its destiny, one who was responsible before God, but who seemingly could also make demands on God.

This 'covenantal' relation with God started, according to accepted tradition, with the Patriarchs, with God's covenant with Abraham, but its full impact in the shaping of the Israeli nation took place with the exodus from Egypt and the – reluctant – acceptance of the Ten Commandments and the Torah by the tribes of Israel.

It was this event which, according to the accepted tradition, created the Israeli nation, hence establishing its identity in a combination of primordial, religious and historical terms. It imbued Jewish collective self-identity with a very strong combination of universal religious and collective historical consciousness – best epitomized in the conjunction, in later Hewbrew prayers, of *Zecher LeMaaseh Bereshit* (the memory of Creation) and of *Zecher Le'itsiat Mitzraim* (the Exodus from Egypt).

The combination of this specific type of monotheistic religion with the covenantal dimension transformed various cultic traditions, legal precepts and ethical commandments from traditional customs into the commandments of God to His chosen people. These commandments showed how the world had to be restructured and denoted also the distinctiveness of this chosen people – giving rise to a great emphasis on the legal sphere or dimension, on the elaboration of the legal codices as one of the major expressions of the will of God, of His commandments to the people of Israel.

These legal codices of the Pentateuch were fully developed and codified only in the period of the Second Commonwealth. Many nuclei of these full codifications – such as probably the 'Torah of Moses', the presumable core of Deuteronomy, found during the reign of Josiah (640–609 BCE) and constituting the pivot of religious reforms and of centralization of the cult in Jerusalem – were, however, of much earlier provenance. They were all characterized by an unusual combination of civil, communal and cultic law and calendaric prescriptions; of religious and ethical commandments together with civil laws, with a very strong emphasis on social legislation – like the laws of the Sabbath, of *Shmita* (the seventh year) in which all debts are to be cancelled and of special attitudes to the non-Jews. These laws were given a principled religious and ethical connotation; and they were more and more open to the public and not confined to small esoteric groups of priests.

The combination of all these elements was most fully epitomized in the figure of Moses – the great prophet–legislator and the great formulator of the Covenant between God and the people of Israel.

It is of course a moot question when these basic conceptions and orientations developed and became fully institutionalized, and to what degree they were widespread and accepted by the different sectors of the Israeli tribes. Whatever the answers to these questions – and historians will probably discuss them forever – it is such crystallization that created the distinctive cultural identity of the Israeli nation, of the Jewish people.

## The structure of elites

These specific conceptions which developed in Ancient Israel were articulated, as indicated above, by the various autonomous elites which were most predominant in these societies and which indeed also evinced some specific characteristics.

Thus first of all there developed a multiplicity of specific types of autonomous elites, of different carriers of these major cultural orientations. The most important among them were the priests, the prophets and the different representatives of the community, such as the elders, the carriers and later on the rulers – the judges, the kings – who also attempted to play this role. They all saw themselves as carriers of the visions, the monotheistic vision and the covenant between God and His People – and between them there developed a continuous competition and a variety of different coalitions.

Three aspects of these elites are of special importance for the understanding of the institutional dynamics of Israeli society. First there is their multiplicity, heterogeneity and volatility. Second is the fact that they were not embedded in the various ascriptive tribal or territorial units, but were symbolically and organizationally autonomous, being recruited and defined by themselves –

even if, as in the case of the priests, in ascriptive hereditary terms – legitimized in autonomous terms as representing visions and values which were not part of the primordial symbols of the local or tribal groups but which were yet accepted among these groups. Third there is the fact that these elites which were the major carriers of the common political, national and religious bonds seemed to cut across the tribes and be, at least potentially, common to all or at least to several of them.

## Political characteristics

The combination of the special characteristics of these elites and of the special religious – monotheistic – conceptions carried by them, in conjunction with the basic characteristics of the social structure of Ancient Israel and its geopolitical situation, shaped a number of unique characteristics of the Israelite institutional structure. They shaped some of its basic political and institutional orientations and characteristics, above all some of the basic characteristics of the centres, that developed within these civilizations and out of which some of its fundamental continuous problems developed.

Thus first of all, in close relation to the basic monotheistic and covenantal orientation, and to the structure of elites, there developed in Ancient Israel several themes of political culture, many of which were to become constant features of Jewish political and communal life.

The first such major political conception, derived from the combination of the monotheistic faith and the 'covenantal' dimension, was the accountability of the ruler to a Higher Law, and also (often against the wish and obvious interests of the rulers) to the various groups – the priests, prophets and leaders of the community – which saw themselves representing and interpreting such Law.

Second, in close relation to the covenantal emphasis, there developed a strong emphasis on the potential free access of all members of the community to the central sacred sphere, and of their participation in this sphere against some of the tendencies and claims of the priests, and later on the kings, to monopolize it in their own hands and to be the sole mediators of such access. Although the latter were, of course, predominant in the period of the First Temple and were reinforced by the ascriptive emphasis of the Davidic monarchy, the stress on such direct, unmediated access to the sacred sphere was upheld by other elites – especially the leaders of the community of tribes or of different territorial groupings – and by the prophets.

The combination of the emphasis on the accountability of rulers to the Higher Law and of the open access of all members of the community gave rise to a strong tendency to a certain lack of automatic acceptance of any 'earthly' authority (best seen in Samuel's famous speech against the establishment of a monarchy). It also gave rise to a very intensive political struggle between various sectors and elites who saw themselves as the true representatives of the Higher, Godly, authority; and to a very strong ideological dimension of this struggle – focused around the structuring of the community boundaries and the interpretations of tradition, of the Higher Law.

## Political and religious centres

These political orientations, combined with the structure of the major elites and the geopolitical situation, shaped some of the basic characteristics of Israeli centres and collective boundaries.

The characteristics of the Israeli religious cultic and political centres were most clearly evident in the pre-monarchic period but many of them persisted even into the period of the monarchy. Some of these characteristics could also be found in other tribal federations in the Near East or Africa, but some were specific to the Israelite situation and it is these that are most important for our analysis.

The first such characteristic was that almost all such centres – political, tribal, cultic – constituted, especially before the era of the monarchy but to some degree even during that era (especially in the Kingdom of Israel), within their broader setting, structural enclaves which were often short-lived and did not develop into permanent, distinct ecological communities with continuous populations and identities of their own.

Second, there was a relative multiplicity of such centres. Even when these centres became more unified under the monarchy – especially the Davidic one – they were always composed of several social elements which rarely coexisted peacefully or merged into relatively homogeneous groups or ruling elites. One such element consisted of representatives of the various tribal or kinship units within the more central organizations; a second one consisted of the various special political and/or religious elites which were somewhat separated from the tribal units and recruited on the basis of different criteria. Between these different elites, which were active in these centres or in sub-centres which continued to exist, there developed continuous tensions and conflicts.

In fact, no fully cohesive ruling class developed; rather, what we find were some embryonic components of such a ruling class which probably only in the periods of consolidation of the monarchy crystallized into a fairly cohesive group, but even then many of the other social elements mentioned above maintained their distinctiveness and relative autonomy.

## Symbols of collectivity –
## religious, national and primordial

It was also in the context of the basic monotheistic and covenantal conceptions, and the structure of these elites, that there developed in Ancient Israel the specific Jewish solution to the problem of the construction of the boundaries of the new civilizational collectivity, and of the relations between its symbols and the more primordial ones of the ethnic and the political collectivities.

The specific Jewish solution of this problem apparently emerged at the very beginning of what became Jewish history, at the start of those processes which transformed the history of different Israeli tribes into the beginnings of Jewish history. This solution was characterized, in marked contrast to what later evolved in other Axial Age civilizations (but interestingly enough, not dissimilar from the Chinese case), by a very positive evaluation in terms of universal religious orientations of the primordial, i.e. 'ethnic', 'national' as well as political symbols. The former were continuously incorporated into the latter, giving rise to continual interweaving of these different symbols – the God, Creator of the Universe, being also the God of Abraham, Isaac and Jacob and the God who had taken the children of Israel out of Egypt. Each of these types of symbols, while not losing their own autonomy, was defined in terms of each other, thus – unlike, however, in the Chinese case – giving rise to continuous tension between them with respect to the concrete manifestations of each and their relative importance.

From the beginning of Jewish history, the structuring of the symbolic boundaries of the Jewish collective identity constituted, probably in close relation to the fragility and volatility of the geopolitical boundaries, a constant and central focus of concern of the major elites of Ancient Israel – and later on of the various elites of the Jewish people throughout their history.

These various components of collective identity combined in different ways with the different religious orientations – the cultic, legal or prophetical–ethical. Different combinations of various religious 'contents' and of different components of the collective identity were continuously articulated by the different religious and political elites mentioned above, giving rise to tension between them.

Thus the cultic elements and the ethnic and primordial identity were probably more emphasized by the local priests and heads of the tribes; but the legal-religious aspects and the historical-national components of the collective identity were probably more heavily stressed by the higher and central priestly groups and some of the monarchic elites, and the religious-ethical and social components of the religious and more universalistic orientations by some of the prophets. But there always existed quite a far-reaching overlap between these various elites which formed different coalitions and which exhibited the different orientations.

But, whatever the differences between them, these tensions were always worked out in the context of attempts to define the symbolic institutional boundaries of the Jewish nation in relation to other nations and to demarcate the parameters of collective identity in terms of its various components and of the basic religious orientations.

This tendency towards the demarcation of the boundaries of the collectivity was accompanied by a strongly ambivalent attitude towards other nations and cultures. Such an attitude was rooted in Judaism's claim to universalism, in the fact that it was the first monotheistic religion, in its attempts to separate itself from its neighbouring pagan nations by claiming to transcend in universal terms their particularistic religious symbols, and in its consequent unfriendly contacts with them.

This ambivalent attitude was, of course, reinforced by the international situation in which the Jews lived and in which other peoples were militarily and politically predominant and culturally attractive. This situation made it more difficult for the Jewish people to maintain, in an environment defined by them as ideologically alien, their political and cultural identity and universalistic orientations. They probably felt they were more exposed than their contemporaries to the possibility of collective dissolution – or at least were more conscious of such a possibility – and the attempts to counteract such a possibility became a major ideological concern of its leaders.

Because of these factors, a continuous tension between the universalistic dimensions of the religious orientation and the particularism of a primordial national community, which defined itself by differentiating itself ideologically and symbolically from its neighbours through the combination of religious and primordial symbols, was incorporated into the construction of Jewish identity from the beginning of Jewish history.

## Conclusions – the basic features of Israeli civilization

It was these basic religious beliefs, cultural and political orientations, and conceptions and characteristics of elites, which emerged in Ancient Israel and in the period of the First Temple, that have shaped the specific contours of Jewish civilization and have also facilitated the development of the unique continuity that has been characteristic of this civilization.

The most important of these beliefs and orientations was, as we have seen, that of the covenant between God and the people of Israel, a semi-contractual relation between them based on God's selecting of His free will the people of Israel as His chosen people – but contingent on their acceptance of His commandments.

Second, there was the emphasis on potential access of all members of the community to the realm of the sacred and the conception of accountability of rulers and of the community to a higher authority – God, Divine Law or the like – and to the emergence of earthly concrete autonomous social groups or categories which represented, as it were, such higher authority, and between which there developed a continuous competition and a variety of different coalitions.

Third, there developed here a continuous tension between cultic and ethical-religious conceptions and a strong emphasis on the legal tradition as combining these different elements.

Fourth, there developed the conflict between the universalistic ethical and particularistic primordial orientations in the construction of Jewish identity, and the continuous combination and tension between political, ethnic, national and religious elements in the construction of such identity and an ambivalent attitude to neighbouring nations.

These general orientations were articulated by elites which developed some very specific characteristics which, in their general form, have persisted – as did those orientations – throughout Jewish history. First of all there developed a multiplicity of autonomous elites in general and of carriers of models of cultural and social order in particular, and their very strong orientation to the mundane – especially political and social – fields. Second, these elites combined political and political–social–religious functions and orientations; even when they specialized in one, they maintained very strong orientations to the others. Third, although they generally had no permanent single centre or organization, they maintained some identity and continuity of orientations and of networks and they continuously emerged anew, even if in changed organizational constellations. Fourth, within all these elite groups, such as the priests or the prophets, there developed great heterogeneity. Between these elites and sub-elites there developed conflicts and tensions connected not only with the representation of different specific interests but also with different interpretations of the tradition, different emphases on its major components – the cultic, legal, ethical. Fifth, they all competed to be accepted as the representatives of the higher authority to which rulers and the community have to be accountable.

It was out of the combination of these structural elements and religious–ideological orientations that there developed some of the major structural-institutional characteristics of the Jewish people and civilization – mainly structural heterogeneity; continuous differentiation and conflict among various social groups within a framework of common but not fully fixed and crystallized boundaries; the volatility and heterogeneity of centres; multiple – political, social and religious – elites; the concomitant restructuring of common bonds between the leaders and the people, often leading to diverse social movements.

The concrete characteristics of these various elites – the political, social or religious ones – varied of course greatly in different periods: between the period of the judges and that of the monarchy; between these earlier periods and that of the Second Commonwealth, and between all these and the period of exile and dispersion. But the basic structural characteristics indicated above continued throughout Jewish history.

It was indeed these characteristics, orientations and social elements that provided the setting for the constant restructuring – usually through incorporation of the older symbols within the new ones – of the contents of this civilization and of Jewish collective identity, and that made it possible to maintain its continuity.

# CHAPTER 2
# The Second Commonwealth

## Introduction – Changing Conditions
### *The development of a Jewish identity*

The basic themes and characteristics of the Jewish civilization analysed above developed and became even more fully articulated in the period of the Second Temple.

Indeed it has sometimes been claimed that it was only during this period that Jewish civilization proper – as distinct from Ancient Israel – crystallized. This exaggerated claim contains two kernels of truth. The first lies in the fact, already mentioned above, that in this period the Jewish people and civilization encountered not only mighty pagan Empires and a multiplicity of pagan nations, but also a new type of civilization – the Hellenistic – and a new type of Empire – the Roman one. These civilizations and Empires were already based on claims to some universal validity – claims rooted not just in conquest or in the mightiness of their gods but on their philosophical and legal tradition and orientations – and it was only through such encounter that the self-consciousness of Jewish people as carriers of a distinct civilization became fully crystallized.

The second kernel of truth lies in the fact that only in this period did there develop a new elite element and new institutional moulds, destined to shape the further course of Jewish history yet continuously referring back to the earlier symbols and traditions. These new moulds developed from the combination of new types of leaderships and social structure, the new ecological setting of the Jewish people – above all the emergence of the Diaspora – and new religious and cultural orientations, all of which continued, even if in different ways, throughout subsequent Jewish history.

## *New elites and geopolitical conditions*

Let's start with the analysis of the new types of social structure, leadership and elites.

There were first of all changes in the composition of the major elites. The Davidic monarchy disappeared; in its place there emerged new types of political leadership, composed of communal, although no longer tribal, leaders – the 'elders' of the community and perhaps the members of the Great Assembly – and also of high priests and the new monarchs. So there were two contradictory tendencies: semi-theocratic priest–rulers on the one hand, and – even more prevalent – a new type of secular kingship or overlordship on the other.

Concomitantly the status of the priesthood was elevated; at least in the beginning of this period, the priests become the most easily identified carriers of national and religious continuity, the keepers of the central focus and symbol of this continuity, namely the Temple and its rituals. The rise in their status was evident in the possibility, mentioned above, of the development of a combined kingship and high priesthood, which, as we have seen, took place under the Hasmoneans – a situation unthinkable in the period of the First Temple. At the same time, within the priesthood itself, different factions and trends developed and became very pronounced. The contrast was especially strong between on the one hand the original High Priesthood in Jerusalem and on the other hand the dispersed, local priests who were probably more connected with various popular strata, and of which the Hasmoneans were probably the most prominent illustration, as well as the secondary or lower echelons among the central priesthood.

This multiplicity of elites – political, cultural and religious – opened up possibilities for new types of political linkages between the political elites and the broader strata, and also for a new type of leadership. This did not consist of priests or kings; nor of 'simple' representatives of the community, nor of charismatic prophets. Its major constituents were the *sophrim* (scribes), the so-called members of the Great Assembly – the exact identity of whom is not well known – and the leaders of a great variety of religious–political sects or movements. The best known of these have been the Pharisees – who, in combination with some of the scribes, were the possible predecessors of the later 'rabbinical' Sages. This development was connected with the concomitant one of numerous semi-heterodox sects.

This new type of leadership and elites probably had antecedents in some of the priestly or scribal sectors in the period of the First Temple. In that period however they were, on the whole, embedded in the more ascriptive groups (as tribal or local communities) and were secondary to the kings, the central priesthood and the prophets. With the return from Babylon, and possibly already in Babylon itself, these new elites became the most active and innovative although they were certainly not the only ones. It was these different types of elites that emerged as the new representatives of the highest authority, the Higher Law to which the rulers and the community were accountable. They were not, however, as the latter historical interpretation based on rabbinical literature suggests, homogeneous. Rather they consisted, probably for a very long time, of quite numerous, sometimes distinct sometimes overlapping, but very volatile elements, continuously evolving, modifying and interacting in various tensions or coalitions with one another and with the more priestly and political elites. Yet, whatever the differences among them, these new elites shared several characteristics.

First of all they were recruited according to criteria which were in principle open to all. Second, many of them were intellectuals, but not purely 'academic' ones; they perceived themselves as articulating basic models of the social cultural order of the Higher Law and hence were intensively involved in political life, whether in the judicial halls of the Sanhedrin, in their own centres of learning and judicial institutions, or in coalition with other more popular groups and leaders more concerned with communal prayer.

It was these elites – or at least some elements among them – that most fully developed the sphere of the Law, as the central focus of Jewish civilization.

It was these elites that started on the work of the codification of the biblical canon – starting probably already in the first periods of the Second Temple with the codification of the Pentateuch, continuing up till around the second century of the Christian era, bringing together the 'Old Testament' and the Apocalypse. This codification was in itself a long and controversial process – attesting to the heterogeneity of groups of elites and sects.

It was also these elites that gradually developed nuclei of new institutions: the centres of prayer beyond the Temple itself – the later synagogues, which could in principle be established anywhere – the various centres of learning, and later on communal courts. These were all destined to be central institutions in the perpetuation of the Jewish civilization.

## The Diaspora

Another crucial structural development in the post-exilic period was the appearance of Diaspora as a constant feature of Jewish existence, giving rise to the emergence of a multiplicity of centres, or, to use Shmariahu Talmon's expression, to a multi-centric situation, adding a new dimension to the heterogeneity of the structural elements in Jewish life and to the volatility of the geographical or geopolitical situation of the Jewish people.

The Diaspora – above all in Egypt, Babylon and Syria, later also in other provinces of the Roman Empire and in Rome itself – developed, of course, continuous relations and contacts with the centre in Palestine and with Jerusalem in particular. The contacts were above all ritual and religious ones, in the form of payment of the shekel and pilgrimages to Palestine, and contacts between the different groups of scholars, sects and priests in Palestine and the Diaspora, and there were also manifold political contacts. Yet, however close these relations were, the communities in the Diaspora were never fully subjugated to the centre in Palestine, not only in the purely political but also in the religious-national sense.

The establishment of the Diaspora attested, of course, to the continuous expansion of the Jewish people and of the Jewish civilization and it was very often connected with strong proselytizing movements and tendencies; at the same time it necessarily sharpened the problems of confrontation with other peoples, civilizations and religions.

The continuous existence of the communities of the Diaspora added a new element to the volatility of the geopolitical situation of the Jewish people which became, in this period, even more pronounced in Palestine itself. The ultimate disappearance of political independence gave rise to a lack of demarcated political boundaries for the Jews and hastened the crystallization of those aspects of the relations between the Jews and their neighbours which led Max Weber to characterize them as pariah people, that is as characterized by ritually fixed social exclusion and by special social and economic placement and low esteem.

Naturally enough within these communities those aspects of the Jewish tradition – whether of learning and prayer, of observance, of ritual perception or of philosophical meditation and study – which were not directly and continuously connected with the cultic observance in the Temple or with independent political activities became most predominant. In the lands of the Diaspora the synagogue, communal organizations, and family networks became the major institutional framework of the Jewish people.

Meanwhile, in the great Jewish concentrations in the Hellenistic–Egyptian Diaspora there developed a growing Jewish philosophical and historical literature written in Greek. The most famous of these philosophers was probably Philo of Alexandria, who lived in the second half of the first century BCE. At the same time the Bible itself was translated into Greek – the famous Septuagint – giving rise to the custom of it being read in the synagogue in Greek.

## New Outlooks and Movements
### Religious and cultural orientations

In close relation to these new elements of leadership, geopolitical conditions and, above all, the encounter with the new Great Civilizations and Empires, there were also in the period of the Second Commonwealth several new movements – religious, cultural, ideological and institutional – all rooted in those of the former period, but going beyond it.

One such movement, with only indirect institutional implications, was in the field of philosophy and ethics – emphasizing the development of philosophical and ethical considerations and themes as a distinct part of the tradition. It was articulated mostly by relatively small, probably mostly aristocratic and priestly, groups – particularly the Saducees, who were strongly influenced by the Hellenistic civilization, and groups in the Diaspora. This orientation found its fullest expression in books like that of Proverbs, but above all in books not incorporated in the biblical codex, like the book of Ben Sirah or the Wisdom of Solomon, the roots of which can probably be found in the Ancient Near East but which were more fully elaborated, with strong philosophical orientations, through the encounter with Hellenism.

Second was the systematization and elaboration of the prophetic tradition with the addition of relatively strong eschatological elements. This development gave rise to individual, prophetic visions and/or to far-reaching attempts at total organization of community life. It was manifested, in literary terms, in the various eschatological visions – some of which, like the book of Daniel, were later incorporated into the biblical canon, while others, like the books of the visions of Baruch Chanoch or Ezra, remained outside.

Some variants of these orientations were adopted but only within some of the sects, like the Essenes and, especially, the various sects of the Judean desert about which so much new information has been obtained through the discovery of the Dead Sea Scrolls.

The third major cultural–religious orientation was focused on the continuous elaboration of the field of legal study, exegesis and codification – as against the ascriptive authority of priests, rulers and the charismatic one of the prophets.

Indeed the very attempts at the codification of the canon – including the prophetic canon – revealed the ambivalent attitude of these elites to the prophetic tradition. On the one hand they fully accepted the tradition, incorporated it into their own learning and to no small degree justified themselves in its terms. On the other hand they rejected in principle the possibility of further individual prophecy as representing the word of God – claiming that it was only the collegial authority of the learned that could constitute the legitimate interpretation of this word.

Fourth was a growing emphasis on individual or communal prayer as a basic mode of religious experience and of participation in the sacred realm.

## Institutional and ideological changes

The rise of the new elites and the new cultural developments were closely related to the formation of several changes in the basic premisses of institutional life.

First of all participation in the central sacred sphere was opened more and more to all members of the community. With the growing stress on potentially free access to the central sacred sphere – and hence to the loci of authority – for all members of the community there developed, as has been strongly stressed by the late Professor Itzhak Baer, the conception of the 'holy community' as a constituent element of the collective religious-political identity.

The second such ideological–institutional change was the concomitant weakening, although not the full obliteration, of the monopoly of access to attributes of sacredness that had been held by ascriptive groups, priests and sometimes kings, as well as paradoxically enough by the more individual and charismatic elements such as the prophets.

Thirdly, new criteria for leadership and membership of the elite were articulated and gradually intensified. These criteria constituted, on the one hand, strong elitist orientations based on the learning of the law and, on the other hand, a broad popular base, emphasizing prayer, observation of the rules and membership in the holy community.

Fourthly, the channels of mobility into the upper religious and civic positions and into political leadership were, in principle, opened to all members of the community.

Fifthly, and in close relation to the former, there was fuller acceptance of the idea of the accountability of rulers to a Higher Law – albeit connected with strong competition among different elites as well as the broader community as to who was the true representative of this higher authority.

At the same time, as we shall see in greater detail later on, there developed among the Jewish people a much stronger collective self-consciousness, as well as a new religious motive – that of *Kiddush Hashem* (martyrdom). This motive probably started to develop in connection with the Hasmonean revolt, gathered momentum with the persecutions by the Romans, and became most fully elaborated in the exilic period.

## Attitudes to the economy

Out of the continuous interplay between the activities of the new elites and groups, the new geopolitical situation and the new cultural movements, there began to emerge during the period of the Second Temple several basic civilizational trends and ideological–institutional premises, a certain attitude to the restructuring of the world and a certain religious evaluation of the mundane worlds.

These trends and premises entailed a generally positive attitude to mundane life, and it was the political and communal aspects of social life and organization that became the focus of religious developments, not unlike those attributed by Herbert Luethy and Michael Walzer to Protestantism. Yet – with the exception of some of the sects – even the great emphasis on the political area was couched here in more this-worldly and communal terms than can be found in Protestantism. This is evident in the fact that the primary focus of the eschatological and apocalyptic visions was not on individual redemption and salvation but rather on collective political redemption, symbolized in the restoration of the House of David, and hence it entailed only a minimal emphasis on duality of spirit and body.

These religious ideas and attitudes entailed also a positive evaluation of economic life, but they did not entail a sanctification of economic activities as falling within the scope of individual or collective salvation.

With all its limitations, it was not – except perhaps in the first decades after the return, during the period of Persian rule – an autarchic self-enclosed economy but was naturally incorporated in many aspects within the broader economic framework. This incorporation gave rise to diversified development of large-scale latifundia, commercial centres, and increased social differentiation and tensions, all of which were probably related to the political struggle that developed within the framework of Jewish society.

The economy which developed was rather small scale, of no central importance to the economic structure of antiquity, although in its own framework it was not negligible. Moreover, on the contemporary scene, it evinced certain exceptional characteristics – especially its relatively smaller dependence on plantation slave-labour than in other parts of antiquity.

Within this relatively limited economic framework – and given the context of the economy at the time – one can identify tendencies to a limited rationalization which probably was related to the systematic organization of daily-life experience generated by the religious orientations. At the same time, the tendencies toward greater social differentiation and large-scale economy were, to some degree at least, limited by some of the communal orientations, and ultimately it was the external political circumstances that undermined many of these economic developments.

But all these economic activities were relatively limited in scope and did not constitute the central focus of the institutional derivatives of the major religious developments. That focus was located, as has been indicated above, in the socio-political arena, in the attempts to construct new types of political–communal institutions and moulds.

# The Crystallization of Different Institutional Moulds and the Conflicts and Struggles among Them
## Political and religious institutions

Out of the combination of the new elites and orientations, there took place, in this period, the development of a new institutional mould or rather of several incipient cultural–institutional moulds – between which there developed continuous struggles, carried by the various elites and their coalitions. These orientations and elites persisted throughout subsequent Jewish history and are of crucial importance for the understanding of its course.

Thus first of all and in a way most predominant, were the different attempts at the construction of some type of political–religious institutions – whether those of the semi-Hellenistic aristocratic polis, built in Jerusalem around the Temple as well as in other cities, those of the semi-theocratic community and monarchy expounded, to some degree at least, by the Hasmoneans, or those of the more secular kingships in coalition with different religious groups of Herod and his successors.

Secondly, there were the more extreme, sectarian moulds developed, as we have seen, by the various organized sects – the Essenes and many other ones documented in the rich harvest of the Dead Sea Scrolls.

Thirdly, there were the beginnings of the institutionalization of the new cultural mould of what later on would be called the *Torah Shebaalpeh* (Oral Law). This mould, articulated by the various scribes – the antecedents of later rabbis – of the various social–religious movements, especially those which were called the Pharisees, was based on a continuous elaboration and interpretation and exegesis of the texts, on the elaboration of the application of the legal–ritual sphere to all spheres of life and on an emphasis on communal prayer. The interpretation itself was based on an increasing systematization of the legal–ritual precepts according to more abstract systematic principles. It was, as we have seen, within this mould that the strong emphasis on the legal sphere, as the focus of Jewish civilization, became fully developed and elaborated – even if such legislation was focused mostly on matters of ritual observance and of what may be called civil law – with much less emphasis on communal and political matters.

This mould was based on a strong emphasis on the collective codification of the basic religious orientations, precepts and injunctions, stressing very strongly the authority of the collectivity – especially the collectivity of learned men, of the sages and of their courts – as against, as we have seen, the ascriptive authority of priests and the charismatic one of the prophets.

## Conflicts and tensions

Between these different elites (the different echelons of the priesthood, the kings, the communal leaders, the leaders of the different sects and the new elites of learning and prayer) and different coalitions (each also usually connected with different social and economic sectors and strata) there developed, as we have indicated above, a continuous struggle and competition focusing around the relative predominance of the different religious and political orientations and of their institutional implications.

The foci of this struggle were first the identification, establishment, codification of the authority of Higher Law, and the specification of the contents of such Higher Law and of its appropriate carriers; second the relations between such carriers and the political authorities, and third the establishment of the boundaries and symbols of collective identity.

The problem of the crystallization of the symbols and boundaries of collectivity did indeed constitute a central focus of these struggles. In their attempts to crystallize these boundaries the various groups of leaders continuously tried to recombine the major components of the basic cultural–religious orientations – such as ritual, legal, ethical and eschatological ones – with the religious–universal, political and primordial elements of Jewish collective identity.

At the same time they tried to restructure the relations of Israel to other nations, a process which began with the very return from Babylon, and to solve the basic dilemmas inherent in structuring of the collective identity, especially that between the universal and the particularistic elements inherent in it.

Both the particularistic and the universalistic orientations and tendencies became much more articulated at this time, especially because of the encounter with the Hellenistic and Roman civilizations, the daily reality of coming together with many nations in Eretz Israel, and the multiplicity of religious trends that developed in the Near East.

Collective segregation – especially as expounded by groups close to the Pharisees and the sects – shifted in this period, in comparison with the period of the First Temple, from an emphasis on adherence to the ceremonies of the Temple and its cult. Now the emphasis was on more dispersed cultic activities, on the monotheistic creed, on very strong limitations on inter-marriage, on calendaric observance and on legal–ritual prescriptions which were seen as binding not only on select groups of priests but ultimately on the whole community. In short the tendency was towards a very strong symbolic and institutional segregation from other nations.

This segregation entailed the continuous combination of the various symbols of primordial, ethnic, national, political and religious identity. But, because of the strong competition of other religions and of other civilizations with universalistic claims, even this solution was not purely particularistic and contained a very strong universalistic orientation. It exhibited strong tendencies to proselytization, which were often in tension with the more particularistic primordial emphases, a tension which different leaders and sects tried to resolve in different ideological and institutional ways. And yet it was probably because of this continuous tendency to the stress on these primordial elements that Judaism lost in that 'international competition'. But this loss was also largely due to the precariousness of the Jewish political situation and to political vicissitudes – and this loss certainly did not obliterate the universalistic dimension in Jewish civilization.

Other elites – the Saducees, other sectors of the elite of learning and the different political elites – developed different ideological and pragmatic solutions to these problems in both the daily encounter with other nations living in Eretz Israel, and the wider encounter with the Hellenistic and Roman civilizations.

Although there was indeed a great multiplicity of sects, groups and movements among the Jewish people in this period, it is difficult to talk about a fully-fledged orthodoxy or heterodoxy. Indeed most of the movements attempted to recombine the major components of the basic cultural–religious orientations (the ritual, legal, and eschatological), with the components of national identity (political, religious and primordial), and with some solution to the tension between the universalistic and particularistic elements in the construction of that identity.

There were only a few exceptions, and these were found in some of the small secluded communities in the Diaspora, in relatively secluded colonies like those in Elephantine, and in some groups in Palestine such as the Samaritans. However great the differences between these exceptions, their common denominator was that they abandoned some of those elements which constituted the crux of Jewish tradition. Because of this, they opted out of the common Jewish framework, and chose to close themselves within more restricted walls.

This contrasted with the other sects and movements which flowered among the Jewish population and which continuously developed and struggled within this broader common national–political–religious framework with all its diverse elements.

All these tensions gave rise to a fuller articulation of the major themes of political culture which had already developed, even if in rather embryonic form, in the late period of the Second Commonwealth, and to an intensification of political struggles. They became very strongly combined with the relations to external powers – to the Hellenistic monarchies in the earlier period and to the

Roman Empire later on – and with the attitudes to the internal political order and authority, to the kings of the Hasmonean dynasty, to Herod, and to the kings and rulers after him until the destruction of the Second Temple.

Ultimately the very intensity of this internal struggle became part of the process which led to the 'Last War' or rebellion against the Romans and the destruction of the Temple in 70 CE and the move of the Sanhedrin to Yavneh.

## Conclusion

Thus in the period of the Second Temple there emerged new patterns of religious orientations, structure of elites and institutional moulds, which were to persist throughout the course of Jewish history. These developments built on the earlier ones but restructured them in a new way – a way which shaped the whole course of subsequent Jewish history.

It was within these frameworks also that the perennial themes and tensions characteristic of Jewish history persisted and even became intensified: the tensions between universalism and particularism; between primordial, ethnic, political, ethical and religious orientations and components; between a primordial and historical identity.

It was in this period that some of the most distinctive characteristics of Jewish society – widespread adult education; the partial exclusion of women from the ritual sphere, and the kernels of the confrontation between Church and Synagogue – became crystallized.*

In this period Jewish civilization was faced with some of its great challenges – namely with the question of its ability to combine such intensive religious orientations to the socio-political sphere with the maintenance of an orderly polity, a fully-fledged and institutional order, and to maintain its broader, universalistic orientations in a situation of active competition with other civilizations.

Externally it did not succeed in facing up to these challenges, but the consciousness of these challenges did not abate. Indeed it was probably after the destruction of the Temple that such consciousness became more fully articulated. The various basic orientations and tensions inherent in the Jewish civilization were transformed by the destruction of the Second Temple and the end of the Second Commonwealth.

* I am indebted to A. Momigliano for stressing these points.

# CHAPTER 3

# Beyond the Second Commonwealth – the Exilic Period and the Predominance of the Rabbinical Mould

## Historical Background
### *General characteristics*

With the destruction of the Second Temple and the move of the Sanhedrin to Yavneh, there began a new period in Jewish history which in a sense continued until the opening of European society to the Jews at the end of the eighteenth and in the nineteenth century.

This long period was not, needless to say, homogeneous or unitary, and one can distinguish within it three major sub-periods. The first sub-period – from the destruction of the Temple to about the seventh century of the Christian era – saw the formation and efflorescence of Rabbinical Judaism. There was the codification and publication of the Mishna around 200 CE in Galilee, and of the two Talmuds, the Babylonian one *c.* 500 CE and the Jerusalem one in the early fifth century. The majority of the Jewish communities lived under the Roman and Persian Empires in Eretz Israel, Babylon, Egypt and to a smaller degree in other provinces of these Empires. The second sub-period – from about the seventh century and the rise of Islam, until about the expulsion from Spain (1492) – was that of 'classical' medieval Judaism; communities were dispersed through Christian and Muslim lands, and there was total predominance in the life of these communities of the medieval Rabbinical mould. The third sub-period is that from the expulsion from Spain until the Age of Emancipation, signalled by the French Revolution; this period marked the beginning, but only the beginning, of the crumbling of the walls of the Rabbinical mould and of the great Messianic movements, above all that of Sabbatai Zevi (1665–6), and of their manifold intellectual and institutional repercussions.

Notwithstanding the great differences between these three sub-periods – the detailed analysis of which is beyond the scope of this work – they shared some basic characteristics which are of great importance for our analysis. Throughout this long period the Jewish people lost their political independence, leading later, with the depletion of the Jewish community in Palestine, to growing dispersion and to growing political passivity and subjugation. Jews everywhere became a political minority, through special permits granted to them (which could be easily abrogated), they were communities of strangers, living by the grace of rulers who were interested in them for fiscal reasons; they were engaged mainly in various middlemen economic activities – above all they were traders, artisans, financiers – and only to a much smaller degree in agriculture; they had relatively circumscribed legal and economic rights and were continuously in danger of becoming objects of popular discontent or of earning the displeasure of the rulers or the ecclesiastical authorities, all this culminating in the possibilities of riots and expulsions.

Closely related to this was, of course, continuous dispersion, continuous migrations, which became a basic part of Jewish existence and the concomitant multiplicity of different centres and shifts in their respective strength.

In the first period, that of late Antiquity and early Christianity, most Jews lived in the countries of the Near and Middle East – in Palestine, Syria, Babylon, Egypt and the Byzantine Empire – and only very few started to move into the realm of Western and Central Europe.

With the expansion of the Muslim Empire from the seventh till the twelfth centuries, Jews lived mostly under Muslim rule in the Near East, Spain and North Africa, but an increasing number (although on the whole a minority among the Jewish people) started to settle into Christian countries – in Christian Spain, France, England and Germany (Ashkenaz). After the expulsion from Spain, till the beginning of the seventeenth century, most Jews continued to live under Muslim – in this case Ottoman – rule in the countries of the Mediterranean and Near and Middle East, but there was still a continuous movement into Christian European countries – Italy, the Netherlands and above all Germany, Poland and other Eastern European countries. Since the seventeenth century it was the Jewish communities in these 'Ashkenazi' countries that continuously expanded and became the major centres of Jewish life.

## Institutional changes

Closely connected with these developments there was a marked shift in the centres of social and institutional organization of Jewish life – a shift to communal organizations, Rabbinical and communal courts and centres of learning and to the networks, contacts and economic relations between them, and between families – and it was these structures that became the major institutional-organizational nexus of Jewish life. The overriding institutions were those of the communities and their courts, which were usually granted by the cities some corporate rights and rights of supervision over Jews and of control over the access to some at least of the economic activities and rights of domicile open to Jews.

Within this framework the basic kernel of Jewish community was the family and networks of families – the synagogue and various communal organizations and centres of study and learning the first in strong contrast to the Church.

It is within these institutional frameworks that there developed the major new types of leadership which were active in the Jewish communities. The concrete structure of this leadership necessarily underwent far-reaching changes after the destruction of the Second Temple. Yet in fact we encounter here a rather paradoxical situation – together with these extensive changes in the structure of such leadership there was also a striking continuity in its basic analytical characteristics.

The changes connected with the loss of political independence and dispersion were obvious. They were, of course, above all manifest in the continuous weakening of relatively centralized political leadership. In fact, whenever the external circumstances were favourable, such leadership – whether that of the Exiliarchs in Babylon or of various equivalents in other places, as for instance in the South of France in the tenth to twelfth centuries – still tended to emerge.

At the same time, under favourable circumstances, there developed a shift to local or trans-local organizations – the famous *Vaad Arba Haaratzot* (Committee of the Four Lands) in Poland or similar ones in Moravia and other parallel institutions. But on the whole the communal leadership was composed of leaders of the communities and sometimes also of the rabbis and students in the major institutions of learning – the various Yeshivot.

It was always some combination of the three elements – the stronger, wealthier, oligarchic elements of the community, the would-be popular political leaders, and the different carriers of learning, the rabbis, scholars and to some degree mystics – that constituted the major elites in most Jewish communities, and it was they who usually composed the major ruling coalitions that exercised control over the life of these communities. Of all these, the latter tended to develop some specialized and autonomous institutions and it was they which constituted the most continuous elements in the supra-communal and even trans-country networks.

These different elites and sub-elites were always composed of numerous elements, so that within each of them, and between them, there developed, as we shall see in greater detail later on, continuous tensions. These tensions were rooted in the fact that with all the change, as compared with earlier periods, in the concrete composition of these elites, they continued to exhibit the basic characteristics of the former ones: multiplicity of elites sharing strong commitment to religious and political realms; belief in the access of all members of the community to the sacred realm and an emphasis on covenantal relations between God and the people of Israel.

All this constituted both a continuation and a break with the Second Commonwealth. There is no doubt, of course, that political independence, after the return from Babylon, was always precarious – even more than in the period of the First Temple; there was not even that degree of political independence and continuity which the Davidic monarchy had enjoyed. Moreover, already in the period of the Second Commonwealth, many Diaspora communities had evolved, primarily in Egypt, Babylon and Syria and they had become a constant feature of Jewish existence, creating multiple centres. But the destruction of the Temple and the loss of political independence had naturally constituted a sharp and traumatic break with the past. Autonomous political power had been lost and, thereafter, relations between the centre and the Diaspora, and the very nature of the Diaspora – of being exiled and in a minority – became not only a continuous fact, but also, as we shall see in greater detail, a continuous problem in Jewish life and in its collective consciousness.

The life of the great majority of Jewish people was, however, probably confined to the exigencies of daily existence; of struggle for survival and escape from persecution. It was focused around family, neighbourhood and the major communal institutions – those of the synagogue, the various associations such as those of study or mutual help, and the various centres, circles and networks of learning – as well as around intercommunal networks, those of family, economic intercommunal relations and networks of scholars and institutions of learning.

## The predominance of the Oral Law

All these developments in the external fate and internal organization of the Jewish people were connected with the growing predominance in Jewish life of the Rabbinical institutional mould, of the mould of the Oral Law, of the Halakha (Law), and it was this mould that became the major framework of Jewish civilization. This predominance was attained relatively slowly – only around the period of the third or fourth century of the Christian era. By that time this mould had displaced – even if only partially – the other institutional moulds, not only the more priestly and political orientations connected with the Temple and with an independent polity, but also the various sectarian tendencies, as carried by the numerous sects and movements and especially by the emerging Christianity.

In the first two or three centuries after the destruction of the Second Temple these sects and groups were still very visible in Judea and in Galilee and were probably quite predominant in the desert in the form of various Hagarist or Samaritan groups, some of the former transforming themselves later on into a new and powerful universal civilization: Islam.

The competition between all these groups and sects, all still related to their common origin within the framework of the Jewish civilization, was very intense and bitter, and it was out of this competition that there gradually emerged the predominance of the Rabbinical mould – a predominance which was to continue up to the modern period. But even then many of the sects and sectarian orientations were not obliterated – they were rather pushed into subterranean levels, into the margins of Jewish societies, or into the interstices between Jewish, Christian and Islamic civilizations.

This mould – that of the Oral Law, the later Rabbinical mould – began to emerge in the period of the Second Commonwealth out of the combined activities of the various communal leaders, the sages and their precursors, and the leaders of the major sectarian religious–social movements. It was characterized, as indicated already above, by increased emphasis on legal–ritual prescriptions, based on the exegesis, study and continuous elaboration of the texts, and/or communal prayer as the focus or arena of Jewish religion and tradition.

This mould was guided by a combination of the predominant this-worldly attitudes and premises together with some of the other-worldly and eschatological ones which, as we have seen above, had developed earlier. The latter did not attain, however, within this mould, the same degree of distinction that they did in other monotheistic or other-worldly religions. The potentially revolutionary and universalistic implications of these attitudes – most visible in some of the sects and later on in Christianity – were here reinterpreted and hemmed in within the emerging tradition of Oral Law.

We have already noted the rather special attitudes that developed toward the prophetic tradition. On the one hand the ethical, rational, and even eschatological, traditions of the prophets were incorporated into the newly emerging paradigm through a process of codification and canonization of the scriptures; on the other hand, the possibility of continuing independent prophecy was denied. In place of revelation, the more structured process of study and legal exegesis and of collegial decisions of the courts and of community organization emerged.

As indicated already above, this new tradition of Oral Law signified a shift from the predominance of ritual cultic elements and prophetic visions to the elaboration of canonic scripture and to the interpretation and elaboration of the emerging Oral Law. The interpretation itself was based on an increasing systematization of the legal-ritual precepts according to more abstract systematic principles. This systematization was codified first in the Mishna and the Tosefta, much later on in the two Talmuds – that of Jerusalem and the Babylonian one – which served as bases for continuous later interpretations, for the great Rabbinical literature which continues to this day. This literature was very rich and heterogeneous. There was the earlier, more interpretative literature of the Middrashim, containing both legal and more 'legendary' (*Agadot*) elements. Later, there was the literature of the *Sheelot Veteshuvot* (Questions and Answers) and of combined commentaries and exegeses of the Law, and of secondary codifications – the most important among which were probably those of the famous 'Misheneh Torah' of Maimonides (composed about 1178 CE), the 'Baal Haturim' of the fifteenth century, up to the last great codification – the 'Shulkhan Arukh' of Rabbi Joseph Karo or Caro (1488–1575). There was the very rich literature of commentaries on the Bible, Mishna and Talmud – the most famous and popular being probably that of Rashi (Rabbi Shlomo Itzhaki) of France (1040–1105), and there was the very widespread 'ethical' (*Musar*) literature.

All this literature aimed to regulate in a systematic way most aspects of the Jews' daily life: in the religious–ethical field, with special emphasis on restrictions on food, and to a smaller degree on dress; in the field of interpersonal relations in general and economic ones in particular; also to some degree, as we shall see, in matters of communal organization and in relations to host nations. Thus it structured the specific contents and boundaries of Jewish collective life and civilization, and provided the justification or explanation of these injunctions in religious and ethical terms.

Thus, throughout this period, it was indeed the mould of the Oral Law, with its combination of 'ritual', 'study' and purely legal aspects, that became, with all its variations, the common binding socio-cultural framework which held the Jewish people together and which provided the symbolic institutional framework of the continuity of Jewish collective-national and cultural identity.

Of special importance in the maintenance of this framework, binding the different Jewish communities together, was the Hebrew language. It was, in common with Latin in Catholic Christianity and Arabic in Islam, the language of prayer and of philosophical discourse. But it went beyond Latin, and to some degree Arabic, in being also the language of ritual-legal discourse and also of correspondence in more mundane matters, such as commercial or family transactions. Although Jews naturally learned the vernacular of their respective countries, and although, at least in the Muslim world, a large part of Jewish philosophical lectures were written in Arabic, yet the multiple uses of the Hebrew language greatly facilitated the maintenance of close relations between different Jewish communities and of the common framework of Jewish civilization as it was focused around the institution of the Halakha.

This mould also articulated and regulated the major symbols of Jewish identity – couched in basic primordial, national or religious terms. While these symbols came before the predominance of the Halakha, yet in this period it was the Halakha – with the manifold communal organizations and networks – that provided the major institutional framework in which continuity of Jewish culture was maintained, and in which all the different elements or components of Jewish collective identity – 'national', primordial, 'ethnic' and religious, cultural and political – were brought together.

Most Jews probably did not differentiate between these different strands of identity; they assumed that these different strands naturally come together and were bound by the Law, and that their basic belief system based on monotheistic and covenantal orientations, and the fact that they were the Chosen people, made the whole structure of the Law legitimate.

## The internal heterogeneity of the medieval Jewish civilization

But, as we have already indicated earlier, the new mould of Oral Law, with its far-reaching institutional implications, was never really as fully institutionalized or as homogeneous as has been often portrayed by the Rabbinical tradition and by subsequent modern historians.

The mould of Oral Law did *not* become the predominant one during the period of the Second Commonwealth, and during this period it was far from being homogeneous. But even later on, when this mould became predominant and most of the other orientations and incipient moulds were incorporated and transformed within it, they were never obliterated. The older elements and orientations – eschatological, mystical or philosophical – persisted within this mould and became transformed within it; moreover they often reappeared as harbingers of various trends – mystical, philosophical and contemplative, and cutting across them the Messianic one – which were extremely powerful even within this mould.

Beyond this, there were also tensions among some of the characteristics that were specific to the new mould. Firstly there were tensions between the elitist attitudes, which were strictly legal, rational and strongly emphasized study and learning and the popular attitudes of prayer, piety and ecstasy, with strong mystical components. There were also tensions between those who placed emphasis on political-communal leadership and activity, and those who emphasized the importance of religious-legal study.

This great internal heterogeneity within the Rabbinical tradition was fed by both internal and external forces. Internally there were the various major religious, intellectual and social orientations mentioned above. True enough, they were never fully autonomous; they were denied symbolic and especially organizational autonomy; they were usually subsumed within the mould of the Halakha as secondary elements; and they were not allowed to develop into heterodox sects; but nevertheless they represented important components of Jewish life, as foci of cultural creativity and of subterranean developments. The struggles between these orientations gave rise to a great variety of interpretations of the tradition – all of them carried by different elites and groups, by the various types of leadership that developed, as we have seen, in the Jewish communities. These struggles – and the closely related variety of cultural creativity – were very closely connected, as we shall see in greater detail later on, with 'external' developments, with the relations of the Jewish communities to their 'host' societies.

This great and varied creativity was, of course, first of all an intellectual one – but it was not only intellectual. Its continuous focus, confirmed by the often intense and vehement disputes and discussions, was the delineation of the symbolic and institutional boundaries of the collective existence of the Jewish people in Exile, and the attempts to maintain them.

# The Relations to the Host Civilizations
## *The patterns of religious and civilizational identity*

The heterogeneous tendencies within the framework of the Rabbinical tradition of the Halakha, were related not only to the heterogeneity and autonomy of leadership that existed within the Jewish communities, but also to the relationship of the Jews to their host civilizations – relations which in their turn reinforced these characteristics of the leadership.

It was not just the political subjugations and the continuous dispersion, the conception of the Jews as basically strangers in the lands in which they lived, that became the decisive aspects of the 'external' history of the Jews. We have already seen that during the period of the Second Commonwealth a large part of the Jewish people developed a strong competitive orientation to other – above all Hellenistic and Roman – civilizations with universalistic claims which they saw as threatening their collective identity. On the whole the Jews did not constitute a direct threat to these civilizations; but, because of the peculiar combination of political, ethnic and religious orientations, they were seen as a rather peculiar type of people or civilization, giving rise to the first articulation, as for instance in the writings of Tacitus, of what could later be called anti-Semitic attitudes and ideologies. These attitudes are seen in the words which Marguerite Yourcenar has put into the mouth of Hadrian:

in principle, Judaism had its place among the religions of the Empire; in practice, Israel has refused for centuries to be one people among many others, with one god among the gods. The most primitive Dacians know that their Zalmonxis is called Jupiter in Rome; the Phoenician Baal of Mount Casius has been readily identified with the Father who holds Victory in his hand, and of Whom wisdom is born; the Egyptians, though so proud of their myths some thousands of years old, are willing to see in Osiris a Bacchus with funeral attributes; harsh Mithra admits himself brother to Apollo. No people but Israel has the arrogance to confine truth wholly within the narrow limits of a single conception of the divine, thereby insulting the manifold nature of the Deity, who contains all; no other god has inspired his worshippers with disdain and hatred for those who pray at different altars. I was only the more anxious to make Jerusalem a city like the others, where several races and several beliefs could live in peace; but I was wrong to forget that in any combat between fanaticism and common sense the latter has rarely the upper hand. The clergy of the ancient city were scandalized by the opening of schools where Greek literature was taught; the rabbi Joshua, a pleasant, learned man with whom I had frequently conversed in Athens, but who was trying to excuse himself to his people for his foreign culture and his relations with us, now ordered his disciples not to take up such profane studies unless they could find an hour which was neither day nor night, since Jewish law must be studied night and day. Ismael, an important member of the Sanhedrin, who supposedly adhered to the side of Rome, let his nephew Ben-Dama die rather than accept the services of the Greek surgeon sent to him by Tineus Rufus. While in Tibur means were still being sought to conciliate differences without appearing to yield to the demands of fanatics, affairs in the East took a turn for the worse; a Zealot revolt triumphed in Jerusalem.*

Thus at this period Jews were probably perceived at most as a local nuisance, not as a basic threat to the reigning civilization. It was when they participated actively in the great competition between different religions that developed in the last centuries of the Roman Empire, that the Jews saw themselves as a basic threat to their host civilizations. This was further intensified and indeed entirely transformed first with the rise of Christianity and its acceptance as the predominant religion of the Roman Empire, and later with the rise of Islam and its conquest of the Near and Middle East. Not only were Christianity and Islam

* Marguerite Yourcenar, *Memoirs of Hadrian* (London 1978), pp. 190–1.

'post-Axial' monotheistic religions with claims to universality, giving rise to attempts to construct civilizations which naturally encompassed all those with whom they came into contact, including, of course, the Jews. Beyond this – and this was above all true of Christianity but, in a somewhat milder version, also of Islam – they were historically related to the Jewish religion and people, and this historical relation was a basic constitutive point of their premises, of their self-definition. The Christians saw themselves as the true children of Israel and the Jews, persisting in their own faith, as deviants, as an aberration of the true faith of Israel. For the Muslims, Muhammad was the last – and the ultimate – prophet, superseding if not necessarily totally negating the validity of his predecessors, and the Jews' non-acceptance of these premisses was also seen as an aberration.

Hence in both these religions and civilizations there developed a basic ambivalence to the Jews which went far beyond the attitude to other minorities. This ambivalence found its expression not only in the 'mere' facts of pogroms, persecutions and expulsions, but in the special ideological dimensions which were added to these acts – to attempts at forced conversion, massacres and in the famous blood libels accusing Jews of killing Christian children and drinking their blood – all these giving rise to heroic Jewish martyrology in sanctification of the Name (of God) (*Kiddush Hashem*).

This ambivalence added a new dimension to the facts of political subjugation or dispersion, interpreting them as evidence for the superiority of the reigning religion.

## Civilizational and religious competition

At the same time, unlike many other minority peoples, the Jews attempted not only to maintain some place for themselves in the tumultuous political and economic reality of that period but also repeatedly to claim the universal validity of their religion and tradition.

Thus, as we have seen, already in the period of the Second Commonwealth the Jewish situation was characterized by the combination of a rather precarious political and economic situation with attempts at intensive participation in the political and cultural life of the period. This participation was based on their attempts to forge for themselves an identity and institutional framework which would enable them to maintain their political, religious and primordial identity and which would at the same time sustain some of their claims to universal validity.

In the long period of the Exile this situation changed quite dramatically; yet the belief of the Jews in the universal significance of their religion did not abate – even if in fact they could no longer openly compete with other civilizations and even if they had to invest almost all of their energies in maintaining their own cultural-religious framework and, through a firm control of their way of life, their segregation from the host people and their symbolic boundaries.

But even in these circumstances the legitimacy which the Jews claimed for themselves was not only religious or 'cultic'. It continued to contain some strong political elements – as was evident in the emphasis, which we shall analyse in greater detail shortly, on collective salvation and political redemption and on the definition, to which we shall refer in greater detail later on, unique among dispersed people, of experience of Exile in metaphysical terms combined with a metaphysical definition in the primordial relationship between the Land of Israel and the people of Israel. It contained also very definite universalistic–civilizational components and premises.

Thus even in this period the Jews were not just a pariah minority who often performed the functions of middlemen. These features of theirs did not define their basic relations with their host civilizations. These relations were defined in terms of common historical–religious origin: the denial, by the Christians – and to a smaller degree by the Muslims – of the legitimacy of the Jewish non-acceptance of Christianity – or of Islam.

All this resulted in Jews being seen as a problematic and ambivalent reference point and as a potential threat to the legitimacy of the hosts' own creed. Hence there developed tense relations between the host societies and the guest communities – each trying to assert the basic legitimacy of its own civilization. (Significantly enough in those civilizations – like China or India – in which this inter-civilizational competition was non-existent, the small Jewish communities have indeed become a sort of religious–ethnic minority.)

It was within this framework that there developed the competitive and ambivalent relations between the Jews and their host people or countries: the continuous – and, up to a point, successful – attempts at conversion; the frequent debates between the Christian priests and theologians and Jewish priests, rabbis and theologians, debates which constituted a regular part of the medieval cultural scene and of the internal scene of each of these civilizations.

All these seemingly external facts – but above all the ambivalent relations between the Jewish people and the two other monotheistic civilizations, especially Christianity – became very closely interwoven with the internal fabric of Jewish life and civilization as it developed in that long period, stretching, as we have seen, up to modern times – and continuing in a new way in the modern period. The civilizational, and not only political or economic, relations with the host civilizations, rulers and people, and the tensions between them and the Jewish communities, were of continuous relevance for the very construction and maintenance of the boundaries of Jewish civilizations for the continuity of Jews as a distinct people.

It was out of these tensions that there developed many spheres of contact – especially in the field of philosophy, theology, mysticism and to some degree law. The contacts that developed in these spheres were sometimes co-operative, but more often conflicting – as evident above all in the famous debates in which Jews were called by the Christian priests and scholars to justify their faith – but there always existed spheres of mutual reference and orientations and they necessarily had an impact on internal developments in

Jewish communities.

Thus, for instance, these debates necessitated by their very nature the elaboration of philosophical and theological arguments, thereby making them into basic arenas for the elaboration of Jewish identity and external tradition – feeding on fertile internal ground, reinforcing the various heterogeneous traditions which existed and continuously developed within the Jewish fold and the multiple arenas of cultural creativity within it.

# Basic Themes and Institutional Implications of Exilic Jewish Civilization
## *Universalistic and particularistic attitudes*

It was these different groups, institutions and networks that articulated in this period, and in the different spheres of cultural activity developed by them, the basic themes of Jewish civilization, the tension between particularism and universalism, between the inward-looking, closed, hyper-provincial xenophobism, and the more outward-looking attitudes based on belief in the universal significance of the specific Jewish view of the world as expressed in its tradition, in the long period of the Galut.

But there was an important and basic difference from the period of the Second Temple. This difference was, of course, related to the fact that the institutional arenas, around which the specific Jewish construction of the world could become articulated, became very limited, and that most of these ideological attitudes and tensions could not be realized in a concrete institutional framework.

Although official Halakhic Judaism never gave up its claim to the construction of a civilization of universal significance, in fact the Jews no longer really competed with the other civilizations – even if these civilizations continued to fear such competition. Jews concentrated mainly on their own frameworks, minimizing their aspirations to a specific construction of the real world and consciously opting for non-participation in contemporary political and civilizational history.

The only institutional reality which was constructed according to the basic tenets of this tradition was that of learning, ritual observance and prayer, and communal organization. By the very nature of this reality and by the nature of the circumstances in which they lived, the Jews could view the concrete economic arenas and the political frameworks in which they lived as the arenas of such construction.

The basic attitude to the mundane world – to economic life and communal organization – was positive, but these spheres were not seen as the arenas of construction of the world according to the premises of this tradition.

The major such arena that was so predominant in the period of the Second Temple – the internal and international political one – disappeared almost entirely. The fact of dispersion and of political subjugation, of having become strangers, made this arena on the whole neutral or even meaningless from the point of view of the basic tenets of the tradition. The existence in the Galut was seen as basically temporal: the Jews in the medieval world lived, as it were, outside history; they opted out of concrete history and defined their existence outside its flow.

Actual assertions of the universal significance of the Jewish religion and the quest for political redemption, were transposed into the distant Messianic future, beyond the scope of the daily activity of Jews – they could in principle hasten it by proper observance of the Law but not by any direct political activity – while the present existed in the confines of a very narrow particularistic solidarity, existing as it were outside history.

Thus the tension between the universal and the particular elements in Jewish culture was resolved, in a sense, by pushing it forward to some future time when there might be the possibility of the realization of the universalistic elements, of a really open dialogue and encounter with other nations, religious and medieval civilizations.

The reality of Jewish life became a very particularistic one, albeit strongly connected with a universalistic orientation. In the reality of pre-medieval and medieval exile, this universalistic orientation could not, because of the nature of the relations with the broader society within which the Jews lived until then, take on any real institutional – as against purely intellectual – dimension.

The universalistic ethical orientations inherent in the Jewish civilization continued mostly in a latent sense, or as a focus for theological disputes, or as a dream. This was connected, of course, with the solution of another dilemma – namely that between the concrete given reality and eschatological orientations and hopes. Again the eschatological – whether universalistic or particularistic – orientations with their strong political ingredients were pushed towards some unknown future, only tenuously related to the temporal, concrete – and seemingly apolitical – Jewish reality. Any attempts to realize them, as for instance in Messianic movements, were seen by the carriers of Jewish orthodoxy as very dangerous to Jewish existence and as going against the basic premises of the Halakhic mould.

## Ambivalent attitudes to host civilizations

It was with respect to the attitudes to the host civilizations that some of the more practical and concrete, as well as principled, problems inherent in the Jewish tradition emerged.

The recurrent encounters between the Jewish communities and their host – Christian and Muslim – civilizations, both in the practice of daily relations as well as the intensive religious controversies, brought out the problem of the principled attitude of the Jews to these civilizations and to the people in the midst of which they were living. With such growing segregation there necessarily developed, as J. Katz has shown, a marked religious intolerance to these civilizations, a strong – although obviously not often openly expressed –

denial of their validity.

Yet both the daily reality as well as the pressure of the environment, the necessity to justify themselves in the eyes of this environment and to counter-attack its allegations, could bring out the more universalistic orientations in the Jewish tradition.

There were here many Halakhic problems – especially as to the extent to which various Halakhic injunctions on proper business relations applied also to transactions with non-Jews. There were the more principled problems of the degree of recognition, by Jews, of Christian and Muslim religions as legitimate ones, towards which the appellations against pagan nations and gods did not apply. The response to this problem – above all to the serious accusations against the Jews of double-morality, of their self-enclosure and of disloyalty to the rulers – was multiple and ambivalent. There was the growth of Halakhic injunctions about the ways of dealing with non-Jews; there was the admittance of the validity of *Dina Demalkhuta* (the Law of the Land), one of the few direct confrontations with the political reality; there was also probably some *de facto* mutual tolerance in daily life. Beyond these there also developed, to some degree among the Halakhic scholars and perhaps somewhat more among the philosophers, the admittance of the partial validity of the other, non-Jewish monotheistic religions and of some incipient – but not insignificant – toleration.*

## The ideology of Galut and Eretz Israel

But in general most of the basic themes of Jewish civilization that developed in this period were ideological, cultural or intellectual, with little application to institutional reality.

The weakness of the institutional applicability of most of these themes did not obliterate them; they persisted and became articulated as intellectual, ideological and symbolic themes defining the symbolic boundaries of Jewish existence, and their potential institutional applications were always latent or dormant.

Moreover several additional themes – the kernels of which could already be discerned in the period of the Second Temple – became more fully articulated, more closely connected with the tensions between particularistic and universalistic orientations. They became an inherent part of the basic constituents of Jewish tradition and collective self-definition, even if, significantly, most of these themes were not allowed, by the carriers of the Halakhic tradition, to become autonomous or predominant.

The most important of these were five closely related, yet not entirely identical, themes: the metaphysical evaluation of Galut, of the situation of Diaspora; the closely related metaphysical and ideological evaluation of Eretz Israel; the fuller articulation of Messianic visions; martyrology; and the solidarity of the Jewish people.

* See J. Katz, *Exclusiveness and Tolerance* (Oxford 1961).

Dispersion was not unique to the Jews – although probably its scope and continuity were. But what was unique and specific to them was the tendency to a strong, metaphysical or religious negative evaluation of Galut. The explanation of the fact of Diaspora Galut became – as the late Professor Itzhak Baer has shown* – a major concern of many, if not most, Jewish philosophers and scholars. Whatever the details of these philosophical expositions, in most cases the fact of Galut was seen as basically negative, explainable in terms of sin and punishment. The existence in Galut was defined as a partial, suspended, existence – but also an existence which had to be nurtured in the hope of the survival of the Jewish people until the time of Redemption.

The essence of this negative evaluation of existence in Galut focused on two, closely connected but not identical, themes: that of the lack of political sovereignty, of *Shiabud Malchuyoth*, and that of a partial, distorted, spiritual or religious existence which was seen as the metaphysical essence of Galut. The two themes were combined – but they were emphasized in different degrees by different scholars or groups – along with an emphasis on the particularistic nature of the existence in Galut as against the more universalistic potential of redemption.

These two attitudes or themes – the political and the metaphysical or redemptive – were also central in the attitude towards Eretz Israel and in the crystallization and articulation of Messianic visions. The attitude to Eretz Israel was, in a sense, the counterweight to that of the Galut, very often enunciated by the same thinkers, but also having some autonomy of its own.

Eretz Israel was defined in both primordial and political terms but – and this was the great innovation, even if it built on earlier foundations – there was also a growing metaphysical religious attitude to it.

Thus Eretz Israel was seen first of all as a national patrimony to which one was attached and from which one was expelled, but it was also seen as imbued with a special metaphysical and religious meaning through which the Jewish people was constituted as a distinct people: and the attainment of this meaning came only with full Redemption.

But whatever the fine details of these definitions and the political–primordial and metaphysical evaluation of the existence in Galut, Eretz Israel became a basic component of the articulation of the Jewish collective identity in the Diaspora, giving to this identity a seemingly non-realistic, yet very strong and articulated focus and dimension, again combining in a rather universal way the particularistic and universalistic orientations.

These orientations to the Galut and to Eretz Israel did not, of course, necessarily shape the daily life of most Jews throughout this long period – a life which was focused on daily existence and survival on the one hand and the maintenance of the legal-ritual observances and prayer on the other hand. Moreover these orientations were not allowed by the keepers of the gates, by the upholders of the Halakha, to become actualized beyond the sphere of the Halakha and its a-political and a-historical attitude to existing reality. But they

* I. Baer, *Galut* (Berlin 1936; New York 1947).

constituted a basic and latent component of such daily existence, especially as such existence was defined in the specific terms of the Jewish tradition; and they were a fundamental constituent of the symbolically more articulated expression of this tradition.

These attitudes to Galut and to Eretz Israel converged around the third theme which, in a sense, subsumed them – namely the Messianic and eschatological one. Its roots are in the early period of the Second Temple – even in the Babylonian exile – and in its many expressions in the various sects of the Second Temple period, and of course in Christianity. The proper interpretation of the Messianic vision – the vision of the Messiah who has already appeared and has saved humanity as against the Messiah who has yet to come at the end of days – became probably the most central focus of controversy between Judaism and Christianity. The salience of this point became, of course, intensified with the reality of the loss of political independence, of dispersion and of expulsion – and hence also the contours of the Messianic vision became much more fully elaborated. They became articulated around the two basic motives or themes – that of political and/or religious redemption. Both of these motives but especially the latter, were wrought with many antinomian potentialities with respect to the predominant mould of the Halakha, and became foci of many elaborated Talmudic and philosophical expositions and controversies.

Rabbinical orthodoxy always tried – without ever denying them – to keep all these visions within very confined limits. It was suspicious of the potential religious innovations inherent in them, and of their power to disrupt the authority of the Halakha as well as the precarious existence of the dispersed Jewish communities. But, despite these efforts, the Messianic visions and hopes were not just intellectual exercises confined to relatively limited circles of cognoscenti, nor just latent, unrealistic hopes.

These Messianic tendencies also erupted, in more or less dramatic fashions, as more popular movements, led by would-be aspirants to the role of Messiah, or of the heralder of Messiah – be it David Hareubeni and Shlomo Molkho in the earlier sixteenth century, or later on in the last and most dramatic appearance, that of Sabbatai Zevi and the development of the Sabbatean movement which shook the walls of Rabbinical Judaism. Naturally these tendencies erupted in times of troubles, persecution, expulsion or great international upheavals which could be interpreted as the harbingers of new times, of the war between Gog and Magog. When such broader movements erupted, however ephemeral they might be, they drew on the rich reservoir of images and visions of the more esoteric or mystical circles, among whom it was more the redemptive rather than the political Messianism that was emphasized. Whatever their foundations, they always threatened the predominance of the Rabbinical mould – not only its specific religious injunctions, but above all its tendency to opt out of the contemporary historical–political scene, its suspension of the Jewish civilizational mission.

The other basic themes which became fully articulated in this long era, a sort of dialectical counterpart or complement of the Messianic hope, were that of martyrology, of *Kiddush Hashem*, and to a somewhat lesser degree that of Jewish solidarity.

The theme of *Kiddush Hashem*, the sanctification of the Name (a theme going back to Roman times, if not earlier), became fully articulated in the wake of persecution and pogroms – persecution which in these periods was always legitimized in terms of the basic religious chasm between Christianity and Judaism and in which the Jews were often called upon to convert on pain of execution. It was in the context of these events that the theme of martyrology developed as a reaction against the more routine existence under the sages of the Rabbinical mould which sanctified the keeping of life and which tried to minimize the overt tension with the host people, but not, of course, at the cost of apostasy. It became a constant theme of Jewish identity, emphasizing the complete commitment of Jews to their tradition.

A complementary but to some degree opposite theme was that of Jewish solidarity, of *Ahavat Israel*, of the necessity to close ranks in face of external threats. This theme, which emerged at both ideological and more popular levels in the long period of the Galut, became, of course, closely related to the self-imposed segregation, to the intolerance of other religions, to the ambivalence to other nations. In its extreme manifestation it could easily become connected with intense xenophobia.

These different themes were continuously interwoven with the different modes – philosophical, mystical, pietist and legal-ritual – of interpretation of the tradition, and constituted the foci of the intellectual and institutional creativity of medieval Jewish civilization, the symbolic boundaries of the framework of Jewish life as it developed in the long period of the Diaspora.

Yet it was these institutions of the Halakha – the institutions and network of prayers, study and legislation – that provided together with those of family and community the major mechanisms of the continuity – and dynamics – of Jewish life and civilization. It was within the framework of these institutions that the new types of leadership which were active in Jewish life – which had naturally undergone extensive changes after the destruction of the Second Temple, and yet had maintained a striking continuity in their basic analytical characteristic – developed, and it was the combination of these different types of leadership, the modes of communal organization and the basic religious and institutional orientations that gave rise to far-reaching dynamics both in the Jewish communal organization, as well as in the patterns of cultural creativity that developed within it.

# Jewish Social Organization and Cultural Creativity – Heterogeneity and Tensions within Common Bonds
## Oligarchic and democratic tendencies

The Jewish communities that developed in the different periods of the Galut were on the whole oligarchic ones, ruled over by the wealthier elements, who also provided the larger part of, although certainly not the exclusive, financial bases – in the form of various taxes as well as donations to institutions of learning – for the many institutions for taking care of the centres of learning and of representation to the authorities.

These oligarchic tendencies sometimes strengthened the development of dynasties among the great, and smaller, rabbis, often interlinked with the wealthier families – a tendency which flourished in the earlier period in Babylon – especially when they were reinforced, as happened also in other cases, by favourable external conditions of long political tranquillity and of economic prosperity.

But these oligarchic tendencies were also counteracted by several others that were inherent in the very structure and organization of the Jewish community and its political situation. Thus, first of all, the vicissitudes of persecution and dispersion often made any continuity of wealth, and of that standing which was connected with wealth, precarious. But second and more important, they were also counteracted by several internal tendencies rooted in the basic premises of the Jewish tradition and the structure of leadership.

Thus, in general terms, these strong oligarchic tendencies which were indeed prevalent in most Jewish communities were counteracted by strong populistic elements in the communities, by the more autonomous institutions of learning, as well as by the existence of other arenas of cultural creativity which developed outside the narrow oligarchic bases of any single community. As a result even the communal, internal political life of Jews, was ridden with tensions, conflicts and social movements.

In greater detail, these oligarchic tendencies were first of all counteracted by the basic 'democratic' or rather egalitarian premises of the Jewish tradition, premises of basic equality and of equal participation and access of all Jews to the centres of the sacred realm, to learning, prayer and the observance of ritual prescriptions, which had become, in contrast to the potentially more oligarchic tendencies of priesthood, the predominant modes of Jewish belief. The egalitarian assumptions of these modes were of course only strengthened by the great need to maintain the solidarity of the community and the adherence to the tradition, in the situation of the Diaspora, and by the openness of learning to all members of the community.

The counter-oligarchic tendencies could also sometimes be reinforced by some of the members of Rabbinical elites, especially those based on autonomous transcommunal institutions of learning, but in most places the Rabbinical elite was closely related to the prevailing oligarchy, often even directly dependent on it.

The oligarchic tendencies were also balanced by the relative autonomy of the centres of learning, as well as by the mobility of the Jews in general and of the scholars in particular. Closely related to this was the fact that ultimately there did not exist any overall single authority binding all the Jewish communities together. This was due, of course, first of all to the very fact of dispersion and to the political status of the Jews. But it was strongly reinforced by the fact that – in contrast, for instance, to the case of the Armenians who shared with the Jews the combination of nationhood, distinctive religion and dispersion – there had not existed among the Jews, by virtue of the basic premises of their tradition, by virtue of the strong emphasis on the equal access of all members to the central sacred spheres and on their semi-contractual relations with God and on the collegial elaboration of the Law, a central ecclesiastical authority.

These oligarchic tendencies could also to some extent be counteracted – not only, as we shall see later on, in matters of cultural creativity but even in the matters of communal organization – by the fact that in general between the different elites predominant in Jewish life, as well as within each of them, there developed constant tensions. These conflicts and tensions were of course greatly influenced by the different and specific interests of each such group or sub-group. But beyond this they were rooted in the persistent multiplicity and autonomy of the leadership and the major elites.

The intensity and concrete outcomes of these communal, internal, semi-political conflicts, were dependent, of course, on a variety of internal and external circumstances. They depended on the relations with the authorities, on the internal legislative power vested by the rulers in the communities, on the economic standing of the community and its different sectors, and on its internal composition.

They depended also on the social position of the different types of scholars – whether they were rabbis appointed by the different communities, more independent scholars, or the relatively isolated ones, surrounded by small groups of disciples or entrenched in independent circles of mystics or philosophers.

Of special importance in this context was whether these scholars, philosophers, poets or mystics, however great their personal distinction, were socially embedded in their communities, usually as parts of their oligarchies, or whether they were, whatever their official position, much more autonomous in their activities and self-perception. Needless to say such autonomy tended to be greater among those who were connected with specialized institutions of learning. But not everywhere was such specialization tantamount to autonomy; there were many (especially small) Yeshivot or circles of learning which were entirely embedded in the life of the community. As against this others, especially the trans-communal ones, were more autonomous.

All these different groups and elements were organized, as we have seen, in different organizations and networks, sometimes co-operating within different elements in the community, sometimes in conflict with them. Even within the central tradition of learning there existed, as we have indicated briefly above and as we shall discuss in greater detail later on, no one, single, accepted authority and the degree of conflict between different authorities was indeed very great.

## Legal traditions and civility

The communal conflicts and tensions were on the whole held within the bounds of the Jewish communities by a combination of the basic solidarity of the communities and of the legal powers vested in them, the most extreme of which was the 'Kherem' – the threat of ostracism, through which people could be threatened with expulsion.

The combination of such solidarity and legal powers was continuously articulated by the tradition of communal arrangements and decisions and communal courts. This communal legislation developed in the Jewish medieval communities, sometimes to a very elaborate degree, above all in the various regulations of community (*Takanot Hakahal*). It became a part, but a very special part, of the Halakhic tradition.

As we have already briefly alluded to above, this sector of law – as against ritual-religious prescriptions and interpersonal, 'civil' law, whether dealing with matters of marriage or of commercial relations – was very weakly developed in the Talmudic tradition. Even less developed were, of course, the purely political aspects of such communal arrangements. Not all of the rabbis and centres of learning wanted to engage in these communal matters and often left the decisions to the representatives of the community and its leaders.

Thus already in the early centuries after the destruction of the Temple, there developed among the Heads of the Yeshivot in Babylon and in Eretz Israel a tendency to shy away from participation in the communal-political authority, in order to be able to pursue studies in an independent way, and in order not to be dependent on the communal powers or to be entangled in the communal conflicts.

Other rabbis – especially, but certainly not only, in modern times, when they felt threatened by the winds of tolerance and modernity – did engage in them, as did, of course, many communal courts. Whatever the degree of their engagement in such affairs, the very existence of these different tendencies on their part, rooted as it was in the basic premises of the Jewish tradition, added to the tensions and dynamics of communal life.

In the context of these numerous tensions – as well as continuous communal problems and conflicts – there grew up a strong tradition of adherence to the decision of courts in general and communal ones in particular, rooted in the collegial framework of the upholding and elaboration of Halakha.

This tradition added a strong element of civility, of the acceptance of the legal framework, as against the more anarchic tendencies in the life of the Jewish communities. The authority of the communal courts, as well as of the trans-local organization, was on the whole upheld, thus adding, or at least reinforcing, a very important component in the Jewish political tradition, and building very strongly on the attitudes of Jewish solidarity.

It was, however, rather limited and circumscribed. It was naturally limited to internal community affairs – usually to the respective localities or to such trans-local arrangements as those of the Council of Four Lands – and to some degree to its relations to the authorities. It did not address itself to the political institutions of a sovereign entity. The courts never faced the problems already prominent in the period of the First Temple, but crucial in the period of the Second Commonwealth, and later on in the State of Israel, of the confrontation between the law and the Jewish State and the higher authority of the Halakha. At most they were concerned with problems of the degree of the validity of *Dina Demalkhuta* (the Law of the Land), stressing usually the obligations to accept it in all secular matters.

Their ultimate sanction, the Kherem, against potential succession, was often upheld not by internal forces but by the authorities. Indeed later on, in modern times, in open modern societies, when the Kehillot became voluntary bodies, the secessionist centripetal tendencies often became very strong within them.

Moreover the decisions of one court were not necessarily binding on others, although they could serve as mutual reference points and bases of precedents. And on the whole – not only in communal matters but also, as we shall see later, in more Halakhic matters proper – there developed a very strong emphasis on the relative autonomy, in matters of interpretation of the law, of different courts and scholars.

These limitations on the power of the courts were in many ways the source of their strength; they allowed for considerable flexibility and provided legitimate arenas for the activities of different groups; but they also underlined the basically apolitical – as against communal or legislative – aspects of these frameworks.

## Cultural creativity and tensions

A similar picture – one of great creativity, heterogeneity and tension yet held within common bounds – could also be found in the major arena of Jewish civilizational creativity, in what may be called, in a very broad sense, the continuous construction, study and elaboration of the Halakha.

Within this realm of cultural institutional creativity there developed differential emphases, different contents or dimensions of the tradition of learning and prayer – those of pure legalistic and ritual learning, those of mystical and pietistic orientation and those of philosophical study and contemplation, as well as different schools in each of these fields. Within all of these there developed continuous and extensive creativity closely connected, as we have seen, with the contacts with the host civilizations – although, obviously, the relative importance of each varied in different periods and there were also frequent conflicts between them.

These tensions and controversies focused, beyond technical details, around the relative importance of these different bodies of knowledge and learning in the construction of Jewish tradition, and of the symbolic universe of Jewish civilizations, and, in close relation to the former, around the concrete details of Halakhic legislation – above all in the sphere of learning and of ritual observance. There was also constant tension between the more elitist traditions of learning of different kinds and the more populist one of prayer with an admixture of mysticism, a tension which later on, in the eighteenth and nineteenth centuries, became explicit in the division between the Hassidim and their Rabbinical opponents.

The concrete focus of these conflicts and controversies was the control of the institutions and curriculum of learning; they also centred around the major Halakhic injunctions, that is around the construction of the symbolic and institutional boundaries of the Jewish communities. These conflicts and tensions often became connected with those more closely related to communal organization and life discussed above.

The combinations between all these elements and the ensuing conflicts varied greatly in different communities and in different periods of their history in ways yet to be studied systematically – as did the relations between the different elites and the patterns of their cultural creativity and the tensions between them.

These combinations and patterns of creativity were influenced by the relative strength and cohesion of the Jewish communities, by their economic standing, by the strength of their constitutions and by the nature of the impact of these societies – both in terms of their level of cultural creativity as well as of tolerance and persecution towards the Jews. Whatever the exact combinations of these conditions, in most Jewish communities, and at least in the greater centres – whether those of Babylon and Eretz Israel in the earlier period, in Spain, North Africa, France and Ashkenaz in the Middle Ages, in Italy, Eretz Israel, the lands of the Ottoman Empire and the Netherlands after the expulsion from Spain, and in Eastern and Central Europe in the sixteenth century – there developed a continuous cultural creativity, and tensions between the different modes and directions of such creativity.

It would, of course, be impossible to tell here the story of all these varied movements and trends in medieval Judaism, but let's mention some of them – just to illustrate the great varied and heterogeneous creativity within this mould.

Philosophical speculation and study has constituted a basic component of creativity – especially since the encounter with Islam and with the heritage of Hellenistic civilization – and we can recall names like Saadia Gaon (882–942), Yehuda Halevi (c. 1075–1141), Maimonides, the Rambam (Rabbi Moshe ben Maimon, 1135–1204), and later, also connected with this secular learning, Isaac Abravanel at the time of the expulsion from Spain and, above all, Barukh Spinoza (1632–77).

During the great period of efflorescence in Muslim Spain a very strong tradition of secular piety also developed, and here Yehuda Halevi, Shmuel Hanagid (c. 993–1056), Shlomo Ibn Gabirol (1026–50), Moshe Ibn Ezra (c. 1055–1135) and Abraham Ibn Ezra (1089–1164) were the most towering figures. They combined in different ways their literary activities with philosophical studies, biblical exegesis or philological and grammatical works. Interestingly enough historiographical study was either lacking or very weak, at least until the earlier modern period.

From early on – probably the tenth or eleventh century if not earlier – there were also various mystical–Kabbalistic trends, as well as strong movements of *Hasidut* (pietism) which first flourished in Ashkenaz. The pivot of all this cultural creativity was the Talmudic learning proper, with all its great variety alluded to above.

## Potential heterodoxies and internal cohesion

All these activities could in principle have become nuclei of 'heretical' trends, of heterodoxies and secessional movements. Such movements had indeed developed in the first centuries after the destruction of the Temple and continued to exist at least in parts of the Near East and in the Christian and Islamic civilizations and the Jewish one. Later on, however, most of them were marginal to, although not without influence on, the mainstream of Halakhic Judaism, which emerged as a fully fledged orthodoxy for the first time in the history of Jewish civilization. Only a few really developed within the central fold of Judaism – perhaps the most articulate being the Karaites who appeared in Eretz Israel and the Near East in the second half of the eighth century, denying the validity of the Oral Law and attempting to go back only to the Written Law – the Torah.

All these potentialities for heterodox developments did exist, even if in a latent way, within medieval Judaism as part of its heritage and its very social structure, its institutions and the composition of its major elites. There were, indeed, groups of mystics, pietists or philosophers; there were many schools of law all of which could have become heterodoxies against the fully fledged orthodoxy of the Halakha. But on the whole, until the threshold of modern times, they did not develop fully either in the religious, cultural sphere or in communal affairs.

These heretical tendencies were all seemingly encompassed within the relatively broad fold of Rabbinical Judaism, accepting, on one level or another, its basic premises. They erupted again with the Sabbatean movement and later in the manifold intellectual and social movements which started to develop from the early modern times and became fully developed with the processes of emancipation in nineteenth-century Europe. Several factors were of crucial importance in assuring their containment within the framework of Rabbinical Judaism.

One was the close internal cohesion of the Jewish communities, due to the combination of internal solidarity and the maintenance of its basic cultural traditions. This solidarity was based first of all in the very strong concord of the family and was extended and reinforced through the close interweaving of all the different leadership elements. Of special importance here was the very close intertwining between the various elements in the communities, between the articulators or the leaders of the community – the leaders of the community and various popular elements within it – and the carriers of the tradition – the scholars, rabbis, mystics, philosophers and poets. However great the tensions between them, they could not survive one without the other and had always to work in common frameworks, thus combining the maintenance of Jewish solidarity with the basic religious orientations and with the overall meaning of Jewish identity focused around its distinctive beliefs, boundaries and symbols.

Second was the fact that many would-be potential apostates did leave the fold, which only served to strengthen the internal cohesion of those remaining and the mechanism of control exercised by the leaders of the Jewish communities.

Thirdly – and in a way most paradoxical – the very fact of dispersion helped to maintain the internal cohesion of the communities, assisting to preserve the boundaries of the faith and keeping many within the fold. It was not only that constant persecution, being driven out from one place to another, strengthened the inward orientation of those, at least, who remained within the fold. Even more paradoxically, in matters of communal arrangements, the dispersion and lack of any centralized, unified authority provided a forum for many of the more independent, autonomous, even semi-anarchic elements inherent, as we have seen, in some of the basic cultural and social orientations prevalent among the Jews.

The same was probably even more true in the field of learning in the broadest sense, in the sphere of Halakha proper. Here also there was no single accepted authority, and different scholars and centres of learning jealously guarded the right of collegial and even individual interpretation and legislation within the common bounds of the accepted – yet also always changing – tradition. Indeed some of the controversy around Maimonides, the Rambam, the most towering intellectual figure of medieval Jewry, was focused not only around his strong philosophical predilections and the concrete details of his Halakhic interpretations and mode of codification, but also against the possibility that he, and later on his work, would attain a sort of monopolistic status in all these fields and would close the gates of interpretation.

Thus in this sphere also the fact of dispersion, of the lack of any single ultimate authority, when combined with the numerous contacts that developed between these communities and centres of learning, provided flexible common frameworks which allowed for some heterogeneity and for different types of creativity.

# CHAPTER 4

# The Modern Times

## General Background – The Decline of Medieval Christian Civilization. The Rise of Capitalism and of the Modern State
### *Introduction*

The walls of Rabbinical Judaism began to shake with the beginning of modern time, with the passing of the Middle Ages and the rise of the early absolutist states – from the late fifteenth through the seventeenth centuries – and crumbled entirely with the spread of the Enlightenment and the French Revolution, and their aftermaths.

This disintegration was precipitated by a series of external upheavals and processes which crystallized in the different parts of the Jewish Diaspora from the end of the sixteenth century through the seventeenth. At the western edge of Europe – in Spain and Portugal – there was, from the middle of the fourteenth century, the period of Inquisition, forced conversion and expulsion from Spain in 1492. This gave rise to far-reaching and intensive outbursts of Messianic hopes; to new intellectual ventures in various fields, above all in philosophy and in Kabbala; to the emergence of new Kabbalistic centres, especially that of Lurianic Kabbala (i.e. the Kabbala of Isaac Luria (1534–72) ) in Eretz Israel in Safed; to the spread of this as well as other related Kabbalistic trends to Turkey, Italy and Poland; to great movements of migration eastward and northward; and to much greater contacts with the non-Jewish population in the different European states.

From the middle of the seventeenth century, the Eastern European Diaspora, concentrated in Poland – one of the Jewish communities which had initially built one of the most prosperous and well-organized Jewish centres with extensive supra-communal organizations and centres of learning – became threatened by the infamous pogroms led by the Ukrainian leader Chmelnitzki in 1648 – one of the most fearful in the history of persecutions of Jews – reinforcing throughout the Jewish communities the Messianic hopes as well as mystical Kabbalistic visions which had followed the expulsion from Spain.

All these tendencies converged in the greatest, and final, medieval Messianic movement – the Sabbatean movement, led by Sabbatai Zevi (1626–76) – which spread throughout all the Jewish communities, encountering fierce opposition from a large proportion of the established Rabbinical scholars and the leaders of the communities, and splitting the Jewish nation in a way unknown in the long period of its medieval history.

The unique spread and impact of this Messianic movement was due to the convergence of several trends and events: the dramatic catastrophic events from the expulsion from Spain to the Chmelnitzki pogroms; the intensification, because of the numerous migratory movements, of the contacts between Jewish communities; the rise, as we shall see, of a new, mobile and very articulate element – that of the Maranos; and the spread of printing.

But while the overt aims of the movement failed (Sabbatai Zevi gave himself up to the Sultan and converted in 1666 to Islam), this overt failure was not – as was the case with most preceding Messianic movements – the end of the story. In many ways it was the beginning. It gave rise to one of the most forceful underground movements and sects, with very strong antinomian tendencies, which claimed amongst other things that the appearance of the Messiah has superseded the rule of the Halakha and opened a new era of freedom. All these movements continued to divide and shake the Jewish communities and the Rabbinical mould, and their repercussions contributed to the later receptivity of Jews to the Enlightenment.

The Sabbatean and post-Sabbatean movements articulated some of the major themes of Jewish tradition. Building on differeent Kabbalistic and mystical visions they combined them with the basic quest for political redemption and for return to the Land of Israel – as well as with the strong antinomian tendencies mentioned above. Later on, in the various subterranean movements, these themes were elaborated and transformed in more mystical directions – reinforcing these strong antinomian tendencies which shook the Rabbinical world to its core, and which were to provide the – direct or indirect – intellectual and historical background to various 'modern' secular themes of freedom and emancipation.

In the developments leading to the Sabbatean movement and beyond it, a new social element became very important in the Jewish communities in these two centuries – namely the Maranos, those Jews who, under the threat of the Inquisition, converted to Christianity. Many of them found their way back to the Jewish fold, but there were also many who, while retaining their Christian faith, maintained some contacts with the Jewish communities. Many of those who came back became leaders of the more mystic and/or the stronger legalistic tendencies to codification of the Halakha. The best known among them was probably Joseph Karo or Caro (1488–1575), the great mystic and the author of the Shulkhan Arukh, the last great code of the Halakha which was to become for centuries the most widespread and authoritative one.

Many of them, especially those who had close contact with the Renaissance in Italy, or with the religious developments in the Netherlands, also participated intensively in secular spheres of cultural creativity – in philosophy and in the sciences – and tried to find some common, tolerant or secular ground with their neighbours which would transcend the old religious divisions. In some cases, as in that of Spinoza, their Jewish identity became attenuated, but usually they maintained it in some form, but very often with a more positive attitude to their host societies.

Whatever their individual beliefs and activities, their position between the two worlds and their great mobility between different Jewish communities made them a new and powerful fermenting element, and to some degree they were forebearers of later developments.

In the Netherlands in general, in Amsterdam and the Hague in particular, and to a smaller extent also in the American colonies, there started to develop the kernels of new types of Jewish communal life or relations – semi-secularized Jews not living in entirely closed Jewish communities but privately, and in open contact with the general community.

All these developments could be seen as harbingers of a new era or at least of a growing tolerance. The readmission of Jews to England under Cromwell, formally acknowledged in 1664 under the reign of Charles II, and later on to the various European Empires, to America – especially to the Dutch and French colonies in North America and to the Caribbean – and briefly even to Brazil was a further indication of this tolerance.

## Shifts in the basic premisses of European civilization

The whole picture of Jewish life changed with the full development of the modern era, especially after the French Revolution and with the rise of modern, capitalist, economies.

The rise of the capitalist economy and of industrialism, and their spread throughout the world – but first of all throughout Europe – opened up new economic opportunities. They were seized upon by the Jews, who had already started to participate – albeit haltingly – in the first stages of these developments, in some of the Western and Central European countries, mainly in finance and large-scale trade, but also to a smaller degree in manufacture.

But the impact of these changes on the whole format of Jewish life can be understood only in conjunction with that of another basic change, namely the change in the ideological premisses of European civilization which took place with the emergence of modernity. These premisses crystallized first of all in the absolutist states and later on in the Great Revolutions, the English, American and above all the French one – and in the consequent social and national movements that developed in Europe throughout the nineteenth and early twentieth centuries. The shift in these premisses, which affected the destiny of the Jews, was a triple one – even though between the three aspects of this shift there developed some significant contradictions, especially as they affected the destiny of the Jews.

First of all, and perhaps most important, was the shift from the traditional religious definition of membership in the civilizational community and of indirect, corporate membership in the political community, to that of a secular universalistic membership in the civilizational frameworks, and a direct, unmediated one in the political community. This conception was inherent already to some degree in the absolutist states, but was most fully epitomized in the French Declaration of the Rights of Man and Citizen of 1789, which declared, as is well known, the universal rights of citizens in purely secular terms – seemingly obliterating, certainly weakening, the strong traditional–religious Christian components in the prevalent definitions of the boundaries of membership of European communities.

The second shift – which did not always run in tandem with the first one, though the two had usually converged together in Western and Central Europe by the end of the nineteenth century – concerned the weakening of the traditional legal power of rulers. The new trend stressed the right of access of all citizens to the very centres of power, and the reformulation of the premises of these centres in an open, modern, universalistic way.

Both these shifts changed the basic relations between the European civilizations and Jews, apparently opening the way for Jews to cease to be strangers in the lands of their settlements. The second shift in particular made them eligible for citizenship in the new emerging political systems, opening the arena of European civilization before the Jews.

But this opportunity of lifting the various restrictions on the participation of the Jewish population in the economic, and above all the political and cultural life of the societies in which they lived, was connected with a new type of demand towards the Jews.

The crux of this demand was that Jews should define themselves only as a religious and not as a national or political community. Their persistence as a distinct and separate national or political identity was seen as a challenge to the emerging civic and national European communities, to the ideas of universal citizenship, as basically incompatible with them. This incompatibility was often stressed by emphasizing the multiplicity of contacts which the Jews in any one country maintained with other Jewish communities – with its implications of double loyalty.

These demands were already inherent to some degree in the policies of many absolutist rulers, like Joseph II of Austria, who were willing to look upon Jews as legitimate domiciled subjects – and not just strangers in their lands – but at the same time abolished the corporate status of the Jewish communities.

These demands became formulated most fully and explicitly in the French Revolution and its aftermath, but were taken up later – even if in different formulations – in other countries, above all in Germany and to a smaller degree in the multi-national Austro-Hungarian Empire.

These trends to the incorporation of the Jews in the modern political life of European nations, based on the two shifts in the premises of European civilization, were to some degree counteracted by the third. This trend was the stress, in the formation of the modern political community of the nation-state, of the more primordial or specific historical bases – be they French, German or Italian – of the emerging political community rather than the more universalistic premises. So the older Christian component, as well as strong primordial elements, often continued to be of importance. The importance of this stress on these components of the modern nation-state was seen in the more formative periods of those countries, like Germany and to a smaller degree also France, where (as against England or the Scandinavian countries) the existence of such national communities and identities had not yet been accepted historically and could not be taken for granted, and where there had not developed a strong tradition of civility, so that the communities often constituted a focus of political and ideological struggle. In such cases the demands on the Jews to give up their national or 'ethnic', primordial and political, as against purely religious, identity not only became very strong, but also became connected with the growth of strong and principled rejection. This rejection was built on the old religious bases but went beyond them, being formulated in modern, secular, national and racist terms – as they developed in modern anti-Semitism, which we shall analyse in somewhat greater detail later on – and denying the possibility of the Jews becoming part of the new European nations.

## Population increase

So the patterns of Jewish history that developed in different parts of Europe throughout the nineteenth century were shaped by the ways in which these forces – those of economic development, and the different combinations of the changing basic premises of the political collectivities – impinged on the Jewish communities, by the opportunities they opened before them, by the Jewish response to these opportunities, and by the reactions to this response of the various sectors of European societies. These necessarily differed between different European societies.

The 'external' aspects of the story are well known. In Western Europe and to a smaller degree also in Central Europe – in Germany and somewhat less in the Austro-Hungarian Empire – the Jewish communities became absorbed relatively quickly, in about two to three generations, into the new expanding economic centres, especially in the urban centres, in commerce and finance, and to a smaller degree in industry and the professions.

These processes were connected first of all with a very rapid growth of the Jewish population. In 1800 there were an estimated 1,500,000 Jews in Europe; in 1825 there were already more than 2,700,000 and by mid-century the number had grown to more than 4,000,000. In 1880, at the start of mass migration of European Jews from the continent, there were nearly 6,800,000 Jews there and at the end of the century the total approached 8,700,000. In 1800, approximately 60 per cent of the world Jewry lived in Europe. In 1880, on the eve of the migration, nearly 90 per cent did. The Jewish population within the Russian Empire grew (notwithstanding the mass Jewish migration at the end of the century) – by 250 per cent between 1825 (1.6 million) and 1880 (nearly four million), and continued to grow to more than five million in 1900; similar patterns of population growth prevailed throughout Europe. In Galicia, the 170,000 Jews in 1825 became nearly 700,000 by 1880, and the Jewish population of Hungary grew from 200,000 to 638,000 during the same period. Between 1815 and 1860 the number of French Jews doubled from 45,000 to 96,000. In unified Germany there were in 1871 more than 500,000 Jews – about three times that of 1837.

There developed a very strong movement of Jewish migration from the small communities in which they had previously been spread into the major urban centres (although sometimes also moving into new rural areas in which economic opportunities appeared), where they concentrated in the new expanding economic sectors. They also migrated westward from Eastern to Central and from Central to Western Europe – and, from all these areas, overseas. While the details varied, of course, according to local circumstances and above all according to the tempo and mode of economic development, the overall trend was very similar throughout Europe and reinforced the migratory tradition which had become so characteristic of Jewish life since late Antiquity.

## Western and Central Europe

But this process of incorporation into the new economic and social structure was not just a demographic and economic one; it was connected with a growing attempt on the part of the Jews to become accepted as part of the emerging political community and civil society, seemingly already based on the new universalistic premisses. The process of this political incorporation of emancipation, as it was called, was, in Western and Central Europe, more arduous and halting than that of Jewish economic and occupational mobility – nevertheless it appeared to be a strong and irreversible process. Gradually the Jews lost their status of strangers, religious limitations on citizenship were lifted, and political emancipation and full rights of citizenship were achieved; but these developments were always closely related to attempts to change the nature of Jewish communal life, taking away from the various Kehillot the overall juridical rights with which they had been vested and attempting to define them in purely religious terms, and often also attempting to alter the Jews' basic way of life.

The first indications of such emancipation appeared in the Austro-Hungarian Empire. In 1771 Joseph II of Austria announced the Edict of Tolerance and in 1789 he applied it to Galicia as well, the aim of which was to remove Jews from specific occupations and integrate them into the society at large. Thus, Jews were no longer allowed to operate inns and engage in tax-farming and they were also – significantly enough – forbidden to send money to the Jewish communities of Palestine. The edict destroyed also the political power of the Kehillot and limited them to specialized religious activities. At the same time, the rules specified that Jews attend public schools and were permitted to attend gymnasia and universities. They were enjoined to conduct their business affairs in German, not in Yiddish, and they had to adopt family names as well; the edict did not, however, remove travel bans and special taxes. These were lifted only after the Revolution of 1848.

This double tendency – on the one hand facilitating incorporation into the European society up to the granting of full citizenship, but on the other hand demanding the transformation of the Jews into religious communities, and removing the special legal and political status of the Kehillot – developed in full force after the French Revolution, spreading later, in different variations and patterns, throughout Western and Central Europe – France, the German states, the Austro-Hungarian Empire, the Netherlands, Belgium and Switzerland.

Large parts of these Jewish communities did indeed, in theory and in practice, accept these demands and started to define themselves as purely religious communities or as associations of purely co-religionist individuals – hoping in this way to open the gates of the general society, to assure their participation in it. As we shall see, these efforts gave rise to far-reaching internal transformations and started an intensive process of assimilation.

But this path was never a smooth one. This relative concentration of Jews in the cities, in specific economic sectors, and their growing visibility in cultural spheres – such as journalism, the arts or radical social movements – produced a very strong reaction: a counter-movement to their actual and potential assimilation, i.e. modern anti-Semitism.

It was not only that many of the Jews were not accepted into Gentile society and *de facto* remained socially separate. Beyond diffuse, seemingly informal even if very effective, social segregation, there started to develop, already in the early nineteenth century, a new form of the old hatred of the Jews, which had been rooted in the Christian faith. This new form was a secular, national, racist anti-Semitism. It was first articulated in the works of scholars – journalists like J. A. Gobineau (1816–82) or Houston Stewart Chamberlain (1855–1927) – who defined the Jews not, as was the case in 'classical' Christianity, just in religious terms, but in secular – racial, biological, at best national – ones. They denied the very possibility of the Jews ever being transformed into a 'mere' religious community and of being assimilable into the political and social body of the new emerging nation-states. This attitude was taken up by many of the modern anti-Semitic movements – culminating, of course, in the Nazi ideology.

## Eastern Europe and migration

The situation of the Jewish communities was different in many, but not all, crucial details in Eastern Europe – in the Russian Empire and to a smaller degree in the Austro-Hungarian Empire – where, as we have seen above, the larger part of the Jewish communities in Europe and the world lived.

Here, and above all in Russia, the pace of economic development and of industrialization was much slower. Small parts of the Jewish community were indeed very active in the forefront of some of the new economic developments and ventures. But in the main centres – especially in Poland and Western Russia – the range of economic activity opened to them was much narrower. The largest parts of the Jewish community were still limited to petty trade and manufacture, to various types of middleman activities in the rural sectors.

But even in these relatively backward countries or sectors, once some processes of economic development, modernization and urbanization started, the Jews began to participate in them very actively – evincing the same general trend to population growth, concentration in urban sectors, and migration. But here they moved into cities in which more cohesive types of Jewish life were maintained, and they concentrated much more than in Western Europe in the small and middle-sized industries, giving rise to the development, towards the end of the nineteenth century, of a very cohesive Jewish working class.

In so far as they succeeded in going beyond these semi-traditional occupations into the modern ones, such as industry or modern commerce, they of course came into conflict with different strata of the indigenous population – be they Poles, Ukrainians or White Russians, or even the Russians themselves – who were also aspiring to these positions or who saw themselves as exploited by the economically and socially mobile Jews.

These negative attitudes to the Jews were reinforced by the cultural–political premises of the East European polities. The Russian Empire defined itself as a traditional, autocratic Christian polity, not allowing, in principle, any free access to the centres of power and defining the Jews as a religiously alien, politically subjugated community, and limiting their residence to the famous overpopulated 'pale' – in Poland and the Ukraine and some western parts of Russia – thus constraining their immigration eastwards and northwards.

At the same time the Tsars greatly limited the powers of the Jewish communities, imposing heavy taxes on them and above all making them at least partially responsible for ensuring the quotas of Jews into the Tsarist army for long periods (twenty years), to become carriers of the Russian–Christian vision to the Jews.

The situation in the Austro-Hungarian Empire was more complex. Already in the eighteenth century, as we have seen above, there had developed a more tolerant attitude to Jews – a tolerance based on demands that the Jews became mostly a religious community and modernized themselves. The granting of some concessions towards the different nationalities of the Empire reinforced this attitude in favour of the Jews, as did also the quicker tempo of economic development than in Russia. There were fewer restrictions on the Jews than in Russia, and – as part of the relative liberalization of the political system of the Empire – these were gradually lifted. Thus many Jews advanced economically, socially and culturally – although there were considerable differences in the situation of the Jewish communities in the various provinces of the Austro-Hungarian Empire. On the whole these Jewish communities exhibited a rather complex mixture of Western and Eastern European elements, with many special characteristics – as for instance the development of very strong semi-modern orthodox organizations, side by side with Reform ones in Hungary. In Hungary itself the Jews did to some degree fill the position of a modern middle class and intelligentsia – although many of them lived in rural towns.

The Russian and Austro-Hungarian Empires were not, however, tranquil or static. They were increasingly exposed to the impact of international, political, economic and ideological forces. The most important among these new internal forces were the many reformist, revolutionary and nationalist movements aiming at the reconstruction of the Russian or Austrian polity, as well as the movements of the various nationalities – above all the Poles, Ukrainians and Lithuanians among whom the largest part of the Jewish population lived – to find some way of national self-definition, even political independence.

The attempts of the Russian Empire to defend itself against these forces only reinforced, especially under the reigns of Tsar Nicolai (1825–55), Alexander the Third (1881–94) and Nicholas the Second (1894–1917), its reactionary attitudes in general and to the Jews in particular.

Both in the Russian and especially in the Austro-Hungarian Empire, the Jews, whose numbers were continuously expanding, were caught between these various, often contradictory, trends. One response was the beginning of a great process of movement of population from within the geographical confines of their respective countries. This process, which started in the 1830s and 1840s in Germany, was destined to change the whole course of Jewish history – a process of migration to new lands, above all to the United States, but also to Latin America, Canada, Australia and South Africa. This movement, which was a part of the general migration of European populations beyond Europe, continued the great migratory traditions of Jewry, especially in medieval times. It had started slowly in Central Europe in the early nineteenth century and gained momentum in Eastern Europe in 1881, especially after the famous pogroms of 1882. In numerical terms, between 1840 and 1880 about a quarter of a million Jews – mainly from Germany and Austria-Hungary, to a smaller degree from Russia and Romania – came to the United States. Then, between 1881 and 1914 about 3,000,000 Jews migrated from Eastern Europe and spread through Europe to Latin America, the Dominions and above all to the United States. About 350,000 settled in Germany and France; about 200,000 in England, where the number of Jews till then was less than 100,000. About 120,000 went to Argentina, 400,000 to South Africa, 100,000 to Canada and almost 2,000,000 to the United States.

This migratory movement bolstered existing Jewish communities in Europe and created new ones. Above all it created a new – and destined to become the greatest – Jewish community in the Diaspora, that in the United States, a community which was no longer a replica of the European Jewish communities, but, as we shall see later, one that developed – even if gradually – in an entirely new way.

## Oriental communities and the Near East

In the middle of the nineteenth century about 500,000 Jews lived in the different parts of the Ottoman Empire – in Turkey itself, in what was to be Iraq, in Egypt and in North Africa, in Syria and Palestine, and in far-away Yemen. Most of them had been there since ancient times, or at the latest since the expulsion from Spain. They identified themselves as different parts of what were later to be called Sephardi or Oriental communities, be they Maghreban or Egyptian Jews, some emphasizing their pure Sephardi origin, very often split into many sub-communities.

The days of economic and cultural glory of these communities were, on the whole, over with the decline of the Mediterranean trade and the continuous weakening of the Ottoman Empire. Many of them lived in relatively closed communities, maintaining their traditional ways of life in some symbiosis with their neighbours, sometimes in relatively peaceful relations, sometimes in very tense and antagonistic ones – but always as a subjugated minority. They maintained the specific Jewish institutions of prayer and learning. Some of these, as for instance those in distant Yemen, constituted not insignificant centres of learning, but on the whole they did not retain the relative centrality in the Jewish world which they had held from the ninth to the twelfth centuries and later, after the expulsion from Spain, in the sixteenth and seventeenth centuries.

From about the end of the eighteenth century, parts of these communities were slowly incorporated into the framework of modern economic expansion and social-cultural movements, which came above all in the wake of European colonial expansion.

The Oriental communities started to undergo far-reaching processes of change and modernization from about the last third of the nineteenth century, with the growing impingement of European colonization and Imperialism and the continuous weakening of the Ottoman Empire. Of special importance here was the French colonization of the different North African countries – Algeria, Morocco, Tunisia – the growing European penetration into Egypt, and the competition of the European pioneers in all parts of the Ottoman Empire.

In North Africa there was an intensive Jewish migration from the hinterland to the coastal cities – about one-third of the Jews of Morocco moved to these cities between 1830 and 1900 – and a similar process can be identified in Tunisia, Algeria and Egypt. New Jewish elements also emigrated to these countries – Italian Jews came to Tunisia, French Jews to Algeria, and Central European and Russian Jews to Egypt.

These processes were combined with a growing weakening of the old traditional milieu and elites – as well as of their dependence on the Ottoman powers. Many Jews attempted to receive the protectorate of European powers; all the Jews in Algeria became French citizens; in other places they tried to be protected by the European powers so as to emancipate themselves from the yoke of the Ottoman state.

All these developments undermined the traditional communities and the authority of their secular and Rabbinical leaders alike, and produced far-reaching educational and occupational changes among the Jews. On the eve of the First World War about 48,000 children in North Africa attended the Alliance schools, and there were several other such institutions. Many of the higher-class Jews in Egypt lived in a very cosmopolitan atmosphere, and this trend became, of course, intensified after the First World War, not only in the communities of North Africa but also in Iraq and Syria, and new, modern types of Jewish organizations, including different Zionist organizations and movements, developed in these countries.

Although this process was probably weaker and less intensive than in the various European countries, it was nevertheless a very dynamic one. There were, however, two elements which were almost entirely lacking, as compared with the experience in Western and Central Europe. There were no attempts to reconstruct Jewish religious life in a new, modern 'non-orthodox' way, and (with the partial exception of some sectors of North African society) there was no ideological attempt at incorporation into the existing ruling society. Quite naturally – given the basic traditional, Islamic premises of the Ottoman Empire and of the colonial situation – there was no special stimulus for the development of such religious movements as the Reform or Liberal one. The traditional Sephardi rabbinate and community organizations prevailed, but losing much of their authority to the more modern or secular ways of life, without at the same time facing any new and powerful ideological challenge either in religious or in liberal or in national terms.

# The Disintegration of the Rabbinical Mould and the Processes of Reconstruction of Jewish Civilization
## Occupational and educational changes

This story of the Jewish communities from about the end of the eighteenth century provides the basic data of Jewish history in the period, but not its internal dynamism and convolutions – dynamics and convolutions which signified the end of a long period of 'medieval' exilic history, the major characteristics of which were analysed in Chapter 3.

As we saw in Chapter 3, the combination of changes in the basic premises of the European civilizations, and of the related, expanding economic opportunities, affected all the basic characteristics of medieval Jewish society; what can be called traditional Jewish society began to disintegrate and the modern era of Jewish history began.

Externally the disintegration of traditional Jewish society was manifest above all in ecological processes and in occupational and educational changes. The Jews lived less and less within the confines of occupationally and economically restricted and ecologically dispersed enclaves. Although Jews continued to concentrate in fairly specific occupations and in certain sectors of cities, they began to live in partially open frameworks and in principle, at least, they could already participate more fully and openly in the various occupational and economic sectors of European societies.

But it was not the degree of economic or ecological concentration that was the crux of the matter – although this in itself was naturally very significant. What was crucial was the combination of these great changes in the ecological and economic structure of Jewish life with those in the premises of the host civilization. This combination gave rise to a more radical change in the life of the Jewish people – namely to the end not just of the ecological but also of the social, cultural and institutional self-segregation of the Jews. The traditional 'medieval' symbolic and institutional style of life and boundaries of the Jewish community, and the type of cultural and social distinction that characterized them in the medieval period, gradually weakened and ultimately disappeared.

The most visible process was, of course, that of the breaking up of the older institutional framework – economic, ecological, educational and occupational – of Jewish communal life mentioned above. Large areas of the Jews' life and institutional activities were no longer confined to a specific Jewish framework. They moved to great cities, engaged in a variety of occupations, sent their children to general schools and were active consumers of general cultural life.

The changes in life-style of the Jews in Western and Central Europe – in styles of dress, housing, in manners of speech, in leisure-time activities, in modes of cultural participation – were rapid, very quickly obliterating the characteristics which had made them so distinctive in their environment in medieval times. They very quickly acquired the languages of their host societies – an acquisition which was part of probably the single most important change in their social-cultural life: their growing access to the general educational institutions (at the expense, of course, of their traditional modes of learning). Thus, to give only one illustration, in 1839 about 40 per cent of the Jewish youngsters in Berlin studied at Jewish schools; in 1850 the percentage had declined to 29 per cent and in 1867 Jews accounted for 15 per cent of the students in the Berlin Gymnasia, four times their share of the population.

## Institutional changes

These changes in the Jews' patterns of life, together with those in their educational and occupational structure, were strongly connected with the weakening of the institutional and symbolic boundaries of the Jewish communities, of the Jewish people. This became evident first of all in the radical changes in the official, judicial standing of Jewish communal organizations. The traditional powers and jurisdiction of the Jewish Kehillot were removed, thus also ending their status as specific, distinct estates of strangers. Instead the Jews became, in principle at least, legitimate inhabitants rather than strangers, and somewhat later on full citizens, of their respective societies.

Their life tended to become more closely interwoven into the institutional matrices of the host societies. Jews were no longer symbolically segregated in distinct communities which defined, under the aegis of the Halakha, the basic boundaries of their collective life and the arena for the implementation of their specific civilizational vision. They started to open their boundaries, to change the definition of their collective identity in relation to the surrounding society, and to see participation in that society as their new role in life, the way to achieve their own civilizational mission – in so far as they were still interested in maintaining it.

Admittedly, many of the institutional characteristics of the Jewish communities – above all synagogues, organizations of mutual help and to some degree the traditional institutions of learning – persisted, and new ones, as we shall see, did develop. But they no longer constituted the central matrix of Jewish life, nor did they define its boundaries.

All this was, of course, tantamount to the weakening, even to the total disappearance in many places, of the Rabbinical symbolic and institutional mould, its premises and manifestations as the predominant institutional and specific civilizational framework.

This weakening of the Rabbinical mould entailed not only changes in the pattern of daily life, but also the possibility of the concomitant transformation and recrystallization of the components of Jewish collective identity and of the symbolic boundaries of the Jewish community, and a basic shift in the conception of the proper institutional arena for the implementation of the specific modes of Jewish civilizational vision. It was not just a question of a general trend to secularism or religious apathy – though needless to say these two processes did take place among many Jews. More significantly there were various attempts – such as the Liberal or the Reformist ones – at reformulation of Jewish religious tenets and of the degree to which ritual–legal prescriptions had to be observed. This was all part of a more general process of the reconstruction of Jewish life and civilization.

Even among the neo-orthodox – first in Germany, then in other countries, especially Hungary – who insisted on total observance according to the Halakha, such insistence was already combined with a very large degree of principled participation in general society and in its civilizational mould, in its educational, economic and cultural structures and organizations.

## The special pattern of Jewish assimilation

In the first wake of emancipation it seemed as if all these transformations would go, as it were, in one direction – assimilation – with possible pockets of orthodoxy remaining segregated from modern life. According to this view – as held above all by the traditionalists, by the orthodox who felt themselves to be on the defensive, but also to some degree by the supporters of assimilation themselves – assimilation was a continuous, unidirectional process on two related levels, those of culture and of the collective Jewish identity.

Indeed, among substantial parts of the Jewish communities, above all in Western Europe and later on in the United States and Latin America, and to a much more limited degree also in the realm of Russian, Polish and Austro-Hungarian Jewry, total assimilation did occur, often connected with inter-marriage and sometimes – especially, but not only, during the first stages of emancipation and assimilation – conversion to Christianity. These processes were also connected, initially at least, with the gradual shedding of 'ethnic', primordial or national components of Jewish identity, its transposition into folkloristic usage or memories, and the initial reformulation of their identity into purely religious terms. There are, obviously, no exact figures, but such trends towards assimilation were certainly not insignificant – although, significantly enough, some of the descendants of these Jews returned later on, after the Holocaust and the establishment of the State of Israel, to admit and even to cherish their Jewish heritage, defining it anew in some combinations of primordial, ethnic, religious, and possibly political, terms.

This process of assimilation was of course not peculiarly Jewish; it has been common to many ethnic groups in Europe as well as, later, in the United States or other countries of immigration and colonization.

What was peculiarly Jewish was that it was not the whole story. It was not the whole story because – unlike in the case of most other ethnic groups – for the Jews there was added to the national and social prejudice between different ethnic and social groups, between host people and immigrants, that special dimension of religious and modern anti-Semitism – the continuous stress on the unique quality of the Jews, their experience and their relation to their host people – which in many ways obviated the possibilities of a relatively peaceful assimilation.

But there were two further, closely related factors which made the Jewish story unique. First of all, in almost all Jewish communities, the challenge of the decomposition of traditional Jewish society and the Rabbinical mould, the search for new arenas in which to articulate the specific Jewish civilizational experience and to reconstruct the Jewish tradition, its contents and premises, and the boundaries of their collective life, were taken up in such a variety of ways by different groups within the Jewish community, becoming a focus of continuous endeavours and conflicts within them, that they attested to the endurance of some crucial aspects of Jewish civilizational orientations and identity. Secondly, the whole pattern of the organization of Jewish life developed in a rather different way from that of many other religious or ethnic groups.

These challenges were taken up on both the level of social-communal and cultural organization, and the more ideological level.

It is of course very difficult to know how much they affected the daily life of different Jewish communities. Certainly this challenge was taken up above all by small groups of leaders and intellectuals, but this has always been the case in such instances of articulated cultural creativity – just as, for instance, the tradition of Halakha was, in the traditional communities, articulated by such leaders. Be that as it may, many parts of the Jewish communities, and especially many intellectuals and leaders, accepted these various challenges to reconstruct Jewish life. The response to them, taken together with the changes in economic situation and in ecological structures, constituted the basic poles of the dynamics of modern Jewish history.

The great variety of ways in which these challenges were met, by different sectors of the Jewish community, and in different countries and periods of modern Jewish history, underlined some of the major themes and tensions inherent in the Jewish tradition: namely those between universalism and particularism, between ethical–legal and cultic elements, tradition, and between commitment to the preceding mould and attempts to go beyond it.

The very multiplicity and variability of these directions constituted the great diversity of modern Jewish history, much more reminiscent of the period of the Second Temple and of the Hellenistic and Babylonian Diasporas, and of its immediate aftermath in the period of the Gaonim, than of the 'classical' medieval Rabbinical era. Nevertheless they did develop directly out of it and did build, as we shall see in somewhat greater detail later on, on many of the foundations of this 'classical' mould – both on some of its official premisses but above all on those orientations and themes which were latent within it.

# The Institutional and Ideological Attempts at the Reconstruction of Jewish Life and Civilization in Western and Central Europe

## Enlightenment – the Haskala

The major movement – intellectual and, to some degree, social – which heralded the incorporation of different Jewish communities into various European societies was that of Enlightenment – *Haskala*.

Its central theme was the reconstruction of Jewish life, tradition and civilization, according to the precepts of Enlightenment, of 'rationalism', so as to make it fully participant in the emerging universal rational, civilizational mould while potentially contributing to this mould some specific Jewish ingredients. While not necessarily in itself anti-religious in the narrow sense – its first heralds, like Moses Mendelssohn (1729–86) or Naftali Herz Weisel (1725–1805), insisted on strict observance of the Halakhic laws – it did negate the exclusive predominance of Rabbinical Judaism as the major institutional framework. It also rejected definitions of the boundaries of Jewish collective identity in terms of radical segregation and exclusiveness from the neighbouring nations. Instead it emphasized the possibility and the necessity of reconstructing many aspects of Jewish life – starting above all from education and encompassing to some extent economic production as well as cultural and social activities – in the direction of greater incorporation into the general European societies.

But the actual orientations of the *Haskala* movement, and the different movements within the Jewish communities which developed in its wake – above all their implication for the reconstruction of modern Jewish life, of its vision of Jewish participation in the new civilization and its possible contribution to it – differed greatly, as we shall see, in the Western and Eastern European Jewish communities.

The first and seemingly most dramatic tendency which developed forcefully in Western Europe, Germany and France, and to a lesser degree in England or Holland, was to redefine the Jewish community as above all a religious community and seemingly to give up entirely its political, national, and in principle also primordial, elements. It could be connected, as among some of the modern neo-orthodox groups, with a very strict maintenance of the religious observances and of the religious collectivity, and in such cases it entailed also the retainment of the primordial or ethnic components of collective identity – but in a rather diluted way.

This trend was also connected with changes and weakening – as compared with earlier Jewish communities in the West – in the whole complex of Jewish institutions and associations. The specific Jewish institutions – the synagogues, educational and philanthropic activities, different communal organizations (many of which developed new centralized patterns like the Board of Deputies in England and the Consistoire in France) and the new institutions of Jewish higher learning or journalistic activities – no longer encompassed the whole of the life of the Jews, nor, except (and even among them, only partially) among the neo-orthodox, were they seen as the major arena of Jewish civilizational creativity.

Similarly, as we have seen above, on the level of daily life, although the largest parts of the Jewish population moved in mostly Jewish circles, yet they found the various specifically Jewish social and cultural institutions and patterns of life secondary.

Moreover, Jews started and continued to participate visibly in some central – academic, literary, journalistic – areas of the general society and their participation and visibility in these fields became – especially in Germany and Austria, to some degree in France and England, and later on, as we shall see, in the United States – very pronounced.

They also started to participate in another field which had naturally been barred to them in the former period – namely general social and political movements. As the more conservative parties of the establishment were usually closed to them, it was chiefly in the more radical political movements, such as the liberal and later on the socialist ones, that they were most active.

## Universal message and participation

In some aspects of the Jews' participation in European cultural and political life, and above all in the more specific Jewish activities and organizations, those among them who did not become totally assimilated or even converted to Christianity (and sometimes even these) developed a series of activities which were specifically Jewish, which tackled the major problems of reconstructing the components of the Jewish civilization analysed above. In these activities the contradictions between, on the one hand, the tendencies to extensive assimilation and, on the other, the concern with the specific problems of Jewish civilization, were often vividly apparent.

Such redefinition of collective identity was necessarily connected with a basic reformulation of the major themes and tensions inherent in the Jewish collective self-definition – above all the tension between the universalistic and particularist orientations, between the eschatological vision and the present; the concomitant identification of the proper arena for the realization of the

Jewish civilizational vision, and the restructuring of the boundaries of the Jewish collectivity in relation to those of other collectivities or civilizations.

It was with respect to these aims that there took place the most far-reaching changes in relation to the medieval Rabbinical tradition. The concrete arena for the implementation of the Jewish civilizational vision was no longer limited to the daily reality of a segregated national–religious community, nor did it point to a distant future. This arena was more and more envisaged as the present, contemporaneous European civilization, to which the Jews were to make their specific contribution, but not in the genre of a segregated community. Here it was, of course, the universalistic orientation that was heavily emphasized, stressing the universal message inherent in the ethical prophecy, as against the more particularistic definition of the Rabbinical mould and the concomitant almost total self-enclosure of the Jewish community.

Even the very attempt at emancipation, or at assimilation, was often couched in terms of the specific premises of the Jewish tradition. Thus, as J. Katz has put it:

The greater part of the community, however, and especially the newly evolved elite of the enlightened, the maskilim, not only accepted naturalization and emancipation as a welcome deliverance from the dire circumstance of the Ghetto, but lent it an historical and spiritual significance. Naturalization and emancipation were hailed as traditionally reserved for the Messianic Age, to the point of identifying kings and princes, the guarantors of the new civil status, with the person of the Messiah. This identification should not be dismissed as an ideological embellishment of the new political and social achievement. It was more than that. As conceived by the original initiators, naturalization and emancipation were meant to provide a new perspective and prognosis for the future of Jewry. The abolishment of alienage was to replace the expectation of a Messianic delivery from the predicament of aliens on foreign soil. According to this conception, the various segments of the nation would be granted a home in their respective environments, thus achieving for the individual, in terms of legal and political status, what the Messianic expectation held out for the nation as a whole.*

This attitude was evident in the way that Jews participated in the cultural and political life of these societies. They concentrated in the more liberal and radical movements, in the more critical academic subjects like sociology (where, for instance, Émile Durkheim propagated a new secular morality and civic consciousness), and in the more critical and liberal parts of the press, and with an intensity seen by many as something specifically Jewish.

It was indeed this universal, liberal, ethical message, seemingly contained in these activities, that was often seen by many Jewish intellectuals – and in a less fully articulated way also by the wider sectors of the Jewish community – as the essence of the Jewish civilization. It necessarily entailed abandoning the idea of Jewish self-segregation, stressing the growing participation in general society as full citizens and participants in its civilization, carrying its special mission to the nations – a mission that was no longer embodied (except among the neo-

* J. Katz, 'The Jewish Diaspora: "Minority Positions and Majority Aspirations",' *Jerusalem Quarterly*, 25 (Fall 1982), pp. 73–4.

orthodox circles) in the more traditional tenets of Rabbinical Judaism.

Indeed many Jews saw in these more liberal and civic attitudes, and in their internal intellectual activities, an articulation of that aspect of universalistic Jewish heritage which had not found a proper expression in medieval times: the emphasis on universal ethical principles uniquely expressed in the prophetic tradition.

## Religious developments

Closely related to these orientations were some of the most specific and spectacular attempts at the reconstruction of the Jewish religion in the light of the more universal tenets of the Enlightenment: there was a move away from the strong emphasis of the legal-ritual dimensions of the Halakha in the direction of the more 'ethical' and prophetic elements of Jewish religion.

Thus there developed from the first half of the nineteenth century the various movements of 'reform' or liberal Judaism, changing the religious practices of the Jews in what seemed to them to be a more modern direction.

These changes were connected with the attempts to define the Jews as a religious community, whose religion was part of a wider universal panorama of monotheistic religions, sharing with them – as with more general philosophical deistic orientations – many common assumptions, moving together into an era of common tolerance and enlightenment.

These attempts at the reconstruction of the religious life of the Jews – often with a strong ideological overtone – although in many ways specific to the Jews, were not always successful in keeping the younger generations in the Jewish fold. The saying among more orthodox or nationalist circles – 'I have never seen a third generation of reform Jews' – may be exaggerated, but contains a strong element of truth, although certainly not the whole of it.

Indeed this attempt to reformulate Jewish identity was paradoxically enough connected with the emergence of a great intellectual movement – that of the *Wissenschaft des Judentums* – a movement out of which modern Jewish historical and philological study and research emerged, represented by figures like Abraham Geiger (1810–74) and Leopold Zunz (1794–1886), the founders of modern Jewish scholarship, and later on the great historian Heinrich Graetz (1817–91).

This great intellectual creativity, especially of the first generations, was guided by a certain paradox. Their official programme and vision was gradually to transform the Jews into a religious community and shed their national identity. Yet their immense scholarship enhanced the historical self-consciousness and identity of the Jewish collectivity, and put the study of Judaism in the framework of modern scholarship.

Of special importance in this context were two types of activities closely related to the dominant intellectual modes in Western Europe in general and in Germany in particular – namely those of philosophy of history and of history proper.

Thus one of the major intellectual activities which developed in the context of the *Wissenschaft des Judentums* was that of religious or historical philosophy. Men like Nahman Krochmal (1785–1840), Geiger or Solomon Ludwig Steinheim (1808–89), and later on Hermann Cohen (1842–1918), Franz Rosenzweig (1886–1929) and Martin Buber (1878–1965), building on the Jewish medieval philosophers but going beyond them to develop a positive attitude to other religious civilizations, attempted to define the specific Jewish contribution to the religious consciousness of mankind and to the unfolding of universal history. Often they emphasized not only the religious, political or national-primordial components of Jewish life, but also its collective identity.

From this point of view Heinrich Graetz provided an important turning-point in Jewish historical research. Instead of trying to explain the course of Jewish history in terms of the movement of some disembodied Hegelian spirit, he wrote his massive history of the Jews as a history of a political, national community – greatly contributing to the development of a collective consciousness among many 'modern', educated, Jews.

## International links

The distinctive characteristics of the Jewish response to modernity were also evident in special features of the occupational and ecological structure of the Jewish communities, as well as of the internal Jewish life and institutions, which, as J. Katz has shown,* evinced from the beginning of the nineteenth century some rather distinct characteristics.

First there was the relatively high degree of social segregation, of endogamy – although of course this did change among the more assimilated. Second was the very multiplicity and scope of activities of Jewish associations or societies – be they religious, philanthropic or scholarly – which on the whole went far beyond those found among other religious or ethnic groups, and many of which were concerned not only with keeping up some remnants of tradition, but in actively redefining it – often, as already indicated above, in the basic terms which characterized it throughout Jewish history.

Moreover – and this is crucial – most of these Jewish organizations were 'international'; they were concerned with helping Jewish communities throughout the world – often enough as 'co-religionists' but nevertheless stressing the international dimension of Jewish existence.

Interestingly enough, the first such development took place in the first country of intensive semi-ideological assimilation, in France. In 1860 the Alliance Israélite, designed for educational, semi-political work in a modern vein among all Jewish communities, was established by more professional Jewish groups from within the periphery, challenging to some degree the assimilated leaders of the Jewish community in Paris, setting a pattern for similar developments in other Jewish communities.

* J. Katz, *Out of the Ghetto, The Social Background of Jewish Emancipation 1770–1870* (Cambridge, Mass. 1973).

Even the more internal religious Jewish organizations, whether those of reform Judaism or the institutions of Jewish learning and scholarship in different countries of Europe, were in continuous mutual contact, helping each other, reinforcing or counteracting each other – but always maintaining a range and intensity of contact between different Jewish communities which was rarely found among other religious or ethnic groups.

## Differences and similarities in various Jewish communities in Western Europe

The concrete patterns of the organization of Jewish life and of the type of intellectual, social and political activities in which they engaged, were naturally greatly influenced by the institutional patterns and intellectual trends prevalent in the respective countries in which they lived.

The following illustrations are chosen almost at random. The centralist mode of organization of French political life gave rise to a parallel centralist tendency in the organization of the major Jewish institutions – especially the Consistoire – while the sharp articulation of political controversies in nineteenth-century France greatly influenced the intensive participation of many Jewish personalities in this field.

The central place of historical and philosophical studies in the intellectual and public life of Germany was very conducive to the rise of the *Wissenschaft des Judentums* and to studies concerned with a philosophical and theological interpretation of Jewish historical and collective experience, while the more decentralized state of German intellectual and also political life – even to some degree after the establishment of the Empire – facilitated the development of more diversified and dispersed Jewish institutions.

Similarly the relatively low degree of concern in England with the philosophical or ideological dimension of political life minimized the scope for such activities among the Jews; the more traditional civic and aristocratic organization of public life facilitated the acceptance of Jews as a quasi-ethnic community and the development of their central organization – the Board of Deputies, the Chief Rabbinate – in keeping with such a civic–oligarchic mode.

Gradually, through education and participation in the civic life of different societies, Jews in different countries acquired some aspects of their hosts' mentality, above all with respect to their conception of public life and their definition of those aspects of this life – such as the relations between Church and State – which were most important for them.

Yet, despite the great differences between the Jews of different countries, they continued to share several crucial interests and orientations. They shared – with the exception of the majority of the totally assimilated – a collective identity which cut across national boundaries and which, notwithstanding the efforts of the groups orientated to assimilation, was not purely confessional.

On the ideological–political level, they shared the concern with problems of

Jewish emancipation and the search for some way of reconstructing their identity and special civilizational vision, and there developed continuous mutual orientations between the Jewish ideological and religious trends. On the more practical–organizational level, they shared the concern with common Jewish educational, philanthropic and semi-political activities.

The flow of immigration and the continuous influx of new immigrants into established Jewish communities – with all the tensions between them – served also as a continuous link between different Jewish communities.

In all these ways the reality of Jewish life, even under the aegis of Emancipation and of incorporation into the general European societies, evinced some combination of social and cultural creativity, multiplicity of activities, mutual contacts, and reactions, that went beyond the attempts to redefine Jewish identity in purely religious or diluted ethnic terms.

And all these processes belied – except for those who succeeded in shedding all Jewish identity – the possibility of full assimilation or of defining the Jews as a purely religious, confessional community.

These possibilities were also to some degree belied by the fact that often the very shedding of the corporate Jewish identity, and even the weakening of attachment to the religious tradition, paradoxically brought out the more primordial components of Jewish identity – often also giving rise to sharp anti-Semitic reactions among many sectors of the general society.

## *Dissociation of cultural activities and communal organization*

These specific characteristics of the institutional cultural activities, as they developed among the Jews in Western and Central Europe, were however characterized by one very specific feature – above all from the point of view of the structure of leaderships and the areas of their activity. On the one hand there emerged a great variety and heterogeneity of types of leadership – political, communal, cultural and intellectual – reminiscent of the period of the Second Commonwealth and the Hellenistic Diaspora.

At the same time there was a strong tendency to some – even if never full – personal and institutional dissociation between the intellectual, or ideological, and the organizational side of their activities, above all between specifically Jewish activities and more general work in the economic, cultural and educational fields. These different types of activities were not on the whole – with the partial exception of some of the new Rabbinical general representative institutions – entirely integrated in common organizational frameworks. Above all these specifically Jewish activities and organizations were not strongly connected – if at all – with the participation of Jews in broader institution-building, in the economic, educational, cultural and political spheres.

The most eminent and intellectual and ideological leaders were either active or visible in general rather than in specific Jewish contexts or, if in the latter, in the new institutions of learning.

The leaders of the different communal and philanthropic Jewish associations – like the Board of Deputies in England or the Consistoire and the Alliance in France, and similar institutions in other countries – were active in these special frameworks which were on the whole distinct from, although often connected with, those in the broader cultural institutions and activities, as well as, of course, from the more spectacular cultural activities in the general society.

Thus, from the point of view of the economic advancement of the Jews in nineteenth-century Western and Central Europe, of their social and cultural creativity, and of their consequent potential integration into the framework of the general societies, a paradox emerged.

The crumbling of the walls of the Ghetto opened up to them many avenues for creativity – fields which were no longer in any sense specifically Jewish. At the same time, however, the intensity and mode of participation of the Jews in these fields increased their visibility as a special, distinct, element, emphasizing some specifically Jewish characteristics.

To some sectors of the general society this activity of the Jews was seen as a positive element in the emerging national or civic cultures. But other elements – the more conservative and populistic elements in periods and places when the activities of the Jews were caught up with far-reaching social upheavals, with the development of national movements, and above all when these processes were, as in Germany, combined with an autocratic regime – evaluated this participation of the Jews in negative terms. Many circles saw in this active and visible participation – especially when allied with very rapid economic and occupational advancement – a manifestation of the pushiness of the Jews and of their rootlessness and 'cosmopolitanism'. These themes were increasingly articulated by the developing modern anti-Semitic movements, which stressed the unique character of the Jews and their inability to assimilate themselves fully, and gradually defined them as an alien caste or race.

It was all these processes – intensive occupational mobility, increased Jewish participation, attempts to reconstruct Jewish tradition and collective identity, cultural, public and economic creativity, and the reactions to all of these – that distinguished the Jews in Western Europe from other religious groups and, later on, in Eastern Europe and especially in the United States from other ethnic or religious groups.

# The Institutional and Ideological Attempts at the Construction of Jewish Life and Civilization in Eastern Europe
## *The Hassidic movement*

The intensity of specifically Jewish experience was even more evident in Eastern Europe where – as we have seen – the majority of Jewish people lived.

All the processes of modernization – the economic, political and educational ones – developed here, as we have seen, in a much slower and above all more convoluted way. The disintegration of the 'traditional' Jewish society was also much slower, and in some parts, such as Poland, that society still persisted, even if in a rather truncated way, in some sectors of the Jewish community in the period between the two world wars.

Yet, from the very beginning of this period some far-reaching changes were taking place. In the wake of the failure of the Sabbatean movement, there arose in Poland and Russia the first massive semi-heterodox, or at least sectarian, movement of Rabbinical Judaism – that of the Hassidim – which, as is well known, developed despite the acrimonious struggles with a large part of the orthodox rabbinate, a part of traditional Jewish society.

While this movement fully accepted the basic premisses of Halakha, it did shift the focus of Jewish religion from learning and legal-ritual observance to religious experience – with strong mystic elements – and vested some mediatory power, till now almost entirely unknown in the fold of Rabbinical Judaism, in the leaders, the *Tsadikim*, giving rise to whole dynasties of such leaders.

The rifts between the Hassidic movement and the 'orthodox' rabbinate split the traditional Jewish community in a way unknown – with the exception of the Sabbatean movement – in the whole history of 'medieval' or 'exilic' Judaism. Later, some common front was established by these different sectors of orthodoxy against the onslaught of the Enlightenment and modernity and later on of Zionism, yet the rift that developed between them was not only indicative of the great changes within traditional Jewish society, but also contributed to the undermining of the walls of this society and of the religious–cultural framework articulated by it.

These walls did indeed start to crumble from the end of the eighteenth and the beginning of the nineteenth centuries with the spread of the Enlightenment and modernization in Eastern Europe in general and among its Jewish communities in particular. But the Eastern European *Haskala* – although greatly influenced by that of the West – nevertheless developed in almost entirely different directions. The relative slowness of economic development, the persistence of traditional–autocratic regimes, the development of revolutionary movements, the existence of a multinational reality and the relative ecological density of the Jewish settlement generated in Eastern Europe some additional dimensions which went far beyond those that we have identified in the responses of the Jewish communities of Western Europe to the challenges of modernity. It was these dimensions which became much more predominant in the Eastern European Jewish historical experience, and it was they which accounted for the distinctiveness of that development.

The Eastern European *Haskala*, and its subsequent movements of religious reform and intellectual and scholarly activities that developed out of it, shared with the Western European one the stress on the negation of the old type of Jewish self-segregation, on a search for a new arena for the implementation of their civilizational vision – an arena which would be part of the modern world – and on full participation in this world. But beyond this it differed greatly from the Western *Haskala* and its consequent movements.

Ben Zion Dinur, the eminent Israeli historian, has aptly defined the difference between the Western and the Eastern European Jewish *Haskala*: in the West, where the whole orientation of the *Haskala* was, as we have seen, towards incorporation into the general society, it was a bridge; in the East it was a lever for the internal institutional reconstruction of the Jewish society.*

Thus, in the East, especially in Russia and Poland, and to a lesser extent in the Austro-Hungarian Empire, the *Haskala* movement was orientated above all to internal reconstruction of the Jewish community itself, to its internal – to use a modern recent expression – modernization, in some type of collective institutional mould. It viewed the incorporation of the Jewish community into the general society in terms of such collective reconstruction; it defined the Jewish community in some national, political or ethnic – and not only religious – terms; it saw the Jewish community connected with intensive internal building of modern economic, educational and social institutions.

Accordingly, the various movements of religious reform, although they did develop there, were on the whole rather secondary as against this broad spectrum of institutional–social, economic, political and cultural reconstruction.

These processes of internal institutional reconstruction were, of course, closely related to special characteristics of the ecological and economic reshaping of the Jewish population in Eastern Europe, to their greater concentration in cities which were relatively heavily populated by Jews, and not only in commerce and artisanship but also in industry, giving rise to a strong, even if highly diversified, working class.

## Institutional creativity

This crucial difference between the Western and Eastern *Haskala* – and of the broader economic process and social movements connected with it – manifested itself on all levels and dimensions of life.

We might start perhaps with the manifestation of institutional creativity. The history of the Eastern European Jewish communities in the nineteenth and twentieth centuries up to the Second World War is a history of continuous modern institution-building which still remained, to a much larger extent than in Western Europe, within the framework of some Jewish communal life. Educational institutions, ranging from kindergartens to vocational schools, modern high schools and institutes of higher learning, teaching in some combination of Hebrew, Yiddish and the major languages of their respective societies; very widespread journalism in Hebrew and Yiddish; later on political parties, social and nationalistic movements, trade unions and labour organiz-

* B. Dinur, *Historical Writings*, Vol. I *Bemifneh Hadorot (On the Crossroads of Generation)* (In Hebrew: Jerusalem 1955).

ations: all developed continuously, and they developed within the framework of – already largely modern – Jewish collective life. Within these frameworks they exhibited some very specific characteristics, reminiscent of the period of the Second Commonwealth: intensive ideological conflicts; the difficulty of accepting any common authority, yet working also in common organizational, political and social frameworks; a very diversified leadership fighting often at loggerheads with one another, coming together in periods of political upheaval or pogroms.

The political activities that developed among the Jews were indeed very varied, comprising a variety of political movements and organizations. Initially, in the last decades of the nineteenth century, up to the First World War, Jews were active above all within the Jewish communities. After the First World War, with the establishment of the various 'succession states' in Eastern Europe – above all Poland, Lithuania, Czechoslovakia, Hungary and Romania – in which Jews were granted full citizenship, they also participated in the general political life. They formed special Jewish parties or blocs (including those of the Orthodox ones), or co-operated with other general political groups, participating in one way or another in parliamentary life and attempting to take care of the specific Jewish interests. It was as Peter Medding* has defined it, a survival of economic and political accommodation. Some Jews participated also as individuals in other parties or blocs – but, with the exception of the socialist movements, were not very prominent within them.

## Wider cultural activity

Not all the modern activities of the Jews in Eastern Europe were, of course, confined to the framework of the Jewish community. Many Jews participated in the different institutional arenas of general society, becoming especially visible in the more radical and revolutionary movements. They were also involved in general cultural creativity, although here their participation was more limited than in Western Europe. In many fields, above all in academic life, and especially in Russia until the First World War, conversion often was a condition of participation.

But against this there developed, within the framework of Jewish communal life, modern Hebrew and Yiddish literature which, in the works of people like Abraham Mapu (1808–67), Judah Leib Gordon (1831–86), Mendele Mokher Sepharim (1835–1917) or Chaim Nahman Bialik (1873–1934) – to mention only a few – attained a very high level of cultural, sometimes even literary, creativity. There also developed modern Hebrew and Yiddish schools, journalism and theatre which, like the internal and extensive communal political and associational life and processes of institution-building, lasted up till the Holocaust.

There was also in Eastern Europe intensive Jewish scholarship, historical

* P. Medding, 'Toward A General Theory of Jewish Political Interests and Behaviour in the Contemporary World' in D. Elazar (ed.), *Kinship and Consent* (Ramat Gan and Philadelphia 1981).

and philosophical, which while building on the achievement of *Wissenschaft des Judentums*, did not necessarily share its vision of Jewish history. In the work of historians like S. Dubnov (1860–1941) and M. Balaban (1877–1942) – building on Graetz but going beyond him – there developed a much more nationally orientated vision of Jewish history, emphasizing not only religious beliefs but also the communal organizations and even various heterodox movements – like the Frankist one. There was also greater emphasis on the study of the economic history of the Jews – significantly enough, contributing also to statistical or demographic studies of contemporary Jewish communities.

## Developments in the orthodox camp

In Eastern Europe there were in addition significant developments – in two directions; one such direction, which was especially evident within the Orthodox camp itself, above all in Hungary and to a much smaller extent in Austrian Galicia, and which was not dissimilar from the development among the neo-orthodox in Germany, although more intensive, focused on construction of orthodox communities organized already in relatively modern ways, sending their sons to general schools, but maintaining a very strong Jewish institutional and communal framework.

The other, more prominent in Eastern than in Western Europe, was the growth among the orthodox group of modern semi-political organization – culminating in the establishment of Agudat Israel in 1922, which developed in the successor states as parliamentary blocs or parties but also led to the establishment of many modern philanthropic and even educational associations.

In some countries, like Hungary, the orthodox groups maintained totally separate communities, barely participating with other Jewish congregations in common activities. In other countries – especially in Poland – they participated in such common institutional and even political organizations.

## Concluding remarks

Thus the restructuring of Jewish life in Eastern Europe was characterized – unlike that in Western Europe – by a very strong connection between specific Jewish organizational and cultural activities and intensive – to no small degree internal – creating of modern institutions.

This intensive building of institutions was connected with the development of specific modes of the reconstruction of Jewish collective identity and of the articulation of some of the perennial themes of Jewish self-definition.

The definition of the Jews as a purely or mostly religious, confessional group was – except, paradoxically enough, to some degree among the more orthodox – rather marginal. Among the majority of the Jews, their own social density, the multinational context within which they lived, the strength of various national movements against the Russian or Austro-Hungarian Empires, and the negative attitude of the autocratic Russian regime, all tended on the whole to reinforce Jewish national, ethnic and primordial and even political identity – although, needless to say, many Jews tried to assimilate themselves in the other national settings or movements. The reinforcement was, however, connected with a redefinition of such national or primordial identity away from its religious–Halakhic terms and towards a more modern secular direction, upholding the viability of Jewish collective existence in the Diaspora. The variety of such secular or semi-secular definitions – some explicitly anti-religious, others not denying the religious component of Jewish tradition but minimizing its predominance – that developed within the fold of Eastern European Jewry was legion, ranging from variations on some concepts of collective, cultural, semi-political autonomy (as developed, for instance, by the eminent historian Simon Dubnov), to the Bundists' populist–socialist definition of such collective identity. Most of these definitions stressed the possibility of maintaining such collective frameworks even without a specific Jewish territorial concentration; others, the so-called territorialists, claimed the necessity of some such territorial concentration as a prerequisite for the maintenance of such autonomy.

Common to all of these definitions was the stress on continuity of creativity in the Hebrew and/or Yiddish language (between the upholders of which there developed, needless to say, bitter and intensive controversies), but combining it with general European education; and the stress on political organization, on some national institutions and organizations, and on some political autonomy – a theme which became perhaps the most central new orientation in the late nineteenth and early twentieth centuries.

The more universalistic components of Jewish collective self-definition were here much more subdued; they were as it were taken for granted as part of the new restructuring of this definition and of this collective identity. It was only in the groups with the more radical socialist orientations that this theme became combined with the reformulation of national identity. In contrast to the Jews in Western Europe, this theme was not defined here as a cultural mission, but rather as a specific Jewish manifestation of a more general historical trend.

It was only among some of the more Jewish members of extreme revolutionary socialist and later Communist movements that there developed a strong denial of the specificity of the Jewish collective identity and of the necessity for the solution of the Jewish question. Among them there grew up an assumption that their contribution to the general revolutionary movement would justify this component of Jewish tradition, and would also solve, by wholly integrating the Jews into the future revolutionary society, the specific Jewish question.

Thus among most of the Jewish movements in Eastern Europe there developed a strong connection between such universalistic orientations and collective internal institution building, without any general belief in a universal religious mission. This connection was in the Eastern European Jewish context strongly interwoven with another theme which was almost entirely lacking among the Jews in Western Europe (except perhaps in the very first wave of Enlightenment in the eighteenth century) namely that of 'productivization' (in the economic sense) and concomitant 'normalization' of the Jewish occupational structure – a theme closely related, of course, to the general emphasis on institution-building.

Such productivization and normalization were seen as a major key to the possibility of creating a viable, creative Jewish existence in the modern world. In a paradoxical way, many of these movements – and later on the Zionist movement – developed a rather negative evaluation of the Jewish occupational structure in the Diaspora – not dissimilar from that of many of the anti-Semitic movements, and urged the Jews to move from parasitic ghetto occupations into productive agriculture and industry. Accordingly they initiated a vast ideological and institutional programme in the form of educational institutions in general and of vocational education in particular, of establishment of agricultural settlements, schools and of migration into new areas (like the famous attempt by Baron Hirch in Argentina) where these programmes could be realized.

This emphasis on economic modernization or productivization was very closely related to two additional themes that developed in the wake of Eastern *Haskala*. The first such theme was that of 'normality', of making the Jews into normal people, not necessarily denying their specific cultural heritage but making its realization contingent on such normalization.

The second such theme was the very strong stress on the physical, demographic and economic aspects of the Jewish question, on the necessity for the search for some proper solution to the economic plight of the Jewish masses – and on the hope that productivization might provide such a solution. It was above all in terms of physical survival and economic productivization that the Jewish question or problem were here defined.

After the late 1920s a very heavy shadow was cast on all these attempts in Eastern and Central Europe. In this period the combination of economic recession, the closing of the gates of the United States, the growth of anti-Semitic movements, and the instability of the political regimes of most Eastern European successor states (with the exception of Czechoslovakia), began to undermine severely the situation of the Jews in these countries.

The search for new outlets of migration and settlement became very intense – especially, of course, after the rise of Hitler to power – but most of it came to naught, and with the outbreak of the Second World War the Jewish communities in Continental Europe – Eastern, Central and Western alike – were pushed into the terrible road of the Holocaust.

# PART TWO

## The Zionist Movement and the Settlement in the Land of Israel

# CHAPTER 5
# The Zionist Movement and Ideology

## Introduction
### *The foundation of the World Zionist Organization*

The development of the Zionist movement and ideology in the late nineteenth century can only be understood within the context of the social and cultural processes, briefly analysed above. In addition, it must be studied against the background of the development of different formulations of the Jewish question, the problems connected with the Jewish communities, and the attempts made to reconstruct Jewish life and civilization in the framework of European institutions.

The first heralds of Zionism, the so-called 'forerunners of Zionism', such as Yehuda Shlomo Alkelay (1798–1878) or Rabbi Tzvi Hersch Kalischer (1795–1874), appeared in the mid-nineteenth century among both Rabbinical as well as among more secular Jewish intellectuals. Those coming from within more traditional circles, under the impact above all of modern nationalist movements and ideologies, held Zionist beliefs which combined traditional semi-Messianic and modern nationalistic elements, stressing either the political aspect of their aspirations, or the practical necessity and possibility of re-establishing a viable settlement in Eretz Israel. It was envisaged as a sort of possible preparatory stage for the coming of the Messiah, which was seen as beyond the realm of human endeavour, and left of course entirely up to the will of God.

A modern utopian–socialist version was developed by Moses Hess, the socialist leader and ideologue, in his *Rome and Jerusalem* (1862), in which the Zionist vision, based on the recognition of the universal significance of the specific type of Jewish religiosity, was already couched in Hegelian terms of the dialectic of universal history.

The Zionist movement itself began to crystallize in the groups of *Hovevei Zion* (the Lovers of Zion), principally in Russia, from about the 1870s and gathered momentum following the pogroms in the early 1880s (the famous Storms in the South). In the wake of these occurrences one of the most important first fully-fledged Zionist tractates was published in 1882: Leon Pinsker's (1821–99) *Autoemancipation*, the title of which speaks for itself.

The Zionist movement then developed into a full-blown political movement with the meteoric appearance of Theodor Herzl (1860–1904) and the First Zionist Congress in Basel in 1897 – the founding of the World Zionist Organization. The same period saw the beginning of settlement in Palestine, under the initiative of the different groups of *Hovevei Zion*. Settlement continued from that point on, first with the help of the Baron Edmond de Rothschild and later under the aegis of the World Zionist Organization.

## Basic Zionist premisses

The Zionist movement and ideology have sometimes been defined as the culmination of modern Jewish nationalism or as the Jewish counterpart of modern nationalist movements. As quite a large part of its ideology was couched in the idiom of a modern nationalist movement – be it that of Mazzini, Cavour or the German Romantics – this definition is of course partly true. Yet it does not exhaust the meaning of the Zionist ideology and beliefs, and it does not do justice to several crucial elements of this ideology.

This definition does not take enough into account the fact that the Zionist movement and ideology, in their full crystallization and articulation, constituted the most radical response to the decomposition of the traditional civilization. Zionism responded to the various attempts that had developed in Europe to reconstruct the boundaries and contents of Jewish civilizations in the modern setting, in the realm of modern civilization in general, and of the modern European nation-state in particular.

It shared with all other responses to this challenge, analysed above, a basic assumption of the possibility, even necessity, of finding an arena in the modern world in which to realize the Jewish civilizational vision. Such implementation would mean full participation in the family of nations, in the realm of history, and the consequent necessity to reconstruct the Jewish tradition and the Jewish collective identity.

It shared also in part, with certain social and political movements that developed within Eastern Jewry, the assumption that such an incorporation into world history, into the family of nations, could only be based on a process of collective reconstruction which defined the Jewish community in some national and not only religious terms. It adopted, as well, the Eastern European *Haskala* theme of collective productivization and normalization of the occupational structure of the Jews, with a strong emphasis on the importance of the building of institutions.

However, one premiss separated it from the whole gamut of Jewish responses to the impact of modernity, and it was this difference which made it the most radical and revolutionary of all the modern Jewish movements. This was its emphasis that the implementation of the Jewish civilizational vision, the reconstruction of Jewish tradition and collective identity responding to the challenges of modernity, was possible only by creating a specific Jewish collective entity in a natural, national, territorial and collective environment. Against all the other attempts at the collective reconstruction of Jewish life which abounded in Eastern Europe, the Zionist movement and ideology stressed that such a vision of collective reconstruction – such a national collective life – could be implemented only in Eretz Israel. It would be a renewal of the covenant between the Land, the People and Eretz Israel. According to Zionist ideology, Eretz Israel, the Promised Land, the historical cradle of the Jewish nation, the land in which the Jewish nation had been constructed, was the only place in which such a Jewish collective entity and environment could be reconstructed, and within which the Jews could re-enter history and become a productive, normal community responsible for its own destiny.

The Zionist rebellion or revolution was thus directed against the supposition that full, meaningful Jewish life and tradition, and even mere Jewish physical existence, could be maintained within the framework of the general society of the modern European nation-state. It was a fundamental tenet of Zionist ideology – going against the mainstream of modern Jewish history – that, within such a framework, the Jews would be threatened, because of both incomplete assimilation and the inability of modern societies to digest them – by either physical or spiritual and cultural annihilation. It was only in Eretz Israel that a new, modern, viable Jewish society could be established and thrive, and the specific Jewish civilizational vision be implemented.

Most parts of the Zionist movement emphasized that only under such circumstances could the simple survival of Jews in modern society be assured (a problem at the core of the 'Jewish question', especially in Eastern Europe); and only within such a context could the full expression the Jewish 'national' genius of civilizational creativity take place. In some parts of the Zionist movement such creativity could be, and often was, equated with the mere establishment of a new national political Jewish community, a place of haven for the Jewish people. Hence it was sometimes claimed that Zionism was just a response to modern anti-Semitism. But this is a very partial and basically distorted view. In large parts of the Zionist movement there was also a stress on some extra, outstanding cultural creativity and/or of institution building which could claim to constitute not only an adequate solution to the concrete problem of settlement in Eretz Israel or to the physical aspect of the Jewish question, but to be also of some transcendental, universal significance. In this way, many parts of the Zionist movement articulated, in a new way, the old pervasive theme of the combination between the particularly Jewish and the universal significance of the Jewish tradition, and stressed the universal elements in that particular tradition.

It was, admittedly, not always entirely clear what kind of a Jewish society would be established and what were the exact implications of this vision. The different answers to this question, found in Zionist literature, are numerous; they comprised various traditional, revolutionary, religious, secular or socialist aspects, themes and dimensions. Perhaps clearer than the positive contents of these ideologies are their common negative elements, such as the kind of society they did not want. They did not want to perpetuate the traditional medieval Jewish society which still existed in many places in Eastern and Central Europe; nor did they accept various types of assimilated Jewish communities, defined only in religious terms as they developed especially in

Western and Central Europe. They looked in different ways for a synthesis between Jewishness and Western enlightenment or modernity. But they did not reject either Jewish tradition or modernity as such. Extremists such as J. H. Brenner (1881–1921) or Micha Josef Berditschevsky (1865–1921), among others, did indeed attempt to deny large parts of Jewish tradition, but even they tended, on the whole, to look within Jewish history for new elements to be revived. And there were but few who rejected any form of modernity. Though many Zionist socialist groups emphasized some sort of 'socialist utopian' society orientated against the evils of capitalist and 'mass society', most of them – especially, but not only, the more Westernized Zionists – envisaged a sort of modern liberal–democratic state with some degree of socialism.

## The Zionist Vision and the Basic Themes of Jewish Civilization
### Exile, return and redemption

The Zionist vision or visions naturally drew on some of the perennial themes of Jewish civilization and reformulated them in terms of their own basic orientations. The strong emphasis on national reconstruction, on national renaissance, necessarily drew on the older Messianic themes of redemption albeit redefining them in mostly secular, political or social terms; as David Vital has put it, 'Exile, Return, Redemption'.*

This secular transposition of the Messianic beliefs seemingly entailed a particular solution to the perennial dilemmas of Jewish civilization. Above all it stressed the possibility of the Jews re-entering the arena of history as autonomous agents. Similarly the Zionist movement also naturally emphasized the theme of Jewish solidarity which had become very pronounced in the medieval period, and imbued it with a strong political dimension.

Closely related to the articulation of these themes in the Jewish tradition, there developed in the Zionist movement a parallel process of the reconstruction of different elements of the Jewish collective identity – political, national and primordial. All these themes were, of course, closely interwoven with what was perhaps the central motif of Zionism, the principled negation of Galut: the hope that the establishment and renaissance of the Jewish nation in Eretz Israel would indeed abolish both the political subjugation, the *Shiabud Malchuyoth*, and the metaphysical fault implicit in the situation of Galut.

Thus indeed, at the beginning of the Zionist movement, and later on with the settlement in Palestine, the Zionist vision of national renaissance, combining all these varied themes, was often portrayed as resolving many of the perennial dilemmas and tensions of Jewish tradition, by bringing them together into a new mould of civilizational creativity, and by imbuing this creativity with broad universal significance, making the Jewish people part of the family of nations

* D. Vital, *The Origins of Zionism* (London 1975), pp. 25–6.

and bringing them back into history.

It was, initially at least, a very naïve and utopian vision. Its purest and most undiluted expression can perhaps be found in the writings of Ahad Ha'am, the pseudonym of Asher Ginzberg, Herzl's ideological opponent, as well as in Herzl's utopian romance, *Altneuland*, which provided a sort of blueprint for the most pervasive, liberal and utopian belief in the peaceful implementation of this vision.

But attempts at concrete implementation necessarily revealed several basic tensions and contradictions inherent in this vision. The most important were those between the universalistic and particularistic approach; between inward-looking segregation and outward-looking, more open orientations; between the political solidarity and the more institution-building and universalistic cultural dimension of the Zionist vision. There was the tension between the aspiration to become a 'normal' nation as against the quest for civilizational uniqueness or a special Jewish state or society, of being, in the words used later by Ben-Gurion, a 'light unto the nations'; between the ambivalent attitude toward the Diaspora and the dependence of the Zionist movement on the Diaspora; as well as the entire range of problems connected with the reconstruction of the different elements of Jewish tradition and identity.

In many ways all of these polarities were connected to a basic tension between the search for a solution to the problem of physical perpetuation, against the more civilizational aspect of Jewish existence – the former of these pulls cutting across the latter in a dichotomy between, on one hand, the political dimension and, on the other, that of the social and cultural creativity of Zionist activity.

The Zionist movement and ideology faced, of course, a rather new intercivilizational situation. The older, 'traditional', religious interciviliz-ational struggle and antagonism became greatly weakened with the onset of modernity and the reformulation in more secular, and seemingly benign, mode of such premises. Hence, the Zionist movement or ideology had to face this problem more and more in terms that were not antagonistic to other – especially Western – civilizations; to find some specific Jewish way of meeting relatively common civilizational aspirations.

## *Inherent tensions*

Some of these tensions and contradictions remained dormant for long periods of time, and only became fully visible in later periods of the development of the Zionist movements in general and of the Yishuv and the State of Israel in particular. Others, those concerned particularly with ideological orientations and to a lesser degree with institutional reality, developed in the very first stages of the movement.

The tension between the emphasis on politics or on establishing economic and cultural institutions appeared at the very beginning of the movement. The stress on autonomous political Jewish entity did indeed constitute one of the main tenets of the Zionist movement and, as we shall see later on, of the State of Israel. But the initial attempts at a quick political solution did not have success. Herzl's efforts to attain a charter from the Sultan failed and this led him to formulate the famous Uganda proposal in 1903, that is to ask the British Government for some territory in Uganda in which to establish the Jewish State. This nearly split the young Zionist movement, and considerably weakened the emphasis on the political dimension. Instead there developed the strong emphasis on 'constructive' colonization and institution-building in Eretz Israel, with rather universalistic orientations. While this was far from being devoid of political significance or implications, it moved away from the sanctification of political activity for its own sake, and from seeing the attainment of immediate political goals as the major vision of the Zionist movement.

Accordingly, at least in the first phases of the development of the Zionist movement and of settlement in Israel, there was not a strong political Messianism, or an emphasis on purely political activity. But the elements of each continued to exist, at least latently, within the Zionist movement and in the process of settlement in Eretz Israel.

It was especially in the late 1930s, with the increasing political conflicts with both the Arabs and the British, that the political dimension of Zionist activities intensified. Paradoxically it was intensified within the Zionist Labour movement, whose initial emphasis was on the 'constructivist' dimension, and it was also in the 1930s that the Revisionist movement, under the leadership of Zeev Jabotinsky, strongly articulated such attitudes. The tension between these elements or emphases continued throughout the history of the movement and of the State of Israel, as did also that between the great political visions and the creation of practical pragmatic politics.

The conflict between becoming a normal society or nation as against being a special type of nation was not very apparent in the beginnings of the Zionist movement and especially of the settlement in Eretz Israel – above all because the very quest for normality was an ideological–revolutionary reaction to the reality of Jewish life in Europe, a reaction articulated especially by the pioneers of the first Aliyot. But here again, with the crystallization of the social structure of the Yishuv and of the State of Israel, the contradictory institutional implications of these two attitudes became more and more apparent.

Concomitantly – especially with the growing political vicissitudes of the Yishuv and of the State of Israel, with the growing Arab and also international opposition to the process of Zionist resettlement in Eretz Israel, with the need to invest more and more resources in security and defence, as well as with the growing impact of the realities of a small country and society – tension on the ideological and institutional levels became also more apparent. These were tensions between the universalistic and particularistic elements, between the inward-looking solidarity and the more open outward-looking attitudes, between the great visions and pragmatic politics, which seemingly should have been resolved by the implementation of the Zionist vision.

The implementation of the Zionist vision was also to bring out in a great variety of ways, as we shall see later on, many of the potential contradictions between the different components of Jewish collective identity – the primordial, ethnic, political and religious ones – and emphasis on each of them or on some combinations between them, often, as we shall see, in rather surprising directions.

# The Zionist Movement and the Reconstruction of Jewish Tradition and Civilization
## Cultural revival

These problems appeared above all with respect to the religious element in the reconstruction of Jewish tradition and collective identity.

The stress on the reconstruction of the Jewish civilizational mould necessarily raised the problem of the relation of the Zionist movement to Jewish tradition in general and to its religious framework, to the Rabbinical mould in particular. Unlike many of the modern nationalist movements in Europe, the Zionist movement did not only have to crystallize traditional, ethnic or linguistic components of collective identity into a modern political framework; it had also to cope with a fully-fledged political–religious–national–historical tradition and identity and with the problem of reconstructing it according to the new Zionist beliefs.

Such reconstruction gave rise first of all to the full articulation of several cultural and ideological themes or emphases which were latent, secondary or taken for granted in the traditional Rabbinical mould, and which were to a large degree negated in the assimilated groups.

The most important among such themes were the rebirth of the Hebrew language, and the re-emphasis of themes connected with the Land of Israel, and of the biblical components in the Jewish historic tradition.

The renewal of the Hebrew language was indeed one of the great accomplishments, first of the *Haskala* period and even more, later on, of the Zionist movements and the settlement in Eretz Israel.

The revival and the modern reconstruction of the Hebrew language, building on the continuous tradition of medieval times, made it, on the one hand, the common national language – the language of the kindergarten, of school and of daily speech; on the other hand, Hebrew proved itself largely capable of meeting the demands of science, of modern technology and literature. Because of this, the Hebrew language now holds a special place among traditional languages and its development has had important implications for the cultural structure of Israeli society. The fact that this 'religious' and 'traditional' language became the national vernacular and the means of communication in a modern society reduced, as we shall see in greater detail later on, the possibilities, first that differences between 'traditionalists' and 'modernists' would centre around different linguistic identities and, at the same time, that there would develop cultural dependence on foreign centres as major and exclusive sources of broader cultural innovation and creativity.

The emphasis on Eretz Israel shifted from mostly religious or metaphysical orientations strongly regulated by the Rabbinical tradition towards a combination of the physical features of the land and its landscapes, often presented in idyllic or mystic terms; the primordial attachment to the land; some secular–metaphysical glorification; and a new mode of religious, semi-mystical sanctification of the holiness of the Land. This new mode developed out of the prevalent Rabbinical orientations, but growing to some degree beyond them, to some degree in line with some of the philosophical and poetic expressions – especially among Jewish poets and philosophers in medieval Spain like Yehuda Halevi.

This emphasis on the Land of Israel as well as the revival of the Hebrew language was very closely connected with the revival of the biblical component in the Jewish tradition – a component which was secondary in the Rabbinical mould, subsumed under the legal and ritual orientation, and the emphasis of Talmudic learning and of prayer, and which was denied among the more assimilated groups. The revival of this element had already begun in the literary activity of the Eastern European *Haskala* – in such works as, for instance, Abraham Mapu's romances, *Ahavat Zion* (The Love of Zion) and *Ashmat Shomron* (The Guilt of Shomron) and became even more pronounced when connected with various more nationalistic movements in general and the Zionist one in particular.

## Reconstruction of collective identity and traditions

The articulation of all these themes indicated the very strong attachment of most of the Zionist ideologies to many dimensions of the Jewish tradition, and their search or quest to find within that tradition those elements or components through which the new Jewish collective identity and civilizational mould could be reconstructed. But at the same time they indicated quite clearly that they went far beyond the basic premises, not only of the assimilationist orientation, but also beyond that of the Rabbinical mould, beyond the specific configuration of the different components of the Jewish tradition as they had become crystallized in the institutions and symbolic moulds of the Halakha. The Zionist movement aimed not just at the continuation of Jewish tradition but at its radical reconstruction.

It was not only that most of the more active among the Zionist groups were not religious and some – especially among the socialist pioneers, above all the members of the second and third Aliyot – were often vehemently anti-religious. Nor that, as we shall see later on, that it was the ultra-orthodox groups who were, together with the semi-assimilated, among the most vociferous opponents of the Zionist movements.

As against this it should be remembered that many of the leaders and members of the Lovers of Zion, as well as of the Zionist movement, were religious, observant, even prominent Rabbis – although they constituted a minority within both the Zionist and the religious camps – and the religious– Zionist party (the *Mizrahi*) developed very early (1902–5) in the history of the movement.

But, however great the strength of the religious groups or of the attachment of other groups within the Zionist movement to the various aspects of Jewish tradition, they all worked within a basic framework which did not accept the symbols and the institutions of the Halakha as the only or even the main framework of Jewish civilizational creativity.

This was, of course, true of all the non-religious elements in the Zionist movement, who constituted the great majority within it; those who did not adhere to the religious tenets or even consciously rebelled against them. But even for those who did adhere to these tenets, the traditional Halakha mould was not necessarily the major source of inspiration for the new symbols of collective identity and above all of institution building; the reconstruction of Jewish life in an autonomous setting constituted, as we have seen, the epitome of the Zionist movement.

True enough the religiously observant sectors within the Zionist movement seemed to have assumed that, once this new institutional reality was established, it would adhere to the tenets of the Halakha. Some of them began also to be concerned with the applicability of Halakha to new problems and conditions. However, only very few, if at all, could derive their inspirations for the new institutions that were to be developed in the Land of Israel from within the existing Halakhic mould. Some great religious figures – like Rabbi Kook, the first Ashkenazi Chief Rabbi of Eretz Israel – developed a new philo- sophical–mystical interpretation of the Jewish existence in general and of the reconstruction of Eretz Israel in the light of religious tenets; others stressed the roots of the Zionist ideology in the religious tradition and symbols. But almost none of them could point out clearly – beyond stressing the observance of the Halakhic prescriptions and the need to include such stress on the tradition (as for instance in the study of the Talmud) in the new curricula – how the Halakhic mould would provide the guidance for the new institutional creativity, for the new political and collective identity.

Later on some rather intensive religious–intellectual activity developed within religious Kibbutz movements – but here again the original, new pushes for institution-building did not necessarily develop from within the existing religious mould – although later of course, they did become legitimized in terms of this framework.

To a considerable extent the ultra-orthodox groups' fierce opposition to Zionism was rooted in their recognition of the fact that the Zionist vision, however strong its attachment to many traditional symbols, went far beyond the basic premises of the existing and predominant Halakhic mould – it wanted to take the collective fate of the Jews in its own hands, in the here and now of history. They also saw such potential secular transposition of the

Messianic elements to Zionism, as well as the possibility of attaining these goals in the present, as very dangerous.

Meanwhile, both in the framework of the Zionist movement as well as in Eretz Israel (many of the first settlers, those of the first Aliya and the founders of Petah Tiqva were observant Jews), a *modus vivendi* was established between the religious and the secular group, which accepted many of the tenets of the religious groups such as the observance of the laws of *Shmita* (the seventh year when all debts are to be cancelled and the land has to be left barren) or the observance of the Sabbath, and later on the vesting of the laws of marriage and divorce in the hands of religious courts.

The fact that the Zionist movement and ideology did, on the one hand, imply the decline of the hegemony of the Halakha as the dominant Jewish civilizational mould but that, on the other hand, there still developed within the movement and in the settlement in Eretz Israel different modes of practical accommodation with the religious groups, helped greatly to prevent a basic rift between modern and traditional sectors of the movement – even if the ultra-orthodox groups were basically opposed to it.

But the very process of such accommodation was, of course, full of tensions and conflicts. The very continuity of this process, as well as of the confrontation between the Zionist vision and the traditional Halakhic one, contained within itself a great variety of possibilities, including the development, from within the religious sector, of trends, reinterpretations and recrystallization of traditional orientations which, as we shall see in greater detail in subsequent chapters, were later on to develop in rather surprising ways.

## The Diaspora in Zionist ideology

All these various tensions became very closely connected with the Zionist attitude to the Diaspora. Here again several strains can be distinguished. In its original and basic conception, Zionism necessarily stressed the negation of the Diaspora as a viable framework for either the physical, or civilizational and cultural, development of the Jewish people.

In reality, as we shall soon see, the Zionist movement was interwoven in the life of the modern Jewish communities within which it was constituted. This combination, of a strong principled negation of the Galut and yet strong enmeshment in the life of the communities of the Diaspora, made the ideological orientation of Zionism to the Galut very ambivalent and often unclear, and gave rise within the Zionist movement to a certain blindness to the ideological implications of its relation to the Diaspora communities.

Many great figures of Zionism, including Herzl and others after him, especially those who saw in Zionism the solution to the dilemma of Jewish existence, assumed that the realization of the Zionist dream would bring to the Land of Israel, to the Jewish State, all those Jews who would be interested in maintaining a special Jewish national identity, while all the others would be able to assimilate peacefully in the lands of the Diaspora. This assumption was very persistent in the public consciousness of Jews and non-Jews alike. It was, for instance, taken up again in the 1960s by the French–Jewish sociologist, Georges Friedmann, whose small book *The End of the Jewish People?\** has elaborated the thesis that the very successful establishment of Israel will bring, through assimilation, the end of the Jewish people.

This extreme position was, of course, reinforced by the very revolutionary nature of the Zionist movement and was, as we shall see, for a long period prevalent in the Yishuv and in the State of Israel. But not all Zionists shared it fully – and even those who did not share it did not face up to the implications for Zionist ideology of continuous Jewish collective existence in the Diaspora. Ahad Ha'am, 'one of the people', the pseudonym of Asher Ginzberg (1856–1927), the renowned publicist who wielded an immense influence in the Zionist movement and who opposed Herzl's political emphasis, evolved a concept of Zionism as a spiritual centre for the Jewish people. This concept did not, contrary to many interpretations, negate the possibility of the establishment of an independent Jewish state in Eretz Israel – but it did assume the continuous existence of Jewish communities in the Diaspora towards whom the spiritual force of the centre in Palestine would radiate. It did not, however – and this was true of almost all Zionist ideologies – provide any special civilizational meaning to the communities of the Diaspora; it did not provide any concrete ways for the construction of meaningful Jewish existence within them. This approach shared, unwittingly or perhaps consciously, with all the other Zionist orientations, the negation of the Galut, or at least a certain evasion of the issue it posed – an evasion which was to become even more pronounced with respect to that new Jewish community which crystallized together with the Zionist movement, that of the United States.

# The Place of the Zionist Movement in the Life of the Jewish Communities in the Diaspora
## Active elements in the movement

Until the Second World War the Zionist movement constituted a minority – albeit a radical and revolutionary minority – within Jewish communities. Indeed it went against the major 'natural' trends that developed among the modern Jewish communities: accommodation to the new and manifold opportunities of modern societies, whether in the lands in which they were settled in Europe or through migration.

Its major carriers and leaders came from beyond the great 'romantic' figures of Western or westernized Jews, like Herzl or Nordau. They came from within relatively new types of socio-economic formations which developed in Eastern and Central Europe, members especially of the middle classes and intelligentsia, who were caught up in the processes of socio-economic and intellectual

---

\* Georges Friedmann, *The End of the Jewish People?* (New York 1967).

mobility into the new sectors of their respective societies, without yet, on the one hand, having attained high status within them or, on the other hand, entirely leaving the fold of Jewish society.

The more active elements in the Zionist movement in general, and among the pioneering groups in particular, came from these socio-economic groups and sectors. Only rarely did they include either the very wealthy or well-established in their respective communities or members of the lower or the purely traditional groups. For the most part they were the young, not yet fully established, or intellectuals. But of course, many of the intellectuals and potential political leaders went either the assimilatory way or joined the more general revolutionary movements – as in the cases of Trotsky, Rosa Luxemburg or, in the bourgeois-liberal field, Walther Rathenau in Weimar Germany, who became some of the most outstanding political figures of their times.

Yet with all its revolutionary orientation, the Zionist movement became part and parcel of the life of Jewish communities in Europe, and later on in the United States and other lands of modern Jewish migration, and to a smaller degree among the Oriental Jewish communities. It is this combination – its basic radicalism and the direction of this radicalism; the heterogeneity of the movement; and its acceptance as part of the public Jewish life – that is important for the understanding of its history and later of some of the most crucial developments in the State of Israel.

The Zionist movement, from the beginning, was organized in many different parties, sects and groups, which were continuously changing. In the late 1920s they crystallized into several major blocs: what came to be called the 'General Zionists', comprising different 'bourgeois' and intellectual elements; the 'Labour Bloc'; and the religious one, comprising *Hamizrahi* and later the Labour-religious branch, *Hapoel Hamizrahi*; and, from the mid-1920s on, the 'Revisionists'. Each of these blocs comprised various, often changing, groups and factions.

Cutting across these political differences, the components of the Zionist movement can be distinguished according to their commitment to the movement. There was first the relatively larger number of sympathizers or supporters – buying the Shekel, donating to the *Keren Kayemet* (the Land Acquisition Fund), and participating in the various cultural, political and educational activities and organizations connected with the Zionist organizations, movements and parties – up to the more committed leadership of these organizations and parties.

Then there were the more radical elements, orientated above all to settlement in the Land of Israel, which organized themselves from the 1920s on, above all in the various pioneering youth movements, and in the camps of the *Hakhshara* (Preparation) – mostly beyond some of the Zionist–socialist groups.

Among those who went to Eretz Israel there were also many, as we shall see, who were not active members of these ideological movements. They were either sympathetic or neutral to them, tended to settle in the cities, but were also quite highly attuned to active components of the Zionist vision.

From the late 1920s and early 1930s there developed within the framework of the Zionist movement another radical group which, while also orientated towards Eretz Israel, did not share the pioneering-socialist orientation of the predominant Labour groups. This was the Revisionist movement under the leadership of Zeev Jabotinsky, which was created in 1925 and then split from the World Zionist Organization. The Revisionists challenged the leadership of Chaim Weizmann in coalition with the Labour movement, in which David Ben-Gurion was becoming a dominant figure, in their more radical political approach. Revisionism called for a political evacuation of Jews from the Diaspora, for a massive political–military action in Palestine, organizing its youth movement in semi-paramilitary formations in the Betar movement, with uniforms and with much of the paraphernalia of military life, stressing *Hod Vehadar* (majesty or splendour and glory), taken from Psalms, and in Eretz Israel creating the germs of the extreme underground movements – the Ezel (*Irgun Zvai Leumi* – The National Military Organization) and Lehi (*(Lohamei Herut Israel* – The Fighters for Freedom). It appealed widely to the Jewish masses in Eastern Europe, who, in the late 1920s and 1930s, became more and more caught between the upsurge of the extreme anti-Semitic policies of their respective governments – especially in Poland – and the closure from the early 1920s of the gates of the United States to massive immigration.

## *Varied patterns of Zionist leadership*

Given the heterogeneity of the Zionist movement it was natural that its different parts should emphasize different themes and orientations. In particular these themes were articulated in different ways by the different sectors of Zionist leadership and 'sects'. Cosmopolitan figures like Herzl, Nordau or Weizmann stressed the combination of the more universalistic orientations – but, in the case of the latter, with strong emphasis on internal solidarity and institution-building. The more local, 'bourgeois', diffuse leadership of the movement and the more religious groups stressed the more nationalist elements. But the Labour groups' pioneers stressed the combination of the more nationalist and socialist-universalistic themes with strong emphasis on institution-building.

As we shall see, it was this third element – that of the pioneers – that became the most active of the formative period of the settlement in Eretz Israel, but it was never the only such element. It always worked in some coalition with all the other ones, and the story of their co-operation and conflicts is the story of the building of the Yishuv and of the State of Israel to which we shall turn in the next chapter.

## Opposition to Zionism, elements of migration

The Zionist movement provoked quite a lot of opposition – some of it very fierce and even vicious. It had four major ideological and political opponents: first the ultra-orthodox, who saw in the attempt to achieve redemption by the hand of man an usurpation of God's prerogative and a threat to the dominant Halakhic mould and who denied the legitimacy of the secular vision of redemption; secondly there were the more 'assimilated' leaders of the Jewish communities in Western Europe, who saw in the Zionist movement a severe threat to their definition of the Jewish people in purely religious–confessional terms, raising the problem of double loyalty and impeding Jewish integration into the general society; thirdly there were the various other Jewish national movements who sought to solve the Jewish problem in a collective way within the framework of the Diaspora, by attaining some national autonomy – with or without a special territorial basis – in their respective societies; and last there were the 'revolutionaries' who, as we have seen, claimed especially after the 1905 revolution in Russia that the universal socialist revolution would automatically solve the Jewish problem.

The intellectual and political controversies between all these camps were vociferous and often vicious. The divisiveness of these controversies within the Jewish communities was, however, to some degree at least, counteracted by several basic factors. First of all by the fact that the opponents were not struggling for any one single centre of power; or, in other words, that they were struggling more for the 'souls' of the Jewish people than for more concrete resources or positions of power – although this latter element was not, of course, entirely lacking in these struggles and problems.

Secondly this divisiveness was muted by the very heterogeneity of the Zionist movement – a heterogeneity which, as we shall soon see, made it easier to maintain many contacts and venues of co-operation with other Jewish organizations.

Thirdly, and closely connected with the former, there was the physical distance between the actual life of large parts of the Jewish communities in the Diaspora and these principled ideological and political discussions. This was not a total break – but enough of a distance for the dynamism of daily life and its problems to develop to some degree in its own way.

This dynamism was, of course, very complex in its own right. First of all various aspects of economic and political struggle and life developed in the different Jewish communities in Eastern Europe. Secondly, and more far-reaching than the experience of the forces of daily life was the great movement of migration, above all to the United States. In a sense this movement was the most strongly opposed to the premisses of Zionism, but nevertheless it rarely came into an ideological confrontation with it, and indeed often kept up many contacts with it. The movement removed some of the – at least economically – potentially active elements from the European Jewish scene and at the same time removed quite a large part, although certainly not all, of the demographic and economic pressure which provided part of the great impetus for more revolutionary orientations before as well as after the First World War.

The migration to the United States was characterized by a strong flow towards the cities and into the educational professional activities. Later a similar trend developed in the Soviet Union. But there, unlike in the United States, there was a strong tendency for total assimilation into the secular Communist (Russian) mould, or a weaker emphasis on some cultural national autonomy, even up to the establishment of the autonomous Jewish republic, Birobijan. The movement was totally and radically opposed to the Zionist premises – emphasizing, for instance, the use of Yiddish as against Hebrew, and describing the Zionist movement as bourgeois and reactionary.

But these developments in Soviet Russia were, of course, later ones. Before the First World War, throughout the Russian and Austrian Empires and later on in the succession states – above all Poland, Czechoslovakia, Romania and Hungary – in which large parts of the Jewish people lived, the efforts of the Jewish communities were directed to the attainment of economic mobility and to the development of the manifold social, political, educational and institutional activities, some of which have been described above. The Zionist movement was caught here on the horns of a dilemma, already evident and fully discussed at the Helsingfors Convention of 1908 under the terms of *Avodat Hahove* (The Work of the Present), whether to participate in all these activities or whether, given their radical negation of the possibility of a viable Jewish life in the Diaspora, to abstain from them.

## Compromise and co-operation

Some of the more radical elements within the movement, especially those who went to settle in Eretz Israel, seemingly opted for the latter solution. But the wider circles of the Zionist movement opted, consciously, for the full participation in these activities. Even for the more radical members the denial of the feasibility of such participation in the organized Jewish activities in the Diaspora was only a principled one – although this more principled stand was to be of great importance in the creation of the symbols and themes of collective identity of the Jewish community in the Land of Israel.

This decision to co-operate in the various collective Jewish activites in the Diaspora, and the continuity of such co-operation, seemingly going against the basic Zionist premises, was due to a combination of several factors, all of them of great significance for the understanding of the history of the Zionist movement, and later on even of the State of Israel in its relation to the Jewish communities in the Diaspora.

The first such factor was the very small number of those who, before Hitler, were ready to go to Palestine, especially after the débâcle of the political vision of Herzl, compared with those who upheld, in one way or another, the tenets of the Zionist creed.

Second was the fact that their very principled stand lost some of its radical vein, of its potential revolutionary power, within the Jewish communities in the Diaspora by the mere fact that their movement did not – could not – attempt to seize the (almost non-existent) centre or centres of power of the Jewish communities.

Third was the seemingly contrary fact that, without participation in at least some of these activities, the Zionist movement would not be able to put down roots in the Jewish community, to mobilize adherents and even the resources necessary for the settlers in Eretz Israel. Thus there developed a continuous dependence of the pioneers, both in preparation for settlement in Eretz Israel and in the settlement itself, on the resources mobilized from the Jewish communities.

Fourth was of course the very heterogeneity of the Zionist movement mentioned above – a heterogeneity which was naturally connected with the participation on many levels of Jewish collective life in the Diaspora.

The opting for the participation in *Avodat Hahove*, and later for partici-pation in all the institutional and political Jewish activities in the Diaspora, was also often facilitated by the fact that many of these activities – especially the educational and political ones – could be seen as being in line with some of the basic Zionist visions of reconstruction of Jewish life, and later on with the efforts to save Jews from impending disasters and persecutions.

Thus, while the principled radicalism of the Zionist ideology in modern Jewish life denied the legitimacy of the viability of such dynamics, in practice the Zionist movement became a part –. even if an ambivalent part – of this dynamism.

Admittedly this participation of the pioneers, the representatives of the Yishuv in general and the Diaspora Zionists in the framework of common Zionist and general Jewish organizations was full of tensions, ambivalence and conflicts, but all this did not negate the very fact of such participation within common frameworks.

These common organizations and activities took on a rather special, ultimately tragic, turn in the 1930s, with the rise of anti-Semitism in Poland which threatened the greatest single Jewish community; with the closure of the gates to the United States, and ultimately with the rise of Hitler and of Nazism and the intensification of the political conflicts of the Zionist movement with the Arabs in Palestine and with the British Government.

Several new world-wide Jewish organizations, like the Jewish World Congress (established in 1936), developed, looking for new venues of migration for European Jews, searching for ways of saving German Jews, and fighting for greater immigration to Palestine. There was a growing co-operation between all of them and the Zionist Organization and the Jewish Agency (established in 1929), this last seeing itself as the fullest legitimate representation of the Jewish people but accepting all the other organizations – including even the ultra-orthodox Agudat Israel.

## Conclusion

Thus the Zionist movement as it developed up to the eve of the Second World War became a part of the broader panorama of modern Jewish life, many of its aspects deeply interwoven in it, even if highly ambivalent to it. On the ideological, political and organizational levels there developed a mixture of intense controversies and mutual accommodation and co-operation; bitter conflicts together with participation in common activities and even in the creation of new educational and cultural frameworks and institutions.

Its more radical element seemingly denied the very bases of such co-operation. But whereas their radicalism called for the phasing out of the existing communities in the Diaspora, these communities nevertheless continued to be a reservoir for the radical sectors and to provide them with the necessary resources, so the edge of this radicalism was to some, but only some, degree limited.

With such a degree of conflict, such multiplicity of competing elites, and such strong solidarity, Zionism exhibited many of the features characteristic of the older ways of Jewish life and also, as we shall see, of life in the Yishuv and the State of Israel.

# CHAPTER 6

# The Settlement in the Land of Israel – the Yishuv

# I · The Historical Development and the Institutional Organization of the Yishuv

## The Background – The 'Old' Yishuv

The Zionist settlers who came to Palestine, to the Land of Israel, found a Jewish settlement already there. In fact there had always existed some Jewish settlements in Palestine; even in the darkest periods of oppression under Muslim or Christian rulers, Jews continued to come on pilgrimage and to settle out of devotion to the Land, often seeing living there as the fulfilment of religious commandments and semi-Messianic aspirations. In particular, after the expulsion from Spain, under the aegis of the Ottoman government and not unconnected with Messianic aspirations, there were attempts at settlement under Don Yossef Hanassi (in mid-sixteenth century) in Tiberias and the Kabbalist-created active centres in Safad. But such periods of florescence were, on the whole, short, and from the early or middle of the eighteenth century on, while pilgrimage and some settlement continued, they were not very extensive. This settlement was based on the perception of settlement in Eretz Israel as a religious ideal. Economically speaking this meant that the Jews in Palestine were totally dependent on Jewry in the Diaspora. Each party regarded itself as fulfilling a religious duty. This support was as institutionalized as it was ideological. Funds were usually collected by special emissaries sent from Palestine to the Diaspora to collect the money needed by them.

But this centrality was only symbolical; certainly at the time, after the weakening of the centre in Tiberias and of the Kabbalistic centre in Safed, it did not constitute a great centre of Talmudic learning or of mysticism. It certainly did not play any central role – beyond the purely symbolic one – in the life of the Jewish communities in the Diaspora at that time. On the whole, with some exceptions like special groups of Hassidic pilgrims and settlers in the early and mid-nineteenth century, it constituted only a sort of extension – and on the whole a weak one – of the more traditional sectors of these dispersed communities.

The actual settlements in the eighteenth century consisted mostly of Sephardic Jews, with very small Ashkenazi ones; economically most of them were not very prosperous. The more prosperous element – mostly Sephardic – dealt in middle-range commerce and landwork, but many eked out a rather miserable existence, through several different *Kolelim* (sort of corporate organizations with housing facilities and places of learning in Jerusalem). They were usually organized on some basis of countries or towns of origin (*Hungaria Kolel* and so on), and were supported financially by the communities in the Diaspora.

This system functioned virtually unchanged until well into the twentieth century. However, important internal modifications were made from the late eighteenth century onwards. Religious developments in the Jewish centres of Russia and Poland brought in their wake a stream of Jewish immigrants from Eastern Europe. Although these were basically motivated by the same religious orientations as the Sephardi ones, their appearance in Jerusalem and Safed marked a change. The communities became more heterogeneous and diversified into European (or Ashkenazi) communities and Oriental (or Sephardi) communities, the latter being more homogeneous than the former. Every Ashkenazi immigrant group organized itself according to its European town or origin, and its appeals for economic support were mainly directed to its home town.

Large parts of them – especially the Ashkenazi – were living on *Haluka* (distribution), contributions arriving from the Diaspora for those studying, learning and praying, and mostly collected and administered through the *Kolelim*.

This increase in the traditional type of immigration continued during the nineteenth and early twentieth centuries, consisting especially of those who literally fled from the ancient Jewish communities of Europe which, they felt, were disintegrating. They hoped to find, in Jerusalem, a last bastion of traditionalism, but were paradoxically already affected by the economic life and ideas of the 'modern' world.

But even in this relatively backward extension of Jewish communities in the Diaspora – albeit an extension with a very high symbolic significance – the waves of *Haskala*, of Enlightenment, started to penetrate, giving rise to new developments among some of the traditional groups in the latter part of the nineteenth century.

Thus more basic changes were introduced around 1830, when several upper-class Western European Jews (such as Sir Moses Montefiore and Adolphe Crémieux) began to advocate a more productive Jewish economy. At first these efforts were mainly directed towards religious activities, such as the setting up of printing presses (for religious books), but later they also included attempts to set up primary services such as flour mills and even the beginnings of agricultural production.

Such a movement to go out of the walls of the old city in Jerusalem and even to settle outside them – thus creating the nuclei of modern Jerusalem – gave rise to the development of new, relatively modern, educational institutions and to the publication of newspapers in Hebrew.

By 1870 two periodicals existed in Jerusalem, one of them openly agitating for productivization. In the same year the Alliance Israélite Universelle founded an agricultural school near Jaffa. A modern secular school was set up by German Jews in Jerusalem and, though promptly banned by the rabbis, it nonetheless found pupils. In 1878 the first agricultural colony was established in Petah Tiqva by orthodox settlers.

Needless to say, all these developments gave rise to rifts and struggles within the old Yishuv – transforming it from a rather stagnant backwater into a very dynamic and intensive arena.

# The Zionist Aliyot
## Characteristics of the first Aliyot

This was the background for the new immigrants, those from the pre-Zionist movement – the 'Lovers of Zion' who constituted the nuclei of the first Aliya and of the later Aliyot.

These new waves of immigration – the modern Aliyot – often became ecologically and to some degree socially interwoven with the previous elements, especially with the more modern elements within them; but in principle these new Aliyot constituted an entirely new element in the landscape of the Jewish settlement in Eretz Israel.

The new Aliyot to Palestine took place simultaneously, as we have seen above, with the major Jewish migrations of the late nineteenth century which led to the establishment of the Jewish communities in the United States, the Dominions and Latin America. A brief comparison of the Aliyot to Palestine with the wider Jewish immigrations may provide a helpful starting point for analysis.

Until the 1920s the various Aliyot to Palestine were of little numerical significance. From 1880 to 1920 they comprised no more than 4 per cent of total Jewish migration. It was only after 1930, and the imposition of severe restrictions on immigration into most Western countries, that the Aliyot mounted to more than 50 per cent. From the beginning, however, they exhibited special and, sometimes, unique characteristics.

Before 1930, immigrants consisted mainly of young unmarried people or of young couples without children or parents. They did not constitute, contrary to the general trend of Jewish immigration, whole communities or even family groups. The Aliyot consisted mostly of younger people, often high-school pupils, university students or 'externs', who had decided not to undertake their chosen careers. They displayed, in many ways, the characteristics of a young 'intelligentsia'. Most of them came from economically stable backgrounds and from families who, though still attached to traditional Jewish life, did not oppose more modern trends. They tended, on the contrary, to encourage their children to study at secular schools and universities. There was relatively little friction in these families between the older and the younger generation on the question of religion versus secularism. These characteristics were most pronounced before the First World War and in the early 1920s but tended to persist throughout the 1930s, and it is only in the late 1930s and the 1940s, with the stream of refugees from Nazi persecution, that the nature of these Aliyot changed markedly.

Thus the first three Aliyot were on the whole – contrary to most other modern Jewish migrations – highly ideological movements in which the formation of ideologies usually preceded the actual migration or 'transplantation' and guided the initial stages of settlement in the new country.

Although a great deal of the pioneering ideology crystallized only as a result of the immigrants' encounter with Palestinian reality, it was firmly rooted in the ideological beliefs developed by the Zionist movement in the Diaspora.

The ideology of rebellion played an important part in the Aliyot to Palestine and the structure of the immigrant groups. The 'rebels' usually formed themselves into small, cohesive groups, connected by various informal and semi-formal ties to associations, social movements and political parties, in which they prepared themselves, both ideologically and socially, for aliya. In these groups they also underwent training in the various vocations which they wanted to follow in Palestine, concentrating on agricultural training. The various *Hakhshara* (preparation) groups, through which practical experience in communal living was gained, were the most outstanding example of this. However, there was also preparation for work in industry, building or the professions. The groups dissociated themselves sharply from their surroundings in the Diaspora and adopted a new and increased mutual social identification. They were similar to various Central European rebel youth movements in that they tended to dissociate themselves from adult society. Unlike those movements they were, however, characterized by a combination of their peculiar type of rebellion, together with migration and colonizing activities, a combination which gave rise to a predisposition to change in all the main directions of social activity – economic, cultural and political.

While it would be a gross exaggeration to suggest that all immigrants who came to Palestine during this period exhibited these special characteristics, there is no doubt that the most active, those who left their mark on the whole country, did so. It should also be remembered that throughout this period a selective process was in operation in the Diaspora, where the various pioneering organizations – especially *Hechalutz* – and the different Zionist parties selected those who were going to Eretz Israel, while in Eretz Israel itself a selective process was in operation and many left the country.

## Basic statistics

It is customary to divide the Aliyot till the establishment of the State of Israel into five:

| Aliyot | Years | Immigrants | |
| --- | --- | --- | --- |
| First Aliya | 1882–1903 | 20,000–30,000 | |
| Second Aliya | 1904–1914 | 35,000–40,000 | |
| Third Aliya | 1917–1923 | 35,000 | |
| Fourth Aliya | 1924–1931 | 82,000 | |
| Fifth Aliya | 1932–1948 | 265,000 | (up to the end of 1944) |

The first Aliya was initiated by the first Zionist movement, *Hovevei Zion*, in Russia and Romania, which had the wave of pogroms which flooded South Russia in 1881 as its main driving power. These immigrants looked on land settlement as a primary condition for the rejuvenation of the Jewish people. During this period of the first Jewish agricultural settlements such as Petah Tiqva, Rishon Lezion, Rosh Pina, Zikhron Yaakov and Hedera, were established and the foundations of the Yishuv were laid. The second Aliya consisted mainly of members of various Zionist labour groups in Russia, who had become disappointed with the social reform movement there (in which they had taken an active part) and which ended in pogroms with the October Revolution of 1905. They came to Palestine in a period of crisis both in that country and in the Zionist movement. Although these 'workers' were in the minority during the second Aliya, it is nonetheless considered as a labour immigration, since the workers' initiative and energy changed the whole structure of the Jewish community. New methods of land settlement were adopted, and the foundation was laid for the whole structure of the labour movement in Palestine. It was during this period that the World Zionist Organization started work in Palestine (1908), and the first mixed farming villages were established. This period also witnessed the beginning of urban development. The foundations were laid for the all-Jewish town of Tel Aviv (1909) and here and there the rudimentary beginnings of industry could be found.

The third Aliya began while the First World War was still raging in 1917 after the Balfour Declaration, which the Jewish world interpreted as the creation of a new start towards the establishment of the Zionist ideal. In this Aliya the pioneering element predominated. It consisted mostly of young people who had been trained through the *Halutz* (pioneer) organizations prior to their departure for Palestine and who were ready and willing to do any work the country might require of them, no matter how hard.

The fourth Aliya, which began in 1924, was activated partly by improved economic conditions in Palestine, which made the absorption of further immigrants possible, and partly by the worsening economic position of the Jewish community in Poland, which was caused by the Polish Government's policy of eliminating Jews from many trades. The main new element in this immigration was middle-class people with small means, most of whom settled in the towns and entered commerce or industry, or became artisans. However, if account is taken of the absolute number of immigrants, the pioneer element predominated in this period also. This Aliya was followed by a considerable emigration from Palestine as a result of the acute economic crisis which broke out during that period of influx.

The fifth Aliya began in 1929 but did not reach its peak until 1932, when a large volume of immigration was resumed and which resulted in great economic prosperity. Up to 1935 about 150,000 Jews – many of them from Germany – came in; they brought considerable capital and helped to develop industry, trade and agriculture on a large scale. From 1936 to 1940, a period of severe troubles in the country, immigration was limited by the Government, and only about 100,000 Jews, including about 15,000 'illegal' immigrants, entered.

# The Decision about the Nature of Jewish Settlements in Eretz Israel and the Relations Between the Mandatory Government, the Zionist Movement and the Yishuv
## *Development of an internal institutional structure*

It was during the period of these Aliyot, that the major institutional formats of the Yishuv developed.* There were various settlements – the Moshavot, the Kvutzah, the Kibbutzim and the Moshavim – their various Federations, the urban centres in the three main cities – Jerusalem, Tel Aviv and Haifa – and in many secondary centres such as Tiberias, Safed and others; major educational institutions, political organizations and the nuclei of the self-defence forces; and the Histadrut, the Federation of Labour, established in 1920, constituting a unique combination of the various settlements, trade-union activities, the Sick Fund, many industrial concerns, and housing, trade and transport co-operatives – all under one central canopy of the *Hevrat Ovdim* (The Company of Workers, the economic branch of the Histadrut) and becoming one of the major, if not *the* major centre of economic and political power in the Yishuv.

The institutional structure that was established during this period was, despite the relatively small numbers involved, a very complex one.

This institutional structure of the Yishuv was shaped by the combination of four major forces or factors which were, of course, very closely related to the basic themes of the Zionist movement and to the concrete situations in which it was active: first, the initial revolutionary vision of the different groups of pioneers, settlers and immigrants; second, the concrete problems which arose out of the necessity to realize this vision in the concrete conditions in Ottoman and British Mandatory Palestine; third, the relations of the different sectors of

* Eisenstadt, *Israeli Society* p. 1.

the Yishuv with the Jewish communities in the Diaspora; and fourth, the momentum of the internal development and dynamics of the emerging structure of the Yishuv itself.

The vision or visions of the different groups of settlers and of the Yishuv were, as we have seen, composed of several components – above all of the basic Zionist tenets and orientations, as well as, at least among the pioneering–revolutionary groups, of a strong admixture of different varieties of socialist visions.

The 'pure' Zionist vision stressed, as we have seen, the establishment of a modern Jewish community where Jews would live among themselves as a normal – economically and politically – modern nation, and the ideology of national renaissance and of the rebirth of Hebrew language. The more specific 'labour' pioneering groups combined these trends with two other themes. One such theme, to some degree shared by all Zionist groups, was a very strong revolutionary emphasis on normalization and production within the Jewish nation. This was to be achieved through the return to agriculture and to industry, and above all through the crystallization of a working class, of a normal occupational structure as against the traditional Jewish concentration in small trade and the like. The second such theme was more a specifically socialist vision – even if in rather vague and utopian terms – stressing egalitarian, non-exploitative communal life and collective frameworks, often – especially after the First World War – in terms of a radical ideology of class.

It was the existence of these radical, revolutionary ideas that explains to some degree the distinct institutional features of the Yishuv, but they can be understood fully in conjunction with the concrete problems which these groups of settlers and pioneers encountered in the very processes of realizing their vision. Problems arose out of the combination of the ideological visions and ideas and the attempt to realize the vision in a small and relatively undeveloped country, a land new both to the founders of the society and to many generations of immigrants and which constituted a foreign and even hostile environment.

These problems – even if their concrete expressions changed – remained relatively similar during all the periods of the development of the Yishuv and later of the State of Israel, and it is they which constituted in a way the major 'environment' of the Jewish settlement in Eretz Israel and of the State of Israel, the major challenges which they had to face continuously. They were connected first with immigration and the absorption of immigrants; secondly with the agenda of productivization, of development of a modern economy and of a productive occupational structure in general and an agricultural one in particular; thirdly with putting down roots in a strange and even hostile environment – especially with settling on the land, and organizing territorial settlement and defence; fourth, with establishing the symbols of a collective Israeli identity in relation to the Jewish identity, on the one hand, and to the Middle East environment, on the other.

## *External and international relations of a small society*

In this context small countries may have to orient themselves towards large, highly developed states, and they usually have to specialize and find areas in which they can promote – or even create – special advantages stemming either from their special location or from their social and economic structure.

This problem was, of course, accentuated by the fact that it was part of the Zionist vision that this new – small – society would become a centre of cultural and social creativity.

Thus indeed the concrete forms in which the various problems enumerated above became crystallized in the Yishuv, and later in the State of Israel, were also greatly influenced by the constant tension between the social and cultural reality of a small, relatively modern society – in the beginning even only of the nuclei of such a society – and its aspirations to be a centre, out of all proportion to its size, of social and cultural creativity of importance both for the Jewish people and for humanity at large.

Thus indeed the Yishuv, and later on the State of Israel, shared some of the basic problems of modern small societies; above all of how it is possible for a society of relatively small scope to maintain a general standard of economic and socio-cultural life, which is more or less on the same level as the one prevailing in its respective international system – a problem which is especially acute given that the internal market of any such small society is not large enough to create enough economic momentum for such development.

The Yishuv, and later on the State of Israel, attempted to develop such external markets and reference points. Indeed, many of the groups in the Yishuv and in Israeli society thought themselves part of and closely related to wider international social networks or movements – whether political–ideological movements or various professional, intellectual and scholarly communities – and also, and perhaps above all, to the Jewish communities in the Diaspora, towards which they developed, as we have seen, a very ambivalent attitude.

Hence the major changes that took place in the relations between the Yishuv and Israeli society and the Jewish communities in the Diaspora were, as we shall see in greater detail later, among the most important causes or indicators of some of the major transformations in the structure of the Yishuv and of Israeli society.

## *Major institutional solutions*

Several basic problems or dilemmas about the nature of the Jewish settlement in Eretz Israel developed from the beginning of the Zionist settlement. The primary question was whether the Yishuv and the Zionist Organization would be willing – as suggested in some British circles – to become part of the upper-class pluralistic colonial society or Western 'colonizers' in an Arab economy.

The decision to create a completely independent Jewish economy as well as to maintain a distinctive semi-political organization, closely related to the Zionist organization, was perhaps the most fateful step in the development of the Yishuv. It created the potential antagonistic relationship with the mandatory power. This was accentuated by the expanding immigration and colonization, raising territorial matters into major political objectives common to all sectors of the Yishuv and a bone of contention with the mandatory government. It also raised self-defence from a matter of local security to a vital political problem.

These developments became closely connected with the search for the best ways of building up the national home. Several alternative ways of settling the country were considered in the early 1920s. The first of these planned rapid colonization by large-scale private investments, as proposed by Justice Brandeis and the Zionists of the United States. This approach was strongly and successfully opposed by Chaim Weizmann and the Labour movements.

The second possibility was the simple expansion of immigration based on private capital and aimed at quick economic normalization. Here the experience of the fourth Aliya was decisive. It proved that, while such immigration could be important, it did not in itself have enough significance to ensure continuous development in face of adverse economic conditions, nor could it develop economic or political power quickly enough to assure continuous absorption of new manpower.

Somewhat later the Revisionists under Jabotinsky attempted to create a political climate suitable for the development of a national home through a purely political movement, concerned with political agitation, organization of the masses and immigration, but not by means of colonization which would, it was asserted, only weaken the intensity of political activities.

The unwillingness of Jews settled in the Diaspora to undertake mass immigration in order to boost the independent economy of the Yishuv and its political power turned the balance in favour of a pioneering solution, based on continuous territorial settlement through lands acquired by *Keren Kayemet*, continuous urban development and the establishment of a relatively closed Jewish economy. This was epitomized by the policies of Weizmann and gradually crystallized in the late 1920s and early 1930s.

It is not easy to settle the historical debate whether all the other possibilities were doomed from the beginning. Nor whether Weizmann's personality captivated the more dynamic elements as claimed by both the Brandeis group and the Revisionists. As with many historical disputes, the answer will probably never be known.

It is a fact, however, that the shifted emphasis in favour of national pioneering and colonizing created the conditions necessary for the predominance of the workers' groups. This did not mean that other sectors failed to play a crucial role in the economic development of the Yishuv. Rather, the continuous expansion of the Yishuv, in its political–economic sectors and political organizations, became dependent on the combination of capital and colonizing movements – thus facilitating the growth and ultimate predominance of the Labour sector.

One should not, of course, minimize the importance of the various groups within the civil sector or the German immigration who did generate, through their private means and efforts, important new economic organizations and activities. But it is doubtful whether even these institutions could be continuously maintained except through some concerted collective effort of the type developed by the major national and Labour institutions, or at least there can be no doubt that it was these groups that shaped the concrete features of the institutional structure of the Yishuv, as it actually developed.

## Internal characteristics of the institutional structure

The interaction between firstly the mandatory government, secondly the different organizations of the World Zionist Organization and the Jewish community in Palestine, thirdly the various waves of immigrants to Palestine, and lastly the ideological and institutional framework established during the periods of the first and especially of the second Aliya, which shaped the institutional and social history of the Yishuv, developed within the frameworks of this basic decision about the nature of the Jewish settlement in Eretz Israel.

Between the mandatory government, the Jewish Agency (or the Zionist Organization with the establishment of the Jewish Agency in 1929) and the other institutions of the Jewish community in Palestine – especially the *Vaad Leumi* (National Council) and the various bodies of local government – there developed rather complex interrelations which are of crucial importance for the understanding of the institutional dynamics of the Yishuv.

The mandatory framework encompassed both the Jewish and Arab sectors. Within the Arab sector, however, no equivalent of the Jewish Agency emerged (although later an equivalent of the *Vaad Leumi* in the form of the Higher Arab Council developed) and the general extent of internal organizational development was smaller. In the Jewish sector internal organizations developed both in the form of the *Vaad Leumi*, which was elected by most of the adult members of the Jewish community, and in the form of numerous local government bodies.

In time there developed a more or less clear-cut division of labour between these different institutions and organizations. The various national institutions of the Yishuv, the Zionist movement, and the Jewish Agency dealt mostly with the following matters: (1) development of Jewish colonization, both rural and urban; (2) arrangements for immigration into Palestine from various countries of the Diaspora; (3) maintenance and development of Jewish defence – the illegal *Hagana*, various semi-legal and legal police groups and, during the Second World War, mobilization in the British Army; (4) development of an active 'foreign' policy – mainly with regard to the mandatory government and the League of Nations – with the object of increasing the scope of immigration and colonization to maintain the political autonomy of the Yishuv and, ultimately, to create the Jewish State; (5) maintenance of an autonomous system of education; (6) maintenance of some social services, especially a wide network of health services. Significantly, the first four tasks were primarily in the hands of the Zionist Organization and the Jewish Agency, while the others were mostly in the hands of the *Vaad Leumi* or of the various Jewish municipalities. In this way the fact was emphasized that the Yishuv itself was, at any time, only one stage in the constant development of the Zionist enterprise.

The various routine tasks of administering the country and maintaining communication services, police, a legal system and, to some extent, local government were mostly in the hands of the mandatory government. Tension developed between the government and the Jewish national institutions both on major issues of policy (immigration, etc.) as well as in spheres where activities overlapped. As the Jewish institutions, and especially the Jewish Agency, dealt mostly with 'colonizing' tasks which were strongly characterized by their connection with future development, the Jewish institutions had no great dealings with routine economic and administrative matters nor with the maintenance of order. The only major exceptions to this were the Jewish municipalities and the allocation of the various funds for colonization and 'constructive' works.

Financial resources of the Jewish institutions were derived mainly from voluntary contributions by Jews all over the world and in Palestine. The main moral and social basis of these institutions was the readiness of most groups in Palestine to accept their political authority and to co-operate in the voluntary participation in common tasks in the process of rebuilding Eretz Israel.

## Relations with the Diaspora

The second crucial aspect of the institutional structure of the Yishuv and its dynamics concerned the relations between the different Zionist parties in the Diaspora and different sectors in the Yishuv, as they crystallized during the mandatory period. The most important of these relations was the peculiar type of federative–constitutional coalition pattern not including the Revisionist and the ultra-orthodox and to some degree the so-called Oriental groups, although even they did, as we have seen, participate in some activities of these common frameworks.

The concrete nature of these relations was, of course, greatly influenced by the basic decision about the nature of the Jewish settlement in Eretz Israel.

Because of this decision, the relations of the Yishuv to the Diaspora showed a rather peculiar dissociation between the two types of resources, finance and manpower, best epitomized in the saying that 'Yishuv – and above all the Labour sector – was developed by Jews without capital and capital without Jews'.

Most of the financial resources were used for the creation of basic infrastructures of settlements, of economic organizations; they were not directly owned by the pioneer groups, but by the various national and other institutions such as the *Keren Kayemet*, the Jewish Agency and by the various collective institutions of the Histadrut.

Thus indeed the most important aspect of these federative–constitutional arrangements was the participation of most of the parties in the central Executive (of the Zionist Organization, the Jewish Agency and the *Vaad Leumi*) and in the allocation of the major resources which it distributed – namely certificates of immigration given by the British Government, and financial resources and manpower which were in the hands of these institutions – for settlement and provision of educational and to some degree social services.

The concrete dynamics of these federative–constitutional frameworks were greatly influenced by the combination of the general Zionist orientations of what has been called constructive activities – a combination which had become predominant under the leadership of Weizmann and the pioneering Labour sectors, and which shaped the Yishuv's fundamental political and economic relationship with both the mandatory regime and the Arab sector.

The predominance of this pattern was connected with the Zionist Organization gradually becoming more powerful than the *Vaad Leumi* and, within the Zionist Organization, the Labour groups gaining predominance. This trend first manifested itself when Chaim Arlosoroff assumed the directorship of the political department of the Jewish Agency in Jerusalem and when, in 1935, Ben-Gurion became chairman of its Executive.

# II · The Institutional Formats of the Yishuv

## The Mode of Cultural Formations and of Cultural Creativity
### Cultural creativity

It was these basic characteristics of the organization of the Yishuv, and the relations with Jewish communities in the Diaspora in general and the Zionist Organization in particular, with the mandatory government and more indirectly with the Arab population of Palestine – rooted as they were in the decision about the nature of Jewish settlement in Israel, and in the encounter with concrete problems of settlement in Eretz Israel – that shaped the development of the social structure and the specific institutional moulds of the Yishuv and the State of Israel, their fundamental and specific characteristics as a modern Jewish society, the ways in which the different themes and orientations were articulated by different sectors of the Zionist movement.

The first such mould to become crystallized in the Yishuv was the cultural one – the format or pattern of cultural creativity and participation which, as compared with many other modern and revolutionary societies, indeed exhibited some rather peculiar characteristics.

This format was influenced by the basic premises of the Zionist ideology: namely that there would be a Jewish cultural renaissance in Eretz Israel. According to this view, the whole rationale of Jewish renaissance in the Land of Israel was, by definition, Jewish, all of it stemming from the attempt to open the gates of Jewish creativity, to reconstruct a modern Jewish society and civilization.

At the same time it would be difficult to pinpoint the exact characteristics, according to the then prevalent view, which would single it out as Jewish – except for the general presupposition that the very homecoming to its own land would bring out all the springs of creativity in the Jewish people that were presumably stifled in the Diaspora. There was much stress – very much in the line of the emancipation period – on the special values and spiritual heritage of the Jewish people which would come into full efflorescence with the settlement in Eretz Israel.

Much of this was very strongly influenced by the different Zionist orientations or ideologies, probably the single most influential one being that of Ahad Ha'am, with his stress on the Jewish community in Israel as a spiritual centre for the Jewish people.

The Zionist theorists and publicists were, as we have seen, very concerned with the relations of the Zionist ideal to Jewish tradition. On the one hand they consciously rebelled against many aspects of this tradition, above all against the premisses, if not the details, of the Halakhic mould.

There was no doubt in the Zionists' minds that the very process of reconstruction would provide most of the answers to the problems posed by the relations of the new cultural creativity to Jewish tradition on the one hand, and to various aspects of modern universal culture on the other; that it would encompass most aspects of cultural life and creativity.

This view was reinforced first of all by the two great achievements of cultural creativity and innovation that took place in this period – namely the revival and institutionalization of the Hebrew language which has been discussed above, and the development and reconstruction of different elements of the Jewish tradition into the institutional framework of Israeli culture – in the emergence of symbols of collective identity, of patterns of cultural creativity and the crystallization of the cultural symbolic dimension of patterns of daily life.

## Reconstruction of tradition

The major development in the cultural field, beyond the revival of the Hebrew language, was the reconstruction and reinterpretation of Jewish tradition in the special Israeli (or rather Eretz-Israel) way.

There was a revaluation of the historical periods of Jewish history, a very strong emphasis of Jewish history as leading to the return to Eretz Israel, an emphasis on the 'secular' aspects of Jewish life and history (such as for instance the Biblical period, the period of the Second Commonwealth and that of the Golden Spanish era), on the political and national dimensions and on the revaluation of the mystical dimensions in this experience.

These tendencies – like the reconstruction of the Hebrew language – were evident on all levels of cultural creativity and participation: in 'High Culture', in modes of cultural participation and consumption and in the crystallization of the symbolic dimensions of daily life.

Research into the history and archaeology of Eretz Israel began, as well as a great revival of the Bible and Biblical studies, as against the rather secondary place they had in the orthodox curriculum of studies.

There was an efflorescence of Hebrew literature, continuing the great creativity in the Diaspora, with the great figures like Bialik, Saul Tchernichowsky or J. H. Brenner or later generations like Shmuel Yosef Agnon, Haim Hazaz, Avraham Shlonsky, Uri Zvi Greenberg or Nathan Alterman – and still later those born or raised in Eretz Israel – each developing different combinations of the basic themes.

Attempts to create traditions were also manifest in the establishment of the national theatre, *Habimah*, and, later on in the mid-1930s, of the Philharmonic Orchestra.

This reconstruction of components of Jewish tradition also spread to several important institutional foci. One such central focus was the establishment of a school curriculum for the new – elementary and high – schools that were established in the different sectors of the Yishuv, first in the Herzlia and Rehavia Gymnasia, the elementary schools, and later on in the whole educational systems of the Yishuv.

The major themes of the curriculum were differential emphases on historical periods of Jewish history; negation of the Galut; emphasis of those periods of Jewish life – as the Spanish period – in which the secular elements were relatively strong; a reinterpretation of Jewish history as leading to the Zionist vision, combining also a relatively strong orientation to general, especially European, history. It was here that the Zionist revolutionary ideology and vision found its fullest expression and in turn became the basis on which the basic identity of the new generations in Eretz Israel was founded.

Beyond the institutionalization of school curricula, the reconstruction of Jewish tradition was also evident in the symbolic components of daily life.

Thus, as we have seen, Hebrew became the lingua franca of the society; Shabbat became the natural day of weekly rest; the Jewish calendar was established as part of the structuring of collective time; the Jewish holidays became public holidays encompassing believers and non-believers, establishing a framework of public life within which different life styles, upholding the tradition or going beyond it, could develop.

Side by side with this was the specific Eretz-Israel orientation: the search for roots in Eretz Israel, the development of new folkways and popular symbols of deep emotional significance, excursions and exploration of the land, its fauna and flora, its antiquities. All of these naturally increased with the growth of a new generation actually born in Eretz Israel, which became part of the youth movements – closely tied to security considerations and the stress on the primordial attachment to the land.

In this context there was a special place for archaeology, as well as for Biblical studies, not only in the academic but in the broader cultural ambiance – all of which became foci of general public interest and subjects of widely attended expeditions and conventions.

Also of special interest were the processes of cultural innovation in the Kibbutzim, and to a smaller extent in the Moshavim, and the impact on the broader format of daily life in the form of new ways of celebrating many of the festivals, with strong emphasis on their relation to nature and to the agricultural cycle, their attempts to create new 'secular' *Pessah Hagada* or the like.

With this emphasis on cultural creativity, a new collective identity developed in the different sectors of the Yishuv. The only exception to this general pattern were the so-called Canaanites from among some younger intellectual and literary circles, who, building on the natural attachment to the Land of those born in Eretz Israel and on the negative attitude to the Galut, attempted to articulate a conception of Eretz-Israeli identity which would be entirely based on a secular attachment to the Land and its early history, with an almost total disjunction from the Jewish people.

The Canaanite movement did indeed have a very strong impact on the latent orientations of many members of the new generations of Sabras; yet it was never fully accepted; the movement itself was rather marginal – although it provided foci of important controversy and although these trends became quite pervasive on the level of daily life. The majority of the Yishuv, with all the negation of the Galut, looked on itself as a part – even if a very revolutionary part – of the Jewish people.

## The impact and place of religion

Another aspect of cultural activity was evident in the ways in which the religious element was incorporated into the fabric of cultural life. Here several levels have to be distinguished.

On the institutional level the most important fact here was the vesting in the Rabbinical courts of all jurisdiction in respect of civil and personal status – this in fact left in their hands the definition of at least the formal, legal boundaries of the Jewish community – as well as, though to a somewhat smaller degree, the religious legislation around Shabbat, Kashrut and the like. This constituted a focus of public–political controversy and struggle which continues to this day, but the very existence of this situation constituted a part of the specific Jewish dimension of the Yishuv and State of Israel.

The religious components were also visible on the level of daily life, as well as in the construction and crystallization of the symbols of collective identity.

On the level of daily life the religious component was indeed very visible in the erection of many synagogues, ritual baths, local religious councils and rabbinates. Although it was independent of the local political institutions to a degree, it was yet part of the general framework, in the development and existence of the special religious educational system, as well as in the various concrete arrangements around the rabbinical courts, in the observation of Shabbat and holidays as the official rest days. It was also evident in the fact that the 'traditional religious' holidays were naturally maintained at least as rest days throughout most of the Yishuv.

As for the reconstruction of a new collective identity, the religious component was not very active in the period of the Yishuv, nor in the first stage of the State of Israel, and the more secular orientations were much stronger. Even within the more religious groups, with all their emphasis on religious observance, there was – with the partial exception of the *Hapoel Hamizrahi* in general and the religious Kibbutzim in particular – but relatively little confidence that the Halakhic mould could serve as a driving force for this process.

So a unique format of cultural life developed in the Yishuv, based on continuous creativity aiming at the reconstruction of the major dimensions of Jewish tradition and of its relation to general cultural values, characterized by relatively great heterogeneity but based, in principle, on the basic tenets of the Zionist vision. A rather special combination of tradition and modernity minimized the rift which could be found later among many new nations, but was also based on far-reaching compromises with the religious groups.

# The Sectorial Organization of the Yishuv
## The three main sectors

One of the major features of the institutional structure of the Yishuv was its organization into sectors – the workers', the 'civil' and the religious ones. The workers' sector comprised the major Kibbutz and Moshav settlements, the various urban economic sectors and the major service-providing organizations, the most important of which was the General Sick Fund (*Kupat Holim*) – all of them organized under the aegis of the Histadrut, the Labour federation. The bourgeois or civilian (*Ezrahi*) sector, less tightly organized, comprised, as we have seen, parts of the urban population, the older (first Aliya) settlements and the new private rural or semi-urban settlements (Moshavot). The Zionist religious sector comprised parts of the religious urban groups under the leadership above all of *Hamizrahi* and *Hapoel Hamizrahi*, and the religious Kibbutzim – the first co-operating more with the civil sector, the latter with the workers, but both emphasizing their distinctiveness especially with respect to religious services and education.

These first three sectors – the Labour, the civilian and the Zionist–religious – constituted the most active elements in the period of the Yishuv, with the

Revisionist groups constituting a competing element within them, without however developing into a fully-fledged sector.

The Revisionist groups cannot be called a sector in the sense of the others. Economically they were almost entirely interwoven in the other – civil and Labour – sectors, and with minor exceptions did not develop any distinct economic institution of their own. The only strong continuous non-political, or non-paramilitaristic, institutions which they have developed were the National Sick Fund – in distinction from and competition with the Workers General Sick Fund – and sports organizations, but these comprised only a relatively limited membership.

It was above all in the political and military defence field that they were very active – from the 1930s on – in marked opposition to the other sectors, especially the Labour one, and to most of the common frameworks of the Yishuv and of the General Zionist Organization.

It was, as indicated above and as we shall explain in greater detail later, the Labour sector that became most tightly organized, but all of them comprised some combination of political, economic and educational institutions. The division of the Yishuv into sectors was particularly apparent in the educational field where there were three major streams of schools – 'the general one', the Labour and the religious ones – with a few private schools being outside any of them. They all shared, even if with different emphases, the basic outlook to the future, the quest to forge out a new Jewish culture and institutions, orientated far beyond their 'natural' clientele. The same was true of the trans-sectoral cultural and educational institutions (the most important of which were the Hebrew University, established in 1925, and the Technion – the Technical Institute in Haifa – established in 1912 but with full-scale teaching undertaken only in 1924), as well as of some of the high schools and, to a certain degree, but until the late 1930s or early 1940s only partially, the organization of self-defence, the *Hagana*.

## Sectors not integrated in the Yishuv: the ultra-orthodox, parts of oriental groups

Besides these sectors there existed the various ultra-orthodox groups which in principle – although not always in practice – denied the possibility of co-operation with the Zionist sectors, and parts of the so-called Oriental Jews who were, as we shall see in greater detail later on, not fully integrated in these sectors.

The various ultra-orthodox groups, the different sects and parts of the old Yishuv, quite strongly divided among themselves – some related to Agudat Israel, others, even more extreme – tried to segregate themselves from the organizations established by the Zionist Organization and those of the Yishuv – establishing their own courts, not registering themselves in the general Jewish census and ideologically strongly negating the basic tenets of Zionism.

But even among them there developed different degrees of non-cooperation with the Yishuv and the Zionist Organization. One stream, connected with the Hassidic groups from Poland, where there existed a tradition of co-operation with other (secular) Jewish groups in common frameworks, developed a rather strong orientation to 'Settlement of Eretz Israel' (Yishuv Eretz Israel) and groups of them settled in various urban centres, *de facto* co-operating in mundane matters with the local organizations. This very stress on settling in Eretz Israel necessitated some agreement with the Zionist Organization in whose hands were parts of the 'certificates' – the permit of entry to Palestine by the mandatory government.

Another part of the Jewish population in Eretz Israel which did not fully participate in the new emerging framework of the Yishuv, were parts of the so-called Oriental or Sephardi Jews.

The term Sephardi originally applied to all the Jews originating from Spain (*Sephard*), who lived in various parts of North Africa, Turkey, Greece and Egypt. The main part of the 'old' Jewish community which lived in Palestine before the beginning of immigration in the 1880s consisted of Sephardim. Chief among these were the following communities (*edot*): Sephardim, Persians, Kurds, Babylonians, Yemenites, Maghrebites (from Morocco), as well as Jews from Bukhara, Haleb, Urfa, Georgia and Afghanistan.

Many Sephardim, however, and most of the other Oriental groups mentioned above, came later with at least about 70,000 after 1918, to add to the approximately 20,000 who were already there. Their arrival, therefore, more or less coincided with the main waves of the European immigration. Though there were many important differences among them, the common denominator 'Oriental Jews' was not only geographical but also, on the whole – with some very important exceptions – had a special sociological connotation.

Their first specific characteristic was that, unlike other groups, they were not – for reasons which we shall analyse in greater detail later on – dispersed in the various economic, ecological and educational spheres. They concentrated disproportionally in certain strata of the spheres, especially in the lower and lower-middle classes, living especially in certain quarters, sometimes slums, of Jerusalem and Tiberias. They also tended to maintain, to a great extent, some parts of their own educational structure. There emerged also a few – not very powerful – political parties based on ethnic identity, such as the Yemenite party and the Sephardic bloc, though by no means all Oriental Jews were identified with these parties. Thus they constituted an important exception to the general high rate of social integration of the Yishuv. Side by side with these characteristics certain behaviour patterns, such as symptomatic non-integration and tension became apparent among them.

At the same time, in the 1930s, there was a great rift between the Labour movements and sector and the Revisionist one – in the Diaspora and in Eretz Israel alike. In the 1940s this rift was transposed into the fight between 'organized Yishuv' and the so-called 'dissident' groups (Ezel and Lehi), constituting one of the major aspects of the history of the Yishuv in the decade.

The focus of this struggle was their relations to the British on the one hand, and the closely connected problems of their acceptance of a common political framework on the other. The organized Yishuv (and its unofficial 'illegal' army – the *Hagana*) and the dissidents shared, to some degree at least, the ultimate political goals: the removal of restrictions on purchase of land by Jews and on immigration and, ultimately, the attainment of political independence. But they differed greatly in the emphasis they placed on these aims. The dissidents stressed the attainment of political independence and especially the 'means' used. The organized Yishuv stressed the combination of continuously expanding territorial settlement, immigration and defended the minimization of direct diplomatic negotiations, above all with the British. Meanwhile the dissidents put greater emphasis on the latter and on political mobilization of the masses of Jews in the Diaspora and Eretz Israel. Moreover – and this in itself was of great importance – the dissidents did not accept the common voluntary political framework of the Yishuv and its implied collective discipline and responsibility.

While there can be no doubt that the activities of the *Hagana* and the *Irgun* alike ultimately contributed to the decision of the British to give up the mandate and to quit Palestine – although it was mostly the *Hagana* that was crucial in waging the War of Independence against the Arabs – yet at that time the conflict between the dissidents and the organized Yishuv threatened to overtake the international struggle, and seemed sometimes to be leading towards civil war and fratricide. This was also the case in the early 1930s, when an acute conflict developed between the Revisionist movement under Jabotinsky and the Labour camp under Ben-Gurion and when the agreement between the two leaders was abrogated by a vote of the Labour sector. The atmosphere of almost civil war that developed on that occasion was intensified when the Labour camp attributed the killing of Chaim Arlosoroff on 16 June 1933 on the beach of Tel Aviv to members of the extreme rightist groups closely related to the Revisionists and, even though those of them who were brought to trial were acquitted, the controversy about this continued to be one of the bitter elements of the collective memory of the Yishuv and later the State of Israel.

## Rivalry between sectors, and the rise of the Labour group

There has always been a struggle between the different sectors of the Yishuv over their relative predominance within the common framework. This struggle and the ensuing conflicts were not always peaceful. There were many small groups of extremists with a high proclivity to violence, and quite a lot of violent outbursts also erupted in the more organized groups in the different sectors. The struggles were over many issues, such as the predominance of the Hebrew language or various economic conflicts, as well as the more general problem of the predominance in the federative arrangements. But gradually a somewhat more peaceful *modus vivendi* emerged, at least within the organized Yishuv, and each sector learned that, given the voluntary nature of the Yishuv, the lack of sovereign power and the continuous influx of new immigrants, any predominance could be only a relative one. From the mid-1930s this predominance became vested in the hands of the Labour sector.

This predominance was evident, however, not only in the fact that the Labour party became the major partner in any ruling coalition; beyond this it was evident in the fact that the institutional–ideological mould created by this sector became the predominant one in the Yishuv. The pioneering Labour sector combined the emphasis of ideology with concrete institution-building orientated specifically (as, for instance, in the case of the Sick Fund) for the absorption and mobilization of manpower, and at least partially supported by various organizations in the Diaspora – above all in the various *Hakhsharot*.

But even this predominance did not obviate the continuity in the Zionist Organization and in the *Vaad Leumi* of the basic pattern of coalition between different parties and sectors, with its mixture of totalistic orientations, of vociferous ideological debates and practical working together in the common federative constitutional frameworks.

Only the so-called 'dissidents', both from the Revisionists who left the Zionist Organization and from the marginal groups of the Yishuv, defied the legitimacy and validity of the 'federative' structure of the Yishuv and hence of its political discipline.

# Political and Economic Moulds; Absorption of Immigrants
## *Sectarianism and constitutional federations*

The political mould of the Yishuv was characterized by a peculiar combination of strong democratic arrangements, totalistic orientation and hard bargaining about the federative (consociational) allocation of the major resources.

The strong totalistic orientations were particularly evident within the workers' sector. They were closely related to the development, albeit secularized – especially by the 'revolutionary' ideological pioneer groups – of themes which had been predominant among the Jewish people throughout its history. Most important of these were the strong transcendental orientations, in the sense of an orientation to a higher human, social or religious ideal; second a strong emphasis on the universal significance of the new Jewish collectivity and institution-building; third, a strong stress on direct access of all the groups to what in the traditional setting would have been called the sacred realm, but what in the modern setting was defined as the proper interpretation of the Zionist vision – resulting from the feeling that every group, sect or even individual had the right interpretation of this vision.

These sectarian tendencies – most clearly seen in the various pioneer movements – were also in many ways reminiscent of both revolutionary movements in Eastern Europe, and many of the religious Rabbinical or Hassidic groups in the Jewish communities of the Diaspora. Indeed many sons or grandsons of these communities became leaders in the different pioneer groups – sometimes, as in the case of some of the leaders of, for instance, *Hashomer Hatzair*, the most leftist secular pioneer groups, replicating some of the relations between the *Tsadik* and his Hassidim.

Given these sectarian tendencies there was of course a strong ambivalence to civility, to the acceptance of the authority of any central institutions and the concomitant continuous development of strong antinomian tendencies in many parts of the Yishuv – often giving rise to violent outbursts and activities. But these were tempered, in the reality of the settlement in Eretz Israel, by several factors – some reinforcing, some contradicting one another – by the necessity to participate in common enterprises and frameworks, and by their dependence on the different parts of the Zionist movement abroad.

They were tempered first by the strong emphasis on internal solidarity and by the broader solidarity of the different movements within the Yishuv, of the Zionist movement; by a very strong, even if often latent, feeling of Jewish solidarity. Secondly they were tempered by the necessity to work together, giving rise to some acceptance of common authority and to some degree of civility. Thirdly they were tempered by the relative segregation of different groups or sectors, by the possibility of each of them finding, as it were, separate institutional and often even ecological niches.

But these niches were not entirely separated. They did come together in the common frameworks and such coming together did on the whole temper the more sectarian totalistic orientations in a federative conditional direction – it could however also generate continuous tendencies of sectarianism and separatism.

These sectarian tendencies were also tempered by the constitutional traditions that developed within the Zionist organization – upheld by various intellectual groups and intellectuals, raised in the tradition of European liberalism and constitutionalism; by the impact, under the mandate, of the British model; by the importance of playing the game, to some degree, according to the constitutional rules of the mandatory power, later reinforced by the influx of German immigration; and by sensitivity to international general and Jewish opinion and institutionalized within the federative–constitutional framework analysed above.

## The semi-consociational model

The concrete format of the political mould that has developed in the Yishuv can best be characterized as an approximation to a consociational model. In such a model, prevalent in small European democracies, like the Netherlands, Switzerland, Austria, and lately also designated as *Proporzdemokratie*, some basic rights or entitlements – such as citizenship and all the duties and rights entailed by it – are, according to universalistic criteria, vested in all members of the broader collectivity (nation). Conversely, the access to the major centres of power, as well as to many of the public goods and the publicly distributed private goods, is mediated to a large degree by representatives of the major 'consociational' segments – be they religious groups, political parties, local units and the like. Within such segments, however, the access to power is open to everyone on a universalistic basis. In the case of the Yishuv, the segments themselves were brought together, as we have seen, within common universalistic frameworks – such as the World Zionist Organization, the Jewish Agency and the National Council (*Vaad Leumi*) of the Jews in Palestine – through which most of the resources were allocated to the different segments. They also served as the representative body of the Yishuv *vis-à-vis* the Jewish communities of the Diaspora and other sectors (Arabs, mandate authorities) of the local society.

These different social–ideological movements created, from the 1920s to the 1940s, separate organizations for agricultural settlement, as well as their own credit, financing and marketing institutions. They controlled a wide range of resources, such as housing and health services, provided to those sectors of their related Jewish population by establishing their own organizations, especially through the use of resources collected among the Jewish communities in the Diaspora and channelled by the Jewish National Institutions. In addition, these institutions constituted, at that period, a very important source of employment.

Out of the continuous interaction between the totalistic, federative and constitutional structures and orientations, and between them and the basic Zionist premises, there developed also some crucial aspects of the Yishuv's political combination of different themes of political culture which were to characterize the Yishuv and later on also the State of Israel and which were also, to some degree at least, related to some of the traditional Jewish themes analysed above – and above all the rather uneasy coexistence of sectarian and antinomian tendencies, predilection to violence and violent struggles, within a common constitutional framework; of highly ideological policies with strong future orientations and of hard bargaining over the allocation of resources; of emphasis on pristine pioneering values and strong power orientations.

Because of this political interaction and tensions, Jonathan Shapiro* has shown that the democratic ambiance of the framework was particularly focused around the right of all groups and sectors to participate in the central frameworks and much less – given above all the totalistic orientation of many of the movements, as well as probably some of the communal traditions – on the rights of individuals, and this special democratic mode tended to become also, as we shall see, quite predominant in the State of Israel.

## Religious arrangements

Within this framework a very special type of arrangement developed with respect to religious questions – an arrangement above all between the Zionist–religious groups (the *Hamizrahi* and the *Hapoel Hamizrahi*) and the other

* Jonathan Shapiro, *Democracy in Israel* (in Hebrew) (Ramat Gan 1977).

parties of the coalition – the Labour camp especially from the mid-1930s – some aspects of which we have mentioned above.

The Zionist–religious groups were, of course, part of the general federative structure, and as such taking part in all the usual federative distribution of resources – certificates, land, public finances and the like – and in the tough political bargaining accompanying such arrangements. The religious groups also took good care of the various local religious institutions, especially the religious councils and local rabbinates which were established in most municipal settings (except those of the Kibbutzim and Moshavim) and which, while closely related to the overall Zionist frameworks, were not yet part of the local political balance of power.

But beyond this there developed specific arrangements, a specific *modus vivendi* with respect to religious matters which affected not only the religious groups, but the whole Jewish population.

One such arrangement was the official observance (even if not always fully upheld) of religious holidays, Shabbat and the rules of *Shmita* (the seventh year) on the national land of the *Keren Kayemet*, that is in most settlements.

The second was the upholding of Shabbat not only as an official rest day – a natural development in itself – but also by introducing various laws restraining shopping, entertainment and public transportation in most cities (Haifa, the bastion of the workers, being a partial exception to the latter) as well as by granting to the rabbinate the powers certifying the Kashrut to those butchers and restaurants which were interested in them (and hence indirectly enabling a relatively strong supervision over the production and consumption of food throughout most parts of the Yishuv).

An arrangement which had an even more far-reaching impact on the whole community was the vesting of the laws of personal status, above all of marriage and divorce – and hence of the boundaries of the membership in the community – in the hands of the Rabbinical courts, which were established in 1922 and which, while not accepted by the ultra-religious, did become a basic part of the institutional structure of the Yishuv.

Here there took place a very interesting, although seemingly natural, development, namely the establishment of an organized Rabbinate – both central and local – under two Chief Rabbis, one Sephardi (the so-called Rishon Letzion, a title which seems to go back to the sixteenth or seventeenth century) and the other Ashkenazi.

Significantly enough the very establishment of such a central Rabbinical structure was not a natural internal development of the religious groups, but rather of the impetus generated within the Zionist and the new Yishuv framework – and was indeed opposed by the ultra-orthodox groups. The first Chief Rabbis – the Ashkenazi Rabbi Avraham Kook and later on Rabbi Isaac Herzog, and the Sephardi Rabbis (The Rishon Letzion) Yaacov Meir and Ben Zion Uziel, as well as the local Chief Rabbis, especially those of Tel Aviv – were indeed seen as an integral part of the common Zionist and Yishuv framework, participating in many of the common – especially political –

activities, and thus symbolizing the integral part (some at least) of the religious tradition in the Zionist undertaking – even if, needless to say, not always agreeing with all the concrete policies and activities of many of the religious or anti-religious groups and leaders.

## Economic institutions

At the same time specific characteristics of the Yishuv economic structure developed, the kernels of the future mode of political economy that developed in the State of Israel. The most important among these characteristics were first the relatively high degree of centralization, and especially the concentration of public capital in the main sectors of economic development, alongside the constant growth of private sectors and the coexistence of public and private sectors in what has been called a 'pluralistic' economic system.

A special way of socio-economic organization also crystallized, especially in the Labour sector. First of all there were the major types of settlements – the Kibbutzim and the Moshavim; then the development of co-operative enterprises in the urban sector; and above all – the main unique feature of Israeli economy – the integration of most of these co-operatives and settlement bodies within unified frames of different sectors in general, and in that of the Histadrut (the General Federation of Labour) in particular. It was this integration that made possible the extension of the workers' sector beyond the boundaries of the pioneering groups' early agrarian orientations and facilitated the development of the major characteristics of the urban social structure of the Yishuv.

The second aspect of the developing social structure of the Yishuv was the strong emphasis on egalitarianism and some opposition to occupational specialization. This found its expression in two ways: in attempts to reduce differentials between different occupations and to minimize visible social differences, and in the assumption that an easy transition from one profession to another was possible.

There developed here also a special type of economic entrepreneurship beyond the relatively usual type of mostly middle- and small-scale capitalists and entrepreneurs – the 'institutional' entrepreneur colonizer.

## The absorption of immigrants

Another very central aspect of the institutional structure of the Yishuv, which developed out of the combination of the basic Zionist ideology in general and the pioneering one in particular, was the rather special type of absorption of immigrants which developed within it and which distinguished it from most other modern countries of immigration.*

The most distinct of these processes was a relatively far-reaching and quick dispersion of different groups of immigrants in the major institutional spheres:

* See in greater detail S. N. Eisenstadt, *The Absorption of Immigrants* (London 1954).

in the occupational structure, in ecological formations, in political structure and in the emerging status systems, and the consequent very weak development of what could be called 'ethnic' identity among most immigrant groups.

While the process of absorption and adjustment could be difficult and in some cases even painful, yet on the whole, as compared with almost any other country of modern immigration, it was relatively quick. The process often developed in less than one generation, almost always in the second.

It was effected through a combination of absorption into the formal political, economic institutions, and into more informal nuclei – especially the self-defence institution like the *Hagana*, the pioneering groups and, for the younger generation, the educational system and the youth movements. It was also effected through the pressure of continuous waves of immigrants on the existing institutions, giving rise to their expansion and diversification. This followed the basic tenets of the Zionist and pioneering vision, for the implementation of which the central institutions of the Yishuv were dependent on the immigrants and on the financing by the central Zionist organizations – on which all the immigrants could exert pressures.

It was only in the late 1930s – with the influx of the German Aliya – and especially in the 1940s, after the end of the Second World War, that new, special institutions were created. The most famous of these was the Youth Aliya established in the 1930s, which constituted a great, unique educational institution which proved to be very effective in integrating young generations of Olim into the central frameworks of the Yishuv.

Till then the process of absorption was on the whole effected through the continuous expansion of existing institutions through the creation of new ones by older and newer immigrants together. The only exception to this were the Orthodox groups who consciously opted out of the Yishuv, and parts at least of the so-called Oriental Jews because of their special historical background. The preponderance among them of more traditional as against pioneering–revolutionary attitudes, and the nature of their educational background meant that they did not become fully absorbed, but developed rather into distinct ecological and occupational sectors. It was within this sector that many social problems – illiteracy or delinquency – also began to develop. Unlike, however, the Orthodox sector, most of the Oriental groups were in principle orientated to the central framework of the Yishuv and the Zionist vision.

Indeed in the new institutional structure of the Yishuv, many of the older Sephardi notables lost their status, while large parts of the Oriental immigrants, old and new alike, became fully integrated occupationally, socially and politically in the predominant sectors of the Yishuv. But many others – who naturally became more visible – did not. Many of the more active among them became, significantly enough, attracted to the various dissident groups, finding a greater affinity to their ambience than to that of the dominant Labour sector.

# III · The Dynamics of the Institutional Development of the Yishuv

## The Dynamic and Stagnating Tendencies in the Development of the Yishuv
### Institutional structure of the Yishuv

The institutional structure of the Yishuv crystallized continuously. This dynamic development was generated by the combination of three broad processes – the very institutionalization of the original Zionist vision in the reality of Eretz Israel; the ideological and power struggle between different parts of the Zionist movement; and the internal growth of the Yishuv itself.

These processes sometimes reinforced, sometimes contradicted one another – and hence the continuous development generated by them necessarily brought out many of the tensions between different forces and orientations analysed above, as well as new ones.

Two aspects of this structure may serve as very good starting-points for the analysis of the dynamics of the development of the Yishuv. One is the analysis of the seeming discrepancy between the reality of daily life in a small society and the very strong dynamics which went beyond such reality; between the concrete reality of the different groups that composed it, with their daily needs and problems, and the very strong future orientation inherent in the Zionist ideology in general and the pioneering one in particular.

The second and closely related point is the continuous existence in the Yishuv of potentially stagnating tendencies – which first became visible in the period of the first Aliya but also existed in all the other periods of the development of the Yishuv – and of the ways in which these tendencies were, at least partially, overcome.

## The dynamics of development

The concrete reality in Eretz Israel, as it slowly built up, was that of a small relatively modern but not very highly developed society with a relatively low level of resources and – by comparison with other modern societies, even the societies from which many of the immigrants come – a relatively low standard of living. The daily flavour of life in the towns beyond the Kibbutzim could be seen as that of a rather provincial small bourgeois society, with a strong ingredient of working groups and a high emphasis on various collective activities and organizations.

Needless to say, in this concrete setting the routine of life centred first around the daily problems of work, education and construction and then of course around political activities and the intense power struggle that existed between the different sectors. But neither this power struggle nor the reality of life in the Yishuv can be understood only – or even mainly – in terms of the concrete problems of these different sectors of the Yishuv. The narrowness and seeming shabbiness of this reality was countered by several basic, strongly inter-connected, dynamic factors and wider issues which really shaped the dynamics of life in the Yishuv. One such issue was the continuous immigration, and concomitant economic expansion discussed in the previous section.

Another crucial, and easily visible, issue was, of course, the heavy political and security dimension, rooted in the confrontation of the Zionist settlement with the slowly rising Arab nationalism in general and in Palestine in particular, and with the closely related policies of the mandatory government.

From the very beginning the Zionist movement and the Yishuv were involved in the international political scene and orientated towards it. It was the achievement of an international political status under the Balfour Declaration and the establishment of the British Mandate in Palestine and Transjordan which provided the frameworks and impetus for the post-First World War settlement. But all these naturally clashed with the nascent Arab nationalism and, from the very beginning, the history of the Yishuv has been a history of conflict, riots and armed encounter which have focused around the Jewish right to settlement, to immigration, to autonomous institution – all of which became intensified from the mid-1930s on.

This strong political orientation or dimension gave rise to the strong emphases on the acquisition – especially by the *Keren Kayemet Leisrael* – of wide stretches of land for the extension of settlements; on building up Jewish territorial blocs; on extension, through such settlements, of the territorial basis of the Yishuv, and on organization of these settlements for defence. This trend started before the First World War, intensified in the 1920s with the acquisition of *Emek Israel* (The Valley of Israel), and culminated in the late 1930s with a whole series of settlements, including the famous Wall and Tower one (*Homa Umigdal*), stressing pioneering, territorial, defence and security dimensions.

These activities added a new dynamic element to the daily life of the Yishuv. They called for the mobilization of manpower; for resources for the settlements and defence; for continuous political activities to assure the success of these ventures. Thus the Yishuv was distinguished from other countries of coloniz-atory settlement or immigration.

More central to the institutional structure of the Yishuv was the Zionist vision of the future – that the Yishuv was built not for itself but for the whole future generation of Jews who will come there, for the whole Jewish nation.

Needless to say such an emphasis could be a simple rationalization for the sanctification of any *status quo*, a justification for demands for help from the outside – almost in the line of the *Kolelim* of the Yishuv.

But the emphasis on future orientation, on the Yishuv being built for the Jewish people, went further; it also gave rise to a special type of institution-building. The most important single manifestation of this tendency was the formation – already analysed above – of various societal and cultural centres, before the appearance of a 'periphery' composed of broader groups and social strata which were not, of course, as creative as the centres in terms of social and cultural innovation.

These centres were thought – by their creators – capable of instructing, absorbing and shaping the periphery, which was destined to develop by means of constant and increasing immigration. As a result of this, most of the institutions developed by these centres were aimed at catering not only for the needs of the population at any given period, but rather for those of a future population.

This tendency was evident in all the major institutional spheres – in education, and in the central economic institutions of the major sectors, especially of the pioneering ones, both in the urban sector and the settlements. The same was true of such organizations as the *Hagana* or the active political institutions, especially of the Zionist organization and of the members of the ruling coalitions. Their major political efforts were continuously orientated, not only to the needs of the existing – yet also continuously expanding – communities, but also towards its extension and the creation of new organizations and frameworks.

## Overcoming stagnating tendencies

This strong future orientation became most fully manifest in the so-called workers' (and religious workers') sectors, in the pioneering groups and their institutions, and in most of their basic institutions. The emphasis on such great creativity – and the consciousness of such creativity – was indeed very central in the self-definition of the Yishuv in general and of the labouring sectors in particular, and in their relation to the Jewish communities in the Diaspora and to the Zionist movement there and the demands made on them. This emphasis was of great potential significance in breaking through the stagnating tendencies inherent in the reality of a small, provincial society.

Also of crucial importance was the continuous incorporation of new elements, as first became evident in the period of the second Aliya, although it continued afterwards. Truly enough the more ideological orientations of the second and later Aliyot, and their organization in social movements, constituted a certain antidote to the dangers of stagnation and provincialism – but only a very limited one. It was not only that the paucity of resources and the smallness of the country and of the Jewish community were naturally conducive to the development of such tendencies. Paradoxically enough, some of the very ideological sectarian emphases of the various movements could also – by self-sanctification, self-enclosure, self-righteousness, clinging to power position – intensify these dangers.

The continuous influx of immigrants and the concomitant expansion and diversification – through continuous struggles – of the institutional framework was vital. But probably of greater importance was the continuous influx of new pioneering and institutional groups and leaderships, breaking through the monopoly of the old-timers and forcing them to co-opt new leadership elements. So the whole institutional format of the Yishuv was changing continuously, increasing both the tensions within it and its creativity.

Overcoming these potentially stagnating tendencies was also of course closely connected with the lack of basic coercive power in the Yishuv, with the voluntary basis of its organization – a fact which was also very closely related to the pattern of absorbing immigrants referred to above.

## The image of the pioneer

This preoccupation with the future and its institutional implications became very strongly connected with the development of a specific human image, that of the pioneer, with its strong elitist and egalitarian revolutionary orientations. For many decades the guiding symbol in the development of the Yishuv, it emerged in the periods of the second and the third Aliyot.

This image contained several basic attributes. The first was the element of self-sacrifice. The pioneer was perceived as a man ready to deprive himself of material comforts and social amenities, to live the life of an ascetic. This deprivation was not, however, undertaken for its own sake as a sort of ascetic renunciation of the world, although ascetic elements often became strong secondary elements. The ascetism inherent in the pioneer image entailed working for a concrete, albeit a future, community. It was upheld mainly for the sake of performing tasks important for the future collectivity which was to develop out of the nuclei of the pioneering groups.

## The high potential of leadership

The multiplicity of centres and the high degree of commitment and concern for the future ensured great reservoirs of political leadership in the Zionist movement and the Yishuv in general, and in the workers' sector in particular. This great number of potential and aspiring leaders was evident above all in the political field and was generated in particular by special frameworks and mechanisms such as youth movements and the *Hagana*.

Many political leaders did find some possibility of expression in the numerous not fully centralized organizations and sectors, but their number also constituted a dynamic element in the creation of new, and growing, sectarianism and of tensions between old and new, different sectors and sub-sectors, and different centres and sub-centres. This was true not only in the political sphere proper, but also in the cultural and educational ones. Thus, to give but one illustration, many of the high schools in the Yishuv were manned by highly qualified personnel of potential academic standing who could not find any academic positions in the very restricted opportunities then existing in the Hebrew University or in the Technion.

The first generation of elites was composed of the leaders of the various Aliyot and the representatives of the Zionist Organization. From the period before and immediately after the First World War they were joined by the first generation of leaders educated in Eretz Israel. These shared some common background, above all that of the special elite high schools or gymnasia – like Herzliya in Tel Aviv, the Reali in Haifa and Rehavia in Jerusalem – and the different youth movements and organizations mentioned above. Most of these leaders did of course specialize in some activities or functions, but on the whole – with the partial exception of the special cultural elites such as writers and teachers – such specialization was not fixed or irreversible. Many of them combined several types of activities; significantly enough it was mainly in the workers' sectors that such leadership activities became semi-professionalized and fully salaried.

There were very few distinct specialized, differentiated, economic, political organizations and activities, and the interrelations between those which did develop were very close. Accordingly most of these elites worked within relatively common frameworks, first of all within each sector, and to a small degree also in frameworks common to the various sectors. Their activities within these frameworks were based on the relatively strong internal solidarity of each sector – especially but not only of the workers' sector – as well as solidarity with the broader common frameworks of the Yishuv or the Zionist Organization as a whole. This solidarity was very closely related to their common ideology as well as to the practical activities in which they engaged.

But there were, of course, also great differences in the composition and function of leadership between the different sectors – related to the respective ideology, orientations and organizations of the sectors.

Here again the Labour–pioneering sector evinced its special, more dynamic characteristic. Its leadership was more ideological, forward-looking and power-orientated and much more concerned with the creation of new institutions. This was evident in its greater concentration in the framework first of the Histadrut and later of the Zionist Organization. In contrast the leaders of the civil sector concentrated in more local, municipal and economic institutions or in the organizations connected with the *Vaad Leumi*.

But this very dynamism of the Labour sector also gave rise to developments in a new direction. There developed within this sector – to a much higher degree than in other sectors – a semi-professional, i.e. specialized salaried, group, a class of emerging political-economic entrepreneurs combining different functions. They were also – as Horovitz and Lissak have shown – more homogeneous in their educational background and career patterns.*

As against the first generation, this second echelon of would-be leaders within the workers' sector was not, on the whole, characterized by high levels of education, although most of them went beyond primary or pre-gymnasia education, nor did it exhibit a broad cosmopolitan orientation. Its major

* D. Horowitz and M. Lissak, *Origins of the Israeli Polity – Palestine Under Mandate* (Chicago 1978), Ch. V.

strength was the combination of ideological visions with the institution-building that developed within their sectors and its very specific type of economic entrepreneurship.

At the same time, because of the continuous expansion and diversification of the structure of the Yishuv new types of leadership beyond the more ideological–pioneering ones developed. Thus there were trade-union leaders, managers of different economic organizations, banks, sick funds, corporations and the like. It was they – people like Aba Khouchi (Hushi) and Yoseph Almogi in Haifa – who started to become very prominent in the second and third ranks of the echelons of the Labour leadership, beyond the earlier, most pristine, ideological–pioneering leaders.

Truly enough the pioneering orientation, the stress on national goals, on the extension of existing institutions, on building institutions beyond the needs of existing population, distinguished them from the usual type of trade-union leader or manager of a co-operative. Yet, in contrast to the more ideological and political leadership, usually in some closed even if ambivalent co-operation with them, the power of these leaders was based far more on the various groups in Palestine and on their concrete interests.

## Fund allocation, bureaucratization and power struggles

Out of these processes, there developed three major institutional tendencies, which were to become very important in the social structure of the late Yishuv and of the State of Israel although they were only incipient up to the mid-1930s.

The first such tendency, closely related to the heavy dependency on public funds and 'national' capital and to a centralized pattern of allocation of these funds, was the growing ideological emphasis on the right of different groups to such allocation – a right vested in their very emphais on pioneering, on the creation of new institutions, on serving in them, even irrespective of their economic productivity.

In the first stages of the great pioneering ventures to establish settlements and new organizations, the irrelevance of pure economic productivity was justified by the necessity to build the infrastructure. Later it became more and more connected with a concomitant emphasis on the right to a rising standard of living, be it in the form of housing or of other amenities, justified in terms of various ascriptive rights of belonging to the different sectors in general and to the pioneering sector in particular.

Closely related to these processes there developed also a growing tendency to bureaucratization – above all in the workers' sector, but also in the more general frameworks of the *Vaad Leumi* and the Zionist Organization; in all these frameworks many organizations developed – such as *Keren Kayemet* and *Keren Hayesod*, local councils, co-operatives and the like. While their heads at least initially were often the leaders of the movements, beneath them there usually developed relatively wide echelons of bureaucrats, dealing with the daily allocation of the public resources, enjoying assured income, and becoming an important channel of mobility and occupational aspirations for many elements of the younger generation and new immigrants.

These tendencies within the Labour sector – and within some of the general Zionist Organization – were, needless to say, paralleled by developments within the civil and other sectors; cutting across the different sectors there developed more economic differentiation with greater discrepancy and inequality.

The process of such future-orientated institution-building generated several additional dimensions of social action and organization. The most important was the internal power struggle between and within different sectors, a power struggle focused around the access to the major resources – economic and manpower – and around the internal power positions in the emerging institutional structure, and the closely connected rise of vested interests growing out of the very process of the successful realization of the Zionist and pioneering visions.

The competition over resources inserted a very strong power element in the relations between the sectors and within the patterns of the leadership that developed in them, above all in the workers' sector. Paradoxically, but significantly, this power orientation was much more closely related to the concrete pattern of institutional building than to pure ideological sectarian visions and differences, and became greatly intensified with the growth of the urban organizations and institutions.

## Changing Dimensions of Political Life and the Selective Institutionalization of the Pioneering Ideology
### Political developments

Out of these processes there developed in the political life first a growing bargaining about the allocation of resources between the central semi-federative organizations and the various sectors and sub-sectors, and secondly, the many trends in the crystallization of social differentiation, incipient class or at least strata differences – albeit, as we shall see later in our discussion of developments in the State of Israel, the combination of relatively non-egalitarian trends with the initial egalitarian ethos.

In this way the strong future orientations and emphases on centre-construction became very strongly interwoven with a growing emphasis on the present, with strong distributive or allocative orientation, with a strong power element and with very intensive political bargaining.

The processes of such interweaving started to shape some of the seemingly more future-orientated aspects of the social structure of the Yishuv, such as the vocational aspirations of the second generation, the processes of social mobility and the orientations prevalent in the various youth movements. All of these became orientated not only to some visionary future, beyond the existing social structure, but also to the attainment of higher social positions in the merging social structure – indeed they became more and more part of the style of life of its higher social echelons.

These processes also became very strongly connected with the growing tensions between the more conservative, provincial, inward-looking orientations and the more creative and outward-looking – both of which could be found in all sectors and in all walks of life.

## Selective institutionalization of the pioneering vision

All these processes necessarily entailed a very far-reaching process of change in the institutional orientations and placement of the Zionist ideology in general and of the Labour-pioneering ideology in particular.

With the growth of the Yishuv, with the development of a relatively complex self-sustaining social structure, and with growing economic and occupational differentiation, the ideology could not be maintained in its purity or simplicity, and there developed many tensions in the institutionalization of the pioneering ideology.

Some stemmed from the encounter of the proponents of the pioneering ideology with other groups in the Yishuv, and from the attempts of the proponents of this ideology to overcome these contradictions and to extend the scope of their power and influence. Others stemmed from the basic contradiction between the general diffuse ideal of the pioneer and the orientation towards a differential economic and political structure entailing a high degree of specialization and individualism – a contradiction which became especially acute with the continuous encounter between the private sectors and the growing economic and professional activities in the workers' sectors.

All these developments gave rise to a process of selective institutionalization of this ideology – a process in which both the more dynamic as well as the more stagnating aspects or dimensions developed.

Such selective institutionalization of the ideology took place in several ways. First there was the predominance of elites who were the bearers of this ideology in the broader social structure of the Yishuv.

Second, of crucial importance for pioneering ideology, was its entrenchment in strategic positions within the educational system of the Yishuv. This was especially manifest in the workers' educational trends and in various pioneering youth movements which held up before young people the ideal of pioneering in a kibbutz as the only, or at least the main, way of pioneering.

Third, and one of the most important aspects of this institutionalization of the labour ideology as the predominant institutional mould, was the pattern of selection of leadership that developed in the Yishuv and which assured some continuity in the development of leadership in the workers' sector but also drew to it large groups of young people from other sectors. The most important mechanism for such selection of leadership were the different pioneering (usually youth) movements – such as the *Mahanot Haolim, Hanoar Haoved, Hashomer Hatzair* and, to a smaller degree, the *Tsofim* (Scouts) – which developed not only in the Diaspora but also, from relatively early in the 1920s, in the Yishuv. These movements were closely connected with the workers' educational sector and later on with the upper echelon of the *Hagana* and especially but not only of the *Palmach*, becoming later on also a part of the establishment of the State of Israel. Some parallels developed in the religious sector, especially the more pioneering parts connected with the religious Kibbutzim and the *Bnei Akiva* youth movement. In the 'bourgeoisie' or 'civil' sector such organizations were much weaker.

The fourth way in which selective permeation of the pioneer ideology into various institutional settings took place was through the crystallization and maintenance of common collective symbols derived from the pioneer image. This tendency was intensified by the external circumstances of the struggle with the Arab population and the mandatory government and the consequent necessity to expand the various settlements.

Fifth the influence of the pioneering ideology permeated in a much more diffuse way the atmosphere and style of life in the Yishuv. It revealed itself in the emphasis on outings, the exploration of the country, the 'return to nature' attitude, youth-movement activity, and the relatively simple pattern of dress and style of living which generally prevailed at this time among most groups of the Yishuv.

Last, this ideology became strongly entrenched in the criteria of allocation of rewards and positions in the Yishuv, in the strong emphasis on egalitarianism, and in the stress on belonging to various collective bodies (especially the various pioneering sects and their offshoots, such as the Histadrut).

In all these settings the pioneering ideology was strengthened by the fact that no counter-myth or counter-ideology of any overriding validity was developed by any other group, while the need for a common symbol was felt by immigrant groups in the process of transition from their countries of origin to settlement in Palestine. The pioneering ideology provided some framework of collective identity and a new symbol of self-identity.

But while these processes of selective institutionalization facilitated the acceptance of the ideology, they greatly changed some of its formats as a focus of collective identity and created many new tensions and problems. The charisma of the ideology was confined to a routine. Its various manifestations became flattened, diffuse, less vivid, and less direct in their bearing on daily relations and activities. Side by side with this there naturally developed a widening differentiation between the purely symbolic expression of the ideology, with its full ideological or doctrinaire expression, and the everyday practice presumably based on this very ideology.

## Changes in the pioneering ideology

All these changes also brought out – especially in the workers' sector – some of the contradictions between the different dimensions and institutional deriva-tives of the pioneering ideology, especially between its elitist and egalitarian components. This ideology, even in its weaker expression among the civil sector, was basically very elitist, stressing the vanguard role of the select pioneers. When combined with various orientations derived from the Jewish tradition – namely with the emphasis on commitment to the ideal order; with autonomous access to the sacred realm; with the non-acceptance of any mediation – it necessarily had a very strong egalitarian vein, but this vein was the egalitarianism of the elect and select, of the sect or of the movement. It was also very much based on a strong combination between duty and right, stressing, initially at least, the dimensions of duty, the pioneering duties of service to the nation and to the community.

But with the growing organization of the social structure of the Yishuv and the pioneering settlements themselves, with the strengthening within this framework of the power elements and continuous bargaining over allocation of resources, another egalitarianism developed, rooted in solidarity and the older Jewish traditions. This egalitarianism stressed much more the distributive–allocative orientation, in which the stress on rights became gradually stronger than on duties. Such emphasis started to develop gradually in the manifold enterprises and housing of the workers' sector, picking up parallel orientations in the civil sector.

In actual reality there developed a rather composite and complex picture connected with the institutionalization of the pioneering ideology and with the struggle between the different sectors. In fact the Yishuv was far from an egalitarian society, and the economic differentials between different occupations and sectors were quite great.

But this inequality, as well as the greater emphasis on the present, on the attachment of high social positions, was mitigated by several forces or factors. It was mitigated first of all by the relative segregation between the sectors, by the continuous expansion of the economic structure, and by the patterns of absorption of immigrants. Second, it was also mitigated by different modes of convergence of the two types of egalitarianism in different social settings. In its more pristine form the elitist–egalitarian ethos reigned in the Kibbutzim, to a somewhat smaller, yet not insignificant, way in the Moshavim and to some degree also in the pioneering phases of the development of the various organizations of the Histadrut, in which wages were originally given on the basis of family situation and to some degree seniority rather than according to task. While this norm was actually applied in a limited way – mostly to the leaders and functionaries of the Histadrut – yet its very prevalence was of important symbolic significance.

But later on, with the growth of the more distributive–allocative aspects of these organizations, with the growth of tendencies to bureaucratization, the contradictory influence of these two egalitarian orientations was to become more visible.

# The Impact
# of the British and their Relations with
# the Arabs
## *Day-to-day encounters*

As has been mentioned, the social structure of the Yishuv developed within the mandatory framework and the relations beteen the Yishuv and the mandatory government, as well as with the Arab population, constituted an important aspect of its structure.

With both the small ruling British community as well as with the Arabs, there developed many informal, daily relations. Those with the English community were usually confined to the intellectual and political elite as well as some of the older Sephardi notables. Those with the Arab community were much more widespread and ranged from traditional daily contact between Arab villagers and Jewish settlers to economic relations between the two communities, including long-established relations between Sephardi and Arab notables and covering co-operation in local administrative matters.

These varied contacts continued throughout the mandatory period despite the growing tension between the communities, but – especially in the later period – they were of course greatly influenced by these conflicts.

Beyond these informal contacts, relations between the various communities also achieved a far-reaching impact.

The impact of the British was felt mostly in the institutional and cultural scene. It was most clearly evident in the legal system, which is maintained in many of the basic aspects of the legal institutions in Israel to this day, and, to no small degree, in the administrative and political spheres.

Beyond these points, the most important impact of the English was the cultural sphere, and especially in the contacts and orientations of the Yishuv with the 'outside' Western world. These contacts focused more and more on English-speaking countries – despite the predominance of an Eastern and Central European background among the pioneers and immigrants during the Yishuv, and later the growing importance of more Latin or Mediterranean patterns evolving through the so-called Oriental immigration. English became and, despite some advances of French, continues to be to this day the major foreign language both in the schools and in the institutions of higher learning, and the number of cultural contacts with English-speaking countries increased continuously.

In many circles the conceptions of citizenship, civil order and propriety were modelled on the English pattern. Though they did not become established and institutionalized in the Yishuv, their overall importance certainly cannot be minimized.

Needless to say, this influence was greatly reinforced by the fact that after the Second World War only very few Jewish communities were left in Central and Eastern Europe (except in the Soviet Union, with which contacts were almost impossible) and that the most important Jewish community was in the United States, with the second largest living in England. For at least the first post-war decade centres of scientific, political and economic power were shifted to the United States, a fact which enabled the further development of tendencies which had begun under the influence of the mandate.

Relations with the Arab community were very different – more diffuse and less articulated. Because of the very basic orientations of the Zionist movement bent on development and because of the growing hostility between the Arab and Jewish communities, there was but little positive identification with the major aspects of Arab culture or ways of life.

Yet, in many ways and on many different levels, activities related to the Arab culture and community did tend to develop. One of the most important developments in this area was the upsurge of Oriental–Arab and Muslim studies in the Jewish educational system, ranging from the university level, where the Institute of Oriental Studies was one of the first and most important schools, to the high school where Arabic was one of the two (French being the second) essential foreign languages.

Beyond this, the younger generation of Sabras and especially those from agricultural regions and settlements tended to acquire a variety of characteristics in dress, daily demeanour and linguistic expressions, closely akin to their Arab equivalents. Similarly, among many of the Oriental communities, patterns of dress, leisure and cultural activities often tended to be rather close to those of the Arab communities.

## Political relations

But the relations with the British – and above all with the Arabs – were not, of course, confined to such daily contacts or encounters. They constituted the focus of the 'external' political relations of the Zionist movement and of the Yishuv, greatly influencing many of their activities and becoming more and more central in their life.

Concern about the relations with the Arab population and the possibility of conflict with them was, to some degree, very strongly stressed by some of the earlier Zionist thinkers, although others failed to see it at all, thinking that Eretz Israel was almost totally uninhabited.

Truly enough, Herzl's *Altneuland* assumed, in a sort of visionary–utopian vein, a natural peaceful co-operative coexistence between the two nations, as did some other Zionist thinkers.

But there were Zionist leaders and thinkers, as for instance Ahad Ha'am and later on Yehezkiel Kaufman, probably the only serious ideologue of the non-Labour camp, who stressed very strongly the possibility of an intensive conflict developing between the two nations or ethnic entities and the necessity to look for ways to obviate such conflict.

Weizmann attempted in his own way to overcome such difficulties by his famous agreement in 1917 with the Emir Feisal in which the right of the Jews to settlement in Eretz Israel was acknowledged in a sort of a pan-semitic pact; but this was, unfortunately, only a passing incident for which there was no continuation because of the division of the Middle East among the Great Powers on the one hand and the growth of Arab nationalism on the other.

The possibility of such conflict and the necessity to find ways to cope with it became, of course, more visible and acute with the settlement in Eretz Israel, with the first continuous daily encounters with Arabs, with the establishment of *Hashomer* (1909) – even if this was sometimes coupled with a rather romantic view of the Arab or the Bedouin which could be found among some of the early settlers, and some of the first Eretz-Israel generation of writers like Moshe Smilanski.

However, after the failure of the Weizmann–Feisal agreement, the consciousness of the direct political dimension of this conflict became dimmed. It was dimmed because of the relative bareness of the land, the sparseness of the population, and the readiness of Arab landowners to sell land to the Jewish Organization; also because of the relative lack of articulation of incipient political organization among the nationalist Arab movements, internal divisions within the Arab camp, and opposition from the Arabs to establish official contacts with the Jews.

It was dimmed by the peculiar setting of Mandatory Palestine which gave international recognition to the Jewish National Home under the mediating function of the mandatory government and, to a smaller degree, of some international bodies (like the League of Nations) between the Jews and the Arabs, thus minimizing the necessity of direct political confrontation. It was also dimmed by the type of economic division of labour that developed in Palestine, by the policy of the Yishuv to minimize the development of mixed Arab–Jewish economic sectors. While the insistence of *Avoda Ivrit* (Jewish Labour), as against the employment of Arab workers by Jews, was very strong in the Labour sector, as part of its vision of the reconstruction of the Jewish national economy, and was often a bone of contention with the civil sector and indirectly with the Arab workers, yet on the whole it made for a greater segregation between the two sectors.

So a rather utopian, 'economic', socialist vision of future relations with the Arabs arose, according to which, with the passing of the feudal character of the Arab society and the modernization of their economy, greater co-operation would naturally develop between the two nations.

The awareness of the necessity to come to such terms with the Arab movement was also dimmed, as we have seen, by the basic Arab intransigence to the Zionist implementation of the Zionist dream. This intransigence came to the surface in the strong Arab reaction to Jewish immigration and settlement in the riots of 1921 and 1929 up to the rebellion of 1936 under the leadership of the Mufti of Jerusalem in which the first Arab military formation – the famous *Knufiot* (bands) – emerged.

Truly enough there were several attempts – by Chaim Arlosoroff, Ben-Gurion and others – to meet Arab leaders but, as from the very beginning they encountered a basic opposition to Zionism, such contacts were on the whole given up by the official Zionist leadership, to be continued only by rather marginal even if influential groups.

Such groups – the most important among them the Brit Shalom Organization – composed mostly of outstanding intellectuals, men like Martin Buber, Ernest Simon and many others, stressed, not only against the seemingly militant Ben-Gurion, but even against the more pacifist Weizmann, the necessity to come to a political compromise with the Arabs. They did not, however, specify how such an agreement would be compatible with the Arab demands on limitation of Jewish immigration and of settlement.

The *Hashomer Hatzair* called for the establishment of a bi-national Jewish–Arab state in Israel – with emphasis on the continuation of Jewish immigration and settlement, and on political autonomy. Again there was no real response from any Arab counterpart.

Very characteristic of the dilemma of those who searched for a realistic accommodation with the Arabs was the case of Arthur Ruppin, the head of the Zionist Office, the major patron of the Labour settlements, who was among the founders of Brit Shalom in 1926 and left it in 1929. But in the end he came to the conclusion that

> I believe that there exist several very serious conflicts of interest between the Jews and the Arabs. At this moment I cannot see how these conflicts of interest can be solved so that the Jews will have the possibilities of unrestricted immigration and unrestricted economic and cultural development in Palestine, which are absolutely essential to Zionism, and will nonetheless not encroach upon the interests of the Arabs.
>
> I have remained exceedingly calm and cool during this time. I have adopted the theory that under the circumstances it is natural that the antagonism of the Arabs to Jewish immigration should find release in periodic outbreaks; that we are living in a sort of latent state of war with the Arabs which makes loss of life inevitable. This may be unacceptable, but it is a fact; and if we want to continue our work in Palestine in spite of the Arabs, we will have to expect such losses. . . .
>
> What is to be done to lessen or to remove the tension between the two nationalities, which can, after all, not go on forever? It is my opinion that no sort of negotiations with the Arabs can get us anywhere at the moment, because the Arabs are still hoping to deal with us above our heads. Not negotiations, but the development of Palestine towards a larger percentage of Jews in the population and a strengthening of our economic position can and will bring about an easing of the tension. When coming to an understanding with us will no longer mean that the Arabs will have to make concessions to us, but only be a question of coming to terms with reality, the weight of the facts will bring about an easing of the tension.*

In Ruppin's case this conclusion – a conclusion which came to be shared by most of the Zionist movements – was tempered by the strong hope of some peaceful settlement with the Arabs. It was more fully explicit in Jabotinsky's and the Revisionist stress that only after a show of force would the Arabs accept the Zionist coexistence. It was, however, also implicitly, but only implicitly, shared by people like Arlosoroff or Ben-Gurion – the latter

* Quoted by Moshe Dayan in 'Afterword' in A. Ruppin, *Memoirs, Letters, Diaries*, edited with an Introduction by Alex Bein (London 1971), pp. 318–20.

emphasizing against the pure military–political stance of the Revisionists the necessity to build up strength through settlement and the bases for power.

At the same time the expressions of Arab intransigence which were to continue – rioting, indiscriminate killing of civilians – made it easier to allege that the Arabs lacked political maturity and to define the conflict, not in political terms, but in terms of 'good' or 'bad', concentrating the political efforts to international arenas.

But at the same time this very confrontation enhanced the political consciousness of the Zionist movements themselves, a dimension which became legitimized in 1937 by the so-called Peel Report (a report of a Royal Commission set up by the British) which in fact recognized the irreconcilability of the Jewish and Arab claims, and the political maturity of the Yishuv, and made a recommendation for the creation in Palestine of two states – a Jewish and an Arab one.

This gave rise to very bitter dispute in the Zionist camp – a dispute between those (like the Revisionists and some parts of the Labour movement, led by members of the Kibbutzim and also by Berl Katznelson) who did not want to give up the right to the whole of Eretz Israel and those, under the leadership of Weizmann and Ben-Gurion and most of the leaders of the religious parties, who saw in it the only possible practical political solution. It was the latter view which ultimately prevailed in the Zionist Congress of 1938, accepting the proposition of the territorial division of Palestine – but giving rise to strong dissension from the Revisionists and the dissident groups, and more latent disapproval from its opponents in the framework of the Zionist Organization.

# The Zionist Vision and the Modes of its Institutionalization in the Yishuv
## Three leaders – Weizmann, Ben-Gurion, Jabotinski

The multiplicity of themes that developed in the Yishuv were also connected with different types of leadership – the more visionary, cosmopolitan one, the utopian institution-building one, and the more power-bargaining one. Needless to say, these various types of leadership often overlapped, but on the whole they were rather distinct, with a lot of tension between them. Nevertheless they tended to co-operate in many common frameworks and, despite the tensions, reinforced one another.

Here two major figures in the history of the Yishuv and the Zionist movement emerged – Chaim Weizmann and David Ben-Gurion. They co-operated for several decades in a tension- and conflict-ridden coalition, the ruling coalition of that period, and are very indicative of the different types of such leadership and of the interrelations between them.

Weizmann – the President of the Zionist Organization from 1920 to 1946 (with a brief period out of office in the early 1930s), later the first President of Israel, a scientist of high standing and a cosmopolitan figure, the man who was instrumental in the attainment of the Balfour Declaration – portrayed in his basic orientation a combination of the utopian liberal vision of Herzl, whose great successor he was, with deep roots in the life of the Jewish people in Eastern Europe and with a realistic appraisal of the international scene as well as of the reality of life in Eretz Israel, with a strong emphasis on the importance of practical settlement work in Eretz Israel. His activities were based, not only on political visionary efforts, but also on the one hand on daily routine diplomatic work and on the other on close co-operation with the practical work of settlement and institution-building in Eretz Israel.

David Ben-Gurion came to Eretz Israel with the second Aliya and emerged, together with Berl Katznelson and others, as the major leader of the Labour movement, and the main architect of the Histadrut and *Mapai*. He was also a visionary but a practical pioneering one, a practical leader who concentrated on organizing the Labour sector and its institutions according to the tenets of the basic Zionist–socialist vision, but with strong totalistic and power orientations. It was he who became, as is well known, the Yishuv's leader in its drive towards independence, in the military preparation for it, and in the establishment of the State of Israel.

His tense relations with Weizmann culminated in the rift in 1946 over the attitude to the British Government. Yet, when he became the first Prime Minister of Israel and wanted to mould its basic character, already based on the institutional achievements of the Yishuv in general and the Labour sector in particular, it was basically the Weizmann vision – stressing the universal mission of the Zionist entrepreneurs, with a strong emphasis on the development of science, a moral mission couched on biblical themes – that guided him; and it was he who proposed to make Weizmann the first President of Israel, even if depriving him of any real power.

These two leaders attained the highest positions in the Zionist movement and in the State of Israel in their own lifetime. In contrast was the more tragic figure of Zeev (Vladimir) Jabotinsky, the leader of the Revisionists and the Betar, who articulated, as we have seen, a rather different interpretation of the Zionist vision. This vision shared, of course, the emphasis on the cultural renovation, and also the secular view of Judaism – but stressed much more the purely political and military activity, with much lesser emphasis on institution-building.

## The paradox of relations with the Diaspora

Meanwhile there was some recognition of the paradoxical aspects of the relations of the Yishuv to the Jewish communities in the Diaspora, and to the Zionist movement as it developed within the Diaspora.

The Yishuv was continuously dependent on the Diaspora for its major resources – financial and manpower. Without these resources it could easily stagnate, as was the case of the first Aliya and as almost happened at the end of the fourth Aliya in the late 1920s. But however much the Yishuv relied on such resources – as well as on the political support of world Jewry in general and of the Zionist organization in particular – yet its relation to the Diaspora was always rather ambivalent – particularly because of the original Zionist negation of the Galut. The Yishuv continuously set itself up as an ideological challenge to the Diaspora.

The result was a paradox, not fully apparent in the period of the Yishuv but to become important later on, in the State of Israel. The ideological claim on the Jewish communities in the Diaspora was, of course, fully evident: in the demand for manpower, in the call for more pioneers, trained in the *Hakhshara*, to continue the rebellion against the Diaspora. But the situation was much more complex with respect to the political and economic resources. These were, of course, largely recruited from those Zionists who stayed in the Diaspora, and the very call on them implied at least implicitly a certain recognition of the legitimacy of the Diaspora's continued existence as Diaspora, and of the Yishuv's dependence on it.

This paradox could be partly overlooked during the period of the Yishuv. First, these resources were in principle mobilized in terms of the basic Zionist revolutionary vision, which made the recipients – at least but not only in their own eyes – morally and nationally superior to the donors, and the call for resources was combined with the call for the mobilization of more pioneering groups.

Second, this implicit legitimation of the Jewish communities in the Diaspora was not fully evident in this period because the resources recruited from them were not administered in a philanthropic way (as was the case with the Baron Rothschild's administration during the first Aliya) but through political organizations, namely the various organs of the Zionist Organization and the Jewish Agency, officially upholding the Zionist vision common to the Jewish communities in the Diaspora, within which the allocation of these resources constituted a focus of continuous struggle and within which the Yishuv acquired more and more power.

The fact that this ideology – and the Zionist movement – constituted as we have seen a controversial and not fully accepted element in the Diaspora only contributed to the crystallization of these premises at least in large parts of the Yishuv. However some groups, especially those close to the Revisionists, saw the establishment of the Jewish Agency, in which even official non-Zionists participated, as a betrayal of the pristine Zionist vision.

Thus in principle the terms of trade between the Yishuv in general and the pioneering sectors in particular and the Jewish communities in the Diaspora were formulated in terms of Zionist ideology: as between a vanguard bearer of the new vision and a broader periphery which did not fully live up to that vision but which should acknowledge its supremacy.

But the negative evaluation of the Galut, of Diaspora, became even stronger in the consciousness of the second generation which portrayed a new Hebrew man, devoid of the many faults of the Galut man. This new prototype had a very strong stress on heroism, with roots in the land, with priorities of working the land and self-defence, and was no longer troubled by the complexes of a member of an oppressed minority. It was around all these themes that the new collective identity of the Yishuv developed.

## New generations – the Tsabras

With the emergence of new generations, those born in Eretz Israel, the emphasis on such creativity, and on the realization of all these dreams, became reinforced. It was conspicuous in daily life, in the youth movements, in the settlements and in the expanding defence activities, although the Yishuv was still far from being a centre of power and influence.

The new generations were called after the cactus fruit *Tsabras* – prickly on the outside and sweet on the inside. They seemed to epitomize the image of the new, 'normal' free emancipated Jew rooted in the land, no longer torn by the insecurities of the Galut, seemingly continuing the pioneering traditions, through the extension of the settlements and the growing needs of security.

This image of the *Tsabra* started to pervade the daily existence in Eretz Israel and became epitomized in the attempts to imbue the traditional Zionist themes and orientations with new specially Eretz-Israeli ones. It was closely connected for instance in the revival of the traditional festivals in the Kibbutzim, all of which contributed to a great upsurge of cultural creativity, not only in its more literary aspects, but also in the daily life.

It was this combination of the new image with the continuation and diversification of pioneering activities that mitigated in the period of the Yishuv what was later to become a very crucial problem – one common to all revolutionary societies – namely that of the perpetuation of a revolution beyond its first generation. It also mitigated the potential rivalry between the older leaders and the *Tsabras* about access to the centres of power in the different sectors and organizations of the Yishuv and the Zionist Organization.

Of great significance here is the fact that relatively few of this generation of the *Tsabras* were active in the creation of new institutional frameworks, or entered into the centres of power. It was only the second *Tsabra* generation of leaders, such as Moshe Sharett or Dov Hoz, who started to make their impact, above all in the emerging security forces.

The crystallization of the image of the *Tsabra* brought out forcefully certain elements of the merging collective identity – namely a territorial-national, semi-primordial, attachment to the land and preoccupation with security or defence. It was not only that it was in the areas of settlement, of defence, and of exploring the land that they were most active. They also emphasized these themes in the literary and political fields.

But whatever their specific orientations and emphases, in this period at least they shared and emphasized the strong future orientations of the Zionist vision.

## The Second World War

The effervescence of the future-orientated charismatic dimension became perhaps most fully crystallized in the Yishuv after the end of the Second World War. The end of the war – with the new hopes and international political mould on the one hand, with the terrible experience of the Holocaust on the other hand, and the waves of the first survivors – raised and intensified all the Zionist visions and the search for a political solution in particular.

The Yishuv and the Zionist movement entered the war in a very gloomy mood. At the international political level the war caught them in a bitter struggle against the British who, under Arab pressure, had backed away from the recommendation of the Peel Commission in 1937. Between 1936 and 1939 the British government, under the impact of continuous Arab intransigence and the attempts to obviate a new war in Europe, set up a series of restrictions on Jewish immigration and purchase of land, culminating in the famous White Paper of 1939, and instead of Jewish statehood opted for the much more restricted federation – all these giving rise to increased Jewish resistance.

The beginnings of this resistance were, to some degree at least, dimmed by the Second World War, by the common front with England against Hitler – but the vision of statehood did not abate. It was only suspended and in 1942 Ben-Gurion, to some degree against the advice of Weizmann, made the famous Biltmore declaration in New York – itself a significant political gesture which emphasized the growing political importance of the United States and the American Jewry. This declaration proclaimed Jewish statehood as the major post-war goal of the Zionist movement.

At the same time the relative economic prosperity in Palestine, the beginning of co-operation with the British in the war efforts leading to the establishment of the Jewish Brigade in the framework of the British Army, the further continuous organization of the *Hagana*, the establishment of the special units of the *Palmach* within it, in a sense prepared the Yishuv and the Zionist movement to take up the political and, if necessary, military struggle more fully after the war.

The main outline of the story of these years is well known: the attempts of the British to limit the influx of immigrants, especially from the camps in Europe; the organization of the illegal *Haapala*; the growing internal military organizations and the growing military activities by the *Hagana* and Ezel against the British; the partial co-operation and the rifts between these organizations; the various attempts of the British to stifle Jewish resistance; the resignation of Weizmann in the 1946 Zionist Congress signalling a shift of power in favour of Ben-Gurion and the American leader Abba Hillel Silver articulating a much more militant stand to the British.

Then came the Anglo-American Commission of 1948 which recommended that 100,000 survivors of the camps be let into Palestine; the non-acceptance of its recommendation by the British and the 'transfer' by the British of the whole problem of Palestine to the United Nations' Commission which came up, against the wish of the Arabs and the British, with a recommendation for the partition of Palestine and for the establishment within it of a Jewish and an Arab state with an international zone around Jerusalem; the 29 November 1947 decision of the United Nations to accept these recommendations; the Arab resistance to this decision; the lukewarm and, on the whole, pro-Arab stand of the British towards the incipient Jewish state; their giving up of the Mandate on 14 May 1948 and the establishment of the State of Israel in a condition of war; the flight of large parts of the Arab population from the Jewish areas; the attack of the armies of five Arab states on Israel; and the repulsion of this attack with the loss of about 6,000 people – mainly by the units of the *Hagana* and *Palmach* (later reconstituted as the Israel Defence Army) – terminating in the armistices of 1949.

But this external story conveys only very partially the great effervescence in this period of the visions for the impending future, all of which are of crucial importance for the understanding of the social structure of the State of Israel.

# PART THREE

## The State of Israel – Crystallization of Institutional Moulds

# CHAPTER 7

# The State of Israel – Historical Setting

## The Historical Setting and Background
### *The experiences of the Jews*

The establishment of the State of Israel was not just a great historical and political event in the development of Jewish settlement in Eretz Israel – it was also a harbinger of far-reaching social transformation and developments.

Before, however, proceeding to analyse the nature of this social transformation and development, it is necessary to point out the profound, dramatic – sometimes tragic – changes in the history of the Jewish people which were historically connected with the establishment of the State. These were the Holocaust and the near total destruction of Eastern and Central European Jewry; the growing isolation of the Soviet Jewry, which became now the second largest Jewish community in the Diaspora; the emergence of American Jewry as the major single Jewish community in the Diaspora – but a community which crystallized in a distinct pattern of its own, a pattern which, as it became more and more apparent, could not be explained in terms of the historical experience of European Jewry; and the reawakening, because of the combined impact of decolonization, modernization and the establishment of the State of Israel itself, of the Oriental Jewry, that is of the Jews in the lands which before the First World War had belonged to the Ottoman Empire.

All these facts had forceful – but also rather paradoxical and contradictory – impacts on the attitudes of these Jewish communities to the Zionist movement in general and to the State of Israel in particular, and they gave rise to far-reaching changes in the nature of the Zionist movement. From the first years of the State, anti-Zionism and even more an anti-Israel attitude (the two were, in principle, still practically indistinguishable) disappeared almost entirely from Jewish public life, except for some groups, like the American Council for Judaism, which were no longer very influential or vocal. The Holocaust – the Jews' most terrible experience in their long history of suffering – seemingly vindicated the basic Zionist premises about the impossibility of even the sheer physical survival of Jewish life in the modern (at least European) Diaspora. The combined experiences of the Holocaust and the Soviet Jewry, which lived under circumstances of pressure to assimilate and of continuous strong anti-Semitism, also undermined the viability of the various 'autonomist'–federalist or territorial solutions of finding some communal national existence in the Diaspora – something which could still be seen as a possibility in pre-Second World War Poland or even in such places as the Birobijan experiment in Soviet Russia. The fact that it was above all in Palestine, and later on in the State of

Israel, that the survivors of the Holocaust – and later on the Jews from Arab countries – would be openly received, strengthened the viability of the Zionist premises and vision.

At the same time these changes in the fate of the different Jewish communities had powerful effects on the social structure of the Jewish community in Israel. First of all it greatly influenced, as we shall see in greater detail later on, the demographic composition of the Jewish population in Eretz Israel. Secondly, the Holocaust deprived the Jewish community in Eretz Israel of its major reservoir of leadership and continuous ideologically orientated manpower – those very elements which counteracted the potentially stagnating tendencies that developed naturally.

At the same time, the very acceptance within the Jewish communities of the Zionist premises, or at least of the State of Israel, the fact that the establishment of the State of Israel added new symbolic and institutional dimensions in the life of the Jewish people in the Diaspora, potentially – and in fact very quickly – weakened the revolutionary or radical component in the Zionist movement and almost totally abolished its place in Jewish life. However, for decades this fact was never fully admitted by the Zionist and Israeli leaders.

Indeed, the whole pattern of the relation between the Jewish community in Israel, the State of Israel and the Jewish people in the Diaspora changed in many ways which greatly affected – although initially almost imperceptibly – the whole internal development of Israel.

This trend was greatly reinforced by the fact, which will be analysed in greater detail later on, that in the United States there developed a new type of Jewish community, a community which established a new pattern of re-construction of Jewish tradition and life – very different from that of the historical experience of Jews in Europe till the Second World War. This new pattern was later on repeated – even if in a milder form – with many variations in those European countries, like England, in which Jewish communities survived the Second World War, or in those, like France, Belgium or Holland, in which new Jewish communities were established.

Also important were the far-reaching changes in the orthodox camp – especially its growth after the 1960s and its adaptation to the new modern settings.

## The international situation

The establishment and the first twenty years or so of the State of Israel took place in a relatively – perhaps very relatively and yet not insignificant – benign international atmosphere. The crucial international act was, of course, the United Nations' resolution of 29 November 1947, which decided on partition and the establishment within it of two states – a Jewish and an Arab one. It was only the Jewish state that was established – its boundaries fixed by the armistice agreements of 1949–50, beyond those of the 1947 decision, and including the

Western part of Jerusalem. Given the opposition of the Arab states to the partition, no Arab state was established in any part of Mandatory Palestine; but the Arab areas, the so-called West Bank of Jordan and Eastern Jerusalem, were annexed by Transjordan which became, in 1950, the Kingdom of Jordan, while Gaza was annexed by Egypt.

In May 1949, about a year after the cease-fire agreements with the neighbouring Arab countries and after recognition by many states – the first being the United States and USSR, Latin America, European and also the Dominion states – Israel was also admitted to the United Nations, thus becoming a full member of the international community.

Throughout the Western world – in the USA, Latin America and Europe – the aftermath of the Second World War, the defeat of the Nazis and the horrors of the Holocaust gave rise to relatively positive attitudes to the Jewish people in general and to the State of Israel in particular. Anti-Semitism, although certainly existing, was not on the whole publicly well accepted, and at least in Europe, but also in the USA, there were many feelings and gestures of atonement towards the Jewish people and the State of Israel – most fully manifest in the German reparations.

This was not to say either that anti-Semitism disappeared or that the international situation of Israel, its security and its relations were a bed of roses. But compared with any other period – either the period between the two wars or, as we shall see, after 1967 – the first two decades of the State were relatively benign. In the words of Fritz Stern:

Israel was born into the postwar era; its birth occurred in the same year as the postwar constellation emerged in Western Europe. It was born of Zionist hopes and European genocide; the former sprang from the belief nurtured in part by the Dreyfus affair, that European nationalism would present a recurrent threat to European Jewry and that only a Jewish national homeland (with its own nationalism?) would offer an acceptable alternative to continued insecurity. The near-extinction of European Jewry made the claims morally irresistible, and in the aftermath of World War II and as a consequence of the collapse of British imperial rule, the United Nations assigned a part of Palestine to Israel and left the state to fend for itself. . . . A pro-Israel policy for most European countries sprang from a felicitous coincidence of political and moral considerations. An offspring of Europe in Asia, Israel evolved what to many at the time seemed a promising new experiment: a democratic-communitarian society. The West Germans acknowledged their guilt – and hence their special relationship to Israel – in a tangible manner: with German billions, Israel could build a modern economy and equip a modern army, with weapons purchased from France, Britain, and the United States . . .*

This benign international atmosphere was reinforced by the good relations of Israel with the emerging Third World – with most of the newly independent countries of Africa and Asia, as well as Latin America – in which Israel developed extensive programmes of economic aid – above all in the agricultural field – riding high on the crest of hopes for development and modernization that pervaded the 1950s and early 1960s.

* Fritz Stern, 'The End of the Post-War Era', *Commentary* (April 1974).

## The launching of a new State

It was within the broad framework of these historical processes that Israel was established and launched on the first stages of its existence.

The launching itself was not easy: the UN declaration was rejected by the Arabs and not wholeheartedly accepted by the British receding from their mandatory custody of Palestine; the bloody and heroic War of Independence ensued, lasting from the day of the UN decision for almost two years, up to the first and second cease-fires in 1949; a war in which the Jewish population of about 500,000–600,000 people had to battle on several fronts with the much more numerous armies of Arab countries, with the less regular Palestinian military forces – while having to cope with the at best passive attitude of the withdrawing British. The outcome of the war, and the fate of the newly emerging State, hung in the balance for about a year, but it ended ultimately in an Israeli victory, and the establishment in 1949 of frontiers beyond those of the UN decision. These frontiers were settled in the armistice agreements and accepted by the international community which established diplomatic relations with Israel – although this recognition did not extend to the recognition of the Western part of the divided Jerusalem as the capital of Israel, an act enunciated by Ben-Gurion in 1949.

But all these victories were won at a very heavy cost. About 6,000 – out of a total population of 600,000 – were killed, most of them young, many from among the potential leadership and elite groups which composed large parts of the youth movements and the units of the *Hagana*, *Palmach* and Ezel, but also from among the new immigrants – some of whom had only arrived in the midst of the war and were immediately sent to the front.

The heroism of the struggle, and the fact that Israel continued not to be accepted by its Arab neighbours with the ensuing situation that the problem of security became central to its existence, were to have far-reaching consequences on the whole institutional format of the new State and its self-consciousness. But despite all these costs the young State started to take its first steps and to undertake those tasks for which most of its population believed it to have been created – the building of the State, of the new homeland which would be open to all the Jewish people and within which the great Zionist visions and dreams would be realized.

It actually opened up its gates, first of all, to the survivors, and then also to many of the Jews from Arab or Muslim countries, those who came to be called 'Orientals', whose status in their countries of origin became increasingly undermined by the various internal processes analysed above: by the growth of Arab nationalism and by the growing anti-Jewish feelings arising by virtue of the very intensification of the Arab–Jewish conflict in Palestine. Many emissaries were sent out of Eretz Israel from after the Second World War to organize the immigrants.

The possibility of the pre-State Yishuv enclosing itself in the new State without the opening of its gates was barely envisaged at all – and under the vigorous leadership of Ben-Gurion the ideal of the ingathering of the exiles was pursued as an initial policy, together with the creation of the army, of the new State.

Many of these immigrants were settled in the areas vacated by the Arabs who fled during the war. Indeed the Arabs who remained in Israel were not only a small part of the original Arab population that had lived in what became the frontiers of the State of Israel; they were also a relatively weak part of this population.

The more active – whether economically or politically – left, some on their own initiative or rather the initiative of their leaders who were sure they would come back after the defeat of the Jewish forces, others under the very impact of the war (in some cases probably also prodded by the initiative of the advancing Israeli forces).

The Arabs who remained in Israel numbered about 156,000 – most of them Muslims (about 107,000), a large number of Christians (34,000), and in addition there were also about 15,000 Druzes and other minorities.

Of the Arabs who left the boundaries of the State of Israel, about 400,000 settled in Transjordan, which annexed in 1949 the Arab territories of the former mandate, and which was declared in 1950 as the Kingdom of Jordan. Many of them went to the Eastern Bank of the Jordan, to old Transjordan, where they became more or less fully integrated although not allowed, along with those who stayed in the West Bank, any specific Palestinian political expression. Others became refugees and moved to Lebanon (about 160,000–180,000), Syria (about 200,000), and Gaza which came under Egyptian domination.

At the time – partly so as to keep them as a factor in the political struggle with Israel, partly because of their unwillingness to accept strangers – most Arab countries were not willing to accept them as full citizens. So they settled in the infamous refugee camps in which new generations were born, maintained in the camps by their 'hosts' and by international agencies – especially by UNRWA. They were to become the first kernels of the future different Palestinian organizations, terrorist groups and national movements.

The State of Israel was established, as we have seen, on the basis of a territorial compromise, the seeds of which were planted in 1936 with the Peel Commission decision on the partition of Palestine and the acceptance of the partition by the Zionist Congress in 1938; a compromise which entailed also the acceptance of the territorial limits of partition of Eretz Israel. This compromise was based on the assumption – not always easily accepted – that this was the most that could be attained, given Israel's strength and the basic attitudes in the international community. For many – including the most prominent among them, Ben-Gurion – this compromise was also essential to keep the fundamentally Jewish nature of the State of Israel as against the possibility of the development of some binational arrangement, and until the Six Day War these premises were *de facto* accepted by all participants in the Israeli political scene, even if officially the *Herut* party did not share them.

# Comparative Indications
*Israel as a small, modern, revolutionary,*
*developing society*

The process of building up the new State was a very dynamic and dramatic one, shaped by a series of problems and by the response of the leading sectors of the State to them.

Some of these basic problems Israel shared with other revolutionary or semi-revolutionary societies – with the USSR, Mexico, many of the new nations and perhaps even early nineteenth-century USA. Israel shared with these societies the problems attendant on the transformation of revolutionary groups from socio-political movements into rulers of states and the concomitant institutionalization of the revolutionary vision within the framework of a modern state. Secondly it shared with them the problem of attaining economic expansion and modernization while coping with the growing social differentiation which results from these processes. Thirdly it shared the problem of absorbing within the framework of such economic expansion relatively underdeveloped sectors of the population.

But the concrete contours of these processes, the problems they engendered, as well as the mode of response to them, differed greatly in different post-revolutionary societies according to their specific historical experience. The Israeli scene necessarily evinced some characteristics of its own which were influenced by the specific historical circumstances of the development of its society on the one hand and by its initial ideological orientations and institutional contours on the other.

Thus, in order to understand more fully the development of the particular characteristics of the State of Israel as a revolutionary society, as they began to develop in the Yishuv and crystallized through the building of the State, it might be worthwhile at this stage of our discussion to compare them with some other modern, colonizatory, immigrant-absorbing, revolutionary and developing societies, as well as with other modern industrial societies.

The Yishuv and later Israeli society shared important characteristics with some non-imperial, colonizing societies, both revolutionary, such as the United States, and non-revolutionary like the white British Dominions societies. They had in common, first, a strong emphasis on equality, at least among the initial settler groups, and the consequent lack of any strong hereditary, feudal, aristocratic landowner class; second, the development of a strong concentration of various types of economic and administrative activities within broad, unified, organizational frameworks, in common with other sectarian colonizing societies; and last, again in common with other colonizing societies, Zionist settlement emphasized the conquest of wasteland through work – as shown in the expansion of productive primary occupations and of the colonizing frameworks and frontiers.

Similar combinations of co-operative endeavours and economic, colonizing enterprises could be found also, for instance, in the settlement of wasteland by the Mormons. The combination of trade unions with the industrial and financial activities of the entrepreneur could also be found in other politically-orientated labour movements, especially in Scandinavia and, to a lesser extent, in England.

However, the fusion of these features as developed within the Histadrut seems to be unique and is explained by the Histadrut's political character and outlook. This also explains its political power, although it has never been economically the largest sector of the country.

These characteristics became closely interwoven with other components of Israeli society, such as the sectarian or social movements, strong totalistic outlooks of the pioneering groups and factions, with their strong internal ideological cohesion and with the institutionalism of this ideology in face of growing social differentiation.

However, unlike many such groups (like the various utopian settlements in the USA), the pioneering groups aimed from the beginning to be the trail-blazers of a modern society, and committed themselves to many institutional frameworks and organizations which might serve as the forerunners of such a development and through which broader groups of Jewish society could participate in the economic, ideological, and political life of the Yishuv.

The Zionist movement – or rather that part of it which became predominant from the 1920s on – differed from most modern social and nationalist movements, however, in that it did not plan for the immediate seizure of power and for the establishment of a new, unitary, political framework – even if this was certainly not beyond its vision. The primary emphasis of the pioneers was on broad rural and urban colonization which, in itself, weakened the political implications of such totalistic orientations. It was only at the end of the period of the British mandate, with the intensification of the external political struggle, that some conception of a self-governing polity developed.

Out of the sectarian and social movements of the Yishuv there developed another crucial trend – the strong elitist ideological bent, aiming at the achievement of a new society through the implementation of an ideological programme most fully epitomized in the image of the pioneer, and in the first communal settlements – above all the Kibbutzim, but also the Moshavim. In this, Israel was akin to some other revolutionary societies, such as the USSR, Yugoslavia or Mexico, which attempted to mould relatively traditional societies into specific modern patterns. However, the ideologies which were developed within the Zionist movement contained more variegated and heterogeneous elements than those of either closed religious sects or revolutionary political movements. This ideological diversity was greatly reinforced, as we have seen, by the coexistence of many different groups within the federate structure of the Yishuv, creating new institutional nuclei orientated towards broader, more universalistic, cultural and social values. Moreover, the Yishuv – unlike later the State of Israel – was not faced with the problem of moulding 'traditional' elements to such ideological visions, as a central problem.

Israeli society also shared many features and problems with other countries which had large-scale immigration. It had to deal with continuous waves of immigrants and with their integration into its emerging institutional framework. But it also developed specific characteristics of its own, rooted in the basic pioneering motivations and orientations among the immigrants and in their strong emphasis on national and social goals.

The Yishuv society – especially later on – also contained many elements and problems similar to those of other developing countries, especially those developing a modern economic framework either in underdeveloped settings and/or with traditional populations. This similarity could be found in the establishment of a new political framework by the elite under a colonial ruler and the consequent transformation of this elite into a ruling class. However, several important differences stand out.

Unlike many contemporary developing societies, the initial institutional framework in Israel was established by modern elites and along modern lines. These elites had a large pool of educated persons committed, by ideology, outlook or creed, to the creation of a modern society. The traditional elements were taken into these frameworks only much later, and the process of their modernization was quicker and more intense than in any other newly independent developing countries. Furthermore, and again unlike most new states, the attainment of independence did not create a sharp break with the past, since the Yishuv and the Zionist movement had already developed manifold political, administrative and economic organizations. The emphasis on the 'Political Kingdom' was therefore much smaller.

In many ways, despite the obvious difference in size, the Eretz-Israel pioneering–ideological experience was closest to the early US experience – with the crucial differences first that, in the latter, individualistic orientations were much more predominant than the collectivistic ones prevalent in Eretz Israel; and, secondly, that the US developed its collective identity in terms of a religious–political ideology and did not emphasize, as was the case in the Yishuv and later in the State of Israel, primordial–historical components of such identity.

Another crucial difference of the Yishuv and later of the State of Israel from all these societies was the very great, probably crucial, importance of the security – later military – dimension in its formation and development.

Last, the Yishuv and, later on, Israeli society can be compared, as we have seen, with other small modern industrialized or semi-industrialized societies, but here also with at least three special differences. One was the above-mentioned importance of the security dimension; the second was the aspiration to become, despite its size, a centre of social and cultural creativity of universal significance; and third was the special importance of the Jewish communities in the Diaspora as one of its major 'external markets'.

All these characteristics of the social structure of the Yishuv and later on of the State of Israel converge around the specific mode in which it developed as a revolutionary society, attempting to institutionalize its vision by confronting the general problems facing modern revolutionary societies – those of modernization, economic development and the establishment of orderly and institutionalized political life as well as the problems specific to it by virtue of its unique revolutionary vision and its historical and political–ecological circumstances.

In Israel the most important of these processes were first, the process of demographic expansion and change in the demographic composition, cultural background and ideological orientations of large parts of the population; second, the concomitant transformation of ideologically orientated pragmatic pioneers, organized in sets of voluntary sectors into a fully-fledged constitutional democratic state; third, economic expansion and modernization; fourth, the intensification of the military–security problem as probably one of the most important problems facing Israeli society and the growing perception, within the major echelons of the society, of this issue as an important and perennial one; fifth were the concomitant changes in some of the characteristics of Israeli society as a small society in general, and of its relations with the Jewish Diaspora in particular.

# Initial Problems
## Demographic expansion

The problems which were immediately apparent in Israel were those of great demographic and economic expansion, giving rise to the concomitant establishment of the basic institution of the new State in general and of those institutions which had to deal with the absorption of the new groups of population in particular. This institution-building began in the late 1940s and early 1950s and crystallized in a definite mould from the late 1950s to the mid-1960s.

The great demographic expansion was not only a quantitative one; it was connected with a great change in the demographic and socio-cultural composition of the immigrants. The basic demographic changes that accompanied the establishment of the State – and especially the changes in the so-called 'ethnic' composition of the population – are well known.

Thus in 1948 the population of the State of Israel was composed of 872,700 residents, in 1958 of 2,031,700 residents, in 1968 of 2,841,100 residents, showing a growth of 456 per cent since 1948. The ratio between Jewish and non-Jewish population was 86.4 per cent Jews to 13.6 per cent non-Jews in 1948; 89.1 per cent Jews to 10.9 per cent non-Jews in 1958; 85.7 per cent Jews to 14.3 per cent non-Jews in 1968; 84.2 per cent Jews to 15.8 per cent non-Jews in 1977, and 83.5 per cent Jews to 16.5 per cent non-Jews in 1981.

The total number of immigrants that came to Israel between 1948 and 1977 was 1,611,058. The number of immigrants to Israel in 1948 was 101,819; in 1958 was 27,082; in 1968 was 20,544; in 1977 was 21,429; in 1979 was 37,222; in 1980 was 20,428; in 1981 was 12,599, bringing the total number of immigrants from 1948 to 1981 to 1,707,700.

The ratio between Jews and non-Jews did not change much between 1948 and 1977, except for a slight increase of the percentage of the non-Jews after 1967 with the unification of Jerusalem. Within the Jewish society there was a change in the composition of the population according to continent of birth.

In 1948 the population of the State of Israel was composed of 86.4 per cent Jews and 13.6 per cent non-Jews. Among the Jewish population, 35.4 per cent were born in Israel, 8.1 per cent in Asia, 1.7 per cent in Africa, and 54.8 per cent in Europe and America.

In 1961 the population of Israel was composed of 88.7 per cent Jews and 11.3 per cent non-Jews. Among the Jewish population, 37.8 per cent were born in Israel (the father's continent of birth was Israel in 5.5 per cent, Asia–Africa in 14.9 per cent, and Europe–America in 17.4 per cent), 15.5 per cent were born in Asia, 11.9 per cent in Africa and 34.8 per cent in Europe and America.

In 1977 Israeli population was composed of 84.2 per cent Jews and 15.8 per cent non-Jews. Among the Jewish population 53.2 per cent were born in Israel (the father's continent of birth was Israel in 11.8 per cent, Asia in 13.3 per cent, Africa in 11.7 per cent and Europe and America in 11.65 per cent), 9.8 per cent were born in Asia, 11.1 per cent were born in Africa and 25.8 per cent were born in America.

In 1981 the Israeli population was composed of 83.5 per cent Jews and 16.5 per cent non-Jews. Among the Jewish population 57 per cent were born in Israel (the father's continent of birth was Israel in 14.8 per cent, Asia in 13.25 per cent, Africa in 12.3 per cent, and Europe and America in 16.5 per cent), 9.02 per cent were born in Asia, 10.04 per cent were born in Africa, and 23.8 per cent were born in America.

The percentage of Israeli-born residents grew significantly from 35.4 per cent in 1948 to 53.4 per cent in 1977 to 57 per cent in 1981. Among the Israeli-born residents the ratio of those whose fathers were born in Israel grew from 5.5 per cent in 1961 to 11.8 per cent in 1977 to 14.8 per cent in 1981. There was a big jump in the percentage of residents born in Africa between 1948 (1.7 per cent) and 1962 (11.9 per cent) and a decrease to 10.04 per cent in 1981, a percentage which has remained almost constant since then. The percentage of European- and American-born residents decreased from 54.8 per cent in 1948 to 25.8 per cent in 1977 to 23.8 per cent in 1981. There were slight changes in the percentage of the Asian-born residents between 8.1 per cent in 1948 up to 15.5 per cent in 1961, and down to 9.8 per cent in 1977, and up to 10.04 per cent in 1981.

This change in the demographic structure in terms of 'ethnic' origin has been often depicted as the most important single massive change which explains many of the crucial social processes in Israel. And yet this is only one – albeit a very important – part of the picture. Of no smaller importance for the understanding of the process of change in Israeli society has been, as we shall see in greater detail later on, the change in the ideological motivation of the immigrants coming to Israel. This change was common to most immigrants, Oriental and Western ones alike, who came after the establishment of the State, and was characterized by a shift from the relative predominance of the pioneering, future-orientated revolutionary types to a more adaptive attitude and motivation – whether one based on a relatively traditional semi-Messianic vision, common to many modern immigrations, or to the attainment of maximum personal and national security.

## The state of hostility

The second most visible aspect of the post-independence period was the continuous state of hostility with Israel's neighbours – the six wars: the War of Independence (1947–9), the Sinai Campaign (1956), the Six Day War (1967), the War of Attrition (1970–1), the Yom Kippur War (1973) and later on the Lebanon War of 1982–3, and predominance of security problems and considerations in the political and social life of Israel.

This predominance was evident in many aspects of Israeli life, some of the most important being: the heavy burden of the defence budget on the total national expenditure; the important place of the security establishment (like the Air Industries) in the economic development of the country; universal military service and reserve up till the age of about 55; the crystallization of a 'security–military' dimension as a crucial aspect of Israeli life; the relatively high prestige – at least up to the Yom Kippur War – of the military (especially the upper echelons) in society; the concentration of almost all Prime Ministers in their activities on the problems of security and external relations. This predominance was also evident in the central place of the security problems of living in a sort of continuous state of siege, in the public consciousness and self-awareness of Israeli society. This could be seen, not only in manifold literary expressions, but also in the fact that three of the most important of the wars – that of Independence (1947–9), the Six Day War (1967), and the Yom Kippur War (1973) – played a very central role as watersheds in the internal development of Israeli society: in its own self-image, in the crystallization of its problems and in the awareness within Israeli society of such problems. They constituted for a long period, especially but not only after the Six Day War, the most central single issue of public debate in Israel.

It was also with the establishment of the State that a major transformation in the status of the Jewish population took place; for the first time since the period of the Second Temple Jews became a majority in their own State; but also for the first time since that period they faced the problem of having other national religious majorities living within the framework of the Jewish State.

# Initial Responses
## The institutional framework of the State

These major problems facing the new State were immediately taken up by the leadership; indeed the very first steps of the State were closely interwoven with coping with the problems.

First of all, the very basic institutional structure of the State crystallized relatively quickly. The State of Israel was established as a unilateral parliamentary democracy, with a government responsible to the parliament, elected by a system of proportional representation. A fully independent legal system of courts – mostly taken over from the mandatory government but largely reorganized – with the Supreme Court serving also as High Court of Justice, often served as an important brake on the executive and the emerging bureaucracy. The office of the State Comptroller was established, and some years later also the Bank of Israel with a relatively independent Governor.

The parties which participated in the political framework were mostly, with some continuous reshuffling, the major Zionist ones from the pre-State period – the only new addition being the Agudat Israel which has continuously participated in the elections to the Knesset in the first government and in some later ones. Its participation – like that of the Zionist religious parties (the *Mizrahi* and *Hapoel Hamizrahi*, later the National Religious Party) – was contingent on agreements which ratified the various arrangements in the religious field. These affected especially the monopoly of Rabbinical courts over marriage and divorce and numerous arrangements about public observance of the Sabbath, supervision of Kashrut and the like, as well as the non-promulgation of any constitution, as according to the religious groups such constitution was given in the Torah or Halakha, and no other constitution could be valid in a Jewish state.

This basic institutional framework evinced a greaty continuity, visible above all in the political field. Up till this very day it is still a constitutional democratic structure as established in the beginning of the State; and up till 1977 there had been continuity of the basic political patterns which had started in the Yishuv in the 1930s, namely a pattern of coalition government – in which Labour was the predominant member, with the National Religious Party (formerly *Hamizrahi* and *Hapoel Hamizrahi*, separately) constituting an almost continuous secondary, but essential, partner.

The State was proclaimed as a demoncratic state with equal rights to all its citizens – Jews, Arabs, Druzes and other groups. The Arab language was declared as an official language of the State and from the very beginning the Arabs participated in elections to the Knesset. At the same time the special Jewish nature of the State was evident: its name, flag and anthem were taken from the Zionist movement; Hebrew became its major official language (and Arabic a second one); and it was conceived and declared as a state open in principle to all Jews – as promulgated in the Law of Return of 1950 in which it was stated that any Jew, barring ones with criminal records, could come and settle in Israel.

## *Absorbing the immigrants and economic expansion*

It was the first governments – together with the Jewish Agency and the World Zionist Organization, but the latter already in a secondary role *vis-à-vis* the government as well as the Histadrut – that undertook the tasks of the absorption of the incoming new immigrants, of national security, of economic development and of provision for the development in the educational and cultural spheres. It was also these governments that developed new institutional frameworks as well as transforming old ones.

These institutions took up first of all the challenge of demographic expansion and coped with it relatively quickly with an impressive, even if only partial, success.

The first years of the State were indeed very difficult. The combination of initially very meagre economic resources together with the influx of new immigrants created some of the most traumatic experiences and times – the period of economic austerity which lasted till about 1952–3 and the very difficult conditions of absorbing the first great waves of immigrants. Special institutions were created for such absorption. There were first of all the famous, or infamous, *Maabarot* (Transition camps) for the immigrants, with very minimal housing conditions (although not necessarily worse, as was to be claimed later, than those of the pioneer settlers in Kibbutzim and Moshavim in their initial periods of settlement); the creation of 'artificial' public works as the main source of employment; the establishment, for many of the new immigrants, of the development towns which, together with the *Maabarot*, were to remain – or were later to become for many groups of immigrants the symbol of hard times, of the distance from the older society, and of discrimination.

The most important among these developments were Kiryat Shmone and Beth Shean in the Galilee, Kiryat Gat or Yeruham in the South, as well as new urban centres created since 1948 – which by 1961 housed about 218,000 people and in 1972 about 541,000, of which about 350,000 were in development towns proper. The major push behind the establishment of the development towns was a combination of the old Zionist pioneering vision of settlement reinforced by the new vision of the necessity to populate all the parts of the State. But the implementation of this vision was already developed in a rather new and convoluted form, as it was based above all on government policy and direction and not on voluntary pioneering; it was probably not viewed by most of the immigrants in a positive way, or at most was seen as an unavoidable necessity or destiny, and it gave rise to the creation (through the very policies of the government and the Jewish Agency) of a new ecological and – as we shall see – social and economic periphery.

The third specific means of immigrant absorption was the new Moshavim – one of the relatively great success stories of the whole process. From 1948 to 1956 about 230 new Moshavim, mostly of new immigrants, were established – successfully continuing till now and comprising till 1961 about 90,000 people.

The Kibbutzim did not, on the whole, participate in such a massive way in this process. They did absorb some of the European immigrants in the late 1940s and 1950s. But, given their ideological closure, they were unable either to absorb a large number of the new immigrants, especially the Oriental ones, or to encourage the creation of new types of settlements by them – a fact of great importance for the transformation of Israeli society.

From the mid-1950s at the latest, with the beginning of the inflow of the German reparations and with the more general restructuring of the economy, there started a period of more intense economic expansion which, with some halts in the middle-1960s, was a relatively continuous one, and which created in a relatively short period of time a modern semi-industrialized economy.

It was through this process of economic expansion, which created the basic economic frameworks, that the increased population, with its own subsequent natural growth, was absorbed. Side by side with these developments, there took place a further extension and diversification of many of the existing institutional frameworks, as well as a growing unification and direct, or indirect, control by the State or by the Histadrut.

Thus, in general, in conjunction with the establishment of the State, there took place the expansion concomitant with that of the economic frameworks: all the public services; the educational system up to the field of higher education; the various social and health services; the regulation of labour relations and the like; the various sectors of the Histadrut and of the public sphere in general. Details of this will be given in subsequent chapters.

## Security

The response to the security problem was the establishment of the most enduring of the new institutions: the new army. The Israel Defence Army, forged in the War of Independence out of the units of the *Hagana* and *Palmach*, was officially proclaimed by 1948 after the famous *Altadena* incident of the first days of independence. A ship carrying arms and volunteers of Ezel, from abroad, was bombarded upon orders by Ben-Gurion, and unintentionally sunk. It was an incident which was to loom large in the history of the State. Following the self-disbandment of the underground military formations of Ezel and Lehi and their transformation into political parties, and after the government's disbandment of the distinct *Palmach* command, the Israel Defence Forces became the only legitimate military force under the supervision of the government.

Very soon after the armistice, the regular peace army was formed under the leadership of the second Chief of Staff, Yigael Yadin. It was based on a general conscription for two to three years and reserve duty till about 50 or 55. The only *de facto* exemption was that of the students of the religious academies, the Yeshivot – an *ad hoc* arrangement agreed upon by Ben-Gurion, in the first years of the State, under the pressure of the several outstanding rabbis who claimed that, given the fact of the destruction of all the Yeshivot in the

Holocaust, special conditions should be arranged to enable them to function in Israel. While in the beginning it applied to a very small number – probably only a few hundred – the number continuously increased, rising in the late 1970s to an estimated 10,000-14,000 men, as well as about 7,000 women, with the whole issue constituting a latent source of contention in the relations between the religious and the secular camps.

The army and the huge defence establishment – the Ministry of Defence, the military industries in general, and the aeronautics industry in particular – also became a major institutional complex in Israel, a major economic sector and a major symbol of the new State, also generating new elites; through them the security problem was contained.

But Israel was not able to achieve peace with its neighbouring countries: they did not accept its legitimacy and there was only a state of cease-fire, not an end of war. Moreover, there was infiltration of Arab terrorist groups – especially those of the *Fedayin* in 1955-6 before the Sinai Campaign – giving rise to great tensions. Meanwhile the repeated bombardment of the settlements in Galilee and in the Jordan valley by the Syrians, and to a smaller degree by the Jordanians, became part of daily life, seemingly a continuation of the pre-State situation.

On the whole, however, the government and the army, under the leadership of Ben-Gurion, were able to control – if not to eliminate – these problems. They managed to secure the borders and to obtain enough international support – especially after the Sinai Campaign and the ultimate withdrawal of Israel from Sinai – if not to eliminate the Arab threat, at least to contain it (even if no such support could be obtained for the more far-reaching objects of the Sinai Campaign).

# The Zionist Vision and the Crystallization of the Institutional Moulds of Israeli Society
## *Institutional structure*

The initial success of the State of Israel seemed to go much further than coping with these problems. Its major test, and its own legitimation was seen, above all but not only by its leaders, in its ability to implement the basic Zionist vision and translate it into a firm, continuous, institutional mould which would be able to cope successfully with all the manifold problems, old and new alike. And indeed, after the first difficult years, it seemed that the State of Israel was able to pass this test, despite many pitfalls, slowdowns and crises, with flying colours.

The very basic institutional structure of the State was crystallized relatively quickly – and, as we have seen above, according to basic tenets of the Zionist vision. The declaration of independence clearly enunciated some of the basic premises of this vision in its democratic, liberal, semi-utopian vein. It stressed the inalienable right of the Jewish people to be a free nation in the Land of

Israel; the roots of this right in the long historical traditions of the Jewish people; the recognition of this right by the United Nations; the consequent opening of the gates of the State to all Jews – at the same time emphasizing the full equality of all its citizens, and its dedication to the ethical elements of the prophetic vision. To quote this document:

The land of Israel was the birthplace of the Jewish people. Here their spiritual, religious, and political identity was formed. Here they first achieved statehood, created a culture of national and universal significance, and gave to the world the eternal Book of Books.

Exiled forcibly from its land, the people remained faithful to it in all the countries of the dispersion, never ceasing to pray and hope for return and restoration in it of their political freedom.

Impelled by this historic and traditional attachment, Jews strove throughout every generation to re-establish themselves in their ancient homeland. In recent decades they returned in their masses . . . They reclaimed the wilderness, revived the Hebrew language, built villages and cities, and established a vigorous and ever-growing community, with its own economic and cultural life, loving peace but knowing how to defend itself, bringing the blessings of progress to all the country's inhabitants, and aspiring toward independent statehood . . .

Accordingly, we, members of the People's Council, representatives of the Jewish people in the Land of Israel and of the Zionist movement are here assembled on the day of the termination of the British Mandate over Palestine and, by virtue of our natural and historic right and on the strength of the resolution of the General Assembly of the United Nations, proclaim the establishment of a Jewish state in the Land of Israel, to be known as the State of Israel.

The institutional framework of the State which was established and developed seemed to be very close to these premises, and it evinced a marked continuity with both the mandatory framework and that of the Zionist Organization. This basic structure has been maintained till today, despite the continuing situation of insecurity from external threats and the changing demographic composition of the population, and it has a marked continuity and stability.

At the same time the basic institutional mould of Israeli society started to develop. The formation of the State and the political economy; the educational and cultural developments; the pattern of absorption and integration of immigrants – all this was perceived, at least by large parts of the older sectors of the population in general, and by the elites in particular, as the implementation of the original Zionist vision – the first step of which had been taken in the Yishuv. The institutional moulds that crystallized in the State, with all the heterogeneity, tensions and contradictions which we shall analyse in greater detail later on, were seen as a continuation, further elaboration and diversification of that dynamic mould that developed in the Yishuv, but already with very significant additions which, on the whole, were seen as both diversifying and strengthening it.

These moulds were justified in terms of the Zionist claims to ensure the safety and independence of the Jewish people as well as to promote socio-cultural creativity in general and institution-building in particular. They were often seen and portrayed as epitomizing the specific Zionist visions in general – the socialist–Labour ones in particular – implemented in a democratic arena, and as being of universal significance.

The older theme of 'constructivism' became more closely interwoven within such themes as economic expansion and development, the modernization of traditional communities, and the ability to forge a new nation out of diverse and heterogeneous elements.

Many of the experiences which developed in Israel were seen as being potentially applicable beyond it. Thus, for instance, the whole complex of the agricultural settlements – especially as implemented in the new Moshavim – was seen as a possible model for developing countries, and so were the general Israeli attempts to forge one nation out of a multiplicity of groups within the framework of a common democratic polity.

All these achievements – the great economic expansion, development and modernization, the great expansion of higher education and its attainment of relatively high intellectual standards – were a crucial illustration of cultural and social creativity with both specific Israeli and universal significance.

## The new collective identity

The emphasis on creative institution-building continued to be a basic component of Israeli collective identity through the attempts to redefine the image of the *Halutz*, the pioneer, and to extend it to new fields – whether those connected with the service of the State, the army, or the absorption of immigrants – thus continuously stressing the importance of commitment to the service of the collectivity.

New themes – such as those of security, military strength, and the search for understanding of Jewish tradition – were added to the crystallizing collective identity; some older ones – such as those of the primordial attachment to Eretz Israel – were more fully articulated; but all were seen as being encompassed by the basic mould of the secular Zionist vision, as being its extension and diversification.

One such theme was, of course, that of security, defence and heroism, which became most fully embodied in the army. Because of the crucial importance of the security dimension in Israeli life, and above all of the composition of the army, i.e. its being an army of universal conscription and of reservists, this element became a very general and widespread one, one of the great innovations in Jewish collective identity.

The element of heroism was also reinforced in a complicated way through the terrible experience of the Holocaust. On the one hand, the experience of the Holocaust and the killing of the defenceless Jews in the Diaspora seemingly vindicated the basic Zionist terms, and initially appeared to give rise among the younger generations in Israel to even stronger anti-Galut feelings.

At the same time the elements of heroism in the Holocaust, as evident in the uprising of the Warsaw Ghetto and of partisans, were seen as that part of the Jewish identity which directly linked Jewish history to Zionism and to Eretz Israel; as a sort of forerunner or epitome of Zionist heroism. The whole experience of the Holocaust was perceived and articulated as a fundamental aspect of the legitimation of Zionism and of the State of Israel as the major stronghold in the event of Jews defending themselves and the place of refuge for the survivors of the Holocaust.

The Memorial Day stressed all these themes, as did the establishment of Yad Vashem, the Memorial of the Holocaust, both introduced in 1953. Such events as the Eichmann trial in 1961 reinforced them, while a growing literature devoted to these subjects deepened – without, initially at least, denying the negation of the Galut experience – the search for an understanding of the historical ties of the Jewish people.

With respect to this exploration of Jewish history and tradition, there also developed new, sometimes opposing themes. There was, on the one hand, a growing stress on the Eretz–Israel dimension of this history, and on the other a greater opening to the tradition of the Diaspora. Whatever the details of this exploration, it did constitute a continuous part of the cultural and public scene.

The same was true, of course, of the addition of the political dimension itself, as emphasized above all by Ben-Gurion in his stress on *Mamlachtiut* (Statehood), seen by him as the epitome of the realization of the Zionist vision against the more sectarian tendencies of different leaders, groups and movements which became a focus for controversy.

Seemingly there were also no great changes in the relative importance of the religious components in the crystallization of the Israeli collective identity. Truly enough, the full ratification of the earlier arrangements in this sphere – the inclusion of Agudat Israel in the Knesset, and sometimes even in the government, the recognition of the Rabbinical courts and their jurisdiction, personal status (marriage, divorce and the like), the ever-crucial position of the religious parties in the coalition – all reinforced the strength of the religious groups. There developed a slow but continuous strengthening of the religious legislation in various areas of life, alongside the growing importance of the Chief Rabbinate, which strove to attain church-like standing, and the growth of the Yeshivot. But in reality there was a compromise and *modus vivendi* between the secular and religious sectors – with the seeming overt supremacy of the secular but acceptance of the special sensitivity and orientation of the religious groups. This was epitomized by the wording of the Declaration of Independence which, instead of the name of God, used the euphemism *Tsur Israel* (Rock of Israel), tantamount to His name for religious people, but a more symbolic expression for secular circles denoting a general reference to Jewish historical experience and solidarity.

One of the major impacts of the religious groups on the basic legislation of the State was their strong opposition to any constitution of the State claiming that the Torah was the only possible constitution. It is however doubtful whether other elements – especially those around the government – were indeed very interested in promulgating such a constitution which would necessarily hamper the government. But from 1964 on, a series of Basic Laws defining the basic constitutional nature of the State were introduced, which ultimately could be seen as almost the equivalent of a constitution, while at the same time the strength of the judiciary fulfilled some at least of its roles.

All these themes, their variations and their relative importance, constituted a focus of continuous struggle, of literary and journalistic discussion, often of public debates. In a sense, this was attesting fully to the strength and viability of the institutional mould within which they developed and to the 'perspective' of which they were all closely related.

Indeed the viability of the basic institutional moulds that developed in this period seemed, perhaps paradoxically but in reality quite naturally, to be reinforced by the fact – as we shall see in greater detail later on – that these moulds were never entirely homogeneous; that there developed within them enduring ideological–political conflicts, disputes and new trends; that the level of political discussions and debates was always quite intensive; and that there were government crises attesting to the basic democratic nature of the State.

Such viability was even more fully visible because of the crucial part played in many of the institution-building by the new generations of the *Tsabras* – those who began to be visible during the late 1940s and especially the War of Independence, and who became even more conspicuous later in the army. Almost all major figures like Yadin, Alon, Dayan or Ezer Weizmann, members of the new academic and economic elite, belonged to this group, which became also more and more visible in academic life, in literature and in many of the newly economic enterprises.

The relative heterogeneity of these institutional moulds was of course reinforced to no small degree by the fact that the State and the institutions attendant on it – the establishment of the army, the foreign service, bureaucracy and academic institutions, as well as the great economic overlap – opened up for the more active elements avenues of mobility and advancement undreamed of in the period of the Yishuv.

This mobility acquired a special international dimension through the extension of the foreign contact – foreign services, the first economic contacts, programmes of economic aid, academic contact – thus combining the image of a small country with the maintenance of some special centrality in terms of institutional creativity.

## The problems of redefinition of Zionism

The establishment of the State of Israel had of course (in the articulation of the different dimensions of the Zionist vision and the different themes inherent in it) many repercussions on the basic definition of Zionism.

On the one hand the establishment of the State could be seen – and indeed was seen by many groups, leaders and intellectuals – as the full realization of that vision, or at least as a most fundamental step towards it.

But at the same time the very beginnings of such realization called forth many questions and problems. First of all it opened up the problem of the relations between the strong future orientation which was inherent in the Zionist vision and the emerging concrete reality of Israel.

Second, the problem of the legitimation of Jewish existence in the Diaspora, as against the Zionist stress on the non-viability of such existence, was potentially opened up, even though the terrible shadow of the Holocaust prevented this problem from fully emerging in public conferences for a long time.

Third, it entailed far-reaching implications for the relations between the Diaspora and the State – which we shall analyse later on.

All these basic changes gave rise to intensive intellectual ideological debates, which abounded in attempts to redefine the nature of Zionist ideology and to some of which we shall refer later on.

## The impact in the Diaspora

However, these debates did not greatly affect the overall identification of the establishment of the State with the realization of the Zionist vision and its acceptance.

This vigorous image of Israel as combining the creation of a new institutional reality with the crystallization of a new Jewish identity, with universal significance, comprising many utopian or semi-utopian visions, was also very prevalent beyond Israel – in the Jewish communities in the Diaspora and in many non-Jewish communities, especially in the West. Anti-Zionism as an active element on the Jewish public scene had almost entirely disappeared, to be supplemented by a general acceptance of the reality of the State.

But it was not only a passive acceptance. For many Jews and Jewish leadership in the Diaspora – with but few exceptions – the State of Israel became an object of pride and identification focused around the themes of heroism, military victory and national sovereignty. It reversed, as it were, the negative image of the Diaspora Jew, and enabled many of them to engage in new types of activities, to participate – through institutional channels, even if vicariously – in these new types of activities and experiences.

Above all the establishment of the State of Israel fully brought out and legitimized the political dimension of Jewish activities, first of all, of course, within the great Jewish concentration in the United States but also in Europe, by weakening the definition of the Jews as a purely religious or confessional or even as an ethnic–philanthropic group. The appearance of Israeli diplomats – such figures as Golda Meir or Abba Eban, various military figures, members of the foreign service and experts, and the host of emissaries who carried the message of the reborn Israel – greatly strengthened this political dimension and identification and it was not an unusual experience to find European or American Jews in distant lands feeling more at home in the Israeli Embassies than in those of their own countries.

At the same time Israeli folklore, songs and dancing spread throughout Jewish communities, and Israeli-orientated activities, especially the mobilization of financial resources and political support for the State of Israel, became more and more a central part of the activities of most Jewish organizations.

There was also quite a widespread – even if not necessarily particularly intensive – acceptance of some sort of pioneering 'social' socio-democratic image of Israel – of which the Kibbutz was usually seen as the apogee. Many Jews attempted to find in Israel the realization of their own view of general or Jewish utopia, whether of a good society, of Jewish solidarity or of some type of cultural renaissance.

There were, of course, many critics of the concrete policies – especially of the international stances – of Israel; there were such critics as Hannah Arendt who, for instance, criticized it during the Eichmann trial for not becoming a sort of symbol for the expiation of the sins of all humanity; there were those – some of whom were on the inside, as for instance Martin Buber and other intellectuals, mostly former members of Brit Shalom – who criticized the lack of any attempts on the part of the Israeli government to initiate peaceful overtures with the Arabs.

There was also, of course, among many Jews in the Diaspora, a muted non-acceptance of many of the premisses or pretensions of Israel; and for a long time the ultra-orthodox camp did not accept the legitimacy of the State, even if increasingly accepting it *de facto*.

But these opinions were not the central stance of the Jewish attitude to Israel. Even for the most assimilated Jews, the existence of Israel – even if without its utopian dimension – became something basic, primordial. As Raymond Aron put it in his outcry against De Gaulle's policy towards Israel in 1967:

> I was never a Zionist first of all because I never suffered being Jewish. It seems probable to me that the State of Israel, for the sake of its own existence, will be dragging along a prolonged conflict. I do not undertake today more than yesterday unconditionally to support the politics of the people responsible for the Israeli state – neither more nor less than those of other governments. But I also know, more clearly than yesterday, that the possibility of the destruction of the State of Israel, (that would be accompanied by a massacre of part of the population) wounds me to the bottom of my soul. In that sense I confess that a Jew could never achieve perfect objectivity when Israel is the subject at hand . . .*

The full realization, as Simone Weil would say in Jerusalem in 1981, that there might be a contradiction between the high universalistic values of Judaism cherished and upheld by Jews as a minority in the Diaspora and the exigencies of running a state, was confined to very few; perhaps it was even accepted, compared to the great experience of the rebirth of the Jewish nation, as being of relatively secondary importance.

Thus indeed the institutional moulds that were developed in the State of Israel in the first period of its history (till about the Six Day War), and which were portrayed by its leaders, and perceived by large sectors in Israel and

---

* Raymond Aron, *De Gaulle, Israel et Les Juifs* (Paris 1968), p. 38.

abroad as at least the beginning of the realization of the Zionist vision in general and the Zionist–Labour one in particular, showed great vitality to begin with.

They also demonstrated viability in coping with most of the problems of the period: the initial stages of absorption of immigrants, the creation of a modern economy, a modern army forging a new nation.

Truly enough, daily reality and emerging institutional trends were of course in many respects quite different from the ideal basic premises of the institutional mould – perhaps even to a higher degree than in the period of the Yishuv, and in many ways similar to many other post-revolutionary societies. In a sense almost every success had another side which could be interpreted as containing at least some kernels of decomposition of this mould, of its ideal premisses.

But initially at least it also showed great – perhaps amazing – continuity. It was not a stagnant continuity but a very dynamic one, within the framework of which there took place far-reaching changes, processes of growth, diversification and opening up, with the wars of 1967 and 1973 constituting watersheds in these developments. Ultimately these processes gave rise to the decomposition of the initial mould and to extensive processes of transformation of Israeli society – in the ethos of which it lives today.

In order to understand these processes it is necessary first of all to analyse in greater detail the basic institutional moulds that crystallized in the initial stages of the State of Israel, the ways in which the major problems of Israeli society were coped with within the framework of these moulds, and the processes of change that developed within them – and we shall now proceed to such analysis.

# CHAPTER 8
# The Political Mould

# I · Political Structure, Institutions and Processes

## The Basic Characteristics
### Initial stability

The political mould that crystallized in the State of Israel was characterized by a series of features derived from the heritage of the Yishuv, the Zionist movement and the mandatory period, and it became transformed in the new reality of the State and its problems.

Its basic institutional characteristic was that of a parliamentary democracy, within which there developed a pattern of coalition government in which one party – until 1977 the Labour party, since then Likud – was the predominant one.

The State of Israel did not proclaim a constitution – largely because of the opposition of the religious parties who claimed that the Halakha constitutes the basic laws of the Jewish people – nor a bill of rights. From 1964, however, the Knesset started to establish a series of basic laws, and the strong standing of the legal system in general and of the High Court in particular provided some, if only partial, equivalent to such a bill or constitution.

This political mould – characterized above all by the predominance of the Labour camp, first of *Mapai*, later on of different Labour blocs – developed in the first years of the State and showed a marked continuity with the political arrangements that were predominant in the Yishuv – as well as a high degree of relative stability and continuity.

The continuity with the pattern developed in the Yishuv could be seen in the fact that the major parties and their leaders were, in one way or another – with some exceptions – more or less the same as in the Yishuv. The two great new developments here were, first the formation of the *Herut* party – which could however be seen as a continuation of the older Revisionist group, and which was often seen (not entirely correctly) a rather special part of the rightist–bourgeois bloc; and, second, the addition of the ultra-orthodox Agudat Israel to many of the coalitions.

The continuity of the initial political mould that developed in Israel itself was evident in the persistence of the major parties and blocs (the Labour, the 'bourgeois' or rightist, and religious ones) – even if, as we shall see, sometimes changing names and often splitting off or reuniting within the major blocs – in a pattern which evinced relative stability for a long period of time – till about the mid-1960s.

This stability was evident – till the late 1960s – in the distribution of votes and power between the major blocs, in the predominance of the Labour party as the dominant party in any reigning coalition until 1977, and in at least the initial composition of the leadership of the major parties and blocs.

Here, of course, the great surprise was that there did not develop any special parties of new immigrants – despite some attempts, mostly by some of the older Sephardi notables, to create such new parties. Such attempts failed – and the immigrant votes were seemingly distributed among the existing parties or blocs almost according to their initial strength and for a long time according to the initial balance of power between them; but gradually more and more of the dissatisfied tended to move into the direction of the major opposition – *Herut*.

This stability was closely related to continuity in two additional aspects of political life: namely the basic socio-political ideologies of the dominant groups, and leadership which lasted at least till the early 1960s – seemingly even later.

## The structure of State institutions

While this continuity applied also to the basic institutional structure of the government, all the formal paraphernalia of a full sovereign state obviously could not be taken over from the earlier period. The major features of these institutions, however, such as the democratic framework, the maintenance of representative institutions and the responsibility of the government to the legislature, were not dissimilar from the situation as it existed at the time of the Yishuv.

Some of the most important formal changes could be seen in the presidency which, unlike the Zionist Organization, became mainly a symbolic office with little real political influence.

Similarly, important changes were effected through the establishment and institutionalization of the judiciary (non-existent within the Jewish institutions of the Yishuv, except for the honorary court of the Zionist Congress, and some sectorial arrangements) and in the controlling and empowering agencies – such as the State Comptroller and the various permanent parliamentary committees.

In spite of the continuity in the nature and composition of the parties and their elites, the establishment of the State of Israel obviously wrought far-reaching changes, not only on the formal–institutional level, but also in the political process and institutions. Most functions of the mandatory government, the Jewish Agency and the *Vaad Leumi* were incorporated within the institutional framework of the state, largely ending the old division of labour that existed between them in the mandatory period. The Jewish Agency continued to deal with problems of colonization, settlement of new immigrants, cultural activities in the Diaspora, and some political and propagandist activities of its own, but most of its political activities naturally devolved on to the State.

A change, parallel to that in the institutional structure, also took place in the relative importance of Israeli and World Zionist organizations and institutions. The situation predominant in the pre-State period – when World Zionists were of much greater importance than their Palestinian counterparts – was completely reversed. Now the centre of gravity shifted to Israel, with the Zionist organs in the Diaspora playing only a secondary role. This could be seen in the composition of the political leadership, with most of the top leaders going over to the government, and in the division of functions between them.

There was also, of course, the development and proliferation of a burgeoning public administration and bureaucracy, above all in the State civil service and those of the municipalities, but also, even if to a smaller degree, in the Histadrut and the Jewish Agency – these last two constituting, of course, a direct continuation of the former period.

Indeed the development of the bureaucracies in general and of the governmental civil service in particular, although building on nuclei established in the period of the Yishuv, went far beyond them and became, with all its good and bad connotations, one of the specific marks of the State of Israel. Gradually the government sector in general, including the military and air industries, the civil service and the employees of the municipalities, became the largest employer in the Israeli economy.

## Political parties

As indicated above, most of the major parties that were active in Israel were continuations or offshoots of those in the Zionist movement and in the Yishuv. However, with the establishment of the State changes took place within them – gradually at first, more rapidly afterwards – resulting in new unified organizations uniting the different movements, sects and interest groups, and with a marked shift in orientation towards the absorption of new elements.*

Some of such changes were also connected with specific events – the most important of which was the Lavon affair.

The Lavon affair goes back to 1954 to the period when Pinchas Lavon was Minister of Defence, and Israeli agents were arrested and convicted with heavy prison sentences for sabotage which was aimed at weakening tension between Egypt and the US.

In 1954 Moshe Sharett appointed an inquiry commission (consisting of the President of the Supreme Court and the First Chief of Staff of the Israeli Army, General Dov) which did not come to any clear conclusion with respect to

* See in greater detail, for the period up to 1965, Eisenstadt, *Israeli Society*.

absolving Lavon, and he resigned.

In 1960 Lavon – who had in the meantime become Secretary General of the Histadrut – claimed that new evidence, which indicated that some of the army officers involved did not tell the truth, existed and that it cleared him, and asked for rehabilitation from Ben-Gurion or the government. Ben-Gurion himself refused to take a stand and the Cabinet – against the view of Ben-Gurion, who wanted the matter to be brought to a judicial authority – decided to appoint a Ministerial Committee which decided that Lavon was not to blame. Ben-Gurion fiercely opposed this conclusion and continued to demand a judicial inquiry. The coalition partners who had taken part in the Ministerial Committee on the affair were offended by their Premier's high-handed behaviour, and together with some veteran *Mapai* ministers now threatened to resign.

*Mapai* now made frantic efforts to reach a compromise in its internal conflict, but Mr Lavon did not agree to the compromise proposed, nor was any *Mapai* leader willing to take responsibility. Finally, in March 1961, Finance Minister Eshkol was forced to decide the issue because Ben-Gurion had meantime resigned and the country was without a government. In a dramatic session of the Party Executive, with pro-Lavon elements demonstrating outside the building, *Mapai* decided to remove Lavon from his position. The Histadrut Executive, led by its *Mapai* majority, carried out the Party's decision.

The final outcome of the vote in the *Mapai* Central Committee was relatively close (159 versus 96). The motion against dismissal was proposed by Moshe Sharett and the result was on the whole regarded as a moral victory for Lavon.

Bowing to public pressure, the coalition partners once more decided to take part in a government headed by Ben-Gurion, thus finally bringing the Lavon affair to its conclusion, with the Knesset dissolving nearly three years before time, and the nation going to the polls again in August 1961. *Mapai* lost four seats, but the resulting narrow coalition government contained an even stronger *Mapai* majority. The whole matter caused one of the most severe rifts in *Mapai* – ultimately, in 1965, causing the rift between *Rafi* and *Mapai*.

Initially the parties could be broadly divided into the Labour camp, the Centre parties, *Herut*, the religious groups, the Communists, the Arab parties, and various splinter groups.

*The Labour camp.* The Labour camp consisted of *Mapai* (Mifleget Poalei–Eretz Israel), founded in 1931 (the party of Ben-Gurion and the major leadership of the Labour camp), and the more leftist *Mapam* and *Ahdut Haavoda*. Even before the establishment of the State, and especially afterwards, these all underwent several splits and mergers, culminating in the establishment of *Avoda* in 1968, comprising *Mapai*, *Ahdut Haavoda* and *Rafi* (the group under the leadership of Ben-Gurion and Peres, and somewhat later Dayan, which split from *Mapai* in 1965), and of the *Maarach* (Alignment), which was originally established with *Mapai* and *Ahdut Haavoda* in 1964, and then continued after the creation of *Avoda*.

In January 1968 *Avoda* and the Labour Alignment promoted a union of all left-wing parties. *Mapai*, under the leadership of Eshkol and basing itself upon the dream of 'unity of Labour', brought about a merger of itself with *Rafi* and *Ahdut Haavoda* to constitute the Israel Labour party (*Avoda*) to which *Mapam* later allied itself to constitute a new, larger *Maarach*.

*The Centre.* Similar changes – perhaps even more pronounced than those within the Labour groups – took place among the different General Zionist groups.

Two major parties developed from the General Zionist movement, the Progressive Party and the General Zionists which, in 1961, merged into the Liberal Party.

Until then the Progressive Party was Israel's closest replica of a Liberal Party, and, though small, it carried considerable moral influence. Evolved partially at least from *Aliya Hadasha*, a party made up mainly of Central European immigrants who came to Palestine after 1933, the Progressive Party was founded in 1948.

The General Zionist Party was made up of a merger of different interest groups, such as the Manufacturers' Association, the Citrus Growers' Association, various merchant groups and the leaders of some municipal groups. With statehood, this party emerged as a champion of private enterprise in an economy dominated by the Histadrut. It also attempted to broaden its appeal by organizing a special wing within the Histadrut.

One of the important results of the Lavon affair was the merger of the Progressives and General Zionists into the Liberal Party, which gained about 14 per cent of the votes and seventeen members in the Knesset in the 1961 elections. In 1965 there was a split in the Liberal Party. Its great majority (almost all the former General Zionists and some former Progressives) founded a parliamentary bloc with *Herut* which received about 21 per cent of the votes. A minority – consisting mostly of former Progressives – founded the 'Independent Liberal Party' which received about 7 per cent of the votes.

*Herut – Gahal –* Likud. One of the main developments in the initial period of the State was the growth of the *Herut* party – the only full opposition party in the spectrum of Israeli politics. It developed from the older Revisionist groups, the 'terrorist' groups of the *Irgun Zvai Leumi* and members of the Revisionist party. (The other dissident group, Lehi, sent one member to the first Knesset only.)

This was the most extensive right-wing anti-government opposition party, being opposed to any economic role by the State, and to the economic preponderance of the Histadrut.

It emphasized – at least officially – an actively expansionist orientation in its foreign policy and was for a time identified with a policy of preventive war against the Arabs as being the best assurance of Israel's survival.

In 1965 *Herut* founded, together with a great part of the Liberals, a parliamentary bloc (*Gahal*) which, as we have seen, received about 21 per cent of the votes; in 1973, with the addition of other small groups, it became transformed into Likud.

*The religious parties.* Similar developments occurred within the National Religious Party, with a growing shift from *Mizrahi* (based mainly on Diaspora elements) to *Hapoel Hamizrahi* (more firmly rooted in Israel).

In 1949, *Mizrahi* joined the United Religious Front (comprising Agudat Israel and Poalei Agudat Israel).

Poalei Agudat Israel, the Labour wing of Agudat Israel, was founded in Poland in 1922. Its objective was to counteract anti-religious feelings among the Polish workers and to defend the place of the Orthodox Jew in industry. The religious base of Agudat Israel and its offshoot, Poalei Agudat Israel, was identical, but the Labour wing put more stress on agricultural settlement.

Its settlement work gradually brought it into closer touch with the Jewish Agency and the Histadrut and, though not a member of the Histadrut, the party participated in some trade union activities. It helped with the organization of illegal immigration, sent workers to refugee camps in Europe, and fought in the ranks of *Hagana*. The Agudat on the other hand, till the establishment of the State, did not maintain too many contacts with the Zionists (except in some political activities orientated to the English), and was based on the older Yishuv.

The most extreme of the religious groups of the 'old Yishuv' were the *Naturei Karta* who to this very day keep themselves apart and do not 'recognize' the State of Israel.

*The Communist Party.* The Communist Party was founded in Palestine in the early 1920s, primarily as an instrument to encourage Arab resistance to British imperialism and Zionism. Since then it was only for the short stretch dating from the UN Partition Resolution in November 1947 to the beginning of the First Knesset in 1949 that this party worked toward the Zionist goal of national sovereignty. Its orientation has, of course, been unflinchingly pro-Soviet.

*Arab parties.* The Arab parties appeared under different names in different elections. In 1965 the most important Arab parties were 'Co-operation and Fraternity' located in the Triangle (the area populated by Arabs near Netanya and Kfar Saba) and among the Druzes, and 'Progress and Development', located mainly in Galilee and affiliated both to the Alignment and to a small group called 'Peace' which was affiliated to *Rafi*.

In addition to the major parties, overall small splinter parties developed, such as the various ethnic lists – which counted five members in the First Knesset, three in the Second, and none thereafter.

*New parties since 1965.* In the 1965 and 1969 elections *Haolam Haze–Hakoach*

**Table 8.1  Results of the Elections for the Knesset, 1949–65 (percentages)**

| Party | First Knesset 25 Jan. 49 | Second Knesset 30 July 1951 | Third Knesset 26 July 1955 | Fourth Knesset 3 Dec. 1959 | Fifth Knesset 15 Aug. 1961 | Sixth Knesset 2 Nov. 1965 |
|---|---|---|---|---|---|---|
| *Mapai* | 35.7 | 37.3 | 32.3 | 38.2 | 34.7 | 36.7[a] |
| *Rafi* | – | – | – | – | – | 7.9 |
| National Religious Party | 12.2 | 8.3 | 9.1 | 9.9 | 9.8 | 8.9 |
| Agudat Israel and Poalei Agudat Israel | 1.7 | 0.6 | 0.3 | – | – | – |
| Other Religious Parties | | | | | | |
| *Herut* | 11.8 | 6.6 | 12.6 | 13.5 | 13.8 | 21.3[b] |
| *Mapam* | 14.7 | 12.5 | 7.3 | 7.2 | 7.5 | 6.6 |
| *Ahdut Haavoda* | included in *Mapam* | included in *Mapam* | 8.2 | 6.0 | 6.6 | 3.8 |
| Progressives | 4.1 | 3.2 | 4.4 | 4.6 | 13.8 (Liberal Party) | 3.8[d] |
| General Zionists | 5.2 | 16.2 | 10.2 | 6.2 | (Liberal Party) | |
| Communists | 3.5 | 4.0 | 4.5 | 2.8 | 4.2 | 3.4[c] |
| Minorities | 3.0 | 4.7 | 4.9 | 4.7 | 3.9 | 3.8 |
| Others | 8.4 | 3.0 | 1.6 | 2.2 | 0.3 | 2.5 |

Notes: a. Including *Ahdut Haavoda*.
b. Including a section from the Liberal Party (*Gahal*).
c. Including the New Communist Party.
d. Under the name 'Independent Liberals'.
Source: Government of Israel, *Election Results 1979–81* (Jerusalem 1981).

*Hahadash* (This World–The New Force), with an extensive leftist orientation, was established by Uri Avneri, the editor of a rather sensational weekly with the same title (*Haolam Haze*), merging later with *Moked* and *Sheli*; in the 1969 elections there developed the *Reshima Mamlachtit* (The State List), an offshoot of that part of *Rafi* which did not join *Avoda*, and *Hamerkaz Hachofshi* (The Free Centre), a rather rightist group led by Shmuel Tamir, former leading member of *Herut*.

In the 1973 election there was also a new list called *Moked*, made up of Jewish Communists and a splinter from *Mapam*, and it won one seat.

An entirely new party, the Democratic Movement for Change (known as *Dash*), which had entered the arena only six months (November 1976) before the 1977 elections, under the leadership of Yigael Yadin, made a spectacular showing on Israeli terms by obtaining fifteen Knesset seats. Its principal appeal

Table 8.2   Results of the Elections for the Knesset, 1969–81 (percentages)

| Party | Seventh Knesset 28 Oct. 69 | Eighth Knesset 31 Dec. 73 | Ninth Knesset 17 May 77 | Tenth Knesset 30 June 81 |
|---|---|---|---|---|
| *Mapai* <br> *Rafi* <br> *Mapam* <br> *Ahdut Haavoda* } Alignment | 46.2 | 39.6 | 24.6 | 36.6 |
| National Religious Party | 9.8 | 8.3 | 9.2 | 4.9 |
| Agudat Israel and Poalei Agudat Israel | 5 | 3.8 | 4.7 | 4.6 |
| *Herut* (Likud) | 21.7 | 30.2 | 33.4 | 37.1 |
| Progressives (Liberal party) | 3.2 | 3.6 | 1.2 | 0.6 |
| Israel Communist Party | 1.2 | – | – | – |
| Free Centre | 1.2 | – | – | – |
| *Haolam Haze* | 1.2 | 0.7 | – | – |
| Democratic list for Peace and Equality (Rakach), Black Panthers and Jewish Arabic Circles | 2.8 | 3.4 | 4.6 | 3.4 |
| Citizens' Rights Movement | – | 2.2 | 1.2 | 1.4 |
| *Moked* | – | 1.4 | – | – |
| Democratic Movement for Change (Dash) | – | – | 11.6 | – |
| *Shlomzion* – Realization of Zionism Movement | – | – | 1.9 | – |
| *Sheli* | – | – | 1.6 | 0.4 |
| Israel Tradition Movement (Tami) | – | – | – | 2.3 |
| Change – Centre Party (Shinui) | – | – | – | 1.5 |
| Resurrection | – | – | – | 2.3 |
| Movement for State Renewal | – | – | – | 1.6 |
| *Flato Sharon* | – | – | 2.0 | 0.6 |
| Minorities | 0.0 | 0.2 | 0.4 | 1.1 |
| Others | 1.1 | 3.8 | 2.2 | 1.6 |

Source: Government of Israel, *Election Results 1979–81* (Jerusalem 1981).

was its emphasis on the need to reform the electoral system. The movement's platform on foreign policy was almost identical to Labour's, minus the explicit reference to returning part of the territories to Jordan.

In the 1973 election there emerged an entirely new list called the 'Movement for Citizens' Rights' led by Shulamit Aloni – a former member of *Maarach* and for some time a member of the Rabin cabinet – and it won three mandates in the election.

Before the election of 1977 a new leftist party – *Sheli* – was also established, which got two mandates for the ninth government. In the 1981 election this party did not get any mandate.

## Election results

Up to 1981 there were ten elections to the Knesset, and consequent changes in the government. The outcome of these elections (as presented in Tables 8.1 and 8.2) confirm the relative stability and continuity of the political system.

# Continuity and Change in Relation to the Yishuv and Changing Internal Features
## *Coalition and oppositions*

This initial political mould within the framework of the basic parliamentary democratic State, dominated by the ruling Labour party (*Mapai*) under the strong leadership of Ben-Gurion and shaped, as we have seen, by the specific transformation of the Zionist vision, was characterized by a strong emphasis on development, security, ingathering of exiles and a largely western-orientated foreign policy, and crystallized in the early 1950s.

The major parties which participated in this mould accepted its basic premises and attempted within these policies to put stronger emphasis on different orientations – most closely related to their ideological orientations or concrete interests.

The 'bourgeois parties' – the General Zionists (mostly composed of the older 'civil' sector of the Yishuv), and the Progressive and Independent Liberals (mostly composed of professionals, intellectuals, probably civil servants) – stressed above all the upholding of law, of civility, of rights of citizens, in general the more civil–universalistic components of these orientations.

The leftist parties – *Mapam* with its two components (the older *Mapam* – *Hashomer Hatzair* – and *Ahdut Haavoda*) – attempted first to direct Israel's foreign policy more in the direction of the Eastern bloc, or at least in a neutral direction; but the Korean War and the growing anti-Semitism during Stalin's last years did not make it easy to find responsiveness to these attempts.

There were only two parties which were initially consciously excluded by Ben-Gurion from participation in this mould – but not, of course, from participation in the Knesset – namely *Herut* and the Communist Party (initially

*Maki*; later from 1965, with the split within *Maki*, divided into *Rakach* and *Maki*, the latter disappearing later). The exclusion of the latter was, of course, easily explained by their non-acceptance of the basic Zionist tenets.

The exclusion of *Herut* – the party which was constructed by the transformation of the former underground Ezel into an open political party within the basic constitutional democratic framework of the State – was rooted in the great historical rift between the Revisionist and the Labour movements in the 1930s; and between Ezel and Lehi underground movements and the *Hagana* during the struggle against the British. This exclusion – manifest in its non-participation in any of the governments until 1967 – made *Herut* into the opposition party *par excellence*, an opposition party which – unlike the more 'bourgeois' parties like the General Zionists (later Liberals) or the more intellectual or progressive ones, like the Progressive or later Independent Liberals – was based not only on differences of interest and social composition and of some social or cultural orientations within the predominant mould, but also on a basically different theme, orientation and conception of the Zionist vision.

The *Herut* party, in partial continuity with the Revisionist view, promulgated a powerful nationalist orientation, a strong emphasis on military strength, a negation – even if for a long time only a *de jure* one – of the basic territorial political compromise on which the State was established. It also undervalued the tradition of strong institution-building and some of the more universalistic emphases in the orientations of the Zionist vision which were, as we have seen, upheld by large parts of the 'older' Zionist Organization in general and the Labour sector in particular.

These themes, and the oppositionary and populistic stances in which they were articulated, started to appeal to several groups which were not fully absorbed within the framework of the dominant Labour mould – especially some of the Oriental groups (who already in the period of the Yishuv had shown some inclination to Ezel), some of the lower economic strata and some new elements of lumpenproletariat that developed, paradoxically enough, in a society ruled by a social democratic party.

The electoral power of the *Herut* party was initially relatively small, but from 1965 on it started to grow continuously. A crucial turning-point in its political fate, and in the whole political format of Israel, was its alliance, mentioned above, in 1965 with the General Zionists or Liberals as a parliamentary bloc, called *Gahal* – and later on, in 1973, the establishment of Likud.

## The religious groups within the political framework

Within this broad political spectrum, the religious groups held a special place, to some degree a continuation of the former arrangements in the period of the Yishuv, but in fact going far beyond these arrangements.

The religious parties – the *Mizrahi* and *Hapoel Hamizrahi* (later, from 1957, the National Religious Party (NRP)) – always played an essential role in the Labour coalitions, being until 1977 a sort of natural partner for the Labour bloc. They accepted most of the premises of the regnant political mould, but were ready to fight with respect to some principled religious issues (such as the question of Who is a Jew, which could imply changes in the laws of personal status), and sometimes bringing down the government on such or similar issues. But till 1977, they always came back and never challenged the basic political or social orientations of the initial institutional mould, or the predominance of Labour within it.

The situation with respect to Agudat Israel was a different one. It did not participate in the Knesset, and after a relatively short period in the late 1940s and early 1950s, it did not participate in the government itself. Basically, it admitted only a sort of *de facto* recognition of the State. It did not share in its basic Zionist premises – as shown, for instance, in its refusal to hoist the national flag or invite the President of State to its conventions – although it accepted the ideal of the settlement of Eretz Israel. It did, of course, exert continuous pressure on the government to grant more and more allocations to its organizations – and *de facto* organized itself as a distinct sector of the population.

The religious parties, as we have seen, were able to obtain a full formalization of the status of the religious courts, and arrangements in religious fields. In addition the *de facto* exemption of the students of the Yeshivot from military service, discussed in detail above, became a basic aspect of the participation of the religious parties in the government. While this arrangement was initiated by the *Mizrahi* leaders, it became even more pertinent with the addition of Agudat Israel and the growing influx of orthodox, even ultra-orthodox, elements into Israel and the growing concentration of orthodox centres of learning in Israel.

In general the power of the religious parties and their influence on many spheres of life grew continuously, even if often seemingly quietly and imperturbably.

Thus in fact there developed here a rather special type of relationship between state and religion (close to the pattern that can be found in many Catholic countries), in which the religious establishments and parties, while not being recognized as an official 'Church', yet exerted a great influence on central aspects of social life – above all perhaps on the definition, through the control of marriage laws, of the legal boundaries of the Jewish (and other religious) communities – maintaining (as could also be seen in, for instance, the wording of the Census) an equation between religious and national boundaries of the Jewish collectivity.

## The crystallization of the new mould

The different political orientations which existed within the basic mould were carried by various social groups but there was no simple correlation between any one group or party and any of these orientations – although, as we have indicated above, there were some natural elective affinities between them. Of special importance in the crystallization and continuity of the several viewpoints was the fact that many of them were carried not only by different social political groups but became also to some degree embedded in institutions – Parliament, the Court of Laws, the army, in professional organizations and the like.

The relative importance of these orientations – and of their concrete derivatives – constituted foci of public debate and of political struggle. The scope of governmental regulation in economic matters, censorship and freedom of the press, the relative place of the older pioneering sectors in the political decision-making, the civilian supervision of the army and the army establishments, and perhaps above all the scope of religious legislation, all continuously attracted such debate and political wrangling – often very intensive and acrimonious.

Yet, despite such intensity and acrimony, these different orientations of political culture and their proponents coexisted in a relatively peaceful yet dynamic way. Peaceful in the sense that all the participants in the struggle seemed to accept the basic premises and themes of the dominant mould: its strong Zionist–Labour orientations; its emphasis on development and in-gathering of exiles; its democratic framework and its specific social democratic ambiance; its emphasis on the universalistic dimension, on constitutional democracy and historical territorial compromise with the State. Most of the opposing tenets of the major parties were set within the frameworks of this basic mould and its premises.

So, interestingly, but significantly enough, there developed but little principled opposition beyond bargaining over allocation of resources to different sectors and welfare activities, and beyond some rather weak, mostly exploratory, attempts by some leaders of the Histadrut sector (like Hillel Dan, the Director of Solel Boneh) to establish, in the first years of the State, an overall Histadrut economy as the regnant one in the State.

The more 'leftist' opposition tended to focus increasingly on relations with the Soviets and the attitude to the Arab minority in Israel – in the latter being joined by some of the Independent Liberal groups which focused also on types of civil rights, on the abolition of censorship, and on military restrictions promulgated on the basis of mandatory orders.

Most of the actual political struggle was focused around the allocation of resources to different sectors and groups, and much less around principled or ideological ones – despite the very strong tendency towards ideological proclamation in the Knesset.

It was perhaps only the *Herut* party – and of course the extreme religious groups – that did not basically accept the premises of the new mould, but even they on the whole in actual political life behaved according to them and the existing rules of the game.

## Marginal political groups

There also continuously developed different marginal political groups and protest movements, such as for instance that of *Tnuat Hamitnadvim* in the early 1950s, which combined voluntary work among the new immigrants with criticism of the growing bureaucratization and possible corruption in the political and administrative realms. Most of these movements cried out against the more restrictive aspects of the regime – whether censorship or the religious restrictions in general – and against restrictions in the laws of marriage and non-recognition in terms of these laws of such groups as the Karaites, in particular; many campaigned for the institution of civil marriage; and many called – together with some of the more leftist groups – for a more liberal attitude to the Arab population. In the early years of the State there existed also several extreme 'rightist', national or religious marginal groups who sometimes came near to breaking the law or actually did so.

Demonstrations and protests, as well as various marginal protest groups, were a continuous part of the Israeli political scene. Significantly enough, until after the Six Day War they only rarely focused on the realm of security and foreign relations. The only partial exception to such relatively lawful protest was the demonstration organized by *Herut* in January 1952 against the acceptance of reparations from Germany – a demonstration which almost came to an assault of the Knesset but was put down by the police.

These movements of protest – and the public debate which they generated or with which they were connected in the increasingly independent daily press – were, even if often indirectly, quite influential. In particular they contributed to the continuous opening up of the initial political and institutional mould, without changing its basic premisses.

## Openings in the political mould

Indeed the development of this mould was characterized by a progressive opening up. The relatively restrictive atmosphere and direction which developed in the first decade or so was characterized by Ben-Gurion's attempts to vest control of most of the power positions in the army and of the major institutions in members of *Mapai* in general and in particular those groups in *Mapai* close to him – especially against the more leftist groups in the Labour camp, such as *Mapam* or *Ahdut Haavoda*. Many attempts were also made by the emerging political elite and bureaucracy to institutionalize relatively strict control over many aspects of social life in line with the more totalistic traditions or orientations of the older movements and sectors now transferred to the State; by the rather heavy paternalistical mode of politics that had developed by then; by the strong orientation to security, especially towards the Arab population – manifest in the establishment in most areas of Arab population of military government which imposed sometimes rather heavy restrictions on the movement of that population. But from the late fifties on all these became gradually weakened. Public discussion and dispute, independent groups' formation and free public opinion were continuously on the increase – thus indicating that this political mould was both continuous, dynamic and opening up.

## The Army and Society
### The basic security policy

The continuous state of hostility with Israel's neighbours and the six wars led to a predominance of security problems and considerations in the political and social life of Israel in the post-independence period, as discussed in Chapter 7.

The very specific Israeli response to this continuous external security threat did not take the form, as was often predicted, of the emergence of a garrison state, but rather of the peculiar Israeli type of an open civilian fortress.

This open fortress was characterized by several major features. First it was characterized by the development of a very strong military and security ethos, and of the marked emphasis on being in a society under stress, as a basic component of the emerging collective identity. The security dimension and military image, as we have seen, became one of the main components of Israeli identity, and to a certain extent it took the place of the pioneering one – to become somewhat weakened after the Yom Kippur War.

Indeed, in the earlier periods the ideal of the *Shomer* (Watcher) – later on of the member of *Hagana* – was seen as part, but only a part, of the general renaissance of the new Hebrew man. It was strongly interwoven with other aspects of renaissance and pioneering – whether work, settlement of cultural creativity or defence – and accepted as a part of all these activities; but now there started to be a marked shift – to no small degree initiated by Ben-Gurion – in which military activities and the security dimension were more and more separated from other fields of activities, while at the same time trying to appropriate the central pioneering status.

Concomitantly there developed, not unlike the Swiss pattern, a civilian army based on national service for 3–3½ years, and continuous reserve duty till about 55 – sometimes later – together with a highly specialized and prestigious core of standing army, composed mostly of officers, giving rise to a situation in which service in the army was part of the life of most Israelis, with both a demarcation and yet a strong interweaving of military and civilian elements. Thus, together with a great military industrial base mentioned above, the army became one of the great achievements of modern Israel.

At the same time, because of the practice of releasing the career officers at the age of 45–55, the core of the army maintained a continuous orientation to the civilian economic and political sectors, and did not develop into a closed corporate unit or an autonomous political force – although it did naturally develop quite strong social relations. Indeed in the political field, although many generals (such as Dayan, Rabin, Barlev, Weizmann, Amit and others) entered into the political arena, mostly in the 1960s and 1970s, they spread out among all major parties.

Last, there developed relatively strong civil control of the army, but coupled with a relatively high degree of autonomy of the (civilian-controlled) security establishment presided over by the Prime Minister or Minister of Defence. There was little effective (as against more formal) control by other parts of political institutions – like the Parliament or the State Comptroller. Truly enough the mechanisms of such control existed, but in fact were rather weak, and were basically limited to reporting by the Prime Minister, Minister of Defence and the Chief of Staff with regard to some of the ultimate decisions about war.

There were, of course, tensions between the military proper – the General Staff – and civilian elements of the Ministry of Defence, which became especially evident during Pinhas Lavon's short tenure as Minister of Defence and Sharett's premiership in 1954 and which had in different ways already existed before.

But on the whole both parts of the security establishment were indeed very closely interconnected, presided over by the Prime Minister and the Minister of Defence, and only to a much lesser degree by other civilian bodies.

This particular civilian type of control over the military was also connected, till after the Six Day War, with a very high level of general political consensus over defence matters and their actual bracketing out from politics, and with primacy of foreign and security considerations.

This consensus, which crystallized around the early 1950s, was based, until the aftermath of the Six Day War, on some basic premisses most fully crystallized by Ben-Gurion – sometimes against the more militant elements in the army, but also against the 'milder' conceptions of some members of his Cabinet, like Sharett, and of the various left army groups. It was based on what could be called the Israeli Defence conception, characterized by two seemingly contradictory, yet in fact closely interrelated, premisses.

On the one hand there was a strong emphasis on the basic necessity of building up military strength and an active defence posture as a condition *sine qua non* of deterrence against Arab intentions of annihilation of Israel. On the other hand there was the emphasis of employing this strength either in relatively limited, even if often very dramatic and internationally not well received activities, such as actions of retaliation against terrorist attacks, or in more expanded overall military campaigns, as in Sinai in 1956 – but here, only in collaboration with some of the great powers.

So employment of this military strength was based – at least after 1967 – on the recognition of their military and political limits of Israel's strength; on the need to find allies in the international field, and to maintain the basic moral stance of Israel or, in the words of Ben-Gurion, to combine strength and justice.

All these elements became evident in the Sinai Campaign, in the initial

Israeli victory – as against English and French withdrawal – and in the ultimate withdrawal from Sinai under the combined pressure of the USA and USSR.

This conception of security was based also on the acceptance of the territorial arrangements of the 1949–50 armistice, of what would later be called the 1967 borders, including the division of Jerusalem: a territorial arrangement in principle opposed by the *Herut* party, but *de facto* accepted even by it.

## The Attitude to the Arab World

This security conception was also based on a rather strong assumption, only rarely tested, of the impossibility of engaging in any real political dialogue with the Arabs – at least for the present – so long as the Arabs would not fully recognize the impossibility of annihilating the State of Israel, would not give up this dream, and would not recognize Israel's existence.

This attitude was also connected with the fact that in this period, up to the Six Day War, the consciousness in public opinion of the problem of relations with the Arabs was at its lowest in the whole history of Zionism.

The successful termination of the War of Independence – at the very high cost of 6,000 casualties – against five Arab armies; the refusal of the Arabs to recognize the State of Israel; the effective closure of contacts with the outside Arab world; the great stress so often laid by Ben-Gurion on the importance of not allowing the assault on Israel to be repeated, and the fear of such an attempt – a fear fed by the declaration of Arab leaders, by their unwillingness to follow the Armistice agreements of 1949 with the conclusion of peace agreements, and by many aspects of the daily security situation; the emphasis on the importance of building up the institutions of the new Jewish state: all these weakened or diminished the awareness of the problem of political dialogue with the Arabs.

Truly enough there were some writers – above all S. Izhar in his *Hirbat Hiza* or A. B. Yoshua, two among the most outstanding writers of the new generation of Hebrew writers – who indeed brought out quite forcefully the problem of the destruction of Arab settlements in the war and of the limits of the relations between the two nations or populations. But, on the whole, as compared with the earlier as well as the later post-1967 periods, there was relatively little preoccupation with these difficulties. Such suspension of any attempt at a political dialogue developed also with respect to the problem of the Arab refugees or those who fled during the War of Independence. Here the experience of the much more successful integration of Palestinians in Jordan stood out against the unwillingness of other Arabs to integrate them in their own midst, and to keep a sort of perpetual threat against Israel.

It was to no small degree the fear of this threat – reinforced later by the fear, often voiced by their leaders, that the refugees might claim back their places which in the meantime had been to a considerable extent settled by new immigrants, mostly indeed from Arab countries, and might undermine, if returned, the whole fabric of the security of the State – that contributed to the unwillingness to engage in any far-reaching dialogues about their problem.

This fear even extended to Israeli Arabs, as shown by the famous case of Ikrit and Baram, two minority (mostly Druze) villages in Galilee. These villages were evacuated by order of the army for security reasons; parts of the lands were resettled by Jewish immigrants, and the original inhabitants were not allowed to return there till now, even when security reasons became quite unimportant.

Needless to say, there were those who did not accept the Ben-Gurion premises – as they did not accept his basic alignment with the West in the wake of the Korean War. The most prominent of these were the left-wing groups – especially *Mapam* – as well as the Communists, who were reinforced by one of the most picturesque public figures, Moshe Sneh, the former great Zionist leader who came to Palestine from Poland to become the Head of Command of the *Hagana* (as distinct from the Military Chief of Staff, Yaacov Dori, who become the first Chief of Staff of the Israel Defence Army).

But the pro-Soviet orientation of these groups became, as we have seen, undermined and lost almost all legitimacy with the anti-Semitic trials at the end of the Stalin era, and with the disclosures of the Stalin atrocities by Krushchev at the 20th Congress of the Communist Party. Since then they remained a rather marginal – even if very vocal – element in the Israeli political spectrum, but of no influence either on policy-making or on wider public opinion.

There was, of course, intense opposition to Ben-Gurion within the Cabinet led by Moshe Sharett, the first Foreign Minister, who advocated a less aggressive stance and sought for some openings to the Arabs, and who often succeeded in having Ben-Gurion overruled in the Cabinet.

Ben-Gurion did in fact withdraw briefly from the Premiership in 1954 – when Sharett became Prime Minister and Pinhas Lavon the Defence Minister. But after the resignation of Lavon because of the famous 'mishap', Ben-Gurion returned as Defence Minister, and ultimately as Prime Minister forcing the resignation of Sharett in 1955. And ultimately, after Golda Meir became Foreign Minister, the Ben-Gurion conception of Israel's security reigned supreme, in fact till 1967, both under Ben-Gurion and, after his final withdrawal from political leadership, under Levi Eshkol. It seemed to be at least partially successful, in that they ensured the security of the borders and obtained enough international support – especially after the Sinai Campaign and the ultimate withdrawal of Israel from Sinai – if not to eliminate the Arab threat, at least to contain it, even if no such support could be obtained for the more ambitious aims of the Sinai Campaign.

# II · The Changing Format of Political Life in Israel

## Political Orientations, Organization and Mobilization
### *Multiple orientations, universalism and restrictive orientations*

The preceding analysis indicates that the political prototype of Israeli society greatly changed from that of the Yishuv, and that more extensive changes in the basic structure and premises of the political mould were continuously taking place in the format that initially developed in the State of Israel.

The establishment of the State transformed the former political voluntary pluralistic frameworks of the Yishuv into a uniform political framework on political sovereignty; and the leaders of the various pioneering movements, organizations and parties into a ruling elite. Concomitantly the various movements and sectors were incorporated into a highly bureacratized network, with the new centre becoming the principal focus of the power structure, the source of distribution of resources, and the focus of expanding and competing demands from the periphery.

At the same time the political fabric which developed within the framework of the basic parliamentary democratic State dominated by the ruling Labour party (*Mapai*) under the strong leadership of Ben-Gurion was shaped by a transformation of the Zionist vision in general and the Labour–Zionist in particular. This transformation was manifest in the shift from the combination of an ideology of national renaissance with a social, socialist or Labour one, carried out by a powerful sectarian and pioneering orientation, and organized in a semi-sectorial and consociational framework. Its place was taken by an ideology of national social ethos articulated within a constitutional democratic–pluralistic State, based on universalistic premises, universalistic citizenship and the access of all citizens to the major frameworks of the State.

This vision combined in a rather varied and complex – but seemingly very viable – way the major themes of the political culture that developed, as we have seen, in the Yishuv, but with some very significant transformations.

The older goals of the various movements and sectors – those of pioneering, of institution-building, of security – were transposed into the major goals of the State, those of ingathering of exiles, of development, of security and military strength, but they naturally persisted also in the different parties – especially in the Labour ones – and their different sectors.

But new orientations were also added and some old ones reinforced. First, and most important, was a strong etatist orientation, buttressed ideologically by Ben-Gurion's stress on *Mamlachtiut* (Statehood) and put into practice with such changes as a unified educational system with two streams, the general and the religious one; the taking out of the different pioneering youth movements from the schools; the development of the army military industries and defence establishments; the appropriation by them of the older security element or orientations, and the appropriation by the State – but also by the Histadrut – of the strong orientations to economic development.

Second there was the development of strong orientations to the formalization and strengthening of civility and of the rule of law. This orientation was evident in the growth of all-encompassing criteria of allocation in the State services; in such institutions as that of the State Comptroller and above all in the establishment and maintenance of the high prestige of the courts in general and the Supreme Court, especially when sitting as High Court of Justice (a process which started in the very first years of the State when the Court often ruled against the government).

The combination of a heritage of totalistic orientations of the different movements with the democratic–universalistic tendencies gave rise to continuous tension between strong regulative, restrictive policies and different more open democratic and universalistic ones.

Indeed, from the very beginning, several restrictions or limitations on the democratic functioning of the State were in existence – most evident in the institution of (military) censorship; in censorship on films and theatre productions vested in a special public authority; in restriction on movements of groups (especially Arabs); in the potential to arrest and hold people under special arrangements – all vested in the government by various mandatory laws and ordinances and usually justified by security reasons.

But even these restrictions could, and often were, reviewed by the courts and, even though the courts often upheld the actions invoking these ordinances, this did provide some – even if limited – safeguard against their too arbitrary use.

## Centralization of power

In order to understand both the initial continuity of this political mould and its ultimate decomposition with the loss by the Labour bloc of its supremacy in 1977, it is necessary to retrace our steps and analyse the forces which shaped the very crystallization of this initial mould and which also, as we shall see in greater detail later, unwillingly generated far-reaching dynamics and transformations within it.

As we have already indicated above, the establishment of the State of Israel constituted not only a major political and historical event, but also a turning-point in the development of the Yishuv's social structure.

All the processes of political transformation described earlier gave rise to far-reaching changes in the structure of the political mould – and they have also generated some of the basic tensions and later contradictions in the initial political mould that developed in Israel.

The crux of all these changes was in the transformation of the pattern that had been predominant in the period of Yishuv. Then the format had been of relatively highly ideological politics in which political bargaining and allocation were very closely related to ideological sectorial issues, and in which such bargaining between sectors and movements was connected with a relatively high degree of participation in each sector within the framework of a federative constitutional semi-constellational democratic format. The new profile was characterized by several new directions and contradictions: first by the development of broader universalistic premisses of the political framework, second by tensions or contradictions between some of the premisses of old and new mould, especially between its federative and centralized aspects; and third by tensions and contradictions between the more universalistic and open premisses of this framework and the strong regulative control and paternalistic orientations of the ruling elite.

Thus, first of all, there occurred a weakening and transformation of the pluralistic structures that existed among the different sectors of the Jewish pre-State Yishuv and a growing unification and centralization of services under the aegis of the State organization.

Truly enough, in some sense, the federal arrangements between the different sectors of the society – the private, the Histadrut, the various political parties, and, with the establishment of the State, the newly emerging government sector (especially the various government corporations) – were even strengthened. The many resources of the State – and of the Jewish Agency through which a large part of the funds was channelled, and often the new immigrants themselves – were allocated on a corporate basis among the major political groups and parties.

In a parallel manner, the different ministries and their administrative services were initially divided – and continued to be so – on a coalition basis between the different parties, according to an electoral system of proportional representation.

However, though such distribution, according to federative arrangements, persisted strongly in the Yishuv and for some period even became enhanced in the State, yet there developed crucial differences in comparison with the former period. Most of the parties or movements lost their independent access to 'outside' resources – be they money or manpower – and these were channelled mostly through the organs of the State or Jewish Agency apparatus. Within the party it was the leadership and apparatus that predominated and acted as mediator in the relations between these resources and the broader groups, sectors and movements.

As a result of these processes the whole format of the relations between the State and different sectors of society as compared with the period of the Yishuv, greatly changed. Many groups – above all the new immigrants, the younger generations, but even older members of various sectors – were transformed from members of relatively independent movements, organized in sectors with autonomous access to the major centres of power and resources, into more dependent members of clientelistic networks and frameworks. This gave rise for the first time in the history of the Jewish settlement to the emergence of a sharp and marked distinction between centre and periphery, and shaped at least initially, the relations between the two in a clientelistic mode and the development of the above-mentioned paternalistic policies.

The development of such paternalistic policies was initially at least greatly facilitated by the incorporation of politically inexperienced elements – without, however, enabling them autonomous access to the centres of power – and by the growing economic expansion, contrary to the 'open' universalistic premises of its legitimation, continuing the more particularistic norms of the movements.

## Universalistic orientations

Closely related to this growing centralization of power in the hands of the State – but also in potential contradiction to it – was the development of the universalistic frameworks of the State, all of them based on the premises of universal citizenship and a democratic form of government, and on strong emphasis on the universalistic premises of the State. One root of this development lay in a rather paradoxical process which enabled the central leadership of the different parties ruling the State and, in particular, that of the Labour Party, to weaken the various sectarian tendencies and movement components of their parties, and the autonomous access of these sectors to the centres of power and of control of resources and which initially enabled, as we shall see in greater detail later on, the development of clientelistic politics. But at the same time these developments also forged out more universalistic premises which guided many of the institutions of the State.

The first most important such institutional derivative was the establishment of widespread administrative services of the State, the access to which was based on universalistic premises. While clientelistic intercessions naturally also developed within large parts of these administrations, they could very quickly become dissociated from those of the parties, and the very multiplicity of such relations weakened not only any such single network, but also the whole clientelistic mode of policies.

## Establishment of the rule of law

The universalistic and civic orientations of the State were also reinforced by the continuous growth of the prestige and strength of the legal institutions. The court system in general and the Supreme Court in particular (especially when sitting as High Court of Justice) acquired an almost unprecedented prestige and standing – closely akin to the US Supreme Court – as a place of resource against government decisions in general and those impinging on civil and political freedom in particular.

Thus, to give only one such illustration from many, when in November 1969 Mrs Meir attempted, giving in to the pressure of the religious parties, to postpone the transmission of television services on Saturday, these were reinstalled by the order of the Court.

While being usually scrupulous not to impinge on the various decision-making prerogatives of the State, from the very beginning of the State it often ruled against many seemingly arbitrary decisions of the government in general and later, after the Six Day War, of the military government in the West Bank in particular. The 'order nisi' (*Bagaz* in Hebrew) has become one of the constant features of the Israeli public scene.

Two additional important aspects of the strength of the legal system were the institution of the Attorney General as well as that of Legal Inquiry Commissions, two of which at least – the Agranat Commission established in 1974 after the Yom Kippur War and the Kahan Commission established in 1983 after the Sabra and Shatila massacres during the Lebanon War – had a far-reaching impact on the political life in Israel.

## Weakening of movements; oligarchic tendencies

The changes – and contradictory tendencies – in the political mould also gave rise to changes in the format of political organizations, of political mobilization and of the decision-making process.

The setting up of such universalistic framework enabled first of all the central leadership of different parties in general, and that of the Labour Party in particular, to weaken the different sectarian tendencies, movements and components of their parties, and the autonomous access of these sectors to the centres of power and of control of resources.

Consequently, in all the parties – but above all in those of the ruling coalitions – there developed a very far-reaching weakening of the access of broader groups to the respective centres of power and of major decision-making. These latter became organized on semi-oligarchic principles, restricted to the small groups.

Participation in the centres of power within the coalition parties – especially the Labour and the religious ones – became more and more limited, highly controlled by the central oligarchies and by professional or semi-professional party 'activists' – whose major source of income was indeed party activity (membership in the Knesset, in the various bureaucracies of the Histadrut or in the parties themselves) – thus continuing a trend which started, as we have seen, in the Yishuv.

Concomitantly there developed a rather far-reaching change in the whole structure of the elite and leadership in general, and of the relation between them and the political process and participation in particular. In most of the older parties the relative closure in semi-oligarchic groups extended to second and third level echelons of political professionals which naturally became very dependent on the centre of the party.

These echelons of political activists were not on the whole among the more active autonomous elements of the population; many of the more active ones went, and were encouraged by the central elite to go, in other directions – to the army, academic institutions and economic life – and these echelons were dependent on the central elites who thus strengthened their control over access to participation in the centre. Very few avenues of autonomous political expression and organization were opened up for many younger or new immigrant elements. On the whole the centres of the parties attempted to control most such activities, not allowing much direct autonomous expression or organization. On the local level they pursued a policy of co-optation. Later on these developed co-optation from above, especially from among the military, usually with little direct political experience and little autonomous access. Thus in most parties there developed a process of atrophization of the internal party-political process in general and of the selection of the political leadership in particular, gradually weakening also the internal solidarity and even self-assurance of the leaderships of many of the parties.

## Patterns of allocation of resources and bargaining

Parallelly political mobilization, mobilization of political support, became more and more based on some combination between co-optation and allocations of resources and intensive bargaining over them.

Within most of the parties there developed a tendency of increased bargaining over the allocation of the major resources without either access of broader groups to the centres and/or direct relation to more ideological issues. The bargaining over resources took place in various party and state channels, dissociated from any ideological orientation, and was indeed perceived as such by broader strata of the population – with the possible exception of the central elites which, while of course exercising and attempting to control such allocation, viewed it as mostly technical matters in service of the broad goals and ideology of the State.

The most extreme type of such allocations and bargaining could be seen in the initial stages of the absorption of immigrants – when votes were directly or indirectly bought through allocation, or promise of allocation, of work, housing and so on. Later on more subtle mechanisms developed and at the same time, however, the growth of State services with their universalistic premises gradually weakened the strength and acceptance of many of these practices.

There developed, however, some crucial differences between the development of this mode of political mobilization within the older and newer sectors of the population. In the older, as well as among some sectors of new immigrants, not only among those coming from the Western but also from the Oriental sector, this atrophization of political activities was connected, especially for the more active elements, with very far-reaching and successful social mobility, of opening up new vistas of activity in the newly developing institutional areas – in the army, in the economic and academic life, and in close social relation to the establishment. Such mobility was more limited, although certainly not absent, among many sectors of immigrants – although here there developed a sense of distance from the centre.

The structure of political participation in the oppositionary parties was more varied. Among the 'older' bourgeois parties, such as the General Zionists, the developments were not very different; the old leadership evinced smaller cohesiveness and there was lesser dependence on the centres of the parties and a lesser professionalization of the middle- and lower-party echelons.

In *Herut*, which had at its disposal much fewer resources of allocation, an oligarchic structure at the centre became connected with principled openness to participation in different political frameworks of the party.

Of course all these tendencies had their roots in the period of the Yishuv, but in that period they were on the whole overshadowed by the stronger participation of broader strata in the centres of the various sectors, as well as by the existence of a more autonomous access of these sectors to the common federative consociational central frameworks. It was the structural and organizational developments attendant on the establishment of the State of Israel and the developments which we have analysed above that weakened the more autonomous and ideological orientations and hence reinforced the strength of orientation to power and allocation over resources and gave rise to continuous struggle over allocation of resources – a struggle undertaken in a great variety of modes.

The existing parties were not able to control or regulate these developments from their respective centres, according to the older premises – whether those of the movements/parties in the period of the Yishuv or the more oligarchic ones of the first decade or so of the State.

Powerful lobbies cutting across parties – such as the agricultural lobby – developed; within parties many sub-groups and cliques developed contending in the various committees of the Knesset or in relation to different ministries. The mere development of such cliques and lobbies was of course a natural trend – the roots of which were to be found in the former times – but there was a growing unruliness of such groups, and a growing difficulty of the parties to regulate them, or even in fact their respective parliamentary sections.

Thus there indeed developed multiple types of political organization – the clientelistic one as well as more open ones – based on intensive bargaining, around different specific issues, with but little integration in ideological settings or even party frameworks.*

Such political bargaining became more and more orientated toward safeguarding the positions of power of the existing frameworks, and was guided more by internal dynamism of the various power groups and by continuously shifting interest groups and lobbies, and less by the ideological impulses orientated towards the realization of the initial ideology in whose name the ruling group claimed to be ruling and the basic premises of which new sectors of the population accepted.

Side by side with these changes was the increased importance of mass media

* Yael Azmon, 'The 1981 Elections and the Changing Fortunes of Israeli Labor Party', *Government and Opposition*, 16, 4 (1981), pp. 432–46.

in general, and of television in particular, as arenas of political debate and appeal, and the closely related strengthening of populistic appeals.

# Changing Modes of Political Organization and Activities; Continuity of the Political Mould
## *The conditions and predominance of the Labour Party*

All these far-reaching changes in political structure, organization and behaviour, which gathered momentum after the Six Day War, were yet, perhaps rather paradoxically, connected with the continuity of the basic political mould in general and with the continuous predominance of the Labour Party as the major dominant political force in the construction of all the government coalitions and in controlling the rules of the political game and the conditions of access to the centres of political power.

The central focus of such continuity was, of course, rooted in the capacity of the Labour, specifically of the *Mapai* (later of the *Maarach* (Alignment)) leadership to rule effectively.

The capacity of *Mapai* and later of the Labour alignment to rule effectively was dependent on three basic conditions. First, was its ability to maintain through its influence on the government, the Histadrut, and the various regulative policies of the government its controlling position in the economy. Second, was its ability to use this power for general economic expansion and development and to assure a continuous rise in the standard of living. Third, was the internal cohesion of its leadership, so that political decisions would be implemented and regulated in face of the diverse and often contradictory pressures of the varied population groups.

As long as these conditions were fulfilled *Mapai* – or the Labour camp – was able to maintain its effective rule and central political position. It was within its central committees that major shifts of policy in the economic, security or educational fields were thrashed out and settled. In such cases all other parties acted as pressure groups or catalysts of the different forces within *Mapai*.

From this point of view it is very significant that on almost all major issues the other parties were usually relatively more homogeneous and unified than *Mapai*, within which a greater variety of attitudes could be found and brought under one, even if really very heterogeneous, umbrella.

Furthermore, no matter how great the opposition to *Mapai* from other parties on any specific issue, such opposition was never unified over any length of time over a broad range of issues, and even changes in the coalition patterns were not always fully indicative of some major shifts of policy.

Although significant changes in economic, social or immigration policy did occur, they were not necessarily proclaimed in the electioneering campaigns, nor even always fully debated in public. The actual development of such policies was usually worked out by mutual adjustment of various interests – especially within *Mapai* and through the pressures of different other factors on groups within *Mapai* – thus reinforcing its predominance in the Yishuv's and in Israel's political system.

Throughout most of the period of its dominance (till at least the early 1960s) *Mapai* – and later on the Labour bloc – combined cohesive leadership, with great flexibility and ability to adjust, through introduction of many new policies, to changing circumstances. These capacities, however, seemed to weaken gradually from the early 1960s, paradoxically, together with the opening up of the initial institutional mould of the State, leading ultimately to the loss of predominance in the 1977 elections.

## Weakening and rifts

Such weakening, which took place, significantly enough, with the continuous opening up of the more restrictive aspects of the initial political mould, was first of all connected with rifts and changes in *Mapai* and in its relations to other groups of the 'leftist' Labour bloc. These changes underlined the weakening of the central core of *Mapai* and of the upper echelons of its leadership *vis-à-vis* other parts of the Labour movement, as well as in the frameworks of the coalition – in comparison with the relationship which had been characteristic from the late 1930s on under the leadership of Ben-Gurion.

The first and possibly most important of these developments was the rift which started to develop relatively early, although it only became viable towards the late 1950s, between the older guard of *Mapai*, to some degree centred around the Histadrut, and younger groups with more technocratic orientations connected with Ben-Gurion and to no small degree encouraged and sponsored by him. Many of these latter younger elements – the most conspicuous among them being Moshe Dayan and Shimon Peres – were centred around the army and the defence establishments. They were sponsored by Ben-Gurion as carriers of the new, dynamic, etatist orientation, of the ideology of *Mamlachtiut*, and of attempts to break through the older, seemingly conservative, 'frozen' leadership of the party and of other leftist parties. At the same time they were almost without any party political experience.

Out of these rifts came the establishment in 1965 by Ben-Gurion of a split party – *Rafi* (The List of Israeli Workers). The events leading to this event were related to Ben-Gurion's ultimate resignation in 1963, which was in a way the apex of developments around the Lavon affair and was indicative of the extensive changes and rifts within *Mapai*.

Ultimately in 1968 these different elements were reunited, together with *Ahdut Haavoda* which had split from the left *Mapam* in 1954, but many of the rifts of the early and mid-1960s were to continue for a long time.

The basic justification for these developments was the attempt of the older leadership of *Mapai*, especially perhaps of Eshkol, to unify and strengthen the Labour camp, but in fact the united party was already much weaker and less cohesive. In fact, however, electorally there took place a certain weakening of the total left bloc. But even more important was the fact that the search for such unification and its ideology was connected with the strengthening of the more leftist groups of *Rafi* in relation to the central *Mapai* sector, often giving these groups the former semi-veto powers within the new alignment, weakening the decision-making capacities of the central political leadership.

This relative weakening of the strength and acceptability of *Mapai* leadership was perhaps best seen on the eve of the Six Day War when Levi Eshkol, the Prime Minister, had against his will, but under the pressure of both the leader of the National Religious party and public opinion – to some degree organized by *Rafi* – to co-opt into the government Moshe Dayan (who belonged in that period to *Rafi*) as Minister of Defence (thus giving up himself this portfolio) as well as Menahem Begin and E. Rimalt representing a new political bloc *Gahal* (*Gush Herut-Liberalim*).

This weakness of the central *Mapai* leadership, and the *de facto* veto powers of *Ahdut Haavoda* or *Rafi* blocs, became most evident, as we shall see in greater detail later on, in the search for military or political solutions after the Six Day War.

## *The break-up of the initial political mould*

While the specific events before the Six Day War were to some degree related to Eshkol's own personality and to the long period of waiting and seeming hesitancy between the closure of the Straits of Tiran by Nasser in May 1967 and the outbreak of the war, yet in fact they signalled a very far-reaching change in the Israeli political scene – namely not only the weakening of the *Mapai* leadership but also the end of the delegitimation of *Herut* initiated by Ben-Gurion.

The end of this delegitimation had in a way started earlier in 1965 when Eshkol, contrary to Ben-Gurion, made a symbolic gesture of passing a government resolution to bring back the remnants of Jabotinsky's body on the twenty-eighth anniversary of his death to be buried in a State ceremony in Mount Herzl. (Jabotinski had stated in his will that his body should be interred in the Diaspora until the Government of the Jewish State would bring it to the Land of Israel.)

But while this could be seen as a symbolic gesture, in line with the general ópening up of the political mould under the leadership of Eshkol, much more important in this context was the establishment in 1965 of a new political bloc – that of *Gahal*. The very establishment of this new bloc, which later in 1973 was expanded to Likud (comprising also some elements from *Rafi*), was an important turning-point in the development of the Israeli political scene and it signalled – because it changed the basic nature of oppositionary politics in Israel – the beginning of the decomposition of the older political mould. It changed the nature of oppositionary politics in Israel by uniting two political forces which till then had been separated not only by political organization but by their very standing within the framework of the dominant political mould or system.

Electorally, initially, these two parts of the new bloc could be seen as almost equal, but in fact it was the *Herut*, under the leadership of Menahem Begin, which managed to neutralize most of the older Revisionist elements, which became more dynamic, giving rise to a strong push to electoral trends to be discussed shortly and which left its basic stamp – strongly national 'rightist' and populist – on the whole format of the new oppositionary politics.

The very joining of these two parties into a unified political bloc (they had remained as separate parties till this very date) necessarily signalled the first breakthrough of the informal but very strong political boundaries of the regnant political framework and mould.

The actualization of these potentialities became possible with the gathering momentum of the electoral trends (which began to be discernible and analysed by social scientists in the mid-1960s and gathered full momentum in the 1977 and 1981 elections*) in close connection with the changes in the Labour camp which were connected with far-reaching changes in the whole format of Israeli society.

But before these events there was an intensification of the various processes of change in the political mould which are analysed above, giving rise to varied conflicts, debates and discussions, above all in the newspapers and media. It was not only protest that was widespread – but also, as we shall see in greater detail, a growing importance of extra-parliamentary movements in Israeli politics.

Growing political fragmentation developed, with a concomitant feeling of the lack of the ability of the parties' leaderships to control them. Very often the lack of such political ability was evident in the abdication of many political decisions (such as those dealing with changes of tax system or even those related to aspects of foreign affairs, or to legal authorities – especially the Attorney-General) or public commissions proclaiming as it were their superiority to the political channels proper.

All these developments could easily – especially with hindsight – be interpreted as indicative of a basic weakness of the initial political mould of Israeli society. But although, needless to say, there existed a widespread awareness of all these different problems, for a very long time (until, as we shall see, several years after the Yom Kippur War), they were not seen as invalidating or undermining the existing institutional mould. In many ways they were seen not only as generated by the mould but also as seemingly becoming contained within its premises. Indeed, the viability of the basic institutional moulds that developed in this period seemed also perhaps paradoxically, but in reality quite naturally, to be reinforced by the fact that these moulds were never entirely homogeneous; that there developed within them continuous ideological–political conflicts, disputes and new trends; that

---

* Indeed in many ways the establishment of the Rabin Government in 1974 could be seen as the first signal of the loss by the Labour Party of its assured place as the dominant party.

the level of political discussions and debates was always quite intensive; and that there were often government crises – all of these attesting to the basic democratic nature of the State.

# CHAPTER 9

# Political Economy and Strata Formation

## I · The Development of the Settlement Map in Israel, 1948–82 (by A. Schachar and E. Razin)

### Introduction
### *The settlement map at the time of the establishment of the State*

Before proceeding to the analysis of the mould of political economy that has developed in Israel, we shall first present a brief outline of the development of the settlement map of Israel, which will provide us with a description of the physical background of economic development.

Basic transformations have occurred in the settlement map of Israel since the establishment of the State, as a result of the policy initiated by the government and by basic demographic trends. These transformations were part of the basic processes of changes taking place in the geographic settlement of Eretz Israel in the last century, as a result of Zionist settlement on the land.

The map of Jewish settlement in Eretz Israel until 1948, as basically planned, included the three large cities of Tel Aviv, Jerusalem and Haifa, hundreds of small rural settlements and an almost total lack of medium-sized Jewish provincial towns. To a large extent, this disposition resulted from the Zionist pioneering ideology which was predominant among the Zionist organizations at the time of the mandate. This ideology viewed negatively, at most neutrally, the urban way of life and stressed the modes of co-operative rural settlement as being the most desirable and best-suited method of bringing about the main goal of the conquest of the land. Attempts to combine pioneering and socialist ideals were indeed made, as we have seen, among the urban workers, through the construction of workers' housing in the periphery of the large cities, but no global urban settlement policy was initiated. The lack of such a policy resulted in the concentration of urban growth almost entirely at the time of the mandate, in the three large cities, especially in Tel Aviv. At the same time however, at the end of the mandatory period there took place, as a consequence of the processes of urbanization which then began in most of the veteran villages (Moshavot), the creation of medium-sized towns in the coastal plain in 1948.

In 1948 approximately 80 per cent of the Jewish population lived in the area of the coastal plain, the major part residing in the section stretching from Tel Aviv to Haifa. The percentage of the Jewish population residing in urban settlements reached, that year, approximately 74 per cent, 78 per cent of which lived in the three large cities. At the time of the establishment of the State, a continuous sequence of settlements, roughly in the form of a capital N, stood out in the dispersal of the rural settlements. This continuity of settlements extended from Metullah, in the north, to the Beth Shean Valley, from there to the Jezreel Valley, on to the Haifa and Western Galilee areas and, thence, southward, to the Judean Valley and the Northern Negev. This distribution of Jewish settlements determined, to a great extent, but not entirely, the frontiers of the State, as they were drawn in 1948-9.

# Spatial Policies in the State of Israel
## *Ideological orientations*

The transformation of the map of settlements in Israel since 1948 has resulted largely from the policy of population dispersal, which has been one of the central goals of the State since its establishment. The aims of this policy were, in the main, political and security-minded, but the aspect of economic planning was also well in evidence. A number of conditions were instrumental in facilitating the application of this policy: first, the massive immigration, which made it easier to determine the place of settlement than would have been the case in the transplantation of population from one region to another; second, the rapid growth of the Israeli economy in the first twenty-five years, as a dynamic and developing economy made it easier to induce such structural changes; third, the very important role played by the government and other public bodies in the Israeli economy in general and the development activities in particular, which were to a great extent financed by public funds, the majority of which were channelled into the country from abroad through the government and the national institutions.

The means used by the government for the dispersal of the population included directing the residence of the immigrants, the construction of public housing and of an economic base, the allocation of national land, the grant of personal incentives and channelling the investments of the private sector.

By the time the State was established, the agricultural sector was well organized to cope with the planning and implementation of the policy of spatial settlement on a wide scale. By 1948-9, over 100 agricultural settlements had already been founded. The main innovations in this settlement operation consisted of penetrating the areas of the Upper Galilee and in the Jerusalem Corridor, in which Arab villages had been abandoned, and in assigning thousands of new immigrant families, who had no previous agricultural training, to rural settlements. The accelerated operations in the field of agricultural settlement proceeded in the first half of the 1950s, the prevailing type among the new settlements being the co-operative village (Moshav Ovdim) which, more than the Kibbutz, suited the social background of the new immigrants. The agricultural settlement was partly directed to the coastal plain but mainly to the new areas opened up to settlement, southwards in the Northern Negev, in the Acre Plain, in the Judean Mountains and in Galilee. In the second half of the 1950s, the rate of settlement slowed down considerably, due, mainly, to lack of land and water resources, and more stress was then laid on urban settlement.

## Shift from rural to urban sectors – new development towns

The shift of emphasis from rural to urban settlement was not caused by a change in ideology of the institutions dealing with settlement, but by necessity deriving from the impossibility of absorbing the major part of the massive immigration in the agricultural sector. The first stage in the process of decentralizing the urban development consisted of populating the abandoned towns and villages with Jews. This stage was already completed by the first half of 1949. The second stage, which lasted until 1951, consisted of the absorption of immigrants in the settlements and villages of the coastal plain. The construction of new urban centres started in 1950, the planning of the layout and size of the towns taking the following objectives into account: first, the settlement of unpopulated and border areas, in accordance with political, security and economic considerations governing the dispersal of population; second, the transformation of the polarized structure of the urban system, by filling out the missing echelons of the urban hierarchy and by the creation of regional systems which would include urban centres to service the rural hinterland. The programme aimed at the establishment of a hierarchy of settlements comprising a number of echelons, the majority of the new towns being intended to fill the missing lower echelons of the urban hierarchy.

The process of building the new towns and directing the settling of immigrants therein, proceeded at a rapid rate from 1950 to 1956 and ended with the foundation of Arad, in 1962, and of Carmiel, in 1964. During that period, entirely new towns were established. However, a number of abandoned towns or urban nuclei which already existed – such as Tiberias, Afula, Beth Shean, Ashkelon and Beersheva – can also be regarded, to some degree at least, as 'new towns' as the extent of the construction then added to them far exceeded the size of the original nucleus.

The achievements in populating the new towns were considerable, but, in contrast to the quantitative accomplishments, the problems in relation to the functioning of the new urban centres and their social stability were still unresolved. According to Cohen, the lack of experience in urban planning of the institutions dealing with settlement resulted in numerous mistakes being made when establishing the new towns. Errors were made in planning the size of the towns, in their siting and in insufficient attention being paid to the social aspect.* The agricultural emphasis of the ideology led to stress being laid on small urban settlements and to a reluctance to plan large cities. In their first years of existence, the new towns were thus given a rural character – low density of building with adjacent auxiliary farms. This considerably hampered the development of these towns: the town residents consequently had a lower social status, and did not enjoy the same prestige as did the inhabitants of the border villages. The institutions dealing with the social planning concentrated their efforts on the agricultural settlements and the new development towns drew relatively little attention in this field. The implementation of the aim of regional integration, the development towns functioning as centres for their hinterland, met with difficulties. The veteran rural co-operative settlements (Moshavim) were more developed, economically and culturally, than the development towns and were united in strong countrywide organizations and, consequently, did not need the development towns. The new towns succeeded, to a certain extent, in becoming centres, mainly in the south of the country, where new rural settlements had also been founded without a stable base. In the course of time, however, certain relations were established between the development towns and their agricultural hinterland, and assumed, in some functional aspects, a definite service role. It can generally be said that the development towns made possible the quantitative implementation of the policy of dispersal of population. However, their very foundation led them to constitute, as we shall see in greater detail later, an economic and social periphery, and not only a spatial one, according to the original goal on which their establishment had been based in the Negev and in Galilee.

## Regional plans

During the 1950s, the lessons drawn from the accumulated experience gained in the establishment of the first development towns and immigrant villages (Moshavim) were learned. A central attempt to implement these lessons was made when planning settlement of the Lachish Region, in the Northern Negev. There, for the first time, comprehensive regional planning was applied, combining the urban and rural systems, and a single administrative framework was established to deal with the settlement of the region. The settlement systems in the Lachish Region was planned as a hierarchy comprising three echelons: the village, the rural centre and the provincial town – Kiryat Gat. An experiment was initiated in that region to combine veteran Israelis with settlers

* E. Cohen, 'The Town in Zionist Ideology', Papers of the Dept of Sociology of the Hebrew University (1970).

who were mainly new immigrants. In general, the Lachish Region constituted a story of success, although the ideal of regional integration was not entirely implemented. The division of the region into areas under local government was not according to the original intentions. Kiryat Gat was granted the status of independent local council, separate from the region, and the limits of the local councils were not determined according to the spatial principles on which the planning of that region had been based. The relative success of Kiryat Gat emphasized the great importance attached to controlling the populating process of development towns and, principally, to the creation of a strong absorbing nucleus of stable population in the first years of existence of a town. These lessons were applied in Upper Nazareth and, mainly, in Arad and Carmiel.

The severe economic and social problems which befell the majority of the development towns led to changes of the urban spatial policy during the 1960s. It was decided not to establish additional new towns and to consolidate the existing ones by increasing their population and developing their sources of employment, mainly in industry. Several strategies were devised in those years. One approach dealt with the need for the development towns to reach a certain minimal size – the 'take-off point' – from which they would be able to evolve on their own. A second approach advocated the need to concentrate efforts on a small number of 'axes of growth' having good potential for development. In practice, these strategies were not clearly implemented and, following the Six Day War, the emphasis shifted, to a certain extent, to the problem of populating Jerusalem and to settlement beyond the Green Line, the borders of the State of Israel until 1967.

## Changes in the Settlement System after 1967
### *The Six Day and Yom Kippur Wars*

The Six Day War transformed the map of the border areas of Israel and resulted in shifting the emphases of the national spatial policies. There was no declared detailed policy regarding the dispersal of population in the territories conquered during the war, but the general principle, which dictated the shaping of the settlement map until the change of governments in 1977, were known as the 'Alon Plan'. In those years stress was placed on the accelerated development of Jerusalem and on settlement in the Jordan Valley, the Golan Heights and the Rafah Region. The new border areas were mainly populated with veteran settlers through the establishment of NAHAL settlements, Kibbutzim and various urban centres. In addition to these areas, Gush Etzion south of Jerusalem (all lost to the Arabs in the War of Independence), as well as Solomon's Region, along the Gulf of Eilat, were also settled. The main innovation in settling the border areas after 1967, the settlement of which was planned and implemented until 1977, was the urban element included in it, accompanied by comprehensive regional settlement. The town of Katzrin as well as two regional centres were built in the Golan Heights. In the Jordan Valley, the area centre Ma'ale Ephraim was founded and Yamit in the Rafah Region.

## New settlement policies in Judea and Samaria

The political changes which took place in Israel as a result of the Yom Kippur War and, mainly, since the changeover of governments in 1977, influenced to no small degree the development of settlement, and the stress was laid on settling the Judea and Samaria areas, which have a dense Arab population. In the past few years, the trend has been shifting towards effecting a basic change in the Jewish settlement system in Eretz Israel through the accelerated settlement of Judea and Samaria. This is based on the establishment of settlements which form part of the enlarged metropolises of Tel Aviv and Jerusalem, as well as of settlements in more distant areas in Judea and Samaria mainly by *Gush Emunim* members who feel strong ideological obligations to settle the whole of Eretz Israel. The new non-agricultural settlement of Judea and Samaria is characterized by relatively numerous small settlements, it being planned that only a few of them would become towns on a significant scale. The characteristics of the Judea and Samaria settlers differed from the ones of the people who, in previous years, had settled in the development towns, established within the borders of the State of Israel. The prominent distinctive features of the Judea and Samaria settlers were their high level of education, a low proportion of people of Asian–African origin and relatively large households. The majority of these settlers were orthodox and the secular sector tended to settle almost solely in places within commuting distance from the Tel Aviv metropolis or the Jerusalem one.

The types of traditional pioneering settlement – the Moshav and the Kibbutz – did not always suit the character of the settlers of the 1970s or the economic base of the settlements. Some new types of rural settlements developed therefore after the end of the 1960s, the most prevalent of which was the community settlement, which was a flexible type, enabling the settler to enjoy great independence and relatively little reliance on the co-operative union. This type of settlement is well accepted by the new settlers in Judea and Samaria and suited to the *Gush Emunim* members and to those settlers of the 'periphery villages' in Western Samaria who do not possess, as a rule, a co-operative ideology. This form of settlement is not bound by a co-operative ideology and a certain economic base, and allows the residents to commute to the large cities. The industrial village is another new form of settlement – a sort of co-operative rural village to be established in areas with poor land and water reserves – a community settlement or co-operative Moshav (Moshav Shitufi) with an economic–industrial base, the accepted planning conception being that these villages would be established in areas, each of which already comprises between five and eight settlements. An additional new type of settlement is the *Mitzpeh* (Temporary Village) which is intended to hold government land in

Galilee by settling in dominant points, the investment in the primary stage being relatively small and an economic base not having to be provided to the settlement.

# Sources of Population Growth in Different Areas
## *Immigration*

The settlement policies changed the whole spatial aspect of Israel, not only that of rural settlements and development towns but also of the urban sectors. However, before describing these changes in the urban sectors, it might be worthwhile to analyse briefly the sources of population growth in the different areas as they acted in conjunction with these policies.

Three components influenced the shaping of the dispersal of Jewish population in Israel: outside migration (immigration and out-migration); natural growth, and internal migration. In the first years of the existence of the State, the model of the first settlement of immigrants assumed a decisive importance in shaping the process of population dispersal. Immigration constituted a main component in the comprehensive growth of the population of Israel and the government exercised considerable influence in channelling the immigrants to the various areas of the country. When the flow of immigration decreased, the importance of the other two components grew, especially that of the internal inter-regional migration, which assumed considerable proportions.

No precise data are available on the sources of population growth in the various areas of the country between 1948 and 1955. During that period, immigration constituted the dominant component in the growth of the population. It seems that the channelling of the immigrants was of significant scale, but that some of the settlers later shifted their place of residence, the internal migration being directed from the village to the city and from the periphery to the centre. Between 1948 and 1951, while the major part of the immigration was still absorbed in the central areas of Israel, only around 11 per cent of the immigrants were being integrated in the new towns, some of which were situated in the centre of the country. But as from 1952 the new towns started to absorb some 30 per cent of the annual immigration and the process of populating the peripheral areas thus became significant.

In the second half of the 1950s immigration also constituted the chief component of the population growth in the development areas and it appears that the main variable which can explain the annual change in population dispersal during the 1950s and 1960s was the percentage of new immigrants in the overall population growth of that particular year. The directing of immigrants towards their primary settlement in development towns diminished in the 1960s. This resulted, first of all, from the decrease in immigration and also from a change occurring towards the second half of the 1960s in the composition of the immigration – namely a reduction in the proportion of immigrants of European and American origin who were not easily amenable to such direction. The decrease of the immigration into Israel in the 1960s and the greater difficulty in channelling the immigrants to the development areas thus constituted the central factors which caused the cessation of the process of population dispersal at that time.

## Natural growth

A second source of population growth which influenced the shaping of the population dispersal process was natural growth. It generally contributed to the dispersal of population in the 1950s, as a result of differences in age structure and origin of the population in the various regions. The natural growth of the Jews in the southern district, in the first half of the 1950s, was more than double the country's average and in the northern district it was higher by some 50 per cent. The contribution of natural growth to population dispersal diminished in the 1960s, because of a decrease in the proportions of natural growth in the peripheral regions although they still remained higher there than in the central district. It should, however, be specifically mentioned that the proportions of natural growth were especially high in the development towns.

The main component influencing the shaping of the dispersal of Jewish population in Israel since the 1960s has been internal migration. The development towns already presented a high negative balance of migration in the 1950s, and between 1956 and 1961; in the 1960s it occurred mainly in the northern district. Conversely, the southern district showed a positive balance of migration, mainly owing to the positive balance of some towns in that district (principally Ashdod and Beersheva). In the 1950s and 1960s internal migration meant that the centre of gravity of the Jewish population in Israel shifted southwards, and the population centralized in the centre of the country. For the purpose of analyzing the trends of change in the spatial disposition of the inter-regional migration in Israel, the spatial structure of Israel can be presented as being made up of areas of nuclei and peripheries. The principal nucleus – the natural area of Tel Aviv – shifted from having a high positive balance of migration in the 1960s to a negative balance in the second half of the 1970s. The place of the primary nucleus as the main focus of attraction in Israel was filled by the peripheral area of the principal nucleus – Rishon Lezion, Petah Tiqua and Kfar Saba. This area, which, in 1961, showed a negative balance of migration, started in the mid-1960s to present a positive one, the components of which gradually increased with time. The peripheral areas of the Tel Aviv metropolis were, thus, the ones that became, in the 1970s, the main beneficiaries of the inter-regional migration currents, the major part of the migrants settling there coming from the inner towns of the metropolis. The area between the nuclei, which comprised the Sharon Valley, the Judean Valley and the Lachish Region, also shifted from a negative balance of migration in the 1960s to a positive one in the mid-1970s. This change was caused by the increased power of attraction of the areas of Hedera, Netanya, Rehovot and Ashdod. The subsidiary nuclei – the areas of Jerusalem, Haifa and Beersheva – shifted from a positive balance of migration in the 1960s to a negative one in the 1970s. It is thus apparent that the towns having second importance in the urban hierarchy of Israel do not constitute an alternative central objective for the migrants coming from the main nucleus and cannot compete against the towns in the periphery of the Tel Aviv metropolis. The area of the national periphery – the northern and southern districts – showed a high negative balance of migration throughout the 1960s and 1970s. It is too early to estimate the influence of the spatial policy of the first years of the 1980s on the currents of internal migration, but it is possible to assume that the attraction of the metropolises will persist, and that the main nucleus and the subsidiary ones will lose population to the benefit of their surrounding areas – including those of Judea and Samaria surrounding Jerusalem, that of Western Samaria in the vicinity of the Tel Aviv metropolis and the hilly area east of the Haifa metropolis.

# Changes in the Urban System in Israel
## Development of a metropolitan ring

The policy of population dispersal and the establishment of the new towns relieved the pressure on the central areas of the country, but did not prevent the rapid growth of the Tel Aviv and other metropolises. The built-up area of Tel Aviv grew rapidly after the establishment of the State and a continuity of built-up areas was formed, comprising Tel Aviv and the towns of the inner-ring of the metropolis: Ramat Gan, Givatayim, Bnei Brak, Holon and Bat-Yam. The city of Tel Aviv, which had grown very fast until the establishment of the State, developed more slowly in the 1950s and, in the middle of the 1960s, its population size started to decrease, a process which has continued up to the present time. In the 1950s and 1960s, the major part of the increase in population occurred in the inner ring of the metropolis. A second ring of smaller urban settlements started to evolve, like Kiryat Ono, Yahud, Savion and Ramat Hasharon, which, although they did not form a continuity of built-up area with Tel Aviv, were still integrated in its systems of urban transport-ation, employment and recreation. It is possible to trace in this ring the start of the phenomenon of the formation of suburbs, having a high level of construction with low density of housing, like Savion, Neveh Magen, etc. It should be mentioned that, contrary to the Western urban experience, the middle-class residents were not the only ones who went to inhabit the suburbs of the Tel Aviv metropolis, seeking low-density residential conditions and high quality of life. The characteristics of the housing and the residents of the suburbs of the Tel Aviv metropolis are variable and include, among others, workers' quarters which had been built before the establishment of the State, as well as new immigrants' housing, built after 1948 in the peripheries of the cities. The suburbs comprise a variegated population of all levels of the socio-economic status, the middle class of Israel not showing a strong inclination to settle in the suburbs.

## Growth of the outer ring

During the 1970s the growth of the population of the inner ring had almost reached the freezing point. As from the end of the 1960s the outer ring of the metropolis acquired impetus. This ring included the veteran towns of Rishon Lezion, Petah Tiqua and Herziliya which, formerly, had to a great extent been independent. As from the 1960s these towns were incorporated in the economic system of the metropolis and the wave of suburb-formation reached them.

In the past few years signs have been evident of the creation of an additional ring, still more external, whose links with the metropolis are growing and strengthening. From Rehovot, in the south, Ramleh and Lod, in the east, to Kfar Saba in the north, the settlements are comprised in this external ring. The new Jewish settlements in Western Samaria, east of the Kfar Saba and Petah Tiqua areas, also seem to be based mainly on a population coming from the Tel Aviv metropolis and living in low-density and cheap housing, while keeping their employment and social links with the metropolis.

Although the city of Tel Aviv has been losing a considerable part of its population, it still preserves its predominance in the employment field. It constitutes a focus for the very strong commuting currents, its economy is relatively specialized, especially in the fields of finance and business services, and it comprises the dominant foci among most of the country's economic activities. A second metropolitan area, which developed at a slower rate, is the Haifa metropolis. Apart from the city of Haifa, it comprises mainly its suburbs (*Krayot*) along the Bay: Kiryat Tivon and Tirat Hacarmel, but constitutes a focus for the commuting currents, also originating from the more distant settlements in the western flank of the Galilee.

A metropolitan area is also evolving in Jerusalem. The new quarters built, after the Six Day War, around the city (Neve Y'akov, Ramot, East Talpiot and Gilo) come within the municipal boundaries of Jerusalem. In the past few years, however, suburban towns, such as Ma'ale Adumim, Givat Zeev and Ephrat, are being built in Judea and Samaria at a fast rate as projects initiated by the authorities. Jerusalem also constitutes a central city in a large Arab metropolis which extends from Ramallah in the north to Azariah in the east and Bethlehem in the south. An additional process which occurred in the Israeli urban system is the urbanization of the villages (Moshavot). This process started even before the establishment of the State but received a strong impetus when a considerable part of the massive immigration was absorbed in the *Maabarot* (immigrants' camps) and, subsequently, in the immigrants' housing built in the periphery of the veteran villages. Later, these villages continued to grow rapidly, especially those which found themselves within the boundaries of the Tel Aviv metropolis.

# II · The Political Economy of Israel – Basic Characteristics

## Introduction
### Background and basic data

The basic socio-political orientations, trends and dilemmas that we identified in the political sphere also naturally found their expression in the development of the mould of political economy that crystallized in Israel.

The specific model of political economy that crystallized in Israel developed out of the confrontation between its initial starting-point – the economic base as it existed at the end of the mandatory period – and the processes of economic development that took place in the State of Israel and the policies that guided this development.

This model, which in several ways was unique among small modern societies in general and post-revolutionary societies in particular, crystallized first out of the transformation and realization of the original visions of Jewish settlement in Eretz Israel, and the power structure which had developed in the period of the Yishuv. It became further transformed, and its major contemporary features crystallized, after the establishment of the State in close relation to the growing concentration of major levels of economic power in the hands of the State and the continuous modernization and diversification of the economy on the one hand and the necessity to absorb many new immigrants on the other.

Let's first of all present some of the basic data about developments of this economy, the major details of the transformation of this economy into the general direction of a relatively industrialized small society.

The following data give us a summary picture of the growth and development of Israeli economy.*

1. The gross national product (GNP) grew from 9,872.3 million IS in 1950 to 27,405.7 million in 1960, to 62,863.9 million in 1970 and 104,738.0 million in 1981 – a growth of 1060 per cent.
2. The private consumption expenditure grew from 6,922.8 million IS to

* Most of these items, except when otherwise stated, are in 1980 prices.

17,726.2 million in 1960, to 37,757.8 million in 1970 and to 68,573.0 million in 1981 – a growth of 990 per cent.

3. The general government consumption expenditure grew from 2,968.5 million IS in 1950, to 6,764.7 million in 1960, to 26,647.2 million in 1970, and to 40,032 million in 1981 – a growth of 1348 per cent.

4. The gross domestic capital formation grew from 5,865.9 million IS in 1950, to 9,340.3 million in 1960, to 21,377.6 million in 1970, and to 23,309.0 million in 1981 – a growth of 397 per cent.

5. The gross national product per capita grew from 7,820 million IS in 1950, to 12,977 million in 1960, to 21,145 million in 1970, and to 26,510 million in 1981 – a growth of 339 per cent.

6. The differentials between exports and imports of goods and services including net factor payments to abroad grew from 5,591.0 million IS in 1950, to 6,129.8 million in 1960, to 21,844.8 million in 1970, and to 27,176.0 million in 1981 – a growth of 486 per cent.

7. The private consumption expenditure per capita grew from 5,464 million IS in 1950, to 8,393 million in 1960, to 12,719 million in 1970, and to 17,356 million in 1981 – a growth of 317 per cent.

8. The national income per capita grew from 32 million IS in 1950, to 171 million in 1960, to 505 million in 1970 and to 49,637 million in 1981 – a growth of 15,511 per cent.

9. The number of employed persons grew from 1955 to 1981 by 218.55 per cent.

10. The percentage of unemployed of civilian labour forces decreased from 7.2 per cent in 1955 to 3.6 per cent in 1965, then increased to 10.4 per cent in 1968, but decreased again to 5.1 per cent in 1981 – a decrease of 70.8 per cent.*

Tables 9.1, 9.2 and 9.3 provide a general picture of the occupational diversity that developed in Israel as well as the place of women in the labour force.

A crucial aspect of Israeli economy has been the heavy burden of defence. Thus the percentage of the security budget in the general budget grew from 19.6 per cent in 1965/6 up to 49.31 per cent in 1973/4 and from then on started decreasing to 33.7 per cent in 1977/8 and was expected to be 28 per cent in 1979/80. At the same time the development of the military industry in general and of the air industry in particular, constituted one of the major aspects of economic development, especially of the development of sophisticated, science-based industries, with a relatively great share in Israel's export.†

Table 9.4 provides some indications about the scope of defence expenditure.

---

* *Satistical Abstract of Israel 1982*, No. 33, 162–4.
† See in greater detail E. Bérglas, *Defense and the Economy*; *The Israeli Experience*, The Falk Institute for Economic Research in Israel, Discussion Paper 83–01 (Jerusalem 1983).

**Table 9.1    Employed Persons by Economic Branch, Population Group and Sex, 1970–81 (percentages)**

|  | Personal and other services | Public and community services | Financing and business services | Transport storage and communication |
|---|---|---|---|---|
| | | Total | | |
| 1970 | 7.7 | 24.0 | 5.2 | 7.5 |
| 1975 | 6.1 | 27.3 | 6.7 | 7.3 |
| 1976 | 6.4 | 27.7 | 6.8 | 7.0 |
| 1977 | 6.6 | 28.0 | 7.2 | 7.0 |
| 1978 | 6.6 | 29.2 | 7.6 | 6.9 |
| 1979 | 6.2 | 29.5 | 7.9 | 6.9 |
| 1980 | 6.2 | 29.6 | 8.2 | 6.9 |
| 1981 | 5.8 | 30.0 | 8.8 | 6.7 |
| | | Males | | |
| 1975 | 4.8 | 19.4 | 5.3 | 9.3 |
| 1976 | 5.1 | 19.9 | 5.5 | 8.8 |
| 1977 | 5.3 | 19.9 | 5.8 | 8.8 |
| 1978 | 5.4 | 20.6 | 6.2 | 8.8 |
| 1979 | 5.3 | 20.6 | 6.4 | 8.9 |
| 1980 | 5.0 | 20.4 | 6.6 | 8.9 |
| 1981 | 4.6 | 20.8 | 7.0 | 8.4 |
| | | Females | | |
| 1975 | 8.7 | 43.4 | 9.3 | 3.0 |
| 1976 | 9.0 | 43.4 | 9.5 | 3.4 |
| 1977 | 9.0 | 44.0 | 10.1 | 3.4 |
| 1978 | 8.9 | 45.2 | 10.3 | 3.4 |
| 1979 | 8.0 | 45.5 | 10.4 | 3.3 |
| 1980 | 8.1 | 45.9 | 11.2 | 3.5 |
| 1981 | 7.8 | 46.3 | 11.9 | 3.6 |
| | | Thereof: Jews – total | | |
| 1975 | 6.0 | 28.6 | 7.2 | 7.2 |
| 1976 | 6.2 | 29.0 | 7.3 | 7.1 |
| 1977 | 6.5 | 29.5 | 7.8 | 7.1 |
| 1978 | 6.6 | 30.3 | 8.2 | 7.0 |
| 1979 | 6.1 | 30.8 | 8.4 | 7.0 |
| 1980 | 6.0 | 30.8 | 8.9 | 7.0 |
| 1981 | 5.8 | 31.2 | 9.5 | 6.8 |
| | | Males | | |
| 1975 | 4.5 | 20.5 | 5.9 | 9.5 |
| 1976 | 4.5 | 21.0 | 6.0 | 9.0 |
| 1977 | 4.9 | 21.1 | 6.4 | 9.1 |
| 1978 | 5.1 | 21.3 | 6.9 | 9.0 |
| 1979 | 4.9 | 21.5 | 7.0 | 9.2 |
| 1980 | 4.6 | 21.3 | 7.2 | 9.2 |
| 1981 | 4.5 | 21.6 | 7.8 | 8.8 |
| | | Females | | |
| 1975 | 8.9 | 43.5 | 9.6 | 3.1 |
| 1976 | 9.2 | 43.5 | 9.7 | 3.5 |
| 1977 | 9.1 | 44.3 | 10.2 | 3.5 |
| 1978 | 9.1 | 45.5 | 10.5 | 3.5 |
| 1979 | 8.1 | 46.0 | 10.7 | 3.4 |
| 1980 | 8.4 | 46.2 | 11.5 | 3.6 |
| 1981 | 8.0 | 46.3 | 12.1 | 3.7 |

Source: *Statistical Abstract of Israel, 1982*, No. 33, p. 337.

**Table 9.2    Employed Persons, by Employment Status and Sex, 1955–81**

| Unpaid family members | Members of Kibbutzim | Co-operative members | Self-employed | Employers | Employees | | Total | |
|---|---|---|---|---|---|---|---|---|
| Percentages | | | | | | | Thousands | |
| | | | Total | | | | | |
| 5.8 | 8.4 | | 22.6 | | 63.2 | 100.0 | 585.7 | 1955 |
| 5.6 | 7.3 | | 19.7 | | 67.4 | 100.0 | 701.8 | 1960 |
| 4.6 | 5.4 | | 17.8 | | 72.2 | 100.0 | 879.0 | 1965 |
| 3.8 | 4.9 | 1.1 | 13.0 | 3.7 | 73.6 | 100.0 | 963.2 | 1970 |
| 3.1 | 4.8 | 1.1 | 12.4 | 3.4 | 75.2 | 100.0 | 1,088.4 | 1973 |
| 2.3 | 5.0 | 1.0 | 13.0 | 2.7 | 76.0 | 100.0 | 1,097.0 | 1974 |
| 2.5 | 5.0 | 1.0 | 12.5 | 2.5 | 76.4 | 100.0 | 1,112.6 | 1975 |
| 2.8 | 5.0 | 1.0 | 12.8 | 2.6 | 75.8 | 100.0 | 1,127.2 | 1976 |
| 2.6 | 5.1 | 0.9 | 12.5 | 2.7 | 76.3 | 100.0 | 1,159.2 | 1977 |
| 2.3 | 5.1 | 0.9 | 11.4 | 3.6 | 76.8 | 100.0 | 1,213.0 | 1978 |
| 2.2 | 4.8 | 0.8 | 10.7 | 4.1 | 77.4 | 100.0 | 1,240.6 | 1979 |
| 2.3 | 5.0 | 0.9 | 10.6 | 3.7 | 77.5 | 100.0 | 1,254.5 | 1980 |
| 1.9 | 5.0 | 0.8 | 10.4 | 3.8 | 78.1 | 100.0 | 1,280.1 | 1981 |
| | | | Males | | | | | |
| 2.0 | 6.6 | | 27.0 | | 64.4 | 100.0 | 443.0 | 1955 |
| 1.5 | 5.3 | | 24.3 | | 68.9 | 100.0 | 521.9 | 1960 |
| 1.3 | 3.8 | | 22.5 | | 72.4 | 100.0 | 637.3 | 1965 |
| 1.1 | 3.5 | 1.4 | 16.4 | 4.6 | 72.8 | 100.0 | 679.8 | 1970 |
| 0.9 | 3.6 | 1.4 | 15.9 | 4.6 | 72.6 | 100.0 | 746.4 | 1973 |
| 0.9 | 3.6 | 1.4 | 15.7 | 4.6 | 73.8 | 100.0 | 747.0 | 1973 |
| 0.7 | 3.7 | 1.4 | 16.9 | 3.6 | 73.8 | 100.0 | 743.8 | 1974 |
| 0.9 | 3.8 | 1.4 | 16.6 | 3.5 | 73.9 | 100.0 | 748.4 | 1975 |
| 1.0 | 3.9 | 1.3 | 16.8 | 3.6 | 73.4 | 100.0 | 753.2 | 1976 |
| 1.1 | 3.9 | 1.3 | 16.6 | 3.6 | 73.5 | 100.0 | 769.6 | 1977 |
| 0.7 | 4.1 | 1.3 | 15.3 | 5.0 | 73.7 | 100.0 | 789.8 | 1978 |
| 0.8 | 3.8 | 1.2 | 14.1 | 5.8 | 74.3 | 100.0 | 799.4 | 1979 |
| 1.0 | 4.1 | 1.3 | 14.0 | 5.4 | 74.3 | 100.0 | 801.9 | 1980 |
| 0.8 | 4.1 | 1.2 | 13.9 | 5.4 | 74.7 | 100.0 | 815.8 | 1981 |
| | | | Females | | | | | |
| 17.6 | 14.0 | | 8.9 | | 59.5 | 100.0 | 142.7 | 1955 |
| 17.6 | 13.0 | | 6.6 | | 62.8 | 100.0 | 179.9 | 1960 |
| 13.3 | 9.5 | | 5.7 | | 71.5 | 100.0 | 241.9 | 1965 |
| 10.3 | 8.0 | 0.3 | 4.8 | 1.0 | 75.6 | 100.0 | 283.4 | 1970 |
| 8.0 | 7.5 | 0.4 | 4.6 | 0.8 | 78.7 | 100.0 | 342.0 | 1973 |
| 7.9 | 7.6 | 0.3 | 4.5 | 0.9 | 78.7 | 100.0 | 347.7 | 1973 |
| 5.7 | 7.7 | 0.2 | 5.0 | 0.7 | 80.7 | 100.0 | 353.1 | 1974 |
| 6.0 | 7.6 | 0.3 | 4.1 | 0.5 | 81.5 | 100.0 | 364.0 | 1975 |
| 6.4 | 7.1 | 0.4 | 4.7 | 0.6 | 80.8 | 100.0 | 373.6 | 1976 |
| 5.5 | 7.4 | 0.3 | 4.4 | 0.7 | 81.8 | 100.0 | 389.9 | 1977 |
| 5.2 | 6.9 | (0.2) | 4.3 | 0.8 | 82.5 | 100.0 | 422.9 | 1978 |
| 4.8 | 6.6 | (0.2) | 4.5 | 0.9 | 82.9 | 100.0 | 441.4 | 1979 |
| 4.5 | 6.8 | 0.3 | 4.4 | 0.9 | 83.1 | 100.0 | 452.2 | 1980 |
| 4.0 | 6.6 | 0.2 | 4.4 | 0.9 | 84.0 | 100.0 | 464.1 | 1981 |

Source: *Statistical Abstract of Israel, 1982*, No. 33, p. 343.

**Table 9.3  Employed Persons and Employees, by Occupation and Sex, 1973–81 (percentages)**

| Year and sex | | Other workers in industry, transport, building and unskilled workers | Skilled workers in industry mining, building, transport and other | Agricultural workers | Service workers |
|---|---|---|---|---|---|
| **All employed** | | | | | |
| persons | 1973 | 6.6 | 29.4 | 7.0 | 12.5 |
| | 1975 | 6.1 | 28.3 | 6.2 | 11.7 |
| | 1977 | 6.4 | 26.1 | 6.2 | 11.1 |
| | 1978 | 5.2 | 26.3 | 6.0 | 11.2 |
| | 1979 | 4.8 | 26.7 | 5.6 | 11.0 |
| | 1980 | 4.3 | 26.2 | 5.9 | 11.0 |
| | 1981 | 4.2 | 25.8 | 5.5 | 11.2 |
| Males | 1973 | 8.2 | 37.9 | 7.9 | 8.4 |
| | 1975 | 7.9 | 37.8 | 7.4 | 8.3 |
| | 1977 | 8.1 | 35.5 | 7.5 | 7.7 |
| | 1978 | 6.8 | 36.2 | 7.4 | 7.6 |
| | 1979 | 6.2 | 36.9 | 6.9 | 7.4 |
| | 1980 | 5.8 | 36.8 | 7.4 | 7.3 |
| | 1981 | 5.8 | 36.4 | 7.2 | 7.6 |
| Females | 1973 | 3.1 | 11.1 | 5.0 | 21.3 |
| | 1975 | 2.4 | 9.0 | 3.8 | 18.8 |
| | 1977 | 2.9 | 7.6 | 3.6 | 17.8 |
| | 1978 | 2.3 | 8.0 | 3.4 | 17.9 |
| | 1979 | 2.3 | 8.5 | 3.3 | 17.4 |
| | 1980 | 1.8 | 7.7 | 3.3 | 17.5 |
| | 1981 | 1.4 | 7.5 | 2.7 | 17.3 |
| **All employees** | 1973 | 7.8 | 29.8 | 3.2 | 12.7 |
| | 1975 | 7.4 | 28.3 | 2.3 | 12.2 |
| | 1977 | 7.6 | 25.6 | 2.4 | 11.6 |
| | 1978 | 6.2 | 25.7 | 2.2 | 11.8 |
| | 1979 | 5.6 | 26.4 | 2.0 | 11.6 |
| | 1980 | 5.1 | 26.2 | 2.1 | 11.6 |
| | 1981 | 5.1 | 25.3 | 2.2 | 11.7 |
| Males | 1973 | 10.0 | 39.2 | 4.0 | 9.1 |
| | 1975 | 9.8 | 38.8 | 2.9 | 9.2 |
| | 1977 | 10.1 | 36.0 | 3.1 | 8.6 |
| | 1978 | 8.4 | 36.8 | 2.9 | 8.6 |
| | 1979 | 7.5 | 37.9 | 2.8 | 8.2 |
| | 1980 | 7.1 | 38.1 | 3.0 | 8.1 |
| | 1981 | 7.4 | 37.1 | 3.1 | 8.4 |
| Females | 1973 | 3.5 | 10.8 | 1.6 | 19.8 |
| | 1975 | 2.6 | 8.8 | 1.1 | 18.0 |
| | 1977 | 3.4 | 7.3 | 1.1 | 16.9 |
| | 1978 | 2.5 | 7.5 | 1.1 | 17.1 |
| | 1979 | 2.5 | 8.1 | 0.7 | 17.1 |
| | 1980 | 1.9 | 7.6 | 0.7 | 17.1 |
| | 1981 | 1.6 | 7.2 | 0.7 | 16.8 |

Source: *Statistical Abstract of Israel, 1982*, No. 33, p. 345.

**Table 9.4    Indicators of Defence Expenditures, 1964–81 (Percentages at current prices)**

| Year | Total non-civilian consumption[a] | Total non-civilian consumption excl. military grants[b] | Weight in GNP Total non-civilian consumption excl. military total grants | Domestic non-civilian consumption | Domestic defence expenditure, foreign currency expenditures and loan repayment[c] | Weight of defence in total wages |
|------|------|------|------|------|------|------|
| | (1) | (2) | (3) | (4) | (5) | (6) |
| 1964–6 | 10 | 10 | 9 | 6 | | 5 |
| 1967 | 18 | 18 | 17 | 10 | | 8 |
| 1968–9 | 19 | 19 | 19 | 12 | | 8 |
| 1970 | 25 | 25 | 25 | 14 | 22 | 9 |
| 1971–2 | 23 | 20 | 19 | 14 | 19 | 9 |
| 1973–5 | 33 | 24 | 22 | 17 | 22 | 11 |
| 1976–8 | 17 | 21 | 15 | 15 | 20 | 10 |
| 1979–81 | 25 | 19 | 13 | 14 | 19 | 10 |
| 1978 | 27 | 22 | 16 | 14 | 18 | 9 |
| 1979 | 22 | 17 | 9 | 14 | 20 | 10 |
| 1980 | 25 | 17 | 13 | 14 | 19 | 10 |
| 1981 | 27 | 22 | 18 | 15 | 19 | 9 |

Notes: a. Columns 1–4 and 6 are based on definition of the National Accounts Department of the Central Bureau of Statistics; the estimates in column 5 are based on government budget data adjusted to calendar years.

b. Grants include the grant equivalent of US government defence loans. The subsidized loans can be broken down into two elements: the loan proper and the grant equivalent, the latter being the difference between the loan proceeds and the present value of the repayments calculated at the going commercial interest rate. This alternative interest is assumed to be 10 per cent for 1964–77, 11.5 per cent for 1978, 12 per cent for 1979, 13 per cent for 1980 and 13.5 per cent for 1981 (see also Oded Liviatan, 'Israel's External Debt', Bank of Israel, *Economic Review*, No. 48–49, 1980).

c. Loan repayments include principal and interest on account of US government defence loans.

Source: Columns 1–4 and 6: Central Bureau of Statistics and Bank of Israel calculations; column 5: Ministry of Finance and Bank of Israel calculations.

# The Specific Characteristics of the Israeli Mould of Political Economy. Strong Regulative Power of the State and Occupational Differentiation
## Basic characteristics

The preceding data point out that, from the point of view of most of the dimensions of economic structure, Israeli economy became very similar to that found in many small, relatively modern or modernizing and industrializing societies – with an intensification of the problems attendant on the absorption of new immigrants coming from relatively underdeveloped sectors.

Yet the data also indicate some special characteristics of this economy when compared with such countries – such as the relatively high concentration in services; the special place of agriculture; the continuously increasing public and private expenditure and rising standard of life, and the heavy burden of security expenses.

The Israeli mould of political economy and the bases for the crystallization of processes of strata-formation and structuring of social hierarchies – with their own specific dynamics and attendant problems – have three basic characteristics. First the development of the very strong concentration of economic resources, and hence also, potentially, of economic power (probably more than in any other non-communist modern society) in the hands of the State. At the same time, second, the State has not become, like in the socialist or communist countries, the major owner of the means of production and of the major industrial and financial enterprises. These were distributed among the three major economic sectors: the Histadrut and the private one, which continued from the Yishuv period, and the governmental one, which was of course new, most of it developing with the establishment of the State, although in part taking also over some mandatory establishments.

The third characteristic of this mould of political economy was the uses to which the government put its large regulative power over the economy – policies rooted in the Labour–Zionist vision of building of a Jewish society in Eretz Israel – but a vision which became transformed with the establishment and development of the State.

The most important aspect of this vision was the decision – naturally following the original one about the mode of settlement in the period of the Yishuv, and combined with the very justification for the establishment of the State of Israel – to open the gates of the State to as many Jewish communities as possible and to create a modern economy, not a small semi-colonial enclave in the Middle East.

The concrete policies which developed out of this vision, and which, in continuous encounter with the economic realities and forces that existed in the State in the beginning, and even more with those which were generated by these very policies, shaped the social and political dynamics of economic development in Israel, were: first, a stress on continuous economic expenditure, modernization and developments; second the relatively strong stress on the regulation of such development by the government (and to a smaller degree by the Histadrut), partially and initially at least in the above-mentioned directions and second in the direction of the development of far-reaching, continuously expanding welfare State services.

Let's explicate all the indications in somewhat greater detail.

## The economic power of the State

The unique place of the State in the economic system was the result of several facts.

First was the fact of the concentration in the hands of the State (or of the Jewish Agency) of those external resources which were important for the closure of the gap between its own productivity and its level of expenditure, which has been a continuous aspect of the Israeli economy. All such major sources – the various contributions from the Jewish communities coming through such agencies as the United Jewish Appeal or the Israel Bonds, the public part of the German reparations and the various forms of external aid, above all from the United States, whether in the form of grants or of loans – were concentrated in the hands of the State (or of the Jewish Agency). Even the private reparations from Germany – which were distributed to individuals – because of relatively favourable conditions given to those who did not convert their reparation into Israeli money, were from the point of view of their use, in fact, under the direct or indirect control of the State. The concentration of all these resources in the hands of the State made it the great repository of capital and the major regulator of the direction of investments in the economy.

Secondly, this control of investments by the State was also reinforced by the very strong regulations by the state of security and pension funds – one of the major sources of capital formation and investment in the Israeli economy – and later also, to some degree at least, of the stock-market exchange.

This government control and guidance was effected through its control of the financial and credit system, through systems of subsidies (to products and to loans), through taxation and through control of foreign exchange – most of which, in one guise or another with partial exception of the foreign exchange control, basically continued, even after the so-called period of Liberalization in 1978, under the Likud government.

While such overall control and regulation was indeed characteristic of all the governments since the establishment of the State, yet there was nevertheless a gradual move from direct detailed administrative control (which was characteristic of the 1950s) to more indirect control through subsidies, special credit allocations, foreign currency exchange and the like.

At the same time, through the extension of the civil service (including of course the teachers), manpower in municipal service, government-owned companies, the military industry (of which aviation was probably the greatest), the State became the greatest single employer in the country. In 1965 there were 54,247 government employees; this number increased in 1975 to 82,576 and to 87,062 in 1981 – an increase of 60 per cent.

This development has indeed been a part of the continuous general increase of the public sector, as illustrated, for instance, by the fact that in 1970, 24 per cent of the labour force were in the public services; in 1975, 27.3 per cent; in 1977, 28.0 per cent and in 1981, 30 per cent – an increase of 25 per cent. At the same time in 1970, 76 per cent of the labour force worked in the business sector; in 1975, 72.7 per cent; in 1977, 72.0 per cent and in 1981, 70 per cent – a decrease of 8 per cent.*

Within the service sector, a continuously growing section was the banking system which, in 1983, comprised about 2.5 per cent of the GNP – the third largest in the world after Luxembourg and Hong Kong.†

In terms of employment this growth of the banks can be seen from the fact

---

* Bank of Israel, *Annual Report, 1981* (Jerusalem, May 1982), p. 63.
† *Haaretz*, 17 August 1983.

that in 1968, 4.9 per cent from the civilian labour force worked in the finance and business sector. In 1975 the figures came up to 6.7 per cent (an increase of 36 per cent); in 1978, 7.6 per cent (an increase of 13 per cent) and in 1981, 8.8 per cent (an increase of 15 per cent).*

This unique development of the banking system was because of the continuous involvement by the government in property development, the unwillingness or inability of the government to control such development directly, and the continuous existence and development of the different sectors, as well as the fact that the banks served as one of the major agencies of mediation and transfer between private households and the public sector in various areas, particularly in savings.

The importance and power of the banks increased even more from the late 1960s with the growing inflation, and the concomitant development of the Israeli Stock Exchange – an exchange which was to a very high degree, although not always successfully, controlled by the banking system and more indirectly by the government.

## Occupational differentiation

The great concentration of resources in the hands of the government and the concomitant possibility of the regulation of flow of capital by the State were rooted not only in the given historical circumstance but also in the ideology of the Labour–Zionist vision and its socialist components. It was the different components of this vision that guided the major orientations and policies of the government, giving a sharp push to development, growth and the assurance of employment.

Thus the State used these various resources, both from external and from the continuously growing internal sources, for continuation of the far-reaching economic expansion and modernization which characterized the development of Israeli economy; that is, for the establishment of the various settlements and encouragement of many, probably most, of the enterprises in the industrial sectors.

The history of the great economic expansion of Israel in the 1950s and 1960s, under the leadership first of Levi Eshkol, later mostly of Pinhas Sapir, was indeed the history of the ways in which these resources were put to use – transforming a rather small underdeveloped country into a relatively highly developed, industrialized and rather different one.

In the first decade or so of the State these policies were orientated towards the initial absorption of immigrants and the creation of minimal conditions of employment. Later on, from the mid- or late 1950s, they were more and more orientated to the extension of the whole economic structure, its growing diversification and continuous increase of standard of living.

Among the first and most continuous outcomes of these governmental policies were, first, a continuously growing process of the diversification and

* *Statistical Abstract of Israel, 1982*, No. 33, p. 337; *Statistical Abstract of Israel, 1974*, No. 25, p. 322.

differentiation of the occupational structure and, second, and closely connected with the former, a transformation of the different sectors among which, as we have seen, the means of production of the major enterprises were divided.

The major trend of occupational development was characterized by growing occupational diversification; by a very strong development of service sectors, by a growth of professional and managerial manpower. Of crucial importance in the development of the occupational structure was the growing demand for educational – high school and university – qualifications for entrance in many occupations, especially in the service sector and in the public service in particular, and for positions which were created, by governmental policies, above all, but not only, through the expansion of the welfare system.

So there developed what could be identified – in rather general and vague

**Table 9.5    Index of Income from Wages and Salary, by Occupation**

| Occupation | Income per hour | | Weekly Income | | Annual Income | |
|---|---|---|---|---|---|---|
| | 1980 survey | 1981 survey | 1980 survey | 1981 survey | 1980 survey | 1981 survey |
| Base total | 100 | 100 | 100 | 100 | 100 | 100 |
| Scientific and academic workers | 148 | 150 | 151 | 149 | 155 | 153 |
| Other professional, technical and related workers | 123 | 126 | 109 | 112 | 109 | 112 |
| Administrators & managers | 140 | 151 | 180 | 186 | 190 | 198 |
| Clerical & related workers | 95 | 94 | 92 | 91 | 92 | 90 |
| Sales workers | 81 | 88 | 79 | 86 | 77 | 85 |
| Service workers | 69 | 65 | 62 | 58 | 61 | 57 |
| Agricultural workers | 71 | 68 | 77 | 73 | 76 | 74 |
| Skilled workers in industry, building and transport, and unskilled workers | 90 | 88 | 97 | 96 | 97 | 96 |
| Other workers in industry, building and transport, and unskilled workers | 68 | 67 | 71 | 71 | 70 | 69 |

Notes: *Income by Economic Branch*: The highest annual income from wages and salary for the period whose mid-point was the beginning of 1981 was, as in previous years, in the 'Electricity and Water' branch, where it was 3 times higher than in the 'Personal Service' branch, in which the lowest income was recorded. Income from wages and salary in the branches 'Industry (Mining and Manufacturing)', 'Public Service' and 'Financing and Business Services' was similar to the average income. In 'Transport, Storage and Communication' income was higher than the average income, and in 'Commerce, Restaurants and Hotels' income was lower than the average income – and this was the case for all years and for both annual income and income per hour.
*Income by Years of Schooling*: The higher the educational level of an employee, the higher his income. At the beginning of 1981, the income per hour of an employee with 16 years of schooling was about twice as high as the income per hour of an employee with less than 4 years of schooling. One of the contributory factors is the concentration of poorly educated employees in occupations where wages are low, like 'services'. Higher educated employees, who had studied for 9–12 years, are employed as clerical workers or skilled workers in industry, construction or transport, which are better paid occupations. The majority of those with 13 years of schooling or more are engaged in high paid occupations, such as the scientific and academic professions etc.
*Income by Age*: Up to the 35–54 age-group, the higher the age of the employee, the higher the income per hour; above age 55, income decreases with increase in age.
Source: Central Bureau of Statistics, *Surveys of Income, 1981*, Special Series No. 205.

terms – a working class, within which the most prominent element was a salaried sector employed above all in the public sector, whether in the government, in the civil service of various kinds, or employees of the municipalities or the Histadrut.

The development of a 'real' industrial working class was much weaker and even here large parts were employed within the government and Histadrut sectors – and not only, or even mainly, within the private sector – although there did also develop, almost for the first time in the history of the Jewish settlement, something akin to a proletariat proper, namely the new industrial workers, as well as lower salaried workers.

There also developed a relatively great concentration of population beneath the so-called poverty line – which in 1965 and 1975 composed about 15 per cent of the whole population.

This process of economic and occupational diversification was connected with the growing wage and income differentials, and, as we shall see in greater detail in Chapter 13, a tendency to a coalescence between class and ethnicity.

Table 9.5 gives us a picture of the trend of development and scope of such differentials.

A marked change in the composition of the labour force developed after the Six Day War with the great influx of Arab labour – especially from the West Bank and Gaza – to Israel, taking over most of the fields of manual labour. This enabled the Jewish labour force to move 'upwards' into service and specialized labour, thus both undermining the older Zionist premiss of Jewish labour self-sufficiency as well as reinforcing some conservative trends in Jewish economy which resisted growing modernization and increasing the service sector in the economy of Israel.

In Israel the workers from the territories are mostly manual workers. This concentration in manual and unskilled work is impressive: 80 per cent of the workers of the territories in Israel work in construction, agriculture and industry, as compared to three-fifths of the Israeli Arabs who work in the Jewish economy, as compared to about half of the Arabs who do not work in the Jewish sector as compared to only 35 per cent of the Jews who work in these three industries.

Arabs constitute approximately a quarter of all workers in Greater Israel (1980). They constitute more than half of the workers in agriculture and construction. In smaller Israel, the Israeli Arabs plus the incoming workers from the territories are 15 per cent of the workers: they constitute a third of the workers in agriculture and more than half of the workers in construction.

As we have seen in Tables 9.1, 9.2 and 9.3, the role of women has been of special importance in the development of the occupational structure. Their concentration, above all in the clerical, professional, technical and related sectors, has greatly bolstered the earning of families in these sectors.

# The Sectorial Division of Israeli Economy – The Governmental, Histadrut and Private Sectors
## Sectorial characteristics and similarities

While the State thus became both the major regulator of investment policy as well as the largest employer in the country, from the point of view of ownership of the major means of production, the economy continued, as we have seen, to be divided into three sectors: first, the so-called private one, composed of multiple private enterprises; second the Histadrut one, which included the major types of collective settlements, the Kibbutzim and Moshavim; and the very widespread industrial concerns of the Histadrut (its Sick Fund, and its major marketing co-operative boards); and, third, the Government one, composed mainly of public services and of numerous government companies in the industrial field, such as for instance the Electricity Company, the Potash Industries of the Dead Sea and many others – comprising roughly about 12–15 per cent of the industrial labour force.

In general the share of the sectors in the net domestic product was relatively stable for the Histadrut sector – about 20–22 per cent; and grew from the 1960s to late 1970s for the governmental sector – from about 20 per cent to 25 per cent – with a parallel decrease in the private sector from about 60 per cent to 55 per cent (if one includes the army, the increase in the public sector was probably even greater).*

The State, through the direction and regulation of the investment policies, exercised an overall control of all these sectors, but at the same time the State gave them a very large degree of autonomy in terms of concrete policies, of ownership of their respective enterprises, and to some degree of the accumulation of their profits.

Indeed the policies of the State greatly strengthened and diversified these sectors and in fact helped to create within all of them new enterprises which became, of course, the bases of employment and of economic development. The different sectors have become, perhaps paradoxically, very strong foci of power – the government greatly dependent on them – albeit within the framework of the basic political–economic orientations established and guided by the State.

These developments also weakened the differences between the different sectors – even if they did not obliterate them entirely.

Perhaps this can best be seen in the Histadrut sector – the most highly organized one and with a seemingly clear, distinct ideology. All parts of this sector – the Kibbutzim and Moshavim, the industrial, marketing, construction or co-operative enterprises of the Histadrut – participated intensively in economic expansion. The 'constructivist' activities of the Histadrut became even more encompassing and its economic 'empire' grew rapidly and became highly diversified, as also happened parallelly, even if unexpectedly, in somewhat different ways in the private and the governmental sectors.

* These rough estimates are based on Table 317 in the *Statistical Abstract of Israel, 1981*.

On the whole it seems that the basic economic policies of different enterprises or groups of enterprises, as well as of the bank (Bank Hapoalim), were guided on the whole by similar economic considerations – even if with the possible admixture of political ones.

At the same time the growing similarity of the sectors often increased the competition between them over scarce resources, while emphasizing the growing importance of political pressure as an instrument of economic activity.

## Sectorial differences

But beyond the tendency of growing similarity between the sectors, several differences between them can be identified – some old ones, some new ones.

First of all there developed some differences in terms of the relative distribution of different economic branches;* secondly, there were also some differences between the different sectors with regard to the relative distribution of innovative or stagnant tendencies, as well as of hidden unemployment among them – although there are not too many systematic data about this.

Thus, for instance, the most developed, highly sophisticated, electronic industry, closely connected with the military industry, was by definition relatively more closely related to the government sector or to industries – like Tadiran – which were connected with it; but lately some very sophisticated science-based industries have also developed in other sectors.

Perhaps the least developed industries were the textile ones, concentrated mostly in the private and to some degree the Histadrut sector.

There was thus naturally the greatest concentration of salaried groups within the sector of the government and the Histadrut, while the industrial manpower was mostly concentrated in the private and Histadrut sector and to a smaller degree in the government one.

The private sector was on the whole bifurcated between various small individual and larger industrial firms and cartels, with the former between the highly developed and modernized; in both there developed far-reaching subcontracting.

But great shifts have also been taking place in the relative importance of sectors in different branches of the economy.

Thus while, for instance, in the early 1950s a very large part of marketing was concentrated in such Histadrut enterprises as *Tnuva* or *Hamashbir Hamerkazi*, later on, from the 1960s on, more and more supermarket chains developed in the private sector. On the other hand, public transportation (by buses) continued to be concentrated in the hands of the various co-operatives affiliated with the Histadrut.

More important, some basic differences between sectors still persisted – differences in overall economic organization, perhaps above all in terms of the

* See D. Shimshoni, *Israeli Democracy* (New York 1982), pp. 234–5.

degree of their amenability to some central-political guidance, as well as in their basic ideological–economic orientations – especially to economic development.

Within the government and the Histadrut sectors there seemingly existed – albeit in different ways – a greater possibility of some more central control generally, and political control in particular, and on internal political consider-ations and allocation, while in the private sector these seemed to play a lesser role.

This was in principle easiest in the Histadrut sector where most of its industrial and some marketing enterprises were brought together under the general canopy of *Hevrat Haovdim* (the Company of the Workers) and in which several overall organizations – such as *Solel Boneh*, the major agency for construction, and *Klal*, which unified most industrial enterprises – developed.

Systematic research on this problem is very meagre but a situation apparently developed in *Hevrat Haovdim* in which, through the relative concentration, it was easier for them than for industries in the private sector to subsidize unsuccessful companies through central funds; moreover some of their funds were probably sometimes channelled into political frameworks of the Labour sector.

Second, some differences between sectors also developed. It was also to some degree with respect to such ideological measures as the participation of workers in the management and profits of companies, that some general decisions were taken – but even here their implementation was on the whole left to the individual enterprises or cartels. But on the whole the amount of workers' participation in the various echelons of the management of the companies was indeed higher and more fully institutionalized in the Histadrut than in other sectors.

Similarly, in the government sector, it was on the whole the specific economic considerations of different enterprises, as well as those of general employment policy which they shared with the Histadrut sector, that were probably most predominant.

As against this, in the private sector, which could not depend to the same degree as the government and sometimes even the Histadrut sectors on direct budgetary allocations, there naturally developed somewhat greater emphasis on profits; but here also, given the strong emphasis of the government on the considerations of employment, much of the energy of the workers of enterprises was necessarily directed to obtaining better credit and exchange conditions from the government.

It has often been alleged, especially in the first two decades of the State, that in the Histadrut and government sectors the emphasis was on 'development' and the readiness to engage in 'colonizing' or national activities.

The representatives of the private sector tended on the whole to deny this allegation, claiming – with particular reference to the Histadrut – that apparent devotion to national goals served only to extend the powers of given political groups, and asserting that the risks were mostly taken by the government and the national economy, and that, given the same preferential treatment by the government, private enterprises would be willing and able to undertake such ventures. In general, it was more and more difficult to discern far-reaching differences between the overall economic consideration of the sectors – with the exception already mentioned above that the private sector, not being able to depend to the same degree as the two other ones on budgetary allocation, had to pay more attention to its profit margins.

Thus it seems that, despite the seeming differences in the respective ideologies between the sectors, from the point of view of economic orientation performance, differences were becoming less and less visible.

Yet, all these similarities notwithstanding, all the sectors, especially the Histadrut one, remained as potential centres of power, and indeed the recognition of this fact has also, lately, given rise, with the Likud government in 1977, to attempts to weaken these centres, either through weakening of the central organs of the Histadrut or through the attempts to undermine some of the bases of their power, such as the proposals to establish a National Health Service which would to some degree at least weaken the monopoly of the Histadrut *Kupat Holim* (Sick Fund) in this arena, or through some preferential treatment to other sectors.

# Major Governmental Policies
## *Economic and social considerations*

The stress on development, and on investment in it, and the maintenance of high levels of employment, constituted one basic pole of the political economy in Israel – providing the momentum for its development. The other such poles were governmental policies orientated at the regulation of some of the natural outcomes of these policies: namely of the continuously rising public and private consumption, and of the continuously rising standard of living.

The considerations which guided the government control were usually a mixture of two closely interconnected components – an economic one and a socio-political one. The economic one was based on the necessity in any modern economy in general, and in Israeli economy in particular, to regulate the flow of money and the accumulation of capital necessary for the implementation of the developing policy, and for the high level of defence expenditure that characterized Israeli economy.

The second component was based more on social ideological considerations with respect to the distribution and allocation of resources. Thus policies were guided beyond economic and concrete expenditure considerations (i.e. the needs of various ministries and the like) by several socio-political orientations. First was the generally strong tendency to regulate the economy which was inherent in the socialist aspect of the predominant ideology and its paternalistic derivatives.

Second such orientations were also rooted in the strong egalitarian and distributive components of the regnant ideology; these egalitarian orientations were implemented through a whole series of tax measures – which brought the Israeli taxation to among the highest in the world, about 56.6 per cent of the GNP – and wage policies, especially in the different public sectors – which initially at least aimed at the minimization of wage differentials between different echelons.

# III · The Dynamics of Israeli Political Economy

## Directions of Control
### Tensions in government policies

The dynamics of Israeli economy in general and their socio-political repercussions in particular developed out of the continuous confrontation between these major policies of the government (and to some degree the Histadrut) – i.e. those orientated to development and modernization on the one hand and those guided by the different regulatory orientations on the other; and by the tensions and contradictions that have developed in these policies.

The first such tension or contradiction was that between the general, continuous emphasis on the rising standard of living and the concomitant growth of private and public consumption on the one hand, and on capital accumulation and economic independence on the other. One manifestation of this tension later on was the contradiction between the intensive flow of money generated by the wage and welfare policies and the attempts to control the growth of inflation.

Second was the contradiction between the egalitarian tendencies and orientations and the process of occupational diversification generated by the policies of development.

Third was the tension between the strong regulatory tendencies and the development, as a result of development policies, of many autonomous economic forces in general and of the autonomous working of the market in particular.

It was these tensions and their institutional repercussions that created the foci of power struggle within the framework of Israeli political economy, and their outcomes greatly shaped the performance of this economy and its major socio-political characteristics.

The first such focus of struggle developed around the major policies of investment and of development, with the tendency to concentrate the control over such investment in the hands of the government.

The actors in this struggle were the different governmental offices (including the Bank of Israel), the major entrepreneurs, investors and the major financial institutions – above all the banks. The major objects of the struggle here were first the amount of governmental subsidies and loans, the terms of such loans, the relative allocation of resources – especially of favourable preferred conditions of credit or foreign exchange allocations to different economic branches and different sectors.

Second a rather similar type of struggle developed around the ownership and control of the investments and capital market – above all the banking sector and the major pension funds; and third – and perhaps in a sense least important – was the disagreement around the overall degree, as against the concrete details, of government regulations.

The outcomes of this struggle were usually determined by the combination of government's strength and purpose; the impact and strength of market forces and the accumulated strength of pressures from the various groups representing different economic interests.

A different, but in fact closely related, set of forces and pressures developed around the wage and tax policies of the government.

Here the major contestants were the various occupational groups and their representatives – especially the different trade unions organized above all by the Histadrut, but which became in fact more and more independent of the control of the Central Committee of the Histadrut.

The major foci of struggle here were the various aspects of wage and tax policies – initially guided, as we have seen, by the egalitarian orientation. Here some of the far-reaching tensions and contradictions between, on the one hand, the egalitarian orientations of these policies and on the other hand the forces generated by the policy of development and economic modernization, became most fully manifest.

The struggle around the different aspects of the welfare state – the provision of different welfare benefits and some of the subsidies for food – was undertaken by some sectors of the Histadrut, the major officers of the National Social Security Authority and by social workers, as well as – especially from the late 1960s – leaders of various parties, more and more competing for the popular vote. One crucial focus of this struggle was the attempt of the Histadrut to maintain in its hands – as proposals came, paradoxically enough from 'liberal' opportunity groups and not from the Socialist camp, to nationalize the health services – the almost total monopoly over these services.

Within the general framework of the basic economic orientations of development, of increasing standard of living, of security and of maintenance of high levels of employment, it was on the whole the government which, despite its overall power in control of resources, proved to be the weaker partner. This was mainly because of its interest in maintaining full employment, and peaceful relations with the major sectors, and also its lack of ability to develop from within itself the appropriate forces to compete with the different sectors. It provided relatively cheap credit to the different sectors and generated through its wage and welfare policies very strong tendencies to high level public expenditure, which, together with the growing importance of the defence budget, generated continuous inflationary pressures. Moreover, it often acquiesced in many of the demands of the various groups.

## Development in the Histadrut

In order to understand the outcomes and repercussions of these policies it is necessary first of all to point out the development of the ideology and activities of the Histadrut after the establishment of the State.

The most important aspect of the transformation of this ideology was the bifurcation of its constructivist socialist and class emphases between on the one hand the stress on the economic and institutional development, as carried out by government and Histadrut elites, and on the other hand a strong emphasis on distributive policies, on different kinds of distributive orientations of welfare policies, of various social entitlements and benefits and on a general increase in the standard of living – with a strong emphasis on governmental regulation of the economy in general and of the wage structure and differentials in a seemingly egalitarian direction in particular.

One crucial aspect of the transformation of this ideology was the growing identification of its socialist or class components with the economic development in general, and with development under the auspices of the government and the Histadrut enterprises in particular. At the same time this ideology did not give any specification in what ways these enterprises – beyond belonging to the government or being regulated by it, or by the Histadrut – would be shaped according to some such 'socialist' orientations. Second the class or socialist components of the ideology became closely related with the growing emphasis on welfare policies and on the general attainment of high standards of living by the workers.

Thus in fact in general the regnant social ideology developed into a broad social democratic direction, without any strong class or socialist connotations, but also without any strong emphasis on participation by various groups in institution-building or on pioneering beyond such transformation.

These transformations of the regnant ideology were very closely related to the development of the activities of the Histadrut in the period of the State in three major directions. One was its growing participation through the expansion of its industrial sector in the process of economic development.

Second was the extension of its basic service framework and organizations – above all the Sick Fund – and a continuous struggle over maintenance of its monopoly of these services.

Third was, of course, the extension of its trade union activities.

With respect to these activities, there developed a certain division of labour between different parts of the Histadrut – in themselves attesting to its changing format and place in the structure of Israeli society. The struggle over wages, indexing, etc. was divided into two parts. The first, general level was about the cost of living index, and general limits or directives of wage policy, and concerned the employers, including the government, and paradoxically also the Histadrut, as the major employer.

The second level was that of different specific sectors – such as public employees, different industrial sectors and the like – and even of specific enterprises undertaken by various trade unions and often even of specific committees, which often did not accept the overall authority of the Central Committee of the Histadrut.

Last, there was of course also the very strong involvement of the Histadrut in the provision of various welfare policies. In all these activities the Histadrut was often caught in a rather special dilemma between being a major employer – both in its service (especially *Kupat Holim*) and in its industrial sector – and being the representative of workers, as well as a provider of general services, especially the health services, to large sectors of the population. In 1983 this dilemma finally erupted, as we shall see in greater detail later on, in a rather intensive force during the famous, or infamous, doctors' strike.

## Welfare and class formations

It was, as indicated above, the outcomes of these policies and struggles that shaped Israeli economy and social structure and their dynamics.

The most general outcome of the government and of the struggle between the various forces analysed above was indeed first of all continuous economic expansion and development, continuous rise in the standards of living and economic growth but with potential contradictions between them, and with stagnative potentialities.

We have already above given general indications about the process of development and growth of Israeli economy and about the continuous rise in the standard of living. This continuous increase in the standard of living in Israel is perhaps best illustrated by the increased use of durable goods.*

In 1958, 37.1 per cent of the Jewish households had an electric refrigerator; in 1970, 95.5 per cent, and in 1981, 99.5 per cent – an increase of 268 per cent. In 1969, 33.81 per cent of the Jewish households had a telephone; in 1974, 52.2 per cent, and in 1981, 70.81 per cent – an increase of 209 per cent.

In 1965, 2.4 per cent of the Jewish households had a TV set; in 1974, 83.1 per cent, and in 1981, 90.9 per cent – an increase of 3,787 per cent.

In 1959, 12.8 per cent of the Jewish households had a gramophone; in 1970, 26.7 per cent, and in 1981, 42.4 per cent – an increase of 158 per cent.

In 1962, 4.4 per cent of the Jewish households had a private car; in 1970, 16.7 per cent, and in 1981, 35.6 per cent – an increase of 809 per cent.

A second major result of these policies was a rather far-reaching shift from the original egalitarian policy orientations.

While no exact data exist, there can be no doubt that the wage and income

* *Statistical Abstract of Israel, 1982*, No. 33, pp. 310–11.

and capital differentials have been continually growing, eroding above all the lower middle echelons but weakening also other middle sectors of the population. Both the tax policies, with their limits on the upper brackets of income tax levels, and the *de facto* wage policy greatly favoured the upper and upper-middle groups – whether the private ones often created by the government policies, or the very extensive salaried professional ones, the managerial sector in general, the upper and middle sectors of the professions, especially the lawyers, the physicians, the upper echelons of the agricultural sector (the Kibbutzim, Moshavim and private agriculture).

Also within this panorama was the professional army whose personnel enjoyed – as compared with other parts of the public sector – high wages and emoluments, as well as very favourable pension arrangements, which made it relatively easy for them to leave the army at around the age of 45 and enter, more or less according to their ranks, different upper or upper-middle occupational sectors.

The sectors which benefited relatively less from these policies were the working class proper – the industrial, technologically unsophisticated man-power, the various middle echelons, whether of salaried or of industrial or private groups.

Between these various groups there developed continuous tensions – tensions between salaried personnel and manual workers on the one hand, and between the salaried and independent professionals on the other; tensions between the higher and the middle and lower groups within each of these broad sectors; as well as tensions about the centrality of the government in the regulation and structuring of all these developments.

All of these groups were competing for their share of the growing income, for access to economic resources and a position of influence on the government – a competition which became even sharper with the growing inflation.

The outcomes of these struggles were greatly influenced by the activities of the Histadrut. Thus first of all out of the combination of changes in the ideologies and activities of the Histadrut and in its relation to the government, its activities became more and more orientated to the more established sectors (especially the higher and middle sectors of the salaried groups in the service – above all public – sector); and much less to the problems of the 'real' proletariat in the private sector or the new rising mobile 'bourgeoisie' groups from within the new immigrants.

Among the workers the Histadrut tended to support very strongly some of the special stronger groups with monopolistic positions in the public sector – the two most extreme illustrations being El Al and the Electricity Company (in certain periods also the part workers) – but also other government corporations and select groups of workers which attained levels of salaries and emoluments much beyond (especially in the case of El Al) those existing levels in Israeli economy.

At the other end there were the lower sectors, the so-called poverty sectors, which tended to become perpetuated through generations. Thus the popu-

**Table 9.6  The Poverty Sector in Israel, 1963–78**

| | 1963 | | 1968[a] | | 1975[a] | | 1977 | | 1978 | |
|---|---|---|---|---|---|---|---|---|---|---|
| | Before getting allowance | After getting allowance | Before getting allowance | After getting allowance | Before getting allowance | After getting allowance | Before getting allowance | After getting allowance | Before getting allowance | After getting allowance |
| Number of Poor Families (1000s) | – | 60.9 | 109.6 | 73.2 | 142.4 | 56.6 | | | | |
| Percentage of Poor Families | – | 11.2 | 17.9 | 11.9 | 18.2 | 7.2 | 9.7 | | 11.0 | |
| Number of Poor People (1000s) | – | 243.3 | 401.0 | 282.8 | 514.4 | 231.0 | | | | |
| Percentage of Poor People | – | 12.5 | 17.9 | 12.6 | 18.0 | 8.1 | 12.3 | | 13.1 | |
| Number of Poor Children (1000s) | – | 124.4 | 189.3 | 142.1 | 236.0 | 119.6 | | | | |
| Percentage of Poor Children | – | 16.0 | 21.6 | 16.2 | 21.6 | 10.3 | 15.4 | | 15.5 | |

Note:  a.  The data from 1968 and 1975 include Arab people and families also.
Source: Bureau of Research and Planning of the Social Security.

lation of this sector comprised in 1968 and 1975 about 15 per cent of the population and the children of these sectors constituted about 22 per cent of all the child population. However, between 1969 and 1977, because of the new reforms in the national insurance policy, which increased the different allowances, there was a decrease in the size of the poverty population, although it started to increase again from 1978. Thus if we look at the poverty population after the distribution of different allowances, we can see that in 1963 every eighth person was under the poverty line, and in 1975 only every twelfth or thirteenth person was in the same status.

Table 9.6 provides a more detailed picture of this situation.

The initial conditions of this sector were in the lowest levels, but at the same time they greatly benefited from various welfare benefits.

In close relation to the changes in the ideological orientations in general and the development of the poverty sector in particular, the Government and the Histadrut developed far-reaching emphasis on welfare policies and services. The scope of these services was continuously expanded, as shown by Table 9.7.

**Table 9.7    Social Security Expenditure, by Branches and Main Schemes, 1960–80 (1980 prices)**

| Year | Total | Old-age and survivors | Health | Family and children's allowances | Government employees' pensions | Public health services | Public assistance services[a] | War victims | Other branches |
|------|-------|-----------------------|--------|----------------------------------|-------------------------------|------------------------|-------------------------------|-------------|----------------|
| | | | | IS millions | | | | | |
| 1960 | 2,197 | 272 | 925 | 54 | 34 | 592 | 170 | 54 | 95 |
| 1965 | 3,526 | 421 | 1,321 | 258 | 110 | 598 | 608 | 81 | 129 |
| 1970 | 6,591 | 1,128 | 2,132 | 685 | 257 | 1,043 | 743 | 389 | 214 |
| 1975 | 12,366 | 2,601 | 3,032 | 2,287 | 453 | 1,486 | 1,006 | 925 | 576 |
| 1976 | 14,425 | 2,502 | 3,548 | 2,909 | 514 | 1,990 | 1,071 | 1,147 | 744 |
| 1977 | 16,486 | 2,767 | 4,241 | 2,794 | 626 | 2,634 | 1,207 | 1,284 | 933 |
| 1978 | 17,653 | 2,816 | 5,098 | 2,617 | 736 | 2,730 | 1,315 | 1,324 | 1,017 |
| 1979 | 18,103 | 2,946 | 5,362 | 2,348 | 753 | 3,120 | 1,218 | 1,257 | 1,098 |
| 1980 | 19,652 | 3,476 | 5,817 | 2,351 | 1,076 | 3,086 | 1,286 | 1,175 | 1,387 |
| | | | | Annual real change, in percentages | | | | | |
| 1960 | 14.9 | 11.0 | 9.1 | 94.2 | 21.4 | 20.7 | 21.4 | 11.0 | 13.3 |
| 1965 | 21.7 | 8.4 | 17.0 | 193.5 | 6.3 | 19.1 | 17.4 | 31.0 | 18.9 |
| 1970 | 14.7 | 17.2 | 14.0 | 19.3 | 14.7 | 16.5 | −0.6 | 18.2 | 26.7 |
| 1975 | 11.2 | 6.1 | −0.1 | 36.8 | −0.7 | 6.2 | −2.4 | 31.5 | 60.1 |
| 1976 | 16.7 | −3.9 | 17.0 | 27.2 | 13.4 | 33.9 | 6.4 | 23.8 | 30.1 |
| 1977 | 14.3 | 10.7 | 19.6 | −3.8 | 22.0 | 32.5 | 12.8 | 12.1 | 25.1 |
| 1978 | 7.1 | 1.8 | 20.2 | −6.4 | 17.6 | 3.6 | 8.9 | 3.1 | 8.9 |
| 1979 | 2.5 | 4.6 | 5.2 | −10.3 | 2.2 | 14.3 | −7.3 | −5.0 | 7.9 |
| 1980 | 8.6 | 18.0 | 8.5 | 0.1 | 43.0 | −1.1 | 5.6 | −6.5 | 26.3 |

Note: a. Employment injuries, disability, unemployment, employees' rights in bankruptcy and equity grants.
Source: Bureau of Research and Planning of the Social Security.

Thus the natural outcome of these policies was that the general growth of distribution of entitlements – especially connected with the welfare system – and struggles around them became a major aspect of Israeli economy.

At the same time this far-reaching development of social service and welfare

policies generated a new social sector, a new type of social stratum characterized by far-reaching dependency on the central distributive offices, and by
growing social demands on the government.

Truly enough, as has been the case in many other countries, many of these
policies, as for instance that of free education, greatly benefited not only the
lower groups, the needs of which were taken care of through special subsidies,
but also the middle or higher groups, who in general had easier access to many
of these services.

Nor did these policies obviate the fact that the level of services of education
and health was much lower in the ecological peripheries – especially the
development towns; yet they did also without a doubt greatly improve the
situation of the poorer sectors.

## Changing normative ambiance and labour ethos

The various struggles and policies also had far-reaching repercussions on
several additional aspects of Israeli society: on its normative ambiance in
general and in the sphere of taxation in particular; on the nature of
occupational struggles, as well as even perhaps more indirectly on some aspects
of the performance of the economy.

Thus given the complicated tax structure – especially the relatively limited
efficiency of the tax authorities, not unrelated to the general difficulties to
recruit qualified manpower to the public salaried sector and to 'hold' it – there
developed a continuous tendency to tax evasion. It was not just outright tax
evasion, often attributed to the private sector; it was, perhaps above all, the
tendency of semi-official evasion, of various under-the-table arrangements in
the form of special fringe benefits or special tax concerns undertaken by the
officials from within the authorities, that necessarily had far-reaching repercussions on the normative ambiance of the society.

Very indicative of these various normative tendencies was the fact that
strikes in Israel developed some special characteristics. Firstly there has been
relative greater concentration of strikes in the public (especially governmental)
as against the private (industrial) sector. Many such strikes – especially the
more visible ones – took place in the upper sectors like El Al or the Electricity
Company. Secondly there has also been a relatively large amount of strikes
unauthorized by the central authorities of the Histadrut, albeit of course with
different rates in different years.

All these developments attested to a very far-reaching transformation of the
original pioneering vision or ethos, moving from the more ascetic product-
ivity-orientated pioneers to the more ascriptive allocation, to the stress on
entitlements, to a heavy service sector and potentially growing dependency on
external sources.

It resulted, as from the middle or late 1960s – but with roots much earlier – in
a growing stress on demands, and gave rise to continuous conflicts, and the
feeling of lack of manageability of wage structure and labour relations – some

of the characteristics of a post-industrial society.

# The Overall Performance of Israeli Economy

It was of course the cumulative impact of all these varied policies that effected the overall performance of the Israeli economy – shaping its strong and weak points alike.

The different developments and tendencies in Israeli economy converged around its major economic dilemmas – those between economic growth and investment and the tendency to rising private and public consumption; between this rising consumption and the possibility of controlling inflation and the dependency on external resources.

Some of the major weaknesses of Israeli economy, closely related to the trends analysed above, were the continuous growth of the service sector in general and the public service one (especially the governmental) in particular. For instance the 1982 report of the Bank of Israel indicated (p. 71):

that in 1981 some 26,000 new labour force participants found work, while about 5,000 joined the ranks of the jobless (both figures are annual averages). Of the total increment, approximately 15,000 were absorbed by the business sector – 9,000 in business and financial services and only about 1,000 in industry. The public services hired approximately 12,000 new workers this year, as against 5,000 in 1980 and 10,000 in 1979. . . . In contrast to the renewed rapid expansion of personnel in the public services (3.7 per cent), industrial employment hardly grew at all, while financial and business services reported an increase of 8.8 per cent. . . . [there is] a long-term rising trend in the weight of the public services in total employed, at the expense of the business sector. In the business sector the most striking feature was an appreciable rise in the weight of financial and business services; the downturn in the rest of the business sector was therefore even more precipitate – from 66 per cent of the total employed labour force in 1975 to 61 per cent in 1981. The data also indicate that industry's share of total employment shrank steadily during the last three years.

Here of course the great expansion of the banking service has been very important.

·Closely connected are the difficulties of recruiting more skilled personnel to the civil service sector as against the private sector or that of government companies, to some extent even to the Histadrut companies.

All these affected the process of economic growth in Israel in which, according to Professor M. Bruno, several periods can be distinguished.*

In retrospect one may consider the period ending in 1972 as the 'golden age' of Israel's economic development. With the exception of a brief slump in 1966–7 (known as the 'Mitun' – or recession), the economic history leading up to 1972 was characterized by very rapid growth. During 1960–72 real GDP grew at 10 per cent per annum (13 per cent during 1968–72), capital stock grew at 9 per cent, labour input at 4 per cent (7 per cent during 1968–72), and total factor productivity at 4 per cent (6 per cent during 1968–72).

* 'External Shocks and Domestic Response: Israel's Macroeconomic performance 1965–1982' (Jerusalem, Falk Institute for Economic Research in Israel, 1984).

This was also a period which – for Israel – was marked by relative price stability, inflation running at a steady rate of around 6 per cent (4.3 per cent during 1965–9), with well-developed institutions to cope with its costs (wage and savings indexation, etc.). Even the balance of payments, which at different points in the past has been an effective bottleneck, did not seem to pose any problem. By 1972 exports financed about two-thirds of imports (compared to one-seventh in 1950, and half in 1960) with the remaining third easily financed by abundant foreign capital in the form of transfers and cheap long-term loans. These came in the wake of renewed immigration signalling the post-1967 euphoria, and on top of a very flexible labour market (due to the 1968 opening up of the Israeli labour market to Arab workers from the Gaza Strip and the West Bank). All this enabled the continued rapid expansion of industry, particularly towards export markets.

The only signs of impending trouble appeared on the internal social front. An Israeli version of a Black Panther movement developed at the end of the War of Attrition on the Suez Canal (1970) and helped divert attention to neglected domestic problems. In the three or four years preceding the 1973 war, Israel allocated an increasing share of domestic resources to the expansion of social services (education, health and welfare), on top of rising defence expenditures, and also developed an income-maintenance scheme which is one of the most advanced in the world. Little, if any, thought was given to the possibility of a major crisis looming ahead, in which the internal political commitments would turn out to be a heavy economic liability.

The 1973 war marked a watershed in almost any field conceivable, and economics certainly took its share. The broad aggregates for the period after 1973 seem to have come from a different economy. Growth virtually stopped. In no year after 1973 did GDP grow by more than 4–5 per cent and in most years it grew by considerably less. Inflation soared – by 30–40 per cent annually during 1974–7, reaching triple digits by 1980. The current account deficit quadrupled during 1972–5 and, although it fell sharply afterwards, it was still relatively high with the foreign debt growing, though at a much slower rate, commensurate with the much reduced GDP growth. While the system apparently adapted to these phenomenal inflation rates with relative ease, the economic and social frictions that it inevitably caused worsened considerably.

The general slowdown of Israeli economy in the early 1970s was probably a natural development after the great upsurge of growth under the impact of the great population growth – and the recession was to some extent also a world-wide phenomenon* – yet there developed also some specific Israeli problems. Thus to quote M. Bruno again:

Israel, like the rest of the industrial world in the 1970s, shows clear signs of a stagflation phenomenon. Its broad characteristics seem similar, leaving aside such special circumstance as the post-Six Day War upsurge in activity, or once we account for the 1974–75 amplitude of the inflationary wave. Israel's adjustment to the shocks seems to have been quite painful, the costs probably worsened over the years and a major puzzle occurs in one area – how to account for the post-1977 hyperinflation.

These specific problems were closely connected with some of the specific pressures on public expenditure, in particular with the immense growth of the

* See J. Metzer, *The Slowdown of Economic Growth in Israel: A Passing Phase or the End of the Big Spurt?* The Falk Institute for Economic Research in Israel, Discussion Paper 83–03 (Jerusalem 1983).

security burden* and the resulting growth of public and private spending which we analysed above (and which received a special impetus, as we shall yet see, in the Likud governments in general and the second Likud government in particular).

## The Israeli Model of Political Economy – Summary

One overall outcome of all these policies was the development of a model of political economy which could not be called either socialist or capitalist or just a welfare state in any of the usual sense of these terms, if there exists such a 'usual' sense.

It was in a way a mixture of these different elements, but the nature of this mixture and its concomitant specific socio-political and economic dynamics were rather special.

From the point of view of its political dimension, the economy was characterized – as already mentioned above – by the combination of the rather indirect, yet very powerful if not always effective, regulation of the economy by the government. Second this mould was characterized by the division of the ownership of the major means of production into three sectors, with diminishing difference between them. Third was the very continuous heavy burden of the defence expenditure.

The dynamics of this mould were shaped by the major orientations of its policies – especially by the continuous orientation of the economy to development, growth and continuously rising standard of living, welfare orientations and the minimization of unemployment, and by the tensions that developed between these different policies and their consequences; by the contradiction between the egalitarian tendencies and orientations and the process of occupational diversification generated by the policies of development and by the tension between the strong regulatory tendencies and the development, as a result of development policies, of many autonomous economic forces in general and of the autonomous working of the market in particular.

As a result of these dynamics there developed several structural economic and social characteristics of this economy.

Thus there developed first of all continuous growth and diversification of the occupational structure, continuous processes of social mobility at all levels of the occupational structure, and the growth of an upper managerial and professional sector in all sectors of the economy.

Second, the Israeli economy was characterized by the special place of, on the whole, a very modern and technologically sophisticated agriculture; the relatively very heavy share of the service sector in general and the public service sector; the rather uneven and continuous difference between highly developed and sophisticated and rather stagnant sectors; and by the special place of military industry and military-related industry in the industrial sector

* See E. Berglas, *Defense and the Economy; The Israeli Experience*.

in general and in the technological sectors and in export in particular.

Last it was characterized by the development of a special type of class-structure – heavily depending on the centre, but with its own autonomous dynamics and characterized by a strong development of different upper and upper-middle sectors on the one hand, and a heavy dependency-orientated poverty sector.

From the point of view of the performance of the economy these various tendencies crystallized around the problem of the continuous trade-deficit and payment, and the continuous gaps between the growth of GNP and the balance of payments, and the concomitant dependence on external sources; and, second, on the possible control of continuous inflation.

From the point of view of the original Zionist, and especially Zionist–Labour, vision of the productivization of the Jewish people, through creation, by pioneering activities, of a basic infrastructure of agriculture and industry, the major problem of this mould of political economy was how to cope with the development of a full, modern, diversified, economic structure. Here this mould was relatively successful in keeping up the special place of agriculture as a leadership, prestigious and highly productive and remunerative sector of the economy. It was less successful from these points of view with respect to large parts (especially the less sophisticated 'lower' parts) of industry. At the same time there developed within it continuously growing service sectors in general and a public service sector in particular – creating on the whole a return to that inverted occupational pyramid against which the original Zionist vision and the Labour–Zionist in particular rebelled. The leading elites who in many ways generated these developments were not able to find ways to imbue them with the more elitist and duty-stressing aspects of the older pioneering elites, emphasizing much more – far beyond their original place in that ethos – the distributive and entitlement orientations.

# IV · Social Organization and Strata Formation

## The Background of the Yishuv
### Basic characteristics

The preceding analysis brings us to that of social organization and the stratification of class structure and relations, of class struggles and consciousness and the structuring of social hierarchies, as they developed in Israel. The patterns of social organization and the dynamics of social stratification, of strata formation and class structure and consciousness in the Yishuv and in the State of Israel have evinced some very special characteristics; they have been shaped by the continuous encounter between, on the one hand, some basic structural situations, especially the occupational structure that developed there, and, on the other hand, the basic ideological and political orientations and mechanisms of control, over the access to the major economic, power and prestige resources, as well as over their use. We have seen that there were some special and rather unusual characteristics of this structure in the period of the Yishuv. Seemingly – given the very tenets of the Zionist–Socialist ideology which envisaged the development of a Jewish working class as the epitome of the realization of this vision – the picture here should have been relatively simple. But, as we have seen, from the very beginning this working class exhibited rather unique features which, together with the weakness of the bourgeois strata in the Yishuv, created a situation in which potential class consciousness and struggle in the classical European sense – although certainly far from being absent – were of rather secondary importance. Although the basic symbols articulated in the ideology of the Labour sector were couched in terms of socialist and class orientations, in fact the major, even the most central, actual emphasis of these 'labour' or socialist orientations was a pioneering one, manifest in a very strong stress in the creation of a new working class and its autonomous enterprises, and in the reconstruction, through such creation, of the economic and political institutions of the Jewish people.

Accordingly the most important referents – although certainly not the only ones – of this 'class' identity, as they developed in the Yishuv, were 'sectorial' ones, focused around the creation of a worker sector and participation with strong national connotations – as best expressed in Ben-Gurion's dictum 'From Class to Nation', in which the socialist construction of a labour economy was seen as tantamount with and leading to the establishment of a viable Jewish national economy.

At the same time, within the civil economy sector, in part anteceding the development of the worker's sector, in part developing concomitantly with it, there developed a much weaker 'class' identity, consciousness or ideology – not couched in such pioneering terms nor in strong sectorial consciousness as in the working sector.

Truly enough in the concrete encounters between private employers and workers there indeed developed quite a bit of 'class' antagonism focused above all on problems of wages and work conditions, to no small degree also fed by European socialist ideologies.

Moreover, from very early on trade union activities – both in the public (i.e. the mandatory government, Jewish Agency and *Vaad Leumi*, etc.) sector and in the private sector – constituted an important part of the Histadrut and of the independent professional organizations, such as especially the Teachers' Union and the Medical Associations (which were not part of the Histadrut); yet these activities did not constitute the major ideological and even organizational focus of the Histadrut.

## Patterns of class consciousness

Of crucial importance in the shaping of the specific characteristics of these activities and their class consciousness were: first that each of the sectors comprised many different occupations across 'usual' occupational groups and class confrontations; and, second, that from the very beginning the workers' sector developed, as we have seen, a series of its own enterprises – co-operatives, marketing and industrial ones – and that it comprised also the agricultural settlements – the Kibbutzim and Moshavim which were often seen as the social and ideological apex of this sector. Thus, from the very beginning, the process of strata formation in the Yishuv could not be understood in usual 'Western European' terms of class formation because the occupational position or economic standing of any social or occupational category did not necessarily reflect the nature of the access to positions of socio-political control, the nature of the frameworks within which such control was exercised, and the ideologies guiding them.

Hence the basic components of class consciousness were here, on the whole, structured in an entirely different way from the usual European one; the major strata divisions were focused not so much around the usual European class divisions, between capitalists and workers, but rather around the divisions or distinctions between the workers and the civil sector, and to a smaller degree in confrontation with them.

Accordingly, the sectorial orientations were initially probably more important than the purely occupational ones – whether of workers, white collars, bureaucrats or agriculturalists. Although some occupational or semi-occupational organizations and consciousness developed, both among the workers and probably even more among the professions such as teachers or doctors, these were certainly not couched in terms of any broader class consciousness.

So from the very beginning – against the attempts of some extremist, but practically not very successful groups – there was little direct overall class confrontation between workers and capitalists. Such confrontations of course existed, as we have indicated, in the 'civil' sector of the Yishuv, but on the whole they were of rather secondary importance in the overall institutional and political activities of the workers' sector in general, and of the Histadrut in particular.

Indeed one of the major foci of something approaching class warfare in the period of the Yishuv developed around the problem of 'Jewish Labour', against the employment of Arab workers by Jewish employers, when the Labour sector, guided by the specific Zionist–Labour vision of the necessity to establish a viable, modern, non-colonial, Jewish economy, as well as by the practical need to find places of employment for the many pioneers, stressed against the employment of Arab workers – an emphasis which, given the socialist orientation of the Histadrut, and especially of some of its more leftist groups, could not be, of course, unproblematic.

# Strata Formation in the State of Israel
## Social differentiation and mobility

The pattern of strata-formation that crystallized in the State of Israel became, of course, greatly transformed in comparison with the period of the Yishuv – although in many ways naturally developing from the situation in the period of the Yishuv.

The starting-point of these developments was the continuously growing and diversifying economic and occupational structure: the growing yet differential mobility, giving wage and income differentials as well as the growing occupational similarities between the different sectors, the general characteristics of which were analysed above.

Within this broad spectrum of occupational development and diversification, several trends stand out. One such trend was the immense growth of the public service sector of white-collar occupations, evident in the government's civil service, in the municipalities and in the Histadrut sectors, making the salaried groups in general, and those in public sectors in particular, the largest in the structure of manpower. Second was the development of many 'higher' occupation groups – managerial and professional ones – most of which cut across, even if not in the same degree, the different sectors.

All these developments were connected with far-reaching and continuous mobility among all the different sectors of the population – both the 'older' ones and those of the new immigrants – generated by the economic development but also by its own momentum.

A crucial new element in this process of mobility was, as we have seen, the growing importance of education and educational certification – whether on the level of high school certificates or of a BA University degree – for access to many occupational positions, especially in the service sector in general and public service in particular.

In many ways, Israeli society in that period could be characterized as a continuously expanding and mobile one. Indeed it was probably such mobility, in its different aspects – the continuous development of new levels of aspiration towards economic and occupational advancement and towards higher standards of living; the concomitant weakening and possible recrystallization of existing patterns of life and of groups' solidarity; the search for new ones – that was probably the most important characteristics of Israeli society in the first three decades of its development.

## Sectorial differences

These patterns of mobility, of course, differed greatly among different sectors of the population.

The older inhabitants, the veterans and their children, the 'first *Tsabra*' generation, very quickly moved into the various upper echelons of most newly developing sectors – such as service, army, academic and business.

Among the new immigrants the process of mobility was greatly influenced by their educational background. The Europeans moved particularly into the middle – some into the upper – echelons of the various sectors and occupations, but many of them remained in the lower-middle rings – in the civil service and the different bureaucracies, in the artisan and small business sectors.

Large parts of the Oriental immigrants started with a greater handicap. Some of them became integrated in the new Moshavim; others entered the lower echelons of the urban sector – some of them moving up later through various educational channels, above all perhaps the vocational one, into the newly developing private sector.

Thus in general there crystallized (as we shall see in Chapter 11) a certain overlap between 'class' and ethnic differences – in the sense that the lower (especially poverty) sector was composed mostly of the so-called Oriental immigrants, the upper sector mostly of those of European and Western origin, while the middle sector became continuously 'ethnically' more mixed.

Another crucial change in the whole format of stratification that developed in the State of Israel was, of course, the incorporation in the framework of the Israeli society of Arab population, which has on the whole developed into a special strata sector of its own.

After the Six Day War there was a further development in this direction, as we have seen through the influx of Arab labour from the West Bank and Gaza into the Israeli economy, mainly as workers in industry, agriculture and construction.

There are several indications that this great almost universal – but naturally rather uneven – process of mobility generated a widespread feeling of relative deprivation among many groups.

## Differential mobility; the ethnic factor

One central aspect of the unequal developments of such mobility and of the concomitant spread of feelings of relative deprivation was the crystallization of some ascriptive tendencies in the structuring of such mobility – but tendencies set within the frameworks of a continuously expanding and mobile society.

Such ascriptive tendencies focused on several, usually reinforcing, criteria, among which 'ethnic' and ecological ones were probably the most important.

Thus, as Matras and Weintraub have summarized:

In Israel there have been sharp ethnic and other primordial differences in distributions by educational attainment and occupation groups, and there have been notable ethnic and other primordial differences in patterns of intergenerational educational and occupational mobility. For the most part intergenerational mobility has not operated to close these educational or occupational distribution gaps. Rather, they have remained stable or even widened intergenerationally *both* because of differential outflow patterns and rates *and* because of very different initial educational and occupational distributions. . . . More generally, and side by side with the ethnically embedded processes, the mobility patterns observed have nurtured the formation of new educational and occupational strata, great expansion of previously quite small or obscure strata, and a general re-ordering of strata sizes and composition. It seems reasonable to conjecture, though we cannot now show directly, that these demo-graphic-morphological shifts in strata have in turn given rise to changes in inter-strata relationships generally. Thus, the mobility regime is itself a prime mover in strata formation processes and not simply a function of exogenously-determined shifts in strata organization and relationships.*

## Internal and external sectors

The processes of mobility in general, the growing intensification and diversi-fication of economical and occupational stratification and of styles of life, the weakening of most of the solid frameworks were greatly reinforced by the development, even if not yet fully understood or researched, of differences between internal and external sectors characteristic, as we have seen, of small societies.

Although no systematic data exist on this problem, there are plentiful indications that the various activities in the externally orientated sectors differed greatly from those more internally orientated ones, and many of the activities orientated to the external markets were not closely related to one another. These differences between the internal and external sectors, although in a way imperceptible and not well researched, continuously emphasized the differences within each occupational group between the more international sets and those more internally orientated, and it seems on the whole these differences between internal and external orientated sectors intensified the distances between different elites and different sectors of Israeli society.

They also contributed to the growing social distance between different groups and strata – and it is important to remember in this context that, at least initially, there was a natural heavy concentration of many of the new immigrants in general and parts of the Oriental ones in particular in these internal sectors.

A common denominator of all these developments was a continuous raising of levels of aspiration, often going beyond the confines of the State, and probably contributing to the phenomena of *Yerida* (emigration from Israel).

While no exact data exist, it has been estimated that about 350,000 people have emigrated from the State of Israel since its inception. The yearly ratio is of 4.5 emigrants per one thousand inhabitants – but 225 per one thousand immigrants – a ratio which is smaller than that found in other countries of modern immigration.†

* See in greater detail Judah Matras and Dov Weintraub, 'Ethnic and Other Primordial Differentials in Intergenerational Mobility in Israel', Brookdale Institute, Discussion Paper 4 (Jerusalem 1977), pp. 22–6.
† Reuven Lamdani, *The Emigration from Israel*, The Falk Institute for Economic Research in Israel, Research Paper No. 159 (Jerusalem 1983).

It is not easy to pinpoint the exact reason for their leaving Israel, or for Israel's relative lack of attraction for them – despite many family and sentimental ties. They can indeed be seen as a natural aspect of any modern migratory movement. Many of the available indications seem to point out that it was the apparently restrictive aspects of Israeli society – whether in the lack of housing for young couples after the military service and at the threshold of their occupational life; in the lack of adequate opportunities for various more skilled or professional occupations; in the relatively restrictive opportunities in academic life – that were behind their leaving or not coming back.

The most general indication is that it is the search for new economic opportunities, the wish to try something on one's own as against the more restricted and regulatory aspects of Israeli society, that has been the most important single factor in such emigration. This has been confirmed by the emigrants themselves.*

## Transformation of the Process of Strata Formation
### Class ideology and struggles

The broad pattern of occupational and strata formation that developed in Israeli society has already been briefly touched upon above in our discussion of the mould of political economy – namely the development of this class structure and processes of strata formation, based on a combination of occupational differentiation, shaped by the centres of political power.

First there were the economic policies of the centre that generated large parts of the – especially new – upper groups as well as the emergence of a special lower class close to the poverty line, to which the multiple social welfare policies were orientated – giving rise to an entirely new sector, defined by growing independence on the centres and its services.

Second, many of the middle sectors – especially those in the service sector in general and in the public sector in particular, were by their very nature also greatly dependent on the centre and above all on the extension of its welfare policies.

Whatever the details of these developments, there can be no doubt that one of their most important characteristics was the transformation of the upper and upper middle groups into a general social democratic direction – yet often still using symbols of pioneering – without full incorporation of the lower groups; all these closely connected with the changing role and orientation of the Histadrut.

Closely related to these developments was the tendency to a coalescence of ethnic and class lines, evident in the fact that the so-called Oriental groups tend to concentrate above all in the middle and lower salaried groups and in the lower, dependent poverty sector – although, as we shall see in our discussion of the processes of absorption and integration of different groups of immigrants,

* Drora Kass and Seymour Martin Lipset, 'America's New Wave of Jewish Immigrants', *The New York Times Magazine*, 7 December 1980.

the overall picture was indeed much more complicated.

The combination of these developments created the probabilities of new types of social distances and 'class' conflicts.

In all these developments the important changes in the nature of the trade union activities of the Histadrut, were of special importance. These activities indeed became very diversified. Some professional organizations – like the primary school teachers' union organization – joined Histadrut – yet at the same time the capacity of the overall Histadrut leadership to direct activities became weaker and, as we have already seen above, it was the different unions and even floor-committees that became the more active elements in the struggles – with the central committee of the Histadrut attempting at most to serve as a sort of last resort, or an empire, in the regulation of some of the conflicts – especially with respect to the public employers.

Moreover the overall orientation to the Histadrut became articulated less in terms of any 'sectorial' or 'class' identification, with outright different economic and/or power considerations becoming much more important.

At the same time a new pattern of organization developed among the different professional groups, especially physicians, teachers and lawyers – often cutting across their employment sectors – evincing very strong corporate organization and interest orientations, with but little ideological orientation.

## *Class struggles and consciousness*

The concrete patterns of strata formation, struggle and consciousness, as they have crystallized in the State of Israel, developed out of the continuous confrontation between, on the one hand, the processes of occupational diversification and mobility which took place in connection with the economic expansion and, on the other hand, the new centres of power and the ideological formations that crystallized in the State of Israel and the policies undertaken by them.

The first major result of this confrontation before the processes of diversification of State policies was the growing diversification of the process of strata formation, the development of a very diversified criss-cross of political, sectorial and occupational formations, of status sets, consciousness and struggle, and the weakening of any overall, especially 'class' or 'social', ideological orientations in the crystallization of such consciousness.

These processes were combined with the development of very complicated differences in life styles among different status groups; of new patterns of status or class conflict and struggles; and of new types of status or 'class' consciousness. These did not develop in the direction of a pure 'socialist' or 'class' formation nor – perhaps even more important – in that of the older sectorial parties which developed in the Yishuv. Accordingly, there were far-reaching changes in the pattern of what may be called strata or class struggle and strata and status consciousness.

The major focus of what may be called class struggles (such as the incidents of strikes and of the struggle about social welfare benefits) was the State, as a distributive, and to a smaller degree also regulative, agency.

By its very nature this struggle was occupationally dispersed with but little overall ideological political orientation. It was dispersed among salaried personnel and manual workers, on the one hand, and between the salaried and independent professionals on the other; within each of these frameworks and the middle and lower groups that remained inside them; between those in key positions and with influence on government and vital points in the economy and those without access to such positions. All of these groups were competing for their share of the growing income, for access to economic resources and positions of influence in the government on the one hand, and for the possibility to develop autonomous approaches and frameworks on the other.

A distinct type class struggle also developed around the various welfare benefits distributed by the State. In many ways these demands cut across those for wages or housing conditions – thus contributing to the further dispersion of the foci of such struggle – and it was only with the poverty-dependent sector that they became connected with the crystallization of a new status sector.

## Strata and status consciousness

So the concrete 'economic' foci of what can be called class struggle became dispersed between the different types of demands of various occupation groups towards the State. Meanwhile the political and ideological expressions of status consciousness became focused less and less around such economic problems and much more, even if on the whole in a rather vague way, around the degree of access or participation in the centre of the society, around the centre/periphery axis, and/or around the development of distinct styles and patterns of life. Truly enough some of the older sectorial elements persisted, but in a very transformed way.

Thus, first of all, the access to the centre of the society, probably even more the feeling of participation in the centre or of relative exclusion from it, constituted one of the major ideological axes of status consciousness beyond the concrete economic demands and problems.

Here a distinction gradually developed – the importance of which varied in different situations – between the different occupational status groups which somehow felt they belonged to the centre as it developed under the auspices of the Labour governments and those, sometimes occupationally very similar, occupational groups who felt they did not or were excluded from it.

The first groups naturally included the Kibbutzim and many of the Moshavim; the upper echelon of the civil service and Histadrut leadership; some sector of the professions, as well as, surprisingly enough, large parts of the newly emerging state-sponsored bourgeoisie and technocratic elements. The second included many of the bourgeois elements of the old 'private sector'; parts of the professions; many of the new immigrants in general and Oriental ones in particular; the lower-middle groups.

On the whole there were but few clear-cut occupational distinctions between these sectors and potentially a very strong fluidity between them. This fluidity would become 'frozen' in periods of political upheaval, but basically it constituted a very important aspect of the strata or class structure that developed in Israel.

Another important aspect was the development, among the higher echelons, especially those close to the centre, of a phenomenon which can indeed be found in many small societies: namely of close networks between the upper echelons of different occupational sectors – the military, business, civil service, some professions. These networks also tended to be relatively strongly orientated to external markets.

And yet, while some of these life styles were indeed common to many groups, yet they came together in different ways in different sectors, greatly influenced by their social background and cultural orientation. Moreover, above all among the members of the younger generation, there developed a growing tendency to privatize these different styles of life – that is to dissociate them from any broader societal visions and legitimation.

## Life styles

The most important differences in the life styles of the various sectors of Israeli society were based on the combination of income and cultural, including ethnic and religious, traditions; on the relative importance of inward- or outward-directed orientations and occupational and economic activities; and, to some degree, on the extent of feelings of proximity to the centre. Except among religious sectors, and to some degree the Kibbutzim, ideological components were less important.

The life styles that developed among different strata were composed of more and more common components. The most important such common elements – with the exception of some of the religious sectors – was a growing emphasis on consumption and participation in cultural events: concerts, picnics, week-end excursions, participation in sport activities, and orientations to the external world in the form of trips abroad, consumption of the products of mass media and participation in various types of cultural activities. This orientation to the outside world and to leisure activities grew continuously.

The high level of mobility also necessarily gave rise to some rather shallow, vulgar orientations and very conspicuous consumption on all levels of the social ladder.

This situation naturally entailed a lot of fluidity in the patterns of life and in the participation of different groups in them – naturally connected with the intensive mobility that took place in Israel.

Yet these common elements and fluidity notwithstanding, the differences in the concrete styles of life of different groups could sometimes be felt very sharply, and contact in some common activities – like sport – could be very explosive. Perhaps gradually, with growing intermarriage and contact, some of these will become less explosive and new mixes of life styles will develop.

Within this whole panorama of different social groups, a certain new element has been exerting some influence: namely that of new immigrants from the West, especially of the United States. While some of them have become highly integrated in the different groups of Israeli society, or have just added some new colours to existing groups, others, particularly the more affluent ones, many coming to Israel at retirement or only as a second home, often living in rather luxurious apartments or hotels, have greatly strengthened the external orientations and the orientation to a high standard of living.

Some changes were connected with the development of a different time-perception in relation to social mobility. Although few specific data exist on this, there are many indicators that, among the higher groups, those in close proximity to the centre, there developed a lesser orientation to the future, a growing emphasis on the present as an important dimension of social activities connected on a wider spectrum of rewards. Concomitantly there was also a relatively far-reaching privatization and differentiation of life styles together with the development of many new types of creativity – not necessarily connected with any overall vision.

At the same time, among some of the upward mobile elements from different sectors there often developed a strong orientation to investment in the future – in occupational advance and also, in some cases, in some collective goals.

These various patterns or life styles became much less ecologically concentrated or ideologized than in the different sectors in the period of the Yishuv. Such ecological concentration, and some degree of ideology could only be found in the Kibbutzim and in the different religious sectors, in particular the more extreme ones (which became more and more prominent as we shall see in Chapter 17). In the more extreme religious sectors most of the common components of the different life styles were missing and the overall segregation from other sectors, including strong tendency to endogamy, was very strong – sometimes total.

Such segregation was less total among many of the more modern religious sectors, which incorporated in their life styles some of the common components, such as sport, use of mass media, participation in cultural events, concerts and theatre, but among large parts of them the tendency to segregation, and especially endogamy, was still strong.

Such tendency to segregation and ideologization was much weaker among other sectors, as for instance in the Kibbutzim – but even within them there developed a far-reaching change which, especially when compared with those in the Moshavim, is indicative of the changes and developments in the processes of strata formation in Israel.

# Changes in the Kibbutzim and Moshavim in the Process of Strata Formation in Israeli Society
## Economic developments

In this period the Kibbutzim as well as the Moshavim – but above all the former – underwent a far-reaching process of internal transformation and diversification. From relatively small communes of young pioneers, establishing the bases of agricultural settlements, they developed into established, on the whole flourishing, collective villages composed of several generations. They established within them a relatively diversified economic structure, first in agriculture, and then spreading over into industry, evincing a continuous economic growth, modernization and specialization of their structure in general, and of their economic structure in particular. Many, if not all, of the Kibbutzim succeeded greatly as economic innovators and entrepreneurs in the industrial sector, in some cases contributing to important changes in the Israeli economy. The picture among the Moshavim was also characterized by continuous economic growth, but with less emphasis on expansion into the industrial sector. Both the Kibbutzim and Moshavim participated in the general trend of economic development and advance in the standard of living that was characteristic of the country as a whole.

Agriculture in general, and in the Kibbutzim and Moshavim in particular, was quite heavily subsidized by the government in several ways – in tax structure (which was especially beneficial for the Kibbutzim), in special prices for water, in allocation of public loans and export quotas, and, in the case of the younger settlements, in long-range subsidies for the establishment of their infrastructure – as was, of course, the case, even if on a grander scale, with the first Kibbutzim earlier on. They constituted a very powerful, but special, part of the agricultural lobby or pressure groups.

Changes in the economic structure of the Kibbutzim were, of course, very closely connected with parallel ones in their internal social structure. Here also, there was some growing specialization in tasks and activities. There took place a continuous strengthening of the familial groups – even of some extended family relations – as against the communal ambiance of the groups of youthful pioneers, as well as a growing *de facto* development of economic specialization, the need of greater technical and professional training.

## Developments in the Kibbutzim

All these far-reaching developments in the realization of the original communal vision of the youthful communes of pioneers were connected with attempts, on the part of the leadership of the Kibbutzim, to regulate them within the continuously changing and yet relatively persistent ideological premisses of the Kibbutz and their major institutional implications – such as the stress on basic equality of members with respect to standards of living, on communal ownership of the means of production and control of patterns of consumption, as well as on the avoidance of dependence on hired labour, and the like. It was indeed this last problem – that of hired labour – which was the most difficult and acute, from the ideological point of view of the Kibbutzim.

On the one hand, hired labour was a very important ingredient of the economic expansion of the Kibbutzim in general and of the industrial expansion in particular. On the other hand, it was, of course, against the basic ideological tenets of the Kibbutz movement and, accordingly, constituted one of the continuous foci of concern within the Kibbutzim and in the public controversy around them.

The exact extent of this phenomenon is not easy to ascertain, but this certainly became a central problem within the different Kibbutz movements.

Various solutions – and subterfuges – were attempted by the different Kibbutz movements. The most extreme – but not very frequent – was the total abolition of such hired labour. A more frequent ploy was to put some limitations on it. Among the more important and frequent subterfuges was that such labour was hired, not by a single Kibbutz, but by the various 'regional' entrepreneurs established by different Kibbutzim or by the Kibbutz federations, often in co-operation with other entrepreneurs.

There also developed many additional problems in the Kibbutz touching on central aspects of its ideology – those between the hierarchies involved in encouraging industrial expertise as against maintaining the ideal of equality; those growing out of the demands of the younger generations for some educational opportunities; and those of inequality between different Kibbutzim.

With respect to most of these problems the Kibbutzim were on the whole successful in finding ways to combine many openings with the maintenance of the overall regulations of the Kibbutz movement. Thus there developed a growing permission for their children to attend institutions of higher learning – especially (but not only) in the fields of agriculture, or in various specialized areas, such as the arts; or for their children, after serving in the army, to go away for a year to 'see the world' – hopefully increasing the attraction of coming back home. But always the Kibbutz institutions maintained overall regulations. They were also very innovative in finding constructive ways of coping with the problems of old age.

This conjunction of the elitist egalitarian and pioneering pragmatic orientations with the internal communal organization transformed the Kibbutzim in the direction of a combination of 'gentleman farmer', with some sort of non-celibate monasticism, a combination which provided both for great innovativeness in general and entrepreneurship in particular, as well as incorporation, in a relatively regulated way, of the new internal developments. But, as we shall soon see, this also created new problems.

## Changes in the Moshavim

At the same time far-reaching changes took place in the Moshavim, both in the older ones, and in the numerous new ones established since 1948, most of which were populated by new immigrants. As D. Weintraub analysed:

In their confrontation with the moshav, each population consequently 'interpreted' the ideology and structure of the blueprint in its own way. The 1960's, a decade after most villages had settled, witnessed the emergence of the consolidated 'modern-western' moshavim, which developed rapidly, agriculturally, and communally, but which were ready to introduce changes in the practices of self-labor and self-employment and in the binding universality of the cooperative. Although the immigrants remained in the moshav movement and adopted much of the normative organization because of its effectiveness and because it was in many respects the best channel for obtaining institutional support and services, the acceptance was largely conditional upon circumstances and alternatives. In this way, they preserved much of the scope and the comprehensiveness of the village cooperation, but did so in a much more open and flexible way. In effect, they tended towards the historical pattern of the 'middle-class' moshav created by non-socialist groups in the 1930's in distinction from the workers' moshav. They promoted multipurpose cooperation based on the community but stopped short of the binding totality of institutionalization. It was a cooperative dealing with marketing, credit, and other farm-supporting services, but was susceptible to internal differentiation and change. . . .

In the 1970's, sustained developmental efforts and a demographic transition changed the picture dramatically in the last type of moshav. In fact, productivity of farms operated by natives of 'oriental' origin does not now fall much short of the level accomplished by their occidental contemporaries. Not only is the gap between the groups in the family farm of the moshav now narrowed, but this sector has become more advantageous to entrepreneurs of 'traditional' descent, in competition with that of urban employees, in which the ethnic disparities are much more persistent. Two factors have apparently contributed most to this process. First, there has been the multiplier effect of the village cooperatives, now functioning increasingly better – on the Western pattern – in villages in which the old conflicts have been attenuated, and now leadership and management have emerged. Second, of focal importance has been the considerable increase in human capital endowment of this group owing to the closing of the secondary education gap in the young generation, brought about by the establishment of special agricultural secondary schools by moshavim and regional councils.

Likewise, the new immigrant villages have been moving to redress also the previous economic and political imbalance within the moshav movement, which had been dominated by the veterans. Using economics and politics of scale and regional cooperative frameworks newly established by them, these villages are getting an ever-increasing share in overall representation and decision-making. . . .

The dairy branch continued to be characteristic of the veteran sector, and its delimitation allowed this sector to grow and hold off the new trends longer. The 1970's diminished these opportunities, however, and specialization has become widespread also here. As a consequence, the moshav way of life has changed. the new branches are not fully compatible with self-employment and self-labor. The emergent village heterogeneity has necessitated a loosening of uniform and universal patterns of cooperation and has brought about organizational restructuring featuring less monolithic and less binding cooperative arrangements.

This increasingly voluntary and differential structure has not meant a decrease in the volume and importance of cooperative activity, however, and has not necessitated a trend away from comprehensive, community-based cooperation as such. Because of the increasing complexity of operations, the potential advantages and scope of voluntary village cooperation have grown rather than declined, so that the lessening of institutionally binding uniformity and dependence have augmented and not attenuated the utility and attractiveness of joint services. Indeed, in the veteran villages, cooperation continues almost unchanged, albeit on a new basis; in the immigrant ones that had earlier undergone a cooperative loosening or had a low level of cooperativization, joint services are now stronger and broader than before. . . .

Among the moshavim there took also, beginning in 1960, important attempts at regional rural organization.

The first nationally sponsored regional project, that of Lachish, was begun in the 1950's, combining newly settled immigrant moshavim. The scheme was designed primarily to utilize advantages of scale and agglomeration so as to provide better, more efficient services under one authority. The region was planned in a traditional, spatial hierarchy: villages were laid out in clusters around two rural centers, providing first- and second-level services respectively; an especially developed regional town had a high school, a hospital, more sophisticated consumer, supply and recreational facilities, and processing plants for agricultural products as well as machme plants and other small industries. . . .

In the following years, this scheme has been acted out in the original region and, with some modifications based on the early experience, adopted for two new areas of settlement. It is too early to evaluate it fully, but indications of the extent to which the innovation has been successful in achieving its aims, and of its main drawbacks and difficulties, are clear. . . .*

## The Kibbutzim and Moshavim in the Israeli political structure

In general, therefore, both the Kibbutzim and the Moshavim developed as parts – truly enough, very special and distinct ones – of the upper echelons of Israeli society, a rather unique agricultural sector of such echelons, developing special styles and quality of life but most certainly belonging to these upper echelons.

But, obviously, they were not only successful agricultural settlements developing specific life styles. They continued to constitute a very important element in the political life of the country in general, and of the Labour sector in particular. The different Kibbutzim continued to be organized in overarching federations or streams, the most important of which are the *Kibbutz Hameuchad* (The United Kibbutz), *Ihud Hakevutzot ve-Hakibbutzim* (The Community or Association of Kibbutzim) and *Hakibbutz Ha'artzi* (The 'Country-wide Kibbutz' – the leftist one of the *Hashomer Hatzair*) combined in 1980 in *Takam* (United Kibbutz Movement).

These federations were, first of all, political–ideological frameworks, each of them articulating its special ideology, developing special political and cultural

* Dov Weintraub with Zeev Shavith, 'Social Issues, Processes and Policies in Israel 1960–1980', prepared for the revised edition of UNESCO, *The Scientific and Cultural History of Mankind*, Draft 3/198, pp. 40–2.

institutions, including schools, publishing houses and a great variety of economic institutions, such as various industrial and marketing enterprises, the latter often common to several such federations and to the economic institutions of the Histadrut.

The *Kibbutz Ha'artzi* (*Hashomer Hatzair*) was affiliated with *Mapam*, the *Ihud Hakevutzot ve-Hakibbutzim* with *Mapai*, and the *Kibbutz Hameuchad* with *Ahdut Haavoda*.

The religious Kibbutzim were, as a rule, affiliated above all with the *Hapoel Hamizrahi*; there were also a few belonging to the Poalei Agudat Israel. The Moshavim were organized in the *Tnuat Hamoshavim* and were, almost entirely, identified with the Labour Party.

These close relations of the Kibbutzim and the Moshavim with the different political parties, and their very strong position within them, further emphasized their interweaving – even if as rather special sectors – in the upper echelons of Israeli society.

## Shift in elite activities

Moreover, this closeness to the upper echelons of society provides some of the best indications of far-reaching changes in the strata formation of Israeli society. These changes were of course connected with the basic fact that the Kibbutzim and the Moshavim were not just another – even if rather special – element in the economic and political life of Israel. They saw themselves – perhaps especially the Kibbutzim – and were, for a long period of time, seen by large parts of the Israeli society, as well as by many people abroad, as the most essential symbol of the Zionist–Labour movement and ideology, as the image of the pioneer and as a special elite group or cadre. This special elite status of theirs was based on the combination of devotion and continuous commitment to pioneering tasks and ideals, of adherence to their pioneering and special communal style of life.

The elite status of the Kibbutzim, within the Labour sector first of the Yishuv and, later on, within Israeli society, was evident not only in some general vague symbolic identification and rhetoric references in ritual situations, but also in some very specific institutional derivations.

The most important of these were: the relatively disproportionate number of the members of Kibbutzim in elite positions in the Yishuv and, at least in the first two and a half decades, of the State of Israel; the importance of membership in youth movements, which made joining the Kibbutz movements and even transitory membership in Kibbutzim a channel to elite status; the high general prestige accorded to membership in Kibbutzim; and the relatively heavy subsidization of Kibbutzim and Moshavim alluded to above. (An interesting illustration of the combination of such symbolic emulation and attachment, together with such subsidization, can be found in the NAHAL formations, as well as in sending volunteers from youth movements and from abroad to work – as a sort of national service – for different periods of time in the Kibbutzim.)

But it is exactly with respect to these aspects of life, that there have been some of the most important changes, shedding light on the transformations of the social structure of the Kibbutzim, on their place in Israeli social structure and on the transformation of the initial mould of Israeli society in general.

The first such change was the relative weakening of the place of the Kibbutz elite – as a distinct ideological group and not only as representative of specific interests – in the Israeli political elite, and perhaps above all their becoming in a sense part of the oligarchic structure of the Labour Party or other leftist parties and of the Kibbutz movements themselves.

Interesting developments also took place in the internal structure of the Kibbutz elites. Here also there developed, although possibly somewhat less than in the general society, a certain closure of the political elite, and the general oligarchic tendencies in the political life had their counterparts within the Kibbutzim. There developed a certain – although certainly not total – bifurcation and differentiation between the political leadership of the Kibbutz (those members who actually participated in the Knesset, in the Histadrut and in party activities) and the ones, mostly from younger generations, who became more visible in the new elite functions. Such functions moved away from political, ideological, and military positions (in the *Hagana*, in general, and the *Palmach* in particular) to other types of positions, such as in select but not necessarily top military formations, for instance among the paratroopers, or many top bureaucratic positions, integrating those of the Histadrut and the government sector. In the latter some members of the older generation of Kibbutz elite could also be found.

## Place in Israeli society

The shift in the relative importance of elite activities within the Kibbutzim was closely connected with a changing relationship of the Kibbutzim to the broader sectors of Israeli society in general, and new immigrants in particular. The crucial facts are well-known – the relatively low level of attraction of the Kibbutzim for the younger groups of older populations and the immigrants, in particular the Oriental ones.

Statistics indicate that the number of people in Kibbutzim rose from 54,208 in 1948 to 123,700 in 1981 – but this indicates a decline from 7.0 per cent of the population in 1948 to about 3.4 per cent in 1981. In 1972 – when their total number was about 189,000 – 4.8 per cent of them were from Asian or African countries.

These figures, as well as the fact that substantial numbers of the younger generation were leaving the Kibbutzim (it is very difficult to get exact data), attested to the weakening of their attraction in general and with respect to new immigrants in particular.

For the members of the older sectors of the society in general, and within the labour camp in particular, membership in the Kibbutzim or even participation in youth movements, whose proclaimed aim was for their members to join the Kibbutzim and to create new Kibbutzim, became a less and less attractive goal. Joining the existing Kibbutzim or creating new Kibbutzim was less and less regarded as an avenue to elite status, and the attraction of the Kibbutzim had more and more shifted to another direction, as we shall soon see.

The Kibbutzim appeared also – in marked contrast to the Moshavim – much less attractive to new immigrants and, beyond some special attempts at attracting new immigrants in the Kibbutzim, relatively few new Kibbutzim were established by new immigrants in general and Oriental ones in particular.

Secondly, and in close connection, there was a shift – already alluded to above – in the attraction of Kibbutzim to new members from the outside, and to the second and third generations of children within the Kibbutzim. Pioneering commitments, although they did not disappear entirely, became less important than a relatively high standard of living, prestigious status and special quality of life.

But the nature of this quality of life, as well as that of the new directions of elite activities, was very strictly set within the adherence to the ideological premises and rather sectarian frameworks of the Kibbutz, which quite large sectors of the population could see as 'aristocratic', distant and self-righteous.

The combination of all these changes was also closely related with a series of shifts, seemingly imperceptible and yet very forceful, in the standing, mainly of the Kibbutz, in the symbolic–ideological universe of Israeli society. The first such shift, which probably developed from the late 1950s occurred from the Kibbutz being a symbol of pioneering – a symbol demanding commitment, emulation and following – to becoming a symbol of the latent, already institutionalized, better aspirations of the society, or of some of its pristine values, commanding high respect and different forms of subsidizing, but with little direct commitment and following.

At the same time, the Kibbutzim fully participated in the economic and political expansion of Israeli society, acquiring strong positions within it and continuing to claim for themselves elite status and importance as symbols of the pristine values of the society. Closely related to this were the new modes of participation of the Kibbutzim, and to some degree of the Moshavim, in the political system which developed after the establishment of the State of Israel. Here, the Kibbutzim remained the upholders of the more sectarian ideological orientations, often attempting to serve as a voice of the conscience or as moral guide, but building their strength more on internal coalitions within the centres of the respective parties, rather than on full participation in the middle and lower echelons of the political game, thus indirectly contributing to their growing decline in the central political elite.

## Sectarian tendencies in Kibbutzim and Moshavim

These contradictory developments within the Kibbutzim – namely their great ability to develop new types of elite activities in general and economic entrepreneurship in particular, on the one hand, and the growing internal self-closure, on the other – were often rooted in the same basic characteristics of the Kibbutzim, in their ideology and social structure, in the basic features of their sectarian, communal ambiance and pioneering orientations or, in other words, in those very characteristics which made them the symbol and vanguard of Labour–Zionism.

But these changes were very closely bound within the basic existing frameworks of the Kibbutzim, within the framework of their rather sectarian tendencies, based on the peculiar characteristics of their elitist sectarian ethos. While the members of these sects were, in principle, ready to extend their egalitarian conceptions towards other sectors of society, such an extension became contingent on the adherence to the basic institutional and ideological mould of the respective Kibbutz movements and to acceptance of all the concrete institutional precepts of Kibbutz life. In so far as these other sectors could not live up to such a standard, the Kibbutzim tended to develop toward a more distant 'tutelary' approach – while maintaining through self-closure their own relatively pristine sectarian purity.

It is here – namely in their ability to combine the elitist commitment together with the growing emphasis on internal quality of life, standards of living and privatization – that the great challenge or question mark about the future of the Kibbutzim lies.

In many cases their great ability to respond to the growing demands, especially by the younger generation, for different aspects of such quality and standards of life – but without combining them with new types of elitist commitment – has given rise, not only to growing privatization and tendencies to leave the Kibbutzim, but also to a great variety of social problems – divorces, addiction to drugs and the like – which seem to have become more widespread within them.

Within the Moshavim, the developments were somewhat different. They shared with the Kibbutzim the general participation in the economic and political expansion and in the rising standards of life, but at the same time they lived up much better to the new social challenges, without stressing the unique, pristine, sectarian elite status.

## Summary

These far-reaching changes in the internal structure and external standing of the Kibbutzim, in themselves and as compared with the Moshavim – the combination of economic success, relatively high standards and special quality of life, elitist self-conception and ambiance; of having become part, even if a special one, of the upper strata of Israeli society; the gradual withdrawal inwards and the loss of many of the central elite positions, together with a high level of commitment to performance of special elite functions – were indeed very indicative of some of the general changes and developments in the elite structure and class consciousness in Israel in general, and in the labour sector in particular.

The Kibbutzim, much more than the Moshavim, have drawn themselves inward, closing up towards the new social, but not economic, reality that has been continuously developing and crystallizing in Israel. They were not able to live up to many challenges posed by this new reality or to influence it. Significantly enough the Moshavim, whose sectarian characteristic was much weaker but which shared with the Kibbutzim the strong pragmatic orientations, were able to combine economic expansion (albeit, given their familistic structure, with weaker orientations to the industrial sector) with a greater openness to other sectors of the society, and to new immigrants in particular. Together they changed the whole ambiance of important parts of the upper sectors of Israeli society and of the overall picture of the symbols of status and of the structuring of hierarchies in it.

All these developments were indeed part of far-reaching transformations of the original vision of Labour–Zionism – a transformation from aims of the more ascetic, productivity orientated pioneers to the strong emphasis on ascriptive allocations and new conception of status and strata formation; to a very far-reaching diversity and complexity of the process of strata formation which differed from either a pure socialist class formation or from the sectorial mode which developed in the period of the Yishuv.

CHAPTER 10

# Educational and Cultural Contours

# I · The Educational System

## The Major Problems of the Israeli Educational System
### *Five periods of educational development*

With the establishment of the State, far-reaching changes took place in the educational system, its organization and structure, and perhaps above all in the way it was interwoven in the social and economic structure. Indeed, many of the major developments, tensions and contradictions in Israeli society – the trend to organizational expansion, the stress on democratization, the problem of the construction of the major dimensions of its collective identity, the tensions between elitist and populist orientation and between internal and external orientations, became crystallized and articulated in the educational system, and in their turn the developments in this sphere had far-reaching developments on the crystallization of these tendencies in Israeli society.

The Israeli educational system was continuously orientated to cope with several problems. The first such problem was, of course, the organization of adequate educational facilities for all strata of the population, and the assurance of incorporation of all the sectors of the population into its framework. Second was the challenge of socialization of the various sectors of the population into the major symbolic premisses and symbols of the emerging collectivity. Third was the assurance, through the educational system, of social and national integration – a problem especially acute with the influx of new immigrants after the establishment of the State and with the growing emphasis on the State's responsibility for education. Fourth was the provision, through the educational system, of the basic skills and orientations expected in the labour market. Fifth was the fostering of cultural creativity in its different aspects and in different fields. Sixth was the coping with the problems of special groups: first of all of the new immigrants in general, of different groups or sections of the Oriental immigrants in particular, and later on of other special groups, whether on the one hand the handicapped ones, or on the other hand the specially gifted ones.

These various problems were closely interrelated, but their relative import-ance greatly varied in different periods. Following Reuven Kahane's suggestion*, it is possible to distinguish five periods in the development of the educational system, the first in the Yishuv and four since the establishment of the State of Israel.

The period of the Yishuv – which itself could, of course, be subdivided into further sub-periods – was characterized, as we have seen above, by a very strong emphasis on cultural creativity. It was also orientated not only to the existing population, but also beyond it. It was only partially – although continuously more and more – orientated to the labour market, and inter-woven in it, and forming a very important part of this system, were the different youth movements which emphasized, at least in principle, a dissociation from this market. In this period there were also a few special programmes for different special groups.

The first period in the State of Israel, which lasted until about the end of the 1950s, was mainly orientated to the absorption of new strata of population into the educational system, the basic organization of this system, and the crystallization of the basic curriculum and its symbolic premises. The next period, till about the mid-1960s, focused more on curricular problems in general and those related to the symbols of Israeli collective identity in particular.

The third period in the State of Israel, from about the mid-1960s, was mainly orientated to the problems of integration, to the special problems of different sectors of the population in general and those of new immigrants in particular. Finally, from the mid-1970s, there has been true educational progress, developing special curricula, and redefining different aspects of the collective heritage.

# The 1950s and Early 1960s: The First Two Periods of the Development of the Educational System in the State of Israel

## Setting up the system and the initial incorporation of the different sectors of the population

The first, simplest and most basic problem in these periods was, of course, the organization of an educational structure and organization which would be capable of absorbing the new waves of population.

It was in this period that the basic structure of the system became fully organized into primary, different secondary – especially academic vocational and agricultural – schools and the various institutions of higher education. Also at this time the basic laws about compulsory free education were promulgated. The State Education Law was passed by the Knesset in the summer of 1953,

* R. Kahane, private note.

thus abolishing the previous multi-trend educational system.

The strongly centralized educational system dealt with all problems pertaining to the curriculum, as well as the employment of teachers, while problems of finance and administration were dealt with in conjunction with the local authorities.

The number of pupils in the primary (up to the eighth grade, at age 14) and secondary (from age 14 to 18) schools grew from 140,917 in 1948/9 to 580,202 in 1959/60 (an increase of 412 per cent) and to 824,432 in 1969/70 (an increase of 142.1 per cent). In later periods the numbers grew to 1,203,836 in 1979/80 (an increase of 146 per cent), and to 1,261,556 in 1981/2 (an increase of 104 per cent). The increase between the years 1948/9 and 1981/2 was 895.8 per cent. The number of pupils in the primary schools grew from 91,133 in 1948/9 to 375,054 in 1959/60 (an increase of 411.54 per cent), to 394,345 in 1969/70 (an increase of 105.14 per cent) to 436,387 in 1979/80 (an increase of 110.65 per cent) to 455,431 in 1981/2 (an increase of 104.36 per cent). In the secondary schools the number of people grew from 55,142 in 1959/60 to 129,436 in 1969/70 (an increase of 234.73 per cent), to 143,810 in 1979/80 (an increase of 111.10 per cent), to 154,193 in 1981/2 (an increase of 107.21 per cent).*

At the same time the number of students in institutions of higher learning increased from 2,572 in 1949/50, to 10,202 in 1959/60 (an increase of 396 per cent); it came up to 18,368 in 1964/5 (an increase of 180 per cent) and to 32,389 in 1968/9 (an increase of 176.3 per cent). In 1976/7 the number of students in the universities was 52,980 (an increase of 163.5 per cent) and in 1982 the student population rose to 60,685 (an increase of 114.54 per cent). The total increase between 1949/50 and 1982 was 2,359 per cent.†

At the same time the three educational streams – those of the workers, the religious and the general ones – which had developed, as we have seen, in the period of the Yishuv, became with the establishment of the State centralized in two sub-streams – the general and the religious ones. At the same time the extreme religious sectors (especially those close to Agudat Israel) were allowed to maintain their own independent stream.

The unification of the educational system into two sub-streams was not only an administrative development. It denoted also a far-reaching transformation of the basic ideological and symbolic premisses of Israeli society. It was here – as in the creation of a unified army, which went beyond its general socializing role to foster many more specifically educational functions, such as teaching Hebrew, various vocational courses and the like – that Ben-Gurion's ideology of *Mamlachtiut* found its fullest expression, incorporating together the older pioneering and state symbols under the aegis of the State.

At the same time the establishment of the distinct religious sub-stream gave recognition to the specific cultural problems of this sector.

---

* Calculated from the *Statistical Abstract of Israel, 1982*, No. 33, p. 624.
† Council for Higher Education, Planning and Grants Committee, Universities in Israel, *Statistical Abstract, 1978/9* (Jerusalem 1980), p. 5.

## Special educational frameworks

Within the broad framework of the Israeli educational system there developed here, side by side with the mainstream of the primary, secondary and high (university) schools, several very important special educational institutions and activities.

First of all most of the Kibbutzim continued with their special educational system – with a very heavy emphasis on combining studies, work and ideology, a lack of formal examinations and, initially at least, non-participation in any of the State examinations (especially the matriculation).

Secondly a very widespread plethora of adult education developed, in the beginning mainly around the workers' sector, based entirely on older traditions of *Volksschulen*, but some of it moving toward more academic directions. Within this framework of adult education, an early and most innovative venture was the development of the *Ulpans*, the special boarding and day schools for adults for the acquisition of the Hebrew language. These have become part of the basic adult-educational scheme in Israel, spreading also to universities, and tens of hundreds have passed through them each year.

The army developed a very far-reaching educational system – starting from special Hebrew lessons for new immigrants, to various types of technical and vocational education, various types of general and adult education, as well as the special paramilitary youth formation: the *Gadna*.

There were also a variety of agricultural and vocational schools which, while part of the formal State education, yet maintained some flavours of their own.

*Aliyat Hanoar* (established, as we have seen, in the 1930s to deal with youth from Germany with at least a semi-pioneering orientation), showed great ingenuity in adapting itself to the new types of student population.

The youth movements continued to be active, but there was a very important shift in their place in the educational panorama of Israel. The relative percentage of their members to the respective age cohorts on the whole diminished. They became more and more – although certainly not entirely – concentrated in the upper and middle strata, initially above all in the older sectors of the population. Membership in them became part of the life style of these strata, and their actual orientation to pioneering activities (joining the Kibbutzim or the like, which as we have seen was part of their ideology), became weaker and weaker.

At the same time, as we shall see in Chapter 12, the educational system of the Arabs was established.

## Curriculum formation

The curriculum that crystallized in these periods was based on the ones that had been formed in the period of the Yishuv, but with several – even if in the beginning rather slow – changes. One was the growing emphasis on Jewish history in general and even of the Galut period in particular, with some very slow weakening of the negative evaluation of the Galut. However a very ambivalent attitude to the Galut persisted for a long time, especially under the impact of the Holocaust.

Second, in the study of Hebrew literature, there was a natural growing emphasis on the incorporation of new generations of Israeli writers. Meanwhile, in some of the more religious groups, especially the more extreme ones, there started a development which gained momentum much later, of growing dissociation from the study of the secular *Haskala* and Zionist parts of this literature.

The turning-point in the development of these tendencies was the programme of Jewish 'consciousness' instituted in 1959 by the then Minister of Education Z. Aranne, and which in a sense constituted the main signpost of the specific problems of the third period in the development of the Israeli educational system, the second in the period of the State. This programme was based on a growing recognition of the importance of deepening a knowledge and awareness of the general Jewish historic and religious customs – especially among the new generation of *Tsabras* who were suddenly found very lacking in this respect.

While this programme itself did not prove a great success, yet it denoted a shift towards the growing incorporation of many elements of the religious tradition into the secular stream. Also in the mid-1950s, the Minister of Education Professor B. Dinur took the first steps to incorporate the heritage of the different *edot* into the curriculum.

## The problem of teaching manpower

The growth and expansion of the system naturally raised the problem of manpower, of the recruitment of different types of teachers, and there was a great expansion of teachers and teacher-training institutions.

The great need to train a large number of teachers in a relatively short period of time, and the proliferation of teacher-training institutions, necessarily gave rise – at least temporarily – to some relatively speedy training courses and a relatively large number of teachers who were not fully qualified. Initially at least this meant a lowering of standards,* and the situation became even more acute until the trend started to change from the late 1960s, and early 1970s.

The general expansion of the teaching manpower is attested by the fact that in primary education there were 22,019 teachers in 1969/70 and 32,700 in 1981/2 – a rise of 148.5 per cent. In the secondary schools there were 10,221 teachers in 1969/70 and 17,000 in 1981/2 – a rise of 166.32 per cent.

There was also a rising proportion of women teachers. In the primary schools in 1958/9, 63 per cent of the teachers were women; in 1963/4 the percentage came up to 68 per cent, in 1969/70 to 75 per cent, and in 1980/1 to 85.4 per cent; in the intermediate schools in 1974/5, 54.3 per cent of the teachers were women and in 1980/1, 69 per cent.

* For further information see *Statistical Abstract of Israel, 1982*, No. 33, p. 639.

Closely related to this was the increasing unionization of teachers, with a growing concentration on wage and working conditions. They also became one of the most strikeprone professions in Israel.

## The interweaving of the educational system in the labour market

The unification and homogeneization of the educational system was also connected with its growing interweaving with the labour market, with the structuring of the occupational opportunities in general and the public service sector in particular.

The major mechanism of this interweaving was the growing emphasis on certification – first of high school matriculation, later of university BA and MA degrees as prerequisites for entry into large parts of the labour market – first in public service and in the public sector in general, as well as in many other service sectors. So, as we have seen in Chapter 9 above, education became one of the main channels of occupational mobility and of status attainment.

Of course this general trend developed in different directions in different sectors of the labour market. General academic certification was prominent above all in the public sector and with some specialization like economics or business administration. More specialized academic education was of course demanded from those going into scientific and engineering vocations. Such academic training was mostly provided in the Technion and in various other technological institutions, such as the Technological Institute in Holon, established in 1962 and partially incorporated in Tel Aviv University.

## The shift from future orientation

The combination of the changes in the place of youth movements in the educational system and in the activities of the youth movements themselves, as well as in the teaching profession, were closely related to the general weakening of the orientation to the future; of the growing orientation of the educational system to the existing groups of population and to its growing interweaving into the existing strata and the labour market. These developments were also connected with the decrease – which had already started in the later periods of the Yishuv – of the importance of the educational system as a locus of cultural creativity or innovation, gradually weakening, although certainly not obliterating, the emphasis on cultural or pedagogical creativity or innovation.

The weakening of the creative functions of the educational system and of the teaching profession was partially reinforced also by the expansion of the universities which absorbed at least some of the potential high school teachers.

Yet with all these problems, in these first two periods of the development of the educational system in the State of Israel, the story is one of relatively great success – especially if the initial difficult situation is taken into account.

The educational system, which absorbed in one way or another large parts of the population, together with the army on one hand and with different special educational courses on the other, seemed to be able to imbue most of the immigrants with the basic rudiments of the Hebrew language (even if large pockets of illiteracy still persisted) with a basic attachment to the country and an acceptance of its premises. Truly enough, it undermined the older traditional settings of many – especially some Oriental – immigrants, but opened up new vistas before them, especially the vistas of full participation in the society and the acquisition of the minimal skills needed in the labour market.

# The Mid-1960s and Mid-1970s: the Third and Fourth Periods of the Development of the Educational System in the State of Israel
## Problems of new immigrants

But this very relative success of the educational system also gave rise to new problems which from about the mid-1960s were the most predominant in the third period of the development of the educational system in the State of Israel.

On the most general level, several major problems developed out of the close interweaving of the educational system with the class structure. Thus, first of all, there was the general problem of social selection as influenced by this process; second, and perhaps more important was the growing discrepancy in the level of educational attainments – and hence also of occupational advancement – first between the older sectors and those of the new immigrants in plural, and later – and much more pronounced – between those of European and those of Afro-Asian origin (the so-called Orientals). The basic data indicate continuous advances of all groups, but also a continuous (even if closing) gap between the Orientals and the Western groups, and a surprisingly greater gap between Israelis born to parents from Asia or Africa and those with parents from Europe or America. But within this general advance there were some very significant differences between different sectors of the population, as can be seen in Tables 10.1 and 10.2.

Thus, in somewhat greater detail, in 1957 students of Oriental origin comprised 52 per cent of the 13–14 age group (comparable to the final year of primary school) and an average 55 per cent in the 14–17 age group (comparable to post-primary education). However, they constituted only 32 per cent of the final primary grade and 17 per cent of the post-primary school population. In 1970, 56 per cent of the pupils in primary school were of Oriental origin; in 1977, 55.7 per cent; in 1980, 52 per cent; and in 1981, 54 per cent; in 1975/6 in the intermediate schools already 57.4 per cent of the pupils were of Oriental origin and in 1979/80 the percentage was 55.2.

Later on, in the post-primary schools, the proportion of the Oriental

**Table 10.1    Jews of both sexes at the Age of 14, by Continent of Birth and Years of Schooling, 1961–81 (Percentages)**

| Continent of Birth | Year | Total | Years of schooling | | | | |
| --- | --- | --- | --- | --- | --- | --- | --- |
| | | | 0 | 1–4 | 5–8 | 9–12 | 13+ |
| Entire | 1961 | 100.0 | 12.6 | 7.5 | 35.4 | 34.6 | 9.9 |
| Population | 1971 | 100.0 | 9.0 | 6.3 | 30.1 | 40.8 | 13.8 |
| | 1981 | 100.0 | 6.0 | 3.7 | 21.3 | 48.1 | 21.9 |
| Born in Israel | 1961 | 100.0 | 2.2 | 1.9 | 26.3 | 54.2 | 15.3 |
| | 1971 | 100.0 | 1.0 | 1.3 | 20.5 | 59.4 | 17.8 |
| | 1981 | 100.0 | 0.7 | 0.6 | 10.7 | 62.9 | 25.1 |
| Born in Israel | 1961 | 100.0 | 4.4 | 3.1 | 34.2 | 45.1 | 13.3 |
| of Father Born | 1971 | 100.0 | 2.5 | 3.3 | 23.1 | 51.0 | 22.1 |
| in Israel | 1981 | 100.0 | 0.9 | 1.0 | 10.0 | 63.9 | 24.2 |
| Born in Israel | 1961 | 100.0 | 4.2 | 4.4 | 52.3 | 34.6 | 4.5 |
| of Father Born | 1971 | 100.0 | 1.1 | 1.6 | 35.0 | 57.5 | 4.8 |
| in Asia or Africa | 1981 | 100.0 | 0.8 | 0.7 | 16.2 | 70.7 | 11.6 |
| Born in Israel | 1961 | 100.0 | 0.6 | 0.7 | 14.5 | 64.5 | 19.7 |
| of Father Born | 1971 | 100.0 | 0.4 | 0.5 | 8.8 | 63.6 | 22.6 |
| in Europe/America | 1981 | 100.0 | 0.5 | 0.3 | 4.4 | 53.0 | 41.8 |
| Born in Asia | 1961 | 100.0 | 31.5 | 10.1 | 36.2 | 19.2 | 3.0 |
| or Africa | 1971 | 100.0 | 23.5 | 8.6 | 36.4 | 26.5 | 5.0 |
| | 1981 | 100.0 | 18.8 | 6.0 | 29.2 | 36.0 | 9.7 |
| Born in Europe | 1961 | 100.0 | 3.2 | 7.6 | 37.9 | 38.5 | 12.7 |
| or America | 1971 | 100.0 | 2.4 | 8.3 | 32.4 | 38.5 | 18.4 |
| | 1981 | 100.0 | 2.4 | 5.7 | 25.2 | 39.0 | 27.7 |

Source: *The Educational System Information in Number, 1982* (Jerusalem, 1982).

**Table 10.2    Students Between the Ages of 15 and 17 in the Post-Primary Educational System, by Type of Schools and Country of Origin, 1963/4–1976/7 (rates per 1000 in Jewish population)**

| Type of Education by Country of Origin and Age | | 1963/4 | 1966/7 | 1972/3 | 1976/7 |
| --- | --- | --- | --- | --- | --- |
| Academic | Age 15 | 163.1 | 167.3 | 144 | 137 |
| Asia/Africa | Age 17 | 96.5 | 102.6 | 98 | 105 |
| Academic | Age 15 | 403.5 | 438.3 | 430 | 374 |
| Asia/Africa | Age 17 | 295.2 | 300.4 | 345 | 336 |
| Vocational/Agricultural | Age 15 | 185.8 | 238.7 | 384 | 453 |
| Asia/Africa | Age 17 | 62.3 | 94.8 | 184 | 255 |
| Vocational/Agricultural | Age 15 | 245.4 | 327.7 | 358 | 405 |
| Europe/America | Age 17 | 116.7 | 149.4 | 247 | 290 |

Source: Bureau of Statistics, *Special Publication*, No. 485, pp. 24–5 and No. 629, p. 13.

children increased from 25.9 per cent in 1963/4 to 28.3 per cent in 1964/5; in 1967 it came up to 35.6 per cent, in 1976/7 to 50.6 per cent and in 1979/80 to 51.9.*

There is, thus, by now almost no difference between the percentage of pupils in the primary school whose parents were born in Asia or Africa as compared to the percentage of children in the age range 6–13 in the general population.

In the secondary schools there was an increase of pupils from Asia and Africa. Most of those pupils studied in the vocational and agricultural schools, and in the general (academic) schools they constituted a smaller part than their part in the population, even though in 1966/7 the gap between their part in the population and their number in the general school was 24.5 per cent and in 1979/80 it went down to 17.4 per cent.

Two other, not unconnected problems, which had begun to spread in the early 1950s, were those of juvenile delinquency and school drop-outs.

## The 'Disadvantaged' and new policies

These problems became central to this period, and a variety of policies, both general educational ones and special ones, were developed from the early 1960s to cope with them. In order to understand these policies it is necessary to analyse the development, in the Israeli educational system, of a special category – probably unique to Israel – the *Teunei Tipuah* (Disadvantaged). To quote Elad Peled:

> There are many definitions of a disadvantaged child: socio-economic, ethnic, geographical and more. Generally, there is a high correlation among the socio-economic variables, the ethnic variables and the geographical variables. The operational definition in Israel's education is based on an analysis of academic achievement in elementary school, illustrated in comprehensive tests (Seker) administered in the high grades of the eight-year elementary school over a period of several years. Following these tests, every social group characterized by definite socio-economic variables was evaluated in terms of 'disadvantaged' and therefore eligibility for special allocation of additional resources in order to improve its prospects of success in school.
>
> Of the elementary school pupils in 1975, 47 per cent were disadvantaged. Of this group 95 per cent were 'Orientals'. Of this group 90 per cent belong to large families and their father's education is lower than the elementary educational level. Elementary schools where their proportion is 70 per cent or more have 55 per cent of all disadvantaged children.†

It was to cope with the problem of these groups that new policies were developed.

---

* *Statistical Abstract of Israel, 1982*, No. 33, pp. 633, 628.
† Elad Peled, 'Israeli Education' in Edward Corsini and J. Raymond (eds.) *Comparative Educational Systems* (Illinois 1981), pp. 222-3.

## Special policies

The special policies were divided into two parts. The first could be brought under the category of complementary education – including special classes, longer school days, special remedial teaching for children who failed in the regular system together with social and psychological services for drop-outs and the like. Within the framework of these policies there were many very innovative programmes – such as those stressing experiments in cognitive development in early childhood or pre-academic preparatory schools in the universities.

The second type of 'special policies' were administrative measures. So the problem of drop-outs was tackled by the simple device of automatic transfer of pupils from class to class in the primary school, thus trying to assure – even if at the expense of maintaining standards – that such potential early school leavers remained within the walls of schools. The decrease in their numbers, which we have noted above, may be attributed at least partially to such measures.

A second important administrative measure – although of a different type – was the semi-formal establishment in the early 1960s of so-called Norm B, the main directive of which was that, whereas a regular student had to score about 7.5–8 (out of ten) to be entitled to state-aid in post-primary education, for an Oriental student a score of about 6.5 plus was sufficient.

## Vocational education

The second type of policies developed to cope with the problems of the disadvantaged, often closely related to the former ones but distinct in their scope, were those which effected far-reaching changes in the whole educational system: namely the reorganization of the vocational stream into a system of non-academic preparatory education; and the policy of so-called integration or reform.

The vocational school type of education was initially marginal to the mainstream of education; until about 1960 it was mostly confined to two years in schooling in different arts and crafts orientated to preparing manpower for relatively small workshops.

From about 1960 on, mainly as a response to the growing needs of groups of new immigrants, there was a very far-reaching widening of the vocational education into a fully fledged system, based on four years of schooling and orientated not only to specific, limited markets, but to the process of more general technical education.

In 1948/9 2,002 pupils studied in the vocational schools. In 1951/2 the number was already 4,315 pupils – an increase of 215.53 per cent, in 1959/60 it increased to 10,167 (an increase of 235.61 per cent), and in 1964/5 to 25,601 (an increase of 251.80 per cent). In 1971/2 the number came up to 60,029 (an increase of 234.51 per cent), in 1978/9 to 67,720 (an increase of 112.79 per cent) and in 1979/80 to 70,361 (an increase of 103.89 per cent).* This population tended to

* R. Kahane and L. Star, *Education and Work* (in Hebrew) (Jerusalem 1983).

be comprised mostly of children from the so-called Oriental groups. Thus in 1956/7 51.8 per cent of the pupils in the vocational schools were of Oriental origin; in 1958/9 the percentage rose to 56.7 per cent but it dropped in 1961/2 to 41.2 per cent and again in 1964/5 to 35 per cent; in 1970/1 the percentage rose again to 41.4 per cent and in 1980 to 64.3 per cent.*

The vocational stream proved to be a very constructive channel of advancement for many such groups – although at the same time it also to some degree became a special tracking for children of Oriental origin – slowly giving rise to growing pressures to grant it fuller academic status. The overall, rather complex, impact of the vocational stream before the full impact of tendencies to academization, has been systematically studied by Y. J. Shavit-Steifler† and his major conclusions have been:

> The academic tracks provide access to higher education and the upper echelons of the social hierarchy. Ashkenazim are disproportionately placed in these tracks. The availability of the lower tracks provides the students of subordinate status with an opportunity to attain greater quantities of post-primary education, thereby both perpetuating the image of equality of educational opportunity and presumably, exposing their students to the dominant value system of society. However, placement in the low tracks prevents students from attaining the matriculation diploma, the major criterion for admission to higher education and positions of privilege. . . .

## Policies of integration

A more far-reaching general educational policy was, of course, that of reform and integration initiated in 1959 by the then Minister of Education Zalman Aranne who appointed the Prawer Committee and later the Rimmalt Committee which made the major recommendations in this direction – and which were later adopted by Abba Eban as Minister of Education.

The new policy was aimed at three goals, closely related to the difficulties of coping with the problems of the disadvantaged: to innovate and modernize the high school curriculum; to democratize secondary education (by extending free and compulsory education), and to create within the school the meeting of children of different economic strata and ethnic groups by imposing, by law, social integration in the junior division of the high school.

The policy of integration was based on the combination of bringing together, in one school setting, groups from different social backgrounds, thus attempting to break the tendency of ecological segregation of education of different classes and ethnic groups, together with the restructuring of the school system itself – and it was also connected with the system of matriculation.

Thus, in greater detail, the system was changed from eight classes in the primary schools and four classes in the post-primary schools, to six classes in

---

* *Statistical Abstract of Israel, 1982*, No. 33, p. 633.
† Yossi Jonathan Shavit-Steifler, 'Tracking in Israeli Education: Its Consequences for Ethnic Inequalities in Educational Attainment', A Thesis Submitted in Partial Fulfilment of the Requirements for the Degree of Doctor of Philosophy (Sociology) at the University of Wisconsin-Madison, 1983 (pp. 122–7).

the primary schools and six in the secondary schools. The first three years in the secondary schools were called intermediate units and their function was to serve as a transition stage between the primary and secondary schools. The system eliminated the formal selection and screening between the elementary school and the junior and senior divisions, replacing it by a system of counselling and guidance. There was a preference for the comprehensive high school and the expansion of vocational education within it, the extension of free and compulsory education for an additional two years (grades 9 and 10).

In 1976, already in the last period of development of Israeli education, another far-reaching change – basically orientated to similar aims – was effected in the matriculation system. The aim of the new programme was to give more children the opportunity of choice: three compulsory subjects (mathematics, Hebrew literature and English) were instituted at different levels, and a very large list of other elective subjects was provided. In some subjects, the pupils were to write papers instead of taking exams.

In this period special programmes have also been established, with the aim to encourage the pupils to volunteer in some activity in the community. New subjects, like the one on the Holocaust, are compulsory subjects. More and more schools on all levels are working with computers in teaching maths, grammar and English.

## Conclusion

It is not easy to evaluate exactly and systematically the results of many of these policies – especially those like school integration, which contain rather controversial and contradictory orientations – and far-reaching controversies have naturally arisen around the evaluation of these results.

In terms of purely quantitative results, the programme has on the whole been rather successful. In the year 1982/3 72,000 pupils from among the Jewish population studied in 128 intermediate units. In 1979/80 only 1.9 per cent of the pupils in primary schools, 40 per cent of pupils in the State-religious schools and 36.7 per cent of pupils in the independent education of Agudat Israel were in segregated schools – that is those where the percentage of the deprived is more than 70 per cent.* So there is no doubt that this policy had an important part in the advancement of the Oriental children and in closing the gap between the Orientals and the Western children.

It is much more difficult to evaluate the overall impact of these policies in terms of educational attainments, as the research results are both complicated and their coverage is far from complete.

In general, much of the research indicates that integration seems to increase the levels of aspirations among different groups of students; that it influences above all the achievements of the upper third of students; and that it is more influential when the number of those in any school from 'deprived' groups is no more than 60 per cent and when the level of education facilities is relatively

* *Statistical Abstract of Israel, 1981*, No. 32.

high. Similarly, some research indicates that, in secondary education, the intermediate framework, above all in families with high academic background, shows enhanced performance, especially in the academic schools.

But, with the passing of time, more and more doubts have been expressed as to whether these policies have indeed attained their goal of growing solidarity and integration. It has even been suggested that these problems might have been intensified by bringing into a common framework pupils from different backgrounds and with markedly different achievements, giving rise to intensification of the feelings of estrangement and alienation between such different groups. It is also questionable whether all this effort has been worth the price of lowering of standards, which – as we shall soon see – has been one of the important developments in the Israeli educational system.

Some of these doubts are in line with the earlier ones about Norm B, when it was indicated

that the beneficial effects of Norm B for the Oriental children has also proved doubtful, since it artificially advances non-qualified students into post-primary education; where no special allowance is made for them. They then face problems of adjustment and are bound to rate high among students who drop out later. The high levels of aspiration are thus first raised – and then frustrated. Further, this policy is likely to attach the stigma of 'second-rate' to most of the Oriental children, most particularly on the few who could achieve Norm A by their own efforts. *

# Educational Policies and Performance
## Contrasting social orientations in Israeli society

Whatever the exact outcome of their evaluation (and it is doubtful whether it would be possible to arrive at a fully objective evaluation), it is of great significance that many of these policies were very closely interwoven with more general tendencies which became predominant in Israeli life and which are very important for understanding the changing format of Israeli life.

These various policies were indeed based on different, sometimes contrasting, premisses, indicative of different social orientations developing in Israeli society. One such orientation stressed the importance of providing the various weaker groups with special additional facilities which would enable them to enter into the educational race, giving rise to a very wide plethora of programmes, above all in the educational and vocational fields and to some degree in that of housing. A second, and to some degree contrary, basic policy orientation was that of granting special privileges to special categories – usually defined as 'deprived' but *de facto* consisting mostly, although certainly not entirely, of Oriental immigrants – and of applying to them special standards.

These orientations and the policies connected with them necessarily had repercussions on the performance aspect or dimension of the educational system.

* Eisenstadt, *Israeli Society*, pp. 277–8.

The first general tendency was a decline in standards, as seen first of all in the relative decline of elite high schools and their growing homogeneization – although some, such as the Reali in Haifa, Tihon Hadash in Tel Aviv, the University High School in Jerusalem and some others, maintained their excellence.

Second, the trend to egalitarianism seemed to bring about a relaxation of standards in the transition from primary to secondary schools. Moreover, although the restructuring of the examinations for matriculation allowed diversification with possible creative innovation in many directions, it also gave rise to a strong decline of standards in the study of mathematics and foreign languages, and in motivation for studying scientific subjects. Thus, while in 1975/6 (the last year before the establishment of the new system of matriculation) about 19 per cent of the students in the last year of high school chose the 'scientific' track, in 1981 there were only 8 per cent!

These last points, as well as the lack of qualified high school teachers in the scientific subjects, were heavily emphasized in the report of the special committee appointed in 1982 by the Minister of Education to look into the problem of scientific education in Israel, headed by Professor Arye Dvoretzky, former President of the Israeli Academy. This report stressed that all these developments constituted a very serious threat for the continuation of scientific development in Israel, and the same pleas were made by the President of the Technion and the directors of several science-based industries.

These different policies were also closely connected with another set of contradictory orientations – especially relevant in the educational field – namely those between elitist and egalitarian orientations, between stress on excellence and creativity and *de facto* lowering of the standards, between future orientation and adaptation to the more immediate present, when the future is seen as just an extension of the present.

Most of the educational policies that developed in Israel through the 1960s thus became as we have seen closely interwoven with the growing emphasis on distributive egalitarianism which stresses rights and entitlements, and minimizes duties and obligations. There was a growing stress on social integration with a much weaker and even ambivalent attitude to the upholding of standards. And there was a stress on excellence and on social or educational creativity – thus going in many ways against the older elitist pioneering orientations – but building on some distributive egalitarian tendencies inherent in them.

## *Attitudes to the Oriental groups*

The absorption of immigrants, and the Oriental groups in particular, meant the development of various policies, general and particular, such as the articulation of the cultural heritage and symbols of the distinct identity of the various ethnic groups.

This was also, on the whole, a relatively new development. Of course in the period of the Yishuv these traditions had been incorporated to some degree in the school curriculum, especially in Hebrew literature and history, which included as its central part the Hebrew literature of the Golden Age of Jews in Spain, stressing above all its secular aspects. These trends continued and became intensified with the establishment of the State of Israel, and gradually their whole ambiance became transformed. In the early 1950s, Professor B. Dinur, the then Minister of Education, emphasized the importance of including more aspects of the 'heritage' and history of the Oriental communities in the curriculum.

All these trends gathered special momentum around the mid-1970s. First of all, there was a further extension of the study of the historical heritage of the Oriental communities in the school curricula. But there were also some far-reaching changes in their basic premisses, in their ideological assumptions and orientations and in their relations to the common Israeli identity.

Thus first of all there was a growing ideologization of the heritage of the different *edot* – of making it an autonomous distinct component of the overall Israeli identity and not just, as before, a rather secondary component.

Second, such ideologization stressed more and more the differences between different ethnic groups, rather than – as in the earlier curriculum – recognizing them as part of a common heritage.

Third, in marked contrast to the earlier negative evaluation of the Galut, there was a much more positive attitude to it, sometimes almost a search for 'roots' beyond the common Israeli scene. This shift became of course connected with the general re-evaluation of the Galut experience after the Holocaust, stressing to a smaller degree future orientation and the construction of new symbols as against stronger emphasis on the present and on the past, and with the parallel growth of the religious component on the educational scene.

## Changes in the religious sectors

Throughout all these periods there were far-reaching differences in the levels of attainment between the general and the State-religious educational sectors, with the latter evincing on the whole lower standards, rooted both in difficulties to recruit adequately qualified teachers and with its great attraction to some parts of the Oriental groups. Yet it was in other parts of this sector that from the mid- or late 1960s some of the most important new developments and innovations in the educational field took place, which, paradoxically, also attracted the most active elements among potential teachers.

First of all the religious youth movement, the *Bnei Akiva*, became the most active of the youth movements, very much more active than any of the older, secular, even the extreme leftist, ones, carrying on much of the ideology of the pioneering era – in a rather extreme religious and nationalist vein.

Second, important educational innovations took place, not within the official State-religious schools nor within the separate trends of Agudat Israel nor within the traditional type of Yeshivot, but above all in a new typically Israeli type of Yeshivot, above all the so-called *Yeshivot Hesder*, the secondary school Yeshivot and vocational Yeshivot, as well as in some of the technologically orientated religious institutions, combining Talmudic studies with modern technological ones.

In general, the number of students of Yeshivot from the age of 14 rose in 1978/9 to about 30,000 from about 400 Yeshivot, as against 4,862 in 1949/50 in 115 Yeshivot. Of these, the secondary school Yeshivot (*Yeshivot Tichoniot*) constitute about 15 per cent, the vocational schools (both confined to ages 14–18) about 10 per cent and the *Yeshivot Hesder* about 6 per cent.

The *Yeshivot Hesder*, catering for ages 14–23, as well as the secondary school Yeshivot, were based on the combination of traditional Talmudic with secular subjects and with military service, thus denying the claim of religious circles that military training is comparable with study in the Yeshivot.

Significantly within these schools there has developed a very strong elitist orientation, evident in rather stringent selection processing, highly tuned to the standards of educational attainment and excellence – and, as far as can be known, the number of Oriental students among them was relatively small, certainly as compared with the 'integrated' schools.

## Developments from the mid-1970s

From around the mid-1970s, beyond the continuation of all the trends and problems analysed above, some new trends developed in the Israeli educational system, and there was a concomitant shift to emphasize some new problems, without, however, belittling the importance of the older ones, especially that of integration.

The weakening of the emphasis on standards, the loosening of discipline and the general growth of permissive atmosphere, manifest, for example, in reports about drugs abuse and violence in schools, gave rise to far-reaching anxieties and to several different counter-tendencies.

One such tendency was some growing emphasis on the maintenance of educational attainments, more stringent discipline in the schools, the development of various counselling services, and more flexible programmes. Several of these attempts coincided with the actualization of the rights of groups of parents to set up 25 per cent of the curricula. Also new programmes were developed for special groups of students – from the mentally retarded to the specially gifted.

There was also continuously growing orientation on Jewish 'traditional' studies in secular schools – sometimes as a possible antidote to the permissive atmosphere and lack of discipline.

At the same time there were further doubts about some aspects of the policy of integration. In the wake of the growing self-consciousness of many groups of Orientals, there was a reaction against attempts to integrate them in 'Ashkenazi' frames – which were seen as a continuation of the older paternalistic one. The policies of integration were also seen as a possible cause of the growing neglect of the lower echelons, perhaps around 20 per cent, and this problem became the subject of public debate.

Thus alongside the growing, pluralistic educational orientations and frameworks, and the encouragement of various innovative programmes, there was a growing apprehension about the lowering of standards.

# Higher Education
## Expansion

The various trends and developments analysed above – especially the expansion of the educational system, its interweaving in the occupational one and the continuous dilemma and tension between the quality and achievement and more egalitarian orientations – also developed in the field of higher education.

From a situation in 1947 in which there existed only one university (the Hebrew University in Jerusalem), the Technion in Haifa and the nuclei of the Weizmann Institute in Rehovot (established on the basis of the former Staff Institute) with a total staff of 2,582, there was by 1983 a very widespread university system comprising seven universities, new faculties and a student population nearing 61,000. Their budgets expanded from 73 million dollars per year in 1974 to 252 million dollars per year in 1981, with a continuously growing part of the Government and the Jewish Agency in their budget.

The expansion of the university system was quite rapid. In 1955 the Bar Ilan University was established, in 1956 the Tel Aviv University, in 1963 the Haifa University and in 1964 the Ben-Gurion University in the Negev. As against the two faculties (Humanities, Science and Pre-Medical School and School of Agriculture) that existed in the Hebrew University in 1948, there are now a great variety of faculties in the different universities: Social Science, Business Administration, Law, Medicine, Computer Sciences, Agriculture and the Sciences, sometimes sub-divided into Biological and Physical Sciences.

**Table 10.3   Growth of Student Population by Faculties, 1969/70–1980/1**

| Faculty | Students by Faculties | | Percentage increase |
|---|---|---|---|
| | 1969–70 | 1980–1 | |
| Humanities | 10,815 | 17,175 | 158 |
| Social Sciences | 8,660 | 15,715 | 181 |
| Law | 1,774 | 2,176 | 122 |
| Medicine | 1,314 | 3,175 | 241 |
| Mathematics and Natural Sciences | 4,918 | 7,618 | 154 |
| Agriculture | 510 | 1,690 | 331 |
| Engineering | 5,392 | 8,291 | 153 |
| TOTAL | 33,383 | 55,840 | |

Source: Based on *Statistical Abstract of Israel, 1971*, No. 22, p. 22, and *1982*, No. 33, p. 648.

Table 10.3 presents a picture of the distribution of the growth of students among different faculties between 1969/70 and 1980/1. Thus we see that the biggest percentage increase took place in two faculties; in Agriculture (331 per cent) and in Medicine (241 per cent), while the lowest increase was in the Faculty of Law (122 per cent).

In the first stage of this expansion, through the 1960s, the three main institutions – the Hebrew University, the Technion and the newly created (in 1949) Weizmann Institute – were successful in establishing many of the departments as academic centres of international standing.* Contacts with the international academic community were continuously extended through post-doctoral sabbaticals and continuous visits abroad, as well as through continuous visits of foreign scholars – Israel becoming a not unimportant intellectual academic centre.

This initial expansion was connected with some important shifts in the orientations of the institutions of higher learning. For the first time in the history of Jewish settlement in Eretz Israel, the academic institutions were no longer small islands of creativity, but opened up to a large student population becoming fully integrated with the social and economic life in the country, as well as in the international academic community. Thus, for instance, the Index of Citation in the Exact Sciences showed that, from among the 100 most cited scientists, there were ten Israelis: six from the Weizmann Institute, three from the Hebrew University (two scientists working in the School of Medicine and one in the Faculty of Sciences) and one from Tel Aviv University. It has been also estimated that in terms of 'production' of scientific publications, Israel holds the sixteenth place in the world (before even Belgium, Denmark or Austria) and in terms of such production *per capita*, it is the first in the world.

Instead of the former studies leading directly to the MA or M.Sc., BA and B.Sc. programmes were developed, attesting to the growing interweaving with the labour market and occupational aspirations of the young generations.

The establishment of the new universities, often under strong pressure of local political leaders, especially the mayors of Tel Aviv, Haifa and Beersheva, was also indicative of the recognition of the growing demands of the local population for easy access to academic institutions.

There was also a slow but continuous expansion of the percentage of students of Oriental origin. In 1969/70 they constituted 3.3 per cent of the students, and by 1978/9 this proportion had grown to 11.7 per cent (an increase of 354.54 per cent).* Of special importance here were the *mehinot* (pre-academic preparatory units) established in the early 1960s (first at the Hebrew University, later at all the others) through which have passed about 35,000 students from diverse backgrounds – but particularly 'Oriental' ones – often through special facilitating arrangements with the army.

In partial response to the high demand for academic degrees, even among those who could not attend universities, there was also a strong development of

* Council for Higher Education Planning and Grants Committee – Higher Education in Israel, *Statistical Abstract, 1980/1* (Jerusalem, August 1982), p. 15.

non-university post-high school higher education. Such institutions were of several kinds: several (about ten) college (but not university) institutions, like the Rubin Academy of Music; special post-high schools for technology and others; as well as regional *Mihlalot* within which some academic tracks under the supervision of universities have been instituted. In the first type, the more fully accredited of these institutions, in 1981 there were about 570 students, of whom 91 graduated, and an academic staff of about 90. Partial academic status was granted to teachers' seminars and similar institutions.

## Problems of maintaining standards

The growing expansion of the universities, and their interweaving with the occupational structure, necessarily raised the problem of maintaining their high standards of study and research.

Quite naturally the very extension of the universities made it difficult to maintain the standards of both students and staff. Although no exact data are available, there seems to have been a lowering of the standards of large parts of the students, connected with changes in the matriculation system and the relatively low attainments of high school students in foreign language and in mathematics. The whole ambience of university studies changed, especially in the Humanities and Social Sciences, in the *de facto* provision – except for smaller select groups – of some type of general education.

Truly enough, from about mid-1970s, the universities attempted to counter-act some of these tendencies by not accepting automatically students with any type of matriculation and by creating special entrance examinations. Although important in themselves, these measures were probably not sufficient to counteract the general trend – as against more select groups of students with high levels of motivation.

At the same time, the persistence, in the curricula of most university faculties, of older orientations to the preparation of cadres of research did not – in its turn – help to cope creatively with the great expansion of the students.

The expansion of the universities also raised the problem of the standard of the teaching staff, and of research and academic attainment reached in many parts of the older institutions. These could not easily be attained in all the departments of the new institutions, and even in some of the older ones. The establishment of the new universities did of course provide creative opport-unities for many scholars who could not find their way into the older ones. But from the 1970s there has been a growing concern among the institutions of higher learning about their inability to maintain their academic standards in teaching and research.

## External problems

The tensions in higher education were not limited to the internal developments in the universities. They became very closely interwoven with – and to a very large extent fed by – the more general atmosphere in the country. There was a growing ambivalence and populist attitudes among many political leaders – very often those close to the political figures who promoted the establishment of new universities – to the elitist ambience and independence of the universities and academic institutions.

While on the one hand there developed great demand for academic manpower and degrees, this very demand generated a strong ambivalence to the more elitist orientation of the universities, to their independence, to the very often independent stand in political matters taken by many faculty members; but at the same time there was a continuous increase of the part of the Government and the Jewish Agency in the budgets of the universities.

This ambivalence to the universities was also related to two aspects of the structure of Israel's academic institutions connected with Israel being a small country: namely, first, to the strong external orientation of these institutions; and, second, to their inability to accept all applicants to the more restricted faculties, especially medicine, some of whom went to study – and sometimes to stay – abroad.

## Budget restrictions

These general developments of the universities, their expansion and their growing dependency on government and Jewish Agency funds, gave rise to the need of some sort of central regulation.

A Council on Higher Education had been established in 1958, appointed by the President on the recommendation of the Government (in itself usually following some of the informal recommendations of the universities) chaired by the Minister of Education. As from 1979/80 he was empowered to approve new departments and faculties.

In 1977 a special Grants Committee was established, chaired by eminent academicians, which supervised the budgets of the universities. Although there were no political interferences in the universities, despite some attempts in this direction, the Universities still had to cope with one of the most important outcomes of the ambivalent attitudes towards them – the severe cuts in their budgets. These started in the early 1970s, and culminated in 1983, when, with an expansion of about 30 per cent, the public allocation remained constant and even went down.

One of the most important effects of such cuts on the standards of the universities is to be found in the changes in the teacher–student ratio. Thus, in 1974/5 there were 52,000 students and a staff of about 6,800, giving a ratio of 0.13 teachers per student and 7.6 students per teacher. As against this, in 1977/8 there were 54,060 students and 6,370 academic staff, giving ratios of 0.11 and 8.4, respectively; in 1983 there was one teacher per 15 students in the humanities and social sciences, and 1:11.5 in the sciences. It seems – as we shall see later on – that this trend is continuing, in many ways undermining the basis of academic work in Israel.

# Conclusion
## Major trends and problems of Israeli education

So the Israeli educational system, as it developed in the State of Israel, was marked by far-reaching expansion, by growing changes and by continuous tensions between different orientations.

The focus of all these changes was the increasing interweaving of the system, first of all in the developing economic-occupational system and the concomitant growth of its importance as a basic mechanism of accreditation needed for occupational advancement, and, second, in the basic socio-political problems of Israeli society, all of which naturally weakening the strong future orientations which had characterized it in the period of the Yishuv.

Both processes of interweaving gave rise to the 'usual' problems of finding adequate means and appropriate organizational frames for such a vast organizational expansion, of over-bureaucratization and of being sensitive to various special pedagogical problems. But there also were some quite far-reaching tensions and contradictions in the basic orientations which guided the major policies in the educational field.

The first such tension was that between the growing interweaving of the educational system into the emerging class system of Israeli society, reinforcing the tendency to growing social differentiation on the one hand, and on the other, the stress on egalitarianism based on premisses of national solidarity and of socialist egalitarian orientations.

This tension became strongly connected with another – perhaps the most crucial one within the educational system proper – between the stress on quality, on excellence and creativity as against the contrary one, closely related to the development of the policies of integration. This problem was very closely related to the many basic trends that developed in the Israeli society, but perhaps above all it was crucial in questioning Israel's ability to maintain a centre of cultural creativity in general and technological and scientific developments in particular, to renew and extend its human capital in all these areas.

This tension between creativity, to some degree future-orientated, so basic to the original pioneering orientations, and the more placid orientation of the present, was also evident in the quality of reconstruction of symbols of collective identity that took place in the educational system and which were very closely related to the whole process of cultural creativity in Israel, to the analysis of which we shall now turn.

# II · Cultural Creativity, Modes of Cultural Participation and Construction of Symbols of Collective Identity

## The Premisses and Patterns of Cultural Creativity and Participation

The establishment of the State also provided very strong momentum to the process of cultural creativity in its manifold aspects, which, as we have seen, began in the Yishuv, but at the same time gave rise to far-reaching transformations in this very diversified and in a way ambiguous field.

The single best indication of these transformations was the growing public awareness and debate, which started relatively early but which gathered special momentum in the 1970s, as to the Jewish nature or characteristics of the State of Israel.

In the Yishuv, and in the first five to ten years of the State, such a question would probably have been seen by parts of the public as rather meaningless or at most marginal, limited to small groups of intellectuals or writers, and not central in the public or even political debate – not because the question was not important, but because it would have been assumed that crucial, even if perhaps implicit, answers were continuously being given.

In the earlier period, in the formative period of the Zionist movement and of the Yishuv, two implicit or explicit answers to this question were predominant. One, negative, was to be found in the Orthodox circles which denied the very legitimacy of the attempt to construct Jewish society, not built according to God's will. The Orthodox extremists saw – especially in the early period of the Zionist movement and settlement – the very attempt to construct such a society as an usurpation of God's will. When later on the existence of the settlement, and later of the State, was gradually accepted, yet it was seen, from the point of view of the extreme religious groups, as at best a series of compromises or a battleground for the implementation of the Halakha.

The other, positive view, perhaps rather simple, was that of the original Zionist ideology – the view that the whole rationale of Jewish renaissance in the Land of Israel was, by definition, Jewish, all of it stemming from the attempt to contribute to the reopening of the gates of Jewish creativity, to reconstruct a modern Jewish society and civilization.

At the same time it would be difficult to pinpoint the exact characteristics, according to the then prevalent view, which would single it out as Jewish – except for the general presupposition that the very homecoming to its own land would bring out all the springs of creativity in the Jewish people that had presumably been stifled in the Diaspora. There was much stress – very much in the line of the emancipation period – on the special values and spiritual heritage of the Jewish people which would come into full efflorescence with the settlement in Eretz Israel.

Although the specific cultural contents of this new, reconstructed Jewish traditional collective life as crystallized between the rebellion against tradition and its reconstruction was not easily specified, yet there was no doubt in the minds of the Jews that the very process of such reconstruction would provide most of such answers – above all the relation of this new cultural creativity to Jewish tradition on the one hand, and to various aspects of modern universal culture on the other – and that in some way this answer would encompass most aspects of cultural life and creativity.

Indeed, as discussed in Chapter 6, in the period of the first settlement of Eretz Israel this very constructive effort was seemingly enough to provide the answer needed to this problem.

This view was reinforced first of all by the two great achievements of cultural creativity and innovation that took place in this period – namely the revival and institutionalization of the Hebrew language and the development and re-construction of different elements of the Jewish tradition into the symbolical institutional framework of Israeli culture. All these continuously – up to this very day – constituted a focus of public–political controversy and struggle, but their very existence constituted part of the specific Jewish aspect of the Yishuv and State of Israel.

At the same time the new Eretz-Israel collective identity, that had been crystallizing in different sectors of the Yishuv, developed. It was of course around the nature of this new identity, as well as the relative emphasis on different themes – such as those of Eretz Israel, of different periods of Jewish history, of the relation to other nations – that many of the differences of emphasis developed, both in public discourse as well as in literature. But most of these – with one exception – developed within the general framework of the attempts at overreaching new creativity through which a new Jewish culture, which would indeed provide basic meaning to the new society, would emerge and become crystallized.

The exact nature of this meaning was, of course, interpreted by various sectors in different ways, yet on the whole they shared – with the exception of the Canaanites – the orientation to the reconstruction of Jewish tradition according to general universal cultural themes.

## The State of Israel – New Developments

The establishment of the State both reinforced many of these trends and also effected some far-reaching transformations in them – the roots of which had already been laid in the period of the Yishuv. Several processes of change took place from the early 1950s on.

Thus first of all there was a far-reaching burgeoning and diversification of cultural activity beyond what could have been dreamt about in the earlier period of the Yishuv – and a participation, what might be called **cultural** 'consumption' in all fields of cultural activity.

The second basic change was, of course, the very formalization of many of the institutional arrangements of cultural life – the school curriculum, the system of education, the revival of the Hebrew language and of the Sabbath and public holidays, the standing of the Rabbinical courts, and slow, initially imperceptible but in fact far-reaching changes in State–religion relations.

Third was the growing diversification, autonomy and privatization of many such patterns of cultural creativity and participation.

Fourth was the development of new cultural themes and the concomitant process of continuous reconstruction of the symbols of Israeli collective identity.

Fifth, there were far-reaching changes in the relations of the various cultural activities to the 'world' outside, both to the various general cultural arenas and to those among the different Jewish communities; this brought the concomitant problem of the relation between the internal and external axes of these cultural activities to greater prominence.

Sixth, there was a change in the connections between different modes of such cultural creativity, and between the symbols and expressions of a national solidarity and the solidarity of different sectors in the society.

# Burgeoning and Diversification of Cultural Activities
## *Creativity*

The burgeoning and diversification of cultural creativity in different spheres were indeed very impressive. We have already analysed the far-reaching developments in the academic field. Similarly in the fields of literature, publications and translations there was extremely varied and intensive creativity carried out by new generations of writers and journalists. In an analysis of UNESCO figures for 1962, Israel showed that it was first in the number of books (different titles) published *per capita*. Recomputing the UNESCO data for 1968 in the same way, Elihu Katz and Michael Gurevitch found that Israel has just barely slipped behind Switzerland and Denmark, but still stood among the highest in the world, with an average of 76 books per 100,000 residents published in Israel.

A very intensive creativity developed in the field of music, where the Philharmonic – and other orchestras – developed a reputation for a very high standard of musical performance. They attracted many outstanding musicians or conductors, be it Leonard Bernstein, Isaac Stern, or Zubin Mehta as well as Israelis like Daniel Barenboim who live mostly abroad, to perform with or conduct them, and made Israel a significant centre of musical creativity.

At the more popular level many performers, singers and artists started to develop a great variety of more local traditions, some building on the tradition of popular songs that developed within groups of pioneers and youth movements or in the army – and many going much beyond it. The army musical and theatrical units, like *Lehakat Hanachal*, became very important in the creation of a new popular culture of relatively high level, and a tradition of popular music and dance festivals developed.

## Participation in the cultural sphere

There also developed a continuously diversified cultural consumption and participation on different levels, crystallizing in very diversified, often quite fluid, patterns.

There was, first of all, the consumption of the different works of 'high' culture; literature, music, theatre, literacy, journalism and the like.*

There was a very wide spread of newspaper reading – of newspapers which on the whole developed and maintained a high level and broad coverage of reporting together with a relatively high level of literary supplements. There has been a continuous growth in the number of newspapers and periodicals that are published in Israel. Thus in 1969 there were 481 newspapers, journalists and periodicals; in 1976, 653; and in 1978, 706 – most of them in the Hebrew language, among them 14 daily newspapers.

A rather special event in Israel has been the *Yerid Hasefer* (Book Fair) usually taking place in the late spring, when the major publishers exhibit their books in 'open fairs' in the major cities. This attracts a very great number of people and has become a great popular cultural event.

Museums have been established: the Israel Museum in Jerusalem which has incorporated the older Bezalel Museum, the Tel Aviv Museum, established in 1930 which was expanded in the 1960s, and many local ones. Although they, naturally, could not compete with the treasures of the great museums of Europe or the United States, yet they managed to acquire – through gifts and purchases – some quite important collections and to organize special exhibitions which continuously attracted quite large audiences. There are also private galleries selling the works of both local and European and American artists.

Within this panorama of cultural activities, of special interest have been the *Iemei-iyun* (Days of study). These are seminars lasting for an evening, day or couple of days, usually focusing around specific topics, such as social, economic and political problems, archaeology, Jewish history and the like.

These seminars, related to the tradition of the various gatherings of traditional learning (such as the *Yarhei Kala* of the Yeshivot), have burgeoned in Israel far beyond the usual range of adult education courses and have become in their scope and often also intensity, a rather special part of the Israeli cultural scene.

The study of the Talmud and the 'Oral' tradition have recently become very popular, especially among religious, but also among other, groups. The two most important instances of such study sessions are the 'Gathering for Oral

* See the detailed analysis in Elihu Katz and Michael Gurevitch, *The Secularisation of Leisure – Culture and Communication in Israel* (London 1976).

Law' and the 'Month of Special Learning', organized by one of the larger Yeshivot in Bnei Brak.

A more popular and spectacular type of cultural event was the *Hidon Tanach* (Bible Competition) organized on Independence Day and drawing competitors from all over the world.

The introduction of television, as we shall see in greater detail, gave rise, in Israel as everywhere else, to a new mode of participation in cultural life and events. The development of radio, of television in 1968, and of video in the 1980s has greatly changed the pattern of cultural participation and 'consumption', giving rise to a weakening of reading habits, and a more passive consumption of the products of mass-media as attested by Table 10.4. There was a general trend away from study and active participation towards more

**Table 10.4   Reading and Entertainment out of the Home, Jews Aged 14 and over, 1969–79 (Percent of Total in Each Cell)**

|  | 1969 | 1975–6 | Total | 1979 Males | Females |
|---|---|---|---|---|---|
| **Book Reading** | | | | | |
| Read at least one book during the month | 50.7 | 45.1 | 52.6 | 49.7 | 55.4 |
| Of those reading books – read during the month | | | | | |
| 1 book | 31.5 | 32.2 | 30.5 | 32.5 | 28.8 |
| 2 books | 28.8 | 25.8 | 26.2 | 26.7 | 25.8 |
| 3 or more books | 39.7· | 42.0 | 43.3 | 40.8 | 45.2 |
| **Reading of Daily Newspapers** | | | | | |
| Read at least one day a week | 79.6 | 78.0 | 82.2 | 86.5 | 78.0 |
| Of those reading newspapers read during the week | | | | | |
| Morning paper only | 24.8 | 20.1 | 17.5 | 13.6 | 21.6 |
| Evening paper only | 39.8 | 49.6 | 52.7 | 51.7 | 53.7 |
| Morning & evening papers | 35.4 | 30.3 | 29.8 | 34.7 | 24.6 |
| Hebrew only | 71.5 | 78.3 | 81.0 | 84.5 | 77.4 |
| only other than Hebrew | 20.4 | 13.4 | 10.9 | 7.2 | 14.8 |
| both Hebrew and other language | 8.1 | 8.3 | 8.1 | 8.3 | 7.8 |
| **Entertainment Out of the Home** | | | | | |
| Attended at least once during the month | | | | | |
| Museum | 8.8 | 16.2 | 20.3 | 19.9 | 20.7 |
| Symphony concert | 3.8 | 4.9 | 5.6 | 5.4 | 5.7 |
| Theatre | 15.1 | 11.6 | 12.2 | 12.5 | 11.9 |
| Light entertainment | 9.6 | 14.4 | 13.4 | 15.6 | 11.3 |
| Sport contest | – | – | 10.9 | 19.9 | (2.2) |
| Cinema (total) | 62.9 | 45.2 | 43.2 | 48.9 | 37.8 |
| 1–3 times | 36.2 | 32.0 | 34.0 | 37.2 | 31.0 |
| 4+ times | 26.7 | 13.2 | 9.2 | 11.7 | 6.8 |
| Average cinema attendances during the month | 1.9 | 1.2 | 1.0 | 1.1 | 0.8 |

Source: *Statistical Abstract of Israel, 1982*, No. 33, p. 720.

passive attitudes to the products of culture; a general secularization and a growing distance from ideological concerns of many patterns of cultural activities. The introduction of television also eventually sharpened the problem of authenticity of Israeli culture.

## Sport and Leisure Events

Another central aspect of entertainment was the development of sport – especially football, but also other forms, such as volley ball, basketball and tennis. Many of the sports organizations had their roots in the sectorial arrangements in the Yishuv and most of the teams were connected with political sectors or parties. Thus, *Hapoel* teams were connected to the Histadrut while *Maccabi* and *Betar* teams were connected to *Merkaz Haherut*. As a result of this, team managements were political and not sportive.

The various football matches constituted a basic part of the leisure life of large parts of the Israeli public, and even though the standard was not very high they attracted large numbers, especially of younger people. Each team usually had its specific adherents, closely related to its political features and constituting important foci for political, local and national groups, thus sometimes giving rise to violent outbreaks.

There were also attempts to organize international sporting events in Israel: the *Maccabiah*, taking place every four years and bringing together Jewish sporting organizations from all over the world; and *Hapoel* (affiliated with the Histadrut) taking place once in four years, and bringing together groups from all over the world. Both these events were usually of relatively high quality. Indeed in some fields – such as athletics and swimming – Israeli sportsmen and sportswomen have attained respectable international standards, competing in international tournaments such as the European Basketball Champion Cup, some Tennis Tournaments and yachting. Such competitions were usually seen as events of strong national identification. They were widely watched on television and many Israelis would even go abroad especially to give moral support to their teams.

Different events connected with a more popular culture also developed, as we have seen. These have continuously expanded and spread to wider sectors of the population, becoming a basic part of the cultural scene and ambiance of Israel.

Weekend and holiday traditions also developed. On the one hand there was a continuous spread of purely secular modes of 'leisuretime activities': picnics, excursions – sometimes connected with the exploration of Eretz Israel – watersports, and the like. On the other hand there was a gradual expansion of some more religious traditions, such as the lighting of candles on the Sabbath or visiting synagogues, even among semi-secular groups. Often such activities were linked with more secular patterns, at other times they were more segregated. The army Rabbinate played a considerable role in strengthening these traditions; recently it has even been seen by more secular circles as rather aggressive. On the whole, these tendencies became closely interwoven in different quite fluid patterns, with clear demarcation only at the two ends of the spectrum – the fully religious and the fully secularized. But in the whole panorama the special traditions of different immigrant groups – especially the Oriental ones – became very prominent, usually cutting across the secular–religious axis.

An additional and increasingly popular leisuretime activity has been travel abroad, by many sectors of the population. For some this has been on the basis of more or less continuous contacts, whether professional, or with friends or family abroad; for others it has meant excursions, often group excursions, of different duration. The numbers going abroad have risen from 83,100 in 1969, through 192,800 in 1972 to 273,000 in 1979.

# Formalization of Cultural Life, and Growing Autonomy and Privatization; New Cultural Themes

This growing diversification of all such activities of the modes and levels of cultural participation and consumption was closely related with the second and third major trends of change; namely with the very formalization of many of the institutional arrangements of cultural life and with the growing diversification, autonomy and privatization of many such patterns of cultural creativity and participation.

## Growing autonomy of journalism

The very institutionalization of the great effervescence of cultural creativity and participation connected with the renaissance of the Hebrew language and the new pattern of holidays and school curricula, and its gradual interweaving into the daily more sober reality of a small, beleaguered society – whose energies were more and more diverted into the security problems on the one hand and the great institutional expansion on the other – created a situation in which many aspects of this effervescence were taken for granted, became part of the daily routine and were no longer perceived as acts of cultural creativity.

The very diversification of all these activities naturally gave rise to growing institutional and symbolic autonomy of many of these spheres of cultural creativity, participation and consumption. Such growing autonomy and new relations to the centre could perhaps be seen best in the academic fields, discussed above, and also in journalism and the media, whose general importance in shaping the cultural field grew here, as in any other modern society.

In this field, the more sectoral ideological dailies and magazines, with their relatively clear, ideological orientations engaging in the construction of the ideologies and symbolism of the new Eretz-Israeli culture, weakened. On the other hand, the independent dailies – *Ha'aretz*, the major independent daily which had started in the Yishuv but which gained great momentum after the establishment of the State, and the two major evening papers (*Ma'ariv* and *Yediot Aharonot*) – gained in strength. A rather similar trend also developed in magazines and journals.

The discussions in the sectoral literature became more inwardly directed and addressed to relatively closed publics with but little impact beyond such publics, while in the more independent press there developed a different mode of public activity. This mode was characterized by a very high degree of independence from political or ideological camps, combined with a very high degree of public responsibility (as can be seen, for instance, in frequent agreements not to publish items bearing on security).

The public debates ranged over all possible issues of internal and external problems and were often very acrimonious. Most of them – albeit with exceptions in matters of external policy – were set on the whole within the broader consensus, but were often very critical of concrete government policies.

## Privatization of cultural activities

Closely related to the growing autonomy of the major organizations in the cultural field was the growing privatization of many of the patterns of cultural creativity, participation and consumption. There was a growing tendency to define such activities in terms of the private spheres of life of different sectors of the population, with a relatively weaker link to an overall vision or orientation – although sometimes connected with the continuation of a search for such a vision.

One of the most interesting developments of privatization was the growing interest in local affairs and life, as seen in the development and popularity of special local supplements to the major newspapers. The contents of these newspapers also attested to the great variety of the levels of cultural and social activities and interests. Some were closely related to relatively 'high' cultural activities and interests, and to attempts to attain a high quality of life – in housing, reading and creativity in different cultural fields. Other social events and gossip revealed the development of what could be called a vulgar mass culture.

The development of such mass culture – often, but certainly not always, noisy, vulgar and in many ways apparently foreign – very often related to aggressive social patterns of behaviour, as for instance in many sport events, but it was also combined with a strong wish to participate in the centre and a feeling of dissociation from it.

These different patterns of cultural creativity and participation have become part and parcel of the different styles of life of different sectors, attesting to a very great variety, diversification and opening up – as well as fluidity – far beyond the picture in the period of the Yishuv.

Within the context of these different patterns of cultural life, the religious sectors in general and the ultra-religious in particular have, of course, developed patterns of their own. While those belonging to the wider Zionist religious groups have on the whole developed patterns which, while naturally putting great emphasis on religious activities and learning, yet participated also in the many broader cultural activities, the story has been entirely different among the various – continuously growing – groups of ultra-orthodox. Here there has developed, as we shall see in greater detail, a rather strong tendency to growing segregation – albeit in different degrees – from the different patterns of 'secular' activities, especially those like theatre, literature, mass media, emphasizing much more traditional learning and developing quite distinct patterns of cultural life.

## The search for broader meaning

Thus all these developments – the institutionalization and the great diversification of the different types and levels of cultural creativity and participation, and the growing autonomy and privatization of these activities – naturally changed the meaning of many such activities in relation to some more general, overall symbols of meaning in general and of collective identity in particular.

This problem necessarily became connected with the major shifts in the development of new cultural and socio-political themes, especially those of heroism, the memory of the Holocaust, and reorientation to Eretz Israel and to Galut alike. They also became connected with the search for a mode in which these themes would be incorporated into the symbols of Israeli collective identity, around different time dimensions – those of past, present and future – into some new parameters, a new overall semantic field, possibly connected with some central vision related both to Jewish and to universal cultural arenas and themes. While most surveys indicated that most Israelis viewed themselves as both Jewish and Israelis yet the mode and nature of the relation between these – as well as of other – components of Israeli identity become more and more diversified, and often blurred.

The relation of these media to the centre shifted from a relatively close interweaving with ideological and political debates to a much more diversified one – with less participation in common frameworks with the political élite in general and in decision-making arenas in particular.

There continued numerous ideological debates – about the nature of Zionism, the cultural format of the State and the like – but they tended to become specialized meetings of intellectuals and ideologists – or in special symposia organized by the newspapers with small participation of active political leaders and decision-makers. While often very indicative of intellectual moods and ideological perceptions, these debates had little relation to actual policies – but they remained an indication of yearnings for the establishment of some connections between these varied activities and some broader, overall, meaning.

# New Cultural Themes and the Reconstruction of Symbols of Collective Identity
## *Israeli identity and changing attitudes to Zionism*

The fourth major trend that started to develop consisted of important shifts, or at least some new developments, tensions and conflicts, around some of the basic themes and symbols of collective identity, and of the symbolic boundaries of the collectivity.

Some of these shifts were connected, as we have already seen in Chapter 7, with several central historical events, especially the Holocaust on the one hand and the establishment of the State on the other, and the concomitant inclusion of some new themes or components in the Israeli collective identity.

The themes of security and heroism, of the Holocaust, of the revision of the relations between the Galut and Eretz-Israel history became, as we have seen, incorporated, even if often in ambivalent ways, into the Israeli collective identity.

Problems began to develop on the level of the symbols of collective identity; could the central symbolic sphere of society absorb new components and redefine the central symbols of Israeli collective identity, both to different Jewish and Zionist themes, and to wider values, traditions and orientations, however inarticulate these orientations might be?

Two elements of this identity became easily identifiable: first there was a strong, local, Israeli patriotism, but, second, the exact contours of Israeli self-identity, in relation to the broad framework of Jewish tradition and Jewish communities, no longer defined Jewish identity in terms of a minority group or culture. Being a Jew in Israel did not necessitate the definition of self-identity in relation to another majority group or culture and did not involve the various problems, uncertainties and anxieties which constituted such an important aspect of Jewish life and identity throughout the modern world.

It was this aspect of Israel's self-identity which constituted its main novelty, and created some of the differences and difficulties in the mutual encounter between Israelis and Jews in the Diaspora which we shall yet analyse in greater detail later on.

The ambience of the greater (non-religious) part of the population in its Jewish or Israeli identity tended to be a secular one – or at least a much more open one than that prescribed by the Halakha. Yet when, in 1958, during one of the disputes with the religious parties over the problem of 'who is Jew', Mr Ben-Gurion took an unprecedented step by putting the problem to the forty-three so-called 'Sages of Israel' all over the world (who included personalities outstanding in religion and the humanities belonging to all schools of thought), the replies of the 'Sages' turned out to be largely in favour of the Orthodox point of view, even if with some modifications.

At the same time, as we have mentioned in Chapter 7, new attitudes to Zionism developed. Above all the problem of the legitimation of Jewish existence in the Diaspora, as against the usual Zionist tenets, came to the fore even though the terrible shadow of the Holocaust prevented it from emerging fully for a long time. Gradually the need for a new meaning or definition of Zionism evolved and came to a head during the Twenty-fifth Congress of the Zionist Federation, when Mr Ben-Gurion declared that, in his belief, it should be the ultimate aim of every Zionist to emigrate to Israel, and that people who could emigrate but did not do so were not Zionists. The Zionist movement had finished its task, he declared; its purpose was reached, its hopes fulfilled.

His adversaries, consisting mostly of the veteran Zionist leaders, including the President of the Zionist Federation Dr Nahum Goldmann, maintained that the help extended by the Jews in the Diaspora to the State of Israel constituted part of the realization of the Zionist idea, while the continuous diffusing and strengthening of Jewish culture and the Hebrew language, and of the Diaspora's ties with Israel provided another important aspect of this process. The debate continued for a long period, at Zionist meetings and congresses, in special symposia and in many journals and periodicals, but no final, fully acceptable solution could be found or formulated.

At this time these debates did not greatly affect the overall identification with the establishment of the State and the concomitant feeling of the superiority of the Israeli-Jewish reality over that of the Galut which, as we have seen, has been very strong among many sectors in the Yishuv, especially among the younger generation of the *Tsabras*. At the same time in this period they developed a rather derogatory attitude to the term Zionism, seeing in it 'just talk' as against the great deeds being done and achievements attained in Israel.

## New developments in State–religious relations

During the first two decades of the State, there were apparently no great changes in the relative importance of the religious components in the crystallization of the Israeli collective identity. Truly enough, the institutional-ization of the earlier arrangements reinforced the strength of the religious groups, and there was a very gradual strengthening of the details of religious legislation, but this was all done under the auspices of the old compromise between the religious and the non-religious, with the latter seemingly predominant.

However further institutionalization of the religious arrangements led to growing confrontations between the religious and the secular or non-religious groups. It was not only the full institutionalization of the judicial standing of the Rabbinate that was important here. In reality it went far beyond it.

One crucial move was the maintenance of Kashrut in the army and, as far as possible under military conditions, the observance of Sabbath and the holidays under the supervision of the army Rabbinate. They provided Sabbath and other religious services for those interested in them, in fact making them a continuously growing part of the atmosphere of large sectors of the army, and hence also a very important socializing agent for younger generations of old and new immigrants alike.

The very establishment of the religious educational sector as the only official one, within the State educational framework, beyond the general one, was another strengthening factor. Similarly, the arrangement for the non-mobilization of the students of Yeshivot was very indicative of possible changes in the religious component of the national collective identity.

Initially at least most of these struggles and arrangements were seen as just pragmatic *ad hoc* arrangements or as part of the natural struggle within the framework of the existing symbols of collective identity and the institutional framework served from it. Yet the very institutionalization of these arrangements, especially of the standing of Rabbinical courts, gave rise to many conflicts, one such conflict being their relative standing *vis-à-vis* the courts of the State in general and the High Court in particular. Here the more extreme religious groups raised the claims that the Rabbinate – while having jurisdiction over the whole Jewish community (including the non-religious majority) – should be exempt from supervision by the state juridical authorities, that is especially by the High Court.

These disputes centred around the possibility of appeal from the Rabbinical courts to the High Court in matters vested in the former – especially in patterns of Kashrut, and in matters of personal law, above all marriage and divorce, closely related to the question of 'who is a Jew'.

In principle the authority of the High Court was upheld even when, as in matters of 'who is a Jew', it ruled in the spirit if not in the exact terms of the Halakha.* In some cases some *ad hoc* measures were made to accommodate actual cases, especially with respect to marriages performed abroad by Reform and Conservative Rabbis – recently giving rise to the claim of the orthodox, especially the *Agudat*, that it would be legislated by the Knesset that only those converted according to Halakha (i.e. by recognized orthodox rabbis) should be recognized as Jews.

Yet, while in general the supremacy of the High Court was upheld, in the crucial problem of the regulation of the boundaries of the Jewish collectivity, there developed a rather strong tendency to uphold what seemed to be at least the spirit of the Halakhic injunctions – even if interpreted in a new way and sometimes by the secular courts.

So in the whole gamut of relations between State and religion there developed here what S. Z. Abramov† has called the situation of the 'perpetual dilemma' – a dilemma between a fully democratic state based on freedom of religion and on seeming separation between Church and State, and the factual growth, rooted both in coalition politics but also in the long history of the Jewish people, of a relatively close interweaving of the two, in the direction of many Catholic countries such as Italy, with the Chief Rabbinate often attempting to obtain for itself a Church-like centralized organization and status.

---

* See in greater detail Eisenstadt, *Israeli Society*, pp. 311–23.

† S. Zalman Abramov, *The Perpetual Dilemma – Jewish Religion in the Jewish State* (London 1976).

# Changes in External Relations
## *Tensions between the internal and external sectors and orientation*

These problems became connected to the fifth major development in the cultural field – namely the growing awareness of several problems or limitations in the patterns of cultural creativity and participation inherent in a small society.

With the establishment of the State and the concomitant institutional expansion, there were increasing contacts with various cultural communities and institutions – academic, literary, painting and music – abroad, together with a very strong orientation to the external world.

Such orientations did, of course, exist before, in the period of the Yishuv and in the early stages of the State, but in those periods they were on the whole subjected and guided by the overall orientations to the revolutionary reconstruction of the new Israel. Jewish cultural renaissance did not accept these external avenues as models, but as objects of rebellion, of possible incorporation into the new cultural mould or as sources of technical knowledge.

This attitude started to change with the development of the various processes analysed above, and also with the changing relations to the Jewish communities in the Diaspora which will be analysed in Chapter 16. All this gradually weakened the attitude to external arenas, and concomitantly gave rise to a certain loss of the former self-assurance, of the clear internal centre of gravity in the crystalliziation of such attitudes. Gradually various external arenas were transformed from objects of rebellion, of incorporation or of technical knowledge, into models of cultural creativity and participation. With these developments came the problem of reconstructing the central axes of the Israeli cultural scene, the major components of its identity and the nature of its authenticity.

At the same time the very institutionalization of many of the cultural and educational activities brought to light some of the dilemmas and tensions inherent in cultural creativity in a small country, especially indeed of such a country which also aspires to be a centre of special, distinct, cultural creativity.

Thus, first of all in many fields of cultural creativity – but perhaps above all in those of musical, academic and literary activities – it became clear that such a small society, given the limits of its natural internal markets and resources, 'exported' many outstanding talents abroad, for example, musicians like Daniel Barenboim or Itzhak Perlman. On the other hand, it attracted many outstanding academic figures and many musicians, including the Israeli ones, to come back as visitors and temporary participants in some of its centres or in various spectacular events – to a far greater extent than could be found in many other countries. So Israel became a centre of attraction for outstanding figures in these fields, without their activities being wholly rooted in the Israeli institutions in the country itself; or – as in most academic fields – where their creativity was naturally more and more orientated to their respective international communities. So Israel became a unique cultural centre. At the same time there was an increasing separation between the external and internal sectors.

The same tensions also became acute in cultural participation and consumption – newspapers, theatre, television or sport. In many of these fields, as well as in the construction of patterns of leisure time in folkloristic events and the like, there developed very variegated internally orientated activities, with strong indigenous roots. But at the same time many such activities were naturally imported from abroad, giving rise to a very great variety of patterns of cultural participation.

To a certain extent the development of such variety was a natural process. Yet many aspects of such development also gave rise to a growing concern about the degree to which the growing orientation to an external world – first in the areas of cultural creativity and academic life, but perhaps even more in those of cultural consumption, above all in its more 'vulgar' aspects – would denote an erosion of specific Israeli authenticity.

So there developed a growing awareness of the dilemmas between the maintenance of high standards, beyond even those of a normal small society and guided now by a non-revolutionary orientation to the external world, and the possibility of losing its own authenticity – even if a very flexible and open one.

At the same time there was a growing, sharpened awareness of the tensions between excellence and creativity and tendencies to provincialism, mediocrity and local chauvinistic orientations – tensions which, as we have seen, were latent in the settlement in Eretz Israel, in the Yishuv, but which became transformed and sharpened with the continuous development of the institutional structure of the State and became especially visible among the new generations of *Tsabras* and new immigrants, coming after the generations of the founders.

## Literary trends

While these developments, problems and concerns found expression in many fields of cultural creativity, it was natural that they became most fully articulated in literature – a field much more rooted in local conditions than music or most academic endeavours.

In literature, as in so many other fields of cultural creativity, there developed a growing diversification of forms and types of literary creativity far beyond what could be found before. In many ways this built on the very rich and powerful works of the great figures of the first generation of Diaspora-Eretz-Israel Zionist-orientated literature – Bialik, Tchernichowsky, Agnon, to some degree, and others who have been mentioned above in Chapter 6. This generation, as well as the second one born in the Diaspora, directed its activity almost entirely to Eretz Israel. But there was a far-reaching change among writers like Avraham Shlonsky, Uri Zvi Greenberg, Haim Hazaz and to some degree Nathan Alterman. The diversified literary activities of both these generations (including also the great works of translation, from the classic literatures of Western civilization, to which several members of both these generations devoted also a great effort) were to a very high degree guided by a conception of cultural renaissance. There was a continuous struggle with the heritage of the Galut, rebelling against and negating it; they also rebelled against the first generation of literary figures, or attempted to transfer some of its components into the new Eretz-Israeli vision of renaissance.

Among the new generation of Israeli-born writers, in the 1950s only two great works appeared which were guided by some such vision, even if naturally expressed in a different mode and addressed to different themes. S. Izhar's *The Days of Ziklag* (*Yemei Ziklag*), an epic focused on the War of Independence; and, in an entirely different vein, Moshe Shamir's *A King of Flesh and Blood* (*Melech Bassar Vedam*), the story of Alexander Iannai, the great Hasmonean conqueror who came into bitter conflict with the Pharisees.

Beyond these two works there developed a much more mixed and complex approach, which can be found in the work of Amos Oz and A. B. Yehoshua, who have probably become the best-known writers of this generation, as well as in the work of many others. Most of the very rich and sometimes powerful works of the new generation of Israeli writers were characterized by a growing acceptance of the new reality – whether the routinized reality of the State, the new types of relations to the Arabs; the very diversified patterns of life which have developed in Israel. There was still a search to find an understanding of this reality, and a meaningful – often problematic and even painful – relation to it. But the search for such a relation was expressed more and more in rather private, often very sensitive, terms with a lesser overall orientation, despite a frequent yearning for some such orientation. There was a rebellion against the attempts to connect such themes to the reconstruction of reality and yet also a yearning for this, which restricted the full artistic expression of various, diversified themes and orientations. It is interesting to note in this context that this generation of Hebrew writers has devoted itself much less to translations of works from other languages and the very abundant and often very powerful and sophisticated translations of many such works have been more and more undertaken by specialist-translators – another indication of the growing specialization in the field of cultural activities and its manifold repercussions.

There was also a growing orientation to external works, sometimes to Jewish writers in the Diaspora, with a certain loss of self-certainty of an internal centre of gravity.* Parallel trends could also be found in theatre or painting.

## New foci of solidarity

Sixth, there developed far-reaching changes, as compared with the earlier period, in the relations between various areas of cultural activities and the symbolization of national solidarity as well as of the solidarity of different

* See G. Shaked, *There is no Other Place* (in Hebrew) (*Kibbutz Hameuhad* 1983).

sectors of the society.

It was, as we have seen above, above all the field of sport – especially football and basketball – that became the single most important area around which such feelings of solidarity were expressed.

Some of the Israeli participation in international contests in this field were regarded as national events. When they were reported from abroad on the television, the streets of most of the cities in Israel were empty, and any Israeli victory was regarded as a great national event. Similarly such events as the *Maccabiah* and the international meetings of *Hapoel*, which brought to Israel many sportsmen from abroad, were very festive and central occasions – even if drawing less attention than Israeli participation in international contests.

At the same time different local and sectoral (*Hapoel*, *Betar*, *Maccabi*) football teams became foci of solidarity and identification of the respective sectors, often with strong ethnic overtones – and the matches between them often became very unruly and violent, foci of expressions of ethnic or political divisiveness.

Many other types of cultural activities – such as various musical and folkloristic events or special days of study and exploration – continued as or became important foci of mutual solidarity and of the solidarity of various sectors of the society. But they did so in a much less visible and overreaching, even if often very forceful and subtle, way than the sports events.

It was the contribution of all these trends that opened up the problem of the nature of the new parameter of the Israeli cultural scene and of the nature of symbols of Israeli collective identity. This gave rise to growing discussions about the Jewish nature of this culture in general, and of the State of Israel in particular, a debate which was earlier confined to relatively small, even influential, circles of intellectuals.

But it was much easier to raise the question than to find any simple answer, or an answer which would be acceptable to all or even most sectors of the population. The very continuous articulations of these various problems implied that there could not be a single answer to them.

# New Trends in the Crystallization of Symbols
## of Collective Identity
### *New problems and conflicts*

All these developments necessarily impinged on the ideological format of Israeli society, and on the construction of the symbols of its collective identity. The most crucial was to make this identity more flexible without the erosion of commitments to wider symbols. The problems emerged at all the levels discussed above, those of the contents of the collective symbols and the pattern of cultural creativity and participation.

On the first level the major problem was the degree to which the pioneer image could continue to be the sole focus of this identity and its bearers to retain exclusive elite status without weakening the very commitments to the basic symbols of Israeli collective identity.

A similar range of problems developed on the second level, that of contents of the collective identity. The original ideology assumed, as we have seen, a great degree of openness in the formulation of this content. Although it laid out some of the directions of cultural creativity, it assumed a continuous, relatively open, process of creativity in all cultural spheres, and it did not specify all of its details. To some degree this emphasis on continuous creativity tended to gloss over both the possibility of erosion of such creativity and commitment, and the development of differences and splits, such as those between the religious and secular groups, between traditional and modern, between different 'ethnic' or cultural traditions. So with the growing expansion and stabilization of Israeli social structure, a marked change took place in this respect.

This first possibility of erosion of such wider commitments became manifest in two major, often interconnected ways: in the narrowing of the scope of wider cultural and social orientation, and in the growth of splits and conflicts in the central symbolic sphere. Such possibilities of erosion were rooted, first, in the attempts of many groups to maintain the predominance of the specific details and injunctions of the older ideology as the only legitimate way of commitments to such broader values. Second, they were rooted in the process of social and cultural disorganization, especially, but not only, among the new immigrants. They were often manifest in the growth of purely instrumental orientations among both the new immigrants and the younger generation of the older sectors of the community and in the resurgence of traditional religious orientations.

On the one hand, there occurred growing differentiations of various patterns of tradition, partial privatization of many of these traditions and a general weakening of the ideological dimension of the adherence to the various cultural contents and traditions. These developments became the foci of possible varied personal identities with variable relations to the overall collective identity. On the other hand, many aspects of such contents became foci of dispute and of possible socio-political splits, and sometimes also of possible erosion of such wider commitments.

Third, there was, of course, the growing awareness of the possibilities inherent in the more negative, 'apathetic' aspects of mass culture, common to many modern societies. The potential expansion of amorphous mass culture and the possibility of resurgence of so-called Levantinism and provincialism could greatly weaken the orientations to wider cultural and social horizons and commitments, and erode their institutional bases and nuclei. This could become connected with and manifested in a narrowing of the orientations to other centres of culture in the West, to a loss of contact with Jewish communities and hence also to an increasingly narrow provincial identity on the one hand and the growth of purely instrumental or adaptive orientations to collective commitments on the other.

Fourth, in all these areas some new splits, which could have very wide repercussions on the format of Israeli culture, also developed. The first such split was in the sphere of secular-religious relations – a split which has recently become greatly intensified and which could restrict the flexibility of the collective identity and its ability to deal with new, modern problems. The second was related to the possible crystallization of ethnic symbols. The third was that between the over-ideological emphasis which restricted the legitimacy of such wider commitments to the older institutional and organizational setting on the one hand, and the attempts at more flexible and independent value commitments on the other.

All these developments gave rise in the late 1950s to growing concerns about the developments of the cultural ambience of the State and the potential development of conflicts within it.

Perhaps the major single concern was that about possible erosion of commitments to collective goals and values, to the overall Zionist vision – a concern voiced, for instance, in the condemnation of the younger, non-ideological generation, the generation which was going to prove itself in the Six Day War as the 'Espresso Generation'.

There was also the fear of loss of the Jewish nature of the State – voiced by such intellectuals as E. A. Simon who feared a general decline of orientations to Jewish values and commitments; the literary critic B. Kurzweil, who derided the overall secular tone of Israeli literature and its turning away from specific Jewish tradition; J. Leibowitz who, as an Orthodox Jew, wanted – in order to keep the religious area uncontaminated – to have a full separation of Church and State.

And yet, despite these concerns, in the first two decades or so of the State, all these developments in all the areas and aspects of cultural activity, the continuous growth, diversification and openings of cultural creativity in different fields of a broad range of cultural interests and participation in cultural areas and fields, were on the whole perceived as taking place under the aegis of the overall Zionist vision of national–cultural renaissance. This view provided, as it were, the overall broader meaning to these activities, as well as to their great upsurge, which was indeed seen as a crucial illustration of cultural and social creativity of both specific Israeli and universal significance. They were perceived as part of that emphasis on creative institution-building that was so strong in that period, and became a basic component of Israeli collective identity.

Truly enough, the intensity and contents of these various – old and new – orientations, and of the boundaries of this collective identity, were less and less conceived in terms of full, explicit ideology, and much more in terms of continuously shifting – and yet persisting – elements, orientations and traditions, values and symbols to which the more active parts of the population tended to adhere and which were only partly expressed in firmly ideological terms.

Yet at the same time many attempts were indeed made by various groups to extend the range of activities and tasks which were subsumed under the collective aspects of the image of the pioneer and to redefine many of the concrete elements of this image – in this way still proclaiming their adherence to it. Various groups – the army, the new economic developers, the absorbers of immigrants and the settlement authorities, the teachers and the like – made strong claims that their activities contained some elements of the collective commitments of the pioneer. Even if such claims have, of course, continuously changed the concrete contents of this image, yet they provided for some continuity to much wider commitments.

# CHAPTER 11

# Absorption and Integration of Immigrants and the Emergence and Transformations of the 'Ethnic' Problem

## Changing Patterns of Motivation among the Immigrants
### *The background*

Almost all the developments in the different spheres of life of Israeli society naturally converged and became most fully articulated in connection with the processes of absorbing and integrating the waves of immigrants into Israeli society.

It was not only that, given the fact of the great influx of immigrants, the process of their absorption necessarily greatly affected all these spheres, being first shaped by the initial institutional moulds of Israeli society and then in turn shaping their further development.

Beyond this was, of course, the fact that this problem, together with that of security, was seen as perhaps the most central one of Israeli society. The broad field of absorption of immigrants and of what was later to become the 'ethnic' problem, or the problem of the *edot* – above all of the so-called Oriental Jews – has been, from its very beginning, one of the most central foci of public concern and debate, of tensions and conflicts in Israeli life and one of the major foci of transformation of Israeli society.

Indeed the ability to cope with this problem – the ability to create one nation out of the different groups of immigrants – was seen from the very beginning of the State, by almost all the sectors of Israeli society, as one most important challenge facing it – and one of its great tests. And, from the very beginning of the State, it was clear that this problem was of a different magnitude and order than the previous experience of the absorption of immigrants in general, and of so-called Oriental Jews in particular, in the period of the Yishuv.

### *Basic statistics*

Let us recapitulate some of the basic data. Table 11.1 shows numbers, years and countries of origin of the immigrants. Between the years 1948 and 1981, 1,707,703 new immigrants came to Israel, most of them from Europe (787,109); 407,977 came from Africa, 349,438 came from Asia and 138,035 came from America. In greater detail, until 1951 there is a stable increase in

**Table 11.1 Immigrants and Potential Immigrants,[a] by Period of Immigration and Last Continent of Residence, 1882–1981**

| Period of Immigration | Total | Europe | America and Oceania | Asia | Africa | Not known |
|---|---|---|---|---|---|---|
| 1882–1903 | 20,000–30,000 | | | | | |
| 1904–14 | 35,000–40,000 | | | | | |
| 1919–14 May 1948 | 482,857[b] | 377,381 | 7,754 | 48,895 | 4,041 | 22,235 |
| 1919–1923 | 35,183 | 27,872 | 678 | 1,181 | 230 | 5,222 |
| 1924–1931 | 81,613 | 66,917 | 2,241 | 9,182 | 621 | 2,652 |
| 1932–1938 | 197,235 | 171,173 | 4,589 | 16,272 | 1,212 | 3,989 |
| 1939–1945 | 81,808 | 62,968 | 108 | 13,116 | 1,072 | 4,544 |
| 1946–14 May 1948 | 56,467 | 48,451 | 138 | 1,144 | 906 | 5,828 |
| 15 May 1948–1981 | 1,707,703 | 787,109 | 138,035 | 349,438 | 407,977 | 25,144 |
| 15 May 1948–31 Dec. 1948 | 101,819 | 76,554 | 478 | 4,739 | 8,192 | 11,856 |
| 1949 | 239,576 | 121,963 | 1,422 | 71,652 | 39,215 | 5,324 |
| 1950 | 170,215 | 81,195 | 1,954 | 57,565 | 26,162 | 3,339 |
| 1951 | 175,129 | 47,074 | 1,286 | 103,396 | 20,382 | 2,991 |
| 1952 | 24,369 | 6,232 | 950 | 6,867 | 10,286 | 34 |
| 1953 | 11,326 | 2,147 | 930 | 3,014 | 5,102 | 133 |
| 1954 | 18,370 | 1,369 | 1,091 | 3,357 | 12,509 | 44 |
| 1955 | 37,478 | 2,065 | 1,155 | 1,432 | 32,815 | 11 |
| 1956 | 56,234 | 6,739 | 1,067 | 3,139 | 45,284 | 5 |
| 1957 | 71,224 | 39,812 | 1,410 | 4,230 | 25,747 | 25 |
| 1958 | 27,082 | 13,695 | 1,320 | 7,921 | 4,113 | 33 |
| 1959 | 23,895 | 14,731 | 1,147 | 3,544 | 4,429 | 44 |
| 1960 | 24,510 | 16,169 | 1,158 | 1,782 | 5,379 | 22 |
| 1961 | 47,638 | 23,375 | 1,969 | 4,149 | 18,048 | 97 |
| 1962 | 61,328 | 11,825 | 2,187 | 5,355 | 41,816 | 145 |
| 1963 | 64,364 | 14,213 | 6,497 | 4,964 | 38,672 | 18 |
| 1964 | 54,716 | 28,124 | 4,188 | 5,057 | 17,340 | 7 |
| 1965 | 30,736 | 13,879 | 3,096 | 5,223 | 8,535 | 3 |
| 1966 | 15,730 | 7,435 | 2,132 | 3,137 | 3,024 | 2 |
| 1967 | 14,327 | 4,295 | 1,771 | 1,987 | 6,268 | 6 |
| 1968 | 20,544 | 6,029 | 2,275 | 4,671 | 7,567 | 2 |
| 1969 | 37,804 | 15,236 | 9,601 | 7,018 | 5,926 | 23 |
| 1970 | 36,750 | 14,434 | 11,405 | 6,904 | 3,785 | 222 |
| 1971 | 41,930 | 20,888 | 12,885 | 5,778 | 2,354 | 25 |
| 1972 | 55,888 | 29,145 | 10,814 | 3,143 | 2,766 | 20 |
| 1973 | 54,886 | 40,492 | 9,522 | 2,025 | 2,839 | 8 |
| 1974 | 31,981 | 23,126 | 6,439 | 1,179 | 1,216 | 21 |
| 1975 | 20,028 | 13,417 | 4,989 | 927 | 689 | 6 |
| 1976 | 19,754 | 12,137 | 5,774 | 1,135 | 697 | 11 |
| 1977 | 21,429 | 12,660 | 6,201 | 908 | 1,620 | 40 |
| 1978 | 26,394 | 16,549 | 6,305 | 1,736 | 1,683 | 121 |
| 1979 | 37,222 | 22,404 | 6,024 | 7,087 | 1,340 | 367 |
| 1980 | 20,428 | 11,792 | 4,350 | 3,202 | 1,007 | 77 |
| 1981 | 12,599 | 5,909 | 4,234 | 1,215 | 1,170 | 62 |

Notes: a. Including tourists who changed their status to immigrants or potential immigrants; as of 1969 including potential immigrants; as of 1970 including non-Jewish immigrants and excluding immigrating citizens.
b. Including about 11,000 illegal immigrants and about 19,500 tourists who remained in Israel.
Source: *Statistical Abstract of Israel, 1982*.

immigration, and from 1952 a sharp decrease. In 1961 there is another sharp increase in the number of the new immigrants which continues until 1965. In 1965 and 1966–7 we can see a decrease of 56.1 per cent (in 1964, 54,716; in 1965, 30,736). In 1968 we can see again an increase of 54.34 per cent in the number of new immigrants, an increase which continues until 1972. Since 1973 there has been a continuous decrease which continues until today.

It is possible to divide the whole period, from the point of view of influx of immigration, since the establishment of the State, into six sub-periods – each contributing a different percentage of the total number of immigrants who came to Israel.

| | | |
|---|---|---|
| First period | 1948–51 | 40.2% |
| Second period | 1952–60 | 17.2% |
| Third period | 1961–64 | 13.3% |
| Fourth period | 1965–68 | 4.7% |
| Fifth period | 1969–73 | 13.3% |
| Sixth period | 1974–81 | 11.1% |

Thus we see that most of the new immigrants came to Israel between 1948–51; from 1952 we can see a large decrease in immigration that goes up only between 1969 and 1973.

These periods differ also with respect to the percentages according to the relative importance of continent of origin of the immigrants.

| Periods | Asia | Africa | Europe | America |
|---|---|---|---|---|
| First | 34.5% | 13.6% | 47.5% | 0.7% |
| Second | 12.–% | 49.4% | 47.5% | 3.4% |
| Third | 8.5% | 50.8% | 34.–% | 6.5% |
| Fourth | 18.5% | 31.2% | 38.9% | 11.4% |
| Fifth | 10.9% | 7.7% | 57.2% | 23.9% |
| Sixth | 9.1% | 4.9% | 62.2% | 23.3% |

Thus we see that during the second sub-period there was a big decrease of immigrants from Asia, a big increase of those from Africa (i.e. North Africa), and a beginning of slight increase from America. During the third period there was a continuing decrease from Asia, a continuing increase from Africa, a continuing slight increase from America and a decrease of those from Europe. During the fourth period there was an increase from Asia, a big decrease from Africa, the beginning of an increase from Europe, and a continuing increase from America. During the fifth period there was a big decrease from Asia and Africa and a big increase from Europe and America. During the sixth period there was a continuing decrease from Asia and Africa, a continuing increase from Europe, and a slight decrease from America.

## Patterns of absorption

We may also recapitulate some of the basic stages in the absorption policy. The first stage, that of the late 1940s and early 1950s, was, as we have seen, the most difficult one – the stage of *Maabarot*, of public works, of the first steps of the development towns.

By the mid-1950s the great majority and the most outstanding of these special organizations – especially the *Maabarot* – almost entirely disappeared; by the early 1960s almost all of them had gone, and only a very few continued.

Of course the settlements in the Moshavim and the development towns continued – a story of relatively great success in the Moshavim with, as we have seen, a more mixed picture in the development towns. But the greater part of new immigrants went into the towns. It was indeed in the towns that there sprang up the various *Shekhunot* (semi-slums), like the Katamons in Jerusalem, Shekhunat Hatiqva in Tel Aviv, Wadi Salib in Haifa or such concentration of immigrants in Rosh Haayin. Here the lower classes of immigrant groups, large parts of those from Oriental origin, to a very great extent from North Africa, but also from other parts, or for instance the Yemenites in Rosh Haayin, congregated and perpetuated their life beneath the poverty line for two generations, sometimes continuing into a third. But the story was, of course, different in other parts of the towns into which most new immigrants went. It was in the different towns, in the Moshavim and the development towns that there took place the transformation of the new immigrants into fully-fledged members of Israeli society. It was there that new social formations, and many of the most salient characteristics of the transformation of Israeli society, crystallized.

The contours of this transformation were shaped by the continuous interaction among the strong initiatives of the centre and sub-centres in creating the many new institutional frameworks; by the mode of entry or absorption of various groups of new immigrants into the central institutional frameworks, economic, cultural and political; by the describing society; by the discrepancies between this mode of absorption and some of the basic premises of the society – some of which discrepancies were perceived by many of the new immigrant groups; and by the natural impetus of developments within the major institutional spheres of the society.

In this continuous, dynamic interaction, all parts of the population participated in a way which was in many ways different from the one that developed in the period of the Yishuv – although one which was entirely natural when compared with most countries of modern mass, non-selective immigration.

## Characteristics of the new immigrants

Two sets of causes or factors were, of course, of central importance in explaining the development of the mode of integration of different groups of immigrants in Israeli society and of its consequent construction, especially as compared with the format that had developed in the Yishuv. First, there were the cultural–structural background and motivation of the different immigrants in general and of the so-called Oriental ones in particular; secondly there was the structure of the 'receiving' society or sectors, with changes attendant on the development and institutionalization of the State. Thirdly, and probably most important, there was the interaction and feedback between these two sets of factors, as evident first of all in the process of absorption of immigrants, and later on in the continuous integration of these various groups of immigrants in the continuously changing Israeli society.

With respect to the first set of factors, the most crucial fact was that the immigrants who came after the establishment of the State did not exhibit the common charactersitics of large parts of those who had come in the period of the Yishuv. They had manifested a relative – admittedly often very relative – common cultural, mostly Eastern or Central European background, of partly traditional, partly assimilated Jews; also a relatively common ideological orientation, in terms of some Zionist and liberal or socialist ideology, to Jewish national renaissance, which rebelled to a large degree against this background of theirs and the consequent far-reaching self-transformation of the various groups of immigrants.

But among almost all the groups of immigrants, European and Orientals alike, who came to the State of Israel itself, there was a general weakening of the 'revolutionary' or pioneering ideological Zionist orientations. Instead there developed, on the one hand (mostly among the Oriental groups) some type of semi-Messianic orientations, although, as we shall see, already of a somewhat different order from the ones that were prevalent among many of the Oriental groups in the period of the Yishuv. On the other hand, there developed, especially among the European groups but also among large parts of the so-called Oriental ones, motivations stressing the search for safety and security, for finding a haven or place to live in their own homeland. Accordingly, in contrast to the earlier more pioneering groups, there was a relatively weak predisposition among most of these immigrants to change their way of life, to revolutionize it in the classical Zionist – and above all in the Zionist–labour – mould.

Moreover, among the so-called Oriental groups there were other far-reaching differences in comparison with the older Oriental sectors.

The first such difference concerned Jewish orientations and identity that developed among the new Oriental immigrants.

The growing assimilation and mobility which developed under the impact of the colonial (especially French, to some degree Italian, as well as British) powers; the growing confrontations with different movements of Arab nationalism; the development of different Zionist movements – pioneering and *Betar* alike: all these added a rather more intensive national, to some degree secular and very often ambivalent, dimension to the self-conceptions of many of the immigrants of Oriental or Sephardi origins regarding their Jewish identity and aspirations. At the same time there was the impact of the Second World War, and the repercussion, sometimes intensive (especially in Libya under Italian rule), sometimes more distant, of the fate of the European Jewry.

Last was the intensification of national and semi-Messianic feelings with the establishment of the State of Israel.

All these indeed greatly transformed the whole orientation to Israel and the general level of expectation of large parts of the Oriental Jewish communities with respect to Israel. Aliya was no longer the older type of traditional pilgrimage, based on the traditional religious, religious–nationalistic emphasis of settlement in the Land of Israel; these themes were already incorporated into the vision of the reborn Jewish State, and with new secular and more active orientations and expectations.

The patterns of motivation that developed among most of the immigrants who came from Europe – survivals of the Holocaust, only a small minority of whom belonging to any of the active Zionist youth or pioneering movements – were different. They came from a great variety of socio-cultural settings – orthodox, traditionalist or to different degrees secular or semi-secular – and were very heterogeneous in their economic background.

Most of them saw in Israel the homeland which was ready to receive them, a place of refuge and safety, and were willing to adapt themselves to the new reality, but only very few were strongly imbued with an active Zionist vision in general, and a pioneering one in particular.

So it was that the Zionist themes and orientations which appealed to the immigrants were above all the more national ones, in combination with personal security, rather than the more pioneering, revolutionary, socialist ones; moreover, the more particularistic as against the more universalistic themes naturally attracted some groups. Nevertheless the other orientations – especially the pioneering, revolutionary ones – were initially very strongly emphasized by the frameworks into which the new immigrants were presumably to be socialized. Thus, in general, most of the new immigrants were less predisposed to change their occupational patterns and aspirations and their life style than the earlier different pioneer groups.

## Different characteristics of the immigrant groups

But within this broad framework of new patterns of motivation and of predisposition to change in general, and in the directions implied by the dominant ideology of the centre in particular, there developed great differences among various immigrant groups in their ability as it were, to 'swim' – especially, but not only, in the first stages of absorption – in the relatively uncharted and very tumultuous waters of Israeli society.

Two sets of variables were of crucial importance in influencing such an ability of different groups of immigrants. First there were the social and socio-psychological background, and second there were the cultural and educational traditions and attainments, of the different groups of immigrants.

Several psycho-sociological variables influenced such an ability: the degree of internal, family and community security and cohesion of different groups of immigrants; the degree to which such groups included active leadership; the different social echelons to which they belonged, and the type of Jewish identification and identity they carried.* On the whole, it was the cohesive groups, comprising strong elements of leadership, different occupations and professions, and carrying a relatively non-ambivalent Jewish identity, that evinced the highest capacity to adjust to the continuously evolving reality of life in Israel.

From the very beginning of immigration some very important differences were identified among the Oriental or Sephardi groups – with the Bulgarians and the Yemenites standing at one end, while many of the North Africans, and especially some Moroccans, at the other end of the scale.

The Yemenites, and to a smaller degree the Bulgarian communities, came to Israel almost in their entirety (as did some North African ones, for instance, that from Marrakesh), bringing their leaders and most of their social echelons. These communities had relatively strong family and community cohesion, as well as strong, positive Jewish identity – very traditional in the case of the Yemenites and some of the North African groups, rather modern among the Bulgarians.

The different North African groups, and to some degree the Iraqis, present a much more complicated picture. A large part of the more active elements and upper social echelon from North Africa went not to Israel but to France, or even to the United States; some came to Israel for a short while and then moved on, perhaps in the early 1950s. Sometimes even brothers of those who came to Israel went to France, where they did socio-economically better in the more open, flexible and variegated French economy, although socially and emotionally they reported as feeling less integrated. The Jewish identity of large parts of these groups was often very complex and ambivalent, for they were torn between traditional Islamic anti-Jewish sentiments in accommodation, Arab nationalism and tendencies to French assimilation, feelings portrayed by Albert Memmi in *La Statue de Sel.**

The picture was, of course, very different among the immigrants from Europe – most of them coming after the Holocaust with the shadow of that terrible experience hanging over them. Many still had strong family cohesion and at least some traditions or memories of cohesive community leaderships, and some had previous attachments to the Zionist movements and organizations in general and the pioneering movements in particular, but many were also socially much weaker, or more isolated.

Closely related to the patterns of interaction was the special structure of the process of immigration which was not characterized, as in the former period, by some predominance of relatively cohesive primary groups and close interaction between the leaders and members of such groups.

---

* See in greater detail Eisenstadt, *The Absorption of Immigrants.*
* A. Memmi, *La Statue de Sel* (Paris 1965).

## The interaction of these characteristics

Motivation, emotional security, family and community cohesion and leadership were not, of course, the only factors influencing the fate of immigrants in Israeli society. Their impact was indeed most visible in the first stage of absorption, when the economy was still underdeveloped and the economic opportunities provided by the absorbing country still very limited.

But with the growth of the economy and of economic opportunities, education level and skills, as well as general cultural background, became more and more important. However, this set of factors did not obliterate the importance of the structure of family and community solidarity and social leadership networks. Indeed their existence or absence was very important in all stages of absorption and integration – especially when there was some 'cultural' distance between the immigrants and the absorbing sectors. Their importance was threefold; first they could provide community support; second they could provide models of activities and advancement in the new setting; and last, they could provide the necessary networks for effective pressure in the absorption agencies, and later on in the various frameworks of Israeli social structure. Initially their existence could even counteract low educational attainment or so-called cultural distance – as was the case in many of the Moshavim.

Thus the different patterns of occupational advance and integration of different groups of immigrants can seemingly be explained by the continuous interrelations and feedback between the levels of education, cultural norms, family and community cohesion, and leadership networks. But this is only a partial, although not invalid, explanation. It is partial because it does not question the impact of the absorbing society, because it takes the structure of this society in relation to the new groups and its impact on them as given, and above all because it does not explain why social mechanisms did not develop from within the absorbing society strong enough to counteract the more negative or weak aspects in the background of the new immigrants.

Such a question may seem – and to some degree probably is – rather superfluous, especially when compared with other societies of modern mass, non-selected immigration. It may indeed be claimed that many of the immigrants successfully integrated into the educational system, the army, even the occupational frameworks, both rural and urban, again particularly as compared with other countries of mass, non-selective migration. The later development of many special programmes in the sphere of education, of vocational guidance and the like also attests to the development within Israeli society of a special sensitivity to these problems.

And yet, given the strong emphasis in Israel on the creation of one nation, on the full integration of all the immigrants into one nation, the question is perhaps not entirely superfluous. And later on, with the growing intensification of the ethnic problem, this question was indeed asked more and more frequently. Hence, even if the development of such overall sufficient mechanisms was in a sense a mission impossible, a sort of utopian vision, it was a utopian vision rooted in the new ideology and symbolism of Israeli society, and hence it is necessary to examine this question.

## Changing Patterns of Absorption
### *Absorbing the new immigrants*

In fact it was, of course, the combination of the various factors analysed above, together with the impact of the absorbing institutional setting, that influenced the nature of the conditions which were important in the shaping of the economic and occupational advance of different groups of immigrants, as well as the mode of their integration into the emerging social system and the consequent transformation of that system.

Here a comparison with the period of the Yishuv is naturally called for, especially with those sectors of the Oriental Jews who during that period were, as we have seen, only marginally integrated into the main sectors of the Yishuv.

Here a rather paradoxical picture emerges. From many points of view – their origin, many of their cultural traditions and patterns of social and cultural life – there was a remarkable similarity between these sectors and the new Oriental immigrants. And yet several crucial differences developed.

First, of course, there was the sheer numerical difference in the scope of this immigration, as well as the relatively greater proportion of the so-called Oriental Jews in the total migration, and their continuously growing proportion within the total Jewish population of Israel.

Second there were the differences in the structure of the process of immigration itself. The process of immigration no longer consisted of trickles of families, or of small family groups of neighbours, as it had in the period of the Yishuv. On the whole, it was now organized under the auspices of the official emissaries and organizations of the Zionist organization, of the State; small parts of these *olim* were organized by the various pioneering movements, often – especially before the establishment of the State – connected with illegal activities and immigration.

Lastly, and closely related to the basic question about the absorbing society, was what probably constituted the most crucial difference between the process of absorption of new immigrants in general and of Oriental Jews in particular, and that process in the period of the Yishuv. The special frameworks of absorption, and the general institutional frameworks within which economic, educational and political absorption took place, were not the result of the more or less spontaneous accommodation of the Oriental groups in a reality which at least was partially alien to them. They were purposefully created by the new national centres, to a very large degree for the express purpose of absorbing the new immigrants and forging one common nation.

Some special organizations of this type had already developed in the Yishuv in connection with the German Aliya in the mid-1930s, but in that period they did not constitute the chief mode of absorption that they became in the early period of the State. From the very beginning all these frameworks – even the *Maabarot* – were not segregated from the centre, but initiated by it and hence also naturally orientated towards it, its premisses, promises and demands, and toward other groups, old and new alike, developing continuous comparison with them and judging the performance of the centre in the light of these premisses and promises.

## *The bureaucratic framework of absorption; power and social distance between immigrants and absorbing sectors*

Thus, although from the point of view of at least some aspects of their background the new immigrants in general, and the Oriental ones in particular, could be compared with the Oriental Jews or other non-pioneering elements in the period of the Yishuv, yet from the point of view of their orientations and expectations the process of their absorption and integration should be compared with that of the different groups of immigrants in the central sectors of the Yishuv.

From this point of view there were some very far-reaching changes and differences which are of crucial importance for the understanding of the process of their absorption and integration in Israeli society.

The first major difference arose because of the very numbers and speed of the first waves of immigrants, especially those of 1949–59, their weight in proportion to the existing population, and the paucity of the economic resources available. The government and the Jewish Agency established special frameworks to tackle the problems of absorbing immigrants, and a highly bureaucratized process of absorption of immigrants developed, directed from the centre. Many special agencies and services were established.

Within these frameworks the new immigrants were, in the beginning at least, the more passive elements which were absorbed according to the premisses of the 'absorbers', of the old-timers, of the absorbing society and of its centres.

Even in the Moshavim, in the beginning at least, it was the officials of the Jewish Agency, and the representatives of the older Moshavim, the Moshav movement, who formed the more powerful element guiding the new ones, and only much later independent cadres of leadership developed from within the Moshavim. This was, of course, even more true in such places as the *Maabarot* and development towns.

Initially neither the informal groups in Israel's social life, nor the political organizations, contributed much to the direct informal social absorption of immigrants. The former became more and more socially self-enclosed, with membership confined to people of similar occupational seniority in the country, or housing vicinity. Only those newcomers who had relatives or friends among the old-timers were able to participate fully within them. In principle the homes of old-timers were not closed to the new immigrants; on the contrary, once immigrants reached the thresholds of these homes, they were usually well received. But most of the veterans did little to bring new immigrants to their door, except inform them of voluntary, even semi-philanthropic activities.

The same applied to most of the old Sephardi organizations. Despite their claims to be the leaders of the Oriental immigrants, the social gap between them and these immigrants was as great as in the case of most other organizations or parties.

Within the political parties, in the Histadrut and its subsidiaries, which became – as we have seen – more and more centralized and bureaucratic, and which gave great economic and vocational help as well as trade union protection for those who had reached some level of occupational skill, attitudes towards the immigrants were usually paternalistic. Immigrants were often viewed mainly as potential voters or as supporters who had to be 'organized' and made 'safe'.

Political pressure, especially at local levels, was often exerted on immigrants, sometimes in very obvious, even brutal ways, by the officials of these agencies. It was also used by the many administrative agencies dealing with absorption which were closely related to different centres of political power.

Meanwhile, immigrants were gradually absorbed through the normal channels of society – the school system, the army (which was of crucial importance in this process), and economic and occupational selection; later, as we shall see in greater detail, new policies were developed, aimed at giving preferential treatment in order to alleviate immigrants' socio-economic and educational disadvantages.

Such special institutions of absorption have now almost disappeared. With the shrinking of the immigration since the late 1950s, some new types of special institutions – such as the centres of absorption established by the Jewish Agency, and various guidance centres established by the government, especially by the Ministry of Absorption – of a more 'educational' preparatory character, dealt with much smaller groups – mostly from Russia and the West – and were much less important in the overall process of crystallization of Israeli society. But they still followed a rather bureaucratic mould and attested to the continuity of bureaucracy in the process of absorption.

As for the earlier immigrant groups, already, in some way at least, integrated into Israeli society, the special policies addressed to their problems – above all those related to 'disadvantaged' or 'deprived' groups or strata – developed to no small degree from the background of absorption but became part of the broader framework of general social policies that crystallized in the State of Israel.

Thus in general, in close relation with the changes in the relative power-relations analysed above, a much weaker continuous reshaping of the formal frameworks developed through the autonomous interaction between the official power-holders and the more informal groups, the newcomers, and as a result of the continuous impingement of the latter in the centres of these frameworks.

Needless to say with the passage of time all these frameworks developed internal dynamics of their own which changed greatly their contours – as seen particularly in the new Moshavim – but this dynamism was already set within the framework of great differences in power between the absorbing elements and the immigrants.

## Development of special policies and recognition of social problems

The very development of such policies of absorption and their quick connection with 'social problems' constituted, of course, a great change in comparison with the period of the Yishuv – not only on the institutional but also on the ideological level.

In the period of the Yishuv, given its basic ideological premises, there was almost no place for the definition or perception of absorption as a distinct separate problem. To a large degree the same was true of the recognition of social problems. It was on the whole assumed that no specific social problem should or could arise in the process of continuous institution-building based on the pioneering labour premises, in a revolutionary 'socialist' community or society.

There was some recognition of the existence of social problems in the margins of society, particularly among the weaker social groups of some sectors of the Oriental groups. Special departments of social work were developed in the *Vaad Leumi* (but not, significantly enough, in the Jewish Agency, the dominant future-orientated Jewish organization), in the various municipalities – mainly in conjunction with the mandatory government. But all these were relatively marginal in the whole gamut of institution-building in the Yishuv, and they were dealing with sectors and problems which were perceived as relatively marginal to the central institutional nexus of the Yishuv.

These broad assumptions about the natural connection between participation in institution-building and the absorption of immigrants also – perhaps paradoxically – guided the initial policies of absorption of immigrants in the State of Israel. Then, given the great numerical influx of immigrants and the very difficult initial economic conditions, it was necessary to organize special frameworks such as the *Maabarot* and special public works (*Avodat Dahak* or emergency works) in order to cope with the central economic problems of their absorption.

But all these were seen as a necessary evil and, by their very nature, transitory; hopefully they would lead naturally to the full integration of the various groups of immigrants into the central institutional – educational, military, occupational and political – frameworks, as was to some degree at least the case of the Moshavim.

Even the development towns, destined, as we have seen, to become tantamount to at least the initial failure of absorption, as sort of second best settlements, were to some degree conceived by their planners as another natural extension of the Zionist pioneering vision of settlement and institution-building.

# The Positive Aspects of the Integration of Immigrants
## *Vision and reality*

But the reality that developed out of these initial plans did not uphold these premises or hopes. The picture of the absorption of new immigrants into Israeli society developed, as is well known, in a rather different direction from this vision and from the developments in the Yishuv.

A new reality started to develop very quickly after the first, transitory years of absorption, a reality shaped by the combination of market forces and social policies emanating from the centre. This reality was set within the context of continuous economic development, and of the new pattern of relations between the centre and the old-timers on the one hand, and the new immigrants in general and some Oriental ones in particular on the other hand.

Within the framework of this new very dynamic, developing reality, out of the continuous interaction of all the factors analysed above, the concomitant processes of the integration of different groups of immigrants developed in the framework of the Israeli society, and the concomitant crystallization of new social formations took place. The picture that emerged was naturally very dynamic and complicated; not only did it develop in directions different from the original vision of integration, of ingathering of exiles, but it also greatly transformed – albeit naturally in conjunction with other processes – the whole format of Israeli society.

## *Economic, educational and political success*

On the positive side, there was first of all the continuous economic and educational advancement of all or at least most groups. Great progress was indeed achieved after the first very difficult years. The initial picture, that of the early 1950s, was, as we have seen, one of great hardships and difficulties, with a growing concern about the possibility of development of two nations. But from the mid-1950s the worst aspects of the initial stage of absorption – the *Maabarot* and the public works – started, at least partially, to disappear. More and more new immigrants were absorbed in the various productive sectors of the economy – even if, as the case has become more and more clear, parts at least of the so-called Oriental groups were on the whole absorbed in the lower levels of these sectors.

Most of the immigrants – Western and Oriental alike – were absorbed in the cities which were greatly expanded; but large parts were also absorbed in the Moshavim and the development towns.

There was a continuous development of new Moshavim, especially after the more critical period of the early 1950s when many such Moshavim were rather unsuccessful and proved to be unviable. Between 1948 and 1956 233 new Moshavim, mostly of new immigrants, were established, and out of the 1961 population of about 125,000 in all Moshavim, at least 90,000 from them were in the new Moshavim. In the development towns there was by 1972 a population of about 350,000 and these towns were seemingly on the way to some economic stabilization; industries and services started to move to them.

Of course this was, as we shall see, only one side of the picture. For a long time many of the development towns were not economically viable, were still dependent on public works and contained a very strong kernel of social cases – and initially at least many of the more active social elements tended to leave them. Many of them remained relatively backward in an economic social sense for a long time and, as we shall show in greater detail later on, there was a general tendency for the mutual reinforcement of ecological distance and low socio-economic status. But beyond these cases and those of the *Shekhunot*, there was a continuous economic and occupational mobility and advancement among most of the immigrants.

Second, and perhaps even more impressive, was the incorporation of most of the groups of immigrants in the basic political and cultural framework of Israeli society. They were granted immediate basic political rights, and continuous participation in the elections; they were admitted into the framework of general education, where Hebrew was the lingua franca of Israel; they were encouraged to join the army. As a result most of them accepted at least some of the basic symbols and premises of Israeli society, especially those of new common Jewish–Israeli nationhood, of loyalty to the State, of a relatively strong identification with the security dimensions of the State, and of at least the basic formal aspect of the democratic political system.

The educational system, together with the army, seemed to imbue most of the immigrants with at least the rudiments of the Hebrew language and to weaken – although not abolish – pockets of illiteracy.

Of course it undermined the older traditional settings of many – especially some Oriental – immigrants, but opened up many new vistas to their children, and the cultural premises and symbols of the centre, as well as the status of life of many of the older groups, tended to become the major reference orientation for most immigrant groups.

This educational process – especially for the Oriental children coming from different cultural–traditional backgrounds – was, of course, sometimes painful. Such painfulness was often compounded, as we shall see in greater detail later on, by the ignorance and lack of sensitivity of the educators to special cultural backgrounds and traditions of many immigrants; by the insistence that they should give up entirely their traditional heritage; by the separation of children from their elders and their traditions. All these attitudes were rooted in the strong self-assurance of the first generation of the different echelons of Israeli leadership that the social and cultural mould represented by the State

**Table 11.2  Persons Marrying, by Groom's and Bride's Continent of Origin (Jews) 1952–80**

| | Total | Groom from Europe/America | | Groom from Asia/Africa | | One spouse Israel-born with Father Israel-born[a] | Endogamy Index[b] |
|---|---|---|---|---|---|---|---|
| | | Bride from Europe/ America | Bride from Asia/Africa | Bride from Europe/ America | Bride from Asia/Africa | | |
| | | | ABSOLUTE NUMBERS | | | | |
| **All Marrying** | | | | | | | |
| 1952–1954 | 14,483 | 7,352 | 885 | 493 | 5,269 | 484 | 0.85 |
| 1955–1959 | 14,196 | 6,320 | 1,199 | 618 | 5,968 | 91 | 0.81 |
| 1960–1964 | 15,303 | 6,273 | 1,354 | 923 | 6,736 | 17 | 0.74 |
| 1965–1969 | 19,681 | 7,559 | 1,278 | 1,436 | 7,304 | 2,104 | 0.70 |
| 1970–1974 | 26,125 | 9,398 | 2,230 | 2,091 | 9,681 | 2,725 | 0.64 |
| 1975–1979 | 26,002 | 7,844 | 2,459 | 2,036 | 10,456 | 3,207 | 0.62 |
| 1978 | 25,025 | 7,245 | 2,376 | 2,007 | 10,188 | 3,209 | 0.61 |
| 1979 | 25,240 | 6,876 | 2,490 | 2,037 | 10,444 | 3,393 | 0.60 |
| 1980 | 24,946 | 6,543 | 2,398 | 1,976 | 10,573 | 3,456 | 0.60 |
| **First Marriages** | | | | | | | |
| 1968–1969 | 18,925 | 7,152 | 1,332 | 1,635 | 6,931 | 1,875 | 0.68 |
| 1970–1974 | 23,064 | 7,905 | 1,973 | 1,890 | 8,801 | 2,495 | 0.63 |
| 1975–1979 | 22,719 | 6,373 | 2,153 | 1,790 | 9,504 | 2,899 | 0.62 |
| 1978 | 21,621 | 5,747 | 2,041 | 1,749 | 9,181 | 2,903 | 0.60 |
| 1979 | 21,747 | 5,458 | 2,139 | 1,758 | 9,394 | 2,998 | 0.59 |
| 1980 | 21,510 | 5,132 | 2,042 | 1,697 | 9,515 | 3,124 | 0.59 |

PERCENTAGES

| | | | | | |
|---|---|---|---|---|---|
| **All Marrying** | | | | | |
| 1952–1954 | | 9.8 | 6.3 | 3.5 | |
| 1955–1959 | | 12.9 | 8.5 | 4.4 | |
| 1960–1964 | | 14.9 | 8.9 | 6.0 | |
| 1965–1969 | | 15.5 | 7.3 | 8.2 | |
| 1970–1974 | | 18.4 | 9.5 | 8.9 | |
| 1975–1979 | | 19.7 | 10.8 | 8.9 | |
| 1978 | | 20.1 | 10.9 | 9.2 | |
| 1979 | | 20.7 | 11.4 | 9.3 | |
| 1980 | | 20.4 | 11.2 | 9.2 | |
| **First Marriages** | | | | | |
| 1968–1969 | 100.0 | 41.9 | 7.8 | 9.6 | 40.7 |
| 1970–1974 | 100.0 | 38.4 | 9.6 | 9.2 | 42.8 |
| 1975–1979 | 100.0 | 32.2 | 10.9 | 9.0 | 47.9 |
| 1978 | 100.0 | 30.8 | 10.9 | 9.3 | 49.0 |
| 1979 | 100.0 | 29.1 | 11.4 | 9.4 | 50.1 |
| 1980 | 100.0 | 27.9 | 11.1 | 9.2 | 51.8 |

Notes: a. Including continent of birth not known.
b. Computed according to combined continent of birth.
Source: *Statistical Abstract of Israel, 1982*, p. 86.

epitomized the full – and probably the only possible – realization of the Zionist vision.

But the general tendency towards the construction of a new common cultural pattern, based on the premisses of the regnant institutional mould and justified by the tenets of the Zionist vision, the integration of immigrants, the forging of one nation out of the ingathering of exiles, seemed to be a great success in Israel – especially when compared with any other modern mass non-selective migration – and it was achieved in a relatively short time.

This was particularly true of those who came from some Western, mostly European, backgrounds – even if their integration into Israeli society in general and the educational system in particular was already connected with the changes in the whole nature and orientation of the Israeli educational system, with its close interweaving with the occupational market, with the weakening of its future orientations and with parallel developments in the cultural sphere. But even for the Oriental groups, even if it was ridden with the problems and tensions they experienced it was this new, continuously changing mould that became predominant.

There was also the continuously growing and active participation of most groups of immigrants in the political life, on the local and central levels alike.

There was also the, in reality surprising, stability and continuity of the political system and framework – evident, as we have seen above, in the composition of the major parties and in the relative distribution of votes among them during this period. Especially significant, from this point of view, was the fact that, despite some *ad hoc* attempts – and some very limited success at the local level, no separate distinct ethnic or new important parties developed. Slowly but surely the new immigrants in general and the Oriental ones in particular were seemingly absorbed within the existing parties, only in the 1977 elections helping to change the balance of power between them.

Throughout this period far-reaching continuous changes in the political sphere were taking place. More and more of the local leaders in development towns and in other sectors came from the Oriental groups – even if initially co-opted in a paternalistic way. So a new generation of such local leaders emerged in the late 1970s, although the number of people from Oriental groups in the higher echelons of bureaucracy remains relatively small.

There was also a continuous rise in the number of 'ethnic intermarriages'. Thus in 1952–4, 9.8 per cent of all marriages were 'interethnic'; in 1960–4 this percentage rose to 14.9 per cent; in 1970–4 to 18.4 per cent, and in 1980 to 20.4 per cent, an increase of 108 per cent; and this percentage has remained more or less at the same level. For a more detailed picture, see Table 11.2.

# The Negative Aspects of the Integration of Immigrants
## *Slow institutional dispersion; perpetuation of poverty sectors; education and occupational gaps*

As against these positive aspects of the process of absorption and integration, to a very large extent unequalled in any other country of mass non-selective immigration, there developed more problematic ones which became centres of growing public debate and concern. Most of these concerns concentrated around the Oriental groups – although in fact similar problems also developed among parts of the Western, European groups.

First there was the continuity, through generations, of poverty pockets,* the great ecological concentrations of such pockets, and the famous *Shekhunot* such as Shekhunot Hatiqva in Tel Aviv, Musrara and the Katamons in Jerusalem, Wadi Salib in Haifa – in which a population of about 200,000 is estimated, composed mostly of Oriental, especially North African, immigrants.

There was also, until at least the mid-1970s, the relatively continuous economic and educational backwardness of many – even if certainly not all – the development towns due, to no small degree, to the ecological distance between centre and periphery, between the central concentration of population in the cities and the development towns.

There was the growth of social problems such as delinquency and crime, large parts of which were concentrated among sectors of new immigrants, attesting to the growing disorganization of many of their social frameworks.

**Table 11.3    Gross Average Annual Money Income in 1975 per Employee's Family, by Year of Immigration and Continent of Birth of Family Head (IL thousand)**

| Year of immigration | Born in Europe/America | Born in Asia/Africa | Israel-born, father born in: | |
|---|---|---|---|---|
| | | | Europe/ America | Asia/ Africa |
| 1965 | 32.3 | 23.2 | | |
| 1966 | 34.4 | 23.4 | | |
| 1967 | 36.4 | 22.2 | | |
| 1968 | 35.4 | 24.9 | 28.8 | 40.7 |
| 1969 | 37.3 | 26.4 | 30.9 | 41.3 |
| 1970 | 40.4 | 29.9 | 31.4 | 48.0 |
| 1971 | 40.4 | 30.1 | 31.0 | 45.6 |
| 1972 | 42.8 | 31.8 | 30.8 | 48.2 |
| 1973 | 42.7 | 31.7 | 36.9 | 52.0 |
| 1974 | 44.6 | 34.5 | 34.9 | 52.2 |
| 1975 | 44.8 | 36.8 | 36.4 | 51.0 |
| 1976 | 46.0 | 37.7 | 35.6 | 52.5 |
| 1977 | 49.8 | 40.4 | 39.3 | 54.6 |

Source: *Statistical Abstract of Israel, 1982.*

Above all, and very often stressed, as Tables 11.3, 11.4 and 11.5 indicate, was the continuous relative occupational (although not necessarily economic) and educational discrepancy between the Oriental (Asian–African origin) immigrants and those of Western (European and American) origin, seemingly culminating in a tendency to a coalescence of ethnic and class components in the very complex class structure of Israel.

* One aspect of this continuity is discussed by Hagit Schlonsky, *Intergenerational Continuity in Poverty*, The Henrietta Szold Institute, Research Report 215 (Jerusalem, September 1980).

**Table 11.4    Jewish Employed Persons, by Occupation, Sex and Continent of Birth, 1980**

| Occupation and Sex | Born in Europe/America Immigrated | Born in Asia/Africa Immigrated | Israel-born, Father born in Europe/ America | Asia/ Africa |
|---|---|---|---|---|
| **Males** | | | | |
| thousands | 236.9 | 215.8 | 113.9 | 97.1 |
| percentages | 100.0 | 100.0 | 100.0 | 100.0 |
| Scientific & academic workers | 13.9 | 2.9 | 15.7 | 2.7 |
| Other professional, technical & related workers | 11.1 | 6.3 | 14.5 | 7.2 |
| Administrators & managers | 7.5 | 3.5 | 9.7 | 3.0 |
| Clerical & related workers | 14.9 | 12.3 | 12.1 | 12.3 |
| Sales workers | 8.4 | 8.9 | 8.9 | 7.8 |
| Service workers | 5.7 | 10.5 | 4.0 | 7.0 |
| Agricultural workers | 2.5 | 6.4 | 10.4 | 6.0 |
| Skilled workers in industry, building & transport, and other skilled workers | 31.4 | 42.1 | 23.3 | 49.5 |
| Other workers in industry, building & transport, and unskilled workers | 3.6 | 7.0 | 1.3 | 4.4 |
| **Females** | | | | |
| thousands | 143.1 | 98.9 | 96.4 | 76.7 |
| percentages | 100.0 | 100.0 | 100.0 | 100.0 |
| Scientific and academic workers | 11.6 | 2.4 | 14.3 | 2.6 |
| Other professional, technical and related workers | 24.1 | 15.0 | 36.2 | 20.2 |
| Administrators & managers | 1.3 | (0.4) | 1.3 | (0.4) |
| Clerical and related workers | 28.0 | 23.2 | 33.0 | 45.6 |
| Sales workers | 9.5 | 7.3 | 3.9 | 3.4 |
| Service workers | 13.4 | 36.9 | 7.5 | 15.3 |
| Agricultural workers | 1.8 | 3.3 | 2.2 | 2.1 |
| Skilled workers in industry, building & transport, and other skilled workers | 8.6 | 9.7 | 1.4 | 8.4 |
| Other workers in industry, building & transport, and unskilled workers | 1.8 | 1.8 | (0.3) | 2.0 |

Source: *Statistical Abstract of Israel, 1982*, p. 349.

**Table 11.5    Index of Gross Yearly Income of Urban Family by Continent of Birth and Year of Immigration of Family Head, 1965–77**

| Date of survey | Born in Europe/America | | | Born in Asia/Africa | | | Israel-born |
|---|---|---|---|---|---|---|---|
| | Total | Immigrated in 1947 | Immigrated in 1955 | Total | Immigrated in 1947 | Immigrated in 1955 | |
| **Males** | | | | | | | |
| 1965 | 100 | 121 | 79 | 72 | 90 | 64 | 109 |
| 1970 | 100 | 111 | 84 | 74 | 84 | 68 | 104 |
| 1971 | 100 | 111 | 81 | 74 | 82 | 63 | 101 |
| 1972 | 100 | 113 | 88 | 74 | 86 | 65 | 101 |
| 1973 | 100 | 113 | 88 | 74 | 85 | 65 | 113 |
| 1974 | 100 | 115 | 89 | 77 | 78 | 72 | 104 |
| 1975 | 100 | 117 | 87 | 82 | 93 | 76 | 103 |
| 1976 | 100 | 114 | 92 | 82 | 83 | 77 | 102 |
| 1977 | 100 | 111 | 96 | 81 | 93 | 80 | 99 |
| **Females** | | | | | | | |
| 1965 | 100 | 116 | 85 | 45 | 61 | 37 | 99 |
| 1970 | 100 | 115 | 90 | 47 | 63 | 40 | 87 |
| 1971 | 100 | 108 | 90 | 48 | 61 | 40 | 85 |
| 1972 | 100 | 115 | 94 | 46 | 63 | 39 | 87 |
| 1973 | 100 | 115 | 94 | 46 | 61 | 39 | 99 |
| 1974 | 100 | 119 | 91 | 50 | 58 | 44 | 90 |
| 1975 | 100 | 121 | 90 | 54 | 65 | 50 | 89 |
| 1976 | 100 | 119 | 93 | 54 | 64 | 50 | 87 |
| 1977 | 100 | 123 | 94 | 55 | 69 | 53 | 88 |

Source:*Statistical Abstract of Israel, 1982*, p. 353.

So we see that a rather complex picture has developed against the general background of continuously high mobility. There has been a growing coalescence of so-called Oriental groups in the lower groups; the broad, continuously changing middle sector has become more and more ethnically mixed, and the higher sector is mostly composed of the European group.

Even within the very broad, middle sector, the picture is more complicated than the official statistics portray. The crucial fact here is that the official statistics deal mostly with educational and salaried income, and much less with the new private sector which has developed such areas as construction, technical works of different degrees of sophistication, and different shops, boutiques and restaurants, areas in which many Orientals seem to be very predominant. At the same time it should be stressed that, from the point of view of occupational prestige, these occupations do not compete with the more academic or salaried even if, from the point of view of economic income, they have often transcended the latter considerably.

These developments were to some degree parallelled by those in patterns of ecological segregation or mixture, where there has been a relatively high – yet somewhat diminishing – segregation between groups of European–American origin and those of Asian–African origin, and also between those from Asia and from Africa. While the general picture did not change greatly between the 1960s and the 1970s, a more detailed analysis of some metropolitan areas (especially that of Tel Aviv) showed that segregation was less marked in the smaller cities than in metropolitan areas.

## The Dynamism and Diversity of Integration
### *The interaction of the immigrants' background and the developing framework of Israeli society*

This slow integration of the different groups of immigrants, especially parts of the so-called Oriental ones who tended to stay in the relatively lower occupational and even ecological sectors, was the single greatest difference from the pattern of absorption of immigrant groups in the Yishuv.

Significantly enough many of the discrepancies were perpetuated into the second generation, that is for the Israeli born, even though it is difficult to evaluate the statistical data exactly, and though the background was one of continuous economic and occupational mobility.

This picture was not uniform – even with respect to the Oriental groups and perhaps even more so with respect to other new immigrants.

The differences between different groups within the broad categories of Western and Oriental immigrants have not been adequately researched, and there are only general indications about the ways in which continuous interaction – between family and community cohesion, cultural background and educational achievements, networks of leadership and influence in relation to the major frameworks of the society – have shaped the process of integration of different groups of immigrants in the continuously developing and changing pattern of Israeli society.

It was but natural that the extreme negative case became most visible – the pockets of poverty in the famous *Shekhunot*, characterized on the whole by the combination of low educational attainments and skills, low family and community cohesion, great distance from leaderships and elite elements of their own countries. Not only have they perpetuated sheer poverty – although cases of overcrowded housing, low income and irregular work, abounded in these sectors – but of no lesser importance has been the growing apathy and continuously growing dependence on the distributive agencies of the State, creating a new culture of dependency, later giving rise also to local populistic leadership orientated to the maximisation of such demands.*

But an initially relative low educational level, as well as cultural distance, could be overcome by the development of relatively strong community cohesion and strong leadership networks in appropriate frameworks of the absorbing society. This can be seen above all in many of the successful Moshavim, in which immigrants without the highest educational qualifications were absorbed, and on the whole successfully; however there were of course many such Moshavim which failed and remained in an economically low stage.†

* Hagit Schlonsky, *Intergenerational Continuity in Poverty.*
† Some earlier stages of this development are analysed in Dov Weintraub *et al.*, *Immigration and Social Change: Agricultural Settlement of New Immigrants in Israel* (Jerusalem and Manchester 1971).

But those who succeeded – and they were numerous – became part of the more affluent as well as politically active and established parts of Israeli society, attesting to the importance of a continued interaction between the frameworks of absorption and the immigrants themselves through a process of mutual selection and feedback. Although this process has not been studied to the degree that it deserves, even a superficial glance at it indicates that this feedback was able to obviate, to no small degree, many of the initial shortcomings in terms of education and lack of 'cultural' background.

Many signs of such success among different groups of Oriental families – those who came both in the period of the Yishuv and after the establishment of the State – could indeed be identified. Among the first, one outstanding example was that of the Levi family which came in the 1930s from Iraq and, living in difficult conditions – which today would be designated as deprived – raised all its children in a constructive and productive way. One of them, Moshe Levi, became the twelfth Chief of Staff of the Israeli Army in 1983.

Many cases of far-reaching success in public service or in industry could also be found among the Oriental immigrants who came after the establishment of the State, and in most such cases it was a strong family cohesion and positive feedback with educational, army and professional frameworks that was of very crucial importance.

But such continuous feedback did not always develop within other sectors of absorption, particularly within the urban sector or – at least until lately – in many of the development towns. Here there have not always been the mechanisms and policies to overcome the combination and mutual reinforcement of the low levels of education, of family and community cohesion, of patterns of leadership and of the developing market forces and of different policies of absorption and integration.

## Overall tendencies

The overall picture is indeed very complicated and not yet fully researched, but some tendencies have emerged. First of all the weaker social elements in all social groups could become more weakened and eroded by the market forces, some of them pushed into areas of poverty with growing dependency on the distributive agencies, or into rather dubious interstices, sometimes criminal or semi-criminal, between different economic sectors.

Second, however, the various stronger more cohesive elements within all immigrant groups started to avail themselves of the various opportunities opened up in the new continuously developing social and economic reality in general and of some of the special agencies and policies mentioned above.

In general, relative cultural similarity between high educational attainments, the development of some networks of influence within the absorbing society and the ability to move into different centres of population have been very important in the advancement of various groups of immigrants. On the other hand, ecological distance from the centre could be rather detrimental, especially when such distance was often concomitant with a low level of educational and public services, relatively weaker educational attainments and low socio-economic status.*

Those ecologically closer to the centre were affected by the special policies developed by the centre. So for instance they benefited from the constitution of a special vocational stream and more specific vocational training schemes. But later on, as we shall see, they also encountered some of the more problematic consequences, especially the growing feeling that the more mobile elements were blocked from full access to the upper educational streams and con-comitant occupational advancement, and even access to the centre.

## Interethnic prejudices, stereotypes and discrimination

It was here that the impact of interethnic prejudice, stereotypes and actual or alleged discrimination became most visible.

Prejudice, social distance and tension between different groups of immi-grants, between new and old-timers, have existed from the very beginning of Jewish settlement in the Land of Israel in general and in the period of the Yishuv in particular. They could be found in the relations between waves of pioneers and immigrants coming from different albeit 'culturally closer' countries, between the Russians of the second Aliya and those from Poland coming from the third and fourth Aliyot, between these first two and the immigrants from Germany from 1933 on. There also existed many derogatory expressions in the 1950s and 1960s orientated to the new immigrants, especially but not only the Oriental ones. Many such stereotypes could also be found in earlier periods, with respect to almost all immigrants.

There can however be no doubt that all such emphases or manifestations of prejudices and the strength of ethnic stereotypes, especially towards Oriental groups in general and the Moroccans in particular, have continued to develop, albeit with some interesting shifts, to a much stronger degree than before.

Beyond the rather diffuse spread of such prejudices and stereotyping, such attitudes and connotations have also become embedded in important insti-tutional niches and key positions, especially in the educational and the vocational fields. Thus several surveys have indicated that teachers tend, often unconsciously, to discriminate against children with names of Oriental origin; and vocational advisers tend to direct such children to the vocational as against academic schools.

Accordingly, feelings of discrimination have also developed, tending to become more and more articulated with the passage of time. There was of course first of all some seemingly 'natural' informal discrimination, evident above all in daily contacts, and the accumulation of such manifestation of discrimination gave rise to feelings of strong resentment. Interestingly enough, with the passage of time and the advancement of many of the new Oriental

* Dov Weintraub and Vered Kraus, 'Social Differentiation and Locality of Residence: Spatial Distribution, Composition and Stratification in Israel' (in Hebrew), *Megamot*, 27, 4 (December 1982), pp. 367–82.

immigrants in various spheres of life or local government, there is a process of reverse informal 'actual' discrimination.

So the overall picture is a rather mixed mosaic. The feeling of discrimination by the new, especially Oriental, immigrants was probably more widespread and later on also more articulated than before, building on the growing tendency to stereotype in dichotomous terms Oriental and Western, or Ashkenazi, immigrants. And the discrimination, in turn, strongly reinforced this tendency.

On the other hand, such prejudices seem to have been gradually weakened through common schooling and intermarriage and one survey made the interesting finding that children of ethnically mixed couples were the most popular among their schoolmates. But this, by its very nature, has been a very slow process, and in the meantime the development of prejudices and stereotypes has naturally become related to feelings of discrimination.

We have already indicated that all these developments were not identical with respect to all the so-called Oriental or Sephardi groups, just widespread enough to become a rather central aspect of the new, emerging reality. Within the framework of these general tendencies there have developed differences between various groups within the broad sub-categories of Sephardi and Ashkenazi.

## Differences between the sub-groups of Oriental immigrants

General indications point out that it was different mixtures of European, Ashkenazi or Sephardi, like the Bulgarians, which advanced relatively quickly, integrated and ceased to be a special 'problem' group, without necessarily losing many aspects of their group or ethnic identity or traditions.

In the middle, between these successful groups and the lower echelons concentrated in the pockets of poverty, there was a more complicated picture, with many groups, especially Oriental ones but also some European ones.

Against the usual assumption, not all the groups of immigrants of European origin were concentrated in the upper echelons; many were in middle, middle lower and even lower occupational positions, and many became well integrated in different levels of the occupational structure.

Similarly the later Western immigrants – those who came from the late 1960s on, those from Russia who remained in Israel, those from Latin America, and those from Europe – on the whole integrated with different degrees of success, but certainly not without initial problems and difficulties. These were probably greatest for the immigrants from Russia. Not only did they, as all the others, have to suffer from the bureaucratic aspects of absorption. They also found a very great discrepancy between their far-reaching expectations and aspirations and the reality of life in Israel; between their semi-'utopian' visions of Jewish brotherhood with concomitant patterns of leisuretime and those of Israeli society; between their basic assumptions about social order acquired in the USSR and the more open, but also less security-providing, framework of Israeli society; and between the levels of professional training in Russia and those in Israel.

Among the Orientals the picture was even more complicated. Within the Sephardi, two exceptions – one a 'full' exception, one a partial one – were identified in the first stages of absorption: the Bulgarian Jews, most of them Sephardis, and to a lesser extent the Yemenites.

The Yemenites, while not advancing very rapidly occupationally, in part evinced a very high degree of integration, but in part were concentrated in some of the slums and in occupationally marginal areas. On the whole they maintained a high level of many aspects of their tradition, without developing a very high level of ethnic militancy.

There were continuously mobile Iraqi and North African groups; many moved into various sectors, both as white- and blue-collar workers, in the public as well as the more private sectors, as well as into the developing diversified new private sector, of construction, mechanics, boutiques and the like.

Many members of the Iraqi intelligentsia and writers became absorbed in universities and research institutes, and continued to write – especially poetry – to a non-existent public in Arabic, a very few – like Sammy Michael – made the difficult transition to writing in Hebrew.

The most dismal picture of discrepancies seems to come from some of the North African groups. The accumulation of certain aspects of their rather specific type of historical experience – of being caught between the disintegrating traditional Islamic society and the rising Arab nationalism on the one hand, and assimilation in the French colonial society on the other; the growing disintegration of the Jewish traditional community and in many cases also of the families; the exodus of many of the richer and modern elite elements to France and America – created among large parts of those who came to Israel the unfelicitous combination of low cohesion, strong ambivalence to Jewish tradition and weakness of leadership networks.

This was not, of course, true of all of North African or even Moroccan Jewry. Many – as for instance the Marrakesh community and other groups from Morocco, or groups from Libya or Tunisia – came in cohesive groups and advanced continuously in Israeli society. Moreover the picture was not static. Even from among those who had initially been placed in relatively bad conditions, above all in different development towns, new dynamic leaders emerged, at least from the 1970s – like David Levi who became Minister of Absorption and Aliya, later of Housing, in the first Likud government and Minister of Housing and Deputy Prime Minister in the second; or like many younger mayors of development towns who became very prominent in the political scene.

But they emerged against the background of the difficult conditions of the inbetween years, against the background of feelings of deprivation and social distance from the existing centres, of the continuity of the pockets of poverty and the predominance of the North African groups in them.*

Thus, through the interaction of the various factors analysed above, there has indeed developed a new reality. The central new aspect was the much slower process of dispersion of different groups of immigrants, especially parts of the Oriental groups, within the different sectors of the society, and above all recently, as we shall see, the development of far-reaching ethnic consciousness, divisiveness and militancy – the like of which was never seen in the Yishuv and certainly was not envisaged by the initial vision of the ingathering of exiles – which has greatly changed the contours of Israeli society.

# Crystallization of New Patterns of Ethnic Identity and Ethnic Protest
## Maintaining ethnic life styles and traditions

Another closely connected process was the crystallization of patterns and life styles in 'ethnic' terms – much beyond what existed in the period of the Yishuv or even in the early years of the State.

Some aspects of such continuity of 'ethnic' patterns of life – the tendency to greater interaction among those closely related in terms of background, maintenance of many daily customs, to some degree religious traditions – always existed, especially among members of the first generations of immigrants. So too did the use of the language of the country of origin or of the special Jewish language (Yiddish or Ladino) both in daily life and to some degree on ritual or religious occasions.

Among many of the new immigrants from Europe, especially from Hungary or Romania, there also developed, from the 1950s on, special Lands-mannschaft (associations) – whether of those from a certain locality or from the whole country – which were concerned with mutual help, and encouraged social occasions, commemorative events and to some degree also political activities, mostly within the existing parties. On the whole these activities did not seem to extend much beyond the first generations of immigrants – except for the numerous commemorative activities, especially those which developed after the Holocaust.

The same was true, even if obviously with differences of detail, of the various Western immigrants from the late 1960s on. Members of each group naturally maintained close personal relations with each other and left some special imprint on the spheres of life in which they became integrated – occupation, leisuretime activities, participation in public activities, voluntary work and the like.

All these levels of 'ethnic' activity were also found among parts at least of the

* The impact of some social factors on feelings of satisfaction and discrimination is discussed in Jack Habib, *Ethnic Gaps in Job Satisfaction in Israel*, Jewish Distribution Committee (JDC) Brookdale Institute (Jerusalem 1983).

different Oriental groups – but among many of them to a much greater degree.

First of all the stronghold of religious tradition was, at least among some of the groups, much more pervasive and continuous. The synagogue and the traditional leadership often constituted important continuous foci of communal organization, sometimes together with or even as a reaction against social disorganization, very often giving rise to continuous recrystallization of religious tradition, memorial days, various cults of saints and of communal symbols, not necessarily in a political direction. Given the fact of sociological segregation and social distance by way of the centre, these activities were also perpetuated in the second generation and often with special emphasis on family and religious tradition – later on serving also as the background for more politically orientated networks.

But the most crucial, relatively new aspect, especially in its intensity, was that of the recrystallization of the ethnic symbolism among many of the Oriental groups – the great and seemingly rather continuous construction of boundaries of social life and social interaction, and interaction in terms of such ethnic symbols, and the growing salience of such boundaries and symbols, despite the growing homogenization of many patterns of life in Israeli society.

There was also the growing development and ideologization of the folklore tradition, especially festivals of the different ethnic groups, up to special ethnic festivals such as the *Mimouna* of the Moroccans – most of which became reshaped in a rather modern way quite often attuned to mass media, developing as major public events often becoming no less – and sometimes more – visible than the more common Israeli festivities.

Somewhat later, from about the 1970s, there was also an added far-reaching ideologization and politization of the ethnic symbols carried and articulated by new types of leadership from the Oriental groups, although not always accepted by all parts of these groups – an ideologization and politization which became couched more and more in very aggressive and divisive symbols of Oriental against Ashkenazi or the like.

## Ethnic protest

This growing continuation of the ethnic problem, its growing ideologization in the various directions outlined above, were very closely connected with the development of ethnic protest. Such protest took a long time to develop – as did the failure of the ethnic political movements mentioned above. There was of course a lot of resentment brimming among many people, but for the first twenty years of the State it was latent. Yet some warning signs developed, each of them intensifying the contours of the problem always leading to the development of often new policies.

The first such dramatic outburst took place in 1959 in Wadi Salib in Haifa. Even in this outburst the themes of ethnic segregation and distinction were strongly emphasized – significantly enough above all by young people after their army service. A State Commission of Inquiry was set up and many of its practical recommendations were for vocational guidance; new vocational plans and channels were to some extent implemented.

The next major such outbreak took place in 1971, above all in Jerusalem, among self-styled Black Panthers coming mostly from within some of the poorer quarters. Foremost among their demands, in addition to those for better housing conditions, was, significantly enough, the one to be incorporated into the army – despite the army's reluctance to call up many of those with criminal records. Indeed, as a result, since then the army has developed some very far-reaching educational activities to deal with these elements.

In fact since then, and especially since the Yom Kippur War, the ethnic theme – the theme of ethnic protest, of growing divisiveness and the expression of this dimension – has become, as we shall see in greater detail, a basic facet of the Israeli public and political scene.

# The Institutional and Ideological Background of the Emergence of the Patterns of Integration and of the Ethnic Problem
## The spread of discontent

Thus we see that, with respect to the integration of the different groups of immigrants, there has developed indeed a very complex, new, reality, differing greatly from the original vision of ingathering of exiles.

The 'objective' sum total of all these processes of integration seems to be rather favourable. Indeed A. B. Yehoshua, the renowned novelist, himself of Sephardi origin, who denies however the validity of the ethnic 'Adati' claim, has stated that, if such a relatively successful incorporation almost twice as large as the original one had taken place in France, it would have indeed been considered a great success.

And yet the picture that emerged at the end of the 1970s, and above all in the 1981 elections, the ingredients of which had existed already before, was a markedly different one; it was a picture of great ethnic dissatisfaction, of the ideologization of the ethnic themes of ethnic separation, distance and hostility.

Not only had there developed a growing emphasis and articulation of the ethnic dimension and ethnic consciousness into a seemingly constant component of Israeli identity, but there had also developed a strong conception of a basic dichotomy of Oriental versus Western groups, a conception which had acquired a strong dichotomous militant and aggressive dimension. Obviously these outcomes and conceptions were not necessarily shared – at least to the same degree – by all ethnic Oriental or Sephardi groups. Neither the Bulgarians and Yemenites, nor probably the Iraqis, were very vocal in it. It was North African groups – and even then only some of them – that were especially vocal. But there can be no doubt that this militant dichotomous perception had become more and more widespread.

## Causes of the ethnic problem

How then can we explain all these developments as against the background of the successful, even if only relatively so, processes of integration?

The explanation of these developments, the key to their understanding lies in the combination of the processes of absorption and integration analysed above with several additional processes which developed from within the centres of Israeli society, and which are very indicative of changes within them.

The first such process was the growing awareness, within the central institutional sectors of Israeli society, of the emergence of an ethnic problem and of the continuous redefinition of this problem, in close relation to changing symbolic and political orientations in Israeli society.

Significantly enough this awareness first became fully articulated – later even in political terms – not among the immigrants themselves, but among many of the 'older' leaders and sectors. It was they who started to define the problem in new ways, thereby contributing to the dynamics of the integration of different groups of immigrants into Israeli society and of the transformation of this society.

The first general reaction to all the new immigrants was to see them as the generation of 'the desert', the culture of which would hopefully pass away with their own full absorption or at least with the integration of their children into the existing mould, with their full and successful socialization in the existing basic premises of the Zionist–labour ideology and the regnant institutional mould – thus overcoming the threat which they constituted to it, which was widely perceived, but not fully or at least officially articulated. The perception and definition of this threat was widespread with respect to almost all the non-pioneering – hence the great majority – of the new immigrants. But within this general framework it was recognized relatively quickly that the Oriental groups – or at least some of them – might constitute a special case. Two lines of thought – one by the official political leaders, the other by intellectuals and educators, the two gradually merging together – began to develop.

In the first stages of absorption, in the early 1950s, the problem of absorption was defined, especially by different political leaders and those dealing with the problem of settlement, as one of cultural backwardness or underdevelopment of traditionality as against the modernity of the older sectors and centres of Israeli society, especially of the more pioneering and revolutionary ones. The new immigrants, especially but at this stage probably not only the Oriental ones, were seen as rather backward and as posing – above all because of their number – a threat to the institutional mould. But it was assumed that this threat could be overcome through proper socialization.

Others believed that these groups had not experienced in their background the Zionist revolution and accordingly that it was necessary to socialize them into the premisses and frameworks of this revolution as developed in the institutional model of the State.

It was at the same time that use of the term *edot* (ethnic groups) became widespread, taken up from the period of the Yishuv, a term which was used mostly with respect to the Oriental groups – but significantly enough not those from the Balkans – and which was picked up very quickly by educators, scholars and journalists.

Some of the scholars and educators stressed the somewhat romantic notion of the possibility of the perpetuation of these traditions in the new settings; others stressed the necessity of finding within the specific traditions of these groups some potential for social innovation or at least adaptation. In the first stages of absorption these emphases were on the whole limited to small groups of journalists and intellectuals and it was the more paternalistic tutelary orientation that prevailed among the political leaders.

In this period also the General Bureau of Statistics coined two technical rubrics in its surveys; it distinguished immigrants of Asian–African origin from those of European or American origin, a distinction which was destined to become the basis of most of the researches on the ethnic problems and which contributed to the tendency for the dichotomization of perception of Israeli society in terms of Orientals and Westerns.

But as we have seen above, very quickly – probably in the middle 1950s but certainly in the late 1950s and early 1960s – it became apparent that the process of such socialization was not an easy one and that it might indeed generate many tensions: lack of participation, passivity and perhaps potential alienation and rebellion.

## Changes in the definition and awareness of the ethnic problem

So new definitions of the problem and a much more vigorous set of policies started to develop. An awareness of the many problems grew with the increasing influx of the new immigrants into the central frameworks of the society and more continuous encounters with them, and this naturally increased with the various ethnic protests. There was also a growing fear of the possibility that 'two nations' might develop, or that the new immigrants might develop a class consciousness in terms of their lower class situation, something which naturally went against the grain of the leaders of a socialist pioneering society. Hence interestingly, and significantly, these problems were not defined as economic or 'class' ones – a definition which seemingly would have been more in tune with the official socialist ideology, but which would have gone against the self-consciousness and legitimation of the centre.

This growing awareness of the problems also gave rise to a new definition or perception of the problem of the Oriental immigrants as mentioned above. Even if imperceptible in the beginning, there developed a continuous emphasis that these problems were not just a transitory phase of the generations of the desert, but something more permanent. The nature of this problem was seen more and more in terms of *edot* (ethnic groups), and the very definition of *edot* changed.

*Edot* were seen as a sort of continuous given problem, but one which continued to be defined in contrast to the wider collectivity which was not *edot* and which was the carrier of the great Zionist transformation and vision and of modernity – later on perhaps even of a different cultural style.

But the attitude to this cultural heritage changed greatly. This cultural heritage and the general problem of the *edot* were more and more perceived as a given basic which had to be accommodated, even encouraged or at least recognized.

Indeed the definition of these problems in terms of *edot* – and not for instance as class or political problems – entailed the acceptance, even the growing legitimation and later even semi-sanctification, of their cultural heritage and distinction, a far-reaching transformation of the whole vision of the basic components of Israeli collectivity. So there was a tendency to a growing dichotomization, not between old and new, but between Orientals and Westerns, between Sephardi and Ashkenazi.

On the one hand, this heritage was accepted as part of the collectivity – and special policies were undertaken to foster it, as we shall see in greater detail later on. But at the same time, even if initially in a relatively amicable way, the policies continued to stress their qualitative difference from the overall non-*edot* collectivity, and their weakness as compared with 'pioneering' self-transformation.

When connected, however, with the widespread stereotyping and prejudice, this approach gradually moved into the direction of a more dichotomous conception of the Western 'pioneering' culture and that of the Oriental *edot*.

This new articulate emphasis on *edot*, coming as it did very much – even if not entirely – from within the centre, was connected in the political sphere with the tendency, within the major parties but above all within the Labour camp, to mobilize or co-opt leaders from within the groups of immigrants who would seemingly act as representatives of the *edot* within the existing parties. Naturally this tendency was even more intensified with the serious outbursts of ethnic protest already mentioned above – those in Wadi Salib in 1959, or by the Black Panthers in 1971 and thereafter.

## New policies

New policies were developed in an attempt to cope with these problems, many of which became part of the broader, more general social economic policies that were crystallizing in Israeli society, and some of which were based – as we shall see – on rather contradictory assumptions.

These policies were of several types. One was the continuation and further extension of some of the policies developed in the first stages of absorption –

such as housing, employment agencies and the like. Within this context, of special importance were many of the social welfare policies – whether those of development, of health unions, of social security, or of special allocation for families with children – which became a part of the basic framework of social policies in Israel, and were mostly orientated towards large sectors of the new immigrants, especially, even if not only, the Oriental ones.

The second type of policies consisted of those in the economic, educational and social fields which were more or less especially orientated to the specific problems of the immigrants. One of the earliest and most innovative among them was the *Ulpanim*, the special boarding or day schools for adults for the acquisition of the Hebrew language, which have become a part of the basic adult-educational scheme in Israel, and through which many tens of thousands have passed.*

Later on, as we have seen, there were many other very diversified policies, above all in the educational field, which were addressed to helping the immigrants to advance in educational and occupational fields.

Two such policies were particularly far-reaching. First, the development of the vocational stream in education, which has indeed been very important in providing many of the socially and occupationally mobile elements among the new immigrants in general and the Oriental ones in particular with channels of educational and occupational advancement.

Second, and possibly most far-reaching, was the policy of integration in the field of education – a policy which has indeed, as we have seen, entirely reorganized the field of primary and secondary education in Israel. This policy of integration was based on the assumption that the stress on attempts to foster intergroup solidarity and interaction, through the provision of common frameworks, would ensure their speedier integration into Israeli society.

Later on, in the late 1970s, a series of special policies orientated to the reconstruction of the quarters (*Shikum Hashekhunot*) and the development towns were undertaken by the Likud government, first of all by the leader of *Dash* – the then Deputy Prime Minister, Yigael Yadin – and continued in the second Likud government by Ministers and Deputy Ministers from the Likud.

## Contradictory assumptions behind the policies

These various policies were based on different, sometimes contrasting, premises, indicative of different social orientations and policies developing in Israeli society.

One such orientation stressed the importance of providing the various weaker groups with special additional facilities which would enable them to enter into the race, giving rise to very wide plethora of programmes, above all in the educational and vocational fields and to some degree in that of housing.

* In 1951, 907 people learned in the *ulpanim*; in 1960 the number was 1,138; in 1970, the number came up to 3,519; in 1980, 6,462 pupils learnt in the *ulpanim*; but in 1982 there was a decrease of the people to 4,092. (*Statistical Abstract of Israel, 1982*, No. 33, p. 656.)

A second, to some degree contrary, basic policy-orientation was that of granting special privileges to special categories – usually defined as 'deprived' but de facto consisting mostly, although certainly not entirely, of Oriental immigrants – and of applying to them special standards. Such was the assumption of Norm B, and to some extent also of policies of integration, of changes in matriculation programmes and the like, which could easily become connected with the lowering of standards, or at least with only a secondary emphasis on the maintenance of standards of attainment in the educational and occupational fields.

Another set of rather contradictory orientations that have guided these policies were those between the more 'paternalistic' or tutelary ones, as against that stress on the development of more autonomous activities and orientations from within the different – especially but not only Oriental – groups. Given the basic fact that most of these policies did develop from the centre, the paternalistic mode was initially very strong and prevalent, and the more autonomous activities were initially at least very weak. With the continuous developments, the picture became of course more mixed, but the more centralized paternalistic trends tended to be very persistent, together with a growing tendency – especially but not only in the political field – to co-opt different leaders in the *Shekhunot*, and they were also very evident in the more recent *Shikum Hashekhunot* project – funded to a large extent by many of the Jewish communities abroad – in which local vocal leaders and intermediaries became very active. Thus many of these policies became very closely interwoven with more general tendencies which became predominant in Israeli life and which are very important for the understanding of the changing format of Israeli life.

First of all they became closely interwoven with the growing emphasis on distributive egalitarianism which stresses rights and minimizes duties and on obligations with a much weaker and even ambivalent attitude to the upholding of standards and to social or educational creativity. Thus many of these policies became part and parcel of the stress on distributive orientations, on growing quests for entitlements, consumption and homogenization of educational channels, on the minimization of the stress on excellence in different spheres of life in general and in education in particular – thus in many ways going against the older elitist pioneering egalitarianism, but building on some tendencies which were, as we have seen above, inherent in it.

## The stress on symbols of Oriental collective identity

Of special interest here are those policies related to the definition of the symbols of Israeli collective identity. These policies – the articulation of the cultural heritage and of the symbols of distinct identity of the various ethnic, above all Oriental, groups – constituted first of all the extension of the different patterns of ethnic traditions. Such traditions, of prayer, of folk arts, music, dancing or singing, derived many of their themes from various Oriental –

especially Yemenite – groups, and included many commemorations of different Jewish communities, a trend which had developed in the Yishuv, but which became intensified after the Holocaust.

Similarly, as we have seen, the high school curriculum – especially in Hebrew literature – included as its central part the Hebrew literature of the Golden Age of Jews in Spain, stressing above all its secular aspects.

As these trends became intensified with the establishment of the State of Israel, their whole ambience became transformed, as we have analysed in Chapter 10.

First of all there were qualitative changes. There was a growing extension of the study of the historical heritage of the Oriental communities in the school curricula. There was also a growing institutional support for research in these fields – ranging through history, folklore, literature and the like. Many funds for scholarship for students of Oriental origin were established. There was a growing stress on the performance of the traditions – especially songs – of Oriental groups in the media, especially on the radio, as well as the encouragement of the folkloristic traditions and festivals of the different ethnic groups. The extension of many of these activities, such as the place of Oriental history in the school curricula, went beyond what seemed to be justified in terms of any objective appraisal of Jewish history.

Beyond these quantitative changes, all these developments denoted, as compared with the earlier periods – whether of the Yishuv or of the first twenty years of the State of Israel – some far-reaching changes in their basic premises, in their ideological assumptions and orientations and in their relations to the common Israeli identity.

All these policies were connected first of all with the development of a more pluralistic pattern of collective identity, stressing to a smaller degree future orientation and the construction of new symbols but with a stronger emphasis on the present and on the past, with a mixture of consensual common–national and divisive themes, whether the latter were couched in ethnic or religious–secular terms.

Second, these trends became connected with a weakening of the connection between the life styles of different groups and strata to any central focus, to some central ideological premisses or symbols. They became connected with a concomitant double development, on the one hand of a trend to growing heterogeneity of such life styles, and on the other hand of the growth of a common popular culture with Oriental themes, visible in music, video and picture.

# Summary
## *The integration of immigrants and the transformation of Israeli society*

We can now bring together the major lines of our analysis and try to explain the development of these new types of integration of various groups of immigrants. Particularly important is the tendency to growing ethnic divisiveness with strong ideological and political overtones and connotations against the background of the relatively great – in many ways unprecedented – success of the process of absorption and integration of the various groups of immigrants.

The starting point of this explanation is the combination of a continuously growing mobility and integration of different groups of immigrants – the fact that through such very mobility they became more and more aware of some of the consequences of the policies of the centre and of market forces which went against some of the basic ideological premises of the absorbing centres, and which were closely related to the changes and contradictions which developed in the regnant institutional mould of Israeli society. These contradictions were indeed closely related to the central processes of change in this society and, as we shall see in further detail later on, also related to the ultimate disintegration of this mould.

Thus first of all these developments indeed became closely interrelated with the changing mode of the political culture and with changes of power relations between different groups or sectors of the society. Here the initial bureaucratic mode of absorption, the great power differences between new and old, the growth of clientelistic political mode, as well as the consequent feeling of social and cultural distance – all set within the framework of the overall stress on common national solidarity and equality – began to be more and more salient and visible.

Here of central importance was the contradiction between the combination of granting to all citizens the rights of full citizenship, including the right to vote, integrating them into the army and school system, and thus making them an integral part of the nation, but at the same time attempting at first at least to direct their political activities through paternalistic, often semi-coercive measures, and through co-opting mechanisms based on the allocation of positions and resources through the central channels of the major parties. Thus it was indeed in the political field that discrepancies between the reality of the process of absorption or integration of many of the groups of new immigrants and the ideal premises of the system and its legitimation could be most clearly seen.

Parallelly and closely connected was the process of crystallization and intensification of the so-called cultural distance, of the alleged basic differences between the Oriental and the Western immigrants and with the developments of new dimensions of ethnic identity.

There can, of course, be no doubt that such differences or distances existed from the beginning – but it is important to stress that there existed at least two different kinds or types of such distance, and the later denotation of 'Western' as against the 'Oriental' does not catch the basic original starting-point of these differences – namely that of 'pioneering' revolutionary orientation largely couched in Western secular terms, but certainly not orientated in principle to the perpetuation of the older Jewish tradition from, above all, Eastern Europe.

Rather, as we have seen throughout our analysis, this ideology was orientated to the creation of a new common Jewish–Israeli culture – as against the much stronger attachment of large parts of the new, especially Oriental, immigrants to their existing ways of life in general and to many traditional, religious aspects in this life in particular.

From this point of view there can be no doubt that the original policies of the absorbing agencies in general, and of large parts of the educational – but also the political – system, often evinced a very strong lack of sensitivity to these problems. The attempts, which must have seemed very brutal to large parts of the immigrants, to make them change their ways of life, often inadvertently also weakened family solidarity and community cohesion, especially perhaps among the weaker elements.

Needless to say, already at this stage, as we have already seen above, there were feelings of cultural distance, of differences between the old and the new – sometimes even then coined in terms of Oriental versus Western cultures. It was also at this stage that some of the strong prejudices among different groups crystallized – but they were not only between Oriental and Western (European) groups, but also between the older forementioned groups and European ones – and these prejudices also persisted, although they didn't actually develop in the direction and articulation of new stereotypes and ideological dimensions.

But the growing perception and articulation (it is difficult even now to judge exactly how widespread it is) of the perception or ideology of a distance between European and Oriental culture or ways of life, was not so much rooted in the 'original' 'objective' cultural differences between the Western and the Oriental groups. Rather it was much more rooted in several aspects of the process and policies of absorption and of integration of the immigrants into Israeli society analysed above, in which the innovative, revolutionary or pioneering vision of the construction of a new secular Israeli culture was continuously weakened, routinized and deflated – moving indeed, as we have seen, into the direction of a modern, secular society with different levels and types of cultural constructs. These styles of life and cultural participation and consumption – especially those developed by the higher elite – became more and more Western and perhaps especially American-orientated. These styles of life, combined as they were with various patterns of the cultural creativity which had continuously developed in the Israeli scene, were not on the whole, because of the lack of cultural common background, fully shared or appreciated by many of the Oriental immigrants, a fact which became compounded by social and political distance as well as by the ideology of *edot*, which developed from within the centre, and of its political repercussions – repercussions which have, against the intention of their perpetrators, also greatly helped in the increase of the feeling of distance from the centre.

It was the combination of these processes within those of growing mobility, the development of different styles of life and social distance between the different sectors, that greatly contributed to the feeling of cultural distance and was of no small importance in the crystallization of the dichotomy between the Ashkenazi and Oriental and Sephardi cultures.

Paradoxically enough, this development does not seem to have been mitigated by the homogenization of much popular culture and of many patterns of daily life. In some ways the meetings in such common frameworks might even have intensified the feelings of cultural distance. It is probably only with the passing of time, with the firm impact of intermarriage among groups and the further weakening of the different styles, that such homogenization might even overcome the feelings of social distance.

All these developments were of course connected with blockages – especially blockages with respect to symbols of status – in the process of mobility in the occupational, educational and economic spheres; with feelings of cultural distance, however justified or unjustified; with blockage of participation in the central areas of the society. Feelings of seemingly far-reaching status distance, of non-access to symbols of status controlled from those very centres which in many ways shaped the structuring of social hierarchies, and from the political centre, seemed to develop among the more mobile groups – whether those going through the vocational system, or those who moved into the new private sector or sectors.

Thus we see that the paradox of the development of the ethnic problem, of its ideologization, and of the growing ethnic tensions, is rooted in the relative success of the process of integration, in the contradictions between the extent and shape of this success, and the vision in which it was rooted and which generated the concrete policies and processes which enabled such – even if relative – success.

This vision was first of all that of the ingathering of exiles, of the creation of one nation, of common Jewish solidarity and nationhood. This vision also implied the hope of combining such absorption together with participation in creative institution-building that was characteristic of the Yishuv and that to some degree at least was assumed to develop also after the initial stages of absorption in the State of Israel.

The basic premises of the vision were very quickly absorbed by many sectors of the new immigrants – as was the realization that the very dynamic reality which developed after the first different stages of absorption did not live up to that vision. And it was in this contradiction that, as we shall see in greater detail later on, some of the basic costs, changes and ultimate transformations of Israeli society can be found.

# CHAPTER 12

# Israel and Minority Populations – the Arabs and Other Minorities in Israel

## General Background
### *Introduction*

The emerging institutional mould of Israeli society was also faced with the problem of the different non-Jewish minorities, above all the Arab minority. It was indeed, for the first time since the period of the Second Temple, that Jews were faced with the existence of minorities among them within a Jewish State.

The fact of Israel being a Jewish State was, of course, emphasized in several ways. First it was emphasized – and fully received by the world – in the very wording of the UN resolutions; in principle the State was established for the Jewish people, as the epitome of their yearnings for the establishment of their own state. The State of Israel was open, at least in principle, to Jews (barring criminal cases) as stated in the Law of Return (1950) which, as we have seen, enunciated that any Jew can come and settle in Israel. The special Jewish–Zionist character of the State was also recognized in several symbolic levels: for example, the hymn and the flag were those of the Zionist movement, and the Chief Rabbis were granted places of protocol as distinguished from the heads of other religious communities.

But within this framework, the Declaration of Independence assured, as we have seen, full equality to all citizens of Israel, irrespective of religion or nationality, and this, of course, also applied to the Arab population. Accordingly citizenship was also granted to the Arab population, and Arabic was recognized as an official language, which could be used in the Knesset and in public discussion.

Arabs participated – as has been briefly indicated above and as we shall see in greater detail – in the elections to the Knesset and entered it, either as members of general (i.e. Jewish) parties – especially the leftist ones (*Maki*, later *Rakach*) or as representatives of special Arab lists (such as *Haklaut Vepituah* (Agriculture and Development) or *Shituf ve Ahdut* (Co-operation and Unity) most of which, till 1977, were close to the Labour party (see Chapter 8).

Muslim, Christian and Druze religious institutions and courts were given wide-ranging jurisdiction in civil matters similar to those given to the Rabbinical courts.

## The distribution of Arabs

The Arabs who remained in Israel were only a small part of the original Arab population that lived in what became the frontiers of the State of Israel, and they were also a relatively weak part of this population.

The more active elements – whether economically or politically – left, some on their own initiative (or rather the initiative of their leaders who were sure they would come back after the defeat of the Jewish forces), others under the very impact of the war, in some cases probably also prodded by the initiative of the advancing Israeli forces.

The Arabs who remained in Israel numbered about 156,000, most of them (about 107,000) Muslims, a large number Christian (34,000) and in addition there were also about 15,000 Druzes and Bedouins. Today most of the Arabs (78.1 per cent) are Muslim. About 13.8 per cent of them are Christian – Latin Catholic, Greek Orthodox, Maronites and others (Protestants, Armenians, Copts) – each organized around their own religious community or church. Later, after the unification of Jerusalem in 1967, this included also the Armenian patriarchs. They deal with the Israeli government through the Ministry of Religious Affairs.

The Arabs who remained in Israel were ecologically concentrated around Nazareth on the Galilee and in the famous Little Triangle (from the Valley of Isreel in the north to Kefar Kassem in the South), with small groups in Haifa, Jaffa and Lydda.

Economically they were mostly composed of peasants with some urban elements – mostly small shopkeepers or workers. Those from the villages who sought employment elsewhere worked mostly as drivers, waiters or non-skilled workers in construction. They worked in the towns during the day, and came back to the village at night. In 1950 50 per cent of the non-Jewish population worked in agriculture, 10 per cent in industry, 6 per cent in construction and 6 per cent in transport.

Their leadership was usually mostly of the more traditional types of family head and of the relatively lower levels of religious leaderships, but one which became isolated from the centres of Arab and Muslim activities.

# The Basic Framework of the Development of the Arab Minorities
## Acceptance as citizens; suspicion and ignorance; benign restrictive semi-colonial paternalism

The general attitude developed by the Israeli authorities towards the Arab population was composed of official recognition and acceptance as citizens in the framework of the basic democratic framework of the State mixed with strong suspicion and ignorance, and a certain blindness to their special problems.

Their recognition and acceptance as citizens was manifest, as we have seen, in the formal granting of citizenship, with the right to vote to the Knesset, the recognition of the Arab language as an official one in Israel and in an extension of basic public services – education, health service, municipal services and the like – to the Arab population. A special department of Arab education was established in the Ministry of Education.

This principled democratic attitude to the Arab population – in the Declaration of Independence – was limited by the consideration of security, by the fact that the Arabs who remained in Israel were of course part of the Arab population, many of which fled from Israel during the War of Independence, which denied the legitimacy of the State of Israel, and by the concomitant apprehension about the loyalty to the State of those who remained.

The combination of all these attitudes gave rise to a special type of relatively benign, but also restrictive, semi-colonial paternalism. On the one hand the Arab minority was assured a very high level of economic development, though smaller than the one in the Jewish sector, and an increase in standards of living which needless to say also led to far-reaching transformations of their social structure. But on the other hand these measures could not efface the Arabs' rather problematic place in Israeli society. This problematic place was apparent in their objective situation but reinforced by the attitudes of the Israeli authorities and the Jewish society, and by their institutional repercussions.

The suspicion towards the Arabs was manifest first of all in their exemption, continuing till this very day, from the army, although some other minorities, such as the Druzes or Circassians, or even parts of the Bedouin, were asked to serve in the army.

The second – more temporary – expression of this suspicion was the imposition in most Arab areas by the military government, of heavy limitations on Arabs' free movement throughout Israel, imposed through a system of permits. Closely related to such suspicion was social distance and ignorance on a daily level – but also, as we shall see, in more official frameworks.

There were also attempts – which we shall analyse in somewhat greater details later – to control, through various paternalistic activities, the political activities of the Arabs.

Added to these security considerations was the lack of any real preparation within most parts of the Jewish community to deal with the problems of a minority population living within a Jewish state, a certain basic blindness to its special problems, which were only gradually recognized through the growing concern among intellectuals, Orientalists and some left-wing and more liberal groups.

The mixture of these different attitudes to the Arabs – especially suspicion on the one hand and their acceptance as citizens with full protection of the law on the other – is perhaps best epitomized by two episodes or incidents, that of Kefar Kassem and the prolonged problem of the two villages of Biram and Ikrit in Galilee.

The incident of Kefar Kassem occurred in 1956, in the beginning of the Sinai Campaign, when Arab villagers of Kefar Kassem, a village in the centre of Israel, returned home after the curfew hours, of the imposition of which they were not aware. They were shot and many killed by a unit of the Israeli Border Police stationed to assure order in the region. Despite the wartime period, and censorship over security items, news of the incident leaked out. Even then attempts were made to hush up the matter 'internally' – but Ben-Gurion insisted on the responsible officers and soldiers being brought before a special court martial, which was presided over by a civilian judge given (as was a usual custom in such cases) a reserve officer rank. Many of the officers and soldiers were given sentences of imprisonment of different lengths of time, on the ground that soldiers have to disobey immoral orders. Although it was claimed that the highest officer involved – directly or indirectly responsible – got off with a light fine, and most of the officers were amnestied after serving parts of their sentences, yet the principle was established that Arab citizens cannot be viewed – perhaps in continuation of the situation of the War of Independence – as enemy population.

The Ikrit and Biram story illustrates another aspect of this problem. These two villages in Galilee, populated by Christian Arabs, were 'temporarily' evacuated in 1948, under the pretext of security considerations. Despite the initial promises that they would soon be returned, this did not occur; they were in fact resettled in nearby Arab towns or villages and most of their lands were requisitioned and taken over for Jewish settlements.

Even when many years passed and the security problem that had existed in that period abated, their claims to be allowed to come back to their villages and renew some settlement on the lands were not – till this very day – allowed. Behind the official security claim, this refusal was based not only on the fear about the necessity to find some proper compensation or perhaps even give them back some of their lands, but also on the much more basic fear that any admission of such a claim might open a flood of demands for resettlement even from Arab refugees outside Israel.

# Demographic, Economic and Educational Development
## Transformation and the traditional Arab society

Within the framework of these basic parameters, a far-reaching social dynamism developed within the Arab population of Israel, evident first of all in the demographic and economic spheres. The high level of health and educational services (high when compared with the Arab countries yet often lagging behind standards in the Jewish sector) gave rise to a concomitant demographic increase – among the highest in the world – as shown in Table 12.1.

**Table 12.1  Increase of the Arab Population, 1948–81**

| | Population at beginning of period (in thousands) | National increase | Migration balance | Immigrants | Total increase | Population at end of period | Yearly percentage of increase | Percentage of migration balance out of total increase |
|---|---|---|---|---|---|---|---|---|
| 1948–54 | 156.0 | 35.8 | – | – | 35.8 | 191.8 | 3.2 | – |
| 1955–71 | 191.8 | 196.4 | 1.8 | – | 266.9 | 458.7 | 4.3 | 0.9 |
| 1955–60 | 191.8 | 47.3 | –0.1 | – | 47.4 | 239.2 | 3.7 | –0.2 |
| 1961–65 | 239.2 | 57.7 | 2.5 | – | 60.1 | 299.3 | 4.6 | 4.2 |
| 1966–71 | 299.3 | 91.4 | –0.6 | – | 159.4 | 458.7 | 4.5[a] | –0.7[b] |
| 1972–81 | 453.6 | 199.4 | 4.7 | 19.4 | 204.1 | 657.7 | 3.7 | 2.3 |

Notes: a. Including addition of East Jerusalem in 1967.
b. Excluding addition of East Jerusalem in 1967.
Source: *Statistical Abstract of Israel, 1982*, No. 33, p. 32.

Second was the gradual growth of an educated intelligentsia, composed of graduates of high schools and even universities. Compulsory education was enacted among Israeli Arabs. In 1973 90.7 per cent of the Arab population in the suitable ages were going to schools, compared to 98.6 per cent from the Jewish population. In 1977 the percentage rose to 92.5 per cent.

Tables 12.2, 12.3, 12.4 and 12.5 present the educational structure of the Arab population in Israel. All these processes brought about a weakening of the 'traditionality' and self-enclosure of the Arab population, undermining many aspects of their traditional social structure and encouraging an inter-weaving with the Jewish economic sectors – but also giving rise to new problems and tensions.

Dov Weintraub and Zeev Shavith have succinctly summarized this development till about 1967. Thus, to quote them:

Rapid modernization and development and political intensification have been the main social trends in the Arab sector and have determined the main problems this sector faces.

From 1960 to 1980, economic processes that started earlier gained impetus. Thus, the amount of land under cultivation and yield per unit of land have increased, owing to mechanization and improvement in methods of cultivation, crop diversification, and development of infrastructure (capital investment, road building, irrigation, and better transportation). Indeed, government policies, the example of the Jewish agriculture, and availability of markets have spurred development that is increasingly sustained. Thus, because fewer persons are employed in agriculture, the value of the produce is constantly growing, and part of it is exported abroad.

The industry picture is totally different. There are practically no factories to speak of, and most Arab industrial workers are employed in the general economy. However, they thus become increasingly skilled and experienced in some branches (auto-mechanics and construction especially); together with the growing number of technical college graduates, they may provide the manpower for future industries, when the necessary local capital can be found.

In addition, the reservoir and number of professionals has greatly increased so that local services – commercial and municipal – are increasingly being run by local people.

Socially, change has paralled economic development, even though many formal structures are unaltered. Greatly spurred by the influence of the overall society, by internal developments and by demographic transition, change has occurred on all levels. Traditional leadership is thus pushed aside by educated young people, leading to a constant confrontation between conservative and modernizing forces.

At the same time, the educational system in the Arab community still has to cope with special problems embedded in the values and traditions of the Arab world. First, in spite of the progress of Arab women, dropout from elementary school was still very high among girls.

Prestige of humanistic subjects is still paramount, so technical and vocational education cannot develop properly. The teachers are still too authoritarian, and their methods of teaching are conservative, tend to rely on rote memorization, and do not encourage the development of independent thinking. These attitudes are hard to change, even though the education authorities have been investing much thought and effort into training programmes and developing new instructional materials, and

**Table 12.2    Pupils in Institutions of Education, 1948/9 and 1978/9**

| Type of Institution | Arab Education | | Jewish education | |
|---|---|---|---|---|
| | 1948/9 | 1978/9 | 1948/9 | 1978/9 |
| Total | 11,129 | 169,952 | 129,688 | 1,000,605 |
| Kindergartens | 1,124 | 17,880 | 24,406 | 244,700 |
| Elementary Schools | 9,991 | 116,859 | 91,133 | 406,925 |
| Special Elementary Schools | – | 727 | – | 12,587 |
| Intermediate Schools (Junior High School) | – | 13,964 | – | 70,610 |
| High Schools | 14 | 17,207 | 7,168 | 58,220 |
| Vocational High Schols | – | 1,850 | 2,002 | 68,164 |
| Agricultural High Schools | – | 747 | – | 5,349 |
| Teachers College | – | 572 | 713 | 11,732 |
| Other Institutions | – | 146 | 583 | 14,141 |

Source: Alouph Harevan (ed.), *Every Sixth Israeli* (Jerusalem 1983), p. 23.

**Table 12.3    Arab Institutions of Education 1948/9 and 1978/9**

| Type of institution | 1948/9 | 1978/9 |
|---|---|---|
| Kindergartens | 10 | (298) |
| Elementary Schools | 45 | 290 |
| Special Elementary Schools | – | 16 |
| Intermediate Schools (Junior High School) | – | 43 |
| High Schools | 1 | 90 |
| Vocational High Schools | – | 13 |
| Agricultural High Schools | – | 2 |
| Teachers College | – | 2 |

Source: Harevan (ed.), *Every Sixth Israeli*, p. 23.

**Table 12.4    Number of Pupils Passing Matriculation Examinations, 1948/9 and 1977/8**

| | 1948/9 | 1977/8 |
|---|---|---|
| Jewish education | 802 | 13,500 |
| Arab education | – | 1,200 |

Source: Harevan (ed.), *Every Sixth Israeli*, p. 23.

**Table 12.5    Non-Jewish Students in Institutions of Higher Learning, 1968/9 and 1978/9**

| Institutions | 1968/9 | 1978/9 |
|---|---|---|
| Hebrew University | 205 | 500 (estimate) |
| University of Haifa | 257 | 662 |
| Ben-Gurion University | 5 | 200 |
| Tel Aviv University | 48 | – |
| Bar Ilan University | 51 | – |
| The Technion | 42 | – |

Source: Harevan (ed.) *Every Sixth Israeli*, p. 23.

various refresher courses. These efforts are probably hampered by the fact that too few Arabs are employed in senior positions in the central educational administration. In this way, the best formulations and communication are not always available, and the perception of the changes and improvements as imposed from above by an external factor, conceivably alien and hostile, is likely to be reinforced.*

## School curriculum

The educational system that developed in the Arab sector evinced at least initially a far-reaching lack of sensitivity to the special problem of the collective identity of this minority – and only very slowly have some openings in this direction taken place.

The curriculum that was developed initially in the Arab schools was rather similar to that of the Jewish pupils, adapted according to the needs of the Arab population but without greatly taking into consideration the problems of the development of its identity. The teaching languages were of course Arabic and Hebrew – studied from the 4th class. The students had also to study some parts of the Bible, and some parts of Jewish Literature, in order to understand the Hebrew language and the Jewish tradition. In the matriculation the examinations in Mathematics and Science were the same as in the Jewish schools but translated into Arabic, and there was also a special examination in Geography (not the same as in the Jewish schools). The English examination was different from 1960 on, before which it was the same as that for the Jewish schools. The history curriculum contained the same syllabus of General History, and a limited version of that for Jewish History.

The crucial problem in the structuring of this curriculum lay in the rather far-reaching differences in the themes selected in the fields of Jewish and Arab history and literature. First of all Jewish history and literature were allocated on a somewhat larger proportion than their Arabic equivalents. Second, and possibly even more important, was the fact that, in the teaching of Jewish history, the National and Zionist themes were stressed – similar to the situation in the Jewish schools – while in Arab literature the emphasis was much more on those classic or modern authors which emphasized such themes as nature or human relations and much less themes related to collective identity. In fact even the syllabus probably served as an important focus of Arab identity. Moreover, Arab history was often included in General History, thus minimizing its distinctiveness.

## Patterns of Political Participation
### Early patterns of political participation

As indicated above, the Arabs were given full citizenship rights, and from the beginning participated in elections to the Knesset – at a relatively high level of participation (see Table 12.6).

* Weintraub with Shavith, 'Social Issues, Processes and Policies in Israel 1960–1980', pp. 39–42.

**Table 12.6    Participation of Non-Jews in the Elections for the Knesset, as Voters and as Elected Representatives, 1949–77**

|  | Participation as percentage of all eligible non-Jewish voters | Percentage of Non-Jewish Knesset members |
|---|---|---|
| First Knesset (1949–51) | 79.3 | 3 |
| Second Knesset (1951–5) | 85.5 | 6 |
| Third Knesset (1955–9) | 91.0 | 7 |
| Fourth Knesset (1959–61) | 88.9 | 7 |
| Fifth Knesset (1961–5) | 85.6 | 7 |
| Sixth Knesset (1965–9) | 87.8 | 7 |
| Seventh Knesset (1969–73) | 82.0 | 7 |
| Eighth Knesset (1973–7) | 80.0 | 4 |
| Ninth Knesset (1977–81) | 75.0 | 7 |

Source: Harevan (ed.), *Every Sixth Israeli*, p. 20.

**Table 12.7    Arabs Voting for the Communist Party and its Chief Rivals (percentages), 1949–77**

| Knesset elections | Communist Party | Ruling Party (*Mapai Avoda*) | *Mapam* |
|---|---|---|---|
| First Knesset (1949) | 22.2 | 61.3 | 0.2 |
| Second Knesset (1951) | 16.3 | 66.5 | 5.6 |
| Third Knesset (1955) | 15.6 | 62.4 | 7.3 |
| Fourth Knesset (1959) | 10.0 | 52.0 | 12.5 |
| Fifth Knesset (1961) | 22.7 | 50.0 | 11.0 |
| Sixth Knesset (1965) | 22.6 | 50.1 | 9.2 |
| Seventh Knesset (1969) | 28.9 | 56.9 | – |
| Eighth Knesset (1973) | 38.7 | 41.7 | – |
| Ninth Knesset (1977) | 50.6 | 27.0 | – |

Source: Harevan (ed.), *Every Sixth Israeli*, p. 20.

Table 12.7 shows the initial strength of the traditional parties, closely related to the Labour party, or formed to no small degree under the auspices of the military government and based on the more traditional forces within the Arab society, as well as some trends of radicalization, evident in the increasing strength of the Communist party (which was also strong in the first election) since the mid-1960s but especially since the Six Day War.

All these developments highlighted the problem of the collective identity of the Israeli Arab population. To quote Weintraub and Shavith again:

This issue is inherent in the geo-political situation, which has placed Israel in a position much more difficult than that faced by other primordially heterogeneous nations. Here there is on the one hand a native minority, characterized by overlapping ethnic, religious, cultural and socio-economic differences resulting from its much lower developmental baseline. On the other hand, the state is itself a small part of a hostile region, of which the minority is, primordially, an integral part. In this way, mutual hostility and alienism could not but accumulate and not be susceptible to any easy, quick solution.*

At the same time, as a result of all the processes of modernization analysed above, and of the gradual emergence of a new generation among the Israeli Arabs, the mid-1960s started also to signal new trends and developments among them.

## Druze and Bedouin minorities

A distinct minority are the Druzes constituting about 50,000 (about 8 per cent of the non-Jewish population of Israel). They are mostly concentrated in Lower Galilee and on Mount Carmel, organized in their traditional communities under relatively strong traditional leadership.

From the very beginning of the State they were positively orientated to it, serving in the army and in the *Mishmar Hagvul* (the Border Police) and thereby following their martial tradition, and it was only after the imposition of Israeli law on the Golan Heights and especially during the Lebanon War, when Israel became involved with the long-standing quarrel between the Druze and the Christian communities in Lebanon, that this loyalty seemed to become somewhat threatened. The same processes of modernization also developed among the Druzes in Israel, although to a smaller degree than among their communities in Syria and Lebanon.

Another special element among the minority population are the Bedouins. In 1960 there were about 20,000 Bedouins in the Negev and 10,000 in Galilee. Since then far-reaching economic transformations, especially in the economic and to some degree also in the social areas have taken place. They have all been affected by the impact of modernization. Schools and medical services were established in all their settlements under the auspices of the State. Some of them advanced educationally, many into the teaching profession, white-collar professions and the medical profession. But beyond the common patterns, there were two major modes of their overall response to modernization, with some variations between them.

One such mode, best exemplified by the Abu Rabia tribe in the Negev, was characterized by attempts to maintain, albeit, of course, with modifications, their nomad way of life and refusal to be resettled in villages. The families of this tribe live in small houses and have land in the village Kseifeh, and some of them do not want to leave this area. They prefer to continue their half-nomad life, with a strong link with agriculture, than to be transferred to the settled

* Weintraub with Shavith, 'Social Issues, Processes and Policies in Israel 1960–1980', p. 32.

village. They want to continue as far as possible their overall tribal way of life and to cope with the problems of modernization in their own way.

The Bedouins in this tribe have been working in agriculture since the establishment of the State in Beersheva and Arad. Some are working in industry and outside work and they do have teachers and white-collar staff from within their tribe. In the whole area of the Negev there are 30 Kindergartens, 26 Elementary Schools and 3 High Schools, and one teacher's seminar.

The status of the Sheikh is here quite strong. The position is hereditary, but does not mean that the son of the present Sheikh is appointed immediately after his father's death. Somebody else in the family may be more suitable, and could be appointed and this appointment needs the agreement of the Government.

The usual tasks of the Sheikh are the solving of inner problems and conflicts within the tribe. During the military government his position was of great importance. Today his tasks are getting fewer, because the Bedouins as citizens have an easy approach to the Government offices, but the overall framework of tribal life, has to a large extent persisted even if with strong modifications. Their insistence on continuing, to a large degree, their nomad life and at the same time to engage in agriculture, has often brought them in conflict with the settlement authorities of the State, as they demand both extensive land as well as a supply of water for irrigation. The demands for land were intensified after the Camp David agreement and the withdrawal from Sinai; new air force bases had to be established in the Negev and large areas of land had to be requisitioned.

The second mode of coping with modernization among the Bedouins, characterized by resettlement in villages and based mostly on non-agricultural work, is best illustrated by the Bedouin village of Rahat in the Negev, in which about 17,000 people, about one-third of the Bedouins in the Negev, live. The planning of this village started in 1965. But in 1978 only two houses were built. Water and electricity are given by the Government.

The village is based on the idea that every *hamula* (extended family group) would live in a different neighbourhood and every neighbourhood would constitute a self-serviced unit, while the schools would be common to everybody. There are 5 Elementary Schools, 1 High School and 1 Vocational School (boys and girls study there).

Fifteen per cent of the people are working in agriculture. But as they do not devote themselves to it, the results are very poor. The rest of the people work outside the village in the Jewish settlements either as truck or tractor drivers, or in services, teaching and white-collar jobs. Each family has approximately 7 members. The young generation marries only one wife. There are mixed marriages among the different *hamulot*, and there have been complaints among them about the development of a new type of social problem, such as drunkenness.

The tribe and *hamulot* continue to exist as social frameworks and networks, but much less as semi-corporate groups, and there are signs of some growing dissociation from the traditional ways of life.

## Developments in the mid-1960s

The 1960s saw the slow but perceptible emergence of the practice and the idea of some partnership between the two communities within Israel, prompted by both sides and by objective processes. There was a gradual development of economic and occupational interpenetration, increasing social contacts, and some intermarriage, even though these gave rise to new tensions and to the possibility of prejudices and social distance.

The political scene was eased with the abolishment of the military government in 1966 by Levi Eshkol, thus indicating the growing – even if very slow – change of the relations towards the Arab minority.

More attention was continuously being given to problems connected with Arab identity, such as education and local government, rather than with their economic advancement. In the political sphere more sensitive positions in government and the army were as yet closed to the Arabs, with the exception of some special groups like the Druzes and the Circassians. At the same time, more Arabs were entering the civil service, Parliament and Israeli political life and parties. All these problems became intensified, as we shall see in Chapter 13, after the Six Day War.

# Israeli Society in the Late 1960s and Early 1970s – the Six Day War and its Aftermath

## I · The Format of Israeli Society in the Late 1960s and Early 1970s

### The Institutional Mould of Israeli Society and the Implementation of the Zionist Vision
#### *General background*

The picture of the crystallization of the institutional moulds of Israeli society during the first three decades of its development – presented in the preceding chapters – is a very complex one.

First of all was the simple fact of the great success in all these fields – success which, when compared with many other modern, especially small, societies, with developing societies with a weak modern infrastructure, or with other countries of modern immigration, was very impressive indeed. From a community of 600,000 people fighting for their independence, in fact for their very life, living in rather strenuous and relatively backward economic conditions, there developed an independent state of 3,500,000 people which succeeded in a very short time in developing a relatively modern, at least semi-industrial economy, with a very successful modern agricultural sector. Its political structure, rooted in rather totalistic movements, organized in a semi-federative or consociational mould, developed into a parliamentary democracy, in some respects restrictive yet continuously opening up, and a strong tradition of law and civility was established. At the same time, the political as well as the whole institutional structure evinced great continuity with its preceding structures, ideas, orientations, visions and ideals.

Moreover, a network of wide-ranging institutions developed in all spheres of life. It succeeded in maintaining itself under relatively difficult security conditions. It built up a very strong army and at the same time maintained a relatively close civil control over the army, albeit – as we have seen – of a rather peculiar type; it certainly did not succumb to the danger of becoming a garrison state or a militarized society – and this army proved itself victorious in 1967. The international standing of the State – precarious in its immediate environment – was relatively good; and the net of its foreign relations, of foreign aid and the like, spread over many continents and countries and it became the general, common focus of identification for most Jewish communities.

It succeeded in developing an impressive and widespread cultural creativity in such fields as music, theatre, or painting, and it created important academic centres of international standing. There was a great effervescence of a new generation of Hebrew literature and Jewish studies; and its general educational efforts were quite impressive, especially when taking into account some of its special problems, above all those related to the absorption of new immigrants.

It was indeed in this area of the absorption of immigrants that – when compared with any other modern countries of non-selective immigration, and taking into account its rather meagre economic starting-point – its success in such a short period of time was, despite the many problems connected with it, very impressive.

In all these ways this society seemed able to cope with what we have seen as the perennial problems that arose out of the combination of the ideological vision of its founders and the attempts to realize this vision in a small and relatively underdeveloped country – a land new both to the founder of this society and to many generations of immigrants, within an alien, even hostile, environment. These problems – even if their concrete expressions did change – remained, as we have seen, quite similar during all the periods of the development of the Jewish settlement in Eretz Israel, in the period of the Yishuv and that of the State of Israel. They were, first, those of absorption of immigrants; secondly, those of development and modernization; thirdly, the problems of defence and of striking roots in a strange and even hostile environment; fourthly, the problems of reconstructing Jewish tradition and crystallizing a new type of Jewish identity.

Through the different institutions developed by it, the State of Israel has shown itself capable of dealing with these various problems in quite adequate, in many ways more than adequate, ways.

## Institutionalization of post-revolutionary societies

Israeli society has shared, as we have seen, many of the processes and problems of such institutionalization with other post-revolutionary societies – the USSR, Mexico, many of the new nations and perhaps even early nineteenth-century USA. The most important of these processes were, first, the transformation of revolutionary groups from socio-political movements into rulers of states and the concomitant institutionalization of the revolutionary vision in the framing of the modern state; second, economic expansion and modernization with concomitant growing social differentiation; and, third, the absorption, within the framework of such economic expansion, of relatively 'underdeveloped' sectors of the population.

Each of these post-revolutionary societies developed different institutional moulds in response to these problems. The starting-point of the development of such different post-revolutionary institutional moulds was the transformation of the revolutionary elite. Such a transformation was connected with the attempts of this elite to direct the post-revolutionary development and to find support and legitimization for such direction, and with the concomitant transformation of the revolutionary ideology. The central focus of such transformation in all revolutionary societies was the restructuring of the relations between the orientation of the ruling – revolutionary and post-revolutionary – elites to power as vested by now in the State and to economic modernization. Such restructuring gave rise to parallel transformations of the more ideological aspects of the revolutionary movement, of the bases of its solidarity and of the bases of legitimization and support of the new regime.

This process and the constant crystallization of different post-revolutionary institutional moulds, of different patterns of modernity, took place in different ways in different post-revolutionary regimes. The totalitarian post-revolutionary regimes opted for the stress on power and coercion, for the appropriation of the revolutionary symbols by the ruling elite, and for the almost total control by this elite of the access to these symbols, as well as to the avenues of mobility opened up by the process of development and modernization: that is, total control of the periphery.

The more authoritarian regimes, like Mexico, opted for the concentration of power and revolutionary symbols in the centre, for far-reaching co-optation of new groups, generated by the process of economic development, without, however, attempting a too far-reaching restructuring of the periphery but also limiting – above all by its demobilization and less by direct coercive control – the access of the periphery to the centre. In the early United States, from before the Jacksonian era, there was the great opening of political access to all sectors of society – an opening which was, even when combined with very strong populistic components, set within the basic American democratic ethos – and relatively open economic expansion and strong individualism, rooted in the transformation of its original religious vision into the political culture of civil religion.

In Israel the central focus of this transformation developed around the possibility of incorporating the orientations of both the older sectors and the new sectors of the population into more universalistic frameworks of the State – together with growing economic expansion.

The specific Israeli post-revolutionary institutional mould, the specific pattern of Israeli modernity, was characterized by a constitutional democratic system with initially strong restrictive overtones, by the seemingly natural granting of principled access to the centre to all sectors of the population – and initially mitigated by development of the clientelistic mechanisms; by the appropriation by the centre of the transformed Zionist and Labour symbols; by the continuous economic development within the framework of a mixed quite heavily controlled economy; by a strong emphasis on the construction of an old new nation with a very heavy emphasis on cultural patterns, on cultural creativity orientated to reconstruction of a new national and cultural tradition and renaissance.

This institutional mould which developed in Israel was, as we have emphasized over and over again, rooted in the Zionist vision. Hence, the development of the State of Israel, encompassing the developments in the various institutional moulds in the major areas of Israeli society, and the methods of coping with the perennial problems of settlement in Eretz Israel, attested to the successful implementation of this vision. It succeeded in proving, for the first time after about two thousand years, the ability of the Jewish people to forge an independent political unity encompassing all spheres of life, to enter history as an active agent, to face the civilizational challenges which were, as we have seen, inherent in its basic self-definition but which had been latent in the long period of the Exile.

Unlike in the period of the Second Temple – the last time that the Jewish people had had such opportunity – they were now much more conscious of it. Indeed, in many ways the Zionist Movement was the epitome of this consciousness or awareness and, unlike in the period of the Second Temple, its civilizational orientation was directed not only to the political arena but also to the social and institutional ones. Moreover, its relations to other civilizations was not necessarily as competitive and antagonistic as in the period of the Second Temple and in the long period of (especially medieval) Galut. The competition was, given the transformation of the civilizational visions in the modern world, more open and seemingly benign – although, of course, many of the antagonistic elements persisted in many different ways.

## The characteristics of the new institutional mould in Israel

This new institutional mould went naturally far beyond what the Jews could have developed in the period of dispersion in the countries of their settlement, in the networks of traditional Kehillot and centres of learning, or the more dispersed and diversified organizations and ways of life of more modern times. It was not only just the development of additional institutional arenas, such as the political and military ones, or the economic one of agriculture and of basic industries that was of crucial importance, but the fact that all these were brought together under the canopy of a new autonomous collectivity, of an overall collective institutional framework. This fact constituted the epitome of the collective entry of Jews into history, into the national community.

Within this broad institutional framework some of the special institutions rooted in preceding Jewish historical experience continued to exist – but obviously in a transformed way. Perhaps most important among these was the relatively high degree of family and kin solidarity: this was manifest in the persistence and reconstruction of family and kin networks as one of the many bases of help and solidarity in almost all sectors of the society; it was a base of support during service in the army, in the relatively weak intergenerational conflict in Israel, and in the relatively high degree of value-continuity between different generations.*

Other institutions – various older communal institutions, as well as networks rooted in the various movements – naturally lost their centrality. They persisted but only in some sectors, such as the religious one with respect to the communal ones, or some of the kibbutz types with respect to the movement networks. Otherwise they took rather secondary places in the overall institutional framework which signalled the entrance of the Jewish nation into history.

This entry was rooted, as we have seen, in a strong rebellion against the Jewish traditional and assimilationist moulds, yet this rebellion was not dissociated from many aspects or dimensions of Jewish history and tradition. On the contrary, this very rebellion against the concrete reality of Jewish life in the traditional and modern Diaspora not only reinforced, renewed or brought out in the open the basic themes and orientations that were latent in the earlier periods of Jewish history, but also greatly transformed most of them. It transformed these themes and orientations from being purely intellectual ones into being embedded into institutional areas and frameworks. All the major themes and tensions of Jewish tradition and civilization – the tension between universalism and particularism, between internal closed solidarity and solidarity as a base for far-reaching social, ethical and cultural creativity; between populist overtones and emphasis upon excellence in different areas of such creativity – became related to the construction and working of concrete institutional formats and overall institutional frameworks of the State. The same was true of the tension between the semi-Messianic future and the emphasis on the present which was no longer confined in the moulds of the Halakha and of communal life; as well as the different orientations to Eretz Israel and to Galut.

This was also true of the basic themes and tensions of Jewish political culture – those related to the issues of solidarity mentioned above, as well as of the tensions between legal order, the strong antinomian and semi-anarchist tendencies inherent in this culture.

The emphasis on solidarity was no longer confined to communal arrangements or to intellectual and literary expressions, but became closely related to the working of overall political institutions and the acceptance of the rule of law, and became closely related to the army and to the civilian control of the army.

Similarly, the emphasis on civility and the rule of law and its tensions with populistic as well as antinomian and semi-anarchic political tendencies, with their emphasis on a Higher Law, went out from the narrow intellectual confines to which it was limited in the medieval period and became closely interwoven

* See R. W. Bar-Yosef and Leah Shamgar-Handelman (eds.), *The Family in Israel* (in Hebrew) (Jerusalem 1984).

with the functioning of the framework of a fully-fledged society and polity with the different dimensions of its institutional format and political forces. The very strong future orientation also became connected with concrete institution-building and hence with the exigencies of the present – giving rise to different forms of confrontations between the two.

The same was true, of course, of the specific Zionist themes – closely connected with the former, general Jewish ones – especially the tension between being a normal nation and a light to the nations and/or a Jewish nation; between the emphasis on the territorial political dimensions and the orientations to institution-building; between the conception of the State of Israel as a place of refuge and security as against an arena of national renaissance.

All these tensions found new literary and intellectual expressions – but above all they became closely interwoven with the working of the overall institutional moulds of Israeli society.

So these institutional moulds crystallized and developed an ability to cope both with the specific ways in which the general problems of post-revolutionary societies manifested themselves within Israeli society and with its own specific problems. This crystallization was connected with the different perennial themes of Jewish life and existence in general and with the major Zionist orientations and themes in particular, and the ability to cope with its own specific problems as well as all the tensions inherent in the Jewish tradition. Indeed there was a continuous challenge before the Israeli institutional mould.

The specific achievement of the institutional mould that has developed in Israel was not that it obliterated these different orientations and tensions. On the contrary, all of them continued to exist within it and their impact on social and political life was – given the fact that they became interwoven in concrete institutional settings – much greater. Rather, the achievement of this institutional mould was in its seeming success in the regulation of all these tensions, so that they both reinforced the working of the mould as well as made continuous changes in it; so that they opened it up, while at the same time their more anarchic potentials were regulated and held in tow, both by the development and continuity of the central institutional frameworks as well as by strong internal cohesion of the elites and their solidarity with the broader sections of the population. The crucial test of the Israeli institutional model came, from this point of view, with its opening up which, as we have seen above, continued to take place.

# The Opening Up of the Israeli Institutional Mould
## The transformation of the regnant ideology

Such opening was, of course, closely connected to the changes in viewpoint – above all in Zionist–Labour ideology. The process of selective institutionalization of the ideology was, as we have seen, already taking place in the Yishuv.

It continued in the State of Israel, far beyond what had taken place in the period of the Yishuv, giving rise, imperceptibly but very forcefully, to a far-reaching transformation of this ideology without, at the same time, this transformation being fully perceived or acknowledged, especially by the ruling elites.

Such transformation developed in several concomitant directions: in the content of the ideology; in the relative emphasis on its different themes; in the relations or connections between them; in the structural placement of the symbols and themes of this ideology, and in the nature of their relations to construction and working of major institutional arenas.

The most general change in the contents and context of this ideology was, as we have already seen above, a shift from an ideology of national renaissance and social reconstruction and institution-building, rooted in strong sectarian and pioneering orientations and frameworks, to the incorporation of these themes into those of a general ethos of national development, of nation-building developing in the framework of the constitutional democratic–pluralistic State, based on universalistic premisses, which attempted to appropriate for itself the older movement's symbols and orientations.

This seemingly innocuous and natural shift was closely connected with some more far-reaching changes in the contents and structure of the Labour–Zionist ideology. Thus, first of all, there was a great dissociation between the various components of this ideology – especially between those stressing creativity in various institutional fields; between the emphasis on elitist pioneering commitment, and autonomous participation in the basic frameworks and centres of the society; between such participation and adherence to symbols of national solidarity; between the latter and the more social or socialistic orientations.

Thus, in greater detail, there took place in the ideological realm and its institutional implication a growing dissociation between the constructivist themes, orientated to institution-building, and the orientation to active participation in such construction and in the respective centres of society.

Parallelly, the emphasis on national symbols, on the symbols of national unity, cohesion and solidarity, became, to some degree at least, dissociated from active participation in institution-building.

There was also a marked change in the general ambience of the contents of the ideology – manifest above all in the weakening of the pioneering elitist orientation stressing duties, commitment and standards of performance, as against the strengthening of the orientation of emphasis on ascriptive rights, entitlements and the distribution of rewards by the centre.

The most important single indicator of these changes in the contents and emphasis of the ideology was in its 'social', socialist labour, or class components. Thus, we have seen, already in the last period of the Yishuv, and, above all, after the establishment of the State, these socialist or class components of the pioneering labour ideology became identified first with the economic development in general – and that under the auspices of the government and of the Histadrut in particular – and second with the extensive welfare policies.

## The development of new conflicts and problems

These changes in the regnant ideology were connected with the institutional-ization of the initial moulds of Israeli society, with the changes in them and with the development within all of them of new conflicts and problems. Indeed, the initial success of the government, guided by these visions and orientations, led to the crystallization of new problems in all major spheres of life in Israel.

Conflicts and tensions developed – as we have seen – in all the spheres of life: in the political mould and its relations to the political economy and strata formation and to the educational system; in patterns of cultural creativity and participation; in the ways in which the society coped with the problems of minorities and of the absorption of immigrants. In all these spheres those conflicts became connected – even if gradually and sometimes inadvertently – with the different orientations and contradictions which developed within them.

In the political sphere, the major problems were to what extent the existing elite would be able to absorb new groups; whether it would be sufficiently resilient in responding to new pressures and new demands to maintain its unity and its ability to deal with new problems, on the one hand, while on the other preserving and developing the pluralistic structure of the centre. In more concrete terms, there arose also the problems of the degree of the political elite's ability to deal with various problems that arose from the major economic trends – such as those of income distribution, demands arising out of the continuous rise in the standard of living, the rising social conflicts that developed with these changes – while maintaining its own cohesion as well as the pluralistic political framework.

These conflicts were closely related to tensions between the older move-ment, consociational patterns and the new centralized universalistic state frameworks and within the latter between clientelistic populistic and civil orientations.

In the economic sphere there developed conflicts rooted in the tension between the strong emphasis on development and the one on consumption – public and private; between the government's very high degree of regulation of the economy and its growing dependency on many new economic forms – most of which it had generated itself; between the stress of egalitarian, welfare and distributive orientations on the one hand, and that of development and the ensuing growing social differentiation on the other.

These problems and conflicts developed at least to some degree out of the policy of partial social security provided in this framework by the Histadrut and the growing social security system – which indeed greatly facilitated the initial absorption of the new immigrants, both in agriculture and in industry, to an extent unequalled in other developing countries. However, these policies did not always suffice to assure the achievement of new levels of economic and technological development, and the State's ability to engage in constant economic growth faced difficulties.

Secondly, many obstacles in the way of continuous development and modernization were the result of the growing conservatism among the leading economic groups. One aspect of such conservatism could be found in the trade unions, which developed tendencies similar to those in England, rather than, for example, those in Sweden. Here such conservatism often constituted an obstacle to the mobility of labour and to the attainment of higher technical and professional standards. In a similar fashion, government policy tended to hinder the development of new types of entrepreneurs not dependent on the protection given to them by the State.

Beyond these concrete issues there loomed the more central problem – namely the growing contradiction between the older pioneering vision focused on the productivization of the Jewish people through establishment of modern agriculture and industry, thus reversing the inverted occupational pyramid characteristic of the Jews of Eastern Europe, and the development in Israel of a modern, diversified economy which in many ways reinstated such a pyramid, even if giving to agriculture and sophisticated industries a special place in it. The major weaknesses of this approach were, first, the relatively low status of simple industrial workers and, second, the burgeoning of service activities in general and bureaucratic civil service and financial sectors in particular.

Thus, the central problem became that of whether a transition would be possible from an economy that emphasized rising standards of living and invested capital in physical developments and in assuring employment, to one in which technological development would be firmly established and which would more and more be able to compete in relatively new open markets and with technologically sophisticated industries abroad.

Similarly, too, the initial success in absorbing broad social strata and groups into the existing structures, within a common political framework, increased on the social scene the acuteness of the problem of egalitarianism on the one hand, and of social divisions and conflicts on the other. The proximity of the various groups to each other and to the centre gave rise to a continuous tendency to mutual comparisons and to an examination of their respective positions in the light of the ideological assumptions of egalitarianism.

There developed new class formations and new conflicts, all of which went beyond the early pioneering vision, beyond the idea of class structure in the European style, and beyond the differences between the sectors in the period of the Yishuv. In this area, the problem of the Oriental communities, as we have seen, became more and more one of the central problems on all levels of social organization.

New problems also developed in the cultural sphere. One of these focused around the nature of Israel's social and basic identity, especially in respect of its Jewishness and the Jewish components of its identity; around the nature of its links with other Jewish communities on the one hand, and its relations with its neighbours, the Arab world and the Middle East, on the other. The second problem in this sphere had its origins in the aggravation of the conflicts between cultural creativity and the danger of provincialism; and of the development of a mass culture without a well-defined form.

Many of these problems were initially at least focused around attempts to redefine the concrete components of the image of the pioneer. Claims made by the various groups that specific new tasks and activities were confirmations or manifestations of this image of the pioneer were significant indications of attempts to maintain such commitments in the new setting, even though such claims continuously contributed to changing the image of the pioneer and to making it more diffuse and often bound to rather narrow interests.

There developed also the increasing tension between the religious groups, who tended towards increasing militancy and more secular groups, and the problem of the reconstruction of the symbols of collective identity began to open up.

Cutting across all these spheres there was also the tendency to the extension of bureaucracy, to over-bureaucratization, the wide spread of rather inefficient bureaucratic organs, often stifling initiative in many spheres of life. While, needless to say, the problem was unevenly distributed among the different sectors of the civil service, some of which were very open and innovative, it was widespread enough to become one of the basic aspects of daily life in Israel.

In some parts of the civil service the situation became, on the whole, continuously worse. This was perhaps best seen in the prison system, which was not attuned to deal with the numerous problems attendant on the expanding prison population, a situation which until recently was not of very great concern to the central policy-makers or to the public.

Indeed it took a very long time – well into the 1970s – for the appropriate sector of the civil service, as well as the broader public, to become aware of many newly emerging issues, especially those of the changed age structure of the population, those of the greater proportion of old people and of their special problems, as well as those related to the place of women in society.

# Routinization of a Revolutionary Society and the Special Problems of a Small Society

These problems and conflicts were of various kinds. They developed out of the institutionalization of the revolutionary ideological society in general and the specific ways in which such transitions were taking place in Israel. A highly ideological society was being transformed into a more routinized, far more diversified, more open and pluralistic one with a strong tendency to the weakening of the impact of ideology on large areas of life. Yet among wide sectors of the population there persisted the search for some such overall ideological vision as best seen probably in the continuous reconstruction of the image of the pioneer and of symbols of collective identity.

Many of the conflicts and problems were similar to those which developed in many of the more 'advanced' societies, as well as in some developing ones, and could be seen simply as the Israeli version of its rather special combination of semi-industrial and post-industrial society. Many were related to the fact that Israel was a small society which at the same time hoped to be a centre of great social and cultural creativity. Indeed, beyond all these conflicts and problems there started to loom a more central, critical problem – namely that of the ability of such a small society, beset with so many difficulties, to maintain such creativity and centrality – especially, but not only, in relation to Jewish communities.

Certainly the Israeli society had shown some far-reaching, rather unusual achievements for a country of about 3 to 3.5 million people, much less in the beginning of the State. And yet those achievements were attained at certain, perhaps inevitable, costs from the point of view of some of the major themes of Jewish history and that of the Zionist vision.

First of all, there was a very important shift – from the point of view of Jewish historical experience – in the loci of cultural and institutional creativity. The building up of the infrastructure of a total society, the necessity to take care of the needs of a whole society, naturally redirected many of those energies which in the Diaspora were directed more to economic activities in selective fields and/or to intellectual and academic endeavours, in the direction of institutional building in general and those of security, agriculture, creating an economic infrastructure, and general public service in particular.

Obviously the cultural institutions created in such circumstances could not, as we have seen – unless by making rather special efforts – compete with the great centres of learning of the United States or Europe, in which more and more Jews were attaining positions of excellence and leadership and which naturally became points of orientation and reference for the Israeli institutions. There also developed the problem, inherent in the nature of a small society in general and one with the specific characteristics of Israel in particular, that many of these academic and cultural institutions and economic enterprises, while successful, were indeed connected with an increasing external orientation, weakening some of their distinct patterns. These developments emphasized the problem and difficulty of how to combine the maintenance of high standards with some distinct patterns of creativity specific to the Israeli scene and gave rise, as we shall see in greater detail later on, to a strong tension between openness and provincialism.

At the same time the experience of *Yordim*, of emigrants from Israel, which became more and more a focus of public concern, attested to the difficulty of the internal sectors to absorb all the manpower – and especially some of the professional and potential entrepreneurial elements – that went through its educational system. It is difficult to estimate exactly how many of those who left could not really be absorbed in the economic structure. But there can be no doubt that – as in any other small country – a part of those who left were pushed out by many of the restrictive aspects of Israeli society – rooted in its small size as well as in some of its specific institutional settings – all of which limited opportunities in Israel in general. Of significance here was the political economy in general and its bureaucratic regulative aspects in particular, its educational system, the difficulties of the housing situation, the prevalence of relative stagnative economic sectors, the bureaucratic patterns of absorption of immigrants and the heavy burden of the security situation.

The experience of the Russian immigrants – the fact that so many of them did not go to Israel or went away from it – was very indicative of some of these problems; it points to the possibility that some sectors of Israelis will feel enclosed within the framework of the State.

This feeling of closure was probably to no small degree reinforced by another aspect of Israeli society which can be found in many small societies: namely the development of close overlapping networks of elites in different fields – the military, economic and the like – and the very strong external orientations of many of these networks.

These problems became more and more acute with the growing predominance of generations born and/or educated in Israel and with the weakening of immigration from Western countries, giving rise almost to a balance between immigration and emigration, moving later on in the direction of growing emigration. They were reinforced also by the anti-elitist tendencies, the lowering of standards in the educational and academic fields.

The development of all these problems underlined the possibility of weakening of some of the creative tensions given in the life of a minority – in this case of the Jews in the – especially modern – Diaspora. Thus they pointed to one very central tension in the Zionist vision – that of the growing routinization between becoming a normal nation on the one hand and a centre of widespread creativity or of a special Jewish society on the other.

## Conservative and Innovative Tendencies in Israeli Society

All these developments necessarily sharpened the tensions and even struggles in Israeli society – sometimes implicit, sometimes explicit – between different approaches to coping with the problem of its being a small society with aspirations beyond its actual scope – and above all between, on the one hand, the more conservative, closed orientations and, on the other hand, the more open ones; between the more stagnant and the more active and innovative ones.

The more conservative approach tended to assume that these aspirations would be realized through the existing social structure and through attachment to Jewish and/or socialist tradition as crystallized in Israeli society, and tended to become connected with more popularistic attitudes, to stress entitlements and distributive policies.

The more open and innovative tendencies stressed that Israel's aspirations could be realized not only through its ability to shine by the mere fact of its existence, but also through its ability to participate directly in social and cultural frameworks beyond itself, in its relations with various Jewish and international, cultural, scientific and political communities; and by reconstructing its own identity through such participation. These tendencies were more connected with orientation to excellence and creativity; with the ethnic emphasis on duties but less with that on distributive policies, entitlements and rights. Such orientations tended to strengthen the internal pluralism of Israeli society, against more monolithic or restrictive tendencies inherent in the more conservative approach often nourished by feelings of superiority and isolation from the outside world, an approach which tended also to reinforce tendencies towards cultural provincialism, populist orientations and rigidity in the definition of collective identity.

Such rigidity and closure could easily express itself in impatience with criticism, a lack of interest in anything not directly connected with Israel, self-satisfaction and the view that Israel had reached the pinnacle of wisdom. It could also have been easily strengthened by an ideological conservatism – both of the secular conservative variety as well as by restrictive and rigid religious tendencies.

## Summary

All these problems and conflicts developed out of the specific pattern of Israeli post-revolutionary institutional moulds, out of the problems of a mixed developing and post-industrial society, and those of a small society.

The processes which gave rise to the development of these problems and conflicts were rooted in the attempts at the institutionalization of the Zionist vision, with the Jewish collective entry into history. Accordingly, these problems and conflicts were also connected with the articulation and transformation of the basic themes and orientations which have developed in Jewish and Zionist history, by bringing them together into the institutional framework of a modern society, thus creating a situation in which these tensions were no longer, as we have seen, purely intellectual ones but became very closely related to social and political frameworks, actions and conflicts.

By virtue of this very fact the 'normal' conflicts and problems, many of which could be found also in other societies, became closely interrelated with these themes of Jewish and Zionist history, and in this way a rather special dimension was added to these conflicts which, in some ways, at least, was unique to the Israeli scene.

Above all, as these problems developed out of the opening up of the initial institutional mould, they posed rather sharply the problem of the possibility of combining the opening up with some of the continuous commitments to the Zionist vision and quest – and with the different patterns of institutionalization that developed in the first two and a half decades of the State of Israel.

Indeed the development of all these conflicts and problems thus posed the question as to whether they could be seen as a dynamic continuation, development, unfolding of the specific Israeli post-revolutionary mould, creating a new social reality and yet faithful to its basic premisses, or whether they signalled the undermining of this mould.

# II · The Six Day War and the Opening up of the Problems and Premisses of Israeli Society

## The Six Day War and its Repercussions
### *The reopening of the problem of territorial compromise and its repercussions*

With respect to all these developments and conflicts, as well as with respect to the larger question about the viability of the internal institutional mould of Israeli society, the Six Day War, and later the Yom Kippur War and its aftermath, proved to be a turning-point concerning the problems and tendencies of Israeli society.

The 1967 war, the waiting period before the war itself and its aftermath, undermined several of the premisses on which the central institutional mould of Israeli society was based. It opened up many of its problems and intensified the various processes, tensions and conflicts analysed above.

Truly enough, first of all it proved the great internal solidarity and power of resistance of Israeli society. One of the most important signs of strength revealed during this period was the high degree of solidarity and unity demonstrated by different parts of the population during the critical period before the war and which continued to a considerable extent after it, apparently rebutting the nightmare of 'two nations' – one of central concern to Israeli society at the end of the 1960s. In general, this period prominently displayed the ability of Israeli society to master new situations – not only in the military sphere, but also in the many new spheres of activity which opened up in consequence of the changing political situation and policy towards the administered areas, in the economic expansion after the period of recession in the two years before the war, and so forth.

At the same time, however, this very success and strength, the great victory in the war, opened up new basic problems, and gradually but continuously and with gathering strength sharpened awareness of these openings. First of all the victory itself undermined the basis of the territorial compromise and frame-work on which the State of Israel was established – the great historical territorial compromise, the seeds of which started in 1936 with the Peel Commission decision on the partition of Palestine and in 1938 with the acceptance of the partition by the Zionist Congress. The State of Israel was indeed established on the basis of this historical compromise – a compromise which entailed also the acceptance of the territorial limits of such partition of Eretz Israel, an acceptance based on the assumption that this was the most that could be attained given Israel's strength and standing in the international community. For many – the most prominent among them Ben-Gurion – this compromise was also essential to keep the basically Jewish nature, as against some binational one, of the State of Israel. These premises were, as we have seen, *de facto* accepted by all participants in the Israeli political scene, even if officially the *Herut* party did not accept this compromise and even if among many groups – whether some of the Labour groups (especially *Hakibbutz Hameuchad*) which were against the partition, or among the groups within the army which were dissatisfied with the existing borders for security reasons – wide territorial aspirations were latent.

All these premises, but especially the political and military ones, were undermined, ultimately even shattered, by the victory in the Six Day War, thus not only opening up the problem of the military and political premises of Israeli society but also potentially reactivating the broader territorial orient-ations and, given their centrality in the whole format of Israeli society, other problems in its self-conception.

## Relations with the Arab world

The developments after the Six Day and the Yom Kippur Wars, also opened anew the problem of the relations between Israel and its neighbours in the Middle East and the implications of these issues for the internal structure of Israeli society.

Thus, the aftermath first of all of the Six Day War and later on of the Yom Kippur War opened up the whole problem of the nature of the political settlement with the Arab countries, the basic problems of Israel's acceptance and standing in the region. The great military victory of the Six Day War, the later, ultimate victory in the Yom Kippur War, attested to Israel's basic military strength, to the impossibility of casting her – as many Arabs dreamed – into the sea; but at the same time these very successes shattered the political bases or premises of what may be called the Ben-Gurion era.

On the one hand Israel showed its military might and reached beyond the territorial settlements of the armistice agreements which were accepted by the international community, but on the other hand this very success sharpened the general awareness – in the international community and within Israel itself – of the necessity to find a more stable political solution, some ultimate political arrangements leading to peace beyond the armistice agreements.

The belief in the necessity of such arrangements, the search for different political solutions, started in the wake of the Six Day War and gathered momentum after the Yom Kippur War and – paradoxically perhaps – even after the peace treaty with Egypt.

The very momentum of all these developments, the reopening of all these problems, gave rise to, and in turn was intensified by, the continuous growth of the Palestinian problem; by the transformation of the problems of refugees into that of the collective political problem of Palestinians. Here, of course, the most crucial process was the development of the PLO and its growing international standing.

Closely connected with all these developments was the growth of internal (especially in the West Bank) and above all international terrorism against Israel, and the at least partial legitimation by such people as for instance the Austrian Chancellor Bruno Kreisky of such terrorism as a part of the Palestinian national movement.

The continuous Israeli military occupation of the West Bank (what was later, under the Likud government in 1977, to be officially called Judea and Samaria, its having become an occupying power ruling over between 1,100,000 and 1,300,000 Arabs, including those in the Gaza District) and the concomitant policy of extending Jewish settlement into these areas gave rise to growing criticism – both internal and international – and to an initially slow but later (especially after the Yom Kippur War) intensified change in the international reaction.

The Six Day War and later, in a changing atmosphere, the Yom Kippur War, and their aftermath, also and perhaps above all reopened the problem of relations between Jews and Arabs – to a certain extent for the first time – in relatively concrete terms. The resulting situation increased the political tension between the two populations or nations, but this political tension differed greatly from the conflict that had existed between the Arab states and Israel before the war. The principal difference, at least for the Arab population of the West Bank, but not only for it, was that Israel ceased to be a myth – merely a symbol of a foreign group injected into the Middle East – and became part of a reality of daily and stable contacts with a Jewish population. Given the nature of these relations – of the continuous military rule of the Israelis over the Arabs – they did not necessarily increase the Arab population's love for Israel. In many ways these contacts, especially those related to the military government, were naturally, as we shall see in greater detail later, liable to increase tensions. But at the same time they added to the mutual relations between the two peoples, in particular through the open-door policy – the relatively open bridges between post-war Jordan and the West Bank and Israel and a certain amount of traffic between the West Bank and Israel itself – a concrete element of reality which had not existed previously.

The same combination of a more realistic attitude to Israel, even a reluctant *de facto* acceptance of its existence, with a growing tension around possible terms of settlement with it, developed in many Arab countries – first of all, but probably not only, in Egypt.

On the one hand there grew – even among the Arabs – at least a *de facto* recognition of the very existence of the State of Israel. Yet on the other hand there developed a gradual but continuous – even if intermittent – deterioration of Israel's standing within the international community: a tendency to a growing political isolation of Israel evinced in the deterioration of relations with the USSR and most of the Eastern bloc (with the exception of Romania) after the Six Day War and with most African countries after the Yom Kippur War; the growing criticism afterwards of Israel's policies within Europe and the development of different European initiatives counter to Israeli policies; the concomitant growing dependence – military, economic and diplomatic – of Israel on the USA, where there also developed growing criticism of Israel. The concern about the necessity of such solutions was greatly intensified both among the Arab countries and in the international community, giving rise to an intensification of diplomatic activities and efforts, such as the various UN mediation efforts or the Rogers plan.

Naturally, these developments also affected the state of the Israeli Arab population. For the first time since the establishment of the State of Israel, the Arab minority – which, as we have seen, enjoyed great economic prosperity and educational advancement, but also social dislocation, disabilities, discriminations and great difficulties in integrating in the urban sectors of Israeli society – was released from its almost heretic isolation from other parts of the Arab world, and contacts were established with that world. The first stages of this meeting sharpened the problematics of the Israeli–Arab identity within the Israeli framework. They also strengthened their feeling of solidarity with Arab nationalism and the ambivalence in their relations with Israel. There developed a trend towards a weakening of differences between the Israeli–Arab minority and residents of the West Bank and a growing intensification of Arab nationalism and of its questioning of the very premises of Israel, and as we have seen with tendencies to growing radicalization. Yet at the same time, as we have seen in Chapter 12, it was also connected with an increasing search among Israeli Arabs of ways to become more fully incorporated, but in a more autonomous way, into the Israeli political system.

There was a change in the image of Israel, both in general public opinion and also to some degree among the Jewish communities in the Diaspora, from that of a small heroic, pioneering country to one of conquerors and military occupants. It was no longer seen as the small David against the Arab Goliath, but as an aggressive expansionist country.

# The Opening Up of the Problems of Israeli Society
## *Security and territorial orientations*

All these developments, of course, had their effect on the internal Israeli scene.
First of all the whole problem of the boundaries – of the State of Israel in

general, of the acceptance of the division of (Mandatory) Palestine, of Eretz Israel, which was, as we have seen, indeed accepted after long discussions, and of the 1949 boundaries – became a focus of both international and internal political discussion.

The problem of the territorial boundaries of Israel was reopened for the first time since the great partition debate in the 1930s, giving rise to a strong demand – based on security, historical and religious reasons – for the extension of Israel's boundaries to the mandatory ones of *Eretz Israel HaShlema* (the whole Eretz Israel). This demand came within many – rather heterogeneous – groups: from within parts of the Kibbutz (especially *Hakibbutz Hameuchad*) and Moshav movements with their strong emphasis on territorial settlements; from within different groups in the army; of course, from the *Herut* party, as well as from many religious circles; especially from within the religious youth movements and above all from the newly developed extremist *Gush Emunim*. This attitude found its concrete manifestation in the policy of the rather extensive establishment of Jewish settlements in the West Bank, undertaken under the Prime Ministership of Levi Eshkol and Golda Meir – but the policy also started to become a focus of public controversy.

Similarly, the problem of the Arab–Israel conflict began to occupy, for the first time in the history of Israel, a central place in public debate, giving rise to continuous discussions and controversies.

The opening up of the political–security problems – and the political–security debate itself – necessarily became closely related to the opening up of the nature of the very central components, especially the religious and territorial dimensions, of Israeli identity.

The war necessarily strengthened the military and defence components of Israeli identity and unavoidably increased the possibility of the militarization of Israeli society. The centrality of the military image became strengthened among the main components of Israeli society and to a certain extent it took the place of the pioneering image, which in turn contributed, as we have seen, to the changes of public opinion abroad to the image of Israel.

All these developments naturally reopened a series of central problems relating to the basic dimensions of the format of hitherto Israeli identity.

## The reconstruction of symbols of Israeli collectivity

But it was not only the territorial component of Israeli collective identity, or the Zionist vision, that was opened up. Other central dimensions of the components of that identity were reopened, especially the one of Israeli society's 'Jewishness' and its links with Jewish communities abroad.

The dramatic encounter – first of all of the Israeli soldiers, then of other parts of the population – with central symbols and places of Jewish tradition, with the Western (Wailing) Wall after the conquest of (Eastern) Jerusalem, with Hebron (the town of the Patriarchs), with larger parts of Eretz Israel which were closed since the establishment of the State, opened up the problem of the historical and religious heritage of Israel – a problem which, as we have seen, was simmering before.

Since then these problems have been continuously in the foreground of public discussion in Israel and more and more central in its political debates.

Developments during the war and after it refuted many of the assumptions current in the Yishuv regarding the nature of the links with Jewish communities abroad and the extent and force of the Jewish component in Israeli identity. On the one hand, they refuted the arguments which stressed the weakness of this component; but, on the other hand, they also indicated that the content of this component and the nature of relations between Israel and the Jewish communities abroad transcended accepted ideological 'Zionist' formulae. They underlined a far-reaching change in the relations between Israel and the Jewish communities in the Diaspora, changes which had been taking place since the establishment of the State but which became more and more visible after the Six Day War.

First, the deep attachment felt by Israelis towards the historic Jewish heritage was revealed, and at the same time the strength of solidarity between the State of Israel and Jewish communities abroad was proven – a solidarity rooted in mutual bonds with a common past, though it is interpreted in different ways by different Jewish groups, and is even strengthened, in a certain sense, by this variety of interpretations. But if these developments showed, on the one hand, the relative weakness of the purely 'Canaanite' element in the new Israeli identity, on the other hand they went beyond the usual view of the nature of the link between the Yishuv and the Jewish communities derived from the original Zionist ideological assumptions. In particular they deviated from the assumption that the only constructive form of this connection was *Aliya* (immigration to Israel) – even though this increased after the War.

Other ways of expressing solidarity – through economic ties with stronger and richer elements in Jewish communities abroad, through varied philanthropic activities, sentimental ties, tourism and family visits – became not only very frequent, but also more visible and articulated, bringing out more fully that the nature of the links between Israel and the Diaspora started to change, focusing less on the older pioneering image and moving more to more primordial and historical religious symbols.

# Continuous Institutional Trends and Changes

The initial responses of Israeli society to all these developments and new challenges were very complex and varied.

First of all was the continuation and intensification of many of the trends – as well as problems – which had started to develop previously in all the major institutional areas of Israeli society. Indeed in many cases many of these trends and the forces behind them were given a new lease of life – but many of the problems were also intensified.

In the economic sphere, the immediate pre-war period was one of recession, of growing unemployment and declining investments. This situation had developed from extensive attempts to break inflation and to restructure the economy which had begun to reveal such danger signs as the growth of the trade deficit, a drop in investments from abroad, and a generally limited ability to encourage export industries or industries of a technical nature.

The situation changed after the June war. The recession ended and, in general, there was industrial development and relatively rapid growth, with shortages of manpower and growing dependency on Arab labour. Especially important were the tendencies towards industrial developments – supported directly or indirectly by defence needs – especially in the metal industries and the beginning of development of sophisticated technological industries. In this, as also in other spheres of industrial initiative, many of the former types of economic activities continued to develop and they expanded with the help of a strong governmental policy.

But while the post-war period in general was one of economic growth, part of this growth – with a few exceptions – was channelled into a framework that perhaps increased the efficacy of many of these enterprises, but did not of necessity change their basic structure and economic orientation. In this period also the conflict between economic growth and inflationary pressures became more severe, the latter aggravating social tensions and problems and damaging particularly the salaried sectors, especially those in the medium levels, more than those of the self-employed or even the working-class proper. The influx of Arab labour from the West Bank and Gaza into the lower – mainly manual – occupations sharpened even more the problem of the viability of the pioneering vision of Jewish economy and productivization.

At the same time in all other fields the continuous opening up that had started before the war continued and was even intensified. Thus in the political field there was a continuation of the diversification of problems of political struggle and bargaining; the beginning of the relative decline of the clientelistic mode;* the weakening of the leadership of different parties and a gradual increase in the strength of parliamentary committees; a continuous reshuffling and unification of parties; the growing impact of the introduction of television and the increase of populistic trends in politics, and also the beginnings of extraparliamentary movements – above all in this period of *Gush Emunim*. At the same time the electoral processes indicated the continuous – even if initially slow – growth of *Gahal*, later of Likud.

A rather important change took place in the mode of civil–military relations, despite the fact that the overall pattern of continuous control of the military continued. For the first time (except for the brief period in the 1950s under Sharett) the Prime Minister was no longer Minister of Defence – creating the possibilities both of more diversified civil control over the military but also of more varied coalitions between different political and top military echelons. The Chief of Staff and senior officers started to attend – with different degrees

---

* Yael Azmon, 'The 1981 Elections and the Changing Fortunes of the Israeli Labor party', *Government and Opposition*, 16, 4 (1981), pp. 432–46.

of regularity – the meetings of the Cabinet and to appear publicly on some aspects of current affairs. While not criticizing the policies of the government or taking clear stands on controversial issues, they yet appeared more and more as presenting some of their own views.

This was not unconnected with the fact that it was in this period that senior officers, including a Chief of Staff (Haim Bar-Lev) and a former Chief of Air Force (Ezer Weizmann) became 'parachuted' into the higher echelons of the different parties, and all parties started to look for possible recruits from the higher military echelons.

In the social field there was also a continuous reshifting and diversification of different status groups – reinforced to some degree at least by the increasing influx of Western and Russian immigration which had been taking place in this period. At the same time, the ethnic problem became more and more visible – especially with the emergence of the Black Panthers – and sometimes intensified by the encounter with the rather privileged treatment given to the former, especially Russian, immigrants. The growing diversification in the cultural field continued, reinforced by the introduction of television. But perhaps most significant was the growing visibility of the intensification of different religious trends; of the renewed *Bnei Akiva*; of the new developments in the structure of religious education; of growing influx of religious migrants in general and of Orthodox in particular, and their growing visibility in all areas of life.

# The Six Day War and the Opening of the Problems of the Cultural Parameters and Format of Israeli Society
## *Institutionalization and diversification of cultural activities*

Meanwhile there was a growing awareness in the cultural field of all the problems analysed above, even if, for a long time, it was widely assumed that the changing pattern of Israeli cultural and collective identity would indeed be able to absorb the various new trends, tensions and problems and that it would be possible to reconstruct some – even if flexible and possibly variable – central axes for the very diversified patterns of cultural creativity and participation that were developing in Israeli society.

But in fact the picture started to change radically in the early and mid-1960s (although the nature of these changes was only dimly perceived at that period), and these changes gathered fuller momentum later on, being given a strong push after the Six Day War.

The first such problem area was that of the components of Israeli identity, and especially that of Israel society's 'Jewishness' and its links with Jewish communities abroad, analysed above.

The various developments after the Six Day War also intensified some of the other internal problems of Israeli society – above all perhaps different aspects of the ethnic problem. In the wake of the first vocal 'ethnic' protest after Wadi Salib – the emergence of the Black Panthers – there was an intensification of the welfare policies orientated to cope with this problem.

At this time, with the great upsurge of the ethnic themes in the 1970s, this emphasis on ethnic identities was much more aggressive and divisive – stressing, as we have seen, the dichotomous perception of Oriental and Western cultures, as well as a very strong militancy against the so-called Western culture of the Ashkenazi centre or central groups.

At the same time there was also a collective confrontation with the Arab reality and the Palestinian question and some growing doubts started to develop among the younger generations, fully expressed for the first time in the famous *Siach Lohamim* (*The Talk of the Fighters*) published in 1967, in which talks and doubts around these problems or at least questions about the nature of the relations to the Arabs and of the predominance of the military relations with them were expressed by soldiers from the Kibbutzim.

Parallelly the processes of diversification of cultural creativity, participation and consumption continued. This growing diversification of cultural creativity and the changes of emphases in the construction of symbols of collective identity as well as the institutionalization of these activities, slowly and unwittingly and paradoxically undermined and weakened the perception that it is possible to bring them together under the aegis of the general orientation to Jewish cultural renaissance and of institutional development of Israeli society. Far-reaching changes have constantly taken place in the meaning of the different patterns of such cultural creativity and participation in terms of some overall vision, thus posing sharply the problem of the possibility of re-constructing their meaning in any such terms, and of the possible loss of any centre or even centres of gravity in this field.

Several processes and changes in this area, which developed earlier and gathered momentum after the 1960s, changed the basic parameters, the basic semantic field of cultural creativity, participation and consumption in Israel, and there started also to develop a growing awareness of these problems.

## *The search for new parameters of cultural activity and collective identity*

It was the conjunction of all these trends that opened up the problem of the nature of the new parameters of the Israeli cultural scene and the nature of the symbols of Israeli collective identity. This also gave rise to growing discussions about the Jewish nature of this culture and of the State of Israel in particular, a problem which was earlier confined to relatively small, even influential, circles of intellectuals.

But it was much easier to raise the question than to find any simple answer or an answer which would be acceptable to all or even most sectors of the population.

The very continuous articulations of these various problems implied that there could not be a single simple answer either to the nature of the Jewish characteristics of the Israeli society, or to the nature of the specific cultural creativity and participation that was developing in Israel and which was characterized by a growing plurality and diversification. It was indeed probably impossible, by the very nature of the problem, to find such an answer. Yet there developed a widespread and continuous search for the construction and crystallization of some such answers, and the very fact that these questions continued to be posed implied that those answers which were given by the different circles were not adequate – or that at least such discussions had become a basic part of the cultural scene.

Indeed all these trends attested to the far-reaching concerns about the problems and tensions attendant on the development of the diversity of cultural creativity and participation and the fear of the possible loss of any centre or centres of gravity in this field. There was a continuous oscillation between the search for such centres of gravity and authenticity and the acknowledgement of the difficulty of providing an open, diversified and pluralist answer to these problems.

It was this continuous oscillation, as well as the erosion of the former common orientations to cultural activities and the search for some new ones, that became more and more connected with the growing change in the relations to Jewish Galut experience, changes to the heritage of the *edot* and also to the growing emphasis on religious tradition – all of which became a basic component of the cultural scene in Israel. In Chapter 15 we shall analyse in greater detail the transformations in the attitudes to the heritage and in Chapter 16 the changes of the *edot*. But now we shall turn to the analysis of new developments in the religious sectors.

# New Developments among Orthodox Communities
## The attitude of the orthodox to the State of Israel

As we have seen, the ultra-orthodox circles were from their beginning opposed to the Zionist vision, denying its semi-Messianic aspirations and its attempts to construct patterns of full collective Jewish life not based on the Halakha. Until the establishment of the State many of them were opposed to the basic premises of the Zionist movement, although some parts participated in the settlement in Eretz Israel, as well as in some common political activities with the Zionist leadership, especially on the international scene.

With the establishment of the State the ultra-orthodox party – the Agudat Israel – has joined, as we have seen, the government for a short while, since then it has continuously participated in the elections to the Knesset and has been on and off a supporter of the reigning coalitions even if not a member of the government.

Such participation did not entail, however, a full *de jure* recognition of the

Zionist State by the Agudat – as could for instance be seen by the fact that national flags were not hoisted in its conventions (to which the President of the State was not invited, as this might give rise to the problem whether the Rabbis should stand up in his presence), or in the non-participation in the celebrations of the Day of Independence, their non-acceptance of special prayers set up by the Chief Rabbinate in honour of the day, and above all in stressing always the higher authority of their own frameworks, the institutions of learning, and the decisions of the Council of Sages to which their members of parliament were responsible.

At the same time they made many demands towards the State, both principled and religious, such as the imposition on the general population of as many religious restrictions as possible, as well as of the various concessions and mundane allocations for their own needs, especially for their separate educational system and later on for their Yeshivot. They also demanded privileges and a sort of partial immunity from many of its laws, such as concessions which in a sense perpetuated their standing as a separate sector. Among the most far-reaching of such concessions were those for the exemption of students of their Yeshivot (the institutions of Talmudic learning) from military service, and the exemption of religious women (girls) from army service. The State acceded to many of these demands, but this did not necessarily ensure the full legitimacy of the State in the eyes of such extreme groups as the *Naturei Karta*, who denied the possibility of any co-operation with the 'secular' Zionist State, nor even of the wider spectrum of orthodox or ultra-orthodox non-Zionist groups. Indeed, in a sense, in their own eyes it increased their own legitimacy *vis-à-vis* the State, making them into at best partial partners in it, but on their own terms, without accepting the basic legitimacy of the Zionist vision.

Thus in fact they attained the status of a semi-autonomous distinct sector within the State, but maintaining their at most ambivalent – and among the more extreme members negative – attitudes to the State.

## *The place of the orthodox in Jewish and Israeli society*

The impact of these trends and attitudes were intensified from the late 1960s – especially after the Six Day War. This intensification was reinforced by a combination of developments in Jewish orthodoxy in general and in Israel in particular, as well as by several major developments in what can be called the Zionist–religious sector – that sector which was a basic partner in all the coalitions with Labour and the New Zionist groups in the Zionist organization and in the State of Israel and in the institutional mould which was created by them.

These developments within the orthodoxy in general (which will be discussed in greater detail, in Chapter 16) went against the basic ideologies – assimilationist, Zionist and even the older orthodox alike – that were predominant in the Diaspora and in the Yishuv till the Second World War. All of these assumed that, in the wake of the presumed general trend to secularization, the position of orthodox Jews would be weakened, perhaps even disappear, that at most they would remain in closed ghettos, completely secluded from modern life, finding some niche in various traditional Jewish occupations like small trade, artisanship and the like.

These predictions were indeed true of some small extreme orthodox groups, but not of the majority of the new orthodox or ultra-orthodox groups in the Diaspora. These sectors went beyond the classical ghetto experience by becoming much more interwoven in the occupational, and even ecological, matrix of modern societies. At the same time, from the late 1930s, but with gathering momentum after the Second World War, there was a very intensive developed reconstruction of the Yeshivot built on the strong tradition of the Eastern European (specially Lithuanian) Yeshivot, and the later development, with the aid of many modern devices, of learning communities and new leadership.*

All in all, the orthodox managed to develop as one of the new variants, a very forceful one of modern Jewish life, and, contrary to the experience of the former generations, they do not seem – here again there are no exact data – to lose out to the secular world.

## Revival of the orthodox groups

At the same time, and in close relation to the general trend in the Diaspora, there was a strong expansion of orthodox groups in Israel itself. The number and visibility of ultra-orthodox circles, as well as of different varieties of types of orthodox circles upholding the supremacy of the Halakha, grew in Israel. This took place especially in cities like Jerusalem, in the centre of Benei Berak, and in Netanya where many Hassidic groups established their own quarters; later, in the 1970s, there were special settlements in Judea and Samaria, often transplanting their patterns of life and symbols, living in relatively closed social, often also ecological sectors. But while some of these were very self-segregated, many others moved in the direction of the more modern patterns of orthodox life which had developed in the Diaspora – although to a smaller degree than there. This expansion was connected with a far-reaching transformation of the standing of Israel within the whole panorama of Jewish orthodoxy.

To quote M. Friedman:

> In Jewish society during the Mandate the selective community had only minimal drawing power. . . .
> This situation changed after the establishment of the State of Israel, especially since the mid-fifties. Israel became a world center of Torah study. The number of yeshivot and kolelim steadily increased. Heads of yeshivot, Torah luminaries and Hasidic rabbis settled in the country with thousands of their followers and founded their own

* See Menachem Friedman, 'The Changing Role of the Community Rabbinate', *Jerusalem Quarterly*, 25 (Fall, 1982), pp. 59–100.

communities. The rise in the standard of living and the system of public housing enabled traditional religious Jews to live in separate neighborhoods. Selective communities based on the leadership of Torah luminaries are today a very common phenomenon. The very presence of luminaries, Hasidic rabbis and heads of yeshivot, as well as of learned religious figures radiating power and of a leader such as the Hazon Ish (Rabbi Abraham Isaiah Karelvitz), had in itself weakened the status of the Chief Rabbinate. Furthermore, the fact that the Chief Rabbinate and the community rabbinate are part of the establishment of the Zionist State, whereas the luminaries and their followers are mostly non-Zionist, if not anti-Zionist, fostered the development of an attitude of delegitimation towards the Chief Rabbinate and its rulings. . . .

Here the circle comes to a close. The selective communities tend to adopt higher standards of religious observance. They become elites which serve as reference groups for the rest of the Orthodox Jewish population, which although it does not behave like them cannot deny that the former are 'better' Jews than they are.

From here it is but one step to a takeover of the religious leadership by these groups. The 'Great Men of Torah', the heads of yeshivot and the Hasidic rabbis come to constitute the front-rank leadership. The corollary of that is a decline in the status of the Chief Rabbinate and the community rabbis associated with it. This is a dynamic situation, which is also sustained by delegitimation, by the spread of kolelim and yeshivot to all parts of the country, by the growing sense of confidence which the yeshivot world draws from the movement of religious return, by the crisis in secular Zionism and more. All of these make clear the problematic status of the Chief and non-selective local rabbinate, especially against the background of the crisis in the status of the community rabbinate we have described.*

All these developments in the more extreme orthodox sector were, from about the 1960s on, and especially after the Six Day War, reinforced in a crucial way by several major developments in what can be called the Zionist–religious sector, and together had far-reaching consequences for the whole cultural ambience of Israeli society.

From the very establishment of the State these ultra-orthodox parties existed for a very long period in a sort of ambivalent relation with the Zionist–religious ones – the *Mizrahi* and *Hapoel Hamizrahi*, later on the National Religious party. These latter parties fully accepted the basic premises of the State of Israel and its demand for the service (at least of men) in the army, yet on the whole they fully supported most of the demands of the ultra-orthodox parties. This was partially because they shared the conviction and many mutual interests in religious matters of the ultra-orthodox groups, even if they did not accept their vehemence and ambivalent attitude to the State. But partly it was because of their feelings of inferiority in matters of religious learning, in representation of the tradition and institutions of such learning, *vis-à-vis* these ultra-orthodox groups. These feelings of inferiority were largely due to the fact that the Zionist–religious parties were not – till the mid-1960s – very active in developing such institutions. The only exception to this were the various *Yeshivot Tichoniot* and *Yeshivot Hesder* which had started to develop earlier, which combined Talmudic study with some secular ones, and which sent their graduates to service in the army, often to some of its elite units, but even here it

* Friedman, 'The Changing Role of the Community Rabbinate', pp. 98–9.

was only later that their full impact on public life in Israel was felt.

Even these Yeshivot tended on the whole to look up – at least in the field of Talmudic scholarships – to the more orthodox circles. But here several far-reaching changes started to develop, especially after the Six Day War.

Several processes, some reinforcing, some contradicting each other, were of central importance. One was the weakening, together with the general ideological exhaustion of the Labour–Zionist vision, of the specific orientation of religious Zionism as developed by the *Mizrahi* or *Hapoel Hamizrahi*. There was less ideological stress on the observance of Halakha, though the basic tenets of Zionism, of looking beyond the Halakha for guidance in concrete institutional building, and many of the civil and ideological premisses of the institutional mould that had developed in the State of Israel, were still accepted.

It was only in the religious Kibbutzim that attempts at continuous ideological as well as institutional innovations were made, but the place of these Kibbutzim in the religious sector was not greatly different from that of the secular Kibbutzim in the general sector, so their special elitist position was also relatively weakened.

This weakening of the ideological self-assurance of the Zionist–religious groups was manifest in their growing dependence in religious matters, especially in matters of Halakhic study, on the more extreme religious sectors and their Yeshivot without developing their own intellectual or ideological orientations. This also weakened their impact on the Chief Rabbinate, which became more and more dominated by Rabbis close to the ultra-orthodox circles.

The opening up of the problem of collective Israeli identity which started to take place after the Six Day War provided a very fertile soil for the emergence of various religious movements in general and of more extreme religious ideological–national movements in particular.

Among non-religious groups it gave rise to a search for meaning of daily life and of its connections to some broader national and cultural patterns – that very connection which the original Zionist vision in general and the Zionist–Socialist in particular claimed to provide, and in which it seemed to have failed.

The most visible vocal sections of this trend developed among so-called *Hozrim Betshuva* (those who return in Repentance), those returning from the secular fold through a variety of preparatory schools or special types of Yeshivot to the field of orthodoxy.

But beyond these extremist trends religious elements and symbolism became continuously more visible in public life. First there was the success, mentioned above, of the religious parties to enforce many restrictions on general public life. These trends were also reinforced by – and in their turn reinforced – the growing expansion and visibility in daily life of religious groups, many of whom, especially the younger elements, were no longer self-apologetic towards the broader non-religious sectors, but saw themselves as the true carriers in a world seemingly losing its centre of gravity.

There was also a growing interest of the general public in aspects of Jewish religious tradition. Courses, seminars and meetings about religious topics seemed to draw a growing public, as did more specifically religious literature, and radio talks addressed to the general public, many of which with passing years assumed a more and more fundamentalistic tone.

## Radicalization of religious trends

At the same time all these trends also gave rise to a growing radicalization within the religious groups. Such radicalization developed in at least two directions – with a common core but also leading in rather contradictory directions.

The common core was manifest in the growing emphasis on the supremacy and validity of the religious tradition in general and of the Halakha in particular, in its symbolic and legal aspects alike, as the epitome of Jewish and Zionist history and essence – as against the seeming bankruptcy of the secular mould.

Institutionally, this common core saw in the generally expanding Yeshivot and the increasingly predominant *Yeshivot Tichoniot* and *Yeshivot Hesder* (against the 'religious' trend) the major dynamic centres of religious education.

It was within parts of these new educational institutions, especially the Zionist Yeshivot, that some of the most important educational innovations were taking place – as against the more conservative official state–religious stream within the separate stream of Agudat Israel or within the traditional type of the Yeshivot to which the majority of the ultra-orthodox went.

Significantly enough, against the mainstream of Israeli education in general and that in the official state–religious sector in particular, these educational institutions tended to exhibit very strong elitist orientations, a strong emphasis on upholding standards and demands and their application to 'old' and new immigrant groups, without outcries of discrimination.

At the same time the strong renewal of the religious youth movements, of the *Bnei Akiva*, against the general decline of youth movements, seemingly attested to the possibility of their becoming a revival of the Zionist vision, a revival focused on the combination of old Zionist themes with new ways of life centred around the new mould of Halakha.

But beyond this common core these trends, although often overlapping in reality, took place in two contradictory directions.

One such direction was firmly set within the Zionist vision – with the development of a radical religious national approach among the youth movements of the religious sector, especially the *Bnei Akiva* and in the special institutions, and of the various *Yeshivot Tichoniot* and *Yeshivot Hesder*, which were the carriers of this new vision, combining settlement, service in the military, extreme national symbolism couched in a very militant mode and a strong emphasis, far beyond the tendency of the older Zionist–religious groups, on the sovereignty of Halakha, albeit Halakha very clearly imbued with strong national orientations and symbolism.

Indeed many – but not all – of these Yeshivot became centres or foci of more extreme religious political activities, such as *Gush Emunim* which, as we have seen, succeeded in occupying the centre of the political stage, proclaiming themselves to be the carriers of the original Zionist vision and of a law higher than that of the State.

For a relatively long time the impression grew that religious Zionism went entirely into this direction – leaving behind the more universalistic dimension of the Zionist vision in which many of its adherents shared before. It was only much later, during the Lebanon War, that this trend started, as we shall see, to change to some degree at least. With the passage of time, and especially from the late 1970s, there were more indications that it was the non-Zionist Yeshivot and orientations that were winning over large parts of these religious circles.

These changes started to gather momentum after the Six Day War – but, as in all the other sections of life, their full significance as well as potentials for change were not fully grasped then and it was only in the 1970s, with the repercussions of the Yom Kippur War, that this happened.

# The Standing of the Arab Communities in Israel
## *Growing awareness of their problems*

Naturally, one of the most far-reaching changes – and openings – concerned the Arabs in general, and the Israeli Arabs in particular.

In the political field, the openings introduced by the Eshkol government before the Six Day War continued, and the Office of the Prime Minister's Adviser on Arab Affairs developed a more open attitude to Arab political activities and cultural and economic rôle.

At the same time there were some new attitudes within the Arab educational system towards the problems of the collective identity of Israeli Arabs and of the Arab component of that identity. Parallelly, continuous contacts with all levels of Arab society – leaders, intellectuals and the different echelons – intensified, in many ways reminiscent of many of the pre-State periods.

But beyond these various developments two complementary problems emerged. The first such problem was that of the growing consciousness of the Israeli Arabs, of their constituting a distinct type of Arab society with specific problems on all levels of social life and of collective identity, and a growing search among them for autonomous collective expression and some integration within the framework of the State of Israel – and beyond it.

The second complementary problem was the growing recognition within broader sectors of Jewish society that the problem of the Arab minority or minorities could not be coped with in an administrative – even if benevolent – setting; that this problem touched on some very central problems of the format of the State and especially on its ability to combine its Jewishness with just a formal incorporation of minorities within its institutional and symbolic frameworks.

These problems were, of course, intensified by the new situation – that of rule over the Arab population in the West Bank and Gaza, together between 1,100,000 and 1,300,000 people who, unlike the Arabs in Israel, were not Israeli citizens. The Military Government was established and ruled over the population in the West Bank, attempting to work mostly through the local authorities but ultimately based on its military power. This added an entirely new dimension to Arab–Israeli relations and to the ambience of Israeli society. Patrolling, control, dispersal of demonstrations, confrontation with a more and more hostile population – certainly this was not a very salutary experience for the Israeli soldier, even in the early years of the benign military rule, and, although much of it became routinized, it could not but add a new, problematic dimension to Israeli life.

There developed also an entirely new economic division of labour between these two sectors, reminiscent of some aspects of the situation during the mandate, sometimes of those very aspects against which the Labour Zionists had cried out; while on the one hand Israeli experts helped greatly to improve agriculture and the level of services on the West Bank, there developed also a new semi-colonizatory relation, in which a not insignificant part of the labour sector in the new as well as some old Moshavim, in the construction works and some part of industry, come from Gaza and the West Bank, much against the older tenets of Labour Zionism, reinforcing very strongly some of the more conservative or stagnative tendencies in the economic structure of Israel.

All these developments added to the growing sensitivity about the relations to the Arab population in Israel and the West Bank, the impact of the military government on Israelis themselves, and these sensibilities became more and more voiced in public debates and in the literature.

Needless to say, such sensibilities could – and did – develop in a great variety of directions. Either the attitudes to the Arabs hardened, or there was a search for ways to open them up. Either way, all these problems featured on the public agenda in a way that had not existed since the establishment of the State.

## The Six Day War and its aftermath – growing problems of integration

Thus indeed, as in all spheres of life in Israel – and actually perhaps more than in others – the Six Day War constituted a watershed in the developments within the Arab population and in its relations with the State of Israel; and the combination of the developments connected with this – and the later wars, the Yom Kippur War and the Lebanon war, as well as at the peace treaty with Egypt – together with the continuation and intensification of the demographic and economic trends that had developed earlier, transformed the nature of the place and participation of the Arab society in the State of Israel.

The central development here was, of course, the encounter with the Arabs of the West Bank, and beyond that with those of the Arab countries, an encounter fraught with ambivalences.

For the first time since the establishment of the State of Israel, the Arab minority – which enjoyed great economic prosperity and educational advancement, but also social dislocation and difficulties in integrating in the urban sectors of Israeli society – was released from its almost hermetic isolation from other parts of the Arab world, and contacts were established with that world. The first stages of this meeting sharpened the problems of the Arab–Israeli identity of the Arab population in the State of Israel.

On the one hand it necessarily gave rise to an intensification of their Arab conciousness, a growing awakening of their links with the Arab culture and people, and strengthened the ambivalence in their relations with Israel. The differences between the Israeli–Arab minority and the residents of the West Bank seemed less important, Arab nationalism intensified, and there was a profound questioning of the very premisses of Israel.

On the other hand there was also an intensification among them of their distinct Israeli–Arab identity – which had become strengthened by the fact that in the meantime generations of Arabs had been born and brought up within Israel, with their whole social perspective set in this framework – however ambivalent they may have been to it. These developments were intensified by the outcome of the internal processes of modernization within the Arab community analysed above, above all by the growing occupational modernization, by their move to industry and construction work on the one hand, and the emergence of an Israeli-born Arab intelligentsia on the other.

The demographic and economic processes gained a momentum in all directions. Thus in 1979 most of the Arab working population (21.6 per cent) worked in construction. Second came those who worked in industry (mining and manufacturing) (21.5 per cent) and the third group was those who worked in public and community services (17.4 per cent).

There has been a significant change since then in the percentage of the different occupations. By 1979 1.7 per cent of the Arab working population were scientific and academic workers; in 1981 it had grown to 2.8 per cent, an increase of 164.7 per cent. At the same time there was a decrease of the Arab workers in agriculture, from 12.3 per cent in 1979 to 11.5 per cent in 1981, a decrease of 93.49 per cent.

In general the Arab Christian population was from the very beginning on a higher educational level than the Muslim one, but the relative advance of the latter was greater, even if the former were still on the whole educationally and occupationally more advanced.

But all these developments threw into strong relief the different tempo of developments between the Jewish and Arab sectors – the dualistic system that had developed in the relations between them, which some of the more extremist Arab intellectuals called a situation of internal colonization. These developments gave rise to growing feelings of resentment among many sectors in the Arab society – a feeling rooted in the greater dependency on the central government, and relative helplessness in the relations to it.

These demographic and economic changes gave rise – both by themselves, and even more in conjunction with the developments after the Six Day War – to new aspirations and frustrations with respect to finding adequate places of employment suitable from the point of view of their educational (especially academic) training and with respect to the difficulties of integration in Israeli society – even if within the latter some openings were gradually appearing. Naturally it was the Arab University students who became vocal in articulating these problems.

Another area of tensions, as well as of growing political consciousness and struggle, and also connected with the Arabs' demographic growth, focused on the problem of land; especially on its relative scarcity in relation to their demographic growth, and the amount of agricultural land at their disposal. The situation was exacerbated by the land settlement policy of the State, aimed at least in principle at the growing Jewish settlement at Galilee where the Jews were losing out demographically to the Arabs.

In the mid-1970s, land policy became a central issue, especially in the Galilee. Considerable acreage had been lost to Arab villages, particularly those near the borders, during and just after the War of Liberation, often under irregular procedures and with inequities in the dates which determined the values for compensation.* In succeeding years, land was taken for public purposes by due process, but the purposes could include the forming of new towns, such as Carmiel and Upper Nazareth in the Galilee, and for industrial sites, as part of the policy of population dispersal and for increasing the Jewish population of the Galilee.† From 1965 to 1975, there was little change in the extent of Arab landholdings. In 1975, however, older plans for intensive development of the Galilee and the encouragement of settlement there were revived and updated. Although they involved the requisitioning of a considerable amount of land owned by Jews, mainly in the town of Safed, a substantially larger amount of acreage was to be acquired by the government from Arabs under eminent domain. Arabs were aware that the government's plans for developing the Galilee were motivated mainly by a desire to ensure a Jewish majority in the area, and they suspected development moves even when these were for the Arab sector; and there were also memories of land losses in the early years of the state. Land became a symbol and focus of protest in the Arab communities, and statements by the government that the intent was to 'develop the Galilee' and not to 'Judaize' it were not convincing.‡

## Political radicalization and the search for an Arab–Israeli identity

These demographic and economic changes, the general trend to modernization, the emergence of a generation of Israeli-born Arabs, created a new situation. The concrete contours of this situation were however shaped by the

* In an inflationary economy, delays in compensation inconvenienced Jews and Arabs alike, and in 1976 changes in the laws were recommended to permit immediate recompense.

† With time, Arab agriculture became intensive, mechanized and highly productive. Between 1965 and 1975, the extent of Arab land under irrigation doubled. At the same time population growth increased the need for more yields.

‡ D. Shimshoni, *Israeli Democracy* (New York 1982) pp. 145–6.

combination of these processes and the repercussions of the Six Day War.

The two major tendencies – complementary and contradictory at the same time – were first, a growing political activization and radicalization of the Arab population and, second, the growing and very ambivalent testing out among the Israeli Arabs of the possibility of developing a special Israeli–Arab identity. Both tendencies had far-reaching impacts on some crucial dimensions of Israeli society.

The political activization and radicalization in general were evident in the rise of participation in elections, and in political demonstrations and different violent outbursts above all perhaps in the Universities (especially Haifa and Jerusalem), as well as around the agrarian question – the so-called 'Day of the Land'.

The Day of the Land (*Yom Ha-Adama*) was first instituted during the influence of *Rakach* in March 1976, after a demonstration during which six Arabs were killed; it has continued as a day of demonstration since then, sometimes in very aggressive tones, later, as we shall see, in more peaceful ones.

These demonstrations were sometimes fed by the concern of the settlement authorities about the problem of Jewish settlement in the Galilee, by the rather hardline attitude of the director of the Ministry of Interior in charge of the Northern District. For example General Ben-Gal (Yanosh), the then-officer commanding the Northern Front, on 10 August 1979 said during a visit of a group of members of the Knesset to the Golan Heights that 'the Arabs in the Galilee are a cancer in the heart of the nation'; later he retracted his words.

The political radicalization was also attested by the results of the elections in 1977, as well as of municipal elections, in which *Rakach* gained growing strength. Moreover the committee of Arab Mayors became established in 1974, becoming more and more active in presenting various demands to the government.

Such political radicalization, both within the internal Israeli scene and with respect to the general Arab front, centred around the question of a Palestinian identity and its possible political expression, and the growing influence of the PLO. So the whole problem of the basic relations of the Arabs to the State of Israel was sharpened and further reinforced by the continuous meeting and encounter with the Arabs in the West Bank and with repercussions of Israeli policies there.

These developments among the Israeli Arabs were connected with the continued opening up of the attitudes to the Arab minority on behalf of the government agencies – a continuation of the Eshkol policy – and a growing sensitivity to the problems of the Arab population among at least parts of the Jewish population.

Problems of the Arab population became more and more publicly discussed – whether in the newspapers, or on the radio and television – often by Arab or Druze journalists, or media specialists, as for instance Attallah Mansur or Rafik Halabi or various spokesmen, to a much larger degree and in a much more open dialogue than before.

Such discussions often naturally and necessarily became closely interwoven with those of Israeli policy in the West Bank – and yet even in such situations the distinction of the problem of the Israeli Arabs has always been understood.

Yet those openings were still very halting. The government policy remained based on relatively paternalistic premisses, on the 'us–them' distinctions, assuming a relatively passive attitude by the Arabs. Actual social segregation, as occupational limitation and discrimination, was in many ways felt more acutely with the occupational advancement of the Arabs.

The more general public discussions about relations with the Arabs also evoked very hard responses – perhaps best epitomized by many of the expressions of the then Chief of Staff (Raful) who significantly enough tended to talk not about the 'enemy' but about the Arabs in general, not always making it clear whether the Israeli Arabs were or were not included in such references.

But such growing radicalization – seemingly often indicating a strong anti-Israeli stand, calling for a separate political identity, sometimes connected, as was the case in the Jerusalem campus, with the desecration of Zionist–Jewish symbols such as those of the Holocaust – was only one possible development of the growing political awareness of large parts of the Arab population.

Side by side with it, other trends developed indicating that among the Israeli Arabs there were also elements searching for new ways of becoming incorporated in the Israel polity and society.

Thus in the 1981 elections a large part of the Arab population voted for the *Maarach*, which, as some other Zionist parties, included in its lists new active political leaders, thus indicating their feeling of the possibility of participating in the political process in Israel, but only through either paternalistic or extreme oppositionary parties. Another indication of such trends was the 1983 Day of the Land, which was much more peaceful. Many public discussions attested to the fact that, among many of the Israeli–Arab intellectuals – and certainly even more among the broader groups of the Arab sector – there was a strong search for some possibility of becoming incorporated in Israeli public life; a testing of such possibilities, often connected with ambivalent attitudes to the Zionist component of Israeli identity; a search for the chance to construct a collective identity within the Israeli framework yet in a strong relation to their Arab identity – and demanding more autonomy in this sphere.

Needless to say no easy solutions were found, and very often new tensions – usually in connection with occurrences in the West Bank – developed. Yet the whole nature of this problem has become greatly changed since the first decade of the State.

## The significance of these problems

All these developments posed more and more far-reaching, principled problems about the nature of the relations between the Jewish majority and the

Arab minority or – to use the title of a symposium on this subject – with every sixth Israeli.

From the point of view of the Arab population, the problem – the possibility of being a minority in a non-Arab country – was a new experience, for Arab history showed a lot of experience with foreign conquerors, but none of being a minority. The Israeli Arabs started to grope with the implications of such a situation, looking both into Israel and also outside, to the other Arab countries, to the 'Arab nation' – in the context of which the Jews were an alien conquering minority.

But this was not only a purely symbolic problem – in itself of no small significance. Nor was it a problem only of getting out from the administrative and political tutelage of the authorities and extending the possibility of autonomous participation in Israeli political life – again a problem of no small importance, but one towards which some, even if slow, advances had been made.

Nor was it just an overt clash of different economic interests – as in the case of the Bedouins and with respect to the land problem especially in Galilee.

This latter problem in fact signalled a much more basic problem or tension – namely the one between the settlement and territorial orientation of the Zionist movement and the legitimate right of the Arabs as Israeli citizens. This was a far-reaching transformation of the Arab–Jewish confrontation in the period of the mandate, and in principle it also differed greatly from the problems on the West Bank, where the Arabs were not granted Israeli citizenship.

Indeed all these developments signalled that Israeli society – Israel as a Jewish State – was faced here with the rather basic problem of the nature of its democracy; not only of tolerance towards non-Jews, not only of its acceptance, in the biblical terms, of 'the stranger within your gates', but also of allowing them a full, autonomous collective cultural and political participation according to modern democratic universalistic premisses.

The mere facts of the situation – above all the close interrelation between this problem and Israel's geopolitical and international status – did not, of course, provide for any easy simple solution, but the very awareness and the growing understanding of this problem were an indicator of the changing format, from the 1970s on, of Israeli society.

## Arab-Jewish relations in Jerusalem

A rather special encounter between Jews and Arabs took place in unified Jerusalem in 1967: the opening of the gates of the different parts of the city, the official reunification in the declaration of the Arab population as Israeli citizens, opened up new hopes for a new mode of coexistence between the two populations. These hopes were not fully realized as the Arabs refused to accept Israeli citizenship, and even to participate officially in the municipal council – although no small number of them voted in the municipal elections.

Many of them did, however, co-operate, especially with Mayor Teddy Kollek, whose imaginative leadership was instrumental in assuring the peaceful coexistence between Arabs and Jews even in moments of tension, such as when terrorist bombs were found in central places in Israel.

It was a relatively peaceful coexistence of basically separate, distinct groups, with but little social contact or common political or semi-political meetings – except at workplaces or some general public or social occasions restricted to a very few groups.

# Patterns of Policies
## *Pragmatics and ideological or conceptual rigidity*

Thus in general after the Six Day War there was a very far-reaching opening in public debate on many of the crucial aspects of Israeli life – indicating, even if indirectly, that the older consensus could not be taken for granted and was at best to be reconstructed.

But many of these problems – especially those related to relations with the Arabs, and international relations but also those seeking answers in other fields – called for answers also in policy terms.

But here the situation was rather different from the one that developed in the realm of public opinion. The policies that developed in this period – especially with respect to the Arab population and foreign affairs – were a combination of pragmatism and relative flexibility on the more daily level, set, however, within the framework of maintaining the *status quo*, and a much less flexible, often quite rigid principled approach towards the much broader problems raised by all the various basic questions and the new developments analysed above.

The pragmatic approach was developed, first of all, by the military government with respect to the West Bank and Gaza. The military government itself was a very liberal one when compared with any other occupying power. It was based on the recognition of the distinct ways of life of the Arab populations and of their connection with the Arab countries. This was evident in the maintenance of the pre-existing educational system and the permission to be examined for entrance in the universities in the Arab countries: in the maintenance of Jordanian (Egyptian, too) law; in the policy of the open bridges instituted by Moshe Dayan; in the *de facto* permission to the former employees of the Jordan government to continue to receive their salaries from Jordan; in the very far-reaching economic development especially in the agricultural sector; in the general rise in the standard of living; in the partial resettlement of refugees – much more than was done by the Jordanians in the West Bank and the Egyptians in Gaza; in the permission for a relatively high level of political expression especially on the municipal level. This was coupled with a firm policy against incipient terrorism – evident in that period in a tendency to what was called by Moshe Dayan 'environmental punishment', such as the destruction or blowing up of houses of families which sheltered terrorists and the implementation of administrative arrests, often based on mandatory security ordinances.

This pragmatic approach could also be found in the negotiations with the USA or through the UN, and later on in the arrangements about the separation of forces with the Egyptians under the Rabin government. On all levels of international diplomacy there was continuous negotiation through various UN intermediaries, with many clandestine meetings with Arab leaders.

But as well as these rather pragmatic and often quite flexible approaches, there were more rigid ones. First there was what was later, after the Yom Kippur War, called the 'conception' of the Israeli military superiority: even a few months before this war, Dayan stressed the inability of the Arabs to overcome Israeli military strength.

Second was the reluctance of most Israeli leaders to face and cope with the fact of rising Palestinian collective-national consciousness and quest for some self-determination; the most extreme example of this was Golda Meir's famous saying: 'I am a Palestinian.'

Third was a very strong clinging to the overall *status quo*. The authorities did not seem ready to express any public acceptance or initiative which would indicate a willingness to change concretely, in the foreseeable future, what was presented as a seemingly good political and military *status quo* – even in the face of growing international pressure.

This attitude was, of course, reinforced by the Arab stance – first by the famous three 'nos' of the Khartoum conference in August 1967, when the assembled Arab leaders declared that any political solutions or settlement must involve no negotiations with Israel, no peace with it, and no recognition of it; by the Rabat declaration of March 1969, which undermined the legitimacy of Jordan which seemed the moderate partner to represent the Palestinian case and declared the PLO the only representative of the Palestinian cause.

But even when some more moderate voices began to be heard after Nasser's death, there was but little official, public (as against informal) response and no feelers were taken up, even from Sadat.

Perhaps the single most important illustration of this attitude can be seen with respect to the Alon plan – a plan formulated by Yigal Alon, the then Minister of Labour, very soon after the Six Day War – for a policy of settlements in the West Bank based mostly on security considerations but containing also some idea of possible political accommodations with Jordan.

Although this plan was discussed in many informal settings and served as the *de facto* guideline for the settlement policy, it was not even formally discussed within the government, as it was assumed that any such formal discussion would weaken the Israeli bargaining position *vis-à-vis* the Arabs and limit its activities.

An even less far-reaching proposal for public initiative, Dayan's proposal to withdraw voluntarily some miles from the Suez Canal, was vetoed by the Prime Minister (Golda Meir) and not pressed by Dayan himself, despite his obvious awareness of the crucial importance of providing some such gesture. Similarly, a suggestion by two Ministers in the Rabin Government – Aharon Yariv and Victor Shemtov – for a possibility of a somewhat more flexible approach to the PLO, was rejected.

Thus, even when voices from within the government made concrete new policy suggestions, yet insofar as they touched both on the negotiations with the USA and the UN, and also on some more basic aspects of the policy, they were not pursued – despite the fact that there was a seemingly contradictory growing recognition, stressed by many people even in the government – especially perhaps by Dayan – of the necessity to attain a *modus vivendi* with the Palestinian Arabs.

In all these matters the image of rigidity was probably much stronger and more persistent than the reality of multiple attempts at negotiations – but this image, perhaps best exemplified by Golda Meir, cast its shadow in internal political discussion as well as on the international scene.

## *Development of a new security conception – the fragility of consensus*

Behind all these developments was the crystallization of a new security conception and its repercussions on the internal and international political scenes. To quote Dan Horowitz:

From a purely military point of view, the most salient outcome of the Six Day War had been that for the first time since its establishment, the State of Israel had some degree of strategic depth. Senior Israeli officers and military commentators repeatedly emphasized two aspects of the postwar military situation: the indefensibility of the 1967 cease-fire lines, and the extended early-warning system against air attacks from airfields in Egypt created by the occupation of Sinai. The broader consequence of these strategic advantages was the adoption of the concept of secure borders which, according to the then Foreign Minister of Israel, Abba Eban, are 'borders which can be defended without a pre-emptive initiative'. In other words, the idea of secure borders implied the abandonment of the first-strike strategies and the adoption of a strategy of absorption followed by counter-attack.

The new concept of secure borders also implied the abandonment of the *casi belli* approach, but not necessarily of the belief in the effectiveness of military superiority as a deterrent. In fact, the readiness to absorb an enemy's first strike paved the way for adopting a relatively 'pure' strategy of deterrence, obviating the need to reconcile such strategy of deterrence with the optional pre-emptive strike strategy. It was only in the course of implementing the new concept of secure borders that the Israeli decision-makers came to learn that the challenge to the legitimacy of Israel's occupation of territories as a result of the war may have a more unfavourable effect on Israel's image abroad and on her international relations than a pre-emptive strike such as that of June 1967. . . .*

Closely related to this was of course the policy of the intensive settlement in

* Dan Horowitz, 'Israel's Concept of Defensible Borders', Papers on Peace Problems (Jerusalem 1975), p. 12ff.

the West Bank, most of it following the Alon plan and guided by security considerations, but some, such as the settlement in Kiryat Arba on the outskirts of Hebron as well as some other ones – initiated mostly by extreme religious–nationalist groups out of which *Gush Emunim* crystallized – guided also by religious and national historical visions.

The crystallization of this new security conception had far-reaching implications on the internal – and international – scene.

Despite the intensive public debate in Israel on issues of foreign and defence policy during the 1967–73 period, there appeared to be a broad consensus among Israel's political parties and factions about the need for secure borders as a pre-condition to any peace settlement. Yet the seeming consensus around this new security concept was connected with several far-reaching developments on the Israeli scene, with *de facto* far-reaching differences of opinion. These touched not only on purely security conceptions, but also on the deeper dimensions of Israeli collective identity – the territorial, the religious and the historical ones, and on the problem of maintaining a Jewish democratic state with a growing Arab population – all of which were opened after the Six Day War. They were indeed opened up but, except in the extreme religious and nationalistic groups and even among them at this period, without full awareness of their implications, no clear conception or plan was articulated by official bodies or by parties; there was not a full recognition of these problems and their implications – and there was also the fear of breaking the seemingly strong, in fact rather fragile, consensus.

The potential fragility of such consensus was evident in the fact that the opening up of these problems also necessarily touched on the other central issues of Israeli collective identity, and also on the security and military one. Very indicative of such developments was the *Siach Lohamim* (*The Talk of the Fighters*), a book of a recording of informal, but very intensive talks among soldiers, members of Kibbutzim, from selections published in October 1967, and in which probably for the first time in the history of the State very serious questions – even doubts – about relations to the Arabs, the justification of war against them, the Jewish claims on Eretz Israel, and the like, were voiced.

Another indication of such a trend was the letter to Mrs Meir from fifty-four high school seniors written in 1970 when the Cabinet did not approve that Dr Nahum Goldmann, the President of the World Zionist Organization, accept an invitation (which later turned out not to be real) from President Nasser to visit him. The writers of this letter accused the government of 'not trying seriously for peace', and even indicated that they would find it difficult to serve in the army. (In fact, all of them later served, some with distinction.)

## *The repercussions of the Six Day War: the framework of optimism*

So these problems and trends crystallized and became articulated in connection with the two wars – the Six Day War and the Yom Kippur War – and their aftermath; but, as we shall see in fuller detail, the impact of these two wars on the institutional format of Israeli society and its self-perception was rather different.

The aftermath of the Six Day War opened up problems which had been dormant before. But at the same time the very fact of the great military victory, the great economic expansion and rising standard of living which developed in its wake, seemingly fully justified the institutional formats which developed within the existing mould. Truly enough, there were many signs of changes and of mounting problems, but the general feeling seemed to be that basically the solution to them would be incorporated into the existing mould. All this, despite the fact that all these developments were connected with the growing atrophy in the political field and the seemingly growing rigidity on many official policies – especially in the security and foreign policy – despite the continuously growing public discussion.

Indeed, the first years after the Six Day War were often perceived, within Israel and beyond it, as the apogee of the implementation of the Zionist vision, as the best testimony to the viability and vitality of that vision and of that institutional and cultural mould which had developed since the establishment of the State of Israel.

Truly enough, neither the mould nor its implementation were ever seen as perfect. Indeed in all the institutional areas and in all spheres of life, there were many multiple tensions and conflicts and contradictions, and Israeli society in the early 1970s differed greatly, not only from that of the late Yishuv and early State, but also from the vision that had guided its implementation.

But the very awareness of these problems; the concern with them; the relative heterogeneity of social and ideological forces which were active within Israeli society; the continuity and relatively high level of public debate and political discussion; the continuous economic development after the war (offsetting the effects of the relative recession just before the Six Day War which had lowered the morale at that period); the success in the war itself; the undertaking of far-reaching policies in the educational field and in welfare aimed to deal with social problems in general and those of absorption of immigrants in particular: all these factors added, in those years, to the feeling of Israeli self-satisfaction.

In particular there was an appreciation of the viability of the Israeli–Zionist institutional–cultural mould. This was seen as dynamic, as more open and flexible, shedding away, as it were, many of the more totalistic and narrow features of the first stages of its crystallization in the early 1950s. It was sometimes expressed, for instance by Yigal Alon and by many other leaders, that Israel was moving to become a new Athens – and not, as had been often feared, a new Sparta.

This feeling was reinforced by the continuous relaxation within Israeli society of the rather tense atmosphere which characterized it in its first stage, and of the development of a rather strong self-assurance, both of which were commented on by visitors from abroad. There was also a continuous improvement in many aspects of what can be called quality of life and of infrastructure – such as road-building and some services – and a continuous opening up of many new avenues of creativity.

The saying, 'We never had it so good', was very widespread then. Of course there were many groups – especially among intellectuals and some Left-wing groups – who claimed that in many ways, and especially in relation to the Arabs, as well perhaps as in the economic field, Israel was living in a fool's paradise. But it seems that these claims were not taken too seriously among the broader public.

Even the fact that Ben-Gurion, now in complete political retirement in Sde Boker, voiced his view that ultimately all the new territories of the West Bank, Gaza and Golan, with the exception of Jerusalem, would have to be returned in order to keep the Jewish nature of the State and assure its international standing, did not make much impression – certainly not on his political successors. It was probably generally accepted that some settlement would have to be attained, but people were in a way 'waiting' – following Dayan's famous saying – for 'the telephone call from Hussein'. In the meantime, even the relative quiet on the West Bank, its continuous economic development under the aegis of the benign Israeli military government and the policy of open bridges, all added only to the feeling of satisfaction and of the viability and strength of the Israeli–Zionist mould.

The major developments in the various areas of life – economic, social, educational and economic – reported above, even in the political field at least until 1973, seemed to indicate that all this might indeed carry on, probably in a dynamic, even tumultuous but basically continuous way, even if it might involve changes in leadership or in many of the ways of life.

And yet very soon this whole mode of self-perception of Israel society changed.

# PART FOUR

## The State of Israel –
## Change and Transformation

# CHAPTER 14

# The Yom Kippur War and its Aftermath – Change and Transition

## The Yom Kippur War and Changing Moods in Israel
### *Political background*

The first years after the Six Day War were often perceived, as indicated above, within Israel and beyond it, as the apogee of the implementation of the Zionist vision, as a period in which the feeling 'we never had it so good' was very widespread.

But in fact this situation was not to last long. The first severe shock came, of course, with the Yom Kippur War of 1973. The seemingly 'external' outcomes of this shock are relatively well known. These included: the outcries against the government in the form of various protest movements; the establishment in 1974, by the Government, of an official judicial inquiry committee (The Agranat Committee, named after its Chairman, the then President of the Supreme Court); its report, which accused the high military echelons (especially the Chief of Staff and the Head of Intelligence) of being unprepared for the war, but which absolved the ministerial level, that is above all Moshe Dayan, the Minister of Defence; the scepticism in the public about this absolution; the resignation of the Prime Minister, Mrs Golda Meir, and the formation, in 1974, of a new Labour government under Yitzhak Rabin (the Chief of Staff of the Six Day War, then Ambassador to the USA, and Minister of Labour in Mrs Meir's last government); the achievement of the agreement of separation of forces with Egypt in 1975; the successful Entebbe raid, which was seen as the epitome of Israeli heroism and military readiness; and the fall – to some degree engineered by Rabin himself – of the Rabin Government over a dispute with the religious parties. All these developments seemed to culminate in the 1977 elections, in which the very prominent part played by a new party, *Dash* (the Democratic Movement for Change) under the leadership of Yigael Yadin, contributed to the Labour party's loss. It lost, for the first time since the mid-1930s at least, its predominant place in the political spectrum and its ability to form the government. This was followed by the formation of the Likud party's government, under the leadership of Menahem Begin – a man who, to Ben-Gurion, was pure anathema and a danger to the future of the State of Israel.

The first Likud government was initially based on a narrow coalition with the religious groups with Dayan as Foreign Minister. Later it was based on a much wider coalition with part of *Dash*, under the leadership of Yadin but without the Shinui group. In 1979 and 1980 Likud's popularity seemed to wane. In the elections of 1981 the non-religious electorate was for the first time in the history of the State of Israel split almost equally between Likud (48 members) and the *Maarach* (51 members), with the weakening of the small parties. So the second Likud government was formed, based on a coalition mainly with the religious group, this time with all the major portfolios (Prime Minister, Defence, Finance and Foreign Affairs) in the hands of the *Herut* party.

## Growing concerns and uncertainty

This series of political events and changes took place in a continuously growing turbulent atmosphere, with very strong feelings of uncertainty and uneasiness and internal conflicts and strong division in the country – all of which was indeed in marked contrast to the feelings of satisfaction and relative tranquillity which had reigned up to the first years after the Six Day War.

This change in the mood in Israel, which was so strong in contrast to the preceding period, was commented on by many journalists, foreign and Israeli alike.* In one way or another they all commented on the growing despondency in the Israeli public; on the growing visibility of, and concern with, economic problems in general and those of unemployment of the younger echelons, especially those leaving the army, in particular; on growing 'ethnic' divisions, and divisions between orthodox and secular groups; on some signs of relaxation of discipline in the army; on the growth of crime in general and on the developments of nuclei of organized crime and of drug problems in particular; on diminishing immigration and growing emigration; and the like. All these developments attested, in the words of the *Time* correspondent, 'to uncertainty about the country's direction'.

Even if such reports were, in the mode of topical journalistic reports, rather exaggerated, and in this instance in a magazine very often not too friendly towards Israel, they yet attested to a mood of apprehension prevalent in Israel, and one in marked contrast to that prevalent only ten or twelve years earlier. And whatever the exaggeration, and although there was no mention of the other side of the story – namely that of the strong internal solidarity prevalent in Israel, of the strong attachment and commitment on the part of large parts of the population to the State, of the fact that quite large parts of these complaints were made in the rather cosy atmosphere of Friday evening social get-togethers in affluent houses – such reports did convey some of the most salient aspects of this new mood, some of the major foci of apprehension and uneasiness prevalent in Israel.

Such reports captured the fact that large parts of the Israeli public – how large it is of course very difficult to ascertain, but large enough to be visible and vocal – had a growing sense, the roots of which were indeed in the Yom Kippur

* See for instance M. Mohs, 'Troubled Land of Zion', *Time*, 18 May 1981, pp. 29ff.

War, of the inability of the society, its leadership and institutions to deal adequately with some of its basic, central, internal and external problems.

## Growing apprehension

It was but natural – given both the great shock of the Yom Kippur War and the continuously growing centrality of the security dimensions of Israeli life – that such feelings of apprehension developed first of all with respect to the area of security and foreign affairs.

Two such areas were most obvious: first, the external relations of Israel in general and with the Arab countries in particular; and, second, the relations with the Arab population of the West Bank – of Judea and Samaria, as they were called for several years unofficially and officially by the Likud government.

The Yom Kippur War and its aftermaths shattered the feelings of relative security. Until then it was widely felt that the policy of relative immobility in the field of foreign relations, with informal diplomatic contacts and contacts through the USA and the UN, together with the relatively enlightened policy of the Military Government of the West Bank and the relatively quiet settlement policy in the West Bank, could provide a basis for some sort of ultimate settlement or could simply continue indefinitely.

Indeed later on the great achievements, in 1980 by the Begin government of peace with Egypt, and before this also (although obviously to a much lesser degree) of the agreement over separation of forces under the Rabin government, provided reasons for great satisfaction in this area.

Yet even these developments were connected with the intensification of the Palestinian problem and the initial denial of its existence by the Israeli leadership. The policy of settlement in the West Bank, undertaken first in a limited way by the Labour and later on intensified and highlighted and aggressively pursued by the Likud governments (especially by the second one), gave rise to growing tensions in Judea, Samaria and Gaza, and to continuous protests from many parts of the world – increasing within Israel feelings of uncertainty, apprehension and tensions within this area.

## The Changing International Atmosphere
### Growing criticisms and antagonisms

These feelings were intensified by the continuously growing rather negative international atmosphere and the changing image of Israel – even if in many cases these developments naturally led to the reinforcement, among parts of the Israeli public, of hard-line hawkish attitudes.

These changes in the international atmosphere – changes which also affected, as we shall see in greater detail later on, the attitudes of parts of the Jewish communities to Israel – started to take place after the Six Day War.

Israel's victory in the Six Day War underlined Israel's military prowess, but also imperceptibly gave rise to a tendency to see the Arabs in general, and above all the Palestinians, as the underdog. It eroded the image of Israel as a small David fighting against the mammoth Arab Goliath. The attitudes towards Israel that have since developed have indeed shown that for many people it went against the grain to see the Jews as victors, as no longer weak, potential victims of persecutions, to be protected. So in some parts of the Western world a latent anti-Semitism was awakened.

Several developments within Israel reinforced these attitudes. The first was the continuous occupation by Israel of the West Bank, of Judea and Samaria as it started to be called officially by the Likud government, which ruled as a military occupying power over a large Arab population. Jewish settlements were established there; first under the *Maarach* in the name of defence; later on and more intensively under the Likud government, under the aegis of a much more ideological emphasis, in which the historical and religious ties to the territory were stressed, and the concomitant growing tension between the military government and the Arab population.

The denial by most official Isreali leaders of the existence of a Palestinian problem – as evident for instance in Mrs Meir's famous saying 'I am a Palestinian' – combined as it was with what looked like a policy of relative immobility or at most a policy of reaction to initiatives coming from others – a situation which only partially changed later in 1979 in the Camp David agreements – also reinforced the negative attitudes towards Israel.

These developments took place at a period of growing strength of the Palestinian movement, its growing radicalization under the leadership of the PLO, with a long record of terrorist activities and with a declaration (The Palestinian Covenant) which denied the very legitimacy of the State of Israel, and which basically aimed at its destruction. At the same time there was growing sympathy in the international community, in Europe and the Third World but with the partial exception of the USA, towards these movements.

All these changes took place in the context of what Fritz Stern* has called the end of the post (second world) war era – in chronological conjunction with the Yom Kippur War – characterized by the weakening of the memory of the Second World War and of the Holocaust; the concomitant decline of the post-war alliances and, above all, confrontations between East and West; the preponderance of detente and its hopes; the weakening of the hegemony of the USA; and the sudden rise in 1973 of oil prices, to be weakened later from the late 1970s but to remain as a constant factor in international relations, attesting to the growing dependence of Western, especially European, countries and of Japan on the oil countries, both as suppliers of oil as well as sources of investment and trade.

These changes in the attitudes towards Israel also took place, in the West in general and the USA in particular, in the wake of the student rebellion of the late 1960s and early 1970s, and during the aftermath of the Vietnam War, with

* F. Stern, 'The End of the Post-War Era', *Commentary* (April 1974).

the development of extreme leftist movements with very weak commitment to institutional democracy, giving rise to continuous new crusades feeding on feelings of self-doubt and with the growing dominance of mass-media by left-wing intellectuals and the development of so-called engaged journalism.

All these developments greatly changed Israel's image among at least some sectors of the international community and necessarily impinged on the internal perception of its own identity inside Israel. The image of an heroic socialist democratic–liberal nation of pioneers – and soldiers – both creating a haven for refugees and constituting a new nation with a special civilizational message based on a combination of national and universal values, gradually changed into one of a self-enclosed nationalist society, with a very strong stress on military martial virtues, a society of oppressors who were unwilling to recognize the rights of others, politically inflexible or moving mainly in a militarily aggressive direction. Before the Six Day War Israel existed in a state of semi-siege, and its military virtues were seen just as a part of the building up of a new nation and of a strong civilian society. But when the direct military threat was at least partially weakened (but as the Yom Kippur War was to show, only very partially), its continuous military orientation was often seen as more and more predominant and, both from the outside but to some degree also from the inside, Israel was seen as living by its sword.

The effect of the Yom Kippur War was rather paradoxical: on the one hand the myth of Israel's military invincibility was weakened, but at the same time Israel continued to be seen as politically inflexible and military orientated.

These images were to become even more intensified under the Likud governments. Even if the peace with Egypt and the withdrawal from Sinai changed the image of inflexibility for some time, it was to be revived again by the expanding settlement policy and the Lebanon War.

Interestingly enough in many cases the supporters of Israel were found more and more among right-wing elements – such as the Movement for Moral Majority in the USA or the Christian Democrats in Germany, rather than in the traditional socialist or liberal ones. On the whole, the older socialists continued to support Israel, while the younger leftists became more and more ambivalent, outrightly critical and even antagonistic. Even many supporters of Israel sometimes expressed feelings of being tired of the continuation of the problem, of the continuous need to support the Israeli cause.

## Worsening of diplomatic relations

Israel's international diplomatic situation also worsened. After the Six Day War the Eastern bloc, with the exception of Romania, severed diplomatic relations with Israel, and after the Yom Kippur War most of the African countries followed suit – although economic relations were maintained and even expanded.

At the same time the problem of the Palestinians became more and more visible in the international scene, especially in the UN General Assembly, as well as in many international organizations. All these organizations became an arena for vicious attacks against Israel, and there were many anti-Israel resolutions, the most prominent and extreme among which was probably that of November 1977, equating Zionism with racism. The advocates of these resolutions hoped to delegitimize the State of Israel, as well as to legitimize almost any attack on Jews and Jewish organizations – often claiming, as was the case on several campuses in England and Canada, that organizations which support a racist State should not be allowed to function.

While the framing of these resolutions in the UN or in many of its branches – such as UNESCO, the World Health Organization or others – attested to the force of the automatic anti-Western majority in these bodies – composed of the Communists, Arabs and large parts of the Third World – it was properly denounced by Patrick Moynihan, serving then as the US Ambassador to the UN, and later by Jeane Kirkpatrick. But it still illustrated the fact that Israel had become an easy target and scapegoat of such anti-Israeli forces. Often it was only the intervention of the USA, sometimes together with some other Western countries, that obviated extreme resolutions against Israel or attempts at its expulsion.

But even in many of the Western countries, there seemed to be a shift in public opinion. Certainly the media was not very favourable towards Israel. While the polls seemed to show a somewhat greater continuity of support for Israel there was more criticism, as well as support for some at least of the Arab countries.

Of very great interest here was the overall reaction of international public opinion – especially in most European and Third World countries – to one of the greatest achievements of this era – the peace with Egypt, signed in 1980 and culminating in April 1982, after a period of very intensive internal turmoil, in Israel's withdrawal from Sinai. While both these achievements were in principle applauded, only in the USA were they seen as central or crucial. Much more vocal, especially in Europe, were such forums as the European Community in Venice, or the Socialist International, which claimed that these agreements were inadequate, because of the lack of a 'total' peaceful solution with all the Arab countries in general, and the lack of a solution to the question of the Palestinians as a collective entity or a nation in particular.

Anti-Semitism, which till then had been latent in many European countries but seemingly publicly unaccepted, from the late 1970s and especially later, in the wake of the Lebanon War, became very vocal, especially among leftist groups. The difference between anti-Zionism, anti-Israelism and anti-Semitism often became blurred, giving rise to an implicit or explicit delegitimization of the State of Israel and of Jewish peoplehood.

All these developments in the international field – whether in different arenas of international public opinion abroad, or in the diplomatic field, the multiplication of one-sided anti-Israeli UN resolutions and continuous international terrorism – naturally weakened that feeling of security and self-satisfaction which had prevailed in Israel, and impinged on the collective self-image of different sectors of Israeli society – leading, as we shall see, to the development among them of different often contradictory developments.

# Growing Apprehension about Internal Problems
## *The problems in the forefront of the debate*

The feelings of uneasiness were not confined, however, to the field of external relations and of security. They developed, especially after the Yom Kippur War, and became more and more widespread, vocal and articulated, with respect to many problems on the internal front, to many aspects of the internal scene.

There was a growing sense of the inability of the society and its leadership to deal adequately with some of Israel's basic, central, internal and external problems which were closely related to the very core of its collective self-identity – problems which just a few years earlier either had not been noticed to such a great extent, or had been seen as being adequately dealt with within the framework of the regnant institutional mould.

Many were problems which had been continuous on the Israeli scene: the increase in the crime rate and the development of organized crime, as reported by a special Judicial Committee set up by the government in 1969 (the Shimron Committee); the continuous growth of inflation; repeated labour conflicts, especially in the public sector and very often initiated by the stronger and more affluent elements in the publicly employed labour – such as the pilots and other echelons of El Al (whose salaries, especially those of the pilots, were far beyond anything comparable in the Israeli private sector), or by the workers of the Electricity company, whose workers enjoyed many privileges (such as an unlimited, tax free, supply of electricity for their homes). Similarly more and more concern was voiced about the proliferation, under the very aegis of the authorities – whether in the Ministry of Finance or the Histadrut – of various semi-official 'under the table' wage and salary arrangements, throwing doubt at the very validity of the public norms and integrity of the norm-setters.

Also voiced in public debates were problems, such as the ethnic one or the social ones of poverty, of the so-called different disadvantaged groups, and of the occupational discrepancies between the Orientals and the Western groups. Moreover the tone of such debates became much more aggressive and militant, and there developed a growing apprehension about their manageability.

Conflicts between religious and secular sectors of Israeli society also seemed to become intensified. There were demonstrations or outright rioting, above all by the more extreme orthodox groups, against the passing of traffic on the Sabbath near their quarters, against archaeological expeditions which they claimed were desecrating Jewish cemeteries, or against the growing attempts by the religious groups to impose more and more of their demands on public life.

Another new development was that of the influx of Arab labour into the Israeli economy after the Six Day War, making them a major part of unskilled and skilled labour and imperceptibly changing the whole ideological basis of Labour–Zionism with respect to the non-colonial aspect of Jewish economy.

## The feeling of normlessness; cases of corruption

However, of crucial importance was the fact that this intensified concern about problems became very closely connected, as indicated above, with a feeling of rather general normlessness and above all with the rumours and cases of corruption in high places. This corruption seemed to differ from the exploit-ation by individuals of their positions for small benefits (such as the employees of some departments of the Jewish Agency, discovered by the then Comptroller of the Agency), or accusations of the use of public funds for various party activities (as was the case of Yitzhak Raphael), which were prevalent in the 1950s. It seemed that the rule of law had become more established in the meantime and the criticism of the public sector on such counts became abated. But in the early 1970s there were much more dramatic cases of corruption of central public figures, of high financial officials very close to Pinhas Sapir, the prominent Minister of Finance; Director General of Kupat Holim. A central figure in *Mapai* and the Histadrut, and an official candidate for the Governorship of the Bank of Israel, were found to be guilty in having misused their positions for the accumulation of private wealth, in some cases contravening the severe foreign exchange regulations. Another high official from the Department of Customs was also found guilty of contravening these regulations. There were rumours and press reports about the investigation by the Police and the Attorney General of the then Minister of Housing, which led to his suicide. Later on, in 1977, there was, on a smaller scale, the contravention of foreign exchange regulations by the wife of the Prime Minister.

## The trend to emigration

Equally important was the growing sensitivity to several problems touching on some of the central nerves of Israel's Zionist vision of a small society which at the same time aspired to constitute a centre of cultural and institutional creativity of some universal significance and a centre of the Jewish people and a point of attraction to them – problems touching on central aspects of the construction of the Israeli collective identity.

First of all – and above all – the relations with the Diaspora became of continuously growing concern and public debate. The most central problem here was the problem of Israel's place among the Jewish people, of its relation to the Jewish communities in the Diaspora; and it was the whole problem of Aliya and *Yerida*, of immigration to Israel and emigration from it, that became a central focus of concern.

The relatively small number of *olim* – of new immigrants – to Israel; the seemingly large (often exaggerated) number of *Yordim* (i.e. of Israelis who emigrated); the fact that in some years the immigration did not even cover the emigration; the very continuity of *Yordim*, including many highly qualified personnel, some from among members of Kibbutzim as well as others who had served in select army units; the many, often of course exaggerated, successes of these *Yordim*, as well as of many North African Jews who went to France, Canada or the USA, which were often portrayed as lands of great opportunity against the drab reality of Israel: all these factors seemed to touch the central Zionist nerve of Israel's self-identity.

Within this context, of special interest was the concern about the Russian Jews, those Jews who were allowed to leave Russia. The central fact here was that over the years fewer of them were choosing to go to Israel, but went instead from Vienna or Rome – their first stepping-stone in the West – to the USA or to other Western countries. This fact gave rise to a rather acrimonious controversy between the Jewish Agency and the Government of Israel and several Jewish organizations, above all the Hebrew Immigration Aid Society (HIAS), when the former accused the latter that their aid to Jews leaving Russia with Israeli visas diverted these same Jews from coming to Israel; the latter implicitly or explicitly claimed that these attacks clearly avoided the main issue – namely Israel's lack of attraction for most immigrants.

Probably of no smaller concern was the fact that Israel did not even seem to be the natural place of refuge for persecuted Jews: those from Iran either remained or moved to Western countries; while of the Latin American Jews, a great many of whom had left their countries of origin where they feared leftist or rightist persecutions, only a few went to Israel compared with those who went to various Western countries, even to Spain.*

# Changing Attitudes Towards Israel among the Jewish Communities
## Israel's changing image

In a wider context, there was growing concern about the changes in the relations between the State of Israel and the Jewish communities in the Diaspora.

These changes first became apparent – often quite dramatically – in the changes of Israel's image among large parts of the Jewish communities in the Diaspora in general, and probably in the USA in particular. For two and a half decades Jewish communities in the Diaspora had on the whole basked in the glory of the image of Israel as a small heroic nation, a democratic–liberal nation of pioneers and soldiers, creating both a haven for refugees and a model society, building a new nation, carrying a special civilizational message based on a combination of national and universal values.

* For greater detail on this trend see Drora Kass and S. M. Lipset, 'Jewish Immigration to the United States 1967 to the Present: Israelis and Others' in M. Sklare, *Understanding American Jewry* (New Brunswick and London 1982), pp. 272–95.

In fact the very nature of this image already denoted in itself a far-reaching shift from the original Zionist vision, from the Zionist premises on which the State of Israel was based and in terms of which it legitimized itself. But whatever this shift, this emphasis, together with a very strong emphasis on overall Jewish solidarity and on Israel as the major epitome and guarantee of this solidarity, constituted the major components of Israel's image among the Jewish communities. And it was this image that was gradually, but often dramatically, eroded – especially after the Yom Kippur War. The aftermath of the Yom Kippur War brought a weakening of the image of military supremacy and strength, a growing financial and military dependence on the USA, a growing criticism of various aspects of Israel's policies – especially with respect to settlements on the West Bank, Judea or Samaria; the erosion of Israel's image in the international community.

There was a weakening of the image of Israel as a centre and focus of security for the Jewish people and of its institution-building capacity or mission. Thus, for instance, in 1973 Nathan Glaser put it in a rather extreme tone:

Thus American Jews are doubly exposed: by the new ethnic frankness domestically, by their need to support with all the influence they possess very heavy assistance for Israel from the United States.

It is not a comfortable position to be in. Jews for the most part have wanted to be like everyone else. Indeed, ironically, the establishment of Israel was an effort to make Jews like everyone else: they would now have a state; they would no longer be an odd, homeless people, but a people like all other peoples. It has not worked out that way. Israel has made Jews more, not less, exceptional. No other state is the object of such nearly universal execration. No other state knows that losing a war means its destruction and disappearance. The pariah people, it seems, have simply succeeded in creating a pariah state. In America the Jews have never been a pariah people, but the special place of Israel forces them into a politically unique situation. It will no longer do any good to point to the fact that the Irish also love Ireland, the Poles Poland, the Greeks Greece. These nations demand little from their ethnic kinsmen overseas, and they thus demand little from the United States. Even American Greeks, who are just now as passionate about Greece, as Jews are about Israel, want nothing from the United States except that it should stop sending arms to Greece's enemy.

Is this picture overdrawn? Mass-media treatment of the Middle East in recent months suggests to me it is not. It is no longer the case that Israel has a good press in the United States, surprising as that may seem when one considers that Israel is an open, democratic society with an almost unparalleled measure of social justice and with a record of remarkably good treatment of its Arab minority, even though this minority must inevitably be considered closely allied to the movements and states that are attempting to destroy Israel. After all, the United States, under a much lesser threat, and with no evidence connecting the Japanese Americans with subversion, removed that entire group from the West Coast, in World War II and confined it in relocation camps. Israel is opposed by dictatorships, one-party states, and authoritarian regimes (leaving aside Lebanon, which is not a 'confrontation state'), whose accomplishments are meager and whose record in oppressing their own peoples, opposition parties, and minorities is great. That these regimes should now be presented by *Time* magazine, by major columnists in the New York *Times* and contributors to its Op-Ed page, and by commentators on the national TV news programs as moderate, desirous of peace, and understandably concerned only with the recovery of conquered lands, while Israel is presented as – the word has apparently now been permanently tacked to the Jewish state – intransigent, is startling . . .*

Such sentiments were to some degree dampened by the growth of anti-Semitism in Europe and even in the USA, yet such anti-Semitic outbursts were often connected with events in Israel, and together with Israel's political orientations and activities, weakened the perception of Israel as a bastion of security or at least made it more problematic.

## Changing patterns of support for Israel

Far-reaching changes also seemed to gather momentum with respect to the evaluation on the part of Jewish communities of various aspects of Israel's life: its institutional creativity and quality of life.

If on the one hand the themes of Jewish solidarity continued to appeal to large parts of the Jewish communities, in other parts – professional, economic or intellectual – there were growing criticisms of the nature of the Israeli economy, of the disappearance in Israel of the Jewish economic genius, of the seemingly greater Jewish academic achievement abroad than in Israel, of the provinciality of life in Israel and the like. Forgotten was the fact that all achievements of Jews in the Diaspora in these fields were achieved within an institutional framework in which the basic economic and political and educational infrastructure, defence and service were taken care of by the general society along with problems of security, of absorption and development. In a rather paradoxical way, these criticisms of Israel were also supported by trends from within Israel. The experience of the *Yordim*, their own view of America as a land in which Jews could seemingly do better than in Israel, could often be quoted to support such a thesis. The same was the case with respect to the contacts of many Israelis with the Jewish communities in which the former looked up to the opportunities available abroad.

Concomitantly the extent and mode of support of Israel among Jewish communities also changed. True enough, most of the Jewish political and communal organizations continuously rallied to the political support of Israel in times of political crises such as the Yom Kippur War, or various political confrontations with the US government. Yet with the passing of time, with the shattering of its image as invincible, with the growing political isolation of Israel after the Yom Kippur War, the whole moral ambience, as well as probably the extent of this support, changed.

Such support was already coupled with growing discussion and debate about the Israeli policies among Jewish circles and groups, and, just as within Israel, there was no consensus with respect to many of Israel's policies, above all those of settlement in Judea and Samaria, the attitudes towards the Arab population,

* N. Glaser, 'The Exposed American Jew', *Commentary* (June 1975).

and the whole problem of the solution of the Palestinian question. In a more vocal and extreme way this criticism found its expression among Jewish intellectuals identified with Israel, who voiced strong misgivings in special announcements signed by leading Jewish intellectuals in the *New York Times*, criticizing the Begin government's settlement policies.

Needless to say, there continued to be strong support for Israel and for its policies among quite large parts of the Jewish communities – but it was no longer as widespread as before, nor could it be taken as given, and the problem of the right of Jewish leadership and communities to dissent publicly from the policies of the Israeli government became a central problem of discussion in Jewish circles and in different types of encounters with Israelis.

There was also a certain erosion or at least weakening of support for Israel among at least some parts of the Jewish communities. It was not necessarily an active erosion. It was manifest above all in weaker participation in different activities in support of Israel; whether it be the Walk for Israel in New York or pro-Israel rallies. Such erosion was probably much stronger among intellectuals and students living in liberal universalistically orientated environments than among the wider groups of Jews; but even among the latter the amount of commitment to active support for Israel could no longer be taken for granted. Significantly enough, whatever Aliya was coming from the West was composed mostly of different variants of orthodox circles, and the older type of 'liberal' or 'socialist' Aliya had almost entirely disappeared.

## Changes in the perception of Israel and Diaspora relations

All these developments led, in one way or another, to the weakening of the perception of the centrality of Israel in Jewish life, or at least to the changing of the mode of this centrality which seemed to have been accepted in the former period and above all largely taken for granted by the Israelis themselves; they also weakened the negative evaluation of Galut which was a central part of the basic Zionist premises implicit in the State of Israel, and which, while not accepted in the Diaspora, had hitherto been rarely challenged openly.

This found its expressions in many different ways and forms. It was expressed in a very civil way in the words of Simone Weil in Jerusalem as she was conferred an honorary degree by the Hebrew University:

Today Judaism's values are integrated in a State, they are integrated in a society, a society which has not existed for more than 2000 years. And we, of the Diaspora, hope that Israel will remain the defender of these values, of this Humanism. We must clearly say that this is certainly more difficult situated in the position of a State, no longer in that obligatory minoritarian position, to continue to carry a flame like this.

And I hope as a Frenchwoman, but as a French Jewish woman, and a Jewish French woman, that our countries will help each other to continue carrying this flame and that they will ceaselessly defend these values, whatever happens. And I know that for every State this is sometimes difficult, that for every State there is a need to mobilize, that

States find themselves confronted with situations which could be 'raisons d'Etat'; but that precisely we have always been proud in a certain way of being above that, of having something more, which has been possibly forced; and today, what I hope is, that the miracle of Israel, the miracle of Jerusalem will reproduce itself, and I am sure that this challenge (I am sure of it and do not just hope it) that this challenge will be your victory and ours . . .

In a more extreme way this new attitude found its expressions in public declarations, made by many Jewish leaders, of the equality of standing of the Diaspora and Israel in Jewish life – a declaration also to be found in a report on Israeli–Diaspora relations prepared for the World Jewish Congress with the active participation of Professor H. Ben Shahar, then President of Tel Aviv University.

In an even more malicious vein the various criticisms of Israel found expression in a series of articles by the late Nahum Goldmann. He was a former member of the Zionist Executive, and later in the 1950s and 1960s became the President of the Zionist Organization, the architect of the reparation agreement with Germany, and for a long period President of the World Jewish Congress. In his time he was one of the rising stars of the Zionist Movement, yet he refused – despite many calls and invitations, and despite his self-portrayal as a great opponent of Ben-Gurion's basic conceptions, especially in foreign policy – to settle in Israel and become involved in its political life. In these articles, published especially in German and French media, he denounced many of Israel's policies as well as many aspects of Israeli life – in one of them, describing Israel as a nation of speculators.

Whatever the strength of the more articulated of these expressions, some of these sentiments became relatively widespread among the Jewish leaders of the Diaspora, attesting to a shift in the image of Israel. Also indicative of such trends were the attempts which developed in the USA in the late 1970s and early 1980s to dissociate the Holocaust from its close relation with Israeli rebirth and make it a central focus of Jewish identity.

## Changes in the attitudes of the Israelis

All these developments, however abhorrent or repulsive to many Israelis, could only impinge on the construction of the components of Israeli identity, on self-perception within Israel itself, both weakening the overall self-assurance of the Israelis and transforming some of the themes of such identity into new directions.

There was indeed a noticeable change in the Israelis' attitudes to such criticism. In the earlier decades of the State, Israelis would not usually accept the possibility of such criticisms, stressing their own 'almost natural' – in terms of the Zionist vision – superiority to the Jews in the Galut, denouncing the *Yordim* not only officially but also in daily life.

The picture has changed greatly since the late 1970s. Some of these attitudes – especially against the *Yordim* – persisted on the official level but not necessarily on the level of daily social contacts. Even on the official level the protests against the pronouncements of the various Jewish personalities in praise of the Galut were not very strong, and in daily life more and more Israelis tended to accept the fact of *Yordim* as well as the existence of the Diaspora (very rarely now called the Galut) as parts of Jewish life, and sometimes even with some envy. There were indeed some far-reaching changes in their own view of the Diaspora.

# Summary
## *Indications of the disintegration of the initial institutional moulds of Israeli society*

The awareness of all these problems – internal and external alike – and the growing sensitivity to them, became more interwoven with public life in general and the politial struggle in particular. First of all it became closely connected with the growing importance of public and political life: non-parliamentary movements; protest movements – which were so vocal after the Yom Kippur War and which contributed to the fall of Mrs Meir's government; the strong extra-parliamentary movements; the extreme religious groups, such as *Gush Emunim*, the left-wing *Shalom Achshav* (Peace Now), and the extreme ethnic movements. All these occupied an increasingly central place in Israeli political life; and all of them articulated in some way the feeling of dissatisfaction with the ways these problems were coped with by the centre.

These concerns and apprehensions became even more closely interwoven with the elections in 1977 and 1981 and the antecedent public debates and discussions, with the growing feelings of divisiveness in the country, and with the growing incidence of violence – above all, but not only, the verbal violence and lawlessness that seemed to characterize public life in Israel after the mid-1970s and which we shall analyse in greater detail later on.

This was all also connected with the growing concern about developments within Israel since the late 1960s, especially on the cultural scene, above all the growth of various types of religious movements, of ethnic consciousness and militancy, all indicating some changes in the basic components of Israeli identity.

This close interweaving of the apprehension about the major problems with extremist political movements, with growing political polarization and violence, with growing attention to the changing format of Israeli identity, indicates that it was not just a simple multiplication or intensification of the different problems that was taking place in Israel. Indeed it is doubtful that it was just the magnitude of these problems that was at the root of the far-reaching changes that Israeli society has been undergoing since at least the Yom Kippur War. In fact were these problems unique to Israel?

Obviously there were some very specific Israeli problems – above all those connected with the security problem, or with the relations with the Arab countries. But it is a moot question whether they were 'objectively' greater than in former periods of the history of the Yishuv or of the State of Israel.

But most of the internal problems could be found in other societies. The intensity of labour conflicts and of economic problems did not necessarily go beyond those of other industrial and post-industrial societies. The rate of inflation was certainly extremely high, but there were many mechanisms – such as the different types of indexing of wages – which cushioned against many of the hardships of inflation. While crime statistics are notoriously unreliable, there is no need to assume that the rates of crime in Israel were higher than in other modern societies.

Again many of the economic problems were very acute, but were not unique – with the possible exception of the growth of Arab labour as a basic component of the Israeli economic structure and which went against the older Labour–Zionist premises, and even that could easily be compared to the *Gastarbeiter* in Europe. Moreover all these problems developed against the background of the continuously increasing standard of living of almost all sectors of the population.

The ethnic problems developed against the background of continuous economic advancement, which in many ways could be compared to the ethnic upheaval that developed in the USA and to some degree in Europe in the 1970s. Indeed the very connotation of 'Black Panthers' points to this connection.

The international problems, the developments in the West Bank, were indeed very acute, but even here, at least until 1981, they were countered by the peace with Egypt, by the very lack of success of the Arabs to overthrow or annihilate Israel with its growing military strength. While the worsening of the international atmosphere was indeed acute, it could be partially countered by the very success of Israel to continue to develop in many ways in spite of it. Even the Yom Kippur War was, from a purely military point of view, a success and paradoxically enough opened up the way to peace.

Thus it is doubtful that it was just the magnitude of these problems that could indeed justify the feelings of apprehension, uneasiness, almost of loss of control that became rather widespread after the Yom Kippur War. Indeed some leaders, as for instance Moshe Dayan, claimed that it was such apprehension that constituted the main failure of Israeli society rather than the alleged failure of the political and military leadership during the Yom Kippur War and after it.

All these developments indicate that what has happened since at least the aftermath of the Yom Kippur War, has not been just a combination of difficult times and political changes. More than this, perhaps above all, there has been a process of decomposition or disintegration of that institutional mould which was regnant in Israel from at least the establishment of the State, of some at least of its premises and basic orientations, of its legitimation and organiz-ational–institutional frameworks.

How can this great change and its timing be explained? In the following chapters we shall attempt to analyse the reasons of the decomposition of this initial institutional mould.

# CHAPTER 15

# The Conditions of the Disintegration of the Initial Institutional Mould of Israeli Society

## I · Institutional Processes; Transformation and Exhaustion of Ideology

### Introduction
#### *The transformation of post-revolutionary societies*

The processes which led to the disintegration of the initial institutional mould of Israeli society were rooted in, or can be fully understood in connection with, several historical and structural processes which developed within that society since at least the first decade of the State. They were touched upon, but only implicitly, in the preceding chapters in which we analysed the major institutional formations which crystallized during the first decades of Israeli society. These processes can be traced to some common root, to a common core or at least to a common denominator, of the processes of transformation of revolutionary societies and of the problems which such transformation engenders. Israeli society has shared, as we have seen, many such processes of transformation and problems with other post-revolutionary societies: USSR, Mexico, many of the New Nations and perhaps even early nineteenth-century USA. The central focus of this process has been the transformation of the leaders of revolutionary groups and sects into the ruling elites, and the routinization of revolutionary visions and ideologies. They have also been connected, in all modern post-revolutionary societies, with the several structural processes attendant on the processes of modernization and economic development – mainly of growing social occupational differentiation and the transformation of the major elites.

But, as we have seen, the concrete contours of these processes, the problems they engendered, as well as the mode of response to them, differed greatly in different post-revolutionary societies and the Israeli scene naturally evinces some characteristics of its own. These characteristics were influenced – as in all such societies – by the specific historical circumstances of the development of Israeli society and by its specific ideological orientations and institutional contours.

The most important such structural processes, of crucial importance for our analysis, that developed in Israel, were, first, the far-reaching changes which took place in the structure and interrelations of the leading elites in general and in their relations to the political one in particular; second, the changes in the relations of all the elites to the broader strata of sectors of the society; third, the weakening, within different sectors of Israeli society, of many frameworks of solidarity, and especially of those frameworks which brought together both different elites and different types of social activities; and fourth – and unique in Israel – the changing relations between the Jewish community in the State of Israel and the Jewish communities in the Diaspora.

## Changes in Elite Structure
### Patterns of solidarity

The first such process was that of far-reaching changes in the structure of the major elites, the interrelations among them and between them. Of special importance here were, first, the growing specialization of different elites and the growing segregation between them, and second the changes in the nature of interrelations between them in general and between them and the political elites in particular. Third, and closely connected with the former, was the weakening of many of the common frameworks of solidarity and relations in which they all participated.

Finally there were changes in the nature of the connection between their respective spheres of activity and their relations to the centre, to the political elite, and in the mode of their participation in the political process.

Thus, from the late 1940s and early 1950s, contrary to the basic ideological premises – even if these premises were not fully implemented in the concrete situation that existed in the period of the Yishuv – there developed in Israel a continuous process of differentiation and growing segregation between the major elites – economic, military, academic, cultural – and changes in the relations between them and the political elite in particular. These developments were in relative contrast to the situation in the period of the Yishuv, although the embryonic elements of these developments had existed then. It was however only in the State of Israel, from about the mid- or late 1950s, that these developments were given full momentum.

Each such elite was indeed granted maximum autonomy within its special institutional arenas. Before all of them – or almost all of them – there opened up far-reaching opportunities of advance, careers and attainment of high standards of life. At the same time they became more and more dissociated from one another, and above all the mode of relations between them changed.

Thus frameworks of common activity and interaction and of solidarity between them became weakened in general, and in relation to the political elite in particular. Most of these elites became dissociated from active participation in the centre, giving rise to the concomitant gradual atrophy of the political process in the central political frameworks.

The growing specialization of different elites – the economic, academic, bureaucratic, civil service, professional, cultural and journalistic – was of course, as in most other modern societies in general and post-revolutionary ones in particular, to some degree a natural result of economic development and modernization and of the development of the State, with its numerous organizational frameworks. Such specialization did, of course, naturally bear in itself the seeds of growing autonomy, and a certain segregation or dissociation of elites. But it seems that these possibilities developed in Israel in a very far-reaching way, while at the same time these developments were also to no small degree contrary to some at least of the basic ideological premisses and self-image of the society.

## Political participation

All these processes of segregation of elites took place also in the relations between all the other elites and the political elite – a relation which was probably the most important of all the processes analysed here.

While, in all the other fields, new arenas of activity and avenues of mobility opened up before large sectors of the population, this was not true of the political field. Instead, in the political field, there developed, as we have seen above, a growing oligarchization of the upper echelons of the political elite and a concomitant professionalization of the middle echelons of party 'activities'.

In most of the older parties, the relative closure in semi-oligarchic frameworks extended, as mentioned, to second and third level echelons of professional political activities, to those echelons whose major source of income was in party activity (membership in the Knesset, in the various parts of the Histadrut bureaucracy or in the parties themselves) and who, naturally, became very dependent on the upper elites of the party.

Moreover, these secondary political elites or activities were not on the whole among the more active or autonomous sectors of the population and, through their very dependence on the central elite, thus strengthened the control of the latter over access to the participation in the centre.

Very few avenues of autonomous political expression and organization were opened up for many younger groups or for new immigrant elements, and the centres of the parties attempted on the whole to control most such activities, not allowing much direct autonomous organization or political expression. The same, to a very large degree, was true of the other elites. Perhaps most significant from the point of view of our discussion is the fact that the various non-political elites – obviously the military, but also the academic, cultural, journalistic or economic one – did not participate and were not encouraged by the central or secondary political elites to participate actively in the central political process, except in rather symbolic ways, such as the election of individuals (who remained rather powerless in the centres of the parties themselves) to the Knesset or some honorific party positions.

Thus, initially, there developed accordingly in Israel what Jonathan Shapira has called an establishment without political power, i.e. a network of upper elites in close social relations and contacts with one another, but without any effective political power. Later on, even the nature of these common social and ideological bonds and bonds of solidarity between the various elites became weakened and transformed, although there developed, of course, a great variety of close personal networks between different groups and sectors. But these networks became more and more focused on the private sphere, on mutual beliefs in various institutional activities, and on distribution of resources, and much less on participation in the political life or in the centre, or in common frameworks of institutional creativity – beyond the sphere of each elite.

The other side of all these processes was the atrophization of the process of selection of the political elites of all the parties and of the internal party-political process, and the weakening of the internal solidarity within the political formations. This weakening became clearly evident in the later attempts to broaden the upper political elite by recruiting new leadership elements from different elite sectors and, above all, directly from the army, without making them undergo periods of active socialization in the political life of their respective parties.

It was the relation between the different elites and the political arena – connected as they were with changes in that arena – that changed the nature of the contacts and interrelations between the different elites in Israeli society.

Naturally enough contacts between such different elites did of course continue, at least on two levels: first, on the purely social one, although even here changes, gradually but continuously, took place; and, second, on the level of decision-making, as bearing on the areas of activities between the different elites – especially between the political and military elite, but to a smaller degree between the political and administrative elites on the one hand and the economic on the other.

But such contacts – especially those bearing on the decision-making process – took place less and less within common settings which were based either on common background and/or on participation in common socio-political frameworks, be they parties, movements or clubs, and became more and more limited to different, often separate decision-making networks.

Such growing dissociation became also more and more visible in the relations between the political and the different cultural elites – the academic, literary, artistic ones and the elites of the media.

## New relations between the elites

All these processes were obviously rather slow to develop. In the first decade, perhaps even the first two decades of the State of Israel, most at least of the upper elites still belonged to a generation or generations which grew up in the different common frameworks and continued to maintain at least relatively close social contacts, although even here the trend to grow apart, to the weakening of such contacts and to the growing seemingly natural closure of each elite, began to be apparent.

Similarly, in the first decade or two after the establishment of the State of Israel, at least some of the different elites continued to meet in some common framework, to maintain common discussions – whether the meetings of Ben-Gurion with leading intellectuals, those in the ideological centres of the different sectors of the Labour Movement, or similar ones of other sectors – as well as through the various personal networks which continued from the previous period. Even though all these discussions and meetings became more and more dissociated from centres of decision-making – and within the latter there was less and less autonomous participation of different elites – yet the ambience of such common participation, of open channels of communication and influence persisted.

With the passing of time, with the growing effects of the structural developments attendant on the great institutional expansion which started in the 1950s, and with the emergence of new generations of elites, the tendency to such relative segregation, to the weakening of common frameworks and to the development of the new modes of discourse became more and more visible.

It became more visible among all elites. First it was seen in the middle, and later on also in the higher, echelons of the military – now more and more coming out of the more specialized military school and formations, tending even, to some degree at least, to live in relatively separate neighbourhoods (like Zahala in Tel Aviv). It also became visible in the academic field, where there was a very rapid expansion of more and more specialized fields and a parallel natural tendency to some de facto social segregation among writers and artists; also in the civil service among the professions and among the economic elites and entrepreneurs. Social contacts between these various elites – very often based also on common school or university background – naturally continued; yet they were more diversified, less extensive and, above all, much less orientated to participation in common spheres of activities in general and in the centre in particular.

Somewhat later on, from the late 1960s or early 1970s, the focus of common debates around public issues shifted more and more from common discussion frameworks to mass-media and, although their public resonance might have been great, in some cases at least, needless to say, the whole mode of relations to the centre changed. This change was, of course, connected with the growing importance of media specialists and with the assumption, by many political figures, of the role not only of participants in a debate, but also of commentators. Moreover this weakened even more the connections between decision-making, possible shaping of public opinion and participation in common socio-political frameworks.

## The elites and the process of strata formation

The full impact of these changes in the structure of elites on the processes of transformation of Israeli society can only be understood if we take into account the connection between them and the processes of economic development and strata formation that were taking place in Israeli society during this period and which we analysed above.

This period was one of rather intensive economic growth and of upward social mobility, of the formation of new strata and status groups in general, and the processes of segregation of elites became closely connected with the crystallization of these strata in general and the upper ones in particular, with a growing difference between the standards and life styles of the upper and lower strata, combined as they were by a growing emphasis on continuous rises in the level and relatively conspicuous standards of life.

Almost all the upper elites participated in this trend even if, of course, in varying degrees – the new economic elites, often created through the very policies of the Labour governments, taking the lead and the others, including some of the political elite, following.

Truly enough, the most outstanding of the older generation of Labour leaders – Ben-Gurion, Eshkol, Golda Meir, Pinhas Sapir (the great architect of economic expansion of the 1950s and 1960s) – maintained a relatively modest life style, not going against the premisses of the older pioneering ethos, or at least not contravening them publicly. But even they, especially perhaps Sapir, legitimized – by their continuous attendance at various social occasions – the conspicuous life style that developed among many prominent professional, economic and also military elites. The younger generation and second level of elites tended to develop much more lucrative and ostentatious life styles, or at least orientations to them.

Thus in fact the various elites – including the political one – which implemented the major policies analysed above became in a way naturally strongly interwoven into the upper economic strata that developed a style of life which stressed a continuous rise in the standard of living and a relatively high emphasis on conspicuous consumption. Moreover, while their solidarity might have become weakened, yet these elites often became – as those elites of many small countries – crystallized into closely related, and relatively closed, networks, thus emphasizing even more their distance from other strata.

Inadvertently, in all these ways, these elites transformed themselves into a sort of upper stratum of a social democratic state, and not an elite of a society with a continuing pioneering vision – thus developing patterns of behaviour which were against the premisses of many symbols of that very ideology according to which they legitimized themselves.

# Changes in the Dominant Ethos
## *The transformation of the Labour–Zionist ideology*

These developments in the structure of elites were closely connected with some of the central aspects of the transformation of the Labour–Zionist ideology – which we have analysed above – and especially with the process of growing dissociation between different components of the ideology. There were very far-reaching changes in its contents in general and in the relative emphasis on the different themes within it in particular.

Thus first of all there was a marked change in the general ambience of its contents – above all a weakening of the pioneering elitist orientation stressing duties, commitment and standards of performance, as against the strengthening of the orientation or emphases on ascriptive rights, entitlements and the distribution of rewards by the centre.

Concomitantly, there developed a marked shift in the balance between individualistic–distributive and the collectivistic elements and components of the ideology – the orientations to commitment, to collective goals. The former orientation became more connected with the various distributive policies, while the second became channelled into the purely symbolic realm.

It was only within parts at least of the military service that the strong commitment to collective goals and symbols and stress on performance were also channelled into specific institutional channels.

The aspect of this transformation most closely related to the changes in the structure of the elites, was probably the fact that almost no attempt was made to find new ways of participation of broader groups or strata in the new institutional expansion, nor of combining such participation of the various emerging specialized elites, as well as of the broader social echelons, with active participation in the centre in general and with respect to the policies through which such institution-building was guided in particular.

In general, this ideology developed, parallel to the transformation of the elites, into a broad social democratic direction, without any strong class or socialist connotations, but also without any strong emphasis on the ways of participation in institution-building or pioneering – thus, indeed becoming rather exhausted in this realm. But at the same time, the pioneering orientation and ethos of elitist participations were those that continued to constitute the pivot of the legitimation of the ruling elite and of the regime.

## *New perceptual mould; new attitudes to the environment*

The combination of all these processes did indeed have some very far-reaching repercussions on the whole ambience and structure of Israeli society and its basic premises. It had far-reaching repercussions on the basic ethos, especially on the basic pioneering ethos, of the society – on its basic modes, attitudes and orientations to the world and to the construction of its own world and environments, on the modes of orientation and thought among the leading sectors of Israeli society, and on the changing patterns of innovation and creativity within it. All this culminated in the exhaustion of the central institution-building, social, political and cultural dimension of the Labour–Zionist ideology, and gave rise to a search – in multiple directions – of new avenues for the recrystallization of these dimensions.

The combination of strong future orientation, social innovation and elitist service with social activity gave way to different patterns of orientations. The strong future orientations that were characteristic of the older pioneer became weakened; there was a growing conflation of the future with the present – or at least a weakening of the differences or tensions between them. The vision of the future was more and more being identified with the present, giving rise – to use the expression of Nathan Rotenstreich, professor of philosophy at the Hebrew University, and one of the main participants in the ideological debates in Israel – to a conflation, whether in the army, in various lucrative careers in the newly created or expanding institutions and even, as we have seen above, in the Kibbutzim, of *Nekhasim* (goods) with 'values'.

This change did not necessarily entail the loss of commitment to collective goals, but such commitment was increasingly channelled into existing social and occupational channels, became closely connected with attainment of higher status and career advances, and but rarely went beyond the existing social and institutional formations – even though some of these, like the Kibbutzim or Moshavim, were originally the carriers of this ideology and ethos.

All these changes were, of course, connected with the growing stress on the increase of the standard of living and on economic development or productivity, with the growing stress on allocation and distributive orientation, and with the stress of entitlements and rights. They became evident in the crystallization of new patterns of life, in the growing conspicuous consumption by different higher echelons, *de facto* legitimized by the elites, and in the patterns of development of cultural consumption analysed above.

All these processes were connected with a far-reaching transformation, within the leading sectors of the society, of the basic attitude to the possibility of construction of the internal and external socio-political environment of its worlds. The creative innovative attitude, stemming from the active construction of such worlds, prevalent in the former period, gave way, seemingly imperceptibly and naturally, to the perception of this environment as given, as one to be 'mastered', conquered or adapted to, but not necessarily shaped anew.

Thus, as we have seen above, Israeli literature of the 1950s and 1960s abounds with expressions of such changes – often connected with expressions of the younger generations's disappointment with the new reality, with its not living up to the grand vision of their youth, or of their parents', a reality which is there, cannot be changed, and has, at most, to be mastered.

It became much more concerned with the explorations of the existing world, its different dimensions and the problems and contradictions in it, than in stressing the possibility of the creation of a new reality – although, needless to say, this last theme did not disappear from the Israeli intellectual or ideological scene.

## The importance of the security situation

Perhaps most indicative of this transformation was the conception of security problems and the growing self-definition of large groups of Israeli society as a society under siege, under continuous stress.

There could, of course, be no doubt about the heavy burden, economic, personal (in simple terms of the days spent in military service) and psychological, the continuing unstable security and international situation in which Israel continuously found itself. It is, however, very difficult to judge whether this pressure was much greater than in the earlier period, except of course for the very fact of its continuity and the concomitant continuous accumulation of stress connected therewith.

Yet a far-reaching change developed – as compared to the Yishuv period when security was seen as part, but only a part, of the basic activity of the pioneer – in the perception and definition of this component of the reality of Israeli society and of its identity.

Thus, first of all, security became the very central dimension of Israeli collective identity. The image of a beleaguered society became a basic component of its identity, in a sense channelling, to a very large extent, the creativity and commitments of large sectors of the population. The very consciousness of this situation and emphasis on this dimension also served as sort of an excuse for not engaging in creativity in other directions.

Here Moshe Dayan's famous saying that it is impossible to carry two flags – both that of security and that of the solution of social problems – is very indicative of this trend, as are the very frequent sayings of many public figures – among them Mrs Meir – of the necessity to open the eyes of those living in the security and relative affluence of the cities to the hardships of service in the army and of the settlement outposts.

## Specialization of elites

The growing specialization and segregation of different elites and the changes in the ideology also had a far-reaching impact on the mode of thinking and perception by the different elites of the major problems within their own areas of activity as well as of major problems of Israeli society. This developed very much in line with the more general mode of orientation to the environment which we have analysed above.

Among most of the elites there developed a tendency on the one hand towards specialization of thinking in their own field, moving in the rather technocratic direction, and on the other towards a rather abstract conception of the major problems of the society.

Within many spheres of life – as for instance in the military and some of the industrial and academic frameworks – such changes in the modes of thinking were connected with a very high degree of specialization and sophistication, with respect to the major problems of their respective spheres, and of high innovation. This usually resulted in the development of but few meeting points or settings within which the problems of the different areas of institutional activities were discussed. Concomitantly, however, there tended at the same time to develop among many of these elites, with respect to broader societal and political problems, either a pristine ideological vision (to be found especially among some intellectuals), or, among the more professional elites, an overall abstract technocratic mode of thinking.

Between these different modes of thinking a continuous pendulum swing developed, often with but little sensitivity to the intricacies and complexities of the concrete problems of different areas of social life and of their interrelations. All these developments tended to reinforce, in a sort of feedback process, the more adaptive as against the more creative attitudes to the construction of the world, coping with the environment, as well as the dissociation of the more adaptive institution-building from the frameworks of broader solidarity.

This mode of orientation found its expression even in the crystallization of daily language. Perhaps above all in the military, but also in other spheres of life, a highly technical vocabulary developed, connected with a rather narrow problem orientation, with the segmentation of life into various concrete problems, somehow weakening the common sense discourse with many sectors of Israeli society.

These processes were naturally connected with a growing atrophy in 'official' social–political thought and discourse as applied to internal as well as external matters. They were also connected to the continuous oscillation of public discourse in general and in political matters in particular, in the Knesset disputes and in other forums, between general ideological platitudes and declarations on the one hand and more technocratic and *ad hoc* arrangements on the other, as well as to the very weak influence of the press media or discussion in more informal forums on policy-making.

This atrophy of socio–political thought was manifest in the lack of ability to forge any coherent guide to policies in such fields as labour relations or the various problems attendant on economic development.

Significantly enough a large part of the internal political disputes was couched in administrative or organizational terms – such as the terms of change of electoral system, some still derived from Ben-Gurion's attempt to cure the ills of the Israeli political system by changing from a system of proportional representation to one of direct district election.

## Changes in collective identity

At the same time there were changes in another aspect or dimension of the Zionist ideology in general and the Labour–Zionist one in particular – namely in the construction of the symbols and components of the new Israeli collective identity and of their relation to the processes of social and cultural creativity that developed within it.

On the one hand the basic Israeli or Zionist components of this identity became on the whole firmly embedded in the collective consciousness of most sectors of the Israeli society – and there also developed within them a process of cultural creativity, participation and consumption. But at the same time these processes could no longer be subsumed under the canopy of simple Zionist, or Labour–Zionist, ideology – as they had been in the periods of the rejuvenation of the Hebrew language and the crystallization of the new components of Eretz–Israel identity in the period of the Yishuv and the first years of the State. The relations of the Israeli identity to Jewish historical tradition and to broader civilizational settings were reopened. The simple and yet strong assumption of the earlier stages, that the very process of cultural renaissance would provide full answer to all these problems, had proved to be at least insufficient – and there developed a consciousness of the exhaustion of these dimensions of the ideology, not dissimilar from that in the social spheres. Such consciousness gave rise, as we have seen, to very far-reaching and diversified upsurges of creativity orientated at reconstructing the central symbols of the society, whether in the historical, religious or ethnic direction, yet with far-reaching changes in their whole ambience – changes from active reconstruction and a strong future orientation to a stronger acceptance of the present and past.

# Weakening of the Regnant Ideology
## *Changing definitions of major social problems*

All these processes led to the growing exhaustion of ideological creativity in the social, political, institutional dimensions of the Labour–Zionist ideology – in the very era of great institutional expansion in all areas of life.

Here again there was a weakening of the innovative transformative orientations, of attempts to shape or transform the givens of the social environment as against the tendency to accept them or, at most, to master them.

This weakening of the transformative innovation can be seen in the very definition of central social problems which developed in Israeli society and of the policies undertaken to cope with them: the 'ethnic' problem, in many of the social problems as well as in other areas, and perhaps above all that central area of security and foreign relations.

A closer look at the various definitions of this problem and at the various policies in this field, indicates that, implicitly or explicitly, these policies were based on the premiss that the root of the ethnic problem lay in the combination of 'objective givens' – especially of cultural gaps, of differences in the original educational levels between the Oriental and the Western groups, and of the concomitant *de facto* – even if certainly not *de jure* – discrimination against the

Oriental groups generated by the misunderstandings rooted in such cultural gaps.

Accordingly, as we have seen, many policies were developed in the attempt to solve these problems. The assumptions of these policies neglected the importance of other more dynamic factors or aspects in the crystallization of the ethnic problems – such as the changing motivational and ideological patterns among all the new immigrants; the fact that many of the so-called Oriental immigrants came without their leadership or socio-economically stronger elements; and a combination of all these factors (together with the cultural distance) with the changes in the absorption of new immigrants in the direction of a bureaucratic–paternalistic tutelary mode, closely related to the clientelistic mode of polities which, as we have seen, developed in this period in Israel. All these factors were, in a sense, taken for granted, and were accepted as given.

Hence these policies neglected to see the significance of the fact that in most institutional spheres there developed but very few formats or ecological settings in which new and old immigrants were bound together. This applied not only in new common frameworks of solidarity, as was the case in the policy of integration in the educational field, it also applied to the stress on commitment and motivation to common endeavours, on achievement or qualitative standards, on common duties, obligations and rights, and on some common attempts to create new types of institutions, and to transform their environments.

Similar premises and policies also developed in the very definition of other social problems, for instance those related to poverty, as articulated by both the politicians and the more professional social workers, or in the sphere of education, as related to the problem of the Oriental groups in general and the deprived ones in particular.

Truly enough, the very articulation or formulation of all these social problems was, in itself, a great innovation in the public discourse of Israel – and indicated great potentialities of creativity and innovation.

But these responses – starting from the very recognition of these facts and containing some very important institutional and social innovations – were in fact tantamount to admitting that these problems could not be dealt with in terms of the premises of the predominant ideology, especially of its constructivist dimension, of its stress on common participation in the creation of social and cultural frameworks and in connecting such activities with some broader overall meaning, with the basic symbols of the collectivity.

# The Changing Mode of Policies
## *The development of dynamic conservatism*

These were not, however, just 'academic' definitions of the major problems facing Israeli society; they were, as we have already seen, very closely interwoven with the major policies which were undertaken by the centre, by the major ruling elites, in the major spheres of social life, such as the absorption of immigrants, economic development, in the political sphere, in the field of security and in the relations to Arab countries.

Indeed, the problems of the new immigrants were never defined as they could have been, given both the basic socialist orientations of the society and their objective economic situation, in terms of class or in terms derived from the pioneering ideology. Instead they were defined at most as the negative counterpart of this ideology. Moreover the ethnic problem was defined as one of *edot*, as against of the wider collectivity which was not *edot* and which was the carrier of the great Zionist transformation and vision. These definitions attested to the exhaustion of the social–political dimension of this ideology, a trend which was also very closely connected, as we have seen, with a far-reaching change in the construction of the symbols of collective identity.

The ideology which guided the crystallization and implementation of these policies was, as we have seen above, that of the 'classical' Labour–Zionism: namely of the implementation of the national goals, of economic development, of the ingathering of exiles and of the forging of one nation out of them, as well as of continuous pioneering in the service of these goals – thus continuing, with even greater impetus and with much greater power and more resources at its disposal, the basic goals of the Zionist movement, and the varied developments in the period of the Yishuv.

Crucial to this ideology – and especially to its pioneering component – was the heavy emphasis on the combination of the implementation of all these goals, together with the participation of social groups in the centres of society and in the process of institutional and cultural creativity closely related to these centres.

Yet in fact most of these policies were guided in part at least by somewhat different orientations and structured in a different mode from the one implied by all these premises – especially from the mode that was most prevalent in the period of the Yishuv – and they developed into a rather different direction or directions.

It may, of course, be claimed – and, indeed with a very strong grain of truth – that, given the conditions in the first years of the State, it was entirely unrealistic to think in terms of the full participation of the various – especially the new – sectors of the population. The great urgency to find solutions to pressing concrete problems – problems of housing and work for the new immigrants, creating the army, starting economic development – naturally gave rise to much more *ad hoc* and pragmatic approaches which could not take into account the lofty premises of the basic ideology.

Yet of crucial importance, from the point of view of our analysis, is the fact that even later on, when the necessity for emergency *ad hoc* measures had to some degree at least passed away, the basic policies became – to an even higher degree than before – moulded in certain modes or directions which, in several crucial ways, differed from some at least of the initial premises of the pioneering ideology, and especially from its 'participatory' aspects and from the emphasis on the close relation between institution-building and commit-ment to collective goals.

The first such mode – to some degree common to many post-revolutionary societies, but which acquired in Israel some specific characteristics – can best be designated as that of dynamic conservatism. The principal identifying characteristic of this type of conservatism is its being guided not only or mainly – as can be quite natural with respect to 'simple' conservative orientations – by the narrow interests of existing groups or organizations. Rather this mode is characterized by being very dynamic in the sense of being ready to give up many narrow vested interests of different existing groups, by openly taking on new problems and by opening many of the existing organizations to new groups, and also by creating new organizations and institutions. At the same time, however, the attempts to solve such new problems, as guided by such dynamic conservatism, have been set almost entirely within the existing power and institutional frameworks.

Thus the policies implemented in this mode attempted to take new groups into existing – or newly created – types of organizations, to solve new problems in terms of the prevalent basic orientations and guidelines, and above all maintain, within the expanding institutional frameworks of the existing elites, the basic existing structure of power and ideology. These policies did not generate attempts to encourage the creation, by different social groups, of new types of social frameworks and institutions, nor did they encourage the development of autonomous participation of such groups in the different sectors of the society in general and in its centres in particular – which could perhaps lead to such creativity.

This was most visible in the field of absorption of immigrants in general – and the illustration of new Moshavim which, as we have seen above, were one of the most successful aspects of this whole endeavour, is very significant from this point of view. These Moshavim were structured and organized, as we have seen, according to the principles of the first pioneering groups which were seen as the basic models appropriate to new immigrants or into which the new groups had to be educated. There was but little effort to look, together with these groups, for some new possible directions.

Similarly the extension of organizational frameworks of the Histadrut and of party activities to many of their areas, which helped these groups to assume their relative positions on Israel's political scene, was undertaken – in a sense quite naturally – almost entirely as an extension of the existing frameworks.

The specific problems of the various new groups – above all, but not only, of the new immigrants – were defined, within these frameworks, mostly in a combination of technical–organizational and educational terms: that is, how to provide them with maximum facilities – housing, work and the like – and how to educate or socialize them, according to the existing premises and, above all, within the existing basic social frameworks, without at the same time envisaging the possibility of changes in such frameworks through the auton-omous participation of different groups, old and new alike.

# The repercussions of dynamic conservatism

The first major result of all these policies – especially those oriented to the absorption of immigrants – was a very great and continuous organizational expansion, the growth and diversification of the major institutional sectors and frameworks of the society – be they ecological, economic, occupational or educational ones.

Moreover, this great organizational–institutional expansion was closely connected with the opening up of arenas of career advance and of social mobility for many groups – be they youth or new immigrants – even if not all of them were able to advance to the same degree. Indeed, in many fields – the army, the educational institutions in general and institutions of higher learning in particular – from the very beginning the top positions were in the hands of some of the new groups, especially the younger generations of the *Tsabras* but gradually also of other select groups.

Thus these organizations – even more than the existing ones – were far from being stagnant: they were indeed, as the very connotation 'dynamic' conservatism implies, continuously developing and changing. But the dynamism, both of older and newer institutions, was structured according to premises which, as indicated above, differed greatly, not only from those of the former period of the Yishuv, but above all also from those of the regnant ideology.

First of all there was but a weak connection between the development of these institutions and the more 'social' aspects of the regnant Labour–Zionist ideology. That ideology did not provide any guidelines – except for the very insistence on economic development and institutional expansion – for the shaping of their distinctive features. Second there were relatively weak connections between the development of such institutions and attempts at institutional innovation in general and participation of the various groups in the major centres of the society and autonomous access to them in particular. Indeed as we have already indicated above, this great institutional and organizational expansion was connected with the growing dependence of all these organizations – old and new alike – despite their diversification, on the centre for the resources needed by them. The centre became more and more a common reference point for all of them, and the relative stagnation creativity in the centre necessarily affected the development and working of these institutions.

# The trend to entitlements – magia li

The full repercussions of such dynamic conservatism can, however, be understood only in conjunction with the second mode which guided many of the policies of the State. This second mode is best illustrated by what has become a very popular pressword in Israeli society: *magia li* (they owe it to me, I am entitled or the like) – namely the stress on the right to obtain various goods or services without any relation to achievements or to performance.

Needless to say, such ideology of entitlements, of rights, constitutes a basic component of any modern welfare state – and as such it became a part of the Israeli welfare state system. But this general attitude of *magia li* had much deeper roots in Israeli reality. Some of its roots can be found in some of the policies and orientations that developed, especially in the workers' sector, in the period of the Yishuv. But probably of much greater importance here was the crucial encounter with the urgent problems that developed with the establishment of the State – especially those of the initial absorption of new immigrants. The severe economic conditions in the beginning of this period – the necessity to find urgent solutions to problems of housing, work and sometimes even the provision of food, at the same time as preventing any far-reaching unrest among the immigrants – gave rise to a policy of, initially very meagre, hand-outs in the *Maabarot*, and of employment in obviously unproductive work, without any attempts to connect these – especially after they had become somewhat more routinized – with too strong attempts at setting some standards of performance. The stories of those years contain many illustrations of this attitude, and the concerns from among the 'absorbers' who cried out against this were not heeded.

Slowly the accumulation of these experiences – the growing orientations in the veteran sectors, possibly also those of the German reparations, the burgeoning ideology of the welfare state and social services, the concentration of many of these policies in development towns – become crystallized into an overall new mode which guided many of the policies coming nicely together with many of the repercussions of the dynamic conservative mode – such as lack of participation in creative endeavours – and becoming part of the general ambience of Israeli society.

## The influx of Arab labour; the reversal of the pioneering occupational structure

Perhaps the most important single indication of the exhaustion or bankruptcy of the older Labour–Zionist social and economic vision was its lack of ability to address itself, beyond a purely adaptive way, to the crucial change in the whole structure of Israeli economy that took place after the Six Day War – namely the influx of Arab labour and the growing dependence of some sectors of Israeli economy – both agricultural and industrial – on this labour.

The flow of this labour into the various sectors of the Israeli economy was, as we have seen, connected with many unpleasant aspects – bad housing conditions, attempts at exploitation – all of which gave rise to attempts by the Histadrut and other organizations to correct them, but not always with full success.

But even when they were at least partially successful, and despite the possibly beneficial impact of these developments on the standard of living of many parts of the Arab population, these developments went against the basic premisses of Labour–Zionist ideology – a premiss which constituted, as we have seen above, a focus of contention in the period of the Yishuv – namely that of *Avoda Ivrit* (Hebrew labour), of the establishment of a normal, self-contained Jewish occupational and economic structure, based on agriculture and industry, and not a 'colonial' one as was to some degree advocated by the British.

In fact the occupational developments in Israel – the growth of white-collar occupations, of bureaucracy, of such traditional Jewish occupations as professions – had in themselves already posed a difficult challenge to these premisses, but at least they could be seen as still developing within the framework of the basic orientation to a self-sustaining national economy.

This could now no longer be true of the great influx of Arab labour which created, in those sectors in which it was important, a 'semi-colonial' structure and above all emphasized the retreat of the Jewish sector from the 'lower' simple manual work, so central in the vision of the pioneers.

In many ways these developments were a sort of natural concomitant of the economic expansion, especially the one that developed after the Six Day War – but it was combined with the lack of almost any willingness to face this problem in terms of the basic premisses of the regnant ideology, thus further attesting to its growing exhaustion.

## Security

This exhaustion was also visible in the field of security. The very fact that this field became the major focus of public attention, and, after the Six Day War, also of public discourse, was in itself indicative of the relative exhaustion of the social institutional dimension of the regnant ideology. But even more indicative of such exhaustion was the relative ossification of at least the official policies – as against to some degree the public discourse – in this field, combined as it often was with the great technical innovation in the military field.

# The Transformation of the Kibbutz as the Epitome of Major Changes in Israeli Society
## Structural and ideological changes in the Kibbutzim

The best single illustration or manifestation of the processes of change analysed above – those in the structure of elites, in their relations to broader strata in the regnant ideology, in the exhaustion of its social–institutional dimension, and in repercussions of all these changes on the transformation of Israeli society – can be seen, in an almost pristine form, in the changes that took place from about the 1950s onwards in the structure and placement of the Kibbutzim (to some degree in contrast to the Moshavim) in the social structure of Israel in general and with respect to new immigrants in particular.

As we have seen above, in this period the Kibbutz and the Moshav underwent a far-reaching process of internal transformation and diversification, and they became on the whole economically very successful, spreading over into industry, and evincing a continuous economic growth, modernization and specialization of their structure. They also continued to be a very important part of the political scene, and became a part of the upper sectors or echelons of the society.

But at the same time there took place some very important changes in their status as an elite group and in the way in which they addressed themselves to the new problems facing Israeli society in general and to the absorption of immigrants in particular.

We have already discussed in Chapter 9 the changing bases of their attraction, and their generally low level of attraction to sectors of the older population as well as – and perhaps above all – to immigrants in general and Oriental ones in particular.

There were some attempts at attracting new immigrants in the Kibbutzim, but very few new Kibbutzim were established by new immigrants in general and Oriental ones in particular. Certainly the different Kibbutz movements did send out emissaries to the youth movements in towns and to new Kibbutzim to help them in their first steps. They participated actively in various programmes of the Youth Aliya, which had shifted their dealings more and more towards new immigrants youth in general and semi-social cases in particular. But their overall impact on the new emergent social reality, as compared with the former period, was rather small.

This was very closely connected with the nature of their elitist–sectarian tendencies, and with the fact that their egalitarianism became more and more inward-looking, giving rise to a 'tutelary' approach to other groups in general and the new immigrants in particular. Whatever new institutional creativity and imagination they did develop was orientated to their own problems, to their economic expansion and to the repercussions of the social consequences of such expansion on their ideological premises – and only marginally to problems of the new sectors of the population. Especially important here was the lack of significant attempts to find ways of participation – of some common framework, beyond the most formal ones on local levels – with the development towns, which were often built very close to the Kibbutzim.

One of the most important indicators of such attitudes was their quite widespread – seemingly natural given their inconstancy on ideological points – reluctance to participate in common regional educational frameworks, an attitude which has only lately begun to change.

At the same time, they fully participated not only in the economic development of Israel, becoming a sort of special type of gentlemen-farmers, but also in its political frameworks, acquiring strong positions within them and at the same time continuing to claim for themselves the status of elites, and symbols of the pristine values of the society, and often attempting to serve as a voice of conscience or as a moral guide. But they built their actual strength more on internal coalitions with the centres of their respective parties, than on full participation with broader strata, thus indirectly contributing to their growing decline in the central political elite.

## The contrast of the Moshavim

Within the Moshavim the developments were markedly different. They shared with the Kibbutzim the general participation in the economic and political expansion and in the rising standards of life, but at the same time lived up much better to the new social challenges, without stressing the unique, pristine, sectarian elite status – thus playing a crucial role in the process of absorption of new immigrants and of Oriental ones in particular.

Obviously even here there were some problems. Thus all the new Moshavim (from 1946) – not only, but mostly, those of new immigrants – were given smaller land allotments than the old ones. Second there developed in the late 1970s and early 1980s various economic problems. These were partly related to the opposition, based on ideological grounds and power considerations, of the leadership of the Moshav movement, which till the late 1970s was mostly composed of veterans, to possibilities of industrialization within them.

There were also tensions between the old and the new Moshavim about the leadership of the movement – as well as of the relatively more privileged positions of the older ones – yet all this was already a struggle within a common framework.

Significantly enough, the first Labour Minister of Agriculture from within the Moshavim (the others from the settlements were from the Kibbutzim) was Aharon Ouzan, a leader of the new ones.

## Summary

These far-reaching changes in the internal structure and external standing of the Kibbutzim, as well as the comparison with the Moshavim – the combination of economic success, relatively high standards of living and of the special quality of life, elitist self-conception and ambience, together with a high level of commitment to performance of special elite functions, and the gradual withdrawal inwards – were indeed very indicative of some of the general changes and developments in the elite structure in Israel in general and in the Labour sector in particular.

The combination of all these factors when connected with close ecological proximity to the Kibbutzim, as was the case of many development towns, could easily become explosive – as it did indeed in the 1981 elections – giving rise, as we shall see later in greater detail, to the eruption of rather vicious outbursts against the Kibbutzim that, as a result, found themselves in a state of shock.

Since then, in many of the Kibbutzim, many attempts have indeed been made to break through this closure, but only the future will tell how successful these will be.

# Exhaustion of the Ideology
## *Changing modes of creativity in the Israeli society*

The development of the Kibbutzim brings together several of the basic processes analysed above – namely the abrogation of the major elites and their relative depolitization; the growing interweaving of the elites in the process of economic expansion and in the upper strata and echelons of the society; their growing distance from the broader sectors of the society; the weakening of links between different sectors of the society; the changes in the regnant ideology; the exhaustion of the social–institutional dimension of the regnant ideology and of its capacity to reconstruct symbols of collectivity according to which the major elites and the political one (as well as the Kibbutzim themselves) legitimized themselves.

The accumulation of all the processes analysed above and the continuous feedback between them gave rise to a growing disjunction or dissociation between the different modes of social activity, above all between active institution-building; the articulation of symbols of overall societal solidarity, as against the solidarity of small sub-centres, and the bringing together of all these in some common symbols of meanings – as against the relatively close association between these different types of social activity that developed in the periods of the Yishuv and in the early stage of the development of the State of Israel. Accordingly all these developments gave rise to the development of new patterns of institutional and cultural creativity and of their relation to the centres of the society and its major sectors.

Thus, in this period, unlike in the former ones, no such great social or institutional innovations as the Kibbutz or the Histadrut, or the renaissance of the Hebrew language which combined these various elements, developed.

Instead this period was indeed basically characterized, in the social sphere, by the combination of a great organizational expansion with the relative exhaustion of the institutional imagination and innovative creativity which had been prevalent formerly.

In the first period of the State, such creativity had been concentrated in several institutional spheres, above all in the military with the development of military industry and, to some degree, in the academic and economic ones which, by their very nature, were, as we have seen, orientated to external markets and models. Somewhat later a very great impetus to innovation and creativity became manifest in many spheres of active economic and educational fields, such as different programmes of special education, in selected fields of economy and technology and in varied fields of cultural creativity.

But all these innovative tendencies were already of a different order from those that had developed in the formative period of the Yishuv and were at least implied in the regnant ideology. These innovative tendencies were less and less closely connected symbolically or institutionally with one another; they were not guided by some central overarching vision, combining national, social and cultural components, and above all their carriers did not participate in the centre and in the articulation of the policies which were formulated in the centre.

This was connected with the concomitant tendency to define many aspects of the internal and external environments and problems of the society as givens. It could be discerned in most fields, in all of which, contrary to the formative periods of the Yishuv and the beginning of the State period, there developed but very few new central institutional formats orientated to the creation of new patterns and goals and to the attainment of qualitative standards – thus, indeed, seemingly moving in many ways in the direction of a 'normal' routinized society.

In other – more 'technical' sociological – wording, the regnant ideology no longer provided models or templates of social action in which technical, instrumental action and power-relation were brought together in some common framework of solidarity and of broader, transcendental meaning, as the older ideology had indeed attempted to do.

It was the combination of these processes and the continuous feedback between them, rooted as we have seen in the very process of institutionalization of these basic orientations and in the policies undertaken by the centre, that explain the inability of the dominant sectors and elites to forge, out of the regnant ideology, a viable symbolic and institutional answer to these new problems.

The regnant ideology was unable to provide guidance for the numerous conflicts, problems and contradictions which developed, as we have seen, within all the institutional spheres of Israeli society, and which became, as we have seen, especially visible after the Six Day War.

The consciousness or awareness of such growing dissociation between all these problems and the regnant ideology and its carriers – the ruling elites – became intensified through the processes of segregation of elites, of weakening of different frameworks of solidarity analysed above – all of which, as we have seen, weakened the connection between broader societal solidarity and trust and different spheres of social activities in general and those directed by the elites in particular.

This consciousness was necessarily intensified by the fact that these developments were presided by a ruling elite, the internal solidarity and cohesion of which became greatly weakened by the long atrophy of the process of political participation and which, in many aspects of its behaviour, gave evidence to the exhaustion of its institutional creativity as well as to bifurcation between the daily levels of political and ideological declarations.

## The resulting paradox

Thus there developed here a rather paradoxical situation but one not uncommon in post-revolutionary society – namely that, on the one hand, through the impetus generated from within the regnant ideology, there developed very intensive institutional dynamics, yet the mode of these dynamics gave rise to the exhaustion of certain crucial aspects of this ideology. Because of this exhaustion, the ideology was no longer able to provide guidance for the shaping of the continuously expanding institutional structures and organizations, for continuous institutional creativity, nor for the regulation of the manifold problems and conflicts which had naturally arisen with this diversified development and which became more and more influenced by their autonomous institutional momentum or by the power orientation of the ruling elites or of different groups rather than by any ideological vision in general and the regnant one in particular.

The mode of policy-formation that we have designated as dynamic conservatism that developed in Israel, in connection with the transformation of the regnant pioneering Labour–Zionist ideology and the concomitant new definitions of the major social problems, was the ideological counterpart of the paternalistic mode of relations between centre and periphery. Ultimately it gave rise to the exhaustion of the dynamism inherent in the dynamic–conservative modes which guided the basic policies and shaped the new institutional structure of Israeli society.

Truly enough, within these broader frameworks, some very important institutional innovations, whether in the field of special education, in new economic enterprises or in military formations, were continuously undertaken. The thrust of the majority of the policies developed in these frameworks was however, in the direction of distributive allocation, on an ethnic or social basis, or, as in the case of integration in the educational sphere analysed above, with a strong emphasis on what was hoped would prove to be new common frameworks of solidarity, but not necessarily orientated to common achievements or to active participation in the reconstruction of the collectivity. At the same time these developments became connected with the continuous construction of new dimensions of collective identity, whether of the ethnic or the religious ones that were developing in Israeli society, thus indicating both the weakness of the·regnant ideology in these spheres as well as some of the possible directions of the transformation of Israeli society.

All these developments attested to the failure of the dominant elites to combine the opening up of the initial institutional mould with some continuity – even in a transformed way – of the older pioneering elitist orientations, which combined a strong commitment to collective goals, to maintenance of standards of creativity and performance, and to obligations inherent in a pioneering elitist self-image.

# II · The Roots of Transformation

## The Bifurcation of Pioneering–Revolutionary Elites

### The transformation of the revolutionary elites

The various processes analysed above had their roots first in the nature of the transformation of the revolutionary elite, attendant on its attempts to direct the post-revolutionary development and to find support and legitimation for such direction. Particularly relevant was the way this elite restructured its orientations to the State, and its impetus to power on the one hand and to the more ideological and participatory aspects of the ideology on the other. Second these processes had their roots in various structural processes attendant on the development of this elite's specific pattern of post-revolutionary institutional mould; and, third, in some changes in the historical situation of the Jewish people.

With regard to the transformation of the revolutionary elites the most important aspect of the Israeli development was above all the attempts of the central political elite in general, and of Ben-Gurion in particular, to free itself from the limitation of the older movement sectors, while, at the same time, basing itself on the symbolic heritage of these movements.

There developed here a combination of, first, a rift between parts of the central political elite, as represented above all by Ben-Gurion, on the one hand, and the older movement sectors, which in the meantime developed into more routinized political machines, on the other; and, second, a growing co-operation between the two elements, in maintaining the power positions of the Labour movement. The first part, led by Ben-Gurion, tried to free itself from both the limitation and obligations of the older movement's sectarian dimension, as well as from the routinization which seemed to have led to its ossification – an ossification which this part of the elite helped to generate by its very attitude to the second part – and by the attempt to base its own power on a more direct appeal to the broader strata and on the basis of general ideology of *Mamlachtiut* (Statism). At the same time this new element shared with the older elite the attempts to control, yet with a democratic pluralistic framework, the autonomous political expression of the broader strata. Thus both elements stressed the commitment of the elite to a democratic order yet combined with strong tutelary paternalistic orientations.

At the same time those parts of the Labour movement who attempted to articulate the tradition of the movements became more and more dissociated from the central political elite – even if often participating in the coalition government.

The first of these developments had taken place in the Yishuv with the rift in 1946 between *Mapai* and *Ahdut Haavoda*. In the history of the State of Israel, the first crucial event in this context was the rift in 1948 between Ben-Gurion and the leftist *Mapam* (especially *Ahdut Haavoda*) and many of the high army officers coming from the Kibbutz movement, around the relative autonomy of the *Palmach* (in which the *Ahdut Haavoda* group predominated) in the framework of the newly established Israel Defence Army.

Ben-Gurion's victory in this field was greatly facilitated by the fact that it was indeed rather difficult to envisage the creation of special autonomous formations, partly responsible for their respective political movements, in the framework of a national army. But it gave rise to the withdrawal of some of the best of these officers, not only from the army but to some degree also from the centres of political power and even participation – Yigal Alon being one of the most outstanding exceptions – while the connections of those who remained in the army with their movements became weaker, even if they continued to constitute one of the most important networks in the army.

Indeed already here the very focusing of the controversy on the army, which emphasized the centrality of security considerations over those in the internal scene, was very indicative of the changes in the ideological orientations.

## Developments within the Labour movement

Such weakening of these orientations was, however, also greatly facilitated by internal developments within the movements themselves, above all by their participating in the process of economic expansion and institution-building in general and the ways in which they themselves have formulated their ideological orientations.

First of all was the crucial fact that the leadership of the Labour party – including that of the Histadrut – became part of the major ruling elite under whose auspices the rapid economic development took place, thus being much more at the centre of economic power and policy-making than the bourgeois or private sectors. The rapidly developing governmental sector of the economy was in the beginning manned by many of these activist elements close to the Labour sector. At the same time, the far-reaching processes of social and occupational change gave rise, as we have seen, to a very differentiated and diversified occupational structure, to a certain change and bifurcation in the activities of the Histadrut – its growing orientation to the more established sectors and to the concomitant transformation of its activities in the direction of a welfare state, minimizing the constructive and participating aspects of its ideology.

Second, and in close connection with the former, was the fact that the 'constructivist' activities of the Histadrut became even more encompassing and its economic 'empire' grew rapidly and became highly diversified.

At the same time, in many of the movements in general, and in the Kibbutzim in particular, there was a bifurcation between on the one hand a growing interweaving in great economic expansion, stemming from their constructivist institution-building orientations, and on the other hand a growing ideological sectarianism and dissociation.

While these sectors in general and the Kibbutzim in particular all participated in the process of economic expansion, often becoming great economic
entrepreneurs, their ideological–political orientations and struggles became
mostly focused around the problem of the relations to the international
socialist camp in general and Russia in particular, all of which became
shattered with de-Stalinisation, and less and less orientated to the internal
dimension of institution-building.

In this last sphere these sectors developed almost no specific themes beyond
those of worker's solidarity or an organization of urban workers or a general
liberal view in the relations to the Arabs, and more flexible approaches in
foreign policy. While these added to the versatility of public discourse in Israel,
they were not of any great importance in founding guidelines for the regulation
of the new dynamic social and economic expansion. Thus indeed in the 1950s,
in the period of great immigration with the manifold challenges it posed for the
country, large parts of the Kibbutz movement were preoccupied in a typically
sectarian split, often within the same Kibbutz, between those who identified
themselves with *Mapai* and those who were affiliated with *Ahdut Haavoda*, and
focused above all around the ideological orientations to Russia. As a result of
this split many Kibbutzim had to be resettled – with a very heavy cost to public
funds – and needless to say this rift necessarily took up a large part of their
social, political and ideological energy.

Whatever would-be ideological centres, such as the educational centre at
Beit Berl, existed in the Labour sector, became almost entirely atrophied; they
carried no new message beyond the general social democratic vision. They
certainly did not carry any new pioneering message or that of creation of new
common frameworks of participation and creativity.

The abolishment of the special workers' educational sector also undermined
the – albeit only very weak – potentialities of any new ideological crystallization, as did the growing interweaving of the 'pioneering' youth movements
in the life of the higher strata and the growing orientation of their members to
the expanding career opportunities.

At the same time the growing segregation of the different elites did involve a
growing dissociation of the various cultural and educational elites from other
ones and from the major areas of institution-building (except in their own
spheres), as well as from the centres of policy-making – reinforcing also the
dissociation of the process of cultural creativity from participation in the
construction of new ideological conceptions attempting to cope with the new
reality.

Thus it is all of these developments that explain, at least partially, why there
did not develop any new ideological orientation beyond the general stress on
economic development, welfare policies and some vague socialist symbols.
Neither the older movement sectors – be they the Kibbutzim or the ideological
leadership of the Histadrut – nor the political elite developed a vision which
could guide these new great developments beyond the expansion of organizational frameworks and the power positions they entailed.

These developments also explain why the continuous opening up of the initially relatively restrictive political mould become disconnected from the pioneering–elitist ethos; why no ways were found to combine such opening up with the continuation of some of the orientations to commitment and elitist obligations.

# The Effects of the Institutional Expansion
## *Structural processes weakening formations of solidarity*

The transformation of the pioneering–evolutionary elites analysed above provided the initial background for the processes of the relative segregation of the upper elites, of the weakening of various frameworks of solidarity and of change in the nature of such frameworks.

The continuous development of these processes, with all its far-reaching impact on the development of Israeli society, was reinforced by several structural problems and trends that evolved in Israeli society in connection with its institutional expansion; with the ways in which the problems of Israel as a small society were coped with; with some of the aspects of the internal structure of the different sectors of Israeli society, as well as with some of the results of the major policies undertaken by the governments of Israel.

Thus, first of all, several aspects of expansion of the major institutional areas, inadvertently but to a large degree, undermined those formations which in the former period constituted some of the most important common frameworks of solidarity out of which the different elites grew and with which they often acted. The most important such formations were the youth movements and the common frameworks and networks of the underground formations, of the small university student body and of the social–political movements themselves, which often cross-cut each other. These were all characterized, in the earlier period, by some combination with the more concrete instrumental and organizational activities in different fields, as well as with the exercise of power and of engagement in power-games, providing at the same time common meanings and orientations which legitimized these activities.

Several aspects of the development and expansion of the major institutional systems and organizations that took place after the 1950s weakened and undermined many of these frameworks and formations, as well as the close personal networks which developed within them. The development of the educational system reinforced, by its tendencies to unification and 'academization', by the growing orientation to quantitative attainments and by the weakening of more specific elite nuclei and orientations, the processes of such segregation of different elites and the weakening of their internal solidarity and commitments. The army reinforced such tendencies, not only by its upper echelons naturally becoming one such specialized elite, but also, more inadvertently, by weakening, during the period of military service, the nuclei of solidarity that might have developed in the school or in the youth movements.

It was only in such formations as the *Nahal* that such frameworks of solidarity were, to some degree, maintained but they were rather marginal and on the whole short-lived.

At the same time the very development of the different elites in general and of the political in particular, the strong orientation of these elites to their specific areas of activities and the atrophy that developed among the political elite weakened, among them, the awareness of the importance of creating such frameworks of solidarity.

The weakening of such frameworks was also reinforced by the strong feelings of relative deprivation which became very prevalent among many groups in connection with the visions of continuing expanding possibilities and of the concomitant continuous multiple comparisons, both with other groups and with their perceptions of their present with their past status.*

The weakening of common frameworks of solidarity and networks within Israeli society was also reinforced by several additional processes that have been taking place there since the 1950s – especially by several aspects of the far-reaching process of social mobility analysed above. The very rapid tempo of this mobility often tended to undermine many frameworks of solidarity, raising expectations often beyond the confines of the Israeli scene, and creating an almost classical anomic situation in which almost all groups, despite their relatively continuous advancement, felt relatively deprived.

Such feelings were, of course, reinforced by the fact that processes of social mobility were also interwoven with the development of great ecological and socio-political distance between centre and periphery, and which in their turn also probably contributed to the weakening of solidary relations between different sectors of the society.

The old division between sectors, as well as the mode of structuring of life within the Labour sector and, to some degree, within the Labour–religious sector, probably also weakened such common frameworks of solidarity. Here, of crucial importance was the existence of relatively few close interpersonal networks, beyond the more formal ones, between the different sectors, as well as the potentially present weakening of the internal solidarity in each of them.

Of some importance in this context was probably also the mode of life which developed, above all, in the Labour and the Labour–religious sectors – namely the tendency to the rather strong concentration around the different pioneering tasks and activities connected with a weak development of arenas of social interaction in other spheres such as social or cultural activities or which could perhaps take the place of the weakened pioneering frameworks.

Most of the patterns of such interaction that did develop, as for instance the many types of voluntary activities, were on the whole limited within the older sectors, except for formal organizational contacts between them. Some of them, as for example most women's organizations, continued to be strongly connected with the political centres of their respective sectors or parties.

---

* See, for instance, Jack Habib, 'Ethnic Gaps in Job Satisfaction in Israel', JDC, Brookdale Institute of Gerontology and Adult Development (Jerusalem 1983).

## Internal and external sectors

Closely related to these processes were the ways in which the problems of Israel as a small society were coped with, some of the effects of the security situation, as well as the results of several aspects of the social structure of the different sectors of Israeli society.

First of all, of special importance here was the growing differentiation within Israeli society – as within many other small societies – between the internal and external sectors, that is between occupational and economic sectors orientated to and connected with the outside, with what may be called external markets of different sorts, economic, cultural, political and the like, and those sectors almost entirely orientated to internal markets and activities.

As we have seen above, many of the patterns of activities in the externally orientated sectors differed greatly from those which were more internally orientated. Moroever, many of the activities orientated to the external markets were not closely related to one another. Thus, for instance, the worlds and reference networks of the academic circles, as against those of the cultural elites – writers, artists and, to some degree, also journalists – were on the whole quite different. Such differences also developed in the economic or professional, as well as in the more political, spheres, where a stronger emphasis was laid on the varied arena of Jewish communal activities in the Diaspora. All these developments seem, even if in a rather imperceptible and not well researched way, to have continuously emphasized the differences both between the more international sets and those more internally orientated with such groups, as well as between the different groups themselves.

Although no exact data are available, it seems that, on the whole, these differences between internally and externally orientated sectors intensified the distances between different elites and sectors in Israeli society; they contributed to the growing social distance between different groups and strata, and weakened their common social frameworks. In this context it is important to remember that, at least initially, there was a rather heavy, even if seemingly natural, concentration of many of the new immigrants in general and parts of the Oriental ones in particular in these internal sectors.

Closely related to these processes was the weakening of some of the potentially more innovative elements in the society through various government policies – especially those of taxation and housing, and the strong general and pervasive impact of the various egalitarian policies above all in the field of education, closely related to the weakening of the elitist–pioneering element in the general societal ethos – and through the general heavy bureaucratization of many aspects of life in Israel in general and in the centre in particular.

## Expectations and reality

The combination of some aspects of a small society, of continuous mobility and rising aspirations and standards of living, gave rise to another phenomenon in

Israeli society which is of importance from the point of view of our discussion – namely to the discrepancy between the expectations from public services and the levels of their performance. The rising aspirations and standards of living, the policy of welfare in its broadest implications, gave rise to naturally high demands for different types of public service – health, education, municipal services, performance and protection of police – especially important in connection with the growing rates of crime in turn not unconnected with the rising standards of living. Even if all these expectations could in principle be satisfied at all, which is perhaps by the nature of the case rather doubtful, the combination of several factors – the great attraction of the various upper occupational sectors often orientated to external markets; the objective difficulties of preparation of adequate manpower for all these services; the natural tendencies to bureaucratization given in a relatively highly regulated economy – made it difficult to attract enough highly qualified manpower to these services, resulting in rather widespread feelings of frustration.

## The impact of the security situation

Another crucial development or aspect of institutional life in Israel – which it seems greatly contributed to this growing dissociation between the crystallization of frameworks of solidarity and the more specialized instrumental fields of activities of different sectors of Israeli society in general and of the elites in particular, and which is also indicative of the new directions of institutional innovation that developed within it – was the security situation.

Several aspects of this situation are of special importance from this point of view. First, there was the continuous burden of the security situation: of the need to be continually alert; of the accumulation, and in a sense routinization, of the stress and insecurity; of the economic strain of wars and of mobilization; of the continuous heavy toll of death; of the constant encounter with the possibility of death. All these became a part of the daily existence, consciousness and awareness of the Israelis, and exerted a continuous pressure, creating some fatigue and possible flight from the calls for creativity in many areas of life, although it also provided new challenges.

Second, there was, of course, the growing specialization of the military elite and the development, natural in itself, of specialized avenues of career advancement which were almost entirely confined within the framework of the military.

Third, some aspects of the social structure of the army seem inadvertently to have reinforced the tendency to segregation between different modes of social activities and of orientations in different spheres of social life. Paradoxically it was those aspects which constituted the special strength of the army, and mainly its reservist nature, which caused this segregation, because very large parts of the male population of Israel were spending quite substantive parts of their time there. Service in the army, especially in the combat units, became naturally the repository of commitment and of solidarity, of sacrifice, of the combination of these orientations with various instrumental activities and with the upholding of standards, at the same time weakening these tendencies and orientations in other areas of life.

Such segregation crystallized into a somewhat broader pattern of life, into what Baruch Kimmerling has called the 'interrupted society':* namely the continuous oscillation between the high degree of solidarity and commitment manifested in times of war and the much more individualistic, to some degree disorderly and even sometimes aggressive behaviour of daily life in normal times, reinforcing perhaps a rather old theme or problem in the structure of Jewish life.

In general, the continuous burden of security and the situation of war or of hostilities strengthened the feelings of solidarity in Israeli society on two levels: that of the primary group, of family and close personal groups and networks, and, at least until the Lebanon War, that of the overall solidarity, of identification with the society as such, with its central symbols. At the same time, they often inadvertently weakened, through the very pressure of the situation, the various networks of solidarity and connection between these two levels.†

In this context it is also important to remember another – tragic – outcome of the security situation, namely the heavy toll of death on potential elite groups in the first wars, especially in the War of Independence, when about 6,000 young leaders and active elements fell in battle.

## Summary

Indeed perhaps the simple major outcome of all these structural processes was the weakening of the various intermediary frameworks – frameworks of solidarity and of common activities, in which the ultimate meaning of such activities was also articulated and which mediated between the 'internal' solidary groups of friendship and family and the broader social frameworks.

Accordingly the accumulation of all these processes contributed to the growing disjunction or dissociation between different modes of social activity, above all between active institution-building, the articulation of overall symbols of solidarity, the construction of the solidarity of small sub-centres – and their legitimization in some common normative frameworks and in common symbols of meaning.

Of special importance in this context was, of course, the dissociation between the political and administrative elites and the various cultural ones – together greatly reinforcing the changes in the modes of creativity, in life styles and in the exhaustion of several dimensions of the regnant ideology that have been analysed above.

* B. Kimmerling, 'Social Interruption and Besieged Societies: The Case of Israel', Amherst: Council on International Studies, State University of New York, 1979.
† R. W. Bar-Yosef and Dorit Pedan-Eisenstark, 'Role System under Stress: Sex Roles in War', *Social Problems*, 25, 2 (December 1977), pp. 135–45.

# The Experience of the Holocaust

The exhaustion of several of the dimensions of the regnant ideology and the growing weakening of the transformative orientations of this ideology were also influenced by several basic historical circumstances or settings – above all by the combination of the effects of the Holocaust and the very establishment of the State of Israel, as well as of changing patterns of Jewish life in the Diaspora.

The Holocaust not only deprived Israel of great reserves of potential manpower in general and of leadership in particular. Beyond this it destroyed that centre of Jewish life within which much of the social and cultural creativity of the Zionist movements developed, a centre which also served, to some degree at least, as an object of revolutionary Zionist orientations – especially those orientated against the existence of life in the *Galut*, against which it rebelled and which it wanted to transform and change.

The disappearance of this object, under such horrible and tragic circumstances, while seemingly attesting in a terrible way to the veracity of the Zionist premisses about the non-viability of Jewish existence in the Diaspora, also deprived the Zionist movement of its major foci of controversy, of revolutionary fervour, orientation and activity. It also destroyed the bases of security which are paradoxically so crucial for the continuity of innovative rebellions and revolutions.

It therefore destroyed the broader cultural and institutional framework within which the rebellion could develop, and accordingly it weakened the revolutionary fervour of the Zionist movement which, to no small degree, had been dependent on the continuous existence of such a centre.

Thus, as we have seen above, one of the most important indications of the impact of the Holocaust on the self-perception of Israeli society was a gradual change in the attitude to Jewish Galut history and past – an attitude which gradually shifted from the almost total denial of the legitimacy of this history to a growing stress on the necessity to reconstruct a more positive evaluation – based perhaps above all on a sort of emotional yearning for this mould which no longer existed.

This attitude gradually came together with some of the ethnic emphases in the growing acceptance, as we shall see later, of Jewish tradition. Existence of the Diaspora became accepted rather than seen as a focus or object of active transformation. Thus the present was conflated with the future, an attitude which was also reinforced by the very establishment of the State of Israel.

Indeed it is impossible to understand the developments within Israel without taking into account basic changes in the relations between Israel and the Jewish communities in the Diaspora. However, before doing this we must dwell on some additional aspects of the processes of transformation of Israeli society, bearing on the exhaustion of the social dimension of its ideology, and bring together the lines of our analysis so far.

# Exhaustion of Ideological Discourse
## *Second generation leadership*

The connection between the processes of the segregation and recruitment of elites and the exhaustion of social and institutional dimensions of the Zionist ideology and of social and political fields can be traced in the process of incorporation of the generation of *Tsabras* or almost *Tsabras* into the centres of society in general and into the social and political arena in particular.

This generation – most of whom were born in Eretz Israel or at least raised in some of the formative frameworks, the youth movements, the elite high schools, the settlements, the *Hagana*, in the second and third decades of this century, epitomizing for many the very realization of the Zionist dream – became from the late 1950s on, very central in many spheres of life in Israel, proving their mettle above all in the field of security, later on in the army. From this generation came the best known commanders and officers – men like Yadin, Dayan, Alon or Ezer Weizmann – epitomizing for many, and often seen by themselves, as the new Jewish or Israeli men.

They also became prominent in other spheres of life such as the academic sphere, although here the number of those not born in Eretz Israel but who came as young people, many of whom had their primary or secondary schooling and especially university education in Eretz Israel, was somewhat greater.

There also arose a generation of Hebrew writers in Eretz Israel, slowly creating, as we have seen above, a vigorous literary activity, although here also it was those born in the Diaspora – like Uri Zvi Greenberg, Avraham Shlonsky or Nathan Alterman – who were for a long time predominant in this area.

They were somewhat less prominent in journalism; it seems that the more towering figures here were from among those born in the Diaspora. But here and in the media, they naturally became more central and visible with the passage of time.

Most – but not all – of these younger elites were from European backgrounds, although some came from Oriental sectors of the society – and much later, in the 1970s, the new immigrants also started to attain positions of leadership.

In the economic sphere there was also a continuous advancement of this second generation, varying in different sectors. The relatively most rapid advancement was in some of the governmental sectors – the 'economic' ministries and government corporations – but to some degree also in the private sector. Such advance was probably relatively slow in the large concerns of the Histadrut, but even there it gradually took place.

In many of these spheres the special impact of this generation was very much in line with the pattern of creativity or of institutional expansion which we have analysed earlier on. Thus they participated in the creation of new institutions and the expansion of older ones – such as the military and academic ones – creating some new models, as in the army, in the academic life and in civil **and** economic sectors, and adapting very dynamically other more general models to the changing, continuously developing, local conditions.

There was however one very central sphere of life in which the members of this generation did not become so prominent. This was the political and what may be called the social–ideological sphere.

It was only in the early or mid-1960s that some members of this generation – Dayan, Alon, Peres (who, being born in Poland, belongs only partly to this category), Yadin (who was for a long time seen by many as the great hope of Israeli politics) and somewhat later on larger numbers from this generation – at long last entered into the centres of politics.

But the mode of entry of most of them – with the exception of Alon who entered into politics relatively early through the central channels of *Ahdut Haavoda* and the *Hakibbutz Hameuchad* – was, as we have already seen above, characterized by some special features. They did not come in through rank-and-file political activity, but mostly through co-optation from above, sponsored as it were by the existing elites.

Later on, especially after the Six Day War, they became relatively central on the political scene, drawing great attention. For many, inside or outside Israel, these men, and probably above all Dayan, epitomized the very essence of the new Israeli.

And yet there has been an element of tragedy in all their political activities. It was not only that none of them – with the exception later on of Yitzhak Rabin – attained the Premiership to which they all seemed to aspire. Beyond this – which might have been accounted for by some weakness of political will – none of them was able to present or crystallize a political or social conception in the internal field, in the field of social and economic development which would go beyond the general premises of the dynamic conservative orientation.

Almost all of them concentrated in the area of security and foreign affairs and – with the partial exception of Alon who, in the famous Alon plan of 1968, attempted to present a pragmatic plan for the establishment of Jewish settlements in the West Bank, based mostly on security considerations – were not able to present a workable policy after 1967. Dayan's famous waiting for the phone call from Hussein certainly did not entail such policy, and even his later insistence on some accommodation with the Palestinians, on the importance of working together with them, did not crystallize into a workable plan, beyond the municipal level.

Truly enough, they were very influential; yet on the whole they were not able to impose whatever conceptions they did develop on their respective governments; and it was not clear to what degree these conceptions would indeed be viable.

Later on Dayan, who in many ways dominated the Israeli political scene from 1967 until 1974–5, played a very important part in the preparation for the peace with Egypt, and he and Weizmann, together with Attorney General Barak, a young scholar born in Poland who came to Israel in 1948 as a child of

12, joined forces in the working out of the Camp David agreement; yet it was Menahem Begin who attained this political fiat and who was able to sway public opinion for it.

Even smaller was the extent to which they developed any new conception or vision in the economic social field or in relation to the Jewish communities in the Diaspora beyond the pragmatic orientations to development and the establishment of a social democratic welfare state, or, as was the case – as we shall see in greater detail – with Yadin and the *Dash* party, beyond purely administrative or organizational dimensions.

It was only Rabin who did attain the Premiership in 1974 after Mrs Meir's resignation; from then and till 1977 he proved to be a rather efficient pragmatic Prime Minister, but much less of a political statesman able to break new ground – especially in the internal field. He showed many weaknesses – such as the lack of ability to withstand the pressures of *Gush Emunim*, due not only (as he claimed) to personal rivalries in his cabinet but also to the general uncertainty within the Labour camp about the nature of a possible political settlement, of being caught in the strong tendency to re-emphasize the territorial and historical attachment to different places in Eretz Israel which were opened up after the Six Day War. (This was also true of Alon who in 1968 was the first Israeli Minister who visited the members of *Gush Emunim* at Kiryat Arba, near Hebron, a settlement far beyond the concepts of the Alon plan – and justified it in historical terms, in terms of the place of Hebron as the city of the Patriarchs in Jewish history and tradition.)

It was indeed in these two areas – those of forging out new viable conceptions with respect to the new security and political situation and the relations with the Arabs, as well as with respect to the newly emerging social and economic reality – that the leadership of Labour in general, and the younger generations of this leadership in particular, manifested basic ideological or conceptual weakness and rigidity.

Unlike the first generations of this leadership, who combined strong but flexible ideological conceptions with very pragmatic approaches and flexibility, there now developed a quite far-reaching pragmatism yet combined with far-reaching conceptual rigidity.

Here the younger generation of leaders – especially Dayan and Alon – although having a certain veto power on political decisions, were on the whole overshadowed by the older one – and were not able to create any alternative conception or even to push too far their own pragmatic initiatives. It was only under the Rabin government that such an approach – the most important manifestation of which was the agreement on separation of forces with Egypt (1975), a forerunner of the peace with Egypt – began to some degree to be implemented.

The failure to develop some new viable conception in this realm was not only, or even mainly, an intellectual failure – although even this aspect was of great importance. Beyond this, a crucial part of the story was the lack of any probability of forging out such a conception because of the *de facto* veto power of two small groups within the Labour group: the *Ahdut Haavoda* represented in the cabinet by the *éminence grise* of the Meir and Rabin governments – *Israel Galili* – and to a smaller extent by Alon and the *Rafi* group represented by Dayan.

All these were, as Yossi Beilin pointed out,* outcomes of the unification of the Labour movements – attempts which did not give rise to a stronger cohesion of its leadership.

And indeed it was also in the period of Rabin's premiership that the breaking down of the internal solidarity and cohesion among the Labour leadership, the great internal division and multiplicity of factions, overshadowed but not readily coped with earlier on by the dominant figure of Mrs Golda Meir, became apparent. It was all these developments, triggered – but only triggered – by his wife's contraventions of the foreign exchange regulations, that made him the Prime Minister under whose leadership Labour lost in 1977 its predominance in the Israeli political scene.

Thus the story of most of the members of this generation in the political arena does indeed contain some elements of tragedy; they who were the great hope of Zionism showed neither a strong political will nor a new social or institution-building vision. Indeed, the impact of all the processes analysed above – the process of selection or specialization of the elites, the growing distance from active political life, their growing orientation to security and the co-optative mode of their later entry into politics, their being overshadowed by the generation of the Founding Fathers – could indeed be discerned in, to use the French expression, their *formation* in the relative narrow scope of the frameworks in which they grew up. And, though the distance from the wider experience of the Diaspora provided them, as compared with the former generations, with security and freedom and firmness, these frameworks seemingly also narrowed their horizons – thus pointing to one of the basic problems and dilemmas inherent in the implementation of the Zionist vision.

It is of course a moot question to what degree all this would have been different if the War of Independence had not exerted its terrible toll of 6,000 dead, many of whom were potential members of the future elite. Be that as it may, the story of this generation provides another – perhaps most indicative and tragic – illustration of the combination of the great activism and expansion together with the exhaustion of the social political dimensions of the Zionist–pioneering vision.

## Attempts at new political visions

But the poverty or exhaustion of ideological vision were not confined to the new generation of leadership, nor to the central core of *Mapai* with its preoccupation with *Mamlachtiut* on the one hand and with great institution-building and maintaining itself in power on the other. It was also, with some

* Yossi Beilin, 'The Political and Social Costs of Unification in the Labour Movement', Research Report (mim.) (Tel Aviv 1983).

sectarian additions, characteristic of the more 'leftist' parts of the Labour camps. Its best expression can perhaps be found in a famous article by Yitzhak Ben Aharon, a leader of *Ahdut Haavoda*, published in January 1963 in *Lamerhav*, the daily of *Ahdut Haavoda*, under the title *Oz Leshinui* (Courage for Change). In this programmatic article Ben Aharon denounced the whole mode of nation- and institution-building that had taken place since the establishment of the State as being non-socialist, giving rise to a new exploitative and parasitic bourgeoisie, to the pursuit of a higher standard of living and to growing class divisions. He recommended some sort of unification of all the different parts of the Labour movement in order to implement a new socialist policy, the essence of which would be a vigorous redistribution of national wealth and restructuring of the economy (including lowering of standards of living) in order to minimize or abolish the growing economic dependence on outside forces.

There was but little pioneering vision in this programme: no answer to the problem of autonomous participation of the different sectors of the population in common creative ventures; no indication of how to reconstruct the pioneering vision in the changing circumstances and how to maintain the strongly elitist emphasis on duties and on attainment of excellence in such various spheres of common endeavour.

All these processes have become connected with the lack of ability of these elite groups to cope with the new problems of reconstruction of the parameter of cultural activity and symbols of collective identity.

The exhaustion of such new visions from within the elites around the Labour camp or closely related to it was also evident in the attempts – mostly within the mid-1970s – to generate new visions or programmes against the ossification of the older sectors.

Of special interest here is the experience of *Dash* – the Democratic Movement for Change – which emerged, as we have seen, several months before the 1977 elections (as well as the nature of those extra-parliamentary politics which developed around the Labour camp – as contrasted with those for the 'right').

The experience of *Dash* was very indicative of the developments of the political field as they bear on the exhaustion of the ideological vision on which the initial institutional mould of Israel was based. It signalled as it were the failure of the most significant attempt to save this mould by 'rejuvenation' of its leadership and by a seemingly new programme within the basic – continuously opening – premisses of this mould.

As we have indicated above, *Dash* was organized after the announcement in 1977 by Yigael Yadin that he was ready to enter the political arena. It drew to itself several existing political groups – the most important of which were the *Shinui* under the leadership of Amnon Rubinstein (one of the developments out of the various protest movements after the Yom Kippur War) and the *Merkaz Hahofchi* (Free Centre), an offshoot of Likud under the leadership of Shmuel Tamir. Both of these groups came from beyond the Labour framework and, as the near future was to show, all these elements were rather strange political bedfellows. But the great majority of the leadership as well as of the second and third ranks of *Dash*, as well as probably of its supporters, came from within social and economic sectors close to the *Maarach* – even from the more successful among them.

They all voiced closely interconnected feelings of not being able to participate in the political centre, as well as the ossification of this centre; of the call of innovation from within it and of the weakness of the political leadership with respect to external security as well as internal matters.

It was these groups, under what appeared to be the dynamic leadership of Yadin, that appealed to the very large population – about 250,000 people – who voted in 1977 for *Dash* and who saw in this attempt the great chance to correct the many failures of the *Maarach*, without in any deep sense going beyond the basic premises of the regnant institutional mould, and who saw in Yadin the man who might indeed achieve this goal. He – and they – saw in *Dash* the force which would be the balancing force, the *Leshon Hamoznaim* without which the *Maarach* would not be able to form the government, and which therefore would be able to impose on the *Maarach* its reformatory orientations.

As is well known, they were to be gravely disappointed and in the 1981 elections *Dash* no longer existed, and most of its votes seemed, as far as one can ascertain on the basis of electoral statistics, to have gone back to the *Maarach*.

Many reasons have been adduced to explain this débâcle and demise of *Dash*. One such reason lies, of course, in the very heterogeneous composition, especially of the leadership, but also of the wider sectors of the movement. Second, and closely connected, was the lack of any political experience of the leadership of this movement and a very naive type of political action and programme.

This lack of political experience was, to no small degree, related to their continuous non-participation in political activities and their naive assumption that goodwill and some broad slogans were more important than such experience and continuous political work and organization.

But probably more basic, though indeed closely related to the former, was the basic political conception that seemed to have guided large parts of the *Dash* leaderhip – Yadin himself and those closest to him. This conception was perhaps best epitomized in the claim that it would be some administrative changes – such as the creation of a special Vice Prime Minister in charge of Internal Affairs (a post which in fact Yadin occupied for several years) or the administrative reorganization of social services, or the appointment of special district Commissioners to mediate between the broader strata of the population and the bureaucratic establishment – that would solve the major social problems, be they those of the 'quarters', of destitute groups, or of the *edot* in general.

This programme was indeed very much in tune with Ben-Gurion's earlier insistence on changes in the electoral system which Yadin had, in its time, supported very strongly, and which, however right or wrong in itself, assumed that such organizational changes would by themselves give rise to some new modes of political participation – without relation to the contents or directions of such participation.

Beyond this semi-technocratic conception, as well as a general emphasis on goodwill and on civil rights, there was not within the central core of *Dash*, especially of what remained of *Dash* when it joined the first Likud government after *Shinui* had left it, any new conception of the ways in which the major stagnative and restrictive tendencies against which they had basically come out could be changed – thus attesting in all these ways to the exhaustion, among many of the groups which had been socially close to the *Maarach* or at least to its institutional mould, of any new dynamic political or social vision.

Some parts of *Dash* – above all *Shinui* – did have a clearer political conception, very close indeed to that expounded by independent Liberal or Progressive groups in their stress on what they called *Zionut Shfuia* (sane Zionism), emphasizing civility, rule of law, rights of citizens; but all these themes, while certainly important in themselves, did not constitute such an overall political programme.

As they, however, had but little to say on other themes which were inherent in the premisses of the regnant ideology and of the initial institutional mould, above all those related to institutional building creativity, it is very doubtful whether they would have been able to create a strong central force – although possibly they could have exerted some influence in the direction of the themes they exposed.

The exhaustion of the regnant ideology, of socio-political vision from around the Labour camp, were also manifest in the case of extra parliamentary politics, which have developed in Israel, above all since the early 1970s, and which we shall discuss in the next chapter.

# The Changing Normative Ambience of Israeli Society
## *Loss of legitimation of the dominant elites; directions of transformation*

The full impact of this exhaustion of the social–institutional dimension of the Labour–Zionist ideology, as well as that related to the reconstruction of collective identity, on the disintegration of the initial mould of Israeli society, cannot be understood except in connection with the changing normative ambience of the Israeli society – manifest in a growing dissociation between the normative specifications of the ideology and the actual social and economic developments leading to a growing feeling of delegitimation of the ruling elites.

We have already seen that the relations between general symbols rooted in this ideology and concrete institutional problems and conflicts became – beyond the developmental and distributive–allocative emphases – weaker and more and more difficult to identify, while at the same time the claims of the elites to provide such regulation continued in full force.

The broad ideological social orientations did not spill over into normative guidelines for dealing with the concrete problems and conflicts which developed within the continuously changing and diversified social structure, and within the continuously opening political and social moulds, and the consciousness and perception of this gap became more and more widespread, and naturally closely related to the changing mode of power relations in Israel.

The origins of this gap were rooted in the prevalence of the clientelistic mode of relations between the centre and the periphery which perpetuated many of the particularistic norms which were indeed prevalent in the former period. But, unlike in that period, these particularistic norms were no longer connected with strong elitist commitment and obligation nor with the strong solidarity of the various movements. Rather, they developed as a result of interplay between the attempts of the ruling groups to buy off the periphery and the pressures of the periphery, thus contravening many of the universalistic premisses of many of the State services and gradually giving rise to a situation of growing normlessness – very often generated by the norm-setters themselves, and most visible in such areas as wage policy, labour relations and taxation, which were closely related to the ideology.

In all these spheres, more and more attempts were made to contravene – out of the interplay of power and groups, of pressures and of the attempts of elites to pacify many groups, especially the stronger ones who were potential troublemakers – the basic universalistic norms set up by the elites.

As these attempts were usually made by the norm-setters themselves and were seen as connected with the power game of the elites, they gave rise to a far-reaching change in the perception of the various aspects of the ideology by different sectors of the society.

While to the new ruling elites this ideology and its relations to the developing institutional structure and its problems were perceived as natural and given, it was not perceived in the same way by the peripheral sectors. They tended to perceive these policies as being directed more and more towards safeguarding the positions of power of the existing frameworks, and as guided more by the internal dynamism of the various power groups and less by the ideological concern and the national goals set by them.

This new normative ambience, the growing feeling of a certain normlessness – at least *de facto* legitimized by the elite – was also reinforced by the continuous mixture, among the elite (as well as among parts of the civil service) and in their relations to the broader strata of the older particularistic sectorial attitudes (often reconstructed in a clientelistic mode) and into widespread networks of 'protekzia' with the more universalistic ones often officially propounded. This mixture created a rather anomic normative atmosphere.

As a result of all these processes, the regnant ideology became more and more identified by broader sectors of the population in general, and by many of the new immigrants in particular, as a mechanism for the maintenance of the power position of the ruling elites in a changing, more open society. The elite started to lose its claims to commitment and was not able to combine such commitments with the continuous opening up of the institutional mould, although the quest for such a commitment, even if certainly not in the older form, continued to be a very important ingredient among large sectors of the public – as well as in the self-portrayal and legitimation of the elites.

Of great importance here was the fact that the various attempts to unify the Labour movement were not connected either with the generation of a new interpretation of the Labour–Zionist vision or with growing cohesion of this elite.

Thus these processes of transformation of ideology – as has been the case in many revolutionary societies – went against the basic ideological premisses of the institutional mould and, above all, against the basic legitimation and self-legitimation of the ruling elites and of the centre. It went in many ways against their self-portrayal, and against the ways in which they presented themselves to the broader strata whom they attempted to mobilize in a democratic manner. Thus these processes contributed to a growing disenchantment with the elites and their vision, and to a weakening of the legitimation of the very ideology which they were portraying themselves as carrying and symbolizing.

All these changes in Israeli society, leading to the disintegration of its initial institutional mould, cannot be understood without taking into account the far-reaching changes in the relations between Israel and Jewish communities in the Diaspora – and we shall turn now to the analysis of these developments.

# CHAPTER 16

# The New Historical Experience of Jewish Communities in the Diaspora and the Place of the State of Israel

## The Emergence of American Jewry
### *A new acceptance by host countries*

The reasons for the very dramatic – even if quiet and in many ways almost imperceptible and seemingly natural – changes in the relations between Israel and the Jewish communities in the Diaspora are many, but two are probably of greatest importance. One was the change in the whole *problematique* of Jewish modern life as it crystallized in the United States and to a smaller degree in Western European countries after the Second World War. The second was the internal changes in the cultural and social format in Israeli society itself, which we analysed above. At the background of both of these processes there was of course, the terrible experience of the Holocaust.

The central focal change, from the point of view of the relations between the Jewish communities in the Diaspora and the State of Israel, was the fact that the historical experience of these communities – and hence the nature of the *problematique* of Jewish life – moved away in directions greatly differing from those that had developed in Eastern and Central Europe and shaped the development of the Zionist movement and of the Jewish settlement on the Land of Israel.

The most important social and political process which changed the nature of the *problematique* of Jewish life in the Diaspora was the crystallization and legitimation in their host societies of a new conception of Jewish collective life. Instead of attempting to restrict Jewish identity and collective activities to semi-private religious and philanthropic spheres – as had been the case in nineteenth-century Western and Central Europe – this new attitude accepted the combination of the communal, 'ethnic' primordial and political components of Jewish identity, and of their peoplehood.

This acceptance and articulation of communal, primordial and political components of Jewish collective identity was combined with the acceptance of the Jews as full, 'emancipated' citizens of their countries, and not just – as had happened in Eastern Europe between the wars – a minority national group among other such minority and majority groups. These developments were connected with the very far-reaching economic and occupational advancements of Jews, far beyond what had taken place in Europe in the nineteenth and first four decades of the twentieth centuries, as well as their growing participation in some of the most central cultural frameworks and activities of their respective countries; and the parallel development of possibilities of relatively troublefree assimilation.

## Background statistics in the USA

This new pattern of modern Jewish existence developed first of all – and even there only gradually and after the Second World War – in the United States, and to a smaller degree in Western Europe; the Jewish communities in Eastern and Central Europe, whose historical experience had generated the Zionist movement, had been effectively wiped out by the Holocaust.

As is well known, the development of the Jewish population in the United States was relatively slow until the great wave of immigration from Eastern Europe. Starting with 1,200 Jews in 1790, the Jewish population increased to about 50,000 in 1848 – composed mostly of Sephardi groups and of some German Jews – and to slightly less than a quarter of a million – mostly from Germany and Central Europe – before the mass immigrations from Eastern Europe. By the turn of the twentieth century the Jewish population in the United States had increased to over one million, by the late 1920s to over four million and by 1950 to approximately five millions. During this period Jewish population growth was greater than that of the American population as a whole, and the proportion of Jews in the total US population increased from 0.1 per cent in 1840 to 3.6 per cent in 1927.

## The early settlements in the United States

The development of the new pattern of Jewish life, of a new type of Jewish historical experience in the United States, was a very slow process – and above all, it was only very gradually perceived as such by the Jews and by the general society alike; yet signs in this direction developed from relatively early on.

The mode of organization of the first waves of Jewish immigrants in the United States – those who were destined to become by the 1880s the upper echelons of Jewish society – was that of dispersed communities, with relatively good relations with their neighbours, seeing themselves as a part of American life – without having necessarily to abandon their Jewishness. Their Jewishness, in so far as it looked for any special expression, found it in the religious field, especially in the Reform and the beginnings of the Conservative movements. The Sephardi and above all German immigrants organized themselves in Reform synagogues – very much in line with the upper and middle class of the broader, still very mobile, society – and started to sponsor the establishment of some new Jewish scholarly institutions, communal and philanthropic activities.

In Nathan Glazer's words:

Thus when one reads the memoirs of the period (for example, the auto-biography of

Annie Nathan Meyers) one gets a picture of Jews with a more integrated relation to America than they have had since (even taking into account Mrs Meyers' very high social position). Reform Judaism, which for a while seemed on the way to unifying American Jewry, was in tune with developments in upper-class Protestant sects. Jews had no important special interests in those years that marked them off from the rest of the population. They did not spend much time worrying about and combating discrimination and anti-Semitism, because these did not become a problem until the end of the nineteenth century. Nor, of course, were they agitated by Zionism or anti-Zionism until well into the twentieth century. On the whole, Jews lived comfortable lives, had large families and servants, entered professions, and met with very little discrimination. Those were the days before Americans in general worried about being respectable – and consequently Jews were more respectable. When the newest multi-millionaire might be some barbarian who had no table manners, it hardly mattered if he was a Jew. Certainly, it did not matter in the West, where the few Jews often seemed to end up as leading citizens.*

These developments were, initially at least, greatly influenced by Central and Western European Jewish approaches, which steered the Jewish community in the direction of defining itself in purely religious terms.

But this definition, as well as the new pattern of Jewish life, were already adapted to the American setting, combining some crucial features which could not be found in Europe. These specific patterns were closely related to their small numbers, and to the fact – the crucial importance of which we shall analyse later – that, given the tradition of religious toleration in the colonies and in the United States, there was much less pressure on conversion. Jewish religion was fully accepted in a society based on the separation of Church and State as fully legitimate. Thus, the reorganization of religious life did not necessarily entail giving up some wider Jewish identity. Although in fact the assimilationist tendencies were very strong, their ideological articulation was relatively weak, and in many of these ideological formulations the maintenance not only of Jewish religious practices but also of some sort of Jewish group life was not seen as being in principle opposition to the participation in American life, but on the whole rather as a part of it. Even when some of them – especially in the South – declared themselves to be Americans of Mosaic persuasion, this did not necessarily have the same apologetic and strong ideological overtones as in Europe.

The ideology of American Reform was based on a very strong rationalistic emphasis which stressed religious reform as something common to all Americans and, although these extreme derivatives of this ideology were not followed in practice by many congregations, the ambience of becoming part of the American scene without giving up some sort of Jewish group identity was rather widespread – even if this identity could become very diluted. It is indeed perhaps no surprise that it was from within the Reform movement that some of the most ardent Zionist leaders later emerged.

* Nathan Glazer, 'Social Characteristics of American Jews, 1654–1954', *American Jewish Yearbook* (1955).

## The influx from Eastern Europe

The nature of Jewish social life, organization, public activity and ideologies of Jewish life changed greatly with the mass immigration from Eastern Europe.

Thus the first generation of Jewish immigrants from Eastern Europe was mainly preoccupied with the problems of economic advance from the rather low initial starting-points, and with becoming Americanized. At the same time, throughout these years, they maintained and developed a variety of communal organizations, as well as of very strong family networks, aided of course by their occupational and ecological concentration. While the struggle for advancement was naturally orientated to the new life in America, the modes of communal organization were, initially at least, often couched in terms of Eastern European ideologies, religious practices and patterns of social, political and communal organization.

The strength of these European experiences was reinforced by the fact that the Jewish mass-migration to the United States was part of a broader European one, which included immigrants from many European nations – especially from Eastern and Southern Europe – with rather strong, deeply rooted anti-Semitic attitudes. So for a long period of time the Jews in the United States lived in close ecological proximity to these European groups.

This tendency was also at least partially strengthened by the fact that many of the Jewish immigrants from Europe came from the lower-middle groups, with a very strong nucleus of artisans with relatively mobile, easily transferable skills. There were among them relatively fewer intellectuals than among either those who remained in Europe or those who went to Palestine. Thus the immigrants naturally hung on to – or developed – modes of communal organization which at least initially were very similar to the ones to which they had been accustomed in their countries of origin, although even some of these (for instance Jewish labour unions) quickly become Americanized. At the same time, the impact of the Eastern European immigrants began to be felt on the earlier, by now more established, Jewish groups, which in the beginning tended to look on this immigration with rather great dismay.

The challenge that the immigrants posed for existing Jewish institutions, and the responses were very diversified. Conservative groups and institutions became revived by them, even Reform was greatly reconstructed by the encounter with them and, as we shall see in greater detail later on, new forms of organization of Jewish life and ideologies, with a distinct American flavour, started to develop from at least the late 1920s.

# Religious Toleration in the United States
## Anti-Semitism

All these developments, especially those of mass immigrations, were of course connected with different modes of anti-Semitism. Some sort of anti-Semitism – although probably more of a populistic than of the very deep religious nature –

was prevalent among wide sectors of American society. Popular anti-Semitism, as is being more and more documented, extended from the colonial times throughout the first century of the new nation. It gathered great strength with the influx of the mass immigrations – by which time many of the 'native' upper Americans had also started to crystallize more fully their new class and national identity – and was naturally reinforced by the influx of foreign elements. Its development was also connected with the coming of many Eastern and Central European groups with strong anti-Semitic traditions. Later anti-Semitism was also probably an important ingredient – although certainly not the only and not even the predominant one – in the closing, during the 1920s, of the gates of America to mass immigration. It re-emerged also in a very extreme way in the 1930s, in wake of the depression. It was also with the influx of this mass immigration that there were far-reaching and extensive social segregations of Jews in clubs, in schools and universities, in housing districts and in different occupations, as compared with the period before that when, given the small number of Jews and their geographic dispersion, it was much less acute. It was in this period that affluent 'upper class' Jews could find themselves excluded from clubs they themselves had founded a generation or so earlier.

Such exclusion and discrimination began to be felt more acutely by Jews in this period of the late 1920s and 1930s, when the second generation of American Jews started to advance very fast economically. More and more of them started to find themselves blocked from universities, from such occupations as banking or from the higher echelons of industry, and it was the Jews with their quick mobility that were more exposed to such practices than other immigrant groups – practices which were indeed often couched in religious– anti-Semitic terms, often based on a conception of the United States as a Christian society.

It was also in this period that, because of all these processes, some of the mobile Jews at least found themselves in a seemingly typical Western–Central European situation, with growing pressures to assimilation – sometimes even to conversion. Such assimilationist tendencies were to no small degree also reinforced by the strong homogenizing tendencies of the predominant civil, semi-secularized Protestant mould and by their orientations towards new immigrants, with the ideology of the melting pot in general and with often strong anti-Semitic tones in particular.

It was a combination – of the fact that the mobile Jews left the confines of the relatively closed Jewish settlements of the first generation of immigrants; of the attitudes and practices of discrimination, concomitant limitations on the educational, occupational mobility of Jews and the fact of their social segregation in their own clubs; and of the pressures to assimilation – that led in the 1930s the Zionist leader Chaim Arlosoroff, and in the late 1940s the poet Shimon Halkin, to analyse the Jewish experience in the United States in the usual European–Zionist terms and to prophesy that Jews would be torn between assimilation and discrimination, if not outright possible destruction.

## The changing problematique of Jewish experience in the Diaspora

And yet, even in this period, the openness of American life and the tempo of its economic development offered the Jews – despite all these restrictions – many continuous opportunities and possibilities of advance, and the whole mode of Jewish historical existence in the USA was moving beyond the premises based on the European experience. Thus, indeed, many of these interpretations were, in fact, superimposed upon a historical experience which was different from the European one.

The crux of this specific American–Jewish historical experience was that all the pressures – to assimilation and Americanization, the reaction of American society to such assimilation, and the threats of anti-Semitism – were of a different kind from those in Europe, so that a new *problematique* of Jewish life crystallized in the Diaspora.

The major characteristic of this new *problematique* was that it defined, even if only gradually and intermittently, the major problem of Jewish existence in the modern world in terms of a search for different ways to express Jewish collective identity, a Jewish peoplehood, in the Diaspora. In this search, the political dimension and civilizational dimension of Jewish identity was stressed within the framework of the continuously changing Western societies (or rather in this case, of the USA), but at the same time the Jews still saw themselves as full members of their respective national collectives.

Basically – despite many misgivings and fears about the ultimate lack of viability of Jewish life in the Diaspora – the consciousness of such a *problematique* took the possibility of some sort of Jewish free collective existence more or less for granted, searching for different ways of expressing its collective identity. The feeling became more and more prevalent among the Jews that it was possible for the Jews in America to look on themselves as both Americans and Jews, and, unlike in the European scene, not to see any basic contradiction between the two identities, even when strongly emphasizing the collective, primordial, historical and political dimensions of their Jewish identity.

## The American political ideology

The explanation of the emergence of this new type of Jewish historical experience is rooted in several basic facts – some of which have often been stressed in the literature. One was the fact that the USA was a country of continuous mass immigration of diverse groups, all of which, especially given the openness of the society, helped to maintain some of the distinctiveness of these different groups.

Second was the fact that the economic and occupational advance of the Jews and their integration were attained, on the whole, in a continuously developing economy, and that – except for the local level – they were but rarely heavy competitors with other groups who could see them as either threatening their economic position or blocking their own advance, as was the case in many countries in Central and Eastern Europe.

There was also the affinity between the American ethos and Jewish economic advance. The general American ethos – imbued by the school and the workplace – stressed educational attainment, occupational mobility and economic advance, all strongly emphasized universalistic and achievement orientations. These 'Protestant' attitudes were easily taken up among the Jews – building on some very strong bases in the Jewish ethos itself. In particular the Jews manifested intensive motivation, evident in the fact strongly stressed by Nathan Glazer that, even when they were still working as labourers, in very dire conditions, their whole ambience, style of life and above all orientations were those of the middle class. All these factors gave rise to a very quick and dramatic process of social and economic mobility, especially, but not only, in the second, American-born generation.* They were helped in this by their strong tradition of learning.

These characteristics of the Jews led some Americans – for instance the renowned American Sociologist Robert Park – to propose in the 1920s that Jewish history should be made part of the general curriculum, as Jews were in a way the prototypical Americans.

All these explanations contain, of course, very strong kernels of truth, and refer to very important aspects of the picture. They are not, however, in themselves sufficient to explain the specific historical experience of the Jewish–American experience – as the comparison, for instance, with another country of mass immigration and of relative economic advancement till about the 1930s of this century, namely Argentina, points out. One crucial difference from Argentina, with its Catholic heritage – even the heritage of the Inquisition – was, of course, the existence in the USA from the very beginning of basic religious toleration.

Some of the highlights of such toleration are, of course, well known. Its first full official articulation can probably be found in Washington's famous reply to the Hebrew Congregation of Newport, Rhode Island in 1790:

Gentlemen:– While I received with much satisfaction your address replete with expressions of esteem, I rejoice in the opportunity of assuring you that I shall always retain grateful remembrance of the cordial welcome I experienced on my visit to Newport from all classes of citizens.

The reflection on the days of difficulty and danger which are past is rendered the more sweet from a consciousness that they are succeeded by days of uncommon prosperity and security.

If we have wisdom to make the best use of the advantages with which we are now favored, we cannot fail, under the just administration of a good government, to become a great and happy people.

The citizens of the United States of America have a right to applaud themselves for

---

* N. Glazer, 'Social Characteristics'. See also S. Kuznets, 'Immigration of Russian Jews to the United States: Background and Structure' in *Perspectives on American History* IX (Cambridge, Mass. 1915), pp. 35–124.

having given to mankind examples of an enlarged and liberal policy – a policy worthy of imitation. All possess alike liberty of conscience and immunities of citizenship.

It is now no more that toleration is spoken of as if it were the indulgence of one class of people that another enjoyed the exercise of their inherent natural rights, for, happily, the Government of the United States, which gives to bigotry no factions, to persecution no assistance, requires only that they who live under its protection should demean themselves as good citizens in giving it on all occasions their effectual support.

It would be inconsistent with the frankness of my character not to avow that I am pleased with your favourable opinion of my administration and fervent wishes for my felicity.

May the children of the stock of Abraham who dwell in this land continue to merit and enjoy the good will of the other inhabitants – while every one shall sit in safety under his own vine and fig tree and there shall be none to make him afraid.

May the father of all mercies scatter light, and not darkness, upon our paths, and make us all in our several vocations useful here, and in His own due time and way everlastingly happy.*

Similarly, in 1810, Congress passed a law, the Sunday mail one (the like of which could not be envisaged in any European country) that mail in Jewish populated neighbourhoods should be delivered on Sundays. To quote Seymour Martin Lipset:

> Although Sunday Blue Laws continued for many decades after the Revolution, the rights of the irreligious found considerable backing, as reflected in the insistence – already noted – by the Democrats that the mails be delivered on Sundays. In 1830 – twenty years after the passage of the Sunday mails bill – a Senate committee report, authored by a future Vice-President and endorsed by a majority of that House, stated explicitly that in the United States religion and irreligion had equal rights, and that laws proclaiming that the government should not provide services on Sunday would work an injustice to irreligious people or non-Christians, and would constitute a special favor for Christians as a group. The report, written by a deeply religious active Baptist, stated these principles in unequivocal terms:
>
>> The Constitution regards the conscience of the Jew as sacred as that of the Christian, and gives no more authority to adopt a measure affecting the conscience of a solitary individual than that of a whole community. . . . If Congress shall declare the first day of the week holy, it will not satisfy the Jew nor the Sabbatarian. It will dissatisfy both and, consequently, convert neither. . . . It must be recollected that, in the earliest settlement of this country, the spirit of persecution, which drove the pilgrims from their native homes, was brought with them to their new habitations; and that some Christians were scourged and others put to death for no other crime than dissenting from the dogmas of their rulers. . . .
>>
>> If a solemn act of legislation shall in *one* point define the God or point out to the citizen one religious duty, it may with equal propriety define *every* part of divine revelation and enforce *every* religious obligation, even to the forms and ceremonies of worship; the endowment of the church, and the support of the clergy. . . .
>>
>> It is the duty of this government to affirm to *all* – to the Jew or Gentile, Pagan, or Christian – the protection and advantages of our benignant institutions on *Sunday*, as well as every day of the week.†

* From *Publications of the American Jewish Historical Society*, No. 3. (1895; second edition 1915), pp. 91–2.
† S. M. Lipset, *The First New Nation* (New York 1963), pp. 164–5.

Indeed the toleration which developed in America was not just religious tolerance in the European sense – based on the limitation or disestablishment of an established Church – although the expressions used were often still couched in European terms.

The full nature of this toleration can only be understood if seen in the framework of the whole format, of the distinct pattern of American collective identity and basic political ideology. The crucial element here was that this collective identity, and above all its political expression, was not based – as was the case in Europe – on primordial historical elements, but on a political ideology derived indeed from religious premises, but transformed in a somewhat semi-secularized way into what R. N. Bellah called 'civil religion', ideologically and institutionally based on the separation of Church and State, and very much future- and not past-orientated.*

The American way of life, even though formulated in terms of the predominant Protestant tradition, was couched in terms of a common political ideology and way of life, with religious overtones and an emphasis on the Christian heritage – often in Biblical terminology, rather than in terms of the combination of religious tradition with historical–primordial, ethnic or national identities – as was the case in Europe. In S. P. Huntington's words:

> For most people national identity is the product of a long process of historical evolution involving common conceptions, common experiences, common ethnic background, common language, common culture and usually common religion. National identity is thus organic in character. Such however is not the case in the United States. American nationality has been defined in political rather than organic terms. The political ideas of the American creed have been the basis of national identity. . . . The United States thus had its origins in a conscious political act, in assertion of basic political principles and in adherence to the constitutional agreement based on those principles . . .†

Accordingly none of the immigrant groups in general and the Jews in particular had to struggle in principle over accepting political rights; they acquired full citizenship relatively easily and naturally as a part of the basic premises of American society, and Jews did not differ in this respect from any other immigrant group. The question of Jewish emancipation never constituted a political problem – and the Jewish question in whatever guise never constituted a central question in the public discourse of America, as it did in Europe.

Similarly the separation of Church and State in the United States was not so much an outcome of struggles against a tradition of tension between the two as a principled derivative from its political assumptions, from the basic fact that the most active elements in the formulation of the ideology of the colonies and of the USA were members of different Protestant sects.

---

* See R. N. Bellah, 'The Civil Religion in America' in Bellah, *Beyond Belief* (New York 1970), pp. 168–193. See also Y. Arieli, *The Future Directedness of the American Experience* (Jerusalem 1964), and Lipset, *The First New Nation.*

† S. P. Huntington, *American Politics – The Promise of Disharmony* (Cambridge, Mass. 1981) p. 23.

Because of these basic characteristics the American collective was potentially open – first of all to acceptance of religious diversity as part of the American way of life and, second, unlike European nation-states, to the incipient possibilities of the acceptance of political expression of such religious, as well as – later – ethnic groups so long as they accepted the basic tenets of the American political creed and adhered to it.

The legitimation of such diversity was initially very partial and weak, especially in so far as the ideology of the melting pot and of the American way of life, strongly articulated in the schools and in the media, stressed the more homogenizing tendencies and demands of American life.

But already, in Washington's address to the Jewish congregation in Newport, the expression of Children of Abraham could have been interpreted as going beyond the purely religious connotation, while the use of biblical terms could also bring out the affinity to the people of the Bible.

Obviously such possibilities of collective expressions in general, and of the Jewish one in particular, were continuously fraught with tensions, with group hostility in general and with – above all religious and social – anti-Semitism in particular. But American anti-Semitism, although it was, as we have seen, often quite widespread and sometimes even rampant, was different in crucial ways from the European one.

First of all it was not connected, as in Europe, with the formation of new national identities and nation-states, and it was not part of the crystallization of the symbolic and legal boundaries of the American political community. In principle, the basic tenets of the American civil religion and political ideology were opposed to it – not only on the formal level, as in Europe, but also because the historical and primordial elements of anti-Semitism were alien to the basic premisses of this ideology.

Second, given the combination of the religious ambience – often formulated in secular terms – of American life, and the self-definition of American people, the segregation of Church and State and the religious tone of many movements of protest in America, anti-Semitism could not hang its hat on the peg of either the denial of the legitimacy of different religions or a strong anti-secularist tone. Because of all this, anti-Semitism in America had, in Jonathan Sarna's words,

to compete with other forms of animus. Racism, anti-Quakerism, Anglophobia, anti-Catholicism, anti-Masonry, anti-Mormonism, anti-Orientalism, nativism, anti-Teutonism, primitive anti-Communism – these and other waves have periodically swept over the American landscape, scarring and battering citizens. Because hatred is so varied and diffused, no group experiences for long the full brunt of national odium. Furthermore, most Americans retain bitter memories of days past when they or their ancestors were the objects of malevolence. At least in some cases, this leads them to exercise restraint. The American strain of anti-Semitism is thus less potent than its European counterpart, and it faces a larger number of natural competitors. To reach epidemic proportions, it must first crowd out a vast number of contending hatreds. . . . The Founding Fathers, whatever they personally thought of Jews, gave them full equality. Hence, in America, Jews have always fought anti-Semites freely. Never having received their emancipation as an 'award', they have had no fears of losing it. Instead, from the beginning, they made full use of their rights to freedom of speech. 'Who are you, or what are you . . . that in a free country you dare to trample on any sectary whatever of people,' Haym Salomon had demanded back in 1784. . . . Non-Jews could respond by pointing to America's supposedly 'Christian character' – a view of American society occasionally recognized by no less august a body than the Supreme Court. Nevertheless, the Constitution has proved to be a potent weapon in the Jew's defense. German Jews could appeal to no similar document. As early as 1784, a 'Jew Broker' – probably Haym Salomon, responded publicly and forcefully to the anti-Semitic charges of a prominent Quaker lawyer, not hesitating to remind him that his 'own religious sectary' could also form 'very proper subjects of criticism and animadversion. . . .'*

Thus social popular as well as upper-class semi-religious anti-Semitism, strong as it often was, had to struggle not only with Jews but with the very principles of American political systems, and it was in the name of these principles and not just of general ideals of Enlightenment and humanism, that Jews could – and did – battle against anti-Semitism.

So it was the continuous tension between the American political credo and the 'natural' anti-Semitism of a society which often viewed itself as Christian, as a Christian nation, that constituted part of the basic parameters of the Jewish historical experience in America. In this battle legitimacy and the official American ethos were on the side of the Jews permitting them indeed to fight anti-Semitism openly, publicly and not necessarily only from a defensive posture – although it could never be eradicated.

# The Legitimation of Diversity in the United States
## *The organization of Jewish life*

The actual experience of life in America permitted some such diversity even with the influx of mass immigration in the late nineteenth and early twentieth centuries.

Thus even in the earlier period of mass migration, the very gradual economic advance of the Jews did not on the whole necessarily lead to the abandonment of their religious and communal activities. Family solidarity and communal cohesion and help remained very strong – as did also positive religious, primordial and even political identification with the Jewish people – even if, among the second and third generation of immigrants, these elements often became, initially at least, greatly weakened, often undermined by the ideology of the melting pot, by the social pressures connected with it and by the exclusive aspects of anti-Semitism. But even in the third decade of this century, when many mobile Jews were experiencing these restrictive aspects of American life, some very significant new developments in the mode of Jewish organization and *ideology* were indeed taking place.

* J. Sarna, 'Antisemitism and American History', *Commentary* (March 1981), pp. 46–7.

Already relatively early – even before that period – Jews started to organize themselves in more diversified ways beyond the more religious, cultural or philanthropic activities, first of all in a very vigorous way on the local level in a series of decentralized communities, later also in various countrywide religious and philanthropic organizations in various clubs.

They started to organize themselves actively against discrimination – as in the Anti-Defamation League founded in 1913 to organize help for Jews in difficult situations, and in the Joint Distribution Committee founded during the First World War – but there never developed here that centralized pattern of Jewish organization characteristic of English or French Jewry.

Probably even more dramatic was the development of new types of Jewish organizations, as well as of ideological definitions of Jewish life – both perhaps best epitomized in the work of Mordechai Kaplan (1881–1982), although certainly not confined to him. It was he who first propounded – although probably building on some former attempts – the programme of transforming the synagogue from a place of prayer to a base for a wide range of Jewish community activities.

This organizational conception, often resisted by the older Jewish religious – Reform and Conservative – establishment, was very closely connected with this ideological conception of Jewishness, with 'Reconstructionism'. While in purely religious terms this went beyond even extreme Reform, yet it was connected in his view with the conception of Jewish peoplehood, with Jews as carriers of a distinct civilization which could, of course, hopefully be part of the American civilization – but not necessarily only of it.

## The crystallization of Jewish–American historical experience – the historical background

However, the full efflorescence of these potentialities of a fully accepted diversity became actualized only from the 1950s, and it was indeed only then that the unique historical experience of American Jewry became fully articulated.

Thus in this period there took place, first of all, a very quick process of educational and occupational advance. Major universities which did not allow too many Jews – which in fact, like Harvard, had instituted the system of a *de facto* quota – became opened to the Jews and Jews started to enrol into them, and to graduate from them, moving into much more variegated economic occupations, above all into professions, into academic and cultural fields, into the media, and other areas. Many sectors, such as banking or top industry, still remained virtually closed to most Jews – but others, above all in professional, academic, mass media and cultural fields, became opened up and Jews became very predominant in them. From about the mid-1970s there were quite far-reaching changes in this respect, and more and more economic areas that were formerly closed became opened to the Jews.

Second, the terrible experience of the Holocaust showed, in a tragic way, the weakness of the possibility of Jewish participation on an individual basis or as purely a religious denomination in another collectivity, without reference to collective Jewish identity; so it strengthened the consciousness of such identity and weakened opposition to it.

Third, the establishment of the State of Israel, which by providing a new focus of collective political identity and a new arena of social and political activities, also played a rather crucial role in this process, which became of crucial importance from the early 1950s on, in the opening up of a new plethora of collective activities, at the same time providing a central focus of collective Jewish endeavour. The image of the State, based as it was on the myth of the pioneer conquering the waste land, with a biblical vision, was very close to some basic component of the American myth and helped greatly to legitimize these activities.

Somewhat later on, this acceptance of diversity was connected with a more general transformation, which took place from the later 1950s on, in the American scene; the weakening ideology of the melting pot, giving rise to the upsurge of ethnic identity in general. While this upsurge was often orientated against the Jews, yet its very development seemed to emphasize the legitimacy of Jewish communal, political and national (or 'peoplehood') activities.

## The characteristics of Jewish– American historical experience

It was in conjunction with all these processes that the specific type of Jewish– American experience became crystallized and articulated. The crux of this experience was the concomitant development of the processes of occupational and economic mobility and advance which gave rise to the restructuring and intensification of new types of Jewish collective activities – paradoxically, together with the possibilities of seemingly smooth assimilation.

But, although such development in the direction of assimilation continued, and even became the major ultimate trend, more conspicuous were the contrary processes which could, however, paradoxically reinforce the more assimilationist ones – a development which was perhaps even more opposed to the basic premises of both the assimilationist or Zionist ideologies.

For large parts of the Jewish communities the processes of economic and occupational mobility became connected with the upsurge of continuously growing collective Jewish activities, on both the local and countrywide levels – a process which became especially strong after the early 1970s, but the roots of which could be found before.

Indeed, the range of such communal political activities and organizations was very wide. They were closely connected with various general Jewish concerns – powerful political lobby activities on behalf of the State of Israel, or those concerned with the rescue of Jews in difficult situations, such as those in Russia.

Even intermarriage could sometimes – against the presumptions of assimilationist, Zionist and orthodox groups alike – have unexpected results,
especially as compared to the European experience. Not infrequently –
certainly much more frequently than in Europe – assimilated Jews who
married gentile women were brought back to some Jewish framework by their
wives who wanted to uphold some sort of tradition, thus revitalizing the
adherence to some aspects or dimensions of Jewish tradition and communal
activities.*

Anti-Semitism of different sorts and different intensity was still not lacking,
manifest as usual in tendencies to exclude Jews from many economic sectors,
or in more diffuse anti-Semitic sentiments, ranging from popular feelings to
ideologies articulated by various – on the whole rather marginal intellectual or
political – groups, and feeding on the strong resentment against their economic
advance and growing visibility in the central cultural arenas.

From the late 1960s on, the great upsurge of ethnicity in the United States
also gave rise to growing anti-Semitism among the 'ethnic' groups and the
demands of different minority groups for positive discrimination were often *de
facto* directed against the Jews. But they never assumed the intensity or scope
of their European nineteenth- and twentieth-century parallels, nor did they
impede, at least till now, the occupational advance of the Jews.

# The Reconstruction of American–Jewish Collective Life
## *The place of the synagogue*

The single most important – although certainly not the only – institutional base
of this new plethora of Jewish organizations was indeed the synagogue. This
was seen no longer only as a place of worship but, much more in the vein of
Mordechai Kaplan's vision, as a centre of multiple communal activities and of
the different expression of Jewish peoplehood – without however accepting
Kaplan's religious views. Thus as Nathan Glazer has commented, Kaplan's
practice was accepted, but not his ideological formulation or his religious
tenets.

This development was especially important among the second generation of
the East European Jewish immigrants, and also the descendants of the earlier
groups of immigrants. It was closely connected with the movement of Jews into
mixed urban suburbs. It was this synagogue centre that became the base of
many Jewish activities, as well as of the type of Jewish education – especially
the afternoon or day school – which transmitted the Jewish collective identity
to the new generations of Jews from the late 1940s on. Organizationally it
followed very much the general American (especially Protestant) congregational mode of religious organizations, but in the scope of its activities or in
its overall conception it went far beyond most of them.

In addition, beyond the synagogue centre but usually based on it, multiple

* See Egon Meyer and Carl Scheingold, *Intermarriage and the Jewish Future* (American Jewish Committee, New
York 1979).

countrywide Jewish organizations developed, above all the United Jewish Appeal founded in 1934, but also the Committee of Jewish Federations and Welfare Funds, the American Jewish Community, and many others, which developed a very wide range of activities, mobilizing financial resources and communal and political support, the like of which could not be found in any other 'ethnic' or religious groups in the United States.

Needless to say, for many Jews, even those attached to the communities, the synagogue was not so central and many other semi-formal forms of interaction between the Jews developed. But on the whole it was the two – the synagogue and the closely related community centre – that constituted the central kernel of Jewish organizational life.

The central place of the synagogue and of religion in Jewish life in America, and the fact that it was so much in tone with the general American way of life, led to the publication in 1955 by Will Herberg of a famous book *Protestant, Catholic and Jew*, stressing both the centrality of the religious component in Judaism, as well as its full legitimation as part of the (religious) diversity of the American scene or way of life.*

But in fact even at the time of the publication of this book, and certainly later on, this view of American Judaism did not tell the whole story. It was indeed right in stressing the full legitimacy of such diversity, as well as the central place of the religious activities. But it did not take into account the very great diversity of collective activities, much beyond the purely religious field, which developed from the religious congregational bases and which emphasized and articulated collective, political components of Jewish identity, of what began to be called Jewish 'peoplehood' – as well as the great diversity of Jewish activities, very much in tone with these varied components of Jewish identity.

## Jewish education

The synagogues and community centres also became the bases for one of the most important Jewish institutions in the United States, the different types of Jewish education; the day schools (relatively rare except within the orthodox circles), 'Sunday' school and afternoon schools – which became one of the most important institutions in the transmission of Jewish identity. These institutions never developed as competitors with the general systems of education, to which the Jews were very loyal. In Walter I. Ackerman's words:

The interplay between Jews, Judaism and life in America has resulted in a system of Jewish education in the United States, the continued growth of day schools notwithstanding, which consists in the main of supplementary schooling conducted in mid-week afternoon schools which meet for 4–6 hours a week and one-day-a-week Sunday or Sabbath schools which offer two–three hours of instruction weekly. This educational enterprise is a voluntary effort of autonomous institutions related to one another more by common aspiration than by ties of formal structure. The virtual demise of secular

---

* A shorter but somewhat broader interpretation can be found in Nathan Glazer, *American Judaism* (Chicago 1957).

Hebrew nationalist and Yiddish schools since the end of World War II has made Jewish education almost entirely an activity of the synagogue; the vast majority of Jewish schools – close to 90% – are sponsored, maintained and ultimately controlled by individual congregations.

Ackerman also provides data about the scope of such education and some possible trends of future development:

The steady rise in Jewish school enrollment which began its ascent immediately after World War II reached a peak in the middle 1960s, and has been declining ever since. During the ten-year interval between 1946 and 1956 the number of children attending Jewish schools of all kinds more than doubled – from 231,028 to 488,432. In the 1957–58 school year, registers counted 553,600 pupils. A decade later (1966–67) the figure stood at 554,468. Data for 1967–71 disclose a decline of 17.5 per cent over the four year period to a figure of 457,196. A 1974–75 school census reported 391,825 pupils enrolled. The most recent tally available places the current total pupil population at 344,251. The pattern is unmistakably clear: Jewish school enrollment has suffered a decline of close to 40 per cent in the period from 1960 to the present. . . .

Further analysis indicates that Jewish education today, as in the past, is by and large elementary schooling. Despite a reported rise in high-school enrollment – that is programs for youngsters above the age of thirteen which meet at least once a week – the majority of the children who attend a Jewish school drop out upon completion of the elementary school level. . . .

. . . One positive factor on the Jewish educational scene today is a discernible trend in the direction of more intensive schooling. In Orthodox circles, one-day-a-week schools have all but disappeared; a similar tendency is evident in the Conservative movement; and the number of midweek afternoon schools in Reform congregations is on the increase. As indicated above, the average number of pupil hours per school year in Jewish schools has risen from 182 to 248, an increase of 35 percent since 1966–67.

The continued expansion of the day school movement, embracing as it now does every sector of organized Jewry, is the major variable in the shift in the direction of more intensive Jewish education. The growth of the Jewish day school is surely one of the more distinguishing characteristics of American Jewish life in our generation. In 1944 there were 39 day schools in the United States, most of them in New York City; today their number exceeds 550. Of that number 86 percent are under Orthodox auspices; 8 percent are Conservative sponsored; 5 percent designate themselves as communal or independent; and 1 percent identify themselves with the Reform movement. Over a 15-year period, from 1962–1977, day school enrollment jumped from 60,000 to 92,000 pupils. Approximately one out of every four children in Jewish elementary schools is in a day school.[*]

The Jewish education that developed in the United States – especially that in the non-orthodox circles – was based on entirely different premises from those of the last great Jewish modern educational system in the Diaspora, that of Eastern Europe. It had no claims to develop a specific overall Jewish way of life or to be part, perhaps the basis, of some collective Jewish institution-building and cultural activity. It was entirely orientated to the American way of life. Its

[*] W. I. Ackerman, 'Strangers to the Tradition: Idea and Constraint in American Jewish Education' in H. S. Himmelfarb and S. Della Pergola (eds.), *World Jewish Education – Cross Cultural Perspectives* (Jerusalem forthcoming).

central aim was to imbue its pupils with a sense of belonging to the Jewish people, of Jewish identity and commitment – but within the framework of American life as a full, legitimate part of this pattern of life.

This basic attitude has been in many ways shared also by the orthodox – with the exception of the ultra-orthodox – education. Their commitment to participation in the American way of life and identification with it was not so central as in the non-orthodox schools – but most of them certainly look on themselves by now as a legitimate part of American society. At the same time they stress, of course, the distinctiveness of their Jewish education which they provide in their schools as indeed orientated to a relatively total Jewish life – yet set, on the whole, within a modern setting, and they do not see themselves as contributing a special dimension to American life.

## Trends in theology

The late 1940s and early 1950s signalled also the beginning of the development of a specific type of Jewish theology in the United States, the first such upsurge since the publication in 1934 of *Jewish Civilization* by Mordechai Kaplan. Such figures as Abraham Heschel (1907–72), who came from a very strong European background, and later on, after the Six Day War, Emile Fackenhaim, Jakob Petuchowsky, Richard Rubenstein and others became very pronounced and influential, and among most of them the memory of the Holocaust, to no small degree heightened by the trauma of the Six Day War, became a central dimension of this thought.

## The Modes of Jewish Participation in American Life
### Cultural, civilizational and political activities

But it was not only the wide-ranging scope of different organizations and activities stressing many different components of Jewish identity that developed within the Jewish community of the United States. Beyond them there developed intensive attempts by many Jews, especially the more active, to find in their host societies a legitimate arena for some cultural and civilizational activities which had specifically Jewish orientations and yet would be accepted in the broader society.

The pattern of such cultural and civilizational activities differed greatly from the nineteenth-century experience of both Western and Eastern European Jewry. There did indeed develop in the United States, as formerly in Western and Eastern Europe, Jewish educational – especially academic – institutions, orientated to the study of different aspects of Jewish history, to the training of Jewish religious and communal leaders, and to the special problem of Jewish education we have mentioned before.

But beyond this, especially from the 1950s, there was widespread partici-pation of the Jews in general academic life, in journalism and the mass media, and also in general social and political activities, much beyond what has been experienced in Europe.

In common with the Western European experience, as against the Eastern European one of the nineteenth century, most of these academic and cultural journalistic activities were not seen in specific Jewish frameworks: there were but few special Jewish newspapers, literary organs, or Jewish academic institutions, and these were not the major arenas of the activity of the Jewish academics, professionals and the like.

This tendency extended into the occupational and political activities of the Jews. Unlike in Eastern Europe, no specific Jewish parties developed, no specific Jewish representatives were elected to the Congress – although many individual Jews became active in political life, Jewish lobbies developed and the Jews did indeed engage in some organized way in many political activities. Similarly, major Jewish writers – Saul Bellow, Bernard Malamud and others – did not create, as in Eastern Europe, a literature written in Hebrew or Yiddish and orientated to specifically Jewish audiences.

As for the non-Jewish intellectuals, writers and journalists, unlike their counterparts in Western and Central Europe in the nineteenth and twentieth centuries, they were not imbued by orientations to assimilation or to rejecting Jewish identity or concerns. Indeed very often it was quite the opposite. They stressed Jewish themes and Jewish personalities as part of the broader American scene: many of them closely identified themselves with Jewish activities and their connections with Jewish organizations, with their more political or communal activities, were often very close.

But beyond all this, there developed among the Jews many new types of public, political or journalistic activities. *Commentary*, the independent monthly published by the American Jewish Committee, is very indicative of this type of activity. The major characteristic of such activities was the creation of specific cultural arenas, openly sponsored by Jewish organizations, but which were orientated to a very large degree to the problems of American society in general, and which combined Jewish themes with open participation in the intellectual life of these societies, providing a somewhat specific Jewish stamp on this life.

Jews also developed several unique patterns of political activity and participation. There were, of course, the numerous political activities of Jewish organizations taking up various Jewish causes briefly described above. But there was also a rather specific open participation of Jews and Jewish leaders and organizations in general socio-political movements – the civil rights movement being the major single most important illustration. Unlike the participation of Jews in radical movements in Europe, this was openly Jewish and often presented participation as a specific Jewish contribution to American political life.

Later on many of the Black organizations did turn against the Jews, and similarly the experience of Jewish students and young radical activists in the 1960s became rather problematic given the strong anti-Israel stand of these movements, in this way stressing the strong component of Jewish identity in these activities. But all this did not abate the feeling, among large sectors of the Jews, of their ability to participate openly – often, although certainly not always – as Jews, perhaps adding some special dimension to American political life.

Of great interest here is also the fact that a large part of this participation of Jews in the political, social and intellectual life of the United States moved away from the 'left' or 'liberal' direction to a more centre or right-wing one. This is evident in the general ambience of *Commentary*, and in the relatively great prominence of Jewish intellectuals – many of whom (such as those close to *Commentary*) were, in their youth in the twenties, members of leftist movements – in the neo-Conservative movement. This was not just a story of individual Jews developing conservative tendencies, or of being ideologues of the centre or right (as could be found – even if to a small degree – in Eastern Europe as seen in the case of Walther Rothman). What is significant here is the relatively large proportion of Jewish intellectuals and journalists participating in this direction – signalling, as it were, that their full participation in American public life need not only take the form of a protest from the left against a conservative or traditional centre, but can also be useful in the articulation of the (American) centre.

From the late 1970s on, there was also a growing participation and mobility of Jews as individuals within political life – in municipal institutions, as congressmen and the like.

## American–Jewish identity

All these developments reinforced the feeling that it was possible for the Jews in America to look on themselves as both Americans and Jews, and, unlike in the European scene, not to see any basic contradiction between the two, even when they strongly emphasized the collective, primordial historical and political dimensions of their Jewish identity. All these developments re-inforced the feeling that the American–Jewish experience was unique. Truly enough, they could sometimes be accused – especially with respect to their attitudes to the State of Israel – of double loyalty, but never in such an intensive and vicious way as in Europe, where the Jewish collective identity, with its primordial and historical element, clashed head on with the parallel elements of European nationalism.

The experience of other immigrant groups – like the Irish or Italians who also were politically active on behalf of their homelands – strengthened these tendencies, and the very establishment of the Jewish homeland helped also in the legitimization of such activities.

Thus the Jews – as many other 'ethnic' groups in the United States, but in fact much more than any of them – tended to develop and crystallize their collective identity, even to articulate it in primordial and political terms, without defining themselves – as was the case in Eastern Europe – as a minority nation coexisting with other such nations, one of which constituted the majority.

Basically most Jews – with the possible exception of the ultra-orthodox – probably tended to think of themselves as participants in the American national collectivity, even if not in its specific American tradition, and the definition of this collectivity in political–ideological ways facilitated such an approach.

Many of these feelings were in fact fully articulated in an ideological way, above all by various Jewish intellectuals. But among wider strata of the Jewish community the apprehension and fear of anti-Semitism, feeding on the memory of the Holocaust and reinforced by any strong outburst of discrimination, was much more prevalent, and even among the intellectuals the story of a very influential and well-established Jewish academic who told his son that he should realize that basically it is a 'Goyish world' might not be exceptional. But in fact most strata of the Jewish population in the United States lived their – private and communal – lives as if accepting the premiss that the Jewish–American experience was unique and as if this premiss was also accepted by the general society.

## Theories of Jewish civilization in the American experience

This new overall pattern of Jewish activities evinced some new characteristics from the point of view of the perennial themes of Jewish civilization.

The degree of separation between specifically Jewish activities and organizations and Jewish participation in general activities was here somewhat weaker than in Western or Central Europe. Even organizationally such separation was not as far-reaching as in Western or Central Europe in the nineteenth and in the first four decades of the twentieth century. Such separation was weakened by the fact that many Jews believed that universalistic elements in the Jewish tradition could be expressed by their participation, as Jews, both in general organizations and arenas and in specifically Jewish organizations.

At the same time the structure of these latter organizations – their 'congregational' patterns, their relative decentralization, and the necessity to take common stands on many matters of Jewish concern – weakened their potential and the anarchic tendencies inherent in the Jewish tradition, although they could also be found here. On the whole, Jewish organizations were governed more by the norms of the broader society, and the specific Jewish organizations constituted only one area, although a very central one, of Jewish political and civic activities. The more intellectual orientations – the mystic, philosophical, political – which could, of course, be sources of great divisiveness, were limited mostly to intellectual discussion, with but a few – if any – implications for Jewish institutional and communal life.

# Jewish Historical Experience
# in Other Parts of the Diaspora
## *Europe*

A parallel, even if weaker, transformation of Jewish activities and identity, from a purely religious to a primordial–political–historical one, and a growing development of commitment to the Jewish people and to Jewish collective activities, took place after the Holocaust in Western Europe, first of all in England, where the Jewish community remained intact (as did also the smaller Jewish communities in Switzerland, Sweden, Finland and to some degree Denmark, the latter saved and transported to Sweden by the Danish population) and in which a long tradition of religious tolerance existed; later on new Jewish communities evolved in France, Belgium and the Netherlands.

It was connected with the weakening, in all these societies – with the partial exception of England where it was never as strong as in other European countries – of the original nineteenth- and early twentieth-century conception of the nation-state, with the weakening of the attachment to historical symbols, with the secularization of daily life and with the readiness on the part of these societies to accept, after the Holocaust, the legitimacy of some sort of communal political Jewish identity and activities. There developed here also – even if probably less than in the United States – new patterns of intermarriage, although here on the whole intermarriage was a much more direct way to assimilation than in the United States.

Here also the range of Jewish collective political activities and organizations was very closely connected with activities on behalf of the State of Israel, or with some general Jewish problem such as the rescue of Russian Jews. It became intensified by bodies of long standing such as the Board of Deputies in England or newer organizations, and through participation in general international Jewish organizations such as the World Jewish Congress, various cultural or religious organizations and the like.

The pattern of these activities, and of Jewish organizations in general, differed from those in the United States, following the specific tradition of these countries. Thus the organizations in England and France were much more centralized and at the same time the attempts to undertake specific Jewish civilization activities were more limited; but here also more and more Jewish intellectuals (the number grew continuously with expanding education) started to emerge and attempted to relate their activities in the arenas of the general society to some Jewish themes in a much more open way than was ever possible before.

But on the whole the new developments among these Jewish communities were, given the specific cultural–political traditions of these countries, less intensive and far-reaching than in the United States. Moreover, the tradition of defining the Jews as, above all, a religious group was still quite strong, as was also anti-Semitic tradition which could erupt in much more intensive and vicious ways than in the United States.

Indeed, given the nature of this tradition in these societies, these anti-Semitic outbursts contained very strong primordial–historical components and themes which could, especially among the new left, become transformed into strong anti-religious and anti-Zionist ones – conflating, as we have seen, anti-Semitism with anti-Zionism. Indeed, it was the extreme left that became in the 1970s the major new carrier of anti-Semitism in these countries, to no small degree building on general anti-religious feelings and on the strong tradition of opposition between the secular and the religious components in the collective identities of many European countries.

Given all these conditions, in most European countries there was not such a strong connection between participation in the general cultural, and above all, political scene and Jewish commitment and participation in Jewish organizations – although even this became relatively more and more prominent, for instance among younger intellectual circles in France. And, in comparison with the pre-war period, there also developed far-reaching changes in the scope and mode of Jewish activities and participation – and in the self-definition and self-consciousness of the Jewish communities.

## Latin America

It was only in Latin America that the pattern of Jewish life in general, torn between mobility, assimilation and anti-Semitism, seems to have been much closer to the older European patterns – although of course even here it was in fact quite different. In Latin American countries special types of Jewish communal life and institutions developed. In Mexico a whole spate of Jewish educational institutions, ranging from kindergarten to high schools, teaching in Yiddish, Hebrew and Spanish, developed, reminiscent of those in Eastern Europe – except that they were not, of course, connected with a flourishing Jewish cultural creativity. It was only in the first generation of Jewish settlement in Argentina that such creativity in the form of literature and journalism in Yiddish, as well as special Jewish educational institutions, developed, but these did not persist in a very significant way beyond the second generation.

Moreover, most of these activities were not generally orientated to their new countries, but more outside, to the old countries in Europe, to the United States or to Israel. There did not develop here that active participation in the general cultural and political arenas and Jewish identity that crystallized in the United States.

In general the younger generation developed stronger assimilatory tendencies, often combined with rather strong leftist orientations. The Jewish communities in Latin America became more and more torn between these tendencies and oppressive regimes with strong ingredients of 'traditional' anti-Semitism.

# Soviet Russia

It is much more difficult to interpret the Jewish experience in Soviet Russia, although some of the basic trends are easily discernible. One, in rather close parallel to the Jewish–American one, was an experience of great ecological and economic mobility and of growing urbanization, moving into tertiary occupations – a trend recognized in the 1930s, with its parallel to the United States, by the Jewish demographer, J. Leschinski.

The second aspect of the Jewish Soviet experience was the mixture of official and semi-official anti-Semitism, manifest in the development of many *de facto* restrictive policies with respect to admittance to academic institutions and to various occupations.

The third aspect of Jewish Soviet experience was that, unlike in the American case, there was a very strong pressure on Jews to assimilate. Hebrew–Jewish cultural institutions were suppressed from the beginning as manifestations of bourgeois–Zionist reactions; there were some attempts to maintain some Yiddish ones, but these were almost totally destroyed; the experiment to establish a special Jewish Republic in Birobidjan, with Yiddish as its official language, was relatively short-lived; and any communal or cultural Jewish life or maintenance of any Jewish tradition was suppressed.

Thus indeed the Jews were the only religious group in the USSR who were not allowed any far-reaching religious organization; and the only ethnic group whose cultural activities were hopefully truncated and whose cultural tradition was not incorporated in some general or specific framework.

Within the framework of these trends some very surprising developments occurred. Not only was there a continuous persistence of some – even if highly diluted – traditional patterns of life, of special family patterns and connections of *de facto* social segregation. Beyond this it seems that the combined effect of restrictive policies and anti-Semitic orientations, attitudes and policies which became continuously intensified, of the establishment of the State of Israel, and to some degree of the growing contacts with world Jewry through many visits of American and European Jews to Russia, activated among parts at least of Soviet Jewry rather strong elements of Jewish identity. This gave rise to movements to leave the USSR with almost 4,000 now (out of 2–3 million) applying for permits to go to Israel (almost the only official way of trying to get out), some going to Israel, but a larger number ultimately to the United States, giving rise to the growth of the *Refusenik* movement and their persecution by the authorities, and growing anti-Semitism and anti-Zionist policies and propaganda.

It is, however, as yet very difficult to analyse the extent and strength of these tendencies and whether the Russian Jews will go in some sort of nationalist direction or in stronger assimilatory directions. There are certainly very strong indications not only of assimilation but also of the strong development of Jewish identity among parts at least of the Jewish population – to no small degree helped by the growing anti-Semitic and anti-Zionist attitudes of the authorities.

## New Developments in the Orthodox Sectors

One of the most interesting aspects of the transformation of Jewish life after the Second World War – again going against the basic premisses of almost all the hitherto predominant modern Jewish ideologies, the assimilationist, Zionist or orthodox alike – took place within the orthodox sectors themselves.

According to the premisses of most of these 'classical' approaches, rooted above all in the experience of the nineteenth century, orthodoxy as such was destined, in the wake of the presumed general trend to secularization, to be weakened, perhaps to disappear, or at most to remain in closed ghettos completely secluded from modern life, finding some niche in various 'traditional' Jewish occupations like small trade, artisanship and the like.

These predictions were indeed true of some small extreme orthodox groups. But even the ultra-orthodox groups in the United States, England or Belgium became, at least economically, much more diversified and 'modernized'. Moreover, these developments were part of a much broader trend of far-reaching changes and recrystallization in the life of the orthodox sector or sectors. The crux of this recrystallization was that large parts of these sectors went beyond the classical ghetto experience by becoming much more interwoven in the occupational, and even ecological, matrix of modern societies, even in several aspects of the secular life style – such as work, reading habits, media watching and the like.

Thus, although no exact data are available, it is easy to see that the orthodox Jews abound in the centres of many cities and their numbers seem to be increasing not only in their traditional but also in new professional or academic occupations. They are very visible in universities in subjects such as chemistry, physics and computer sciences, which earlier on seemed to them – unlike pure mathematics – to be beyond the plane of orthodox Jews. Special general academic institutions, orientated primarily to orthodox publics, such as Yeshiva University in New York and to a smaller degree Bar Ilan University in Israel, emerged in the orthodox sector. In fact many of these modern institutions and somewhat more modern ways of life were not accepted by the ultra-orthodox – they were indeed an anathema to them.

In general, from the 1930s on – and especially after the Holocaust, when some of the leading orthodox scholars came to the United States and established there strong Yeshivot and centres – these became more powerful and dynamic. Their own specific educational institutions were extended and diversified, sometimes combining some secular subjects or allowing their students to combine the study in the Yeshiva with education in general schools. Many of these circles were of course still strongly opposed to such ventures, even when they had to obey the laws of the land and send their children to schools or provide them with an education in which such secular subjects had to be studied.

In their private life, many of them lead a very affluent style of life, and to some degree also an intensive cultural life of their own, with a very ambivalent, often hostile attitude to the secularized Jews, sometimes attempting proselytizing activities among them. They also developed a special type of relationship with the State of Israel and their central organizations.

Contrary to the experience of former generations they do not seem – here again there are no exact data – to lose out to the secular world. On the contrary, it seems that there is a quite visible movement of younger Jews coming from more secular backgrounds turning to some variant of orthodoxy – even though it is probably less prevalent than claimed by the orthodox circles.

These orthodox groups do not see themselves on the defensive, and they do not 'hide' their orthodoxy in their public activities. On the contrary they are very open about it. The older saying of the European Heskele – 'be a Jew in your home and a man in public life' – certainly does not apply to them. Most of them – except for the very ultra-orthodox ones – do not hesitate to appear openly as do secular Jews, but of course with much greater visibility (manifest first of all in their wearing of *yarmulke*).

Thus in a way they articulate yet another variant of the possibility of development of collective Jewish life, both in America where they are becoming an accepted part of the American scene, and to a smaller extent also in Europe.

Among the various sectors of Jewish population they are probably the most divided among themselves – into different Hassidic communities, into different sectors often at loggerheads with one another. Yet there can be no doubt that in the mid-1980s they provide the most internally compact sectors within the panorama of Jewish life, developing educational and communal institutions and providing, as we have seen, a large part of the Jewish day schools.

Their central organizations have been very vocal in internal and general Jewish affairs, as have many of the individual Rabbis, at the same time exhibiting their usual great internal divisiveness. Many of the orthodox Jewish leaders have become more central in general Jewish institutions – a fact also possibly connected to the growing movement of the younger generation of university-educated Jews into more general areas of American society, including the political ones. They seem to provide a very important centre of Jewish life and a reservoir of Jewish leadership – thus also potentially changing the basis of support for Israel and of relations with it. Whatever the future may hold for them, these various orthodox groups have, as of now, developed as one of the new variants – and a very forceful one – of modern Jewish life, in which the combination of themes of religious community and peoplehood, and even political activity, both within their countries of residence as well as in relation to the State of Israel, have become crystallized in a new pattern which went far beyond that of the European 'modern' or traditional orthodoxy.

# New Patterns of Crystallization of Jewish Experience
## *Collective Jewish activities and smooth assimilation*

It was all these far-reaching transformations in the structure and organization of the Jewish people in the various communities of the Diaspora – especially in the United States and to a smaller degree in Western Europe – that changed, as we have briefly indicated earlier, the *problematique* of Jewish collective existence as it was perceived among the Jewish people – and especially of course among their intellectuals, beyond the premises of the European nineteenth- and twentieth-century experience in general and of classical Zionist ideology in particular – that very ideology which shaped the revolutionary and ideological premisses of Israel and which guided and shaped much of the Israeli perception of and attitude to the Diaspora.

To reiterate what has been said earlier, the change in this *problematique*, intermittent and not always fully articulated, and yet very forceful and above all almost all-pervasive, was in formulating the problem of Jewish existence in the modern world, not in terms of the dilemma between assimilation on the one hand and the maintenance of a collective Jewish life in a purely Jewish environment on the other – whether the closed one of orthodoxy or the in principle open one of the Zionist variety or as one minority nation in a state composed of many such nations, with one nation being the majority. Instead there developed more and more a search – of course only among those who cared about this at all – for finding different ways of expressing Jewish collective identity and Jewish peoplehood – stressing both political dimension and civilizational aspirations within the framework of the continuously changing Western societies – while at the same time being full and equal members of their respective national or political collectivities.

Basically – despite many misgivings and fears about the ultimate lack of viability of Jewish life in the Diaspora – the formulation of such *problematique* took the possibility of such free collective existence more or less for granted, searching for different ways of expressing Jewish identity. Truly enough, part of these Jewish activities – like those of the anti-Defamation League and different types of vigilantes – were on the whole defensive. Parts of these activities were philanthropic, seemingly in the tradition of such activities in the nineteenth century. But most of them became crystallized in more dynamic and variegated patterns of the new collective Jewish activities, sharing the implicit assumption of the possibility of developing such activities and frameworks within the communities of the Diaspora – even if in close relation with Israel.

It is, of course, a moot question to what extent all these tendencies make invalid the basic Zionist tenets about the inevitability in such circumstances of assimilation, or demographic decline or, in more extreme cases, of anti-Semitic persecutions and perhaps destruction – and the vision of the Holocaust has indeed been more and more prevalent in the collective memory of American Jewry.

Yet, despite all these possibilities, those among the Jews concerned with such matters were seemingly able to find in the new setting and the countries in which they lived not only possibilities of maintaining communal identity and activities which were based on primordial and political activities and civilizations and of combining these with full participation in the societies in which they lived. It does indeed seem that the majority of American Jews – and especially those who actively upheld their Jewishness – refused to see any basic contradiction between their American identity and their Jewishness, and refused to see in anti-Semitism (some even tried to deny its very existence) a basic threat to their incorporation as Jews in that society.

Thus, instead of the old 'classical' problem of the possibility of physical and cultural survival of the Jewish people in the modern world within this *problematique*, the crucial question, as viewed by the more active and positively conscious of their Jewish identity, became how to find new ways of Jewish collective authenticity in the modern setting.

Among many of them there developed a growing concern about the possible assimilation of Jews through ecological dispersion and intermarriage and a growing interest in strengthening Jewish educational institutions – but all this was firmly set within the framework of their Jewish existence in the Diaspora, even if on the whole to a very high degree orientated also to Israel.

For others – perhaps ultimately a majority – this quest may go together with growing assimilation, sometimes even paradoxically helping such assimilation. Indeed there has here developed a rather paradoxical situation – namely that these very processes which enabled the intensification of Jewish activities and organizations could also move for a relatively fast and smooth assimilation – just because such assimilation could take place without demands for changing religion or even denying one's Jewishness of any sort whatsoever. Such assimilation could of course also be helped by the demographic decline which the Jews – with the exception of the orthodox sector – shared with the population of many other highly industrialized societies of the United States or Japan.

## Expressions of Jewish identity

In close relation to the development of this *problematique*, there developed within the different Jewish communities a great variety of ways, a great heterogeneity, in articulating patterns of Jewish life and identity.

First, there developed a situation in which the simple correlation between shedding traditional ways of life and giving up elements of Jewish identity no longer held. Many Jews were continuously changing their ways of life, and most of them in the Diaspora did not lead lives which are primarily or fully Jewish, but they might not want to lose their Jewish identity. They attempted to reformulate this identity, even if it was no longer their only exclusive and perhaps also not even their predominant one.

Second, and closely related to this, was the continuous restructuring of the components of this identity. Here two processes were continuously taking place. The first was that, in addition to shedding away certain of these components, there were continuous attempts to reconstruct them and their symbols and to recombine them in different ways. Second this entailed, in most cases, both the reformulation and recombination of most of the 'older' elements – primordiality, religious attachments to something which is seen as a religious tradition – together with some element of 'peoplehood'.

Third, there was a strong return to certain traditions or customs which had religious origins, but which had become symbols of collective identity, such as candle lighting on *Hannuka* and on the Sabbath, or celebration of those aspects of the tradition which were related to the most primordial facts of life: circumcision (which is obviously the choice of the parents), *bar mitzvah*, marriage, funerals. These different patterns of reconstruction of religious symbols were not necessarily related to a return to orthodoxy, to the acceptance of the Halakha as the basic framework of Jewish life – although such a process was taking place to some extent. The upsurge of orthodoxy and neo-orthodoxy constituted a closely connected but obviously not an identical process.

Another new element which developed in its fullest way in the period after the Second World War was that of the emergence of legitimate collective Jewish political activity within the political frameworks of their respective societies. For the first time in exilic history, Jewish communities throughout the world became politically active and conscious as Jews. The pinnacle of this development was, of course, as we shall see in greater detail later, the establishment of the State of Israel.

This process of reformulation and reconstruction of different elements of Jewish identity was naturally, in most Jewish communities, very closely related to a parallel process in the selection of different elements of Jewish tradition.

Here also there was a continuous search and exploration – about which we know systematically relatively little.* The most interesting aspect of this process is that there is, contrary to the previous conception, no simple relation between attachment to different Jewish customs and traditions and commitment to Jewish identity. Even within the orthodox circles, seemingly the ones in which the older components should go together, the picture is very complex. Thus, as we have seen, the upsurge of neo-orthodoxy was connected with a growing participation in 'general' spheres of life – such as higher education and other occupational spheres – which would have been an anathema or at least alien to the older, Eastern European traditionalists. It was also connected with a growing participation in some political Jewish activities of the new kind.

The picture is, of course, even more complex among the non-orthodox. Beyond the going back to some of the *rites de passage* and the other symbols of identity mentioned above, there is no simple relation between such 'contents' and the nature of Jewish identity and commitment.

Yet another new element – connected with Jewish civilizational activities or aspirations – became predominant. In many cases, most Jews who were

* See for instance, Dominique Schnapper, *Jewish Identities in France* (Chicago 1983).

searching for the expression of their identity tended to combine this search with those problems which were, as it were, 'repressed' in the medieval patterns and which, in the early assimilationist period, were taken beyond the scope of Jewish communal activity – namely, with the search for some sort of resolution of the tension between the universal and particularistic element in Jewish collective identity. In some cases the older semi-assimilationists' 'ethical' – liberal, socialist or nationalist – attitudes persisted, but significantly enough even these attitudes were more and more connected with a more positive Jewish identity and commitment. In many cases they were related to some activity in Jewish communal activities, institutions and organs, seeing them as a constructive, positive component of the general setting. Certainly these specific Jewish institutions, unlike those in Eastern Europe up to the Second World War, were – and still are – set within a predominantly non-Jewish environment; they were mostly focused in the leisure time space of the Jews. These activities were mostly conducted in the language of the country – English, French, German and the like – but at the same time they were presented both as expressing the different dimensions of Jewish identity and as a legitimate part of the broader society.

Today different Jewish communities differ as to how they go about this task – or even each community may change the patterns of its activities. There are different emphases of various components of identity. For different communities, the hierarchy or the combination of such components may differ and there is nowhere a full definitive crystallization of some new combination of the elements. Rather in every Jewish community there is a continuous process of experimenting with the different elements of Jewish identity; no community has settled for a 'solution' or endpoint, and all communities are in a constant state of flux. The unifying elements, however, are the very variability, the act of experimentation, the continuous search, and the mutual awareness of these different Jewish communities that they share a common heritage and this common search, the details of which are of course greatly influenced in each community by the specific circumstances in which their members live.

Thus, today, one can be – and feel – Jewish without having a fixed and set notion of what this actually means in terms of actual contents. Since flux is difficult to capture organizationally, Jewish institutions – and education – lag considerably behind these developments and tendencies, although certain issues, such as those connected with the State of Israel or the problem of Soviet Jewry, do serve as major themes for focusing on the activities.

Thus indeed a new, paradoxical element has entered into Jewish life: namely the growing multiplicity of what in terms of traditional patterns would be seen as heterodoxies with seemingly heretic orientations and very often it is these orientations which become the point of growing sensitivity and common awareness among different Jewish communities – without, however, having any institutional implication.

Needless to say, as we have already pointed out above, this situation may, of course, lead to 'total' assimilation, to the abandonment of the Jewish fold – and this may indeed be the ultimate outcome of these processes.

But this certainly is not the whole picture or at least certainly not to the degree that it used to be assumed in the 'classical' literature on assimilation, and, paradoxically, such assimilation and the development of intensive Jewish activities can even in some situations reinforce one another.

## The paradox of modern trends

All these developments and possibilities gathered further momentum from the 1970s on, especially in the United States. In general there was a continuous educational and occupational advance of Jews, evident in a generally higher return among Jews on investment education due to the consequence of their having fewer siblings with whom to compete for parental attention and also probably to their benefiting from greater parental input of resources, as is suggested by the lower Jewish female participation in the labour force. Thus all in all about 70–80 per cent of young Jews in the United States went through college, with all the occupational implications of this fact.*

At the same time, the developments in the 1970s highlighted the different contradictory and yet often mutually reinforcing possibilities inherent in the Jewish–American historical experience. Thus on the one hand there continued the different patterns of specific Jewish organizations – new ventures in Jewish education and the like. In many ways the synagogue community, even if in continuously changing forms, continued to provide the major basis for such activities.

On the other hand there was a continuously growing participation in various general areas of American (and to a smaller extent European) life. Thus many Jews started to move into various occupations and economic sectors which had hitherto been on the whole closed to them, to become more and more active in political life – on the local, State and national level.

Some of these developments may also bear within them the seed of future developments – in the direction of assimilation. The ecological movement to small communities and the general demographic decline of Jews – that same decline which at least partially accounts for their strong economic advance-ment – may make the maintenance of Jewish communal life and activities more difficult. The growing participation in general areas of life of their respective societies may deplete the reservoir of leadership for specific Jewish activities – as shown by the growing influx of orthodox Jews into them. Similarly the great attraction of many of the new religious sects – like for instance the Moonies – to Jewish college youth attests to a similar possibility.

So the possibility of gradual, painless Jewish assimilation, a slow shedding of many components of such identity, became stronger – to no small degree facilitated by the fact that no principled demands for such assimilation were made on the Jews and paradoxically also reinforced by the very fact that it was

* Barry R. Chiswick, 'The Labor Market Status and American Jews: Patterns and Determinants', *American Jewish Yearbook, 1985*.

possible to maintain some such identity in the relatively – even if only relatively – non-problematic ambience of American–Jewish life, and to a smaller extent in many of the Jewish communities in Europe.

Demographic trends reinforced such possibilities. Recent demographic projections predict 'a long-term' dwindling in the number of Diaspora Jews, from 10.7 million in 1970, to 9.7 million in 1980 and a projected decline to 7.9 million by the year 2,000 – due to 'migration, secularization, modernization and assimilation'.*

So there is a very paradoxical picture with respect to the trends of development of the Jewish people in the Diaspora. The relatively great success of Jews to be accepted on a group basis in many countries of the Diaspora and above all in the United States and the development of manifold Jewish activities, as well as diversified patterns of participation in the different spheres of activity of the societies in which they live, do not by themselves assure the continuity of the Jewish and civilizational activities and creativity. Indeed this very success – if not changed by developments in their host societies – together with trends to demographic decline, may lead to an exhaustion of such activities and creativity and to a continuous weakening of Jewish identity and collective cohesion.

It may lead to the possible development of three sections of Jewish people. The first is composed of various orthodox communities which would move more and more into a rather narrow, sectarian direction, abandoning the more universalistic or civilizational orientations of the Jewish heritage.

The second section would be a small hard core from within the great non-orthodox majority, which would attempt – mainly through attachment to Jewish education – to maintain a strong Jewish identity, while not abandoning their broader civilizational orientations and active participation in the general society.

This sector could however be continuously threatened both by the orthodox group and by the third section, the great majority who will, after a generation or two, move into different directions of relatively painless assimilation.

# The Place of the State of Israel in the Historical Experience of Diasporan Communities and Changing Patterns of Israel–Diasporan Relations
## *The political dimension*

The State of Israel played a very special role in the crystallization of these new patterns of Jewish identity.

First of all, it was instrumental, as we have already indicated above, in the revival of the political dimension of Jewish existence and the orientation to the State of Israel, which could be found in almost all Jewish communities and

* R. Bachi in an interview with Yosef Goell, *Jerusalem Post*, 11 August 1983.

THE TRANSFORMATION OF ISRAELI SOCIETY

their sectors, constituted a central pivot of this dimension.

Thus, for instance, in a country like France, with its relatively long tradition of assimilation and of the emphasis of Jewish identity as a religious community, it found its expression in such events as Raymond Aron's polemic against de Gaulle, the Chief Rabbi's sermon during the Yom Kippur War, and later on in the 1970s the growing political engagement of large parts of the Jewish community in connection with French policies towards Israel – an engagement which was intensified by the influence in the French community of younger generations, as well as of North African Jews who became very active in Jewish activities and organizations.

The articulation of this political dimension in relation to the State of Israel was no less far-reaching in other Jewish communities. The English community has a much longer tradition of such activity, especially through the Board of Deputies and through the fact that for many years London was the head-quarters of the World Zionist Organization. It was particularly visible in the United States, in the activities of such bodies as the Board of Presidents – the major Jewish organization; the United Jewish Appeal; the various Jewish political lobbies and the like. It also found expression in activities related to Soviet Jewry.

Significantly enough, however, within this whole plethora or panorama of Jewish activities, the place of the Zionist Organization proper became, to say the least, less and less central. Membership in the Zionist organizations seems to have depleted; the Zionist Congress has even lost some of its more ceremonial and symbolic functions which it had retained in the first two decades of the State. But the Zionist Organization and the Jewish Agency have continued to be the major avenue of channelling funds from the Diaspora to Israel.

## A centre of Jewish life

The State of Israel also provided a geographical centre, a symbol of common heritage and common solidarity which large parts of the Jewish people accepted, the only pivot which was indeed common to all or most of the Jewish people. It provided also a central – not always an easy, simple, very often a very ambivalent – focus of collective Jewish identity.

It became the natural meeting-place for most Jewish organizations; a sort of natural place for family gatherings and events, and there are by now but very few organizations of Jewish communal life which are not connected in some way or another with Israel.

Many Jews attempted to find in Israel the manifestation of the dimensions for which they longed; not only those of political and military strength and collective identity, but also those of social justice, of full religious fulfilment or of some great civilizationary vision – as well as those of 'simple' Jewish solidarity.

The demands made on Israel from such points of view were often utopian, exaggerated, unrealistic – and very diverse – but all of them attested to the fact that the State of Israel constituted a continuous, central focus of such orientations. Even the strength of ambivalence and of criticism against Israel which became more and more vocal from the mid-1970s attested to the relatively central place of Israel in the construction of contemporary collective Jewish identity.

Similarly the possibility of a distinction between Jewish nationhood and Zionism, which constituted a central focus of ideological debate in Eastern Europe, abated almost entirely – aided by the fact that the anti-Semitic outbursts in the 1970s continuously identified the State of Israel and Jewish nationhood. Such anti-Semitism did not only reinforce the Zionist orientation – as was, of course, one of the original Zionist assumptions – but could also give rise to more ambivalent attitudes to Israel.

Indeed in many ways the orientation to the State of Israel – even if of a critical vein – became the basic common focus of Jewish activities and identity, beyond the orthodox or rather the ultra-orthodox sectors. Even from these circles, although they never accepted the Zionist tenets, there was a *de facto* recognition of the State with growing demands on it in terms of their own premises; many settled in Israel and even more developed very close relations with those in Israel.

Significantly enough the old controversies around Zionism, around the viability of the Zionist vision which, as we have seen, abounded within the Jewish communities in Europe – and also in the United States – from the very beginning of Zionist and Jewish settlement in Eretz Israel, have almost entirely abated. The terrible experience of the Holocaust, the fact that Palestine, and later Israel, was initially at least the only place which readily accepted the Jewish refugees from Europe and Asia, the very fact of the successful establishment of the State of Israel, have made most of these controversies meaningless. Even when some groups, as for instance the American Council for Judaism in the United States, attempted to continue in this vein, they found but little resonance within the Jewish communities. In so far as controversies developed – as they did especially from the early 1970s – they became focused on questions pertaining to the degree to which Israel did indeed live up to the various ideals which were expected from it; on the degree of support to be given to it and lately, as we have seen, around the right of Jews to dissent publicly from the policies of the Israeli government. Only among parts of the orthodox and especially the ultra-orthodox has there recently developed a growing distance from the State of Israel, especially in its Zionist dimension but also in its central focus of Jewish existence in general.

Thus Israel has become fully accepted, fully legitimized, not only as a place for Jewish refugees, but as a central aspect of Jewish existence.

## Changing relations and terms of trade

Yet all these variegated developments went far beyond the tenets of Zionist ideology and to some degree of the practice, up to the end of the Second World War, of the Zionist movement in general and of the pioneering groups in particular. It also altered the problem of the relations between Israel and the Diaspora as it had been perceived in Israel up to the Six Day War. In fact, unwittingly but very forcefully, the 'terms of trade' between Israel and the Jewish communities in the Diaspora became transformed in a far-reaching way, in many ways undermining all the Zionist tenets. Israel had been receiving from the Jewish communities of the Diaspora economic resources, political support and diffuse solidarity, manifest in a great variety of ways – attachment, support, visits and the like. At the same time Israel gave to them the symbols of political sovereignty, the political dimension of a collective existence, the pride in Jewish statehood, independence and military strength, and became a central focus of Jewish organizations in general and in those connected with Israel in particular – often opened up for large parts of Jewish leadership channels of participation in the political activities of their own countries. Even if with the passing of time many of these leaders began to take the activities in Jewish organizations in general and those connected with Israel for granted as ones which could be got relatively cheaply as compared with participation in the political or cultural centres of their respective societies, yet these activities continued to be symbols of Jewish solidarity and attachment.

For many within the Jewish communities the participation in activities connected with Israel, visits to Israel on semi-official missions (such as the UJA mission of young leaders) provided them with the excitement of participation in creative works and of access to central political figures which they could rarely attain in their own countries.

These relations between the various active Jewish groups in the Diaspora and Israel were not, as has already been indicated above, always easy. There developed many potential and actual points of tension – and conflict – which became intensified from about the mid-1970s. Yet they were all set within the basic framework of the new terms of trade that developed between Israel and the Jewish communities in the Diaspora.

## The shift and changes in Zionist ideology

But, whatever the details of these terms of trade between Israel and the Jewish communities in the Diaspora, two complementary elements, which were indeed predominant both ideologically and institutionally in the pre-State period (although even then they were not the only ones) were now missing – namely the semi-revolutionary interpretation of the Zionist vision and the principled ideological denial of the legitimacy of Galut life, culminating in the call for Aliya as a revolutionary movement.

As we have seen, the classical Zionist interpretation of this *problematique* and of the concomitant demand to rebel against the experience of the Galut was that Jewish life in the Diaspora was neither safe nor full; that it was only in Eretz Israel that Jews could be safe, free and live a full creative modern life;

that it was only there that they could create a full modern Jewish culture and institutions which would be of some universal significance, which would make them full, even if unique, participants in the family of nations. While the relative importance of these different elements varied in different interpretations of Zionism, they usually tended to come in some way together.

It was, as we have seen, this ideological vision and these premises that were predominant in the Yishuv and in about the first two decades of the State of Israel, in the school curricula of history and in literature, and it was these premises that constituted the basis of perception, especially by the younger generation of *Tsabras*, of Israel's relations to the Diaspora. But in fact this vision became less supported by reality, by the real contacts and terms of trade that developed between Israel and the communities in the Diaspora.

Even on the ideological level some shifts took place. One of the first such shifts was Ben-Gurion's insistence that only those Jews and Jewish leaders who immigrated to Israel could indeed be called – and were entitled to call themselves – Zionists, which had the paradoxical effect of legitimizing the widespread activities of Jewish organizations on behalf of Israel without any commitment on their part to Zionist tenets.

Later on, throughout the 1950s, there developed a growing shift among the Zionist ideologists from the denial of Galut to a definition of the relations between Galut and Israel in terms of the primacy or centrality of Israel – whatever the exact meaning of such primacy or centrality. The term Diaspora was used more and more frequently than Galut, and even these claims of centrality tended in the late 1970s and early 1980s to be sometimes denied by parts of the leadership of the Jewish communities. They often tried to depict Diaspora Jews in general and American Jews in particular as the New Babylon – a new great centre of Jewish life and creativity.

In the seminars on relations between the State of Israel and the Diaspora, organized since the mid-1970s under the auspices of the President of Israel, the Diaspora existence was usually taken for granted – as seen for instance in the title of one of them, 'The identification of the Nation with the State'.

Certainly the old Zionist claims, tenets and visions – the continued stress on the incompleteness of any Jewish life in the Diaspora as against that in Israel and on the dangers of Jewish life in the Diaspora – continued to be made for a long time by the various official or semi-official representatives of the Yishuv – such as the different emissaries of the Jewish Agency, the *Schlichim* who were sent only from Israel to the various countries in the Diaspora, as well as in many of the encounters of Israelis with the Jewish communities in the Diaspora.

But on the whole these claims did not fall on very receptive ears, either in the United States or in other Jewish communities. They did not even become foci of central public controversy in the Jewish community, in the ways that the parallel calls for Aliya were in Europe and even in the United States in the pre-Second World War period. These claims and the debates which they could in principle engender did not become, as against activities in support of Israel or other Jewish national concerns, a central focus of the internal life of these communities.

The various *Schlichim* from Israel became *de facto* closely interwoven in the life of these communities, reinforcing the existing activities in the Jewish field. They did participate quite actively in many such activities, like Jewish Sunday or afternoon school programmes, in special summer camps and the like; yet it was but rarely that these activities of theirs went beyond the existing patterns of Jewish life; certainly only rarely did they forge some new types of activities. Even when they were successful in organizing Aliya, this was seen as only a small part, and certainly not necessarily the central focus of the relations between them and Israel.

The various educational programmes and other activities of the Zionist organizations, although continuing to function, certainly did not play a central – and even less a controversial – role in the Jewish collective life as they had before. They were often overshadowed by the plethora of other Jewish activities; and this was even more true with respect to activities related to Israel.

This trend could also be discerned in Jewish education as it developed in the United States – and which was, as we have seen, of crucial importance in keeping up Jewish collective consciousness. Even some of the new more intensive programmes of Jewish education which started to develop in the 1970s did not contain any specific Zionist message, nor did they deny the legitimacy of the Galut experience or call for a revolutionary break from it. The concern with Israel did not become a central aspect or focus of these curricula, although many aspects of Israeli life, especially various traditions of folklore and special celebrations like the Day of Independence, became an important part of their activities. In a way, all of them, even those which relied heavily on teachers or inspectors from Israel, were much more orientated to strengthening Jewish life in the Diaspora and stemming the waves of assimilation, than to directing it beyond the Diaspora to Israel.

Indeed there developed a strong paradox in the official and actual policy of the preparation of many of these *Schlichim*. Thus, for instance, the Pinkus Fund of the Jewish Agency (named after Arye Pinkus, its chairman in the late 1960s) concentrated on training *Schlichim* in Israel and potential leaders in the Diaspora, in order to strengthen the Jewish component in Jewish communal organizations and education in the Diaspora and so stem the tides of assimilation. Thus, paradoxically, Israel here became a basis for strengthening Jewish existence in the Diaspora.

In most of these institutions the tension between two orientations – between maintaining Jewish institutions in the Diaspora and the Zionist call for Aliya and the denial of the legitimacy of the Galut – was almost entirely absent. Indeed there developed here a rather paradoxical situation that, while in the activities of the adults the concern with Israel and its problems constituted a central focus, it found only a very weak echo (beyond some celebration such as the Day of Independence) in the curricula of the different Jewish schools.

All these activities orientated towards Israel became an accepted part of the dynamics of Jewish life in the Diaspora. The symbolism of the State of Israel became interwoven in the framework of the Jewish communities in the Diaspora, contributing – even during controversies about Israeli policies – to the maintenance and continuity of these frameworks, as did also the more folkloristic aspects of Israeli experience.

## Acceptance of the Diaspora

The acceptance and at least *de facto* legitimization of the Diaspora was also reinforced because of the growing dependence and need of Israel for economic and political support. Many Israeli institutions – universities, schools, museums, sports centres, medical centres and the like – were helped by Jewish organizations or by individuals from the Diaspora. The fact that in many cases such donations were relatively smaller than those given by Diasporan Jews to various Jewish and non-Jewish institutions in the Diaspora (even if these organizations, like the United Jewish Appeal, gave large parts of their funds to Israel) was also a very important indicator of the changing mutual attitudes between Israel and Diaspora – as was the growing dependence of the Israeli institutions on these donations.

The acceptance also became reinforced by the fact that not only could the Jews in the Diaspora participate in many central institutions of their societies – economic, academic or in the media – but that these institutions became points of attraction – and even models – for many groups in Israel, thus weakening the claim of special creativity of Israel in this field. In many of the academic, professional or cultural institutions in the Diaspora which were frequented and visited by their Israeli counterparts, it was the Jews of the Diaspora that quite clearly held the upper hand. There were more distinguished Jewish scientists in the Diaspora than in Israel, and many of them attained peaks – like Nobel prizes – which the Israelis did not. It was they who could extend help to the Israelis, and this very often gave the Diasporan Jews who visited Israel a standing beyond that which they could have got had they settled there.

In a few, even if very outstanding, cases Jewish businessmen from the Diaspora invested in Israel or Israeli enterprises as the much stronger partners – although often also getting special concessions from the government.

The acceptance of the Diaspora was also strengthened through the natural mutual attraction between Israeli diplomats and emissaries and the higher circles of Jewish society in the Diaspora; by the fact that many of the former, upon retirement, became business representatives of the latter in Israel or sometimes even abroad. In a more general way, this acceptance was strengthened by the fact of the development within Israel of many activities orientated outside to external sectors – the most natural being the Jewish communities in the Diaspora.

This Jewish existence and activities in the Diaspora were often accepted, not only as a fact, but also paradoxically as an aspect of the articulation of overall symbols of Jewish national identity and its political dimension, thus strengthening the vitality and dynamics of the Diasporan organizations.

## Lack of Israeli response to the problems in the Diaspora

This change in the relations between the Jewish communities in the Diaspora and Israel was also evident in, and reinforced by, the lack of understanding in Israel of many aspects of the internal *problematique* of Jewish life in the Diaspora, and consequently of a lack of concern and response to it.

This *problematique*, which focused, as we have seen above, on finding ways of expressing Jewish collective identity in their countries, developed in two directions. The first was the organization of manifold Jewish activities and organizations and fields of activities – communal, organizational, political and the like – and in the concomitant crystallization of different symbols of Jewish identity. The second was the participation of Jews in the cultural and political activities of the societies in which they lived, often also stressing the specific Jewish dimension of such participation.

Significantly enough, within Israel there were few activities – beyond those stressing Israel as a focus of Jewish solidarity and nationhood and of the strengthening of the Jewish component in their life – which were related to these aspects. Perhaps the most important illustration of such lack of response from Israel to the specifically Jewish *problematique* of these communities can be found in the field of religion, religious thought and practice.

The major non-orthodox trends, especially among American Jews, the Conservatives and the Reform, could find in Israel no real resonance – beyond some symbolic support and the establishment of a few communities in Israel, even if their number has lately been growing – as part of the more general opening up of the cultural scene in Israel. It was not just that the whole format of the religious institutions in Israel was different from that of the Diaspora, and that they continuously encountered the outright political monopoly in the religious field of orthodox establishment. Of no less crucial importance was the fact that till now there were but few responses in Israel to the search, which was so central in the Jewish communities in the Diaspora, for meaningful reinterpretation of some aspects of Jewish tradition in religious or theological terms. Beyond a common emphasis on the development of some traditional practices, which developed to a large extent independently in Israel and in the Diaspora, there was little common ground in this area. Even the experience of the Holocaust which became so central in Jewish theological thought in the Diaspora was less central in Israel – and there were no far-reaching attempts among intellectuals or educators and the manifold cultural and academic institutions in Israel and in the Diaspora to look for some common starting-points in the interpretation of the Jewish historical experience in general and the new one that has developed in the United States – and above all to maintain some continuous common activities in this direction.

The same applied to the problem of Jewish participation in general, especially American, activities. There were but few common cultural activities or endeavours in literature, journalism or mass media. Those which did develop in the United States – as for instance *Commentary* – had almost no resonance in Israel; no real dialogue developed between them and the Israeli public or intellectuals on such problems. It was only in academic life that more intensive contacts developed between institutions of Jewish learning in the Diaspora and those in Israel – but in many ways these did not differ greatly from contacts with general academic institutions.

Moreover even here, while Israel naturally become the centre of Jewish studies, especially those, like archaeology, closely connected with Eretz Israel, in particular, yet with the growing development of different centres of such studies in many universities in the Diaspora, especially in the United States, the latter started to develop themes beyond those emphasized in Israel. They stressed, for instance, the interrelations between Jewish communities and their broader settings and the civilizational aspects of Judaism in all the periods of its history; they based themselves much more on an interrelation between Jewish and general studies, as against the more national and Eretz Israel emphases relatively more predominant in Israel. While they could not compete with the great scope of Jewish studies in Israel, yet they did not necessarily accept the latter as the unique model, and were less apologetic towards it.

## The role of Jews from the Diaspora in Israel

This new relationship between the Jewish communities in Israel and in the Diaspora was also manifest in the pattern of Diasporan Jews' participation in the social and political life of Israel. The crucial new development here, in marked contrast to the period of the Yishuv, was the strong tendency to the marked depolitization of the participation of the Jews from the Diaspora. This was seemingly a natural outcome of the very establishment of the State with its own citizenship and government, with the lessening importance of the Jewish Agency or World Zionist Organization, in relation to the organs of the State. But while some marked changes in these directions were, of course, inevitable, it is a moot question whether they had to go so far as they did.

The crucial event or process here was probably the rift between Ben-Gurion and the American Zionist leadership of Abba Hillel Silver, which was already evident, despite their momentary alliance, in the Zionist Congress of 1946 before the establishment of the State of Israel. The rift was intensified later when Ben-Gurion claimed that only those living in Israel could participate in affairs and effectively withdrew Silver – and probably many others – from active participation in the affairs of Israel and even in those of the Jewish Agency and the Zionist Organization.

Although, as in all 'if only' historical questions, this one is difficult to answer, yet it seems that at this period there was some possibility of more active participation on the part of Americans and others, although certainly differing in many concrete ways from the patterns of participation of Eastern European

Jews in the period of the Yishuv. This possibility might have activated, within the American–Jewish community and in other communities of the Diaspora, some forces which could have become more closely interwoven in the political social life of Israel.

But this was not to be. The combination of pressures to help the State in its many concrete – political and economic – endeavours and the unwillingness of the Israeli leadership, and especially of Ben-Gurion, to accept any 'outside' interference – which constituted to no small degree a part of the general tendency to minimize the movement aspect of political life – gave rise to the development of a new pattern of such participation of Jews from the Diaspora in Israeli institutions and life.

This new pattern of participation was set within the new basic terms of trade that developed between Israel and the Jewish communities in the Diaspora. It was, accordingly, characterized by a relatively limited active participation in Israeli affairs; it provided political and economic support for Israel, even when voicing private criticism, and public criticism was kept to a minimum –although even this began to change markedly after the mid-1970s.

There was also a rather special pattern of involvement of Diasporan Jews in economic affairs of Israeli mobilization of aid through campaigns such as the United Jewish Appeal or selling of Israel Bonds, coming in contact with some very selective and preferential industries in Israel, and in other various economic frameworks, but in relatively few common enterprises. When such enterprises were established, the Diasporan elements often loomed as separate, distinct and strong, even if in fact they were often bolstered by special concessions from the Government.

Many – probably most – of the major Jewish organizations developed some contacts in Israel, very often organizing their conventions in Israel, but very few really found ways to participate in life in Israel – except perhaps for some type of semi-philanthropic involvement, even if couched already in more modern ways. Nor were there many signs that Israelis in general, and the Israeli establishment in particular, were very eager to find some such ways.

There developed many dialogues between Israelis and Jews of the Diaspora – organized by such organizations as the American Jewish Congress or American Jewish Committee; lately also, as we shall soon see, by organizations sponsored by circles of intellectuals of Oriental origin in the Diaspora. But these did not involve any continuous participation in Israeli life or of Israelis in the life of the Jewish communities in the Diaspora.

There developed also, of course, far-reaching personal contacts, especially among academics and professionals, or on purely a personal or family basis, as well as through communal activities; but there were relatively few cultural enterprises established in common by Jews from the Diaspora and Israelis. A few outstanding Jewish musicians – Leonard Bernstein, Arthur Rubinstein, Isaac Stern and others – contributed, as we have seen, to the development of musical life in Israel. Many academicians would come to lecture or participate in academic activities in Israel. But the centres of their work were outside, as was also the case with many musicians born or raised in Israel, such as, for instance, Itzhak Perlman or Daniel Barenboim.

The pattern of intervention of Jews from the Diaspora in Israeli life which has recently developed among the so-called Oriental communities, has on the whole followed a similar trend. This trend was characterized by the growing intervention of the Oriental – above all, but not only, North African and Egyptian – Jews, who settled in Europe (above all in France and Switzerland), and also in the United States, on behalf of the Oriental groups in Israel. The former consisted mostly of those Jews from these Oriental communities who opted to go to Europe instead of to Israel; they constituted mostly the stronger, more skilled, more intellectual, more confident elements for whom it was 'natural' – in the words of Albert Memmi,* the North African Jewish French writer settled in Paris – to go to the West, as it was natural for the weaker elements to go to Israel where they would be assured of being taken care of, at least minimally.

Many of them prospered in the West as businessmen, professionals and intellectuals in the framework of that very Western civilization against which their brothers in Israel – and even they – seemingly cried out; they found in this framework – again as Albert Memmi has attested with respect to himself – the natural arena of their creativity, all that time maintaining some kind of Jewish identity and activity and also contacts, often family contacts, with Israel.

From around the mid- or late 1960s, when these groups were established in their countries, there developed, however, a new pattern among them, in the wake of the growing articulation of ethnic themes in Israel. There was a new participation in Israeli affairs and they started to support more and more the claims of the various Oriental groups in Israel.

Already earlier, in the early 1960s, there had been some active groups, like *Oded*, which stressed Aliya, but they comprised relatively small numbers. Later on, much more frequent was the growing support such different organizations or leaders gave to the various activities of Oriental groups – whether through organizations like the World Sephardi Federation with its claims to seats on the boards of the Jewish Agency or the World Zionist Organization; or through many other activities – thus creating a new framework of such contacts between Israel and the Diaspora. There was, however, basically very little new in this framework as compared to other such frameworks – except that it probably contained somewhat more paternalistic overtones on the part of the Jews in the Diaspora. These frameworks (with the partial exception of *Oded*) did not entail the continuous participation – beyond symbolic or semi-paternalistic semi-philanthropic gestures in Israel – in activities, institution-building or cultural activities in Israel and, in so far as it changed the terms of trade between Israel and the Diaspora, it was in the direction of weakening even more the position of the Israeli side.

---

* In an interview in *Haaretz*, 31 March 1983.

## New conceptions of Aliya

The changing pattern of relations between the Jewish communities in the Diaspora and the State of Israel can best be seen in the changing place of Aliya (immigration to Israel) in the life of these communities and in its very motivation.

First of all in this period immigration to Israel became only one of the links connecting the Jewish community in the Diaspora and the State. It was no longer unlike the most important or traumatic event it had been in the formation period of the Yishuv. Many of the historical, primordial, national and religious elements binding Jews together, and not easily given to definition, continued to exist and were even renewed – but they did not necessarily give rise to Aliya. Even in Israel itself – and in spite of the concern with immigration and the problems of its absorption – the stress on Aliya was only one of the ways by which connections with Jewish communities were formed. Other ways of expressing Jewish solidarity developed, as we have seen, through economic ties with stronger and richer elements in Jewish communities abroad, through varied philanthropic activities, sentimental ties, tourism and family visits.

Israel indeed became for a very large part of world Jewry (almost as in the period of the Second Temple and to a smaller degree even later, until the disappearance of the centre in Eretz Israel) a centre of different types of pilgrimage – religious, sentimental, expressing national solidarity or a search for symbols of collective identity, and the like. This aspect became more prevalent, perhaps more important, than immigration, than Aliya itself. Probably wide circles in the Diaspora accepted Aliya as the epitome of attachment to Israel, although many parents were probably rather ambivalent if it affected their own children (even if not daring to express such ambivalence).

Even when it took place, Aliya was rarely conceived as a revolutionary experience, as the transformation or reconstruction of the patterns of life in the Diaspora. It was rather an act of affirmation of the attachment to Israel, of seeking some framework for living among Jews, of expressing Jewish solidarity or an attachment to Jewish tradition; or, for some orthodox groups which became relatively more prominent among the *Olim* after the late 1970s, of being able to live a fuller religious or religious–national life.

It was only among some of these 'modern religious' or orthodox groups, especially those who identified themselves within the more extremist political movements in Israel, that some ingredients of a revolutionary experience could be identified – and even they were probably a small part of this Aliya.

Aliya, especially from the West itself, was relatively small, although it did increase in the late 1960s, consisting in no small part of modern orthodox – often of non-Zionist – circles. The older pattern of a pioneering–liberal–socialist Aliya had almost entirely disappeared.

A relatively new pattern of Aliya that developed in this period was a sort of extension of life in the Diaspora – Jews who retired to or, above all among the more affluent elements, established a second home in Israel, dividing their time between their homes in the Diaspora and in Israel – becoming very closely interwoven with the different patterns of life of various, usually higher, circles in Israel.

All these patterns of connection between the Jewish communities in the Diaspora and Israel became very variegated – but they all were very far from the perception of Aliya as a revolution against Jewish life in the Diaspora, as a process of radical reconstruction of the pattern of that life.

Whatever the composition and orientation of these Aliyot, one element or dimension which had been relatively strong in the previous periods (namely their impact on the central institutions of Israel, on their basic format in general and the provision of leadership on all levels of public life in particular) here became rather weak, if not non-existent – thus moving into the natural direction of most immigrant countries.

Needless to say, some of the new immigrants became prominent in the academic and in the professional life; some established new Kibbutzim and even more innovative types of settlements. But all these activities were not directly orientated to the central institutions of the society, nor did they impinge on the centre. Thus, unlike in the period of the Yishuv, the Diaspora ceased to serve, with few individual exceptions, as a reservoir of leadership, of groups and of movements with direct access to the centre, which could break through its limitation, through possibly stagnative tendencies of the Israeli social structure and become agents of its possible invigoration and reconstruction.

## Yordim

An entirely new – and very significant – element in the panorama of the Jewish Diaspora was the rising prominence of *Yordim* – their number ranging according to different estimates between 300,000 and 350,000 people since the establishment of the State.

Many of them tended to concentrate in several great centres – New York, Los Angeles and in more minor centres in the United States, Canada and Europe. Many – although certainly not all – of them tended to live a rather separate life of their own, not wholly integrated in the Jewish communities, because of mutual reluctance and suspicion and because of the rather negative labelling of them in Israel. A significant number of them have indeed become integrated, marrying into Jewish families, often bringing to them many aspects of Israeli life, folklore and the like, and have started to participate in various Jewish activities and to be engaged – despite some official outcries in Israel – in local Jewish communities and in institutions of Jewish education. According to some estimates, in many of the great Jewish communities like Los Angeles or New York, they constitute about 40 per cent – if not more – of teachers in such institutions. Special cultural activities, like special Hebrew broadcasting oriented to them, have developed in many of their centres. Some of them have become 'naturally' very visible when caught by the law in some illegal or semi-legal activities.

But whatever the details of their life and organization, their very existence, their relatively great numbers, their having seemingly become a permanent part of the Jewish scene, went against the basic tenets of the Israeli self-perception. This is all too obvious in their negative labelling, as for instance that of the then Prime Minister Yitzhak Rabin who called them *Nefolet Nemushot* (fallout of weaklings), as well as the continuous attempts to find ways to bring them back.

The different groups of the *Yordim* have also added a new dimension to the relations between Jewish communities and Israel – above all very variegated personal and family contacts, combined with more ambivalent relations or attitudes.

The experience of the *Yordim* can be looked at – as it has indeed been often looked at in Israel – from the point of view of the possibility of Aliya, of the potential attraction of Israel to Jewish groups in the Diaspora. Often the *Yordim* were looked upon as potential *Olim*, although usually with a very strong ambivalence rooted in the general opprobrium directed at them – an opprobrium based, of course, on the basic ideological tenets and totalistic and solidarity orientations and components of Israeli identity, the like of which it is rather difficult to find in other small countries like Switzerland or Holland with out-migration.

## Israel as a place of refuge

But it was not only with respect to the more 'revolutionary' dimensions or aspects of Aliya that the appeal of Israel seems to have abated and changed its nature. No less important, and in many ways quite shocking for many Israelis, was the fact that for many Jews in search of security, Israel was not even the natural first place of refuge.

The first shock was that many – in fact most from the mid-1970s – of the Jews who left Russia with an Israeli visa, officially proclaiming their intention to go to Israel, in fact opted to go not to Israel but to other countries in the West – above all to the United States. Thus the percentage of drop-outs in Vienna, which was very small (less than one per cent) in 1971 and 1972, started to increase from 1973, reaching about 50 per cent in 1977, around 65 per cent in 1979 and 1980 and about 81 per cent in 1981. The fact that in this they were helped by Jewish organizations such as the Hebrew Immigration Aid Society (HIAS) gave rise, as we have seen, to rather acrimonious debates.

Probably even more shocking from the point of view of the Zionist tenets was the fact that, out of the Iranian Jews who were confronted with the Khomeini revolution, only a very small part opted, despite the obvious dangers, to leave Iran and that, even from among those who left, a not insignificant part seemed to have gone to countries other than Israel.

The same was the case, though less visible among Latin American Jews, many of whom – especially as far as one can ascertain the younger professional or academic ones – tended under the pressure of the oppressive regimes (especially in Argentina) to leave their countries. Most of them tended to go to the United States, to Europe – for instance to Spain, where, given the common language they could relatively easily become absorbed – and only a relatively small number went to Israel. A similar picture could be found among many North African Jews, amongst whom the more educated ones opted, from the 1950s on, to go to France, Canada or the United States, and not to Israel.

Thus indeed it seemed that Israel's place in the map of Jewish immigration, even of immigration from countries in which Jews felt threatened or were persecuted, became rather secondary so long as other countries were ready to accept them. Its symbolic place notwithstanding, it became an ultimate, but only an ultimate, place of refuge – even if paradoxically its very existence as a place of such refuge may have helped these other migratory processes.

## Conclusions

Thus, Israel tended to become a central component of Jewish life throughout the world, but this very centrality – not unlike that of the Second Temple and later on the period of the great Mishnaic Talmudic centre – greatly weakened its potentially revolutionary impact on these communities, on seeing it as a place in which to reconstruct their life as modern Jews.

On the one hand Israel was a major symbol and centre of Jewish identity, a focus of solidarity and primordial sentiments, of hopes and dreams, a potential haven from oppression, even a symbol of the civilizational potentialities of Jewish life, a symbol of pride because of its achievements or of criticism because of its failures.

On the other hand, however, it was not – as presumed in classical Zionist ideology – the sole centre of Jewish creativity, the only place in which new types of social, educational and cultural activities and creativity of the Jewish people could develop. The creative impulse of many Jewish communities did not necessarily become focused on life in Israel, and the pattern of Jewish renaissance developed in Israel was but one pattern of such creativity – even if a central one.

Controversies around Israel shifted from the older views about the viability of the Zionist vision, to those about Israel – but not other Jewish communities – living up, in its life and policies, to the tenets of this vision. It was indeed against the background of this paradoxical change of the place of Israel in the life of Jewish communities that there developed also the various trends of denial of its centrality in Jewish life, and of ambivalence to it.

The effects of this change in the relations between Israel and the Jewish communities in the Diaspora in general and in the United States in particular, on the developments in the Jewish communities in the Diaspora are not easy to ascertain. Almost any such appraisal would be in the realm of conjecture or at best a question for further research. Perhaps the most intriguing of these questions would be the effect of these processes on the selection of Jewish leadership, its style and orientation; whether it is possible that more active and autonomous relations with Israel could have drawn into the realm of American Jewish organized activities new more variegated leadership elements and themes. All these are, of course, matters of conjecture, but at least worth pondering about.

The impacts of these developments on the structure of Israeli society are somewhat clearer. In Israel these trends naturally reinforced the various processes of transformation of the Israeli political mould, of the structure of its elites, and the atrophization of much of its political activities that we have discussed earlier – especially those tendencies and tensions inherent in Israel as a small society between openness and closure; between some of the tendencies prevalent in Israel to populist–nationalist provincialism inherent in it and those to a more open democratic society, the tendencies to stagnation and to creativity.

On the one hand these trends seem to have developed and maintained a plurality of avenues of contact with the outside world, thus in principle strengthening the openness of Israeli society, although some of these contacts also reinforced the tendencies to provincialism and closure. On the other hand, however, these trends, unlike those in the former period, did not contribute to the restructuring of Israeli society and its centres.

Thus, just as with many of the internal problems of Israel analysed above, so also with the Israeli responses to the patterns of Jewish experience in the United States and in Europe, there has not till now developed a new institutional imagination and creativity which could break through the initial mould which developed, naturally as it were, in the first decade or two of the State. At the same time there are indeed many signs, which have become even more evident in the last two decades, that among the new generation of Jewish businessmen, academics, intellectuals and professionals there has emerged some search for new imaginative ties with Israel, the likes of which they could not find in the United Jewish Appeal or the existing Jewish organizations.

There has indeed developed here a rather paradoxical situation – on the one hand Israel has become a very central focus of Jewish identity, and probably also one of the major points of reference of Jewish activities and organizations . On the other hand, however, the very dim recognition in Israel and the Diaspora of the nature of the new patterns of such activities and of new potentialities; a certain blindness to the full implication of this fact in many communities in the Diaspora as well as in Israel; the taking for granted in Israel of the 'terms of trade' that have developed between them, all these may lead to changes in the nature of contacts between different sectors of Jewish population in the Diaspora and Israel, weakening the contacts with sectors more active in American life, and ultimately leading to the drying up of these springs of creativity, both in Israel and in the Jewish communities in the Diaspora.

# CHAPTER 17

# The Late 1970s and the 1980s – Change, Transition and Confrontation

## The Background to the Elections
### *The disintegration of the Labour– Zionist institutional mould*

In the preceding analysis we have analysed the reasons for the processes leading, in Israel, in the Diaspora and in the relations between them, to the decomposition of the Labour–Zionist institutional mould. This analysis pointed out that the crux of these processes was the contradiction between the basic ideological premises of the regnant institutional mould – especially between the emphasis on institutional and cultural creativity, autonomous access to the centre and participation in the centre on the one hand, and the more open universalistic orientations on the other; and between the development of the paternalistic mode of relation between centre and periphery in general and of political participation in particular.

These contradictions were intensified and reinforced by their interconnection with the transformation of the carriers of the ideology into a ruling elite; by their strong interweaving with the upper strata of the society, some of whom were acting against many of the premises of this ideology; by the transformation of the regnant ideology in general and the exhaustion of the social institutional dimension, as well as the construction of symbols of collectivity of this creativity in particular.

Many of these processes of transformation – at least in their general outlines, if certainly not in their concrete details – were indeed common to many post-revolutionary regimes, but in each post-revolutionary society they crystallized in a specific way.

All these developments seemingly attest to the fact that the basic programme of these elites rooted in the Labour–Zionist ideology – that programme which had guided the development of Iraeli society in the first twenty-five years of its existence – became, to use Johan Galtung's words, a 'spent' one, while at the same time these elites continued to legitimize themselves in terms of the vision behind this programme.

The single most important aspect of the contradictions between the emerging social reality and the basic ideological premises of the regnant institutional mould was the emphasis on participation, creativity and access to the centre on the one hand, and the growing feeling, among large sectors of the population, of exclusion from the centres of the society on the other. Such centres seemed to have lost their meaning, as had the ideology in the terms of which many Israelis, and the major elites within them, portrayed and legitimized themselves.

## The effect of the 1967 and 1973 wars

All these developments gave rise to the weakening – even shattering – of the cognitive map of the leading sectors of the society.

The first transformation of this map was evident in the changes from a more creative to a more adaptive attitude to internal and external environments; the leading sectors of the society were not really conscious of this transformation, or probably would not have admitted to it.

The Six Day War reinforced this adaptive attitude, strengthening the feeling of ability to master these environments and further weakening the transformative attitudes. But the Yom Kippur War shattered the self-assurance about the ability to master these environments. All in all the feeling of self-assurance, of self-confidence was shattered, and the long-term creative and yet pragmatic vision was weakened.

It was the combination of all these processes that explains the prevalence of the feelings of uneasiness, apprehension and uncertainty which became so prevalent in large sectors of Israeli society after the Yom Kippur War. This was so different from the feeling of self-satisfaction and self-assurance which had characterized it on the whole in the previous period, especially in the period immediately after the Six Day War. So it is indeed in this context that it is possible to understand the acute sensitivity to major problems that developed in Israel in the 1970s, as well as the ways in which this became manifest in the political arena and combined with the elections of 1977 and 1981. It was in these elections – in themselves, as we have seen, the culmination of long-term electoral processes – that the Labour bloc lost its predominant place in the Israeli political system. It was the Likud that formed the governments which changed in many ways, as we shall see, the formats of political life in Israel, although still within the basic frameworks of Israeli constitutional democracy and its Zionist legitimation.

All this does not explain, of course, the special timing of this outcome of these elections. Here of special importance was the coincidence and the accumulation of first the effects of the Yom Kippur War, second the impact of various cases of corruption among high echelons close to the *Maarach*, and third the maturation, as it were, of the social processes analysed above, especially of the various processes of social mobility and of the variegated developments in the cultural field.

The aftermath of the Yom Kippur War and the various cases of corruption generated the loss of confidence in the ability of the establishment to deal with the crucial, central problem of security and cast several doubts on the probity of many of the members of the establishment. These events were not perceived in purely technical or personal terms, but as manifestations of the ossification of the centre, of the inadequacy of security, and of internal corruption or weakness. These were themes which were abundantly stressed in the various movements of protest that mushroomed after the Yom Kippur War.

So these occurrences, when set against the background of the various long-term processes analysed above, greatly added to a growing sense of the inability of the society, and its leaders, to deal adequately with some of its basic, central – internal and external – problems. These were the problems which were very closely related to the very core of its collective self-identity. Earlier they had either not been noticed so much or had been seen as being adequately dealt with within the framework of the regnant institutional mould.

In the 1977 as well as in the 1981 elections these problems became closely interwoven with the political process. So in these elections the regular political struggle became closely connected with one about the viability of the initial institutional mould that was regnant in the State of Israel and about the possibility of developing a new one. This combination, of course, added a new, very intensive dimension to the political struggle.

**Table 17.1    Results of the Elections for the Knesset, 1977 and 1981 (percentages)**

| List | 1977 | 1981 |
| --- | --- | --- |
| Alignment (*Maarach*) | 24.6 | 36.6 |
| Minorities connected with Alignment | 1.4 | – |
| National Religious Front, *Mizrahi* and *Mizrahi* Workers | 9.2 | 4.9 |
| Israel Tradition Movement (*Tami*) | – | 2.3 |
| Agudat Israel | 3.4 | 3.7 |
| Agudat Israel Workers | 1.3 | 0.9 |
| Democratic Movement for Change (*Dash*) | 11.6 | – |
| Likud | 33.4 | 37.1 |
| Rebirth (*Hatehia*) | – | 2.3 |
| Movement for State Renewal (*Telem*) | – | 1.6 |
| Shlomzion Realization of Zionist Movement | 1.9 | – |
| Independent Liberals | 1.2 | 0.6 |
| Citizens' Rights Movement | 1.2 | 1.4 |
| Democratic List for Peace and Equality (*Rakach*), Black Panthers | 4.6 | 3.4 |
| Other minorities lists | 0.4 | 1.1 |
| Platto-Sharon | 2.0 | 0.6 |
| Other lists | 2.2 | 1.6 |

Source: Government of Israel, Press Bureau.

## The Elections – The Feeling of Exclusion from the Centre and the Quest of Access to it
### Shift away from the Labour camp

In order to understand the nature of these processes in greater detail it might be worthwhile to start with an analysis of the results of the 1977 and 1981 elections, so as to explain the reasons for the downfall of Labour and the victory of the Likud.

We may start with the analysis of the electoral data, and in particular the socio-economic ethnic and age bases of the electoral shifts. Here there are of course important differences between the 1977 and the 1981 elections, but in many ways it was the 1977 elections that provided the watershed, the end of the predominance of Labour in the political scene in Israel.

Table 17.1 reiterates the comparative results of these elections. The usual interpretation of these electoral trends was to stress the so-called 'ethnic' factor: the fact that the Oriental Jews (i.e. those of Afro-Asian origin, above all Moroccans) tended to vote more and more for the Likud. Even if many members of these groups voted for the *Maarach*, the trend was seen as evidence of the fact that these groups were alienated from the Labour institutional mould, its values and ideology.

Such alienation was usually explained in terms of two closely combined factors – a cultural and a class one. From the class point of view it was stressed that most of these groups belonged to the lower occupational strata. From the cultural point of view it was stressed that their cultural traditions were alien to the semi-secular, westernized, ideological premisses of the dominant mould.

Another, later, explanation of the predominance of the Likud, especially of *Herut* in general and of Begin in particular, was in terms of the attraction of populistic and national-chauvinistic slogans and orientations to lower-middle petty bourgeoisie and *déclassé* proletarians.

While these explanations do indeed provide important pointers for the understanding of these electoral processes, they do not provide a fully adequate explanation. They take into account the fact that on the whole the Alignment appealed more to the well off, older, better educated people born in Europe, while the Likud appealed more to younger people (especially from the Oriental groups, and from those born in Israel), to the less educated and to those born in Asia and Africa. But a closer look at these electoral trends in general, and at the Oriental vote in particular, shows that these interpretations do not explain the special intensity and dynamics of the electoral trends which culminated in these elections, and their institutional repercussion.

There were, first of all, other social elements which were crucial in the toppling of Labour in 1977, and at least one of them was also very important in 1981.

One, relatively continuous, such element concerned various categories of youth. All the survey data since at least the late 1960s indicated that the appeal of Likud was greater, often even growing, among the younger people between the ages of 18 and about 26–27, especially those of Oriental origin and those born in Israel but to some degree also those of Western backgrounds.

In the 1977 elections there was another such element which crystallized around *Dash* (The Democratic Movement for Change), although there are disputes as to the degree of its importance. Support for *Dash* comes from within the social-economic strata, even from within Kibbutzim and Moshavim, of rather typical *Maarach* voters. They were probably the most 'modern' of such voters, even if they were not from Labour's core political groups. Most of them seem to have 'returned' to the *Maarach* in 1981 after the complete bankruptcy of *Dash*. But there is no doubt that they were of great importance, not only in the specific outcome of the 1977 elections but also – and perhaps above all – in the weakening of the 'historical' legitimacy of Labour as the dominant coalition party.

Most of the voters of *Dash*, as well as many of the younger generations, did not share either the class or the presumed cultural characteristics of the Oriental supporters of the Likud and hence the explanation in such terms cannot be applied to them. They did, however, share one common denominator with many of the youth and the Oriental groups – namely the feeling of exclusion from full and equal participation in the central loci of the dominant institutional mould in general and of its political and cultural centres in particular; of a lack of access to them; and, as a consequence, a very intensive feeling of alienation, as well as concern that these centres had become more and more ossified.

The common denominator of all these sectors was indeed the feeling of exclusion from autonomous access to political and cultural centres, from being able to become part of these centres and of the central, political and cultural elites – of being the object of paternalistic policies which, while greatly varying in the details as applied to these various groups, were yet common with respect to all of them.

Each of these social sectors perceived this exclusion from participation in the political and to some degree cultural centres from a different vantage point. Many of the supporters of *Dash* were indeed part of what may be called the broad Labour spectrum. They were closely related to it in terms of social background, career patterns and broad socio-political orientations, and many of them had attained their positions owing to the policies of development undertaken by the Labour government. Many of them were socialized in the premises of this mould, as it had constantly developed and changed in the State of Israel, had grown up within its frameworks and shared many of its premises as they had changed with the transformation of the regnant ideology.

Some of them came from within the higher echelons of the army whose colleagues were co-opted – often 'parachuted' – into top political positions. Yet neither they, nor many from the younger generations, could find a place for themselves within the existing centre. While quite obviously there could not be enough top places for all the primadonnas, they also saw the centres of decision-making as ossified and inefficient. Most of their demands and programmes were very much coined as the corrective of the *Maarach*, and it was in this way that most of them saw themselves.

Among large parts of the younger generation, as well as those of the 'Liberal' elements of the older bourgeois whose process of initial political socialization had been different from that of the different Labour groups, the criticism of the *Maarach* also became connected with the non-acceptance of some, especially the so-called socialist, premisses of this mould and of their concrete institutional manifestation – such as centralized economy, heavy control, over-bureaucratization. In this they had the backing of many of the core *Dash* supporters and leaders.

They did, however, accept other premisses of this mould – such as the national security and development – but attempted to transform them in the direction of more civil, universalistic premisses, of maximization of paternalistic policies and demands, the opening up of great flexibility of the central echelons.

There existed also, among many of the 'European' groups, so far as can be ascertained among relatively wide echelons of the more 'traditional' elements of the private sector, as well as many groups in the public sector, a feeling of alienation from the political pattern developed by the centre, as well as the cultural pattern evolved by the Labour camp, a feeling which naturally became intensified with the development of this pattern into a sort of general secularized social democratic one, without special pioneering or seemingly even Jewish eléments.

## Geographical influences

This feeling of alienation and exclusion was probably shared by the several more traditional parts of European immigrants and even more by large parts of the so-called Oriental groups – but in order to understand more fully the nature of these feelings it is necessary to have a somewhat closer look at the nature of this vote in these elections. There were indeed the inhabitants of the *Shekhunot*, who were the traditional voters of the Likud. But it seems that much more important in the increase of the votes for the Likud were the more mobile, relatively affluent groups, partly self-employed in the various new sectors of economy analysed above, partly employed in public sectors, who felt themselves being blocked from fuller and autonomous participation in various political, cultural and social centres.

An analysis of the geographical aspects of the elections brings out this point succinctly.

The recent growth in the electoral support for the Likkud, occurring mainly in geographical concentrations of the population of Asian-African origin and of lower socio-economic status, has assumed a pattern of geographical diffusion from the core of the country to its periphery. In 1965, the electoral support for the Likkud surpassed **that** for the Labour Alignment in only a few, old inner-city neighbourhoods of the three large cities, such as Nahla'ot in Jerusalem, Hatikva in Tel Aviv–Yafo and Wadi Salib in Haifa. In the rest of the concentrations of the Asian–African population, the Labour Alignment parties led the Likkud parties by a 2–2.5 to 1 margin. In the 1969 and the 1973 elections, the support for the Likkud spread to the outlying housing suburbs in the older cities and towns within the core of the country, as well as to the nearby new immigrant towns, such as Or Yehuda near Tel Aviv–Yafo and Tirat Hacarmel near Haifa. Only in 1977 did the electoral support for the Likkud surpass that of the Labour Alignment in the new development towns on the periphery of the country.

A possible explanation for the pattern of geographical diffusion of the electoral support for the Likkud lies in the geography of the urban political economy. In the immigrant housing suburbs and particularly in the development towns, where housing, employment and services were largely initiated and controlled by Labour-dominated agencies, the electoral swing to the right took place at a later date than in the core areas. In the core areas, the lower-status population of Asian-African origin faced a diverse political economy when in search of employment, housing and services, and was thus more flexible in its political behaviour than its counterparts on the periphery.*

So it was not just lower-class groups that were important here. Perhaps the most important aspect of this process was that it took place in the core geographical areas as well as in the periphery. And the more mobile and affluent groups were of crucial importance in the electoral shift.

Thus all these data indicate that it was above all these (very often rather affluent and mobile) Oriental groups, living close to the various concentrations of affluent old-timers with no common social frameworks with them, who were important in the political shift.

Probably these various more mobile elements found their status aspirations and their aspirations to participation in the centre blocked, and developed a growing feeling of cultural distance from the patterns of life of wide sectors of the upper strata and elites that up to then had been most important, vocal and active.

## Demands from within Oriental groups

The concrete demands that were voiced in these elections by or on behalf of the Oriental groups constituted a continuation and intensification of ones that had been articulated earlier.

Thus one demand was for access to positions of authority, power and prestige. The second was for the recognition of the specific Oriental tradition or the symbols of that tradition within the framework of the common symbols of their identity, whether of styles of prayer, family life, attachment to tradition or styles of life. Finally there were demands for the closure in some ways – up to some vocal demands for positive discrimination – of the occupational gap between the Oriental and the Ashkenazi groups.

* Amiram Gonen, 'The Geography of the Electoral Competition between the Labour Alignment and the Likkud in Jewish Cities of Israel, 1965–1981', *Medina, Mimshal Veyehasim Benleumiyiim* (in Hebrew), 19–20 (Spring 1982), pp. viii–x.

The intensification of all these demands, often very vocal, often with strong aggressive orientations – while probably exaggerated through the media, even if this very exaggeration was, of course, in itself a very important fact – attested to the fact that they went far beyond 'simple' demands for better positions or for more resources. Indeed at the time of the 1981 elections there were some extreme ethnic demands. The newspapers and media became filled with articles and letters which focused around this theme – some of them by people, usually intellectuals, who identified themselves as Orientals, and stressed their feeling of being discriminated against, of alienation. The experience of the *Maabarot* in the 1950s, of the neglected urban sectors, of the developments towns, became a major symbol of such feelings of alienation, even of discrimination or exploitation by the Ashkenazi; the basic division between Orientals and Westerns was voiced, often in a very extreme way and in violent expressions.

Some of the most extreme formulations of this theme were developed by intellectuals, Ashkenazi and Orientals alike, many of them gathering around *Tami*, the ethnic list created in 1981 by Aharon Abu-Hatzeira, former member of the *Mafdal* and Minister of Religious Affairs, who, when accused of misappropriation of public funds when Mayor of Ramleh, felt abandoned by *Mafdal*. These intellectuals claimed that the bad situation of the Orientals was the result of a conscious exploitation by the Ashkenazi and called for the establishment of a separate Oriental society and culture – a theme that also became widespread among some of the younger Orientals in the universities.

There were even some who complained about the performance on the wireless or television of old (i.e. 'pioneering') Israeli songs which, according to the complainers, were alien to many of the Oriental groups.

Those among the Orientals who came out against such ethnic stress, like one of Israel's most prominent writers, A. B. Yehoshua, or J. Bechar, a journalist of Bulgarian origin, were in a relative minority.

Whatever the real strength of these feelings, there can be no doubt that they were relatively widespread in daily life, very loudly articulated, all giving rise to a growing feeling of divisiveness up to a point when the President of the State, himself of Sephardi origin, had to speak out against it.

But a closer look at these debates and diatribes indicates a rather more complex set of themes than just the demand for an Oriental social or cultural entity. These themes could be discerned as early as the 1970s, in such movements as the Black Panthers who protested against the non-inclusion of certain semi-criminal elements in the army – a policy which was at least partially reversed later with the establishment of many special educational programmes in the army for the more deprived sectors.

In fact, as indicated by the relative failure of *Tami* which gained only three members of the Knesset against the two great blocs, the most central theme was the combination of the feeling of exclusion from and the very strong wish to be included in the centre.

Later on, in 1981, this theme was highlighted in a controversy around a television series, 'The Column of Fire', which portrayed the history of Zionist and Jewish Settlement in Israel. A group of Oriental intellectuals appealed (unsuccessfully) to the High Court against what seemed to them to be an unjustified underemphasis of the part of Oriental Jews in that history.

This emphasis became very vocal in the often stressed comparison, again made often in an obviously exaggerated way in the 1981 elections campaign, between the 'local' type of leadership and that which developed in different development towns; between the 'authentic' local leaders who were active in the Likud and the seemingly co-opted leaders of the *Maarach*.

Very indicative from this point of view was the claim made in a radio interview in early 1983 by Aharon Uzan, who came from Tunis and settled in one of the new Moshavim which became quite prosperous; who became one of the major leaders of the Moshav Movement, Minister of Communication in Mrs Meir's last government and Minister of Agriculture and Communication in the Rabin government. On the eve of the 1981 elections (literally a few days before the date for the submission of the electoral lists) he left the *Maarach* and joined *Tami*, to become later – after Aharon Abu-Hatzeira's indictment by the Tel Aviv court of misappropriation of public funds when he was Mayor of Ramleh – Minister of Labour and Absorption in Mr Begin's second government. In that interview he said that, although he never suffered economically and could not complain of economic hardship, yet he was more and more aware that he had never matriculated in the High School, did not speak English, and somebody – presumably by implication the *Maarach* Establishment – had to be responsible for it. He claimed also that, although the establishment immediately found a job for the former Chief of Staff Mota Gur, nobody took care of him.

Of great interest also, from the point of view of our discussion, are the claims made by many of the activists, the carriers of the distinct Oriental culture, that those North Africans who went to Europe or the United States did well there, not only in business but also in the professional and intellectual life and universities – the very bastions of Western culture.

The strong quest for participation in the centre could also be discerned in the transformation, from the late 1920s to the early 1980s, of the great Moroccan Jewish festival of *Mimouna* (held one day after Passover) – in itself a new public feast, a new construction created in Israel – from a rather divisive–ethnic to a national one, stressing the brotherhood of all tribes of Israel. Similarly, later another, probably competitive, festival of *Shorashim* (Roots) brought together in the summer of 1983 many North African families in Israel, stressing their common solidarity and the fact of Israel being the natural place and centre for the expression of such solidarity.

## Criticism of the Kibbutzim

The strength of those feelings of exclusion from the centre as probably the most important and potent catalysts even of the ethnic themes, can be seen in several additional facts which became visible in the elections and are of great importance for the understanding of the relation between these elections and the process of decomposition of the initial institutional mould that was regnant in Israeli society.

Of special importance was the sudden eruption of diatribes – above all among some parts of the Likud – against the Kibbutzim, that very central symbol of the Labour–Zionist mould. The concrete themes were those of the preferential treatment given always to the Kibbutzim, the fact that in all the regional industries owned by the Federation of the Kibbutzim (so as not to concentrate all hired labour into any single Kibbutz) all the upper managerial positions were in the hands of the members of the Kibbutzim (even if the general working conditions were among the best in the country), and of meagreness of common frameworks and contacts (except when during the elections the members of the Kibbutzim would come to the development towns to try to mobilize votes for the *Maarach*).

But the underlying theme was the seeming deep alienation from and hostility towards the Kibbutzim. Needless to say, as far as one could ascertain, this was not necessarily shared by all the population of the development towns or beyond. Many of them seemed to accept accusations, voiced also by the Prime Minister on his wireless New Year address, of the *Hitnasut* (of looking down upon the Kibbutzim) – an accusation which was interpreted as attempts to delegitimize the symbolic and institutional bases of the Labour mould.

## The situation of the Likud

The second important fact was the rather paradoxical situation of the Likud, as against the *Maarach*, with respect to the articulation of the ethnic theme. In this context it is first of all interesting to note that the number of Oriental deputies in the Likud was smaller than in the *Maarach*. Thus in the 1981 Knesset there were thirteen deputies of Oriental origin in the *Maarach* groups as against only seven in the Likud – and the Likud had only two Oriental members of government (two others were from *Tami* and *Telem* – Dayan's group), as against three such Cabinet Ministers from the *Maarach* in Mr Rabin's government.

Second, and of crucial importance, is the fact that, although the Likud did indeed attract many of the Oriental groups, it did so, not under the aegis of the 'ethnic' theme, but rather under the aegis of common participation in the national collectivity, in the name of the basic solidarity and equality which were part of the original ethos of the Labour–Zionist mould in which many of these groups were relatively successfully socialized in Israel.

Indeed, unlike in the *Maarach*, from within the leading echelons of which there first developed the theme of *edot*, the Likud barely articulated this as a basic ideological theme, stressing instead themes of national unity. This came out rather dramatically in the last two days in the 1981 election campaign.

Two days before the election, in the *Maarach*'s final rally, Dudu Topaz, a popular entertainer, alleged that most members of the *Maarach* were members of the select units in the army, while those of the Likud were *Chach-Chachs* – a rather derogative term, in this context orientated to *Jobniks* in the army, and understood to refer mostly to Orientals.

Next day Menahem Begin, at the Likud's final rally, came out intensively against this term. He claimed that he himself had learned about its existence only that morning, and stressed that – giving the illustration of two members of Lehi and Ezel (Moshe Feinstein and Meir Baranzani, executed by the British in April 1947) – all parts of the nation, Askhenazi and Sephardi alike, had participated equally in the national struggle.

Similarly David Levi, one of the 'authentic' Oriental leaders of the Likud – and one who like so many others initially went over to the Likud after unsuccessful attempts on his part to become accepted within the local leadership of the Labour camp in Beth Shean, the development town in which his family was settled on arrival from Morocco – who became in 1977 Minister of Housing and Absorption in the first Likud government and Deputy Prime Minister of Housing in the second, talked about *edot* only in terms of *shehavot metzuka* (deprived sectors), 'destitute' groups or the like.

Whatever the truth about the very widespread allegations, against the leaders of the Likud in general and the Prime Minister in particular, of using demagogy orientated – above all – to ethnic sectors of the electorate, yet it is of central importance to the understanding of the political scene in Israel that such demagogy was couched not in ethnic but national or social or to some degree religious themes.

It was also – and perhaps above all – couched in terms of anti-establishment; of recognition of exclusion from the centre of, as it were, being outsiders, and in the offer to bring the people into the fold of the centre.

Truly enough in the 1981 elections the two major parties developed into relatively ethnically homogeneous blocs – about two-thirds of the supporters of Likud being Orientals and about 70 per cent of the Alignment being Ashkenazi. However, as studies of the electoral process in 1981 have also indicated, the political articulation and identification was couched above all in foreign-policy orientations – the more hawkish attitude to the Arabs and to settlement in the territories – as well as a strong positive attitude to religious traditions, that were crucial in the attraction of the Likud to large parts of its supporters in general and Oriental ones in particular.*

# The Elections and Struggle About the Format of Israeli Society
## *Differences between 1977 and 1981*

There were, however, some important differences between the 1977 and the

* Michael Shamir and Asher Arian, 'The Ethnic Vote in Israel's 1981 Elections', *Medina, Mimshal Veyehasim Benleumiyiim* (in Hebrew), 19–20 (Spring 1982), pp. 88–105. For a different view, stressing more the purely ethnic view, see Y. Peres and Sarah Shemer, 'The Ethnic Factor in the Elections to the Tenth Knesset', *Megamoth* (in Hebrew) (1983).

1981 elections.

The 1977 elections signalled the end of Labour as a dominant party – the first sign of which could be found in the resignation of Golda Meir in 1974 and in the establishment of the Rabin government. Yet in many ways this outcome was still seen as accidental. It came as a surprise even to the leaders of the Likud, especially as in the 1977 elections one major group, *Dash*, was basically orientated not so much to the undermining of this mould as to reforming it, as it were, from within.

Indeed even the first Likud government was seen – and on the whole, portrayed itself – as mainly representative of a different political orientation, but not of a new political or institutional mould. Key positions within the government were held by persons close to the Labour camp, or at least not fully identified with a totally different orientation from that of Labour: Moshe Dayan was Foreign Minister from 1977 till 1980; Ezer Weizmann the Minister of Defence, although a member of *Herut*, was not really part of its original core; and Yigal Horovitz, formerly member of *Rafi* who became Minister of Finance in November 1979 after Simha Erlich, was himself a member of the Liberal Party in the Likud.

They all, with the exception of Erlich – who remained as Deputy Prime Minister – resigned from the first Likud government and their respective places were taken by people much closer to the original *Herut* core: Yitzhak Shamir who resigned from the Speakership of the Knesset to become Foreign Minister; Yoram Aridor, a young member of *Herut* with a record of long service in the party and of loyalty to the Prime Minister, who became Minister of Finance in early 1981, and the architect of the new 'correct' or 'good' economic policy, a policy which, in sharp contrast to Horovitz's insistence on restraint of consumption, encouraged it through imports of various goods – especially conspicuous ones like television sets and cars – and which was seen by many as being very instrumental in bringing the victory of the Likud in the 1981 elections, and, of course, Mr Begin himself who became Minister of Defence after the resignation of Weizmann until after the 1981 elections when Ariel Sharon was given the post.

Thus towards the 1981 elections it became much clearer that the political struggle was not just a regular electoral one. Indeed the 1981 elections – in which *Dash*, which had shared many of the premises of social background of the *Maarach*, had disappeared and most of its voters returned to the *Maarach* – signalled that the close political context had indeed became closely connected with the basic contours of the institutional mould of Israeli society. For the first time in Israeli politics there emerged, in the non-religious sectors, two large almost equal political blocs. Thus these elections to no small degree become interwoven with a contest about the shaping of this mould, and of a potentially great divisiveness – a divisiveness which also fed on the weakening, analysed above, of the networks of solidarity in Israeli society.

The crucial importance of the combination of electoral struggle and the process of reconstitution of the format of Israeli society in the 1981 elections, and to some degree already in the 1977 elections, can be seen in the fate of the National Religious Party.

In 1977 the party, in which the younger groups were led by Zevulun Hamer and Yehuda Ben-Meir, who were close to religious youth movements and to *Gush Emunim* and who were seen as the carriers of the renewal of the Zionist pioneering vision, succeeded in gaining.

In 1981, as a result of the rift between Aharon Abu-Hatzeira and the establishment of the *Mafdal*, the consequent establishment of *Tami* on the one hand and the growing religious militancy of Agudat Israel, and on the other hand the appropriation of the national symbols by the Likud, which was also seen as basically sympathetic to religious tradition and therefore did not call for a strong stand on specific religious issues, the National Religious Party lost heavily, almost halving its Knesset membership.*

## *Extraparliamentary politics and political visions*

These elections also highlighted some important differences between the major camps.

We have already commented on the significance, from the point of view of the vision represented by the Labour camp in the broader sense, of the programme and activities of *Dash*.

The differences between the visions of different sectors were also highlighted in the different protest and extraparliamentary movements that had recently become very prominent on the Israeli political scene.

The importance of these movements began to increase after the Six Day War and gathered strength after the Yom Kippur War. Immediately after the Yom Kippur War there developed many protest movements which, although not necessarily identical in their political orientation, stressed the ultimate responsibility of the government and its political conceptions in the lack of preparedness for the war. These groups, as we have seen, were instrumental in creating the atmosphere which made Mrs Meir resign. Many of these movements were rather transitory, although some did continue to erupt.

At the same time two broad extraparliamentary groups developed or gathered momentum and they can be distinguished in the usual inaccurate Israeli political parlance – leftist and rightist.

The most important among the movements on the left side was *Shalom Achshav* (Peace Now), a movement which became formally constituted as such around 1976.

It was mostly orientated to problems of relations with the Arab world, both in the West Bank and with Arab countries, emphasizing what would usually be called a dovish attitude. It was against the ideology of *Eretz Israel Hashlema* in general and the policy of settlement in the West Bank in particular, and supported peace approaches to the Arabs, including the Palestinians. It

* See M. Friedman, 'The National Religious Party in Crisis', *Medina, Mimshal Veyehasim Benleumiyiim* (in Hebrew), 19–20 (Spring 1982), pp. 105–23.

exposed many misbehaviours of the army in Judea and Samaria, in some cases forcing the Chief Army Prosecutor to bring them to court.

It was very visible during the Camp David peace negotiation, when it went out against the extremists in *Herut* who opposed the Camp David agreement, and when it supported Begin in the Lebanon War, when it was very instrumental in organizing demonstrations – often giving rise to counter-demonstrations.

It also generated controversies among Jewish communities abroad, finding support especially among some Jewish intellectuals and giving rise to controversies within the Jewish communities.

The very development of such oppositionary extraparliamentary movements was, of course, very indicative of the disintegration of the initial institutional apolitical mould and of the change in the whole format of this mould. The differences between the two extraparliamentary trends – the left and the right – were very indicative of some of the dimensions of such transformations.

The leftist movements – especially *Shalom Achshav* (Peace Now) – seemed to recruit most of their supporters from groups relatively close to the Labour sector in the broadest sense, and in many ways they epitomized some of the basic weaknesses and problems of this camp. The major focus of their concern and activities were security and foreign policy, together with a very strong emphasis on the importance of maintaining a Jewish democratic state – as against becoming an occupying power with the consequent danger to the moral fabric of Israeli society. At least until 1983, when they started to try and co-operate with leaders from the *Shekhunot*, they did not stress any internal problems or any of the constructive institution-building aspects of the Zionist vision – those very themes which originally constituted the major core of the Labour-Zionist mould.

Their major adherents – and especially leadership – seemed to come from well-established groups, whether in various sectors in the urban cities or even in some Kibbutzim, as well as some new immigrants – above all intellectuals – who devoted quite a lot of time to the activities of the movements, without however in any way attempting to change their ways and life styles, or to create new institutional formations which would attract either sectors.

Only rarely did they call on their members for continuous, sustained activities beyond petitions and demonstrations, many of which – such as for instance their claims about the misbehaviour of army officers in Judea and Samaria – were indeed very effective.

The story of the extremist movements on the right is of a different mode or type. Its centre was that of *Gush Emunim*, based in many of the Yeshivot, especially in the *Yeshivot Hahar*. It built on the new extremist national religious orientations that developed in the religious groups, and for a long time gave them their most articulate expression – their message being the religious–national commandment of *Eretz Israel Hashlema* and its settlement. It was instrumental in the establishment of new settlements in Hebron, in the

West Bank, very often against the policy of the government, sometimes even against that of the Likud government to which it was very close (especially to Ariel Sharon), very often contravening the Law of the State or the commands of the government.

Its followers propounded an extreme national–religious ideology, claiming to be the true carriers of the Zionist vision and by virtue of this often claiming to represent a higher law than that of the State and hence also of being allowed to contravene the latter.

They also became very close to the new extremist right-wing party *Hatehia* which, in the 1981 elections, won three mandates, and, together with several other elements, they were extremely active in the events before the withdrawal in Sinai (April 1982), organizing not only demonstrations but also many illegal activities against the army and the government, but seemingly with some silent backing or at least encouragement from some circles close to the government.

Thus the picture of the rightist extraparliamentary movements seems in many ways to have been the very opposite of those 'on the left'; their ideology stressed the combination of the old Zionist constructivist pioneering orientation, albeit with a strong nationalist and often extreme religious bent and almost without any social one. Truly enough – as many of their opponents claimed – some of their pioneering may have sometimes been rather dubious, for they often retained at least their apartments, sometimes their jobs elsewhere. Yet on the whole they imbued a rather pioneering atmosphere; they seemed to be, as Yaakov Hazan, the veteran leader of *Mapam* and their staunch political opponent, called them, 'a pioneering tribe' – drawing on that basis quite a lot of public sympathy.

Their social composition also seems to have differed greatly from that of the leaders of *Shalom Achshav*. They came from less established, more mobile elements – quite a large number of new immigrants with strong religious orientations – as well as from within some Kibbutzim, thus combining some of the older pioneering Zionist orientation together with new themes and symbols.

## Consensus and divisiveness

These processes of decomposition of the regnant institutional mould and the concomitant attempts to point out the possibility of developing a new one were not peaceful ones – as they rarely can be especially when they are connected with electoral and political struggles. The fact that they took place through orderly democratic process, within the constitutional framework, and that even during this period many civil aspects of this framework, such as the authority of the High Court, were continuously upheld, were both surprising and encouraging for the future.

Indeed both elections attested to the strength of the democratic tradition in Israel – the first, in 1977, because a major change of regime was indeed peacefully accomplished; and the second, in 1981, because, despite the confrontation entailed, the basic democratic framework continued to function.

Moreover both elections, and perhaps especially those of 1981, also seemingly attested to a relatively broad range of consensus around several central themes. Thus during the electoral campaign – especially in the official television programmes of the different parties, as against the more divisive themes and violent outcries in the large rallies, especially those of the Likud – one could discern an astonishing consensus around some of the major social and national themes, a consensus attesting to the attempts of almost all the major parties to incorporate in their programmes some of the major themes of the original Labour ideology and mould.

The themes of settlement, economic development and institution-building, as well as those of social justice, extension of education and housing schemes, and taking special care of the deprived groups, were voiced not only by the Labour camp or by the National Religious Party but also – rather surprisingly – by the Likud (and to some degree by Agudat Israel). Indeed many in the Labour camp claimed that the Likud in its propaganda appropriated for itself all the achievements of the last decades.

It is, however, significant that, when the Likud stressed these themes, it combined them with its specific 'revisionist' and even 'populist' orientations, and attempted in this way to dissociate them from the specific Labour mould, denying as it were their natural connection to the Labour camp and its socialist orientations.

Menahem Begin often attempted to portray himself as the inheritor not only of Jabotinsky, but also of Ben-Gurion or the more activist leaders of the Labour camp – especially those like Berl Katznelson or Itzhak Tabenkin who in the 1930s were against the partition of Palestine.

Such emphasis was, of course, even more visible with respect to the theme of security, where the Likud could naturally stress that in many ways the *Maarach* stand – even going back to Ben-Gurion – appropriated to itself many of the older revisionist themes, and perhaps above all it would be even more constant in this direction.

Moreover the great achievement of the peace with Egypt in 1979 was, of course, used to indicate that this direction was not incompatible with the attainment of peace – that, on the contrary it was the only one which can lead to it.

And yet, behind this broad consensus, beneath the surface, there were signs of deep divisiveness between these camps – far beyond the natural divisiveness between different political orientations and parties. These differences became more evident around the period of the 1981 elections, although needless to say, such differences were not fully dispersed and only gradually reached some different sectors of the population. To some degree at least this explains the volatility of many 'free voters' reported by many surveys, especially until the last period before the elections.

The vision of the *Maarach* was portrayed by some of its politicians and by intellectuals and literary figures close to it as that of 'nice Israel', of a good quality of life perhaps best epitomized in the Kibbutz, of an orderly civil and democratic society.

The vision of the Likud, which much less articulated, at the same time denoted a much higher level of activity – a fact stressed, for example, in a newspaper interview given some time later by the writer A. B. Yehoshua, himself a very strong opponent of the Likud.

Such divisiveness became connected with the relatively high level of at least verbal violence and lawlessness on many levels that accompanied the 1981 elections, and which continued – as we shall see later – in many different areas of public life, such as daily behaviour in the streets, driving, and the high rate of accidents.

Such violence was closely connected with a growing intolerance of opponents, with tendencies to label them in rather extreme derogatory terms, to put them as it were beyond the pale, to delegitimize them in terms of the seemingly common Zionist themes in the growth of divisive – whether ethnic, political or religious – slogans, thus potentially at least undermining the bases of the democratic constitutional order.

No lesser persons than the President of the State and the then speaker of the Knesset, and the President of the Supreme Court, as well as many journalists and commentators, commented on this growing violence. A special public organization for the furtherance of mutual toleration was established. But all this did not abate the strength of these developments which continued and even became intensified after the elections.

These feelings of divisiveness and hostility, voiced in a violent way, could be found above all among the groups close to the Likud. They were often voiced in the encounters of such groups with the political activities of the Labour camp or of *Shalom Achshav*, where they fed on the feeling of exclusion from the hitherto regnant institutional mould and its centre, and of distance – even of alienation – from it, and on the breakdown of links of solidarity to it.

But these feelings of divisiveness and of alienation were not only prevalent within the Likud. To some degree it was reciprocal. Some of the leaders of the *Maarach*, or at least some of its major supporters among literary figures, stressed the confrontation of two cultures. They did not stress the ethnic division (although it was to some degree interpreted in this vein); they spoke instead of a Labour culture, based on the premisses of pioneering, as against the Revisionist one stressing might and glory. Truly enough their expressions were on the whole much less violent or aggressive, but the feeling of divisiveness was still very strong, fed to no small degree in its turn by the feeling of being as it were dispossessed from the centre.

All this gave rise, during the elections of 1981 and after them, to the widespread feeling that the country was divided into two opposing camps, which were not just political but also social and cultural, each trying to delegitimize its opponents and legitimate itself in terms of some of the basic common Zionist themes and values. Even though these elections also attested, as we have seen, to the prevalence of many common themes, yet these facts did not always abate the feelings of division and polarization and the various expressions of violence connected with such feelings, attesting to the fact that Israeli society was indeed undergoing a very far-reaching process of change – far beyond 'mere' changes in governments – with the direction of the search for the crystallization of a new institutional mould.

## The unique characteristics of Israel's post-revolutionary development

Many of the ideological and institutional changes which we have analysed above were not unique to Israel, not even to modern revolutionary societies in the narrower sense. But it was in such societies that they were more visible.

But, while most of these developments are common to all post-revolutionary regimes and were connected with the problems attendant on the institutionalization of the initial post-revolutionary mould and the changes which take place in it, yet the concrete ways in which these problems develop, as well as the responses to them vary greatly in different post-revolutionary regimes.

Thus, naturally, all these developments crystallized in Israel in a rather specific way and it is this specific way which provides the starting-point for the understanding of its specific dynamism, for the direction of change and transformation beyond this initial institutional mould.

The specific characteristics of the Israeli transformation of the revolutionary ideology and of its institutional implications can be understood only if we take also into account some dimensions of this transformation, no parallel to which can be found in other post-revolutionary regimes – except perhaps partially the very first ones, those of the first great European revolutions and perhaps above all the American one.

One such transformation – not to be found anywhere else to such an extent – was the growing emphasis, rooted in the basic national Zionist orientations, on national solidarity and on the continuous recrystallization of the national tradition. Second was the strong emphasis on equality of participation in the new national framework. Third – closely related to the former yet perhaps an even more astonishing aspect of this transformation – was the rather widespread, even if often perhaps rather shallow, acceptance of democratic constitutional frames and practices in general, and of rule of law in particular, as basic premises of the new institutional format.

This transformation was indeed astonishing if we remember the social historical roots of the original Zionist movements and especially the totalistic orientations prevalent on the one hand, and the more communal–solidary aspects of the traditional Jewish community, as well as the strong ideological sectarian element in Jewish political culture, on the other.

This element was rooted in some very basic premises of Jewish cultural orientations and persisted, in a more articulated form, in the Zionist movement and in Israel in particular, and could become itensified with the attainment of independence.

The democratic federative arrangements that developed in the Zionist movement and in the Yishuv were not derived so much from the ideological models set up in these movements, from the political culture inherent in them, but rather from the historical context of the emergence of the Zionist movement, in the context of Western and Central Europe; from the necessities of the different Zionist groups to live together in one common framework; from the relations between the Yishuv and the Zionist movement in the Diaspora; and to some degree from the British model portrayed during the mandate.

Yet these universalistic–democratic–constitutional arrangements – together with a strong emphasis on the rule of law (which did have strong roots in Jewish historical experience) even though undermined by the contrary sectarian and populist tendencies – did strike roots in the Yishuv and the State of Israel. Truly enough, as Jonathan Shapiro has indicated, these arrangements aimed more to assure the participation of different groups in the centre than to uphold rights and liberties of the citizens. Yet with all these many limitations such constitutional arrangements became, as we have seen, interwoven in the very basic institutional framework of the State and became an important, even if certainly not the only, component of the legitimation of the State.

All these developments were, of course, closely related to the rather paradoxical transformation of the ideology of national reconstruction, from being embedded in potentially 'totalistic' movements and sectors and the search of power engendered by them – above all in the Labour Party, into the more democratic frameworks of the State based on full voting and represent-ation and with continuous opening up of the initial institutional and political mould. While this transformation weakened the participatory dimensions of the ideology, yet it assumed a very marked continuity with the Zionist national vision and with its initial constitutional democratic framework. At the same time, however, it stressed more and more the national components of this ideology, the element of national solidarity, and weakened its social insti-tutional, 'constructivist' dimension, as well as potentially its more universalistic orientations, thus necessarily entailing also the reconstitution of many of the components of the Jewish social and civilizational orientations and of the Zionist vision.

It is this unique combination that indicates the specific characteristics of the Israeli response – as distinct from other post-revolutionary regimes mentioned above, such as the totalitarian, authoritarian or early democratic ones – to post-revolutionary developments. They are epitomized by rather non-routine changes of government, made within the framework of orderly constitutional changes, yet connected with relatively far-reaching confrontations and divisiveness.

It is this unique combination of transformation and continuity of ideology that helps us to understand both the decomposition of the initial institutional mould and the partial at least delegitimation of the regnant elite, as well as the far-reaching repercussions and further developments that have been taking place in Israel since then.

Given the specific characteristics of the Israeli scene, these developments have naturally become connected with the growing articulation and reformulation of some basic themes in the Zionist ideology – an articulation which first of all took place on the ideological level, but needless to say, has some very far-reaching institutional implications, posing strongly the question of the possibility of the crystallization of a new mould in Israel, its characteristics and its viability.

# CHAPTER 18

# Israeli Society in the 1980s – Trends, Developments and Problems

## I · New Trends

### The Likud Government
### *New orientations and policies in transition*

The late 1970s and above all the early 1980s were a period of new developments and great changes in Israeli society. While many of these developments – especially the various demographic and some structural ones – were continuations of former ones, and the same can to some degree be said of many of the changes, yet the latter often involved also far-reaching transformations which often changed the meaning of the structural developments. Most of these changes were connected with the great political change which began in 1977, and was reinforced in the 1981 elections, when Likud became the dominant party in Israeli politics, until September 1983 under the Prime Ministership of Menahem Begin.

It was after the 1981 elections that the Likud government in general and the *Herut* party in particular came into their own, concentrating in their hands, especially in the hands of the *Herut* party, the central ministries – those of Defence, Finance and Foreign Affairs – in addition, of course, to the Prime Ministership.

Truly enough, this government was based on a rather shaky and narrow coalition. The religious party – the NRP – had only six seats and Agudat Israel four, and two of the central positions, that of Chairman of the Coalition in the Knesset and that of Chairman of the powerful Finance Committee of the Knesset, were put in their hands. Later on *Tami* (the list headed by Aharon Abu-Hatzeira), two members of *Telem* (the Dayan list) and *Hatehia*, the extreme right-wing party (three members) joined the coalition. But there can be no doubt that it was the Likud, or rather the *Herut* party, that set the dominant tone in this government. It was only in the areas of religious affairs that the religious parties, and especially Agudat Israel, became more and more influential and demanding.

Thus it was indeed during the second Likud government that the full impact of new orientations, both in the political as well as in the more general ambience of Israeli society, was beginning to be felt, and could be clearly identified – although some such implications, especially the vigorous settlement policy in Judea and Samaria, could already be observed in the first Likud government in 1977.

During the elections of 1977 and of 1981, and the turbulent period around them, several themes and orientations from within the repertoire of basic Jewish and Zionist orientations, some of which had been latent or secondary in the first two or three decades of the State and some of which started to become articulated in the period after the Six Day War, were more fully articulated and more central in the political life of Israel. Such articulation also became closely related – although not always necessarily in a simple way – with the development of different policies. These policies had some far-reaching institutional implications, even if on the level of policy the impact of these orientations was not always clear or unequivocal – thus raising very sharply the question whether they heralded the crystallization of a new institutional mould.

The very possibility of the development of such a new mould, or rather the question of such a possibility, was, of course, rooted both in the decomposition of the former mould, that of Labour–Zionism, in its manifold transformations which we have analysed above, as well as in the fact that the *Herut* Party, as well as – in an extremely different mode – the extreme religious ones, indeed portrayed themselves as carriers of different Zionist or Jewish visions or themes, accepting as given the accomplishments of the former period in such spheres, and even attempting, as we have seen, to subsume these accomplishments under their own canopy.

## Security and foreign policy

The three major areas in which such new orientations and their institutional implications were most fully visible were those of security, military and foreign policy; those related to the religious spheres, and also – even if in a less clearer direction – the economic sphere.

Truly enough, many of the ingredients of these new developments – and especially of some of the policies which were undertaken by this government – could be found in the earlier periods. But under the Likud government these ingredients were not only expanded but in many ways transformed in a very far-reaching way in their overall meaning.

In the security–military–foreign policy the first new development was the attainment in 1979 by the first Likud government, still with the participation of Dayan and Weizmann, of the peace with Egypt, together with the later withdrawal, in the Spring of 1982, from Sinai, according to the details of this agreement. While this achievement was not necessarily connected with the Revisionist vision or ideology, it could be – and was – portrayed as attesting the basic correctness of this ideology as leading, after a show of strength, to possible peace with the Arabs.

Second was the continuous extension of settlements in Judea and Samaria and Ramat Hagolan. It was indeed here that the confidence of the *Herut* leadership, albeit supported also by other groups, and its belief in the possibility of translating its ideological orientations, especially that of *Eretz Israel Hashlema*, into concrete policies, became most prominent.

With respect to the Golan Heights there was a change of legal status when the Golan Law was passed in December 1981, proclaiming the imposition of Israeli law on it (but not its formal annexation to Israel).

On the legal level there was also the earlier formal proclamation on 31 July 1980 of united Jerusalem as the capital of Israel – resulting in the withdrawal of the few foreign embassies hitherto situated in Jerusalem (the Dutch and several Latin American ones) to Tel Aviv; while the Golan Law gave rise to a far-reaching entanglement with the Druze population.

There was no overall legal change with respect to Judea and Samaria, despite the vocal demands by more extreme rightist groups for imposition of Israeli Law on all of it – or for outright annexation. Neither of these demands were acceded to by the government, most probably out of consideration for foreign relations, especially with the United States, and possibly also with the Arab countries.

## Settlement policies

There was, however, a very strong and continuous attempt at massive – both rural and urban – settlement in these areas, which in many ways changed the map of the area.

The settlement process in Judea and Samaria indeed took new directions after the Likud government came into power* and also became a focus of national controversy. These new developments were an outcome of the ideological and political legitimation given by the Likud government to settle all parts of Eretz Israel, even to abolish the Green Line (the Armistice lines established at the end of the Independence War) and to allow and attract a maximum number of Jews to move and live in these areas, thus diminishing the chances of withdrawal from Judea, Samaria and the Gaza regions. These ideological and political motives were in sharp contrast to the considerations of security which influenced the Alignment government in its settlement policy.

The settlement process under the Likud governments can be characterized by several features. First there was its magnitude. While in the period between 1967 and 1977 about forty new settlements were established, in the period from 1976 to 1983 the number of new settlements almost doubled. The increase in the number of the Jewish population was even higher because of the predominantly urban nature of the latest new settlements, bringing the total Jewish population in the West Bank to about 30,000 people (although, significantly enough, during the preparation for the municipal elections in the

* This survey has been prepared by A. Schachar.

fall of 1983, it became apparent that only about 2,000 were registered as residents there).

The second feature of the settlement process under the Likud government was in the location of the new settlements. During the Alignment period settlements had been established in areas which were empty of Arab population, the vast majority concentrated in three blocks of settlements: the Golan Heights, Northern Sinai and the Jordan Valley. All three blocks of settlements were regarded as 'buffer zones' against military action from Syria, Jordan and Egypt. The location of settlements in the Jordan valley followed on the whole the Alon plan which was based on the principle of separating the West Bank from Jordan by the establishment of a line of settlements in government land along the Jordan valley. Very few settlements were located in other parts of Judea and Samaria, and those were an outcome of heavy political pressure from *Gush Emunim*.

The location of new settlements changed to a large extent in the period of the Likud governments. The goal of locating new settlements became the maximization of Jewish presence in all parts of the West Bank. Instead of refraining from settling in areas of dense Arab population, the location policy intentionally established new settlements within areas of dense Arab population, and even within the large Arab urban concentrations such as Nablus, Ramalla and Hebron. The actual sites of the new settlements were determined by the identification of a particular site as a Biblical settlement (Shilo, Bet El) or by the capability of acquiring land or expropriating it through the legal system. The geographical outcome of this new location policy was a dispersed pattern of new settlements, many of them of small size, by achieving maximum Jewish presence in all parts of Judea and Samaria.

A third feature of the settlement policy since the Likud period relates to the nature and economic base of the new settlements. During the Alignment period almost all settlements established were of a rural nature, with a strong agricultural base. These rural settlements were established through the strong and efficient operation of the national organizations of the Kibbutzim and Moshavim movements. The nature of the new settlements of the Likud period was a very different one. Most of them were urban settlements, with various sorts of community organization; local employment was quite meagre; thus most of the employed persons commuted to the major employment centres in the Tel Aviv metropolitan area and in Jerusalem. It is most significant that many of the new settlements of the Likud period were within commuting range from Tel Aviv and Jerusalem, and their population relied heavily on the extensive labour markets of the largest urban agglomerations of the country. In many respects, the new settlements in the Likud period were an extension of the suburbanization processes at the peripheries of the Tel Aviv and Jerusalem metropolitan areas, carried out by middle-class population who were utilizing a rare opportunity of massive governmental support to achieve a suburban way of life, single family housing and high environmental quality. Thus, many of the new settlements of the Likud period were an outcome of private enterprise, supported by massive government incentives, while the traditional settlement movements became in this recent settlement process rather inactive.

The settlement policy of the Likud government was carried out vigorously and with a feeling of urgency, the major thrust being to reach as fast as possible a point of irreversibility with regard to permanent Jewish presence in the West Bank. The governmental support was not limited to the establishment stage, but carried a standing commitment to support the high costs of the provision of the various services to the new settlements – the high costs resulting from the dispersed pattern of the new settlements. There was very intensive investment in the construction of infrastructure, roads, electricity, telephones and the like, to an extent much greater than could be often attained in older areas. An important part of this policy was the development of the settlements around Jerusalem; many began either on or after the unification of Jerusalem, but extended far beyond it, to some extent against the view of Teddy Kollek, the Mayor of Jerusalem, who claimed that these developments may depopulate Jewish Jerusalem.

There was also the continuous extension by the settlers, mostly from *Gush Emunim*, often against the directions of the Government, but which usually gave in to them, of the Jewish settlement in Kiryat Arba and Hebron. This continuously expanded its borders, encroaching on many places in Hebron itself, some of which were indeed owned by Jews before the 1929 riots.

The general policy of settlement was part of the *Herut* party ideology and that of other supporters of the ideology of *Eretz Israel Hashlema*, but it became, as indicated above, a focus of national controversy. It was directed by the dynamic leadership of Ariel Sharon, Minister of Agriculture and Chairman of the Joint Committee on Settlement of the Government and the Jewish Agency in the first Likud government, and Minister of Defence until early 1983 in the second one.

All these activities created, as we shall see, far-reaching changes in the relations with the Arab population in these areas, having also far-reaching impact on the whole ambience of Israeli society.

## The Lebanon War

This policy of settlement was closely connected with a new more active stance in security matters, with a strong ideology of active struggle against terrorism in general and the PLO in particular. The development of this new conception towards security culminated in the Operation Peace for Galilee, starting in early June 1982, which became the Lebanon War. As is well known this had far- reaching repercussions on the internal format of Israeli society, as well as on its foreign relations and standing.

The war started in June 1982 as the Operation Peace for Galilee, which was officially destined to last only 48 hours. In fact it was the longest of all Israel's wars, and the only one – according to Begin – which was undertaken out of choice and not of necessity imposed upon Israel.

The bare chronicles of the war are well known: the expansion of the war beyond the originally officially proclaimed goals to the Beirut–Damascus road and beyond; the bombardment of Beirut; the strong internal and international reaction to this bombardment; the destruction of most of the bases of PLO in Southern Lebanon and in Beirut; the withdrawal of the PLO in September 1982 from Beirut; the election of Basheer Jemayel – supposedly an ally of Israel – as the new president of Lebanon; his assassination a few days after his election; the entrance of Israeli forces into Beirut; the massacre of Palestinian refugees and guerrillas in Sabra and Shatila by the Christian phalangists – seeming allies of the Israeli army – just a few days after the entry of the Israeli army into Beirut with the declared aim of maintaining order in the area.

This massacre gave rise to strong outcry in Israel, culminating in a demonstration organized by the Alignment, *Shalom Achshav* and other opposition groups, of about 400,000 people in Tel Aviv, demanding – following the President of the State, Yitzhak Navon – the establishment of a judicial inquiry committee to investigate the circumstances of the massacre and the degree of Israeli responsibility. The commission was ultimately set up against the wishes of the Prime Minister and a large part of the government.* Several months later (in February 1983) it published its report (usually called the Kahan report) – the like of which, in its criticism of the government, had no parallel in any democratic country and which has evoked sometimes even far-reaching criticism. The report† absolved Israel from any responsibility, but pointed out the indirect responsibility of the Minister of Defence, the Chief of Staff and many army officers (including the Chief of Intelligence and several field commanders), recommending the removal of the Minister of Defence and the Chief of Intelligence, and not making any direct recommendations about the Chief of Staff only because he was going to retire very soon anyhow.

It used also very forceful language about the Prime Minister's conduct of affairs and the behaviour of the Minister of Foreign Affairs Yitzhak Shamir, Begin's successor in September 1983.

The publication of the report came as a rather severe shock to the Prime Minister and the government and to the higher echelons, and it took them several days before deciding on the implementation of the recommendations of the Commission. The repercussions were the resignation of Sharon from the Ministry of Defence, but not from the government where he remained as Minister without Portfolio (although the Commission at least hinted, if not more, on the feasibility of his removal from the government); the appointment of Professor M. Arens, one of the major figures in *Herut* and then serving as Israeli Ambassador to the United States, as the Minister of Defence; and later the 'normal' resignation of the Chief of Staff; the lengthy period of negotiations with Lebanon and the protracted entanglement of Israel with the different

* It was composed of two members of the Supreme Court – the President Yitzhak Kahan and Aharon Barak (the former Attorney-General) – and General (retired) Jonah Efrat.
† The Commission of Inquiry into the Events at the Refugee Camps in Beirut, 1983. Final Report (Authorized Translation) published in the *Jerusalem Post*, 9 February 1983.

factions (Christians, Druzes, Shiites and the like); the signing of a peace treaty with Lebanon on 17 May 1983 which was not, however, ratified by the Lebanese Parliament, especially under Syrian pressure. All this made it the longest of all Israel's wars, with a mounting number of fallen soldiers (518 as of mid-September 1983), and the continuous protest against the war by many groups, including mothers of soldiers and army reservists who were going to the front and coming from it. It also gave rise, as we shall see, to far-reaching division in the country. Israel withdrew to the Awali river in South Lebanon in September 1983, probably causing at the same time the resignation of Mr Begin from the Prime Ministership and having far-reaching repercussions on the internal Israeli scene as well as its international relations which continue up to this very time.

## The religious arena

The second major area in which far-reaching developments took place under the Likud governments – especially the second one – was the religious one.

It was not only that, following long-standing tactics, the religious parties used their crucial position in the coalition very effectively and extended it beyond anything that could be imagined in former periods. So the religious parties, and especially Agudat Israel, got increasing financial allocations for their institutions, often arranged in ways contravening standard budgetary procedures and even in periods of far-reaching budgetary restrictions in education, social services and the like.

Beyond this they also became very influential in setting the general tone with respect to the place of religion in general public life, so extending its scope as to change the whole ambience of State–religion relations and the place of religion in the structure of Israeli society. Thus there was a continuous extension and strengthening of the supervisory powers of local Rabbinates with respect to laws of Kashrut, extending to far-reaching (beyond the specifics of Kashrut) control of, for instance, observance of Shabbat in many hotels. There were many new restrictive laws. To give only some of the most notable illustrations: the religious groups succeeded in passing the pathology law, which greatly restricted the scope of autopsies; revoked the relatively liberal law of abortion; increased the scope of exemption of religious girls from the army; obtained the closure of El Al flights on Shabbat and Jewish Holidays; and have been attempting to limit greatly the freedom of archaeological excavations (in so far as they may discover old Jewish cemeteries) – as well as to pass the Law 'Who is a Jew?' which would state that, so far as converts were concerned, it would apply only to those who were converted according to the Halakha – i.e. according to the Orthodox, and not Conservative or Reform Rabbis.

These developments did not seem always to go against the mood of the government – or at least of the Prime Minister. The Liberal ministers and members of the Knesset, while murmuring their dissatisfaction, on the whole –

with some exceptions – usually gave in, claiming rightly that all this was part of the coalition agreement.

## Economic policies

It is rather more difficult to pinpoint, as clearly as in the religious or especially the security and military areas, the clear ideological underpinnings of the economic policies of the Likud. The first stage, that of liberalization under Simha Erlich, was obviously connected with a rather naive liberal conception of economy as against the former emphasis on government regulations. Its major single outcome was the effective abolition of most of the regulations of foreign exchange, especially those with respect to imports; but on the whole many of the central aspects of the government's regulation and investment in economic life – the share of government's civilian expenditure in GNP and the share of government in employment – were higher than ever before; real wages increased, inflation and deficit in balance of payment increased.

The second stage came with the appointment of Yigal Horovitz as Minister of Finance. He had in mind strong restrictive policies, with demands for sacrifices – which did not go very well in an election year and he resigned in early 1981.

It was then, with the appointment of Yoram Aridor as Minister of Finance, that the new specific Likud or *Herut* economic policy, the 'good' or 'correct' economy was instituted – with the declared objective of curbing inflation and renewing economic growth. Food subsidies were sharply increased, taxes on consumer durables were reduced, and budgetary constraints were relaxed. Consequently, private consumption and real wages naturally soared in 1981, the elections year, and continued to do so later, leading too, in 1984, to an inflation of about 400 per cent.

The usual connotation of this ideological underpinning was that it was a 'populist' economy – and in some ways it very much resembled such policies as those of Peronist Argentina and, as we shall see, it did indeed have further far-reaching repercussions on the ambience of Israeli society.

## Zionist and Jewish Themes; Changes in the Centre
### Strength and territory

Most of these policies were closely connected, as we have indicated already above, with attempts at far-reaching reconstruction of some of the major themes of the Zionist vision and also implicitly or indirectly, of those of the Jewish civilizational orientations.

Almost each of these themes existed also, of course, in the former, but mostly in a rather secondary and latent form. But in this period of the late 1970s and early 1980s there was a far-reaching transformation of their overall format and of the combinations between them, as well as an overall tendency to 'flatten out' or to deny the tensions between them.

The first such major theme inherent in the old Revisionist vision was that of emphasis on strength, on military strength and struggle and attempts at its partial sanctification.

Closely related to this was a far-reaching strengthening of the territorial component of the Zionist – and also of traditional Jewish – orientations. There developed many attempts at the sanctification or semi-sanctification of this component in historical and religious terms, a sanctification which did not constitute a very strong component of the older Jabotinski Revisionist vision.

The conception of territoriality had greatly changed, from perceiving territory as a means to the realization of the national reconstruction or an expression of the special relations of the nation to its land, or as a basis of national security, to the almost total, secular or religious, sanctification of territoriality and settlement as an end in itself, as the very epitome of the Zionist vision.

The more secular terms of such sanctification were to be found among many of the supporters of *Eretz Israel Hashlema* in the Labour sector, and in many sectors of the Kibbutzim or Moshavim, as well as among wider sectors in the cities. They combined a secular primordial emphasis with a strong emphasis on settlement and on security.

The religious–national terms of such sanctification were developed above all among the *Gush Emunim* and those close to them, stressing above all the religious, historical, sometimes almost mystical dimensions of the territorial component, very often giving rise to a sort of conflation of this territorial dimension with political–mystical Messianism – supposedly derived from the teaching of Rabbi Avraham Kook, and highly elaborated by his son, Rabbi Yehuda Kook and other rabbis connected with several of the *Yeshivot Hesder* (especially Mercaz Harav) and *Gush Emunim*. They were very aptly described by the writer Haim Bar as 'Canaanites with Tefilin'.

Such sanctification of the territorial component gave rise to a rather far-reaching reaction, not only from 'secular' universalistic orientated elements from within the Labour groups, but also from some, above all non-Zionist, religious circles. Thus, for instance, Rav Avraham Shach, one of the members of The Council of Sages of Agudat Israel, in its last convention in Jerusalem, ridiculed such claims to sanctification of territory, stressing that Israel had become a nation through its acceptance of the Torah and that only this acceptance legitimized its entry into Eretz Israel.

## Solidarity *and* Lehetiv im Ha'am

Perhaps the most widespread Jewish and Zionist themes were those of Jewish solidarity, the strong emphasis on the religious dimension of the Jewish tradition and historical experience.

Closely connected with this there developed a very strong emphasis on the purely solidary aspects of this tradition. This was strongly related to an emphasis on particularism, on looking inwards and cutting oneself off from the outside world, on the inherent morality of the Jewish or Israeli collectivity, on the weakening of the civilizational and hence also universalistic – as against the national and particularistic – dimensions of the Zionist or Israeli identity, as well as of the 'revolutionary' institution-building ones.

There developed also a far-reaching transformation of the basic social themes, or at least an intensification of some of the former ones. Above all there was the continuous weakening of the elitist conceptions of the stress on duty and obligation, as against the more distributive orientations on rights and titles.

This orientation was very succinctly expressed by Prime Minister Begin in one of his sayings, in which he contrasted his own policies with those of his predecessors. He stressed that they were tough inside towards the people of Israel and weak in their relations to the outside, while his position would be the opposite one, in his insistence on doing good with the people (*Lehetiv im Ha'am*), which constituted a very good background for Aridor's 'good economy' policy.

## Movement of new sectors into the centre

The close interrelations between many of the policies undertaken by the Likud government and the attempts at the articulation of a new constellation of themes into the Zionist vision had far-reaching repercussions on the whole ambience of Israeli society, and perhaps above all on the question whether a new institutional mould was indeed emerging here.

In order to understand more fully these repercussions, it is necessary to take into account the fact that the implementation of these policies – connected with a far-reaching change of regime, as well as with the articulation of various hitherto latent themes inherent in the Zionist movement, and in Jewish civilizational orientations – was connected not just with a regular routine change of government, but with what came very close to a change of regime. Such change necessarily involved several important processes – of which the two most important were first the far-reaching influx and mobility of new personnel into the centres of the government and different positions connected with the centre, and second the far-reaching attempt by the new regime at delegitimation of the old one and of legitimation of itself.

First of all there was a very far-reaching movement of new echelons – from *Herut*, from the Liberal groups, and also from *Tami* – into the various central positions, not only political and civil service positions, but also many economic ones in the government sector and in many public companies, in the Jewish Agency and the like.

There was an extensive search for such positions, a great turnover of manpower and a gradual dispossession of parts at least of the old establishment from many such positions. In some cases these changes infringed the civil service regulations and were justified by the claims that in the preceding regime very few from these sectors were taken into these positions. There were many claims, especially from around *Tami*, to make such nominations according to ethnic and cultural background, while among the *Herut* and the Liberals as well as the NRP there developed a rather natural tendency to put more of their adherents into such positions.

These movements signalled a widespread process of mobility, not occupational or economic but into the centre. Very closely related to this process was the development of a new active and constructive leadership in many of the development towns, with close relations to the centre, and with aspirations and feelings of the possibility of participation, of not being dispossessed.

A natural counterpart of this movement of new groups into the centre was the continuously growing feeling of dispossession among the *Maarach* leadership proper and even more within its broader periphery.

Many of those formerly in high positions retired into private business; others just retired; and for the broader strata or groups it became clearer that the *Maarach* had lost many of its strongholds. It was indeed naturally very difficult for many of them to come to terms with the fact of its not being in the centre and central positions, except in the Labour economic sector.

## Legitimation and delegitimation

Such feelings of dispossession were intensified by the closely related attempts by many of the new leaders of the Likud of at least partial delegitimation of the former regime, and at the appropriation of many symbols of Zionism – even of 'constructive' Zionism, the very epitome of Labour–Zionism – for themselves as representatives of the whole nation.

Many claims about the neglect of the importance of Ezel and Lehi undergrounds in the histories and symbolization of struggle for independence were voiced – for instance in the fact that no guards of honour stood at the graves of their members in the Day of Independence, a situation changed by Mr Begin. There were claims that the place of these Revisionist movements, as well as of these undergrounds in the Diaspora in general and Oriental one in particular, was neglected. There were many attempts to rectify this situation, often in very exaggerated and very aggressive and vocal ways, including rewriting the histories of the struggle against the British and the struggle of Independence – a rewriting which above all minimized the role of the *Hagana* in all these events.

Perhaps the most curious yet very significant step in this direction was the constitution by the government of a special Inquiry Commission into the murder in 1933 of Chaim Arlosoroff – an event which had, as we have seen, divided the Yishuv. It seemed that the intention here was to 'absolve' totally those members of the right-wing group which, while freed by the mandatory court, were yet often held in suspicion in the Labour sector; to finish once and forever this 'blood-libel' story; thus also potentially or at least indirectly, to delegitimize the Labour establishment and rule, usually based on divisiveness and not on national unity.

As against this, the Prime Minister always attempted to portray himself, and his party, as representing national unity, encompassing all patriots. So, for instance, on his first visit to Egypt, he took with him representatives of all undergrounds – the *Hagana*, Ezel and Lehi alike.

Similarly the Prime Minister often tended to present himself as continuing the work of Ben-Gurion and the more activist leaders of the Labour camp, going out against the socialist aspect of Labour ideology, but at the same time claiming – pointing out the pockets of poverty and ethnic groups – that they were never really serious about their socialism.

Another interesting indication – one out of many – of such attempts of some partial delegitimation of the Labour camp, or at least of its central place in the history of the Yishuv, could be seen in the Independence Day celebrations of 1983. In the traditional ceremony of torch-lighting at Mount Herzl, which that year was dedicated to 100 years of Jewish settlement of Eretz Israel, the place of the Labour settlements – both of Kibbutzim and Moshavim and of the new Moshavim – was belittled as against the various private settlements (Moshavim and urban settlements) on the one hand, and the new settlements in Judea, Samaria and the Golan on the other.

Meanwhile large sectors close to the *Maarach* or to the various protest movements could not easily accept – perhaps still cannot – the full legitimacy of the new government, the fact that the Zionist vision could be legitimately expressed by Mr Begin and the Likud.

# Realignment of Political Forces
## *New government–opposition relations*

One of the important results of these developments was a far-reaching change in the structure in Israeli political life – namely the development of a new type of opposition and of government–opposition relations.

It was not only that for the first time in the history of Israel there was an opposition which had almost as many seats in the Knesset as the coalition (in fact the *Maarach* had three seats more than the major party, the Likud); what was of special importance was that this opposition did not see itself just as a corrective to the government, but as an overall, principled opposition which did not accept the basic premises of the government and most of its policies – coming out quite sharply even if not always too effectively against them. Slowly it became more and more apparent that such an opposition was indeed emerging.

Truly enough it took a long time for the Alignment to get used to the idea that they were not in the government. In many cases, like the Golan Law, the Jerusalem Law and in the beginning of the Lebanon War, they – out of what they claimed as considerations of general national interest and responsibility, as well as the pressure of the hawkish elements within them – voted with the government. (Indeed in the case of the Golan Law some of these elements were among its strongest protagonists.)

There developed also continuous voices from the Alignment for the establishment of a government of National Unity, and they became even more vocal after the resignation of Mr Begin. It was only the more extreme left-wing members of the Alignment, Yossi Sarid, Shulamit Aloni (head of *Ratz* group), who joined the Alignment as a parliamentary bloc, and some members of *Mapam*, who continuously opposed such a possibility.

But towards the end of 1982, with the worsening of the situation in Lebanon and the deterioration of the economic situation, a far-reaching principled opposition against the government crystallized within the Alignment. At first it did not always know how to present itself, too often proposing votes of no-confidence (which never gained the requisite majority), and often seen as being in very great haste to replace the government. With the formation of the government by Mr Shamir, the possibility of the formation of a government of National Unity, although discussed, was turned down by Labour (to be realized, as we shall see, after the 1984 elections).

The lines of such opposition became more and more drawn around the basic political and security conception – around the policy of territorial expansion and continuous Israeli presence in Judea and Samaria, with the consequences of ruling over 1,000,000–1,300,000 Arabs, as against a conception of some sort of territorial compromise which would assure the democratic and Jewish nature of the State.

This new situation of a principled opposition – a situation which did not exist before – created an entirely new development on the Israeli political scene.

In all the period of the *Maarach* – especially under Ben-Gurion and Mrs Meir – the tendency to equate the government with the State had been very strong, given the acceptance, even if only *de facto*, of the basic premisses of the government by large parts of the opposition, who demanded at most a somewhat stronger stance. So the problem had been much less acute. But, with the development of the new situation, it became very acute indeed.

## Changes in economic strongholds

The development of such opposition was of course reinforced by the fact that several of the concrete policies, closely connected to 'regime change', attempted to undermine, or possibly to take over, even if not very successfully, several of the economic strongholds of the Labour camp, above all, but not only, the Histadrut.

One illustration of such attempts was the reorganization of the El Al company, for long one of the major symbols of the tendency of the Histadrut to support the stronger groups in Israeli society. This put the Histadrut into another unpleasant and weak position, and has certainly changed the whole mode of labour relations in the company. It could perhaps also have been relatively successful in economic terms, but for the fact that it was connected with the abolition of flights on the Shabbat.

The second even less successful attempt was the one to reorganize the health services, to nationalize most of them, thus undermining the monopoly of *Kupat Holim* of the Histadrut.

An initial attempt in this direction in the first Likud government had been unsuccessful, resulting only in some restructuring of hospital services and ultimately leading to the famous or infamous doctor's strike in the early summer of 1983. This strike proved disastrous not only for the health services, but also for the whole moral ambience of the society, but it did also put the Histadrut in a corner in its triple role as employer of the doctors, as their representative in the trade union activity, and as the provider of health services to the general public.

In general the Histadrut was more and more losing its place as a partner in the formulation of economic policies to the government. It was indeed often put in a corner, from where it could not easily – given the objective situation as well as the lack of imaginative leadership – regain its position or exercise any far-reaching leadership in the economic and social spheres.

Parallelly the Likud faction in the Histadrut developed strong oppositionary tendencies, sometimes under the leadership of David Levi, giving rise in the Histadrut Convention to some very unruly behaviour which could be seen as part of the new political ambience that was developing in Israel.

# The Repercussion of New Policies
## *Repercussions of settlement policy*

The combination of the new policies and the new themes, the movement of new social groups into the centre, and the realignment of political forces had, of course, a far-reaching impact on the possibility, degree and mode of development and crystallization of new institutional moulds in Israeli society. Such repercussions developed first of all in connection with the policy of settlement in Judea and Samaria – a policy which went, as we have already seen above, far beyond that of the Alignment in this area.

This policy was guided by a new political orientation – that of *Eretz Israel Hashlema* and of the creation of a situation in which no other entity except Israel could rule over the territories. This entailed a strong posture against the PLO – which also guided the Lebanon War – aimed at the destruction of its influence in Judea and Samaria, and at the establishment of its own, very limited, conception of autonomy for the Arabs in these areas.

This political orientation gave rise to several far-reaching concrete policies – beyond the establishment of the settlements but, of course, very closely connected with them. First of all, it involved far-reaching appropriation of public and sometimes private lands from Arabs, as well as encouragement of private entrepreneurs to buy such lands. It also minimized, as compared with the former period of the military government, the possibility of political self-expression of different Arab groups, giving rise to detention, arrest and deportation of many Arab public figures, including mayors of several towns, and to the establishment of very far-reaching, often ridiculous, censorship on books and journals. It was also connected with attempts to find pro-Israeli elements, especially among the so-called *Agudat Hakefarim* (the Association of the Villages).

All these activities naturally gave rise to continuous tensions with the Arab population, who often tried to stop the appropriation of land by appeals to the High Court which sometimes were indeed successful. Some of the more extreme attempts at rather dubious forms of buying or appropriation of lands were also, at least to some degree, limited by injunctions from the Attorney-General's office.

But on the whole these appeals could affect only marginally the whole process of appropriation of land – and above all, the whole new political ambience in the relations between the government (especially the military government) and the Arab population.

This new political stance towards the Arab population was even more evident in the attitudes of many of the Jewish settlers in Judea and Samaria – who became organized in self-defence units and often expressed very extreme anti-Arab attitudes with a very strong show of force, not fully controlled by the army or by the police, often developing – as was claimed for instance, by a former chief of the Internal Security Service – into a new sort of underground. (The scope of this underground, and its potential great danger, were discovered in May 1984, as will be discussed in the Postscript.)

The most extreme occurrences were probably those in Hebron, where the most militant elements among the Jewish settlers in Kiryat Arba extended their settlement, often against the directives of the government which however usually gave in to them – developing very tense relations with the Arabs, culminating in a series of occurrences in the summer of 1983, when first a Jewish student was killed and then, on 26 July, a group of masked men, strongly suspected to be Jewish extremists, killed three Palestinian students and wounded many others, in a random gun and grenade attack on Hebron's university – giving rise to an explosion of violent riots and Israeli counter-action.

Thus, indeed, there developed in Judea and Samaria a situation of continuous – even if naturally characterized by ups and downs – tensions and demonstrations – often violent ones; of stone-throwing on the army and police; of shootings on passing Jewish cars; of arrests and deportations; of closure of colleges and universities – and as we shall see, often very tough, often brutal behaviour of the army. All these signalled a change in the whole ambience of the military government in its relations with the Arab population. They also signalled a shift in the basic Israeli orientation from an ideology of temporary to permanent occupation, settlement and conquest – best epitomized in the partial transition from military to civil government; Israeli rule over Judea and Samaria was no longer temporary. And all these had far-reaching repercussions on internal life in Israel.

## The internal repercussions of the Lebanon War

Even more far-reaching were the internal and external repercussions of the Lebanon war. It was the first of Israel's wars which was not supported by national consensus. It was also the first of Israel's wars which was based on a security conception deviating from the centre of national consensus – and it gave rise to far-reaching cleavages in the country.

Truly enough, the first stages of the war, when the Prime Minister declared that the aim of the war was to assume a security zone of 45 kilometres in Galilee, were taken seriously. It was supported by most parties, except the left opposition (several members of Labour and most of *Mapam*) who turned out to be much more far-seeing than those who accepted the official statements.

But with the extension of the war beyond its initial aims, there was a growing feeling of a lack of veracity on the part of the Minister of Defence (Ariel Sharon) and many of the army spokesmen (including the Chief of Staff). Even the soldiers often saw in the field that the official announcements were not true. The dissent within the society became stronger, becoming intensive around the bombardment of Beirut, and even more so the Sabra–Shatila massacre. After that, as we have seen, dissent was continuous.

There even developed splits within the army, giving rise to protests of officers, the most noted among whom was Col. Eli Geva who asked to be relieved of his command before the bombardment of Beirut (which he was) and to continue to serve with his unit (which he was not). It also gave rise to vicious personal abuse by many top people, including to some degree the Prime Minister.

There developed also a growing tension between many higher echelons of the army and the then Minister of Defence, Sharon, which became intensified after the publication of the Kahan report, and somewhat alleviated by changes in the Ministry.

The dragging on of the war, the longest of all of Israel's wars; the mounting number of fallen soldiers; the growing awareness of the impossibility of a settlement in Lebanon; the bankruptcy of the 'global' security conception and of the pretension to impose a new order in the Middle East in general and in Lebanon in particular, so often announced by Sharon, the deterioration of relations with the loyal Druze minority in Israel; the fact that, far from eradicating the trauma of the Yom Kippur War, as claimed by Begin in the beginning of the war, it probably reinforced it among many sectors of the population – all these factors may, according to various reports, have played a significant part, in addition to failing health, in Begin's decision to resign in September 1983.

# *International relations during the Lebanon War*

The international repercussions of the war were also far-reaching – in several different directions. The operation started with the seeming blessing, or at least with the tacit agreement – at least for its more limited objective – of the United States, especially of the then Secretary of State, Alexander Haig, who possibly shared Begin's and Sharon's posture against the USSR, and the belief in Israel's possible role in some sort of containing force in a 'global' strategy, as well as the view of Israel as the only reliable military–political element in the Middle East.

But even this stance was not shared by other political factors – whether the European states, most of the media in the United States and in Europe, or many other political sectors in the United States. Later on, with the bombardment of Beirut and the massacre in Sabra and Shatila, the support of the United States began also to wane – giving rise, in September 1982, to the Reagan plan which was for a total peace in the Middle East based on negotiations with Hussein for a territorial compromise in Judea and Samaria – a plan immediately rejected by the Israeli government.

The outcries in the media and against Israel, during the war in general and the bombardment of Beirut and the Sabra and Shatila massacre in particular, did not lack strong anti-Semitic overtones which conflated anti-Israel, anti-Zionist and anti-Jewish themes. They have also contained no small degree of hypocrisy – as became evident a year later, in 1983, when, with the withdrawal of the Israeli forces from Lebanon, the mutual killing of different factions in Lebanon went far beyond what had happened in Sabra and Shatila, but with no outcry from the media. (This can be compared with the earlier period, when the PLO erased the Christian village of Damour – again with no outcry from the media.)

This was due to no small extent to many of the western journalists stationed in Beirut, who are either under pressure from the PLO or indeed became very strong sympathizers, providing a very one-sided picture of the developments – not reporting the outrages committed through the years by the PLO in Lebanon; and in one case even using a picture of a mother and child from Damour taken several years earlier to depict Israeli cruelty.

But, notwithstanding these facts, there can be no doubt that for quite a long period, until the beginning of the peace negotiations in Lebanon, the atmosphere with respect to Israel greatly deteriorated. Even later such atmosphere contributed to a change in the nature of acceptance of Israel – accepting it as a military presence but implicitly, and often explicitly, criticizing it and even attempting to some degree to delegitimize it. The same was true with respect to the portrayal, often by journalists whose countries were the leading exporters in this field, of Israeli sales of arms to various countries ruled by military cliques, like Argentina, the Congo (Zaire) and the like, and to South Africa – to no small degree feeding on the very showy advertisements of some of these deals by Mr Sharon.

The outcries against the war were very problematic and became more so as the war dragged on. On one side was the destruction of the military, and to some degree political, bases of the PLO – even if, with the withdrawal of Israeli forces in September 1983, many of them started to return to Lebanon under Syrian and Druze protection. There was also the achievement of peace for Galilee – where the inhabitants of the settlements now feel secure after many years of exposure to attacks. On the other side, there was the growing entanglement in Lebanon: the growing dependence on the United States; the collapse of the 'great strategy' of the new global strategic conception.

The relations with the United States, after a very low period, improved towards the end of 1982 and the beginning of 1983 – especially after the weakness of the 'moderate' Arab camp and its inability to get the PLO's endorsement of Hussein's participation in the proposed talks with United States and Israel about the future of Palestine, and Hussein's concomitant withdrawal from them. In this period Israel was also successful in establishing some of its relations with Africa – with Zaire and later in 1983 with Liberia.

The general level of support for Israel, as indicated by the polls especially in the United States, seemed to remain the same, albeit becoming connected with some tiredness among Israel's supporters, and a somewhat general loss of interest. In Europe also, after the great demonstration and the publication of the Kahan report, and the peace with Lebanon, there was a growing acceptance of the new situation – but with much less interest or commitment to Israel than before. In general the whole atmosphere towards Israel – especially in Europe – became more detached and less involved, often accepting it, to some degree, as a 'normal' state, without any claims to being something special or as having special claims on others.

## Repercussions of the Lebanon War on the Diaspora

In Europe, the war gave rise to far-reaching anti-Semitic outbursts and terrorist assassinations in Rome, Paris and Brussels, in which anti-Israeli slogans, often conflated by many leftist groups with anti-Semitic ones, gave rise to sharp reactions on the part of the Jewish communities. Thus, in Rome it was only after some negotiations that the President of the Republic was allowed by the Jewish community to participate in the funeral of the small boy who was killed in the synagogue – as the Jewish community claimed (as did also that in France) that the general pro-PLO policy of the Italian (or French) government, as well as the whole tone of the press, created an atmosphere very conducive to the development of such terrorist outrages.

In general there developed a closer identification, sometimes rather negative, of Jewish people with Israel. This often increased the insecurity and anxiety of many Jews, as seen for instance in cases when Jews did not dare, in the autumn of 1982, to attend Holiday prayers, and also in attempts on their part to dissociate from Israel.

Thus in Europe and in the United States the war naturally had a far-reaching and often contradictory impact on the Jewish communities in their relations to Israel. It gave rise to far-reaching splits within Jewish communities. On the one hand there was strong denunciation of Israel's policies by Jewish intellectuals (including such prominent figures as Sir Isaiah Berlin), many of whom were closely related to the opponents of the war in Israel, but perhaps even more to the more leftist or Labour circles of Europe. On the other hand, there were also many expressions of solidarity with Israel from some of the sectors of Jewish populations.

Thus there developed the potential of a split within the Jewish community, as well as a shift in the bases and nature of support for Israel.

The dissension within the Jewish communities, and the opposition to the Israeli government's policies with respect to the settlements as well as the Lebanon War, could be seen in the facts that, in the official declaration of support, Jewish organizations could often discern a rather ambivalent attitude to many aspects of these policies, and the Zionist Congress, for the first time since the establishment of the State of Israel, did not fully endorse a resolution supporting the policy of the government.

In general – whatever the exact stance towards Israel among most Jewish communities and whatever the degree of support or criticism, of association or dissociation – one element became very weak, almost entirely absent: namely that of looking on Israel as a place for some common ventures, for activities and undertakings which would involve their own needs – beyond philanthropy, Jewish solidarity, support or dialogue. There was also a weakening of the element of pride in Israel; particularly after the great demonstrations in Tel Aviv and the publication of the Kahan report.

## Repercussions in the religious and economic spheres

There were also repercussions of policies in the religious field. There was the continuous extension of various aspects of religious or traditional education in the general schools – the various religious study groups, common courses and the like – very often moving into a very fundamentalist direction.

In general this was connected with the continuous strengthening of the orthodox sectors and with the changing mode of their relations to the State. Indeed, in all spheres of life, the impact of the religious sectors in general and of the extreme non-Zionist ones in particular, was felt more and more, necessarily having, as we shall see in greater detail later on, far-reaching implications on the format and ambience of Israeli society.

There was also the more far-reaching involvement of the official religious establishment, especially of the then Chief Rabbi Shlomo Goren (the first Chief Rabbi of the Israeli Defence Army). This involvement went in two directions. The first, best exemplified by the declaration of the Chief Rabbinical Council during the controversy over archaeological diggings that the 'ways (customs) of life' in Israel were to be determined by the Rabbinical Council, attested to the growing ideological militancy of the religious groups and their attempts to impose what they saw as the rule of Halakha on the whole nation. In the same direction were also, for instance, Rabbi Goren's strong expressions against the erection of a football stadium near religious quarters in Jerusalem, bringing up the image of Hellenistic gymnasia as anathema to real Judaism.

The second mode of such involvement was manifest in the very frequent pronouncements – especially by Rabbi Goren – on current political matters, in the spirit of *Eretz Israel Hashlema* often attempting to present this approach as sanctified by the Halakha. This point was not necessarily accepted by other Rabbinical groups, especially perhaps those of Agudat Israel, but they were on the whole much less vocal in these matters.

Another indication of this type of involvement were the attempts of the army Rabbinate, during the first steps at least of the Lebanon War, to provide it with Biblical legitimation (especially referring to the book of Joshua, which tells the story of the Israelite conquest of Canaan).

The more extreme demands of the religious groups have given rise to great divisiveness in the society, to violent outbursts ranging from throwing of stones on vehicles passing near religious neighbourhoods on the Shabbat up to those around the archaeological diggers in the City of David in Jerusalem.

The repercussions of the economic policies – especially those of Yoram Aridor's 'correct economics' – were also far-reaching, especially on the whole ambience of Israeli public life in Israel as well as on the whole process of institution-building in the society.

The overall result of these policies – the combination of an increased standard of living, and the growth of speculation on the Stock Exchange which burgeoned in 1982 (to be reversed in 1983) – was the creation of an atmosphere of free for all, of *enrichissez-vous*, of quick grabbing and spending. This was also reinforced by such occurrences as the huge compensations to the settlers of *Yamit* after a period of protracted, rather unruly and undignified negotiations. At the same time, however, there developed an atmosphere of growing uncertainty, of looking at things with a very short time perspective, and this atmosphere continued up to the 1984 elections.

# II · Changes in Formats of Political Life and Patterns of Institution-building

## Changes in Symbols of the Centre and of Collective Identity
### *The influence of Begin – pride and defiance*

All these developments had far-reaching repercussions on the format of Israeli society in general and political life in particular, on the construction of the centre and its symbols, and on the possibility, degree and mode of the development of some new institutional mould.

First of all there developed significant changes in the themes and symbols of the centre and of Israeli collective identity.

The Likud in general and the Prime Minister (Mr Begin) in particular were, initially at least, successful in articulating some new symbols of the centre, based on the Revisionist symbols of strength, as well as those of Jewish pride and defiance – and there can be no doubt that these symbols found a far-reaching resonance among many sectors of the population. Indeed, many observers – Israelis, supporters and opponents of Begin alike, and foreign ones – attested to this oratorical power.

Thus in 1983 David Shipler, the *New York Times*'s correspondent in Jerusalem, wrote that in every Israeli there is a little bit of Begin.* And an article published in the Opinions section of the *Jerusalem Post* stated:

Menachem Begin retrieved and reasserted the Israelis' national self-confidence and their conviction that they can, at least partly, determine historical circumstances . . .

Much of Begin's foreign policy contributed in various ways to the *Arabs cautiously adopting* a sober image of Israel. Without that image, Arab warfare against us could become a daily and deadly affair . . .

As a Jew who believed in the truths of the Bible, Begin had the strength and motivation to contend with the everyday Middle East tug-of-wars.

As Prime Minister, he represented the vitality of Jewishness and Judaism as ingredients and requirements necessary in the make-up of an authentic and effective Israeli leader.

All this found expression in his undisputed oratorical capacity in making 'Judea/Samaria' the working political term, and to uplift and give hope to his people.

He, like all true leaders, had a mysterious and magnetic link with his followers, who trusted in him like they never trusted any man . . .†

Truly enough, others – many others – hated his guts. Thus, for instance,

---

* See, for instance, 'The New Israel', *The Economist* (30 July–5 August 1983), pp. 35–41.
† Mordechai Nissan, 'The Begin Legacy', *Jerusalem Post*, 11 September 1983.

Shulamit Hareven, a noted writer and publicist, wrote at Begin's resignation that he was 'the High Priest of the Fear', alleging that he had built his whole political conception, as well as his appeal, by emphasizing the theme of fear of another Holocaust – and many similar voices could be heard.

But even those who were themselves strongly opposed to him, seeing in the symbols and themes annunciated by him a great danger to the State of Israel, could not but admit the existence of such resonance – even if bewailing it.

This resonance was of course also greatly reinforced by the continuous movement of new personnel into the centre; the growing feeling of belonging to the centre, of no longer being dispossessed, among large sectors of the population in general and in the development towns and many of the more mobile sectors in particular.

Thus indeed these themes or orientations become greatly strengthened and incorporated into the centre – even if the militant note with which they were connected waned somewhat with the continuation of the Lebanon War.

## Changes in ethnic and religious symbols

These changes in some of the symbols of the centre and in the relations between the centre and parts of the periphery and the opening up of the centre to new sectors in the society also had important repercussions on the incorporation of several – such as ethnic and religious – themes and symbols which had already gathered momentum before.

The crystallization of these themes developed in two different directions. On the one hand, there was a continuation and even intensification of their divisive aspects, often giving rise to rather ugly outbursts. One was in the Hatiqva quarter in Tel Aviv, where an illegally built house was demolished by the police, on the order of the municipality, giving rise to an outburst against the police. Afterwards, in the north (affluent, Ashkenazi) suburbs of Tel Aviv, there were many graffiti 'Ashke*nazi*' (thereby connecting Ashkenazis with Nazis), and many of the older divisive slogans continued to appear and be voiced. On the other hand, some of these themes continued to be incorporated into the centre, and accordingly there was also a growing tendency among Oriental leaders or intellectuals to stress their unifying and not divisive aspects.

Thus, some at least of these divisive orientations changed. Some of the standard-bearers of the Oriental culture, who had presented it as an alternative to the Ashkenazi one, started to stress that this should be true not only for the Orientals, but as a legitimate part of the common centre; others stressed the search for different ways of bringing Oriental and Western themes together; while still others tended openly to deny the validity of any such distinctive Oriental culture.

The ethnic festivals and gatherings – the Moroccan *Mimouna*, the Kurdish *Saharana* and the like – stressed more and more the theme of national unity and solidarity, of their being part of the whole nation. The revival of many ethnic traditions – as for instance of the North African cults of saints – was often seen as an affirmation of the sense of belonging to Israeli society.*

The development of religious themes and the mode of their relation to the centre and to the symbols of society, and of collective identity was rather more complex. In general there was the growing visibility of religious symbols, symbols of religious tradition, as well as the viability of religious groups, both in the centre as well as in the daily life of many sectors of the population.

But beyond these trends there continued to develop far-reaching changes in the principled place of religion in the society and in State–religion relations. These changes went, as we have already seen above, into two rather opposing, but often mutually reinforcing, directions.

One was the growing ideological and political militancy of the Zionist–religious group, both in the political and in its Halakhic claims against 'secular' Zionism.

This direction – which, as we have seen, developed with the rise of a radical religious national approach among the Youth Movements of the religious sector, especially the *Bnei Akiva*, and in the special institutions, the various *Yeshivot Hesder* – was firmly set within the Zionist vision. The carriers of this vision combined settlement, military service, and an extreme national symbolism couched in a very militant mode with a strong emphasis – far beyond the tendency of the older Zionist-religious groups – on the sovereignty of Halakha, albeit imbued with strong nationalist connotation.

For a relatively long time the impression grew that religious Zionism went entirely in this direction, leaving behind the more universalistic dimension of the Zionist vision – in which many of them shared before. It was only during the Lebanon war that this trend started to change, at least to some degree.

The second major trend in the religious field was represented by Agudat Israel, and was combined with the growing delegitimization of the Zionist premises and symbols – with the growing attempt to impose not only the rule of the Halakha but also the specific non-Zionist ambience.

With the passage of time – especially from the late 1970s – there developed more indications that it was the non-Zionist orientations that were winning over large parts of these religious circles, both from within the Zionist religious circles and from the *Hozrim Betshuva*. This was to no small degree due to the fact that it was from within these more ultra-orthodox circles that many of the 'teachers', with the more extreme religious, non-Zionist orientations, had to be recruited, and were accordingly influencing their students. Many younger people coming from religious Zionist homes moved beyond the Zionist fold, in order to attain fuller realization of the Halakhic mould.

But it was not only within the religious sectors that the tone of Agudat Israel – and even of more extreme orthodox sectors – became predominant. In fact their whole central place in the coalition seemed at least partially to legitimize their anti- or at best non-Zionist orientations.

Thus, for instance, during the occurrences around the archaeological digs in the City of David of Jerusalem, there were strong undertones of opposition to

* Information provided by Dr Yoram Bilu.

modern, secular, academic research, to the necessity of controlling or censoring it, and to the special symbolic place of archaeology, of the attachment to the land as a central component of the new Israeli collective identity – as against the themes stressed in the Halakhic rule.

## A shared acceptance

However varied, often mutually contradictory, were the ways in which both the religious as well as the ethnic component became incorporated into the symbols of Israeli collective identity, they all shared – as could be seen in the construction of curricula, in many festive events, in popular festivals and in the general ambience of popular events – the acceptance of tradition (even of reconstructed tradition); the sanctioning of the past against attempts of reconstruction; and the concomitant weakening of the reconstructive, revolutionary attitude to cultural traditions and symbols. This tendency to weaken the reconstructive aspect of orientations of the Zionist vision was paradoxically shared by the sectors socially and culturally close to the opposite camp, the *Maarach* (Alignment). In these sectors, the major emphasis was on the open characteristics of political culture, of tolerance and of democracy and on the more humanistic elements in Jewish tradition, on the traditions built up by the long settlement in Eretz Israel – but with very few attempts at new modes of reconstruction of Israeli culture and symbols of collective identity, of new patterns of creativity.

Many of the protagonists for this sector strongly emphasized the need for 'sane' Zionism, and the necessity to accept reality as against visionary dreams, and, while indicating many crucial political problems and weaknesses in the quality of life in Israel, they yet seemed to accept this reality in its 'nicer', civilized, universalistic aspects as given, and in no great need of change or renewal.

And yet of course, the differences between these camps were very far-reaching. The trends from within the Likud and some religious sectors were, initially at least, connected with a growing inward-looking orientation – away from the more universalistic Jewish and Zionist orientations, from reference to other nations and from the civilizational conception of Jewish tradition, from the recognition of the tensions which such orientation entailed with the particularistic national conception. They were connected with a very strong tone of self-justification, most fully epitomized by the Prime Minister at the height of his oratorical power, by references to the experience of the Holocaust and the promise not to allow its recurrence.

This tone was often used by him even in relations to foreign Heads of Government, like Chancellor Schmidt (even if he also often referred to the great civilizational contributions of such events as the French revolution, or to principles of international law), in justifying many of the policies against the PLO and refusing to accept the legitimacy of criticisms from the outside.

Similarly, from within some of the religious groups there arose also a legitimation for extreme xenophobic behaviour, based on biblical injunctions against Amalek, going against the recognition of the tensions between the particularistic and the universalistic orientations which was characteristic of the older religious Zionist movements, as well as, of course, of the other 'secular' Zionist groups.

This inward-looking attitude found one of its most significant expressions in the attitudes to the Arabs in Judea and Samaria – becoming closely related with the policy of settlements there and the ideology of permanent Israeli rule over the Arabs.

The more extreme expressions of this attitude could be found among many of the settlers of *Gush Emunim*; among some persons from different old settlements depicted by Amos Oz in his reportages for Israel of 1982* in the person of Zadok; among the extreme voices from some of the orthodox groups referred to above; and above all among the Jewish Defence League under the leadership of Rabbi Meir Kahane who used biblical and post-biblical references to justify the denial of any rights of the Palestinian Arabs, even advocating their evacuation. Meanwhile the then Chief of Staff, Gen. Rafael Eitan (Raful), referred not to the enemy but to Arabs in general, and the Prime Minister depicted the PLO as animals walking on two legs, this dehumanization implicitly often – especially during the Lebanon War – drawing ideological distinction between the blood of Jews and non-Jews.

One of the most significant repercussions of these stances were many instances of brutal behaviour on the part of the army and security forces – not to say anything about some of the settlers – towards the Arab population in Judea and Samaria. Most indicative of these tendencies were the rather far-reaching, quite brutal instructions by the then Chief of Staff, Raful, about the treatment of demonstrating, stone-throwing or protesting Arabs. These instructions were publicly disclosed in the trial of several army officers, who were brought to court through the initiative of *Shalom Achshav*. Some of them were indeed sentenced by the Military Court, which also condemned, even if in a mild way, the instructions themselves. These instructions were later rescinded by his successor, Gen. Moshe Levi, and the new Minister of Defence, Professor Arens.

The spill-over of such attitudes could also be found in such expressions as *Mikhlaot* (pens) used by the army to designate the dwelling units in the camps for prisoners, many of them members of the PLO during the Lebanon War.

While it is, of course, very difficult to measure the exact influence of such sayings and orientations, yet there can be no doubt that all these pronouncements found some attentive audiences. And even if their impact waned with the dragging on of the Lebanon War and the deterioration of the economic situation, yet they probably remained as a very powerful element or component of Israeli public life. Closely related to them were the results of many polls and journalistic interviews which indicated both that the commitment to democratic values was being eroded, and that the Israeli occupation

* Amos Oz, *In the Land of Israel* (London, 1983).

over Judea and Samaria was being taken for granted among huge sectors of the population in general and of younger people in particular.

It was against this inward-looking orientation, the Ghetto mentality combined with military power, that the sector around the Alignment, the *Shalom Achshav* and other protest movements, cried out, stressing the values of human life and of democracy, thus continuing the division that had already developed around the 1981 elections.

# Changes in the Formats of Political Life and in Political Culture
## *Introduction*

These changes in the symbols of the centre did not, however, despite some of the claims of the leaders of the Likud and their protagonists and despite the far-reaching changes they effected in the symbolic ambience of Israeli society, crystallize into a new institutional mould.

Indeed, most of the repercussions of these developments, especially when taken together with the continuation, or even intensification, of many older trends in the major institutional spheres of Israeli society, indicate rather the opposite – namely the weakness of the crystallization of any new viable institutional mould; weakness in central institution-building and in the implementation of many policies; low level of effectiveness of the government – all of which became more and more visible towards the end of the Begin government in September 1983, together with the great divisiveness within the country which reached its peak around the time of the publication of the Kahan report.

On one level, Israeli society continued indeed to develop in the major directions which we have analysed in the preceding chapters. It continued as a small modern society with its own characteristics, a combination of post-industrial and industrialized society, and with great diversity and pluralism in its social and cultural life, a diversity enhanced by the mobility into the centre of new groups, by the recrystallization of new ethnic and religious themes, and by growing contacts with the external world – as manifest for example in the continuously growing number of trips of Israelis abroad, of import of goods from abroad, and the like.

There accordingly developed many conflicts and problems. Many of the older problems continued – labour conflicts, especially in the public sector, problems related to its being a small country, the very intensive concern with problems of Aliya, *Yerida* and the like. And some new social problems and patterns – such as, for instance, ageing of the population – became more visible.

But many of these problems were related to a different level of social life, to some of the new developments – especially to the realignment of political forces and the movement of new social echelons into the centre, and to the new ideological and political themes – which greatly transformed many of the specific conflicts and problems into very strong confrontations.

The test of the crystallization of a new viable institutional mould lay, of course, in the ability to regulate these conflicts and to direct, to some degree at least, the forces generating them – and it is here that many of the weaknesses of this period became visible.

## Weakening of the centre

This became evident first of all in political life. The pattern of internal political life continued in several directions which had started to develop before – namely the continuous weakening of central party organs and leadership and their inability, except partially in the security field, to regulate or direct the political process, which became even more diversified than before.

There continued the confrontation between parliamentary committees – even between members from within the coalitions – and different ministers, most of which, except for the Prime Minister, did not command much authority. The level of debates in the Knesset became lower and that of abuse – especially between members of the coalition and opposition – higher; at the same time, the members of the Knesset were extremely hesitant to impose restrictions on themselves, as for instance in the case of traffic violations by them. The bargaining and bickering among the coalition parties continued, and the level of political discussion became lowered. Parallelly, an intensification of populist and media policies developed, with a growth of leakages from within the government.

At the same time, there was also the intensification of extraparliamentary politics – of demonstrations and outbursts. In many cases and situations – especially those related to foreign security or settlement problems, the withdrawal from Sinai, the Lebanon War, or various events around settlements in Judea and Samaria, or in Hebron – it was the various protest movements, instigated by *Shalom Achshav* or on the other side by *Gush Emunim*, the settlers in Judea and Samaria, and the underground terrorist anti-Arab groups, that occupied the centre of the political scene, attesting to the weakening of the central political organs and especially of the parties in the Knesset.

The government showed, especially after the Kahan report, and the growing deterioration of the economic situation in 1983, less and less cohesiveness and more and more internal bickering, and leaks from within the government, even between members of the same party, especially among the Liberal ministers but also among those of *Herut*, became quite usual.

One focus of such quarrels was the attempts of the Minister of Finance, Yoram Aridor, to centralize in his hands supervision over the finances of different institutions. This was resisted by other ministers, as became especially visible during the doctors' strike in 1983, and, when the bad outcomes of his general economic policy became apparent, a new policy of budgeting cuts was in principle decided upon.

Many of the ministers had but little political or administrative experience and, with some exceptions, did not carry much authority. After the publication of the Kahan report, even the authority of Mr Begin seemed to wane – or at least he did not choose to exercise it in such crucial situations as the doctors' strike or during the uglier manifestations of divisiveness and lawlessness. Even when he did exercise it, as in the case of the election of the President, the successor of Yitzhak Navon, he was unable to assure the success of his candidate and instead, Chaim Herzog, the candidate of the Alignment, was elected in the secret ballot of the Knesset.

## Relations with the opposition and with the press

The full impact of these trends on political life can be seen in their relation to the various policies – especially those in Judea and Samaria and of the war in Lebanon. These highlighted the great division between the two great blocks, the Likud and the *Maarach* and their supporters, as well as between the religious and the secular – the two sometimes converging together, sometimes each divisiveness going in its own direction.

This division between the two blocs became more and more focused around the question of the basic political solution of the problem of the Arab population in Judea and Samaria and of its implications for the format of Israeli society. The political stances of the Likud, with its emphasis on continuous Israeli rule over these areas even if not necessarily on their immediate annexation, brought out in a very sharp way the dilemma between granting the Arabs full citizenship which could easily undermine the Jewish nature of the State or granting them special status (for instance as proposed by Yuval Neeman, one of the leaders of *Hatehiya*), that of resident aliens.

The Likud leadership did not face up fully to these problems; the more honest among them, as for instance Moshe Arens – the new Minister of Defence – admitted that he did not have any single solution. More simple and straightforward was the ideology of many of the settlers of *Gush Emunim* (not to say anything of the more extreme view of Rav Meir Kahane of the Jewish Defence League) who had a clearer vision of keeping the Arabs, often according to what they understood to be biblical injunctions, in a situation of second-class residents or subjects.

This assumption of the continuity of Israeli rule – not only, as we have seen earlier during the Alignment rule, as a temporary exigency – over an alien and on the whole hostile population, and in fact behaving in many ways as a conquering people had, as we shall shortly see, far-reaching repercussions on the whole format of life in Israel.

It was against this orientation and ideology that the Alignment (or at least parts of it), *Shinui*, the extraparliamentary opposition groups such as *Shalom Achshav*, and many public and intellectual figures stressed the necessity for some territorial compromise, or even the acceptance of a Palestinian State in Judea and Samaria. They did not accept that full rule over Judea and Samaria was necessary for security reasons, and emphasized that a compromise solution was necessary, not only in order to come to some settlement with the Arabs, but also for the maintenance of the Jewish and democratic nature of the State, avoiding all the undemocratic, brutalizing aspects of remaining or ruling over a conquered population.

Thus the lines between the two great blocs, which had become apparent in the 1981 election, became in many ways even more sharply drawn.

These developments sharpened the problem of relations between government and opposition, and between loyalty to the State and to the government – a theme which was, of course, very much stressed by the government against the opposition, especially during the Lebanon War. The Likud compared their own loyalty to the former Labour governments (not mentioning that this was based on fundamental agreement to their policies), as against the presumed disloyalty of the opposition – especially of *Shalom Achshav*, but also of parliamentary groups – accusing them of disloyalty to the State, even, in the heat of discussion or in the outbursts on the streets, of helping the PLO.

Later on, in one of the debates in the Knesset about the situation in Lebanon and the economic one, the Prime Minister, while admitting that it was a bad time for Israel (not mentioning who was responsible for it), claimed that in such a time it was appropriate to close ranks and not to attack the government.

The accusations against the opposition's attitude to the government greatly influenced the general tone of public debate. This had started to change during the first Likud government, continued during the 1981 elections and gathered momentum afterwards. This new tone was set above all by the Likud – especially during the Lebanon War – by the Prime Minister, by the then Minister of Defence, Ariel Sharon, and by the Chief of Staff, Raful.

Both before the war, and even more during its first and later more controversial phases, criticism of the government and of the Chief of Staff was often equalled by many top echelons of the Likud with treason,* an attitude which spread widely, giving rise to some even – if milder – outbursts from the sectors opposing the government.

This stance towards the opposition was reinforced by the fact that concurrently with the development of these new government–opposition relations, there were far-reaching changes in the relations between the government and large sectors of the literary, artistic, journalist and academic community.

Although the claims that there was a total alienation between these groups and the government were, on the whole, exaggerated, yet they contained more than a kernel of truth. There were only a few outstanding literary or artistic figures who wholeheartedly supported the government; the academic sectors were more split, but even here those against the government were probably more visible; the government did not on the whole receive a good press – especially with the continuation of the war in Lebanon and the breakdown of the 'correct' economic policy.

* See, for instance, the leader 'Making Criticism Treason', *Jerusalem Post*, 30 March 1982.

The lack of success of Likud to found a daily newspaper of its own, and the continuation of some independent and critical reporting even on the television, where the government – or rather the Broadcasting Authority – created a rather restrictive atmosphere, only reinforced the anti-intellectual, populist attitudes within large sectors of the Likud. Moves towards imposing restrictions on free expression became at least very vocal, and quite a restrictive atmosphere, even an atmosphere of fear, developed in many echelons of public life.

There were many outbursts against the media within the entourage of the Prime Minister and members of the Knesset, above all by Sharon and Raful who became the torch-bearers in these campaigns, both before the war and even more during and after it.

Thus, during the imposition of Israeli identity cards on the Druze in the Golan – one of the unhappy political events of this period – as well as during the withdrawal from Sinai, the press and the media were either not allowed in or were severely limited. Similar initial attempts during the war in Lebanon were unsuccessful, although they were enough to antagonize large parts of the foreign press. The war became one of the best covered, not only by the foreign press but also by Israeli commentators, the most outstanding among them probably being Ze'ev Shiff, the military correspondent of *Haaretz*, a fact singled out also by the International Press Institute. After the publication of the Kahan report, Sharon's diatribes against the press and the Commission became even more intensive. These outbursts against the media became connected with growing divisiveness and sometimes intensification of ethnic and religious conflicts, of conflicts between the government and its opponents; they became indicative of the growing intolerance towards opposition and attempts at its delegitimation; and connected with the lowering of the tone of public debate. Such debates, especially during the debates around the Lebanon War, but also before, continued to no small degree the atmosphere of the 1981 election's demagogic slogans, and contributed to the enticement of different sectors of the population to divisiveness within the society. At the same time the resignation of Begin in the autumn of 1983 was often attributed to his growing awareness that he was not fully informed, even possibly deceived, about the military plans and the concrete situations – a situation which, of course, contributed to the weakening of civility.*

## Weakening of civility

The combination of all the trends analysed above had a far-reaching impact on the whole structure and ambience of Israeli political culture – weakening the scope of civility and of the rule of law, weakening the norms of public behaviour and giving rise to the development of anarchic politics of Higher Law.

The first aspect of the weakening of civility was evident in the deterioration –

* See Ze'ev Shiff and Ehud Yaari, *Israel's Lebanon War* (New York 1984).

after the attempts of the first Likud government, in the beginning phases of its rule, to institute some norms – in the behaviour of ministers and public figures. The norms proposed by a special committee were in many ways not upheld, and the influx of new personalities into the government was often accompanied by contravention of civil service regulations. Parallelly, allocations – especially to religious groups – became connected with the contravention of proper budgetary control.

These contraventions were sometimes justified by the fact that this had been the situation under Labour – which was to some degree true of the 1950s – but disregarded the fact that since then the universalistic rules had become more and more prevalent; and that within the Alignment – as several occurrences at the end of the Rabin government, especially the suicide of the Minister of Housing, and Mr Rabin's own behaviour attested – there was a very great sensitivity to the upholding of such norms and a very strong feeling of shame at being accused of their contravention.

During the Abu-Hatzeira case, there were many outcries both that it should be necessary to accept the existence of different norms within different ethnic groups, and that the particularist norms and/or patterns of behaviour which still persisted in the older sectors were no better than those for which he had been sentenced. These, often rather violent, outcries were not rebuked by the Prime Minister or other persons of authority.

There also took place the weakening of many autonomous public bodies. For instance, the new Governor of the Bank of Israel, initially at least, behaved in a much less independent way towards the Government than all his predecessors. There was also the appointment of A. Shapira, Chairman of the Coalition and himself an industrialist, to the Chairmanship of the Bank of Israel. There was also some weakening of the autonomy of the public but not government bodies, such as the Broadcasting Authority, and the imposition of a rather restrictive atmosphere within it.

Yet another aspect of the weakening of civility, which emerged particularly during the Lebanon War but the kernels of which had existed before, was the growing involvement of some army echelons in politics.*

The most extreme manifestation of this was the unprecedented public declarations of the Chief of Staff, Raful, not only on some general educational principles, but also on specific political issues. He often came out in defence of the basic policy of the government, publicly attacking the opposition – an involvement unheard of by any former Chief of Staff, even if they also tried to influence policy. There was also the disregard by Sharon and Raful during the war of the parliamentary committees.

Second, less visible and naturally not fully documented, was the involvement of various higher echelons of the army with different political coalitions.

---

* See Y. Peri, *Between Battles and Ballots: Israeli Military in Politics* (Cambridge 1983).

## Weakening of the rule of law

Another aspect of the weakening of civility could be seen in the application of law, both within Israel proper and especially in the relations between Arabs and Jews in Judea and Samaria.

Within Israel itself, especially until the Kahan Committee Report, the authorities had tended to be more lenient towards religious and politically right-wing sectors. This was very evident in the silken-glove treatment given to the demonstrators against the withdrawal from Sinai, to religious demonstrators, to the settlers in Judea and Samaria and especially in Kiryat Arba, at least until after the murder of Emil Grinzweig; and in the treatment of the rightist, as against leftist, anti-government demonstration. It was only after this that the picture changed.

Perhaps the most extreme illustration of such unequal application of law to different sectors of the population could be seen in relation to the Arabs in Judea and Samaria, where many of their complaints against the settlers or the army were not given attention. A special committee was set up by the Attorney-General (the Karp Committee) to investigate the enforcement of the law with respect to Jews engaged in conflicts with Arabs in Judea and Samaria.

There was also the tendency of the then Chief of Staff, Raful, to reduce sentences imposed by the military courts in cases of soldiers accused of, and sentenced for, various types of misbehaviour towards Arabs. Many claimed that this attitude was also reflected in the behaviour of military courts, noting in this context that the recommendation of a public commission headed by Supreme Court Justice Shamgar, a former Chief Army Prosecutor, that the military court sphere be headed by a jurist was postponed for some years.

The atmosphere of selective implementation of law was also enhanced by the fact that many of the perpetrators of criminal acts against Arabs (as for instance planting of bombs against several mayors of Arab cities) were not found for a very long period of time.

Last, there was the development of what may be called the politics of Higher Law. Many groups – especially the religious and the extreme orthodox ones, above all the *Gush Emunim*, the settlers in Kiryat Arba, in Judea and Samaria, some members of *Hatehia*; and many other upholders of the ideology of *Eretz Israel Hashlema* – presented themselves as representatives of a law higher than that of the State to a much higher degree than before, thus bringing in a very strong anarchical element in the Israeli political life, which culminated in the organization of an underground terrorist group which was discovered in April and May 1984.

In all these developments which influenced the ambience of the political life in Israel, the Liberal party had but little influence, despite its alleged 'liberal' credo. Their liberal postures were sometimes upheld with respect to matters bearing directly on the economic interests of the groups they represented, but with very little, if any, respect for the upholding of a rule of law, or rights of citizens – themes which were much more stressed by *Shinui* or *Ratz* or parts of the Alignment. It was only with respect to some of the more extreme demands of the religious groups, as for instance with respect to the Archaeology Law and the 'Who is a Jew?' question, that some elements among the Liberals were up to now* successful in postponing the requested legislation. But on the whole most of their political activities were focused on bargaining, on assurance of positions for their members.

The only exception was the case of Itzhak Berman, a former Speaker of the Knesset and Minister of Energy in the second Likud government who resigned after the Sabra–Shatila massacre. This act of his, supported by a few other Liberal MKs, was probably important in inducing the Prime Minister to appoint the Kahan Committee.

## Violence and divisiveness; lawlessness

The combination of all these trends – the weakening of civility; the divisiveness within the society; the split between the two great blocs; the breaking down of many of the normative restraints on public behaviour; the weakening of feelings of shame – gave rise to a growing intolerance, an intensification of violence and violent outbursts, as for instance the one in the Hatiqva quarter in Tel Aviv mentioned above.

There it was some public personalities, especially journalists, who came out against the violations of the rule of law. Even after the ugly inscriptions of Ashke*nazi*, the Prime Minister was silent. But some voices in the leadership of the *Maarach* came out against the too stringent application of the law in such 'social cases'.

This normlessness and the violent behaviour connected with it became more and more visible in daily life – on the streets or in offices – abating somewhat only after the murder of Emil Grinzweig. Such normlessness could even be seen in the behaviour of many Israeli tourists, in Israel and abroad alike, who perpetrated acts of vandalism in the hotels in which they were staying, stealing sheets, carpets, curtains or anything.

The culmination of such normlessness was probably in the doctors' strike in the summer of 1983. On the one hand, there can be no doubt that the government showed great ineptitude in the management of the health services in general and during the strike in particular, and the Histadrut was almost entirely immobilized by being caught between being the employer of the doctors; the would-be professional representative, and the provider of health services to a large sector of the public.

On the other hand, however, the behaviour of the doctors – the way many of them abandoned the hospitals and went on a profit picnic on the Sea of Galilee; the later hunger strikes which meant they were unable to treat patients; the very violent expressions verifying an incitement to disobey laws – had no precedent in labour relations in Israel and created a very demoralizing atmosphere.

* September 1983.

Another serious instance in that period of lawless behaviour by well-established groups was that of parents in Rishon Lezion, who in the beginning of the 1983/4 school year blocked many schools and did not send their children to them, in opposition to the implementation of the policy of reform and integration, and gave in only when, after rather prolonged and hesitant negotiations, the Minister of Education made a final decision to implement the law.

The weakening of the various aspects of civility brought out more forcefully some of the original themes of Jewish political culture – especially those of intransigence, of the politics of Higher Law, and of the stress on distributive allocations in the name of solidarity of various groups in the society. These attitudes had been very strong, as we have seen, both in the medieval period and in the first twenty-five years of the State of Israel – but were regulated by their respective institutional moulds. Paradoxically enough, the development of the State of Israel had seemed to relieve many of the carriers of these orientations of any feelings of responsibility for the overall running of the society.

The weakness of many of the central normative regulations and frameworks in Israel had indeed enabled the articulation by various standard-bearers of many of the more extreme Jewish or Zionist themes – of strength; of sanctification of territoriality or of normless solidarity. These themes had previously been articulated in relatively closed groups or sectors – in some units in the army, in various sectors of the older settlements or in more traditional sectors – or had been latent within wider sectors of the public, enclosed in a central institutional framework, which segregated them from autonomous articulation and impact on the centre. Now they became much more vocal, visible in the public scene and in the centre.

This situation has been very forcefully portrayed by Amos Oz in his 'Here and Now in Eretz Israel'* in which it is the various extreme groups – the ultra-orthodox, *Gush Emunim* or the articulators of ethnic divisiveness – that are the more dynamic and articulate ones, as against some of the inward-looking, segregated old settlers; or as against the vibrant, almost entirely present-orientated town of Ashdod, thus attesting, maybe against the author's intention, the lack – within the Labour camp or around it – of any central, dynamic, future-orientated vision, to counter the visions of these extreme groups. At the same time however, most of these visions were connected with a very weak capacity for institution-building.

# Patterns of Institution-Building

The processes of institution-building that developed in this period were very weak on the macro-level, even if they were often counteracted by many creative developments on the micro-level. Thus indeed many creative attempts continued in industry – especially in science-based, technological industries.

* In *In the Land of Israel*.

There were attempts at new technological ventures: the Lavi airplane; the plans, even if controversial, about the *Taalat Hayamim* (the Channel of Seas), which was to connect the Mediterranean with the Dead Sea.

Important educational innovations were made in the army, initiated or encouraged by the Chief of Staff, Raful, as well as in many other areas of education and culture.

But all these were to a very large degree counteracted by the various processes in the centre, or by various attempts or proclamations made by it.

The most grotesque of these attempts was probably that enunciated by Yaacov Meridor, one of the leaders of the Herut and one of the Ministers of Economy in the second Likud government. Before the 1981 election, he declared that teams of scientists working with him had found a new source of energy which would replace oil, which later turned out to be a rather dubious affair. He made further grandiose declarations without any foundation, while more humble attempts in his Ministry, for instance to improve the levels of government, ended in failure.

But the more creative tendencies of institution-building were counteracted above all by the repercussions of the 'correct' economy, which greatly intensified the negative tendencies in Israeli economy, giving rise to growing consumption and imports, growing trade and payment deficits, foreign debt and stoppage of economic growth, as shown by the following report by the Bank of Israel of 1983, and the further deterioration since then.

In 1982 the central problems facing the economy in recent years became more acute: high inflation combined with a sluggish level of activity, and the growth of the current account deficit and the external debt. Gross national product rose by a mere 1 percent, a low rate even compared with the average for the past decade (3.3 percent); the business sector product did not grow at all. The import surplus expanded by about $400 million; less defense imports (which declined this year), the civilian import surplus increased by $1 billion. The net external debt rose for the second consecutive year by 15 percent to stand at $15.5 billion. Despite the stagnation of GNP and the larger balance of payments deficit, inflation not only failed to weaken but it returned to its 1980 level (130 per cent). The slight increase in economic activity was accompanied by continued slackness in the labor market – for the third straight year unemployment ran at 5 percent of the civilian labor force.

The marginal increase in the domestic product despite an 8 percent expansion of domestic demands can be attributed to special factors which this year dampened exports and stimulated imports. Exports retreated 2.6 percent, the first time they suffered a setback after many years of very rapid growth. The downturn was due to the combination of global recession and Israel's diminished ability to compete in foreign markets. In the last two years world markets were depressed and international trade slumped. The weakening of European currencies against the U.S. dollar and the real appreciation of the sheqel in relation to a basket of foreign currencies made it harder for Israeli goods to compete abroad. These influences were moderated by some reduction of taxes on labor and by the exchange rate insurance arrangement, which *inter alia* provided for the compensation of the country's exports to Europe for the strengthening of the dollar.*

* Bank of Israel, *Main Points of the Annual Report, 1982* (Jerusalem, May 1983), p. 1.

These trends gave rise to a deterioration of major services, the abolishment of many social services and special programmes – such as many of those for handicapped children, the continuous deterioration of the educational situation of the lower echelons, and a severe threat to the institutions of higher learning, a threat which could be disastrous for the future of scientific and scholarly work in Israel.

The low point of all these developments in the political sphere and in institution-building came towards the end of the Begin era. The doctors' strike, the economic crisis of 1983 and the rather lukewarm attempts to halt or even reverse this current and the low level of the functioning of the government all indicated the lack of any clear direction in internal matters or even in those of foreign policy and security.

The feeling of the weakness of the overall policy of Likud was well expressed by Herzel Rosenblum, editor of *Yediot Aharonot* and a sympathizer of Likud, in a leading article in which he said that the great mistake of the Begin government was to develop an activist external policy while entirely neglecting the internal front – and thus also the strength of the nation. This weakness became most visible in the autumn of 1983 with the crisis of the bank shares on the Tel Aviv exchange.

## Counter-Tendencies
### *Continued constructive tendencies and changes in the periphery*

As against these various tendencies towards the weakening of civility and the processes of institution-building, the continuous divisiveness within Israeli society, and the inward-looking ambience and orientation, there were also many structural and ideological counter-tendencies, both in various sectors of what may be called the periphery as well as in the centre.

Two of these tendencies were particularly important. First was the continuous crystallization of constructive creative tendencies, especially among many of the younger generations between the ages of twenty and forty, searching and attempting for new avenues of constructive work and creativity. Parts of these echelons, many of them products of the Israeli educational system, as well as small groups of new immigrants, were active in many of the creative activities – whether in the technologically sophisticated industries, in scholarly, educational and cultural areas, or in the construction of varied styles of life.

Second, there developed far-reaching structural changes in various hitherto dormant or passive peripheries of Israeli society – especially but not only in some of the development towns, as well as among the more mobile and active elements in the cities.

It was not only the growing symbolic attunement of many sectors of the society to the themes articulated in the centre or the movement of new groups – processes which could quite easily be connected with the more problematic aspects of the recent developments – that were important in this context.

Of much greater importance is the fact that in many parts of the hitherto dormant, passive, to no small degree alienated periphery, especially but not only the development towns, a new very constructive mode of institution-building and creativity, especially on the local level, was developing. These activities were carried out mainly by a new generation, born or raised in Isreael, whose members evinced high motivation to such constructive activities, a high level of social commitment, and a desire to shake off the shackles of dependency that had developed in the earlier period.

These efforts were also often connected with the clamouring among the younger generation in many hitherto successful development towns. They had successfully been through the educational system and the army, and were searching for more diversified and sophisticated economic opportunities – thus continuously posing new challenges before the centre.

Among some of the Oriental groups such tendencies were often connected with the above-mentioned transformation of many of the ethnic symbols and orientations – in the direction of stressing their belonging to and active participation in the society.

This feeling of belonging found its expression also in the Lebanon War. Far more than in any of the former wars of Israel, soldiers and officers from development towns not only became much more visible (a fact due to simple demographic process), but also evinced, according to several researches as well as more direct testimonies, a very high, perhaps the highest, level of motivation. This was higher than the soldiers and officers from the Kibbutzim, who had previously held the pride of place in this respect, but whose place dropped significantly in the Lebanon War.

Thus, indeed, all these trends indicated the development of a very high level of potential for new types of linkages of solidarity within principle pluralistic and more open centre or centres.

## The legitimation of protest and opposition

Several very significant counter-tendencies developed also with respect to the weakening of civility.

First of all, there were some quiet tendencies to accept some aspects of greater pluralism in many spheres of life, even in the centre of the society, thus weakening some of the divisive aspects of such pluralism. There started to develop tendencies against the divisiveness of lack of tolerance and delegitimation of protest, and towards a stronger insistence on the upholding of the rule of law.

The turning-point in these trends and developments was the murder – by unknown and hitherto not found person or persons* – during the demonstration organzied by *Shalom Achshav* at the publication of the Kahan report, of Emil Grinzweig.

* In early 1984 a suspect was arrested by the police and brought to court.

During the demonstration itself, the hatred of the so-called 'street mob' which gathered at the pavements against the demonstrators reached unprecedented dimensions. But immediately after the murder, although it did not evoke a very sharp reaction from the Prime Minister or the Minister of Police, a sharp turn seemed to take place in the public. Thus, already at Emil Grinzweig's funeral, attended by the Speaker of the Knesset and the Deputy Minister David Levy, a wreath on behalf of all Zionist youth movements was laid by the representatitve of *Betar* – the Revisionist (Likud) youth movement.

Since then many attempts on behalf of the more rightist groups to find ways of contact, of *Hidabrut* (talking together) with protest groups against the government, have been developing. Some of the members of these groups – for instance Zachi Hanegbi, one of the leaders of the students and of the protestors in *Yamit* – publicly admitted to being wrong in their delegitimation of *Shalom Achshav* and stressed the importance of protesting within the limits of the law.

The attempts at delegitimation of opposition and of protest became much weaker and many demonstrations or happenings against the war in Lebanon no longer – at least for the time being – evoked strong outbursts of hatred or attempts at violence.

There was also a calming down at the university campuses, where the semi-terrorizing atmosphere of the late 1970s and early 1980s subsided, and where the groups close to the Alignment won in elections to student organizations.

After Mr Begin's resignation there were negotiations between Likud and Labour about the possibility of establishing a government of national unity, which according to the polls was favoured by large parts of the public. These were conducted in a very civil atmosphere and, when they were ended without any agreement, the tone of civility and mutual acceptance by both parties was maintained.

Also of great significance in this context was the stance developed by the new Chief of Staff, General Moshe Levi, who, as we have seen, rescinded the instructions of his predecessor with respect to treatment of Arab demonstrators; and who also – in one of his appearances before soldiers – stressed that there is no such thing as the army's view, that the army represents all the variety of views existing in Israeli society. There was also a general calming down of the rather heated atmosphere among some of the higher echelons of the army, and a restoration of mutual trust in it.

## Upholding the rule of law

Parallelly there also developed many important reaffirmations of the rule of law.

Of first importance here was the upholding of the rule of law with respect to the publication of the Kahan report, as well as the fact that most of its recommendations were, on the whole, implemented, even if sectors of the public protested against the fact that Mr Sharon remained at all in the government (the Attorney-General ruled that this was not against the spirit of the recommendation of the Committee).

Unlike most Royal Commissions or other commissions of inquiry in democratic regimes, and unlike the Agranat Commission after the Yom Kippur War, which, as we have seen, absolved the political level, the Kahan Commission criticized very sharply the political and military levels alike.

While their conclusions also evoked criticisms as well as continuous abuse from Ariel Sharon, without any public figure rebuking him, yet the very fact that the report was basically accepted and implemented, constituted a testimony to the strength of the rule of law.

The strengthening of the rule of law was also effected in several directions by the Attorney General, as well as by the High Court.

Thus for instance the latter has ruled against the Television Authority which banned any interview with PLO or anti-government Arab leaders. Similarly, against the wish of the police, the Supreme Court ruled to allow a demonstration commemorating thirty days after the murder of Emil Grinzweig; stressing the duty of the police to assure the exercise of the basic democratic right to peaceful demonstration. Later the Attorney-General (after negotiations with the Inspector General of Police) issued directives to the police that it is their duty to undertake the security of legitimate oppositionary demonstrations, even if a large part of the public may be opposed to them and they thus seemingly threaten the public order.

Similarly, it was from the Attorney-General's office that the initiative came for the establishment of a Committee (the Karp Committee) to investigate the application and implementation of law – especially towards Jews in conflict with Arabs – in Judea and Samaria.

A not unimportant turn in this direction also took place in the case of Aharon Abu-Hatzeira after his case was appealed to the Supreme Court and he was sentenced to three months of imprisonment. Unlike the first time he was brought to court when there were, as we have seen, quite vocal outbursts against the legal system, this time the reaction was much quieter and subdued – even if the facts that he did not resign from the Knesset, and his party *Tami* intended to make him again a member of government, were not indicative of the most stringent norms of public behaviour.

## Ideological developments and the maintenance of the democratic frameworks

There were also some very new important ideological developments. First of all, during the Lebanon War, many religious intellectuals, who had been relatively silent over many years, came out strongly against the war and against the seeming monopolization of the Zionist–religious standpoint by *Gush Emunim*.

Perhaps even more significant was a similar very strong stance against the war from within the *Yeshivot Hesder*, by such persons as Rabbi Avital and others, giving rise even to the public expression of rather far-reaching second thoughts by the Minister of Education, Zevulun Hamer, one of the leaders of the younger groups in the NRP, which was one of the major standard-bearers of the ideology of *Eretz Israel Hashlema*.

Similarly among some Oriental intellectuals could be heard criticism against the image of the Orientals as war prone, sometimes even claiming that this was part of the Ashkenazi plot to denigrate the Orientals, and various attempts at new movements and organizations of Orientals for peace were made.

Above all, there was of course the fact that the basic democratic framework and most of the rules of the democratic game – despite the many threats to them, and the polls which indicate doubts about democracy – were maintained. So too was the continuous openness of the society and the lines of communication between the strata of population and the authorities – even during the height of the war, a war not based on consensus. Moreover, the lack of such consensus did not impede the efficiency of the army and the basic loyalty of the citizen. There was the fact that, despite some initial efforts, the Lebanon war was the most fully reported one in the media, sometimes probably even beyond the legitimate limits of military censorship – thus creating a sharp contrast, for instance, with the Falklands War.

Needless to say all these trends were not the only ones. Many of the trends towards the weakening of civility, divisiveness and intolerance continued, and sometimes even intensified, and there were only the beginnings of overcoming some of the structural conditions and institutional frameworks which have led, as we have seen, to the weakening of overall solidary linkages in Israeli society.

## Overview

Thus the picture is indeed very mixed. This mixture was very well captured by President Chaim Herzog in his Rosh Hashana address, in which he pointed out all these weaknesses and problems against the background of the great achievements of the State of Israel. In his words:*

> During the period of my incumbence [of the office of Presidency] I have become every day aware of the beauty of our land and the greatness of the people living in it. I have become aware that the positive aspects of our life – the constructive work and intelligence and wisdom – far outweigh the negative aspects.
>
> During my trips in the country I am often astounded by the great achievements, the spirit of volunteering and the creativity which I encounter . . . This does not mean, however, that there do not exist shadows in our public life which, if not dispersed, may endanger our very existence. . . . Despite the many dangers from the outside, the greatest danger is from the inside. This danger is rooted in shaken human relations, in lack of consideration for others, in a non-civilized mode of public debate, which sometimes deteriorates into violence. This danger derives from the polarization between different parts or sectors of the people, a polarization which finds its expression in enticement and physical violence. The blood of Emil Grinzweig is still calling to us from out of the earth . . . This danger derives from disregard of others, of the rights of

* English translation by S. N. Eisenstadt.

individuals, of the citizen and the strangers in our gates,* of the rights in natural justice and in the commandments of the Torah. It derives from tensions betwen different sectors which often base their acts and arguments according to their own interpretation of what is good for the people – disregarding the opinion of others.

And in all this cauldron which threatens our security, there have also lately developed some indications – in some opinion surveys – that perhaps it is possible to give up democracy.

Perhaps one of the most dangerous signs that have developed lately is the tendency to undermine the authority of our legal system. Such an attitude is of immense danger for the nation, and constitutes indeed an outright violation of the injunctions of the Torah: 'Thou shalt do according to the law and to the judgement which they shall declare to thee; thou shalt not swerve to the right hand nor to the left hand from any sentence which they shall report to thee.' (Deut. 17: 11.)

Rashi† comments on this: 'Even if they tell you that right is left and left is right', and the Ramban‡: 'Even if you think that he is wrong and that the matter seems simple to you, as you know the distinction between right and left – you have to obey their orders.'

If today in our society people talk against democracy and let the same voices be heard which attempt to undermine the authority and independence of the legal authorities, we face one of the most dangerous developments which, if not stopped, may – God forbid – bring to anarchy and destruction.

You may say that all this is dependent on leadership, on the opinion makers and on the media. This is correct, but it depends also on everyone of us . . . and [this situation] often derives from disregard of small matters and disobedience of law, of elementary precautions . . . Since the establishment of the State, 15,000 people have been killed in road accidents, 2,000 more than in all of Israel's wars. Since the establishment of the State, about half a million people have been injured in accidents on the roads, and most of these were due to negligence, disregard of laws, arrogance, exaggerated self-assurance and disregard of others – and these attitudes slip over into the public arena and debates and give rise to a very dangerous deterioration in our society.

Yet with all this self-criticism and mortification, we are entitled to look around us and be proud of the society we have built. Out of the 160 members of the United Nations, only about 35 solve their problems in the way that we do . . .

Often I think about the majority of the nations, underdeveloped, with low levels of education and health, with lack of free expression, without a free press, with the concentration camps and the Gulaghs – regimes in which fear is a major factor in human life, with hundreds of millions of people who never knew and till the end of their life will not know what freedom is. I compare them with our small State which we built with our own hands, which excels in many fields: in medicine, in education, in technological development, in agriculture and research; with the great wonder of the Ingathering of Exiles and building of the nation – and all these despite the threats to our very existence, and despite the great social and economic difficulties. Without for a moment disregarding the failures, the things which have not yet been achieved, the grave problems facing us, we are entitled to be proud of the achievements of our people and our Land and of what we have built. . . .

---

* The biblical expression 'ger'.
† Rabbi Shlomo Itzhaki, the great medieval commentator on the Bible and Talmud.
‡ Rabbi Moshe ben Nahman (the Nachmanides), a great medieval scholar and philosopher.

# III · Postscript

## The 1984 Elections

As I indicated in the preface, the manuscript was finished in the autumn of 1982, more or less at the time of Begin's resignation, and it is not my intention to analyse the period after that in any great detail. I would like only to make a few brief comments on some recent events – especially the July 1984 elections – as they bear on some of the major points of our analysis.

## *Some events in 1983 and 1984*

Before, however, turning to the analysis of the elections, it might be worth while to mention two events which took place between the resignation of Begin and the elections.

One was the threatened crash of the bank shares on the Tel Aviv stock exchange in the autumn of 1983. Until then the bank shares, by being actually subsidized by the banks with at least silent co-operation of the government, had provided throughout this period a continuously high yield beyond the rate of inflation – and beyond their actual worth. They constituted one of the major areas of investment in the rather peculiar Israeli capital market.

In the autumn of 1983, the artificiality of their high values on the stock exchange became more and more obvious, and their possible collapse more and more imminent.

A very large sector of the population was involved and, as the collapse of the bank shares touched on some central nerves of the system, the government and the Bank of Israel stepped in. Trade in the shares was stopped for some time and a rather particular arrangement was made – which promised a high future yield if the shares were not traded immediately but became, as it were, frozen.

These developments greatly shook the confidence of the public in the financial policies of the government. They led ultimately to the resignation of Mr Aridor as Minister of Finance and the appointment of a new one, Mr Cohen-Orgad, who tried, but not very successfully, to implement a more restrictive economic policy.

The second important event – on a different front – which took place a few months before the elections, was the arrest, after a very long surveillance by the internal security service, of more than thirty members of the 'Jewish underground' – mostly settlers in Judea and Samaria, many of them reserve officers and very close to *Gush Emunim*. They were brought to court, accused of planning many subversive, terrorist, activities against the Arabs. Their very arrest was seen as an important indication of the rule of law, while the discovery of their acts gave rise to some soul-searching among the settlers and among members of *Gush Emunim*.

Yet, at the same time, the arrested members seemed to evoke a lot of sympathy from the general public – even when they did not agree with their concrete activities. Thus there were but few clear-cut denunciations of them by public figures – be it the Prime Minister or the Minister of Interior whose declaration indicated some sympathy with them. This attitude of sympathy spilled over to some of the prison authorities so that the conditions of their stay in prison were relatively lenient.

## The election campaign

The elections were called by the Knesset, before the 'usual' expiration of its term, as a result of the initiative of the Labour opposition and of *Tami* – the 'ethnic' list under the leadership of Aharon Abu-Hatzeira – with the support of some other small parties, against the wish of the ruling Likud party and the government headed now by Yitzhak Shamir, Begin's successor.

The election campaign itself was much less vocal, violent and divisive than those of 1977 and, especially, 1981, and it was conducted in a much more subdued way. This relative calmness was to some degree due to the insistence of many public figures – the President of the State, the Chairman of the Election Commission, Supreme Court Justice Gabriel Bach and many others. Their appeals were heeded by the major and minor parties alike, both because of the more prevalent fear of divisiveness as well as because of the closely connected uncertainty about the mood of the electorate.

This uncertainty was to some degree evident in the numerous polls, although on the whole most of them predicted a victory of Labour, of the Alignment, seemingly a natural outcome against the background of the Lebanon War and the deteriorating economic situation – with inflation hovering close to a yearly 400 per cent. Yet, with the approach of the elections, the Likud seemed to be gaining strength in many polls – and this was, as we shall see, certainly borne out by the results of the elections themselves. Whatever the results of the polls, the mood of uncertainty was indeed prevalent, and there can be no doubt that it contributed to the relative calm of the election campaign.

Although themes that were ethnic, religious and anti-religious (or rather against religious coercion, i.e. against the imposition of restrictive religious laws), themes as well as differences in policies, were obviously stressed in the campaign by the different parties, yet this was done in a very subdued tone. There were few violent outbursts as compared with the 1981 elections.

Indeed, many of the major concrete policies or themes as advocated especially by the two major parties – the Likud and the Labour – could often be seen as not too dissimilar. There were, of course, differences in emphasis and above all in the overall symbols of identity presented by the different parties. The Likud propaganda stressed that it represented the 'National Camp' and called on everybody to join it – implying that those who did not vote for it were not part of this 'real' national bloc. It stressed also very strongly the theme of Eretz Israel – of not giving up any part of it. Labour stressed more of its heritage of constructive and sane policies, obviously implying that the policies undertaken by the Likud were neither constructive nor sane.

The various other parties appealed above all to their own constituencies: the religious to various parts of the religious camp; the *Ratz* (CRM) group headed by Shulamit Aloni to the more leftist or secularized parts of the Israeli public, and so on.

Two new lists appeared – at either end of the political spectrum. First there was the 'Progressive List' group, combining Arab and Jewish leaders – with a much heavier emphasis on the former – with a strong emphasis on Jewish–Arab coexistence, and appealing mostly to the Arab population (and hence strongly opposed by *Hadash* (former *Rakach*) ) and to some of the far more leftist and dovish elements in the Jewish population.

At the other end of the political spectrum was the list *Kach* headed by Rabbi Meir Kahane (the leader of the American Jewish Defence League and still holding an American passport), voicing the most extreme Jewish nationalistic, almost racist, militant anti-Arab stand.

Both lists were initially banned by the Electoral Commission – the first seemingly on the basis of security allegations (allegations that their leaders were close to the PLO and hence constituted security risks), the second seemingly on the basis of its electoral manifesto. Both appealed to the Supreme Court which in an unanimous verdict of five judges reversed the decision of the Electoral Commission and permitted them to run in the election.

## Election results and the formation of the Government of National Unity

Table 18.1 shows the results of the elections. From the point of view of the

**Table 18.1   Results of the Elections for the Knesset, 1984**

| List | Seats | | Votes | | Percentage |
|---|---|---|---|---|---|
| Alignment | 44 | (47)[a] | 724,074 | (708,107) | 34.9 |
| Likud | 41 | (48) | 661,302 | (718,299) | 31.9 |
| *Tehia* | 5 | ( 3) | 83,037 | ( 44,677) | 4.0 |
| NRP | 4 | ( 6) | 73,530 | ( 95,423) | 3.5 |
| *Hadash* | 4 | ( 4) | 69,815 | ( 64,452) | 3.4 |
| *Shas* | 4 | ( 0) | 63,605 | | 3.1 |
| *Shinui* | 3 | ( 2) | 54,747 | ( 29,834) | 2.6 |
| *Ratz* (CRM) | 3 | ( 1) | 49,698 | ( 27,875) | 2.4 |
| *Yahad* | 3 | ( 0) | 46,302 | | 2.2 |
| Progressive List | 2 | ( 0) | 38,012 | | 1.8 |
| Agudat Israel | 2 | ( 4) | 36,079 | ( 72,322) | 1.7 |
| *Morasha* | 2 | ( 0) | 33,287 | | 1.6 |
| *Tami* | 1 | ( 3) | 31,103 | ( 44,431) | 1.5 |
| *Kach* | 1 | ( 0) | 25,907 | | 1.2 |
| *Ometz* | 1 | ( 0) | 23,845 | | 1.2 |

Note: a. The numbers in parentheses are those of the 1981 elections.
Source: Government of Israel, Press Bureau.

contest between the two major parties, the results of the elections were inconclusive: both lost in comparison with the 1981 elections, although the Likud lost more and, on the whole, the 'leftist' bloc gained. None of these parties was able, however much it tried, to form a government – leading indeed to the formation in September 1984 of the government of national unity (or national coalition).

There were also some other rather interesting, potentially even very significant, developments in the political scene.

First, there was the growth of different extremist groups. Rabbi Meir Kahane did muster enough votes to enter the Knesset, staging with his followers, after the election, many provocative public appearances – even if all this did seem to give rise to a growing dissociation from him by all the other groups not only of the left but also of the right.

*Tehia* – headed by Professor Yuval Neeman and the former Chief of Staff, Raful (Rafael Eitan), who, together with his supporters, joined the list – representing the more radical elements of the right, increased its seats in the Knesset from three to five, to no small extent through the votes of younger people including soldiers in the army.

The Progressive List gained two seats probably at the expense of both *Hadash* (which retained its members but had hoped to gain more) and some of the groups in the Jewish sector, whose votes in the former elections probably went to *Sheli*.

Some interesting developments also took place among the ethnic and religious groups. The major, more or less openly 'ethnic' (Sephardi) party within the Zionist sector, *Tami* (its leader Aharon Abu-Hatzeira was formerly a member of the National Religious Party and a member of the Cabinet on its behalf) lost heavily – to the weakening of the direct ethnic appeal.

At the same time a rather dramatic development took place in the ultra-orthodox sector, hitherto represented by Agudat Israel. Within this sector, there developed a very strong rebellion of Sephardi elements against the hitherto monopoly of positions of leadership – seats in the Knesset and the budgetary allocations – by different Askhenazi groups. A new religious ethnic group crystallized, *Shas* (Sephardi Tora Guardians), composed almost entirely of Sephardi, and whose spiritual leader was the former Sephardi Chief Rabbi, Ovadia Joseph. It was very successful in the earlier municipal elections in Jerusalem. In the elections to the Knesset it gained three (four) seats at the expense of Agudat Israel, who lost two seats and remained with only two.

A split also took place in the National Religious Party: a more militant national and religious *Morasha* group left the party getting two seats in the Knesset, while the NRP was left with only four compared with six in the 1981 elections.

A new group, *Yahad* (Together), was formed under the leadership of Ezer Weizmann, the former Minister of Defence, proclaiming itself to be in between Labour and Likud, but leaning more towards Labour, in some ways reminiscent of *Dash* in the 1977 elections.

After protracted negotiations, when it became clear that neither of the two major parties could form a government, and probably helped also by the feelings of both the new (Shimon Peres) and the outgoing (Yitzhak Shamir) Prime Ministers that this was their last chance of retaining the leadership of their respective parties, a Government of National Unity was formed in September 1984.

This government was supported by nine parties: Labour, Likud, *Yahad*, *Ometz*, National Religious Party, *Shas*, *Shinui*, Agudat Israel and *Morasha*, all of which, except Agudat Israel, were represented in the mammoth cabinet of twenty-five (but not in the inner cabinet of ten), many of the small parties by Ministers without Portfolio.

The government was based on a written agreement between the two major parties which stipulated, among other conditions, that the Prime Ministership would rotate between Shimon Peres and Yitzhak Shamir for periods of twenty-five months (i.e. half of the term of the Knesset), with Peres being the first Prime Minister with Shamir as Deputy Prime Minister and Minister of Foreign Affairs – positions which would go to Peres when Shamir became Prime Minister.

The coalition agreement included also several items about internal and external policies, with a strong emphasis on the importance of coping with the economic problems and rather general statements about the policy of settlements and possibilities of peace negotiations with the Arabs. These statements leaned somewhat – indeed only somewhat – towards a rather modified Labour stance, but on the whole they were too general to give any clear indications of future policy.

Within the cabinet the key positions were allocated as follows: Labour took the Ministries of Defence, Education and Culture, Police, Agriculture and Health and Energy; Likud (Liberal) took the Ministries of Finance, and Justice; the Likud took the Ministries of Construction and Housing, Labour and Social Affairs, and Industry and Trade. Other positions were distributed more or less equally between Labour and Likud and various minor parties. Ezer Weizmann became a Minister in the Prime Minister's office.

One of the great gainers in this group was Ariel Sharon, who after the Kahan report was Minister Without Portfolio but has now become Minister of Industry and Trade.

One of the first outcomes of the formation of the government was a split within the Labour camp – *Mapam* and one *Avoda* member, Yossi Sarid, did not join and left the Alignment. In addition, the government was not supported by *Ratz* (CRM), by *Tehia*, by *Tami*, by the Progressive List, and by *Hadash* – thus possibly indicating the crystallization of new developments both on the left and on the right of the political scene.

The first steps of the government were in the economic field; there was a series of seemingly drastic signs – a rise in the prices of subsidized foods, an announcement about far-reaching cuts in the budget, and increases in taxes – the effects of all of which have, of course, yet to be seen – especially whether they will be able to effect far-reaching economic changes without intensive social upheaval and turmoil.

At the same time, when presenting the government to the Knesset, the new Prime Minister came out with a very strong appeal to the Arab world in general and to King Hussein in particular to enter into peace with Israel, and the new Defence Minister, Yitzhak Rabin (Prime Minister in 1974–7) came out rather strongly in a meeting with the settlers in Judea and Samaria against the conflation of settlement and security – stressing that he does not see any necessary relation between the two.

## Some repercussions

It is extremely difficult to predict how successful and effective these policies will be, especially given the rather far-reaching differences and former enmity between the different groups composing the government. There seem, at least at this point, but few indications as to how long it will last, how effective its policies will be, and to what degree it will be able to overcome the immobility which may be inherent in its very composition, as well as the internal bickering within and between different parties comprising it.

But although, needless to say, the answers to these questions will greatly influence the further development of Israeli society, especially its ability to overcome the various divisive and stagnative tendencies analysed above, yet some tentative observations which bear on our analysis earlier in this chapter may not be out of place.

The pre-election campaign, the results of the elections and the formation of the Government of National Unity do indeed attest to the point stressed in our previous analysis – namely that Israeli society is undergoing a process of far-reaching transformation and recrystallization. They attest also to the fact that the directions and outcomes of this transformation, the different themes, old and new, will come together. What exact new institutional formats, political groups and conflicts will develop, and to what extent Israeli society will be able to overcome the divisive and stagnative tendencies analysed above, are as yet very difficult to know – even if some of the major problems it is facing are well known.

And yet some very tentative indications can, as we have mentioned above, be pointed out. First of all, the very formation of the broad coalition government, and the muted tone of the elections, do attest to some attempts to minimize the divisiveness and conflicts that were so visible before.

Although the very establishment of this government was a consequence of the stalemate in the elections, yet the fear of the renewed divisiveness was very much in the background. The call for the formation of such government immediately after the election was first made by four eminent authors, all of them identified with the Alignment, two very well known for their dovish stance. It was taken up by many public personalities, and was expressly indicated by the President of the State when he summoned Peres and entrusted him with the formation of the government. It was also stressed as a condition of their joining or supporting the government by several political groups – especially by Weizmann's *Yahad*.

Perhaps the most important outcome of the formation of this new government is the weakening, at least for the time being, of the mutual delegitimation of the two camps – Labour and Likud. This may perhaps – especially if the government will last for some time and will show some effectiveness – signal the beginning of the establishment of some new framework of solidarity, possibly of new rules of the game. It may also provide important support for the continuity and strengthening of democratic institutions; to halt the erosion of the commitment to them.

But, needless to say, this is only a possibility – it certainly is as yet far from being assured – and the ability of the new government to maintain itself, and to be successful in the implementation of its policies in general and in the first period of its rule in particular will be of crucial importance from this point of view, and for the future of Israeli society.

# Concluding Reflections

## The Jewish Re-Entry Into History and its Problems
### *A unique story*

We have come to the end of our story – but the story itself is continuously unfolding.

The story told in this book has many dimensions. On the seemingly simplest level it is the story of a small society built up by groups of revolutionary pioneers, by a movement of colonizatory settlement in order to create a place of refuge and of national security for an old–new nation. Accordingly, this society has, as we have seen, shared many of the characteristics of other revolutionary, pioneering, settler societies and of other small modern societies.

Many of the developments and changes in the format of Israeli society – such as the transformation of revolutionary pioneering elites into ruling ones, the process of the routinization of the original revolutionary vision, the various processes of development and modernization, the differences between internal/external sectors – were to some degree common to other post-revolutionary, developing or small modern societies.

So the ways in which this society coped with many of these problems and its consequent institutional dynamics, the processes of the crystallization and change of its institutional moulds, could easily be compared with those of other, relatively similar societies. Obviously these processes differed here, as in all other such societies, according to the specific historical, geopolitical and socio-economic forces and circumstances of Israeli society, but these were in a way 'normal', understandable differences – relatively easily amenable to a comparative analysis.

On this level of analysis, the single most distinctive characteristic of Israeli society was the combination of all these characteristics with a strong national movement and with settlement in an alien environment which became more and more hostile to it – making the security problem one of the most important aspects or dimensions of this society.

But the unique feature of the developments in Israeli society was their close interweaving with the history of the Jewish people, with Jewish history. It was, of course, this close interweaving that brought all these pioneers to Eretz Israel, to Palestine, and to the specific encounter with Arab nationalism. But it was not 'just' the development of a modern national movement and of the clash between two nations or two national movements that was unique – although, needless to say, these facts were in themselves enough to explain many of the specific characteristics of Israeli society in general, especially those derived from the special significance of the security dimension in its basic formation in particular.

But of crucial importance for the understanding of this society was the fact that the nature of this national revolutionary movement was greatly shaped by its specific relation, its close interweaving, with a broad civilizational vision – the Jewish civilizational vision – originally couched, as was the case with most of the Great Civilizations, in religious terms, and with Jewish religion and tradition as developed in the history of the Jewish people. The story of the Jewish people is not, however, just a story of a religious tradition in the narrow sense; or of attempts to maintain religious sects or groups. It can only be understood in terms of their having been carriers of a civilizational vision, and of their concomitant attempts to reconstruct the world in terms of the basic premisses of this vision.

## The development of the Halakhic mould

The old Israelite and Jewish civilization was, as we have seen, among the very first of the so-called Great Civilizations, certainly the first in the realm of the Mediterranean and among the monotheistic religions, and accordingly a very complex vision developed within it with very strong universalistic orientations and very distinct institutional premisses and frameworks. The implementation of this vision became closely interwoven with one people, giving rise to a very complex construction of collective identity – comprising, as we have seen, primordial, political, religious and ethical components. The implementation of this vision – creating a new society at the crossroads of many nations and of great empires – took place also in very specific geopolitical conditions, a situation which repeated itself with the Zionist settlement in Eretz Israel.

The conjunction of these geopolitical conditions together with the specific combination of civilizational and national collectivity gave rise to the very turbulent history of the Jewish people and to a very peculiar pattern of national continuity and civilizational changes, of shifts in the modes of implementation of its specific civilizational vision.

This turbulent history stretched from the early settlement in Eretz Israel through the period of the Judges and of the Kingdom of Judah and Israel; the destruction and disappearance of the former; the later destruction of the Davidic monarchy in Judah and the Babylonian exile; the return from Babylon and the turbulent history of the Second Commonwealth period, up to the destruction of the Second Temple; the loss of political independence and the dwindling of the centre of Eretz Israel and the dispersion of the Jewish people.

These political changes comprised far-reaching changes in the nature of the implementation of its civilizational vision. The first such major shift took place as we have seen, in the period of return from Babylon and during the period of the Second Commonwealth; the second major shift occurred after the destruction of the Second Temple and the gradual crystallization and predominance of the Rabbinical mould, the mould of Halakha.

This mould, which started to crystallize during the period of the Second Commonwealth, was certainly not predominant during this period, nor was it a homogeneous one. Even when this mould became fully crystallized and the predominant one in the life of the Jewish people, it was not homogeneous; it comprised many heterogeneous orientations derived from other earlier moulds, as well as a great heterogeneity in its own components.

All these components – the philosophical or mystical orientations, the different emphases on learning and study as against more popular ones of prayer; the political orientations, the different combinations between primordial, national, religious and ethnical orientations, the continuous tension between universalistic and particularistic orientation and many others which we have discussed above – did not disappear with the crystallization of this mould; they became hemmed in within its basic framework, often erupting from within it.

The historical circumstances in which this mould became predominant and institutionalized – namely, those of the loss of political independence and of dispersal – did however imply a far-reaching shift and change of the institutional area in which this civilizational vision and the institutional mould generated by it could be implemented.

Because of these circumstances, the Jewish civilizational vision could no longer be implemented in the political arena nor in an overall societal-institutional complex of a territorial society. Such implementation became confined to the area regulating the daily life of Jews in their private, communal and cultural–religious settings; in the centres of prayer and of study and in the internal arrangements of their communal life – although within this framework it was very creative and innovative. At the same time the Jews lived as a dispersed minority, in a situation of political subjugation, in the institutional margins of other societies and civilizations. In these circumstances, the more universalistic, as well as political and Messianic, orientations became relegated to a distant future and not related to any of the concrete institutional settings in which they lived, while the host civilizations treated the Jews both as a pariah people as well as potential competitors.

It is, of course, a moot question whether there was any 'necessary', logical relation or connection between the full crystallization and predominance of this mould and the loss of political independence and dispersion, or whether the conjunction was accidental or at most implied as in the Talmudic portrayal of Rabbi Yohanan Ben-Zakai's move to Yavneh, the attempt to save whatever could be saved from the possibility of implementing this vision in an extremely adverse political situation. Whatever the answer to this question – if there is indeed one such answer – there can be no doubt that there developed a conjunction between the two – between the loss of political independence and dispersal and the growing predominance of the Rabbinical mould, a conjunction which necessarily also narrowed the scope of the applications of the

Halakhic mould and of its basic orientations.

## The Zionist movement and settlement in Israel

This specific civilizational mould, the mould of the Halakha, started to break down with the beginning of the modern age, with the triple process of secularization and enlightenment; of political and ideological universalism; and of modernization. The conjunction of all these weakened the traditional collective boundaries of the Jewish people and culture, and also opened up before them both the potentiality of finding new areas for the implementation of the Jewish civilizational vision and the possibility of disappearance as a collective identity, through assimilation or annihilation.

The Zionist movement and the settlement in Eretz Israel constituted, as we have seen, the most revolutionary outcomes of this opening up. They were orientated both against the assumption of the traditional orthodox way of life, and against the different modern patterns of life and movements that had developed among the Jews in Western, Central and East Europe. Implicitly, ideologically, they were in principle also strongly opposed to great migratory movements of Jews from Europe – even if actually there was but little encounter or confrontation between them.

This rebellion, this revolutionary orientation against these realities of Jewish life in the nineteenth and twentieth centuries, made the Zionist movement into one of the modern revolutionary, as well as national, movements, albeit a rather special one – with a strong emphasis on pioneering settlement, on migratory movement and on carrying a civilizational vision – the closest to which was probably, as we have seen, the earlier Puritan settlement in North America. The crux of this rebellion and revolution was an attempt to bring the Jewish people – and civilization – back into history; to establish a place of security for the Jewish people, to solve the 'Jewish problem'; to reconstitute for them a territorial–political country and one arena in which they could attempt to implement the civilizational vision in a 'total' institutional setting, in the setting of a national territorial community, and ultimately of an independent state.

These attempts to implement the Jewish civilizational vision differed however to a very great extent from those in the period of the Second Temple – the last time Jewish people had had such an opportunity – although many of the basic orientations and premises of this vision had indeed persisted, even if in changing forms and content, and although the geopolitical situation in which they found themselves was – perhaps with a vengeance – very similar to that of that earlier period.

Unlike the period of the Second Temple, these attempts to implement the Jewish civilizational vision were orientated not only to the political arena, but also to the social and institutional one. Moreover, the relations to other civilizations were not necessarily as antagonistic as in the period of the Second Temple, and in the long period of the (especially medieval) Galut. The civilizational competition, as against the national or 'racial' encounters with their tragic culmination in the Holocaust, was, given the transformation of the civilizational visions in the modern world, more open and seemingly benign – although, of course, many of the antagonistic elements existed on many different levels.

Moreover, the carriers of this vision were now much more conscious of the problems involved in such implementation; indeed, in many ways, the Zionist movement was the epitome of this consciousness or awareness.

Thus Israeli society had in a sense taken up a double task, a double burden: that of finding ways of building a viable modern society in a rather hostile as well as underdeveloped environment, as well as that of combining such institution-building with some of the basic themes of the Jewish civilizational vision.

It was this combination that provided, as we have indicated throughout this book, many of the specific dynamics of the Israeli society which distinguished it from other post-revolutionary, modern, national, colonizatory, migratory or developing societies, in addition to those of the specific characteristics which were related to its geopolitical setting.

This combination became institutionalized in several of the characteristics of Israeli society. First of all, it became closely connected with the attempt to build a small society which at the same time aimed to be a centre of great creativity – a creativity rooted in the Jewish civilizational vision.

Second, this very rebellion against the concrete reality of Jewish life in the traditional and modern Diaspora not only reinforced, renewed or brought out in the open the basic themes and orientations that were latent in the earlier periods of Jewish history, but also greatly transformed most of them. It transformed these themes and orientations from being purely intellectual ones into being embedded into institutional areas and frameworks. All the major themes and tensions of Jewish tradition and civilization – the tension between universalism and particularism, between internal closed solidarity and solidarity as a base for far-reaching social, ethical and cultural creativity; between populist overtones and emphasis upon excellence in different areas of such creativity – became related to the construction and working of concrete institutional formats and overall institutional frameworks of the State. The same was true first of the tensions between the semi-Messianic future and the emphasis on the present which was no longer confined in the moulds of the Halakha and of communal life; and second of the different orientations to Eretz Israel and to Galut. These tensions became connected with new ones which developed with the implementation of the Zionist vision – those between the emphasis on the territorial political dimensions and the orientations to institution-building, between the conception of the State of Israel as a place of refuge and security as against an arena of national renaissance.

All these tensions found new literary and intellectual expressions also in large parts of the modern Diaspora, first in Europe up to the Second World War and then, and above all, in the United States. In Eastern Europe, and to a much smaller degree in the United States, they were also connected to some degree with new patterns of institution-building, but it was only in Eretz Israel that they became closely interwoven with the working of the overall institutional moulds of Israeli society.

It was thus indeed not only that in Eretz Israel there developed variegated patterns of creativity. It was above all the different cultural and political themes, those connected with the constitution and running the territorial, national society of a State that constituted the epitome of the Zionist revolution – and its greatest continuous challenge.

In this context, of special importance were the dialectical relations of Israel with the Diaspora, as a focus of rebellion, as a reservoir of leadership, against the stagnative tendencies inherent in any post-revolutionary or small society; as a source of support as well as seemingly another possibly competitive avenue for the implementation of the Jewish civilizational vision. And gradually there also developed, as we have seen, a new type of encounter with Jewish orthodoxy.

The first stage of this attempt to create a territorial, ultimately politically independent, Jewish entity which would also be an arena for the implementation of the Jewish civilizational vision – the process of settlement of the Yishuv, and the first phases of the State of Israel – was, as we have seen, a story of relatively great success. During this stage a viable, institutional, modern, democratic society was set up, a framework which combined the construction of a national society with some of the themes of Jewish tradition and civilization and which developed a distinct, specific pattern or mode of modern society.

This specific Israeli institutional mould, the specific pattern of Israeli modernity, was characterized by a constitutional democratic system with certain strong restrictive overtones; by the seemingly natural granting of principled access to the centre to all sectors of the population – and initially mitigated by development of the clientelistic mechanisms; by the appropriation by the centre of the transformed Zionist and Labour symbols; by continuous economic development within the framework of a mixed, quite heavily controlled economy; by a strong emphasis on the construction of an old-new nation with a very heavy emphasis on creativity orientated to reconstruct a new national and cultural tradition and renaissance.

This new institutional mould naturally went far beyond what the Jews could have developed in the period of dispersion in the countries of settlement, in the networks of traditional Kehillot, communities and centres of learning, or in the more dispersed and diversified organizations and ways of life of more modern times. It was not only just development of additional institutional arenas – such as the political, the military, or the economic one of agriculture and of basic industries – but above all, of course, the fact that all these were brought together under the canopy of a new autonomous collectivity, of an overall collective institutional framework that was of crucial importance. It was this fact that constituted the epitome of the collective entry of

Jews into modern history.

Within this framework the perennial themes and orientations of Jewish civilization were closely connected with the basic themes and tensions of Jewish political culture – those related to the issues of solidarity mentioned above as well as the tensions between legal order, and the strong antinomian and semi-anarchistic tendencies inherent in this culture.

The emphasis on solidarity was no longer confined to communal arrangements or to intellectual and literary expression; it became closely related to the working of overall political institutions and the acceptance of the rule of law, in particular to the army and to the civilian control of the army.

Similarly, the emphasis on civility and the rule of law and its tensions with populistic as well as antinomian and semi-anarchistic political tendencies, with the emphasis on a Higher Law, went out from the narrow intellectual confines to which it had been limited in the medieval period and became closely interwoven with the functioning of the framework of a fully-fledged society and polity with the different dimensions of its institutional format and political forces. The very strong future orientation also became connected with concrete institution-building and hence with the exigencies of the present – giving rise to different forms of confrontation between the two.

The same was true, of course, of the specific Zionist themes closely connected with the former, general Jewish ones – especially the tension between being a normal nation and a light to the nations and/or a Jewish nation; between the emphasis on the territorial, political dimensions and the orientations to institution-building, between the conception of the State of Israel as a place of refuge and security as against an arena of national renaissance.

The specific achievement of the institutional mould that developed in Israel was not, as we have seen, that it obliterated these different orientations and tensions. On the contrary, all of them continued to exist within it and their impact on social life was – given the fact that they became interwoven in concrete institutional settings – much greater. Rather, this achievement lay in the fact that this institutional mould, with its specific characteristics was relatively successful in the regulation of these tensions. As a result these tensions reinforced the working of the mould, while their more anarchic potentials were regulated and held in tow by the development and continuity of its central institutional frameworks as well as by the relatively strong internal cohesion of the elites and broader sections of the population. The crucial test of the Israeli institutional model came, from this point of view, with the opening up of its initially rather restrictive features.

## The disintegration of the Labour–Zionist institutional mould

As has been the case in all post-revolutionary societies, the success of this mould exacted its prices. The toll of routinization; of the exhaustion of many of the dimensions of the original vision; of the transformation of revolutionary elites into the ruling class; of growing dissociation between different elites; of the weakening of solidary frameworks, all gave rise, as we have analysed in great detail above, to the disintegration of this mould.

The processes leading to this disintegration – as well as their repercussions – evinced several characteristics common to other post-revolutionary and small modern societies. Israeli society shared with these societies the tendencies to the routinization and demystification of the original revolutionary vision – the stagnative and inward-looking tendencies of both revolutionary and small societies.

But the ways in which these processes and their repercussions crystallized in Israeli society evinced some specific characteristics. Here was a small and a revolutionary society, with a specially important security dimension. The impact of these factors on the relations between inward- and outward-looking orientations, and the heavy toll on the structure of solidarity, lent a very special intensity to these processes – making even more surprising the continuity of the democratic frameworks, the like of which could be found, among such societies, only in the United States.

Thus indeed, the processes leading to this disintegration highlighted, in Israel perhaps even more than in other such societies, some of the choices inherent in the very institutionalization and dynamic development of such a mould. Above all it was a choice between commitment to a vision – with its monolithic potentialities and potential power orientation – as against openness and pluralism; between elitist and against populist orientations; between the stress on obligations as against rights and entitlements; between active participation in the central frameworks of societal and cultural creativity as against the more passive or privatized ones – and the great challenge of finding continuously new ways of combining these various orientations without entirely giving up any of them.

The sharp articulation of these choices or dilemmas in Israeli society was largely due to the fact that the institutionalization of this mould and of its disintegration were closely connected with, and intensified by, the problem of implementing the Jewish civilizational vision in the specific setting of a small, beleaguered society. So it also highlighted the problems and dilemmas of the Jewish re-entry into history.

So the growing dissociation between different elites and the weakening of frameworks of solidarity gave rise to the emergence of different themes of Jewish civilization and of the Zionist vision – the Messianic, territorial, solidary, or primordial components of the collective identity all emerged, each claiming its autonomy from the other themes, challenging the validity of the other themes and the tensions with them, and claiming total predominance in the direction of the institutional formation of the society.

In parallel, there took place the weakening of the institutional frameworks and ideological symbols which brought together the various themes of Jewish political culture, regulating and controlling the more anarchic or distributive–

bargaining ones. It was easy for a tendency to develop combining the anarchic politics of the Higher Law and the solidarity of small sectors. Paradoxically enough, because of the existence of the Jewish State, such a combination could become connected with the giving up of the responsibility (which was quite strong in the medieval communities) for the whole community and for the maintenance of some order within its frameworks.

Indeed there were many indications that these political tendencies, when transposed into the setting of a territorial state, and a modern democratic one in particular, might undermine the very viability of its institutional frameworks – as they probably did in the period of the Second Commonwealth.

## The challenge remains

These developments, attendant on the disintegration of the initial institutional mould of Israeli society, posed in a very sharp way the problem inherent in building a small society in a hostile environment to carry the burden of some mode of the implementation of the Jewish civilizational vision.

The growing awareness of this problem gave rise to some ruminations in different directions. Would Israel do best to become just a 'normal' nation? Would the implementation of the Jewish civilizational vision in the free communities of the Diaspora be viable? Would orthodoxy be the best assurance of the survival of the Jewish people?

And yet, the varied experiences of Jewish modern history in general, and of the development of Israeli society in particular, point out the great improbability of the success of any of these directions.

The development of Israel into a normal small society, dissociated from the Jewish civilizational orientations, is rather doubtful, as it might give rise to many of its stagnative tendencies, to a weakening of motivation and an unwillingness to carry its apparent burden. It might also become very closely connected with the development or combination of politics of Higher Law and religious fundamentalism, and the concomitant weakening of its institutional fabric.

The story of the non-orthodox Diaspora, especially in the United States, is indeed a story of great success in terms of the different modes of participation of Jews in many areas of activity in their host societies, and in developing special Jewish activities. Yet as we have seen, the loss of creative tension in their relations to Israel may indeed slowly erode their Jewish identity and the springs of their specific Jewish activity – even if they do not lead, as in Europe, to their physical extermination – just as the loss of such tension within Israel may give rise to tendencies towards stagnation within it.

With respect to the new type or types of modern orthodoxy, there is indeed, as far as one can see now, a great feasibility that this sector of the Jewish people may be able, demographically as well as culturally, to survive in the conditions of modern society. But this type of survival is predicted on an entirely different premiss from those which were predominant in the medieval times, in the periods of the predominance of the Halakha. In the conditions of a modern, open society, such survival involves giving up the civilizational vision; development into a rather closed religious group or groups or sects; with some emphasis on specific Jewish 'peoplehood'.

But at the same time the attempts to impose an orthodox solution for Israeli society would face the difficulty both of combining it with the working of a complex modern society in general and a democratic one in particular, and of it serving as a focus of creativity, motivation and attraction for many – indeed most – of its inhabitants and the Jews in the Diaspora.

Thus indeed, all these developments belie that accusation made by Hermann Cohen, the outstanding Jewish–German philosopher, against the Zionists, that 'the lot wishes now to be happy' – that is to be a normal people, not torn by the tensions which, according to him, are of the essence of Jewish living.

Indeed, the story of the implementation of the Zionist vision has shown that such happiness was not to be theirs – not only because of the difficulties of colonization and security, but above all because the very process of the implementation of the Zionist vision depended on the continuity of such tensions, not only, as described by Hermann Cohen, on the intellectual level, but also on the institutional and geopolitical levels.

It is perhaps some, albeit dim, awareness of these problems, difficulties or tensions that looms behind one of the texts from the Talmud included in the closing prayer of Yom Kippur, the Neila, which says:

> Thy people's needs are large, their knowledge broken,
> Their wants and wishes they can scarce express.

Many people may have thought that implementation of the Zionist vision would do away with this tension by diminishing the needs of the Jewish people, but the process of this implementation has indicated that this did not happen. This process has indicated that the real challenge of this implementation – which seems indeed to be very closely related to the very survival of Israeli society, and in many ways also of the Jewish people and civilization – lies in finding institutional frameworks and symbolic meanings within which some continuously changing, moving balance between all these tendencies would enable the development of the creative potentialities inherent in them while at the same time curbing the anarchic and stagnative ones. This challenge looms still and continuously before Israeli society.

# Select Bibliography

## Jewish History

GENERAL TREATISES ON JEWISH HISTORY

Baron, S. W., *A Social and Religious History of the Jews*, 2nd ed. (New York, Columbia University Press, 1966).

Ben-Sasson, H. H. (ed.), *A History of the Jewish People*, contributions by A. Malamot (London, Weidenfeld and Nicolson, 1976).

—— and Ettinger, S. (eds.), *Jewish Society Throughout the Ages* (New York, Schocken Books, 1969). (A collection of studies first published in the *Journal of World History*, vol. XI, no. 1–2 (1968).)

Finkelstein, L. (ed.), *The Jews; Their History, Culture and Religions* (New York, Schocken Books, 1970–1).

Goldin, J. (ed.), *The Jewish Expression* (New York, Bantam Books, 1970).

Gross, N. (ed.), *Economic History of the Jews* (New York, Schocken Books, 1975). (A collection of articles by Salo W. Baron, Arcadius Kahan and others from the *Encyclopedia Judaica*.)

Kedourie, E. (ed.), *The Jewish Worlds* (London, Thames and Hudson, 1979).

Seltzer, R. M., *Jewish People, Jewish Thought – The Jewish Expression in History* (New York, Macmillan, 1980).

WORKS ON SPECIFIC PERIODS OF JEWISH
HISTORY UP TO MODERN TIMES

Baer, I., *A History of the Jews in Christian Spain*, Vols. I–II (Philadelphia, Jewish Publication Society of America, 1966).

Dubnov, S., *History of the Jews in Russia and Poland*, 3 vols. (Vol. II) (New York, 1937; also Philadelphia, 1946).

Goitein, S. D., *A Mediterranean Society, the Jewish Communities of the Arab World as Portrayed in the Documents of the Cairo Geniza* (Berkeley, University of California Press, 1967–78).

Hengel, M., *Judaism and Hellenism*, 2nd vs. (London, SCM Press, 1979).

Kaufmann, Y., *The Religion of Israel* (New York, Schocken Books, 1972).

Neusner, J., *First Century Judaism in Crisis* (Nashville, Alingdon Press, 1975).

—— *Ancient Israel After Catastrophe – The Religious World View of the Mishna* (Charlottesville, University Press of Virginia, 1983).

Roth C., *A History of the Marranos* (Philadelphia, Jewish Publication Society of America, 1932).

Safrai, S. and Stern, M. (eds.), *The Jewish People in the First Century* (Assen, Van Gorcum, 1974–6).

Tcherikover, V. A., *Hellenistic Civilization and the Jews* (Philadelphia, Jewish Publication Society of America, 1959).

Urbach, E. E., *The Sages – Their Concepts and Beliefs*, 2nd vs. (Jerusalem, Magnes Press, 1975).

SELECTED ASPECTS OF JEWISH LIFE AND CIVILIZATION

Baer, I., *Galut* (New York, Schocken Books, 1947).

Baron, S. W., *The Jewish Community: Its History and Structure to the American Revolution*, 3 vols. (Philadelphia, Jewish Publication Society of America, 1948).

Finkelstein, L., *Jewish Self-Government in the Middle Ages* (New York, The Jewish Theological Seminary, 1924).

Guttmann, J., *Philosophies of Judaism, the History of Jewish Philosophy from Biblical Times to Franz Rosenzweig*, Introduction by R. Werblowsky, Trans. by David Silverman (New York, Schocken Books, 1973).

Katz, J., *Exclusiveness and Tolerance – Studies in Jewish–Gentile Relations in Medieval and Modern Times* (Oxford, Clarendon Press, 1961).

Katz, S. T. (ed.), *Jewish Philosophers* (Jerusalem, Keter Publishing House, 1975).

Parks, J., *The Conflict of the Church and the Synagogue – A Study in the Origins of Antisemitism* (New York, Atheneum, 1969).

Scholem, G., *Major Trends in Jewish Mysticism*, 3rd ed. (New York, Schocken Books, 1954). (Originally published in 1941.)

—— *On the Kabbalah and Its Symbolism*, Trans. by Ralph Manheim (New York, Schocken Books, 1965).

—— *The Messianic Idea in Judaism and Other Essays on Jewish Spirituality* (New York, Schocken Books, 1971).

—— *Sabbatai Zevi: The Mystical Messiah 1626–1676*, Trans. by J. Zwi Werblowsky (Princeton, NJ, Princeton University Press, 1973).

—— *Kabbalah* (New York, Quadrangle/The New York Times Book Co., 1974). (Based on his articles in the *Encyclopedia Judaica*.)

Werblowsky, R. and Karo, J. Z. J., *Lawyer and Mystic* (Philadelphia, Jewish Publication Society of America, 1977). (First published in 1962.)

### MODERN TIMES

Hertzberg, A., *The French Enlightenment and the Jews* (New York, Columbia University Press, 1968).

Katz, J., *Out of the Ghetto – The Social Background of Jewish Emancipation 1770–1870* (Cambridge, Mass., Harvard University Press, 1973).

—— *Anti Semitism – From Religious Hatred to Racial Rejection* (Cambridge, Mass., Harvard University Press, 1979).

—— 'The Jewish Diaspora: "Minority Positions and Majority Aspirations" ', *The Jerusalem Quarterly*, 25 (Fall 1982), pp. 68–78.

Mendelsohn, E., *The Jews of East Central Europe Between the World Wars* (Bloomington, Ind., 7 Indians Press, 1983).

Mendes-Flohr, P. R. and Reinharz, J. (eds.), *The Jews in the Modern World – A Documentary History* (New York, Oxford University Press, 1980).

Meyer, M., *The Origins of the Modern Jews: Jewish Identity and European Culture in Germany, 1749–1824* (Detroit, Wayne State University Press, 1967).

Pinson, K. (ed.), *Essays on Antisemitism* (New York, Conference on Jewish Relations, 1946).

Poliakov, L., *The History of Anti-Semitism*, 3 vols., Trans. from the French by R. Howard (New York, Vanguard Press, 1965–76).

Rotenstreich, N., *Jewish Philosophy in Modern Times: from Mendelssohn to Rosenzweig* (New York, Holt, Rinehart and Winston, 1968).

Sacher, H. M., *The Course of Modern Jewish History*, updated and expanded ed. (New York, Dell, 1977).

### THE HOLOCAUST

Cohn, N., *Warrant for Genocide, The Myth of the Jewish World Conspiracy and the Protocols of the Elders of Zion* (London, Eyre and Spottiswoode, 1967).

Dawidowicz, L. S., *The War Against the Jews, 1933–1945* (New York, Holt Rinehart and Winston, 1975).

—— (ed.), *A Holocaust Reader* (New York, Behrman House, 1976).

Massing, P. W., *Rehearsal for Destruction: A Study of Political Anti-Semitism in Imperial Germany* (New York, H. Fertig, 1967).

THE ZIONIST MOVEMENT AND IDEOLOGY

Avineri, S., *The Making of Modern Zionism, the Intellectual Origins of the Jewish State* (New York, Basic Books, 1981).

Halpern, B., *The Idea of the Jewish State*; 2nd ed. (Cambridge, Mass. Harvard University Press, 1969).

Hertzberg, A. (ed.), *The Zionist Idea, a Historical Analysis and Reader*, Foreword by Emanuel Newmann (New York, Atheneum, 1970).

Katz, J., 'The Jewish National Movement – A Sociological Analysis', *Journal of World History*, Vol. 11 (1–2), pp. 267–98.

Laqueur, W., *A History of Zionism* (London, Weidenfeld and Nicolson, 1972).

Vital, D., *Zionism, the Formative Years* (Oxford, Clarendon Press, 1982).

*Zionism, Encyclopedia Judaica*, Vol. 16 (mainly the following headings: Forerunners, Roots of Hibbat-Zion, Background to the Emergence of the Movement, Ideological Evolution, Non-Zionist and Anti-Zionist Trends).

## History of the Development of the Yishuv and of Israeli Society and its Various Facets

GENERAL WORKS

Bein, A., *The Return to the Soil, a History of Jewish Settlement in Israel*, Trans. by Israel Schen (Jerusalem, Young and Hechalutz Department of the Zionist Organization, 1952).

Curtis, M. R. (ed.), *Israel, Social Structure and Change* (New Jersey, New Brunswick, Transaction Books, 1973).

Eisenstadt, S. N., *Israeli Society* (London, Weidenfeld and Nicolson, 1967).

Eylon, A., *The Israelis, Fathers and Sons* (New York, Holt, Rinehart and Winston, 1974).

Lucas, N., *The Modern History of Israel* (London, Weidenfeld and Nicolson, 1974).

Sacher, H. M., *A History of Israel – From the Rise of Zionism to our Times* (New York, A. Knopf, 1982).

Safran, N., *Israel, the Embattled Ally* (Cambridge, Mass., Harvard University Press and The Belknap Press, 1978).

Segre, D. V., *A Crisis of Identity, Israel and Zionism* (Oxford, Oxford University Press, 1980).

Shimshoni, D., *Israeli Democracy, the Middle and the Journey* (New York, The Free Press, 1982).

COLLECTIONS OF DATA

The best continuous collections of statistical data on most aspects of Israeli society can be found in *The Statistical Abstract of Israel* (Jerusalem, Central Bureau of Statistics).

The best continuous surveys and analysis of economic data can be found in the Bank of Israel *Annual Reports* (Jerusalem).

READERS

Very useful material can be found in the following readers (most of which are in Hebrew but which also contain substantial material in English).

Adler, C. and Kahane, R. (eds.), *Israel – A Society in the Making – Values, Religion and Culture – A Sociological Analysis of Sources, Material*, Vol. B. (Jerusalem, Academon Press, 1975).

Bar-Yosef, R. and Adler, C., (eds.), *Integration and Development in Israel* (in English) (Jerusalem, Israel University Press, 1970.)

Bar-Yosef, R. and Shelach, I. (eds.), *The Family in Israel – A Reader* (Jerusalem, Academon Press, 1970).

Dar, Y. (ed.) *Education in the Kibbutz: A Dual Faced Socialization* (Jerusalem, Academon Press, 1982).

Doron, A., Ninio, L. and Pishoff, I. (eds.), *Welfare Policy in Israel – A Reader* (Jerusalem, Academon Press, 1970).

Eisenstadt, S. N., Adler, C., Bar-Yosef, R. and Kahane, R. (eds.), *The Social Structure of Israel – A Reader* (Jerusalem, Academon Press, 1966).

——, ——, —— and —— (eds.), *Israel – A society in the Making: A Sociological Analysis of Source Material*, Vol. A (Jerusalem, Magnes Press 1971).

——, ——, Kahane, R. and Shelach, I. (eds.), *Stratification in Israel – A Reader* (Jerusalem, Academon Press, 1963).

Hauder, A., Kahane, R. and Rosenfeld, H. (eds.), *The Arab Society in Israel* (Jerusalem, Academon Press, 1983).

*Immigration and Absorption in Israel*, a collection of summaries of studies and surveys; regulations, laws and information concerning immigrants; Statistics 1950–1971 (Jerusalem, Academon Press, 1972).

Kahane, R. and Kopstein, S. (eds.), *Israeli Society 1965–1967 – A Reader* (Jerusalem, Academon Press, 1974).

—— and —— (eds.), *Problems of Collective Identity and Legitimation in the Israeli Society – A Reader* (Jerusalem, Academon Press, 1980).

—— Lital, N. and Homsky, E. (eds.), *Israel, a Society in the Making*, Vol. III: *Patterns of Corruption and Deviance from Common Norms in Public Institutions in the Israeli Society – Sources from Documents and Newspapers* (Jerusalem, Academon Press, 1984).

—— and Sochi, R. (eds.), *Youth Associations in the Israeli Society* (Jerusalem, Academon Press, 1980).

Lissak, M. and Gutman, H. (eds.), *Political Institutions and Processes in Israel* (Jerusalem, Academon Press, 1971).

—— and Kimmerling, B. (eds.), *Armed Forces, National Security and Society in Israel – A Reader* (Jerusalem, Academon Press), forthcoming.

——, Mizrachi, B. and Ben-David, A. (eds.), *Immigrants in Israel – A Reader* (Jerusalem, Academon Press, 1970).

Schachar, A., Weintraub, D., Cohen, H. and Shelach, I. (eds.), *Towns in Israel* (Jerusalem, Academon Press, 1973).

The English reader can find many interesting articles on all aspects of Israeli life in the *Jerusalem Quarterly*, published in Jerusalem by the Middle East Institute since 1976.

## Demographic Structure of Israel

Bachi, R., *The Population of Israel* (Jerusalem, Institute of Contemporary Jewry, The Hebrew University in Co-operation with the Prime Minister's Office, 1977).

## Economic Structure and Development of Israel

Barkai, Ch., *The Public, Histadrut, and Private Sectors in the Israeli Economy*, The Falk Institute for Economic Research in Israel, 6th Report (Jerusalem, 1954), pp. 13–90.

Barkai, Ch., 'The Israeli Economy in the Past Decade', *The Jerusalem Quarterly*, 32 (Summer 1984), pp. 16–17.

Ben Porath, Y., *The Arab Labour Force in Israel* (Jerusalem, The Falk Institute for Economic Research in Israel, 1966).

—— (ed.), *Israeli Economy, Maturing through Crises* (Cambridge, Mass., Harvard University Press, forthcoming).

Berglas, E., *Defense and the Economy: the Israeli Experience* (Jerusalem, The Falk Institute for Economic Research in Israel 1983).

Bruno, M., *External Shocks and Domestic Response: Israel's Economic Performance, 1965–1982* (Jerusalem, The Falk Institute for Economic Research in Israel, 1984).

Halevi, N. and Klinov, M. R., *The Economic Development of Israel* (New York, Praeger, 1968).

Hanoch, Q., *Income Differentials in Israel*, The Falk Institute for Economic Research in Israel, 5th Report (Jerusalem, 1961), pp. 37–132.

Metzer, J., *The Slowdown of Economic Growth in Israel: A Passing Phase or the End of a Big Spurt* (Jerusalem, The Falk Institute for Economic Research in Israel, 1983).

Pack, H., *Structural Change and Economic Policy in Israel* (New Haven, Yale University Press, 1971).

Patinkin, D., *The Israeli Economy – the First Decade* (Jerusalem, The Falk Institute for Economic Research in Israel, 1958).

Rubner, A., *The Problems of Israel Economy, the First Ten Years* (London, F. Cass, 1960).

See also the Reports of the Bank of Israel.

## Political Institutions and Processes

Akzin, B., 'Codification in a New State', *American Journal of Comparative Law* 5, 1 (Winter 1956).

—— 'The Role of Parties in Israeli Democracy', *The Journal of Politics*, 17 (1955).

Arian, A., *Ideological Change in Israel* (Cleveland, Press of Case-Western Reserve University, 1965).

—— *Consensus in Israel* (New York, General Learning Press, 1971).

—— *The Choosing People Voting Behavior in Israel* (Cleveland, Press of Case-Western Reserve University, 1973).

—— (ed.) *Israel, a Developing Society* (Tel Aviv, Pinhas Sapir Centre for Development, 1980).

—— (ed.) *The Elections in Israel, 1977* (Jerusalem Academic Press, 1980).

Aronoff, M., *Power and Ritual in the Israeli Labour Party: A Study in Political Anthropology* Assen Van Gorkum, 1976).

Birnbaum, E., *The Politics of Compromise, State and Religion in Israel* (Rutherford, Fairleigh Dickinson University Press, 1970).

Dror, Y. and Gutmann, E. (eds.), *The Government of Israel* (Jerusalem, The Hebrew University of Jerusalem, The Eliezer Kaplan School of Economics and Social Sciences, 1961).

Etzioni, A., 'Kulturkampf or Coalition, the Case of Israel', *Sociologia Religiosa*, 4 (1959).

Etzioni-Halevy, E. and Shapira, R., *Political Culture in Israel, Cleavage and Integration among Israeli Jews* (New York, Praeger, 1977).

Fein, L., *Politics in Israel* (Boston, Little Brown and Co., 1967).

Freedman, R. O. (ed.), *Israel in the Begin Era* (New York, Praeger, 1982).

Galnoor, I., *Steering The Polity: Communications and Politics in Israel* (Beverly Hills, Zaqs Publications, 1982).

Horowitz, D. and Lissak, M., *Origins of the Israeli Polity – Palestine Under Mandate* (Chicago, Chicago University Press, 1978.

Isaac, R. J., *Party and Politics in Israel* (New York, Longman, 1981).

Merhav, P., *The Israeli Left* (San Diego, Cal., Barnes A. S. and C. Inc., 1980).

Newman, D., *The Role of Gush Emunim and the Yishuv Kehilati in the West Bank, 1974–1980* (Durham, University of Durham Press, 1981).

Shimshoni, Daniel, *Israeli Democracy: the Middle of the Journey* (New York, The Free Press, 1982).

## Army and Security

Allon, Y., 'The Arab–Israeli Conflict: Some Suggested Solutions', *International Affairs*, 40 (April 1964), pp. 205–18.

Baehr, K., *Arab and Jewish Refugees: Problems and Prospects* (New York, American Christian Palestine Committee, 1953).

Horowitz, D., *Israel's Concept of Defensible Borders* (Jerusalem, Hebrew University, Leonard Davis Institute for International Relations, 1978).

—— 'Israel's war in Lebanon: New Patterns of Strategic Thinking and Civilian Military Relations',

*The Journal of Strategic Studies*, Vol. 6, No. 3 (September 1983), pp. 83–102.

—— and Kimmerling, B., 'Some Social Implications of Military Service and Reserve System in Israel', *European Journal of Sociology*, Vol. 15, No. 2 (1974), pp. 262–276.

—— and Luttwak, E., *The Israeli Army* (New York, Harper and Row, 1975).

Kimmerling, B., *The Interrupted System: Israeli Civilians in War and Routine Times* (New Jersey, New Brunswick, Transaction Books, forthcoming).

Lorch, N., *One Long War* (Jerusalem, Keter Publishing House, 1976).

Peri, Y., *Between Battles and Ballots: Israeli Military in Politics* (Cambridge, Cambridge University Press, 1983).

## Education

Ackerman, W., 'Education in Israel 1959, *Jewish Education*, Vol. 30, No. 3 (1960).

Adler, C., 'The Israeli School as a Selective Institution' in A. M. Kazamias, *Schools in Transition* (Boston, Allyn and Bacon, 1968), pp. 209–11.

Harburger, P., *Vocational Education in Israel* (Jerusalem, Ministry of Labour, 1964).

Hyman, A., *Education in Israel: A Survey* (New York, Israel Education Fund, 1965).

Kahane, R. and Starr, L., 'The Impact of Rapid Social Change on Technological Education: an Israeli Example', *Comparative Education Review*, Vol. 20, No. 2 (June 1976), pp. 165–78.

Kleinberger, A. F., *Society, Schools and Progress in Israel* (Oxford, Pergamon Press, 1969).

Minkovich, A., *An Evaluation of Israeli Elementary Schools* (Jerusalem, Hebrew University School of Education, Magnes Press, 1977).

——, Davis, D. and Bashi, J., *Success and Failure in Israeli Elementary Education* (New Brunswick, Transaction Books, 1982).

Peled, E., 'Israeli Education', in Edward Corsini and J. Raymond (eds.), *Comparative Educational Systems* (Illinois, F. E. Peakock Publishers, 1981), pp. 23–185.

'Vocational Training in Israel', *Modern Labour Review*, 86 (September 1963), pp. 1067–69.

## Absorption of Immigrants and the Ethnic Problems

Adler, C., 'Absorption of Immigrants', *Journal of Educational Sociology*, Vol. 36, No. 8 (April 1963), pp. 386–7.

Ben-Gurion, D., *First Ones* (Jerusalem, Government Printing Press, 1963).

Ben-Simon, D., *L'Integration des Juifs Nord-Africains en France* (Paris, La Haje, Mouton, 1971).

—— *Immigrants d'Afrique du Nord en Israel* (Paris, Anthropos, 1971).

Cohen, E., 'Social Images in an Israeli Development Town', *Human Relations*, 21, 2 (May 1968), pp. 163–76.

—— 'Development Towns – The Social Dynamics of "Planted" Communities in Israel' in R. Bar-Yosef and C. Adler, (eds.), *Integration and Development in Israel* (Jerusalem, Israel University Press, 1970). pp. 587–617.

—— 'Black Panthers and Israeli Society', *The Jewish Journal of Sociology*, 14 (1972), pp. 93–107.

Cremer, G., 'The Israeli Black Panthers: Fighting for Credibility and a Cause', *Victimology* 1, 3 (1976), pp. 403–13.

Deshen, S., 'Political Ethnicity and Cultural Ethnicity in Israel During the 1960s' in E. Krausz (ed.), *Studies in Israeli Society* (New Jersey, New Brunswick, Transaction Publications; 1980).

—— and Shokad, M., *The Predicaments of Homecoming: Cultural and Social Life of North African Immigrants in Israel* (New York, Ithaca, Cornell University Press, 1974).

Eisenstadt, S. N., *The Absorption of Immigrants* (London, Routledge and Kegan Paul, 1954).

Goldberg, H., 'Culture and Ethnicity in the Study of Israeli Society', *Ethnic Groups*, Vol. 1, No. 3 (1977), pp. 163–86.

Horowitz, T. R., 'Integration and the Social Gap', *Jerusalem Quarterly*, 15 (Spring 1980), pp. 133–44.

Inbar, M. and Adler, C., *Ethnic Integration in Israel* (New Jersey, New Brunswick, Transaction Books, 1977).

Katz, E., and Zloczower, A., 'Ethnic Continuity in an Israeli Town: Relations with Parents', *Human Relations*, 14 (1961), pp. 309–27.

Kraus, V. and Weintraub, D., 'Community Structure and the Status Attainment Process of the Jewish Population in Israel', *Zeitschrift für Soziologie*, 4 (Oct. 1976), pp. 346–78.

—— and ——, *Social Differentiation and Locality of Residence Spatial Distribution, Composition, and Stratification in Israel* (Rehovot, Settlement Study Centre, 1981).

Krausz, E. (ed.), *Migration, Ethnicity and Community* (New Jersey, New Brunswick, Transaction Books, 1980).

Lissak, M., *Social Mobility in Israel* (Jerusalem, Israel University Press, 1961).

Marx, E., *The Social Context of Violent Behaviour* (London, Routledge and Kegan Paul, 1978).

Matras, J., 'Intergenerational Change in Occupational Structure of Immigrant Groups in Israel', *Jewish Journal of Sociology* 7, 1 (1966), pp. 31–8.

Peres, Y., 'Ethnic Relations in Israel', *American Journal of Sociology*, 76, 6 (1976), pp. 1021–47.

Peretz, D. and Smooha, S., 'Israel's 10th Knesset Elections – Ethnic Upsurgence and the Decline of Ideology', *Middle East Journal* (Autumn 1981).

Shokeid, M., *The Impact of Migration on the Moroccan Jewish Family in Israel* (New York, Steven M. Cohen, Holms and Maier Press, 1982).

Smooha, S., *Israel Pluralism and Conflict* (London, Routledge and Kegan Paul, 1977).

Spilerman, S. and Habib, J., 'Development Town in Israel: The Role of Community in Creating Ethnic Disparities in Labor Force Characteristics', *American Journal of Sociology*, Vol. 81, No. 4 (1976), pp. 781–812.

Weingrod, A., *Israel: Group Relations in a New Society* (London, Pall Mall, 1965).

Weintraub, D. and Parness T., 'Rural Life, Orientation to Change and Modernization: A Pilot Study of Farm Youth in Israel', *Rural Sociology*, Vol. 33, No. 3 (September 1968), pp. 285–99.

## The Arabs in Israeli Society

Kahane, R., Herdan, A. and Rosenfeld H. (eds.), *Arab Society in Israel, Jerusalem – A Reader* (Jerusalem, Centre of Documentation and Research of Israeli Society, the Hebrew University, Academon Press, 1982).

Landau, J., *The Arabs in Israel: a Political Study* (London, Oxford University Press, 1969).

## Social Structure and Organization – Selected Aspects

### GENERAL

Ben David, J., 'Professions and Social Structure in Israel', *Industrial Relations*, 5, 1 (October 1965), pp. 48–66.

Ginor, F., *Socio-Economic Disparities in Israel* (Tel Aviv, David Horowitz Institute, 1979).

Habib, J., *Transfers and the Poverty Problem, an Evaluation* (Jerusalem, Falk Institute for Economic Research in Israel, 1974).

Lissak, M., 'Patterns of Change in Ideology, and Class Structure in Israel', *Jewish Journal of Sociology*, 7, 1 (June 1965), pp. 46–62.

—— *Social Mobility in Israeli Society* (Jerusalem, Israel University Press, 1970).

Matras, J., *Social Change in Israel* (Chicago, Aldine, 1965).

### KIBBUTZ AND MOSHAV

Blais, J. R. (ed.), *Kibbutz Studies Series* (Darby Pa., Norwood Publication, 1979–).

Dar, Y. (ed.), *Education in the Kibbutz, a Dual Focused Socialization* (Jerusalem, Centre of Documentation and Research of Israeli Society, the Hebrew University, Academon Press, 1982).

Krausz, E. (ed.), *The Sociology of the Kibbutz* (New Jersey, New Brunswick, Transaction Books, 1983).

Rosner, M., *Democracy, Equality and Change; the Kibbutz and Social Theory* (Darby, Pa.; Norwood Publications, 1980).

Weingrod, A., *Reluctant Pioneers, Village Development in Israel* (New York, Ithaca, Cornell University Press, 1966).

Weintraub D. and Lissak M., 'Problems of Absorption of North African Immigrants in Small Holder Cooperative Settlements in Israel', *Jewish Journal of Sociology*, 3 (June 1961), pp. 29–52.

——, —— and Atzmon, Y., *Moshava, Kibbutz, Moshav; Jewish Rural Settlements and Developments in Palestine* (New York, Ithaca, Cornell University Press, 1967).

### PATTERNS OF CULTURAL LIFE

Adler, C. and Kahane, R., *Israel: a Society in the Making, a Sociological Analysis of Sources*, Vol. II: *Values, Religon and Culture* (in Hebrew) (Jerusalem, Academon Press, 1975).

Eisenstadt, S. N., 'Israeli Identity: Problems in the development of the Collective Identity of an Ideological Society', *Annals of the American Academy of Political and Social Science*, No. 370 (March 1967), pp. 116–123.

Halkin, S., *Modern Hebrew Literature, from the Enlightenment to the Birth of the State of Israel: Trends and Values* (New York, Schocken Books, 1970; reprint, 1974).

Halpern, B., 'Zionism and Israel', *Jewish Journal of Sociology*, Vol. 3, No. 2 (December 1961), pp. 155–173.

Kahane, R. and Kopstein S. (eds.), *Problems of Collective Identity and Legitimation in the Israeli Society – A Reader* (Jerusalem, Centre of Documentation and Research of Israeli Society, The Hebrew University, Academon Press, 1980).

Katz, E. and Gurewitch, M., *The Secularization of Leisure – Culture and Communication in Israel* (London, Faber and Faber, 1976).

Segal, E., 'Israel and Zionism', *Nation*, Vol. 197 (November 1963), pp. 293–96.

## Contemporary Jewish Communities in the Diaspora

Good surveys of contemporary Jewish communities can be found in the volumes of the *American Jewish Yearbook* (New York and Philadelphia, American Jewish Committee) and in the Jewish Publication Society of America.

### AMERICAN JEWRY

Cohen S. M. *American Modernity and Jewish Identity* (New York and London, Tavistock Publications 1983).

Dawidowicz, Lucy S., *On Equal Terms – Jews in America, 1881–1981* (New York, Holt Rinehart and Winston, 1982, 1984).

Gittler, J. B. (ed.), *Jewish Life in the United States: Perspectives from the Social Sciences* (New York, New York University Press, 1981).

Glazer, N., *American Judaism*, 2nd ed. (Chicago, University of Chicago Press, 1972).

Halpern, B., *The American Jew: A Zionist Analysis* (New York, Theodor Herzl Foundation, 1956).

Howe, I., *World of Our Fathers: The Journey of East European Jews to America and the Life They Found and Made* (New York, Simon and Schuster, 1976).

Liebman, C. S., *The Ambivalent American Jew* (Philadelphia, Jewish Publication Society of America, 1973).

Neusner, J., *American Judaism; Adventure in Modernity* (Englewood Cliffs, NJ, Prentice-Hall, 1972).

—— (ed.), *Understanding American Judaism: Toward the Description of a Modern Religion*; Vol. 1: *The Rabbi and the Synagogue*; Vol 2: *Sectors of American Judaism* (New York, Ktav

Publishing House, 1975).

Sklare, M., *America's Jews* (New York, Random House, 1971).

—— *Conservative Judaism: An American Religious Movement*, new ed. (New York, Schocken Books, 1972).

### SOVIET JEWRY

Kochman, L. (ed.), *The Jews in Soviet Russia since 1917* (London, Oxford University Press, 1970).

### RELATIONS BETWEEN ISRAEL AND THE DIASPORA

Davis, M. (ed.), *The Yom Kippur War, Israel and the Jewish People*, Foreword by Prof. E. Katzir (New York, Arno Press, 1974).

—— (ed.), *World Jewry and the State of Israel* (New York, Arno Press, Herzl Press, 1977).

—— (ed.), *Zionism in Transition* (New York, Herzl Press, 1980).

# Index